THE MANY MEANINGS OF MYTH

Martin S. Day

UNIVERSITY
PRESS OF
AMERICA

LANHAM • NEW YORK • LONDON

All University Press of America books are produced on acid-free
paper which exceeds the minimum standards set by the National
Historical Publications and Records Commission.

Table of Contents

iii

Plumbing the wellsprings of myth
Mythic thinking
Myth and symbol
Psychology of some mythic concepts: the
    word, cannibalism, sacrifice, death

Preface

This volume attempts, as far as present knowledge and speculation (and the length of this volume) permit, to answer three questions:

(1) Why and how did myth originate?

(2) What functions does myth fulfill in human life and human society?

(3) How can we interpret myths, how understand the often puzzling and alien character and themes?

After the first chapter defining and discussing some basics of myth, the second chapter summarizes the significant theories about the origin of myth as proposed from Thales of the 7th century B.C. until the late 19th century. The remaining chapters of the book consider myth through approaches especially pursued within the last 100 years:

Religion and Myth (Chapters III - VI)
Social science and myth (Chapters VII - VIII)
Psychology and myth (Chapters IX - XII)
Natural and physical sciences and myth (Chapters XIII - XIV)

The second question above is intertwined with the origin of myth but is an especial concern in the chapters below:

III (myth and the power of personal religion)
V - VI (myth and the impact of community religion)
VII - VIII (myth and man as a social creature)
IX - XII (myth as an expression of the inner life and as a benefactor of the psyche)

The third question, interpretation of myth, is the overarching purpose of the entire work. Many theorists (as the second chapter certainly reveals) claim to have the one sovereign explanation for myth, but, truthfully, the totality of myth is far more complicated than Middle Eastern politics. Please note the following important stipulations:

(a) Interpretation of myth is highly speculative. Archaic peoples accept myth without analysis and, if pressed for an interpretation, usually assert that it means what it says. Acculturated peoples are all too willing to agree with an intellectual from an advanced society; such interpretations are wholly suspect. As outsiders to the archaic world of myth-fabrication we can never speak with certitude.

(b) All fruitful approaches should be explored. Wendy Doniger O'Flaherty has proposed the "toolbox" technique,[1] carrying about a sizable range of tools to employ upon myth and selecting the most applicable tool for each myth. She offers sound pragmatic advice:

> Often the explicit content of a myth will give a broad hint as to how it might be interpreted: if it is about castration, try Freud; if it is about heresy, try theology. In the first analysis it pays to be literal-minded; after that (and particularly if the head-on approach fails to bear fruit), one can indulge in the search for more arcane meanings.[2]

(c) All potentially viable approaches, it follows, must receive a full hearing. This volume is not espousing any one approach but seeks to find the significant contributions of each tool in the "toolbox." In the text proper and in the footnotes appear criticisms and caveats for each approach. Considerable space is devoted to psychology and myth because recent generations have emphasized the psychological exploration of myth. We are fascinated and challenged by these revelations, but we must admit that much psychological probing of myth is wholly hypothetical and that other, perhaps less exciting, proposals may be at least equally worthwhile.

(d) Myths must be interpreted within the context of the culture that created them. Romantics deficient in knowledge of Elizabethan life made some woefully inaccurate judgments about Shakespeare's "second-best bed." Even the most knowledgeable of anthropologists can certainly err in interpreting myth from an enigmatic archaic past.

(e) Myths are symbolically charged, and reading symbols can be difficult. A glance at any competent study of symbols[3] will indicate an almost bewildering spectrum of meanings for the same symbol. Myths from totally different cultures may deceptively employ the same symbols but have quite different meanings.

(f) Claude Lévi-Strauss advises even more exacting techniques. He asserts that every myth must be interpreted on two or more levels simultaneously. He asks that every myth be considered in relation to other myths, both of its own society and of other cultures.[4]

The vast body of myth and the herculean task of interpreting it render most unlikely any definitive study of the subject. This work is merely an introduction, hopefully blocking out the significant areas and organizing and clarifying a number of mythic elements. The themes and problems of myth are far from exhausted, but I try to encompass the major questions arising during more than 20 years of teaching mythology.

Each of the scholarly divisions treating of myth has its own specialized terminology. Where such technical vocabulary seems indispensable I have employed it, but for the most part I use my own idiom addressed to the general reader.

The bibliography consulted by any specialist in mythology is so large that a fullscale list would be rather appalling and uncomfortably cumbersome. Accordingly, I have generally omitted all collections of myths and individual studies of bodies of myths (e.g. Hindu, Greek, Amerindian, Australian). Also absent for the most part are the invaluable anthropological works upon archaic societies (e.g., E.E. Evans-Pritchard, Witchcraft, Oracles and Magic among the Azande) which deal extensively with myth. I must acknowledge my deep indebtedness to scores of such works and must refer the reader to the British Museum Catalogue or the card files of any research library. "Bibliographical notes" and the entire documentation appended are therefore to provide citations not for the mountain of factual material but for questions of interpretation. Lists of books on specialized topics do not exhaust the field but are confined to works I found helpful and stimulating. Many worthy volumes I have read are left out because, so far as my search extended, they presented little illumination in myth interpretation beyond what is noted.

To prevent confusion, the term Indians will always refer to the peoples of south Asia, and the term Amerindians will always mean the aborigines of North and South America. Western refers to the civilization of Western Europe which now has ranged through much of the world: North and South America, Australia, etc.

Transliteration of words from foreign tongues presents especial problems. The treatment of words from European languages is reasonably elucidated in standard dictionaries of the English-speaking peoples, and readers recognize that Heracles or Herakles (Greek) and Hercules (Latin) are interchangeable. Where accepted forms (e.g. Shiva, Koran) of alien tongues are familiar, they are employed even if many specialists prefer other and perhaps more precise forms. For numerous less well-known languages the forms given in this text may sometimes appear cryptic (e.g. N!odima, G//awama, Mahārāṣṭra). Explanation of the sounds involved would be too lengthy here. The reader is referred to <u>The Principles of the International Phonetic Association</u> (London, 1949) for a reasonably detailed analysis of these symbols as employed in specific languages. Also helpful is Peter Ladefoged, <u>A Course in Phonetics</u> (New York, etc., 1975). It is imperative that the practice in transliteration of a particular language be consulted, for the same diacritical markings are often employed in different fashions for different languages.

I sincerely appreciate the invaluable assistance of the University of Houston, which granted me a semester of developmental leave to write most of this book and also generously awarded me a grant towards completion of the typescript. Superbly patient and helpful even when I addressed to them the most exotic of bewildering questions have been University of Houston, Rice University and University of Texas (Austin) libraries, as well as the Jesse Jones Medical Library (Houston) and the Houston Public Library. Most patient and most helpful of all has been my wife, Dr. Elizabeth Eikel Day.

University of Houston, Texas, 1983

Chapter I Some Basics about Myth

Extra-terrestrial sentience! The chiming syllables, redolent of high-level learned discourse and etherial scientific research, can evoke in many of our contemporaries the sense of awe and wonder summoned up in days of yore by the Hebraic archangel Zadkiel hovering on colossal pinions, by Hermes the swift-winged messenger of Greek gods, by the enormous soaring bird Garuda bearing Vishnu of India as rider. Modern man will dismiss these myths of the past as mere fancy, but he will enthusiastically espouse parallel or identical myths encrusted with today's technological hardware dreams. UFO's are genuine and probably altogether natural phenomena; by a quantum leap multitudes imagine UFO's as mechanical Garudas bearing within incredibly brilliant creatures from some remote star system.

The itch has affected our scientists themselves. For some time huge radiotelescopes have probed the heavens, seeking some vestige of intelligent communication. If there are numerous civilizations in the cosmos, many far advanced beyond us, the whole universe should be pulsating with all sorts of sentient signals. But as yet the cosmos offers no such communications, just as UFO's have produced no concrete particles of inorganic or organic matter. In very human fashion the scientists persist in this cosmic search, for none of us wants to be alone in all this cosmic vastness.

If we should actually make contact with extra-terrestrial sentience, we are almost certainly in for a terrifying jolt. Our mythic assumptions will be devastatingly shattered. Creatures from another star system will not look like Charlton Heston in radiant robes of white samite. The laws of chance rather effectively rule out human-like form. Whether some-what resembling us or grotesquely exotic, these beings from space will be repulsive, even disgusting, to us. Contemporary myth sprinkles the universe generously with reassuring humanoids and, as in Star Trek, has them all obligingly converse in American-style English.

If these celestial visitors are as fantastically "advanced" beyond us as the myth proclaims, they are likely to puncture our mental balloon far more cataclysmically than did Copernicus or Einstein. The sentients from space would probably dismiss virtually all our thought. Wickedly they would point out that in the Age of Enlightenment, when men resolutely demanded a no-nonsense world of unswerving yard-sticks, Newtonianism proffered a universe of clock-work precision and invariability. In our own age, these nasty creatures from space would note, man's irresolution and vacillation cause science to find the universe operating by Einstein relativity and Heisenberg uncertainty. Our brash travelers from elsewhere in the cosmos would insist that all human thought basically is mythic.

This profoundly disturbing experience might cause mankind to realize that mythic thought is not some story-book fossil of the childhood of our species or some rare and curious aberration of homo sapiens. Mythic thought has been the prevalent form through all human existence, is vigorously alive today, and for the foreseeable future will probably continue to dominate human thinking. How, then, can we properly define and explain such an enormous area of our human response?

Definers of myth are as varied and irreconci-lable as delegates to the United Nations, but all theorizers about myth[1] agree on one point: myth is non-rational. Romantic enthusiasts of the late 18th century and early 19th century rapturously embraced myth as irrational, deeming reason quite inferior to a glorious realm of fine fabling.

Rationalists contemplating myth seem to fall into two camps. One division of rationalists appraises myth as pre-rational or sub-rational. These rationalists consider myth preliminary to the eventual triumph of reason in the individual and in society. They tend to praise or at least tolerate myth in its earliest sphere but regret its continuance in advanced societies. Hence a book title such as The Myth of Independence (1969) by Z. A. Bhutto of Pakistan declares that the nominal freedom of former colonies cannot be taken at face value; a myth here is deemed a deceptive propaganda ploy, ignoring facts and reality. The extremists of this wing impatiently dismiss all myth as mere false-hood, unacceptable in this pragmatic era. The title "Myths about Hunter-Gatherers" in Ethnology[2] asserts that we have held erroneous ideas about early human ecology and must jettison these false notions and perceive the actual facts. This first category of rationalists tends to concentrate upon such myths as the bearing of the world upon his shoulders by Hercules. "Utter hogwash," snort the extreme rationalists who call myth nothing but falsehoods, while most rationalists of this first type will observe with mild disparagement how effective though naive is such testimony to the strength and steadfastness of Hercules. The second broad division of rationalists considers myth as supra-rational, i.e. beyond reason. Such rationalists dearly respect the great domain of reason but recognize essential functions that myth performs for mankind, functions for which reason will not suffice. These rationalists will dwell upon such myths as the account of Ishtar and Tammuz. Nothing else, they admit, can so potently celebrate deathless love, intrepid penetration to the profoundest fears and pains, and the triumph of resurrected life.

Not merely is myth different to different observers. The problem is compounded fourfold because few theorizers discriminate adequately among the four major forms of myth arising from separate cultural levels.

Myth I (archaic myth). Archaic myth arises from a non-literate tribal society of food-gatherers, hunters, nomads, or rudimentary agriculturalists.[3] Such myth is usually crude, naive, awkward; nonetheless, all who tell these tales and all who listen agree that this is sacred material, genuine truth. Lévi-Strauss and other social scientists of our age work extensively with the archaic myth of precivilized peoples, finding in these myths the basics of human thought and behavior that are blurred or muted in later sophisticated accounts. Such archaic myth, now available in great volume from South American Indians, African bushmen, Borneo headhunters, Polynesians from remote atolls, and Eskimo fishermen from coastal Greenland, offers probably our best opportunity to plumb the fundamental nature of myth. Such illuminating material, however, could never have engaged the rapt attention of countless readers as have the superbly narrated myths of Greece, the Middle East, and India. Some translators, possibly improving upon the native originals, have produced poetized versions of archaic myth, but they can never compare with the Mahabharata from India, The Epic of Gilgamesh from Mesopotamia, and a multitude of Greek and Roman poems ultimately based upon archaic myth.

Even among archaic peoples there are distinct strains of myth production:

Myth of the observant layman. In all cultures the layman is a pragmatist, the shrewd factual scrutinizer of the world immediately around him. Such laymen produce the Chinese myth of the cicada as experiencing resurrection and immortality, or the Egyptian myth of the dung-bred scarab as ceaseless renewal of life. Such myth will form subsequent folklore.

Myth from the religious specialist, the shaman or other religious functionary. The Winnebago Amerindians of Wisconsin postulate the creator deity sprawled in space inert, inwardly pondering. Spontaneously tears fall from his eyes and form a glistening mass. The previously passive deity now realizes that he is wholly capable of creating things, and he proceeds to construct the universe. Unlike the earth-bound layman, the philosopher-religionist who conceived this account was deeply concerned with the nature and actions of primal deity, the relations of the supernatural and the natural. Myth of this type leads onwards to theology and philosophy.

Aition, conveying a lesson or message in story form instead of bald didactic statement. Instruction, indoctrination, teaching, are basic to man as a human, and the aition has apparently been a key form of instruction as long as man has had articulate speech. The myth of the hero has admonished millions of young males to live the heroic life not by exhortation but through the enthralling account of the mythical dragon-slayer and invincible warrior. The Japanese rice-planting ritual celebrates the marriage of the Water-goddess of the Realm of Water to the Sun-god. The child born of this union is the god of the rice field. Thus in mythical fashion is stated the fact that rice is born of sunlight and water. Myth of this type leads on to education and eventually to dreary textbooks.

Myth II (intermediate myth). Psychologists and social scientists of our era may resolutely pursue archaic myth, but most of us today, as almost all devotees of myth for the past two millenia, are powerfully drawn to intermediate myth. Even the most sober of scientists, like Francis Bacon, and the most prosaic of philosophers, like David Hume, have been

4

attracted by the art of intermediate myth. Such myth is founded almost wholly upon archaic myth, but intermediate myth is skillfully shaped by highly conscious writers in a literate era. During the period in which intermediate myth is produced, the populace or the author or both still believe in the sacral nature of the myth. Aeschylus seems a devout worshipper of almighty Zeus, and Lucian of Samosata appears as sceptical as Edward Gibbon or Thomas Henry Huxley. The accomplished Greco-Roman purveyors of myth ranged from the sturdy agriculturist Hesiod to the ultra-sophisticated urbanite Ovid, but scholars agree that uniformly these ancient writers, even the pious Aeschylus, deemed myth a plastic substance that they were free to mold and interpret. Our century has spread before us a growing hoard of impressive mythological accounts from the ancient Middle East, e.g. the Sumerian "Dumuzi and Enkimdu," the Akkadian "Enuma Elish" (Creation Epic), and the Ugaritic poems upon Baal and Anath. Scholars are not certain whether these anonymous poets regarded Middle Eastern myth as wholly sacrosanct or exercised some of the freedom assumed by Greek writers. The ancient poets of India from the early Rigveda onwards seem far more religion-centered than their Greek counterparts, but often, as in the Bhagavid-Gita, display an explora-tory mind more characteristic of Greek philosophers than Greek poets. Whatever the mind-set of the writers producing intermediate myth, their aesthetic power will probably insure that the future like the past will look to them as the great repository of myth.

The strong self-consciousness in intermediate myth produces several strains:

Myth of the highly conscious artist, dominated by aesthetic impulses and intent upon neat, attrac-tive telling of a good story, like the masterful Ovid. In the hands of Aeschylus, Sophocles, and Euripides mythological themes are the means of probing the basic characters of god and man, the enigmas and putative truths of the relationships between the divine and the human. Such myth remains what most readers of millenia have enjoyed and have deemed the supreme examples of mythology. Thus literature originates, proceeding eventually to non-mythological accounts but always retaining some features of its sacral past.

Myth from philosophers and moralists. Myth is the vehicle to expound ideas, even profound abstractions, in a milieu still rampant with mythological material. Indian myth tells how Garuda, the gigantic bird mount of Vishnu, discusses with the crow Bhushundi the proper roles of knowledge (jñāna) and devotion (bhakti), the latter personified as Sita, the consort of Vishnu.⁴ Especially the Puranas in India demonstrate mythology developing into philosophy and theology.⁵

Propaganda myth to substantiate the position of the power elite. Tribesmen of the New Guinea Highlands to this day will shout to nearby enemies rather lengthy narratives of their own exploits (somewhat exaggerated), of their father's mighty deeds (considerably exaggerated), of their ancestors' fabulous feats (exaggerated to mythic proportions). Such were the flytings of Anglo-Saxon warriors and the boastful harangues of Homeric fighting men. With more composure myth tellers recount the tribal heroes responsible for the greatness of the entire tribe, and each Greek city-state told of its illustrious founder who cast lustre ever since upon every citizen.

Various tinkering with and concocting of myth by intellectuals in an era when many archaic practices and references were wholly cryptic. The ancient Greeks probably invented most of the eponymous heroes, the supposed early worthies who gave their names to tribes and cities, e.g. Dardanus, reputedly the founder of Dardania, later Troy. Since the name Rome is probably very ancient Etruscan, Romulus may be a fabrication. In Palestine the place name Lehi means "jawbone of an ass." Probably smarting from outsiders' levity over so plebeian a name, local citizens apparently sponsored the stirring saga of Samson resolutely demolishing Philistines with the jawbone of an ass. Existing personal names, sometimes distorted, would be explained by a dramatic account. The name Apsyrtus for the younger brother of Medea is suspicious, for it means "swept downstream." The account in the Argonauts legend of the dismemberment of Apsyrtus and the jettisoning of his fragments into the water may graft upon the Jason account a sacrificial rite of fertility remote from the Witch of Colchas. From the end of the Euripidean drama Hippolytus seems a male virgin (possibly destroyed by a sex goddess, as Ishtar summarily dealt with those she trapped) celebrated rather sentimentally by modest maidens. His name meant "of the stampeding horses" (it may be the twisting of another name to provide this form), and such is the tragic fate of the puritanic youth. It is also possible that behind the account that intrigued the elegant Racine in Phaedre is a savage primitive slaying of a sacred king by stampeding horses.

Robert Graves believes that many of the myths descending to us were misconstruings of pictures and sculpture of earlier myth.[6] For example, Graves conjectures that the stories of Theseus killing Sciron and Cercyon were misreadings of the ritual of the sacred king as depicted in archaic representation. Notoriously, the emblems of one era will be taken with lamentable literalness in a subsequent age. A Japanese myth has a hero Momotaro born of a peach. In modern slang a "peach" is an attractive girl. In Japanese figurative language the peach stood for the female genitals. Classic Greece deemed Eros a flaming, youthful god of love, but in late Hellenistic times the transformation was made into the putti-like cupids, dear to St. Valentine Day greeting cards.

An immense chasm separates Myth I and Myth II from Myth III and Myth IV. The two latter categories are no longer sacralized; potent and often quite impressive, they are held sacred by no one.

Myth III (derivative myth). No one will exalt derivative myth as the basis for examining pure myth, but for multitudes it is the chief, perhaps only, contact with mythological accounts. Ever since the Middle Ages, Western civilization has known extensive retelling or citing of myths outside the Judeo-Christian tradition. The Greco-Roman myths and mythological personages were well exploited by medieval artists, but the Renaissance released such a torrent of mythological material by poets, painters, sculptors, and artists generally that no one can properly understand Western art before the bourgeois triumph in the early 19th century without a rich knowledge of classical Greek and Roman myths. In the 18th century a renewed interest in ancient Teutonic myth resurrected tales about Wotan, Thor, Loki, and their fellow Aesir and Vanir.[7] Celtic lore staged a spectacular but hoax-burdened surge in the "Fingal" poetry of MacPherson, a poetry that enthralled Goethe and many contemporaries. All of this material is derivative myth. Neither the artistic creators nor the observers of this art ever experienced religious stirrings in these renditions. The primary concerns are aesthetic and secular, frequently remote from the interests of the ancients. While the foundation for derivative myth is essentially intermediate myth, these recent artists demand complete liberty for any treatment they wish, producing in works like Prometheus Unbound by Shelley violent and unrecognizable modifications of an ancient theme. Everybody will dismiss Tiger at the Gates by Giraudoux and the continuation of The Odyssey by Kazantzakis as merely "suggested by" the ancient accounts. But outside of Finland very few people are acquainted with the Kalevala except from the music of Sibelius. Wagnerian operas and music provide information about Teutonic mythology for scores of people to every reader of the Eddas. I encounter university students today who claim that their only exposure to classic mythology has come from cinema and television dramatizations of Troy, of the wanderings of Odysseus, of the labors of Hercules (often bizarrely remote from classical reports), of the founding of Rome. Specialists may continue to approach myth solely through archaic myth, but, for all beyond this handful, derivative myth is today the major supplier of myth and probably will dominate the future even more fully.

The most radical form of derivative myth is narrative fiction ostensibly set in contemporary or future surroundings but relying upon immemorial patterns of myth and folklore. Hercules seems quaintly old fashioned, but Tarzan and Superman are tailored to the 20th century, while going through paces old to heroes before Gilgamesh. Some ingenious authors have successfully pawned off their creations as folk myth. Apparently the Lorelei, a water nymph who lured sailors to destruction in the manner of the ancient Sirens, was a fabrication of Klemens Brentano in 1800. The American super hero, Paul Bunyan, seems largely the creation of W. B. Laughead, author and illustrator of the first publication on Paul Bunyan in 1914. It is impossible, however, to imagine these mythical figures, devised in our age, except with the cultural heritage of age-old myth. Science fiction may, as its label suggests, seek to imagine genuine possibilities of future research and exploration; it may also be fantasy, wishful thinking, or probing criticism of current tendencies which by extrapolation demonstrate their viciousness or vacuity. Much which is termed science fiction actually employs

themes of archaic myth such as the heroic quest and
even specific images such as hostile monsters and
divine intercessors (now termed "sentient beings far
more advanced than humans").

Myth IV (ideological myth). Myth is protean.[8]
Modern man is usually politely patronizing towards
"myth," for, he confidently asserts, he knows what is
factual and lives by it, and he knows what is
imaginary and enjoys it playfully. While recent man
may dismiss as fiction the god Perkunas and the epic
Shahnamah by Firdausi, mythical notions and mythical
concepts continue to control modern life and
behavior.[9] Even though today's psychoanalysts
predicate even pre-natal sexuality, multitudes still
assert the total "innocence" of the very young. Even
though careful research reports that in every physiological aspect, except muscularity, women are
stronger than men, many still refer to women as "the
weaker sex." Marxism is defiantly "scientific," but
the blissful perfection of its ultimate goal,
anarchy, follows the party line of Elysium, Islands
of the Blest, Valhalla, Utopia, New Atlantis,
Erewhon, and the Big Rock Candy Mountain. Shorn of
his rhetoric and his pretenses, modern man may follow
different mythical dreams but he is just as governed
by his Myth IV[10] as Trobriand Islanders and Kwakiutl
Amerindians were governed by Myth I.

Living without myth is not viable.[11] Modern
urban life has spawned many cynics who believe in
nothing except hedonistic pleasure for the self.
Ironically, this nonmythical "realism" seldom
produces any sustained satisfaction. Deprecate myth
as he may, man nonetheless finds the mythical view of
life indispensable. Of course, only Romantic extravagance can justify myth as sheer irrationality.
Rationally we can interpret myth as controlled or at
least structured intuition in words. Overall, myth
is the als ob ("as if") of Vaihinger.[12] In a
bewildering cosmos man must construct the mythical
views that offer meaning and order. Even if
grotesquely contrary to fact, myth grants community
stability and psychic assurance. It is humbling to
realize that generations of the future will probably
deem our cherished Weltanschauung as benightedly
mythical as we label the als ob of our ancestors.

The broadest possible term for all shaped verbal
intuition is the myth-making faculty, mythical
thought, or mythical creativity. Bergson called it

the _fonction_ _fabulatrice_.[13] The myth-making faculty
ranges from the majestic _Rigveda_ to the incantations
of Gypsies and Pennsylvania-Dutch hex doctors. All
versions of the myth-making faculty display three
essential elements:

(1) Hosts of people believe it to be valid.
Belief can range from fanatical insistence that the
account is divine and eternal truth to "willing
suspension of disbelief," the feeling by many readers
of fiction that while imaginary the tale is wholly
true to life, a genuine reading of experience. A
sizable number must concur in belief. Each human has
his own private notions, what might be called a
private mythology, but the myth-making faculty
ignores the idiosyncratic ideas restricted to an
individual and demands a larger and more general
acceptance. A forceful personality within a very
limited area and with a receptive audience may impose
upon a group his mythmaking faculty, even if it is
insane and suicidal. In spite of lay and clerical
protests, thousands of young people in the early 13th
century followed the German peasant Nicholas and the
French shepherd Stephen to death or to slavery in the
so-called Children's Crusade. Our own era has
demonstrated that such aberrations are shockingly
present today; in 1979 almost a thousand of his
parishioners in Guiana were swayed by the Rev. Jim
Jones to commit suicide en masse. For real effectiveness the myth-making faculty must have genuine
staying power. According to Indian classification
there are two types of lasting mythical thought.
Deshi ("local," "ethnic") is the mythical hold upon a
specific community, binding its members together in
common tenets. For at least two centuries the idea
of progress (perhaps now expiring) dynamized Western
civilization and set it apart from all other
societies present or past. _Marga_ ("road," "way") is
myth applicable to all mankind. Buddha used the word
marga to mean freedom from the world; we would see
marga as freedom from the world of cold measurable
facts. Man's myths about the afterlife and rebirth,
for example, are widespread throughout the world, and
their prevalence testifies that such myths are _marga_.

(2) Scientifically, it cannot be proved.
Crucial to all consideration of the myth-making
faculty is its postulation of events, objects, and
beings that scientific scrutiny simply cannot confirm
or cannot find endowed with the remarkable attributes
claimed in myth. Birth of humans from the armpits of

10

Ymir, the flying carpet of the Arabian Nights, and the six-armed deities of India are all creations of the mythmaking faculty and are all contrary to any objective observation. Even the most scientifically scrupulous will recognize as rhetorical heightening for effect the extraordinary feats of Hercules, Beowulf, and Rustum, although real men certainly seem to loom behind these larger-than-life heroes. Nonetheless, the fundamental issue here is how one defines truth. Certainly the myth-making faculty cannot be properly reconciled with phenomenological facts, but mythical thought, if it is to endure, must be reconciled with the inner life of man. The engrossing dreams and the radiant visions, the lancing fears and the recurrent hopes of every man's inward existence are genuine realities. When the myth-making faculty taps these universal inner realities, the result is extremely potent marga, universals that will touch multitudes of psyches and outlast many dynasties.

(3) Symbolism.[14] The words emblem and symbol are too often employed today as synonyms. A national flag, for instance, is properly an emblem, for it suggests a country, with multitudes of personal associations, to each viewer. An emblem, therefore, is a sign which the conscious mind recognizes as a device to identify some other concrete object. Symbol represents not an external reality but a psychic and spiritual reality.[15] Hence, the participant in a sacred drama or sacred dance is actually living the sacral experience. Hence the statue of a god truthfully has the god within it. Christian statuary is emblematic, according to church doctrine, and the worshipper is said not to be addressing the deity in the statue but is granted direction and encouragement through the image. Most intelligent professed Christians of today similarly regard as emblematic much biblical material, such as the creation account or the Garden of Eden tale; some "fundamentalists" still astonish us by rabid protestations of the absolutely literal truth of Christian myth. For such souls the myth is truly symbolic, reflecting a wholly divine truth.[16] If we have such examples before us today, we should certainly understand the transcendent and incontrovertible truths that Vedic worshippers of old India, devotees of Osiris in ancient Egypt, and natives of Africa, Australia, and the Americas regularly perceived in the symbols of myth."[17]

11

But we must note how sophisticated can be members of a non-literate society. The Gikuyu of Kenya tell a myth of the good Gikuyu god in dire conflict with the bad Maasai god in storms and in the phases of the moon. How could the Gikuyu relate such a tale when they are avowed monotheists! The Gikuyu shrug their shoulders and say that this quarrel is "just a way of saying it." The Gikuyu are wholly conscious of the nature of figurative speech.

We would say that ancient Egyptian myth emblemized the inundation of the land by the Nile, which brought rich nutriments and fertility.[18] To the ancient Egyptians themselves Osiris "floating" or "drowning" in the river and the ritual act of lifting up a jar of fresh Nile water were the awesome symbols of the god's actual presence and the living benison of the benevolent power of the deity.[19]

Our central concern is with just one section of the vast realm of the mythmaking faculty, the area of archaic myth and intermediate myth. We must extensively consider intermediate myth because it is our sole source for much mythological material and because until quite recently it was the only myth contemplated by most theorists and scholars. Structuralists like Lévi-Strauss in analyzing myth will consider all versions of a myth.

Archaic myth (Myth I) displays the characteristics of the entire myth-making faculty but in addition has its own particularizing aspects:

(4) It is sacred.[20] One is tempted to define myth as all sacred tales alien to the reader's cultural tradition.[21] Western civilization is most respectful to the ethical, devotional, and mystical literature of India, but it still tends to brush aside as bizarre fantasies the sacred stories of Hinduism and Buddhism. Since almost all Greco-Roman myth has been transmitted as intermediate myth, its sacral nature is often minimized or ignored. Generations of Western civilization deemed education to be knowledge of Latin, and the most impressive collection of ancient myths from one Latin author is the Metamorphoses of the flamboyant Ovid, who revelled in brilliant descriptions and spectacular episodes, but displayed no appreciable religiosity. Until recent generations Christians unhesitatingly dismissed all sacred accounts outside their tradition as falsehoods or self-delusions. For more than a century anthro-

pologists have been collecting archaic myth from undeveloped cultures, but as yet not a one of these sacred myths has a fraction of the attention still accorded the siege of Troy. Today we are getting larger and larger doses of the holy stories of primitive people, but the general public receives most of these accounts in coffee table books or in other popular media which emphasize the quaint, the exotic, the fantastic. Myth generally appears to us as art or as pleasant diversion; we too often forget that to the original narrators it shone with the awesome radiance of the divine.

We must not impose our idea of the sacred upon others. Protesters will politely ask if Homer isn't considered a pious devotee of the gods and then will dramatically point out the passage in the Iliad where Hera nags Zeus like a situation-comedy harridan. Although our idea of divine dignity has been grievously assailed, the ancients, certainly of Homer's era, felt the sacred element undiminished. First, the Homeric epics were aristocratic literature about aristocrats and directed to an aristocratic audience. All such aristocrats claimed deities in their genealogies and stood on quite familiar terms with the gods whose social status was but a turn of the screw above theirs. Second, just as willful Achilles behaved as he pleased and none could challenge him, so the gods follow their own inclinations with a fine disdain for any plebeian reproach. Third, while the peasant of Homer's time may have given more allegiance to chthonic gods than to the lofty Olympians, the whole age was homogeneous in its unquestioned acceptance of the being and the power of the gods. Such an era, when there is no criticism of the gods, never demands the consistently impeccable conduct enforced upon the deities in a heterogeneous age.

(5) It is narrative. Although the early Greeks probably used mythos in the sense of "word" or "speech," classic Greeks employed mythos to mean "story" or "plot" just as Aristotle did in his Poetics. Long before Aristotle defined mythos as conflict, the tellers of archaic myth made their tales dramatic struggles of opposing forces. Early men saw the outward world as an arena of deadly conflict; they similarly in their inner lives, from the electric circuitry of the human brain, perceived existence as a confrontation of opposites.

13

Aristotle has disturbed us by exalting plot (mythos) over personality, but archaic mythmakers would wholly agree with him. Today we will lengthily contemplate heroes and deities, flat like photographs on the page of a book or posed like statuary. Archaic peoples along with Aristotle are primarily concerned with deeds, and they would sensibly assert that character becomes meaningful only in actual performance. Thus a representation of Apollo armed with bow and arrows would suggest to us the brilliant god of light and art; we might fancify his arrows as emblems of sunbeams. The ancients would be stimulated quite otherwise; they would launch into the slaying of the Python by, Apollo, or Apollo shooting Tityus for attempted defilement of Leto, or Apollo and his sister Artemis killing all the children of Niobe.

(6) The setting for a myth is frequently timeless. Never is it set in present tense, the time of the mundane and the physically demonstrable. Even the pious of today usually doubt contemporary alleged miracles, while they confidently and dogmatically assert miracles in the long ago. Men of traditional societies behave similarly. William Lessa secured almost 1500 responses to the Thematic Apperception Test (TAT) from natives of the Ulithi Atoll. In vivid contrast to their wondrous myths set in the distant past, the Ulithians in TAT improvisations portrayed the everyday life of everyday people today with, of course, a normal human dollop of the scandalous and melodramatic.[22] For most peoples the usual setting of myth is in illo tempore (Lat. "in that time"). Some tribes ascribe their myths to the days of "the old ones," "the elders," "the grandfathers"; they always mean a long, long time ago.

For the great majority of myths everywhere the time is the remote and misty past. Very clear cut is the Mythical Age celebrated by American Indians throughout Canada and the U.S.A. (except for parts of the southwest). This Mythical Age is a specific era predating the first appearance of human beings. In this pre-human world all the animals, birds, and forces of nature talk, act, and occasionally look like human beings. Coyote, Raven, Buffalo, Eagle, and their like during this Mythical Age create the world and establish much of the geography and life behavior still extant. Especially along the Pacific coast from Baja California to Alaska, the Mythical Age terminates sharply by summary punishment of its primal creatures or by their grudging acquiescence to the superseding human period. The Australian aborigines have no such incisive end to the Mythical Age, variously termed alcheringa (or alchera) by the Arunta, bamum by the Murngin, tjukur by desert tribes of West and South Australia. In the remote era of this "Dreamtime," say Australian aborigines, the world was created and formed to its present contours. Especially the culture bringers of that distant epoch established once and for all the techniques and customs of man. Any query about tribal practices receives the calm and irrefutable reply, "As it was done in the Dreamtime, so must it be done now and for evermore."

For prophetic and eschatological myth the setting is sometime in the future. Even if one becomes increasingly blasé about the past, the days ahead still seem openended, and all sorts of fantastic things can be predicated of the boundless future. Some of man's most exalted and wondrously imaginative visions have been set in the eons yet to come. In bygone days myth of the future tended to the horrendous prophecies of colossal and universal catastrophe at some remote time. Our dynamic society, experiencing and expecting constant change, can suggest bizarre and melodramatic mythic events posited even a few years hence. The favorite locale of much science fiction is in the timeless future in the measureless depths of space where heroic deeds burgeon more extensively than in ancient Greek legend, especially when on planets of Fomalhaut or across the tractless wastes surrounding the Magellanic Clouds lurk monsters more appalling than the chimeras and hippogriffs of old.

(7) Highly respected supernatural powers are participants. Some purists would restrict myth to tales in which deities are the central figures, but the heroic accounts of Ulysses, Sigurd, and Maui certainly call for important involvement by deities and certainly belong with the great myths. The lowest echelons of the supernatural may lack the social status needed for proper recognition in myth. According to Norse accounts the maggots feeding upon the corpse of Ymir transformed themselves into Light Elves and Dark Elves. Such inauspicious origins restrict elves, and kindred beings like pixies and gremlins, to folklore rather than majestic myth. Of course, the chief reason for barring these lesser supernatural creatures from myth is their lack of

power. The peasants who tell about undine, leprechaun, kobold, brownie or bucca picture such beings as mischievous or churlish or kindly in a rather trivial fashion, without any of the awesome clout of the great gods.

(8) Myths are held to provide valuable knowledge and guidance. Accepting all the foregoing, even noting that myth is sacred to earlier man, many today would still espouse a centuries-old attitude of Western society that myth is a cultural decoration, an aesthetic embellishment. We must realize that every myth was originally treasured as a repository of real knowledge and sublime truth.[23]

(9) Myth is believed with profound intensity. Ultimately it is not the substance of the narrative that makes a myth, but the burning conviction of teller and listener. Our coffee table collections of myths provide from remote and archaic peoples accounts that seem preposterous or ludicrous to many Westerners. Chinese intellectuals, for instance, have often felt the same about Judeo-Christian myth. Kali, the gaunt blood-stained goddess of India, is every whit as real and operative to the true Indian believer as any of the Christian supernatural Figures to a medieval European.[24]

Vast and far roaming as archaic myth is, it still represents only part of the narrative resources of archaic peoples. Among the American Navaho, Clyde Kluckhohn found myth-like accounts ranging from "simple entertainment" to "intellectual edification."[25] Many archaic societies carefully discriminate "true," "serious," "important" narratives from "false," "frivolous," "trivial" tales even if gods, heroes, and other mythic elements are common to both types. The North American Pawnee and Cherokee as well as the African Herero and many other peoples will relate the "trivial" stories to any audience at any time but will scrupulously reserve the "true" accounts solely for adult male audiences (i.e., the truly initiated) especially at sacred times of the year or at avowedly sacred gatherings.[26] Among the Trobriand Islanders, Malinowski observed a threefold division carefully labeled:

> liliu--venerable, sacred, highly revered;[27]
> libwogwo--well-regarded, supposed true recitals of notable achievement;

16

kukwanebu--facetious or engrossing anecdotes, the repertoire of a capable raconteur.[28]

Quite possibly the early Greeks recognized similar categories. We might be more accurate in our appraisal of classic myth if we realized that the original narrators of the farcical bed-trapping episode involving Aphrodite and Ares may have considered the whole charade as kukwanebu.[29]

The classification system of the Trobriand Islanders is significantly parallel to our familiar scheme: myth, legend, folklore. Many commentators frequently dismiss such classification as too fuzzy and overlapping to be meaningful. Nevertheless, there does seem to be a genuine progression in cultural history from the divine to the heroic and thence to the realistic, as Vico, Comte and other theorists of history have observed.

"Myth" (liliu),[30] as it involves the sacred, is reverentially ascribed by archaic societies to the shadowy past when gods roamed the earth or to the visionary future when the entire cosmos will be wrenched asunder.[31] For most myths absolutely the most recent setting is in the time of "the grand-fathers" (a term often meaning remote ancestors). For many peoples mythical accounts ignore persons and events recognizable today and treat wholly of super-natural beings, talking animals, culture bringers.

"Legend" (libwogwo) tells of military and spiritual heroes in the past, not the remote past of myth but from the time of "the fathers" or even from our distant youth now transfigured with roseate glow. Nestor in the Iliad sounds indeed like the super-annuated warrior who is nobly gracious to Achilles and Menelaus and Diomedes of the Trojan War but will dilate without much persuasion upon the real, genuine heroes, the Argonauts of his now misty early years. We who soldiered in World War II were pointedly told by World War I veterans that we had it soft in mechanized, elegantly provisioned warfare, while they had been the truly tough heroic fighting men early in this century. Legend, saga, epic, heroic tale proclaim that in former days they were men but, indubitably, they were far stronger, more valiant, more intelligent, more moral, more everything commendable, than the mundane fellows of this era. Ajax could heft a rock that three men of our puny day couldn't budge; but he was a mortal, ending rather ignominiously in madness and suicide. Beowulf swam three days and three nights in full armor (and no modern gold medal winner of Olympic swimming can match that feat), but Beowulf experienced mortal death, expiring from a prevalent medieval ailment, dragon attack.

Perhaps more than one legendary hero has been fashioned from mediocrity or worse, much as the fictional Sartoris family of William Faulkner glorified Bayard Sartoris I (who was killed while perpetrating a tawdry "harebrained prank" during the American Civil War) into a splendiferous hero, "altering the course of human events and purging the souls of men."[32] All tales oft-repeated tend to improve and inflate quite wondrously. Oldsters, who in their hearts really know better, hasten to magnify past exploits "for the family honor" or "for the glory of our tribe." They can also reassure their consciences that they must exaggerate just a bit to impress the new generation and set up a truly splendid example for the young to admire and emulate.

The categorizing as "myth" or as "legend" is slippery and disputable. It would be convenient to apply a rigid yardstick: gods are the central characters of myth, men the central figures of legend. Such a neat scheme is shattered by an account like that of Perseus, presented as a mortal but wholly enmeshed in the wildest of supernatural goings-on. Consider the Volsungasaga from Iceland and the Middle High German Nibelungenlied, which both celebrate the career of the same hero. The Sigurd of the Icelandic version is embroiled in the dense Wagnerian myth of Valkyries and rings of magic fire. The Siegfried of the German account would be an appropriate companion for Chaucer's Knight amongst the Teutonic Knights of medieval Christendom. If a label must be applied, the Volsungasaga can be placed with myth and the Nibelungenlied with legend; but many might find such classification rather arbitrary.

"Folklore"[33] (kukwanebu), "folktale," "fairy tale," or Märchen always have a "let's pretend" air to them. Even the most gullible juvenile realizes that the sugarcandy chalet and the gingerbread wall in Hänsel und Gretel simply aren't for real. The narrators of folktales usually adopt a manner of smiling whimsy or mock-serious solemnity. Even those who dearly love the Märchen and those who treasure a sizable repertoire for future telling will deprecate

such narratives and will consider them quite inappropriate for grand, full-dress occasions. Notwith-
standing, myth and folklore can almost merge like two
gametes; consequently, authorities like Ruth
Benedict[34] and Stith Thompson[35] deem it bootless to
attempt any rigid separation.[36] Folktales often
share with myth (and legend) the supernatural and the
heroic, even the very same themes.[37] But in folklore
the supernatural tends to revel in witches, ogres,
giants, hobgoblins, rather than the straightforward
deities of myth. In folktales the heroic usually
surges forth from humble folk rather than from the
blueblooded aristocrats of myth and legend. Folklore
tends to the tragicomedy pattern with all sorts of
cliffhanging episodes until the usually happy ending,
whereas myth frequently concludes in tragedy or cold
sobriety. Myth plays a sort of grand opera to the
operetta of the folk tale. But perhaps the outstanding differentiation between myth and folklore lies in
mood. In kukwanebu the Trobriand Islanders emphasize
the spirit of play, of frankly epidermal terrors, of
amused attention to the tale, and generally the final
laughter of relief.

Certainly the Eros-Psyche tale has genuine
mythic themes such as the challenge to the unknown
night lover and the imposition of an apparently
impossible task. Even without the easy laugh at the
shooter of Love's arrows snagged by his own weaponry,
the entire business exudes such a Walt Disney cartoon
quality and such sentimental patina of a grade B
woman's periodical that any self-respecting Pawnee or
Cherokee would relegate the account to the
"frivolous." And what can we make of the bizarre
riastradh ("bodily distortion") of Cuchulainn? His
body swirls around inside his skin, his hair stands
up stiff with a gleam of fire at every tip, one eye
narrows to the size of a needle's eye, while the
other eye is grotesquely enlarged. Of course it is
conventional to simulate "fired up" for battle by
physical fires and anatomical gyrations, but it all
sounds like an insinuating brogue from a winking,
smirking Irishman who has extensively bussed the
Blarney stone.

In addition to the "fun" quality, for Western
society a major feature of folklore is its concentration upon the lower social class. Archaic myth,
certainly, is an uppercrust preserve, its recital and
transmission entrusted to the most prestigious of
society. The Orpheus-Eurydice story is a notable and

tragically elevated myth of ancient Greece. In medieval Europe it was transformed for aristocratic tastes to an heroic romance with a happy ending. In the popular ballad "King Orfeo" the transformation is complete to folklore with Orfeo playing a "gabber reel" (a sprightly popular air) and claiming his missing spouse, "An dat's me Lady Isabel." This pattern displays the familiar sociological phenomenon of an upper-class practice descending to the lower classes with corresponsing modification to lower-class manners and language.

While folklore frequently utilizes themes from myth and legend, folklore notably reveals far less orthodox religiosity. The realm of myth and legend seems an establishment world whether of virtually the entire community as in myth or distinctly the aristocratic elite as in the heroic legends. The gods are wholly dominant in myth, and the world of legend is still a world governed by eminent deities and cosmic fate. In folklore, however, conventional religion is largely ignored or, as in many of the Virgin Mary tales of the Middle Ages, modified to archaic motifs (e.g. the earth mother).

Folklore, in its lower-class orientation, may properly represent not a mere vulgarizing of elitist myth but a very ancient strain of anti-establishment tales. The Trickster stories of Amerindians seem quite archaic, but even in Mesolithic times there were elite figures in tribal shamans. The "excrement advisors" of the Trickster look like the common man's scatological burlesque of the spirits that bring solemn counsel to the shaman. Birds and animals occasionally turn the tables upon the Trickster, suggesting coarse laughs at the shaman, who asserted wondrous control over birds and animals.[38]

Revealingly, Robert W. Jacobs in 1970 thrice heard the same tale about the first breadfruit tree on Alau in the Pacific. Spanish and later German missionaries concentrated on ridiculing the archaic religion of the area, and in 1910 the Germans destroyed all the native shrines and exiled the shamans. The oldest narrator had reached young manhood before the German persecution, and his account was truly myth, a reverential recounting of a sacred event. The second narrator was a younger man, but mature. For him the same account had become a legend, told with respect. The youngest narrator, a teenager, was determinedly modern and related the story as folklore, a quaint and amusing business.[39]

20

Any attempt to classify mythical topics is dubious, for the borderlands are vague at best, but some working designations can be helpful:

(1) Etiological myth[40] and miscellaneous tales of the gods. Etiology means "causation" and therefore tries to explain the origin of things and the reason for things. Etiological myths throughout the globe start with the creation of the world and proceed to propound the beginnings of everything from ants and whales to human procreation and ritual taboos. Usually lumped with etiological myths are all the activities of deities, since these supernatural beings presumably cause most of the events of human life. Many peoples treat of their gods in grave solemnity, as the Babylonians chanted about their heavy-jowled tyrannous deities and the Central Americans recounted the bloodthirst of their violent, scary gods. Other peoples, such as Africans and Pacific Islanders, often report their supernatural beings as puckish or quite earthy. Perhaps some of the informality of these treatments arises because natives often try to go along with the attitudes of European visitors, deprecating their own heritage. Much of our material on the ancient Scandinavian mythology comes from Christian writers who frequently make some of the old Northern gods look like drunken navvies. Though gods generally monopolize this area of myth, the multitudinous South American Indian myths assembled by Lévi-Strauss explain the origins of numerous plants, animals, and social customs with only minimal references to the deities.

The search for causation in myth may be even more pervasive than we realize. Moderns tend to interpret the myth of Oedipus as a quest for identity and therefore shrug off as a minor plot mechanism the plague which precipitates the entire action. We must remember, however, that before 18th century rationalism a disease epidemic was generally explained as divine intervention. If your besieging enemy was struck down by pestilence, like the Assyrian cohorts of Sennacharib before Jerusalem, God was vigorously supporting you. If your city of Thebes was being ravaged by disease and you had witnessed heartbreaking deaths of family and friends, you would shudder at the dire anger of the gods and vehemently demand the reason for this monstrous reprimand. Your panic-stricken fellow citizens can understand the divine wrath only as punishment for the most outrageous of sins in the highest places. Somehow the

21

scurrilous rumor starts to circulate that your beloved king Oedipus, who vigorously asserts his grievous concern about the health of his subjects, is himself unwittingly the horrific cause. It is whispered that he--well, you know the rest of the salacious report. While to us the Oedipus story is a heart-stopping psychological drama, to archaic peoples it quite possibly was essentially an etiological myth, revealing a horrifying cause for a devastating catastrophe.

(2) Ritual myth. Much of the English-speaking world faithfully reads the biblical account of the nativity or Dickens' "Christmas Carol" in the celebration of Christmas. Such a practice, combining a rite with a narrative, produces ritual myth. Almost as enigmatic as the hen-and-egg problem is the question whether ritual spawned myth or myth engendered ritual. Specialists in Middle Eastern mythology are especially led to consider most or even all myth as originated to accompany ritual; from Egypt to Mesopotamia much of the ancient body of myth is found in temple libraries and is closely associated with religious ritual. Elsewhere myth usually seems less tightly associated with specific rituals.

Nonetheless, ritual acts may be the wellspring of far more myth than the average observer might surmise. Hera delayed the birth of Heracles by tying knots and tying knots while Alcmene was in child-birth. Thereby Eurystheus was born first and sub-sequently, as the overlord of Heracles, commanded the famous twelve labors. Today's readers gloss over the ritual acts of Hera as merely a story device, but the consequences of Hera's knot-tying are truly momentous. Conceivably, the colossal tasks of Heracles were imagined or carefully attached to demonstrate the efficacy of the ritual. Knot-tying has an almost universal folk significance of restraining or thwarting an enemy. To prevent conception or child-birth the practice has been employed by the ancient Hebrews, the Yao of Africa, Galician peasants, and Moroccans.

(3) Heroic myth or prestige myth. All of us bask in reflected glory by recounting the superlative deeds of ancestors and supposed relatives, or the magnificent accomplishments by past notables of our tribe, community or nation. Canny Homer mentioned numerous places and people in the Iliad so that

practically anyone in the Greek world of his time could exultantly proclaim, "See, some of our chaps were in the Trojan fracas!" Especial prestige arises from an illustrious mythical atmosphere surrounding the founding fathers. The first king of Egypt was none other than the sun-god Re. In theory every ancient Mesopotamian city-state was the original property of its god. Probably an artisan of Ur could impress visitors by remarking that he leased his pottery factory from the god Nannar, while a burgher of Babylon could awe outsiders by reporting as his landlord the great deity Marduk. The founder of mighty Rome, Romulus, appropriately had an aristocratic mother in Rhea Silvia and a divine father in Mars, the god of war. The first king of Athens, Cecrops, was half-man, half-dragon. Although a mortal, Cadmus was the dragon-killing founder of the city of Thebes.

Myths of the giant founders and the glorious origins of any people are especially suspect of exaggeration or downright hoaxing. Modern scholars hazard that Ozolae Greeks along the north coast of the Corinthian Gulf obtained their designation from Oze, "bad smell," from sulphur springs in the area. Their own account ascribed an extraordinary bitch to King Orestheus. She gave birth to a wooden stick that Orestheus buried in the earth. The people of the community were named from the shoots (ozoi) surfacing from the buried stick. Orestheus also supposedly named his son Phytius ("Plant Man"). An interpreter of this myth can certainly dwell upon phallic symbol, vegetation motifs, possible plant totem, even tree deities; but it is difficult not to see a painfully labored attempt to evade the unsavory label of "the stinkers."

Some zealous students of mythology would exclude from the category of myth the tales of heroic supermen because herein the gods are not the central characters. Joseph Campbell, however, would assert the heroic quest as the monomyth, the one and central myth of which all others are segments.[41] The archaic heroic accounts truly breathe throughout the globe the heady air of the supernatural whether celebrating Wainamoinen of Finland, Ilya Murometz of Russia, Rama of India, Rustum of Persia, Gilgamesh of Erech, Dietrich of Bern, Maui of the Society Islands, Quetzalcoatl of Central America, and the numerous heroes of the Greek and all other mythologies. Homer is the prime example of how much energy and art have been expended in celebration of mythical heroes.

(4) Soteriological myth is the myth of saving,
of salvation. Etiological myth explains how humanity
got into its present plight, and eschatological myth
will promise a merciful end to contemporary woes. In
between the start and the finish it is reassuring and
necessary to have divine assistance to rescue us from
imminent disaster and miserable total failure.
Soteriological myth chronicles a momentous saving
which is explicitly or implicitly supernatural. The
saving may be quite physical and material, for
archaic man insisted upon a divinity that produced
practical results in the real world. Consider the
stratagem of the Trojan Horse which finally snatched
victory for the Greeks from a decade of frustration.
We might hazard that the wily Odysseus opportunis-
tically hired an itinerant siege platoon to breach
the walls of Troy with a battering ram. Myth,
however, deems the episode so awesome that it can be
explained only as shrewd advice from Pallas Athene,
the goddess of wisdom.

More palatable to the modern standards of salvation, soteriological myth can reveal spiritual salvation, perhaps most magnificently in the path of
Siddhartha towards enlightenment of the soul. The
Devas filled the universe with the concept of his
mission and guided him to the Bodhi tree; after
prolonged meditation in the lotus position he arose
as the Buddha, the enlightened one. Soteriological
myth also notes sorrowfully the tragic collapse of
would-be salvation. In the Babylonian account Adapa
is offered the bread of life and the water of life in
the celestial court of Anu, god of heaven, but,
forewarned by his father Ea, he refuses and thereby
forfeits the boon of immortality.

Contemporary man is most likely to seek his
salvation in medical research and in the Gross
National Product, but many people still claim
specific divine guidance in marriage partners,
health, business transactions, and multitudinous
other actions. Archaic myth details numerous
examples of soteriology, often as powerful and
beautiful as the gifts of Prometheus to benighted
mankind or the reassembly of the fragments of Osiris
by Isis and her restoration of Osiris to life. If
archaic societies had known dikes, the famous little
Dutch boy with his finger preventing a flood would
have been inspired to the deed by a goddess of earth
or of the household, or the lad could have been
transformed into some ministering god benignly

repelling the sea merely by a determined divine digit.

(5) <u>Prophetic</u> <u>myth</u> and <u>eschatological</u> <u>myth</u>. What is past has been mythologized vigorously, but what might lie ahead in this world and what might be occurring in a spirit realm above have fascinated mythologizers even more, as they grasp the imaginative possibilities of vision and prediction. Of all myth the prophetic and eschatological myths are declaimed with the most intense conviction and can achieve the most hypnotic effects upon listeners. These myths are also the most remote from human experience and usually the most heavily laden with symbology.

Unlike mysticism, prophetic myth is an external vision: "With mine own eyes I saw this glory," "The Great God called to me from his throne and spoke thus." The American Plains Indians especially cultivated prophetic myth, some tribes even demanding that male initiates experience visions of Old Man Coyote or Thunderbird to be admitted to manhood. The prophets of Old Israel constitute the most impressive national group of such visionaries--Isaiah,[42] Jeremiah, Ezekiel, David and a host of lesser prophets. Zoroaster of Persia, Shankara of India, and Mahomet of Arabia continued the tradition of prophetic myth. Today narration and imaginative visions are often minimized in favor of spiritual meditation as in "The Prophet," Kahlil Gibran. In secular guise, however, prophetic myth is rampant today as science fiction, perhaps the strongest claimant to "myth of the 20th century." Traditionally the "dreamtime" of myth has been the remote past; hosts of modern myth-makers from Jules Verne to Ray Bradbury are projecting our "dreamtime" of myth to the future.

Eschatological myth is prophetic vision carried to the ultimate, for eschatology treats of "last" things as etiology treats of "first" things. The "last" things may assign individual humans to final eternal positions in an afterworld or may consider the ultimate end of the world and the cosmos. In either case eschatological myth differs from prophetic myth in positing a rigid, static finality, a changeless condition in contrast to the unceasing change of the world we know.

"Last" things for individual humans, according to eschatological myth, mean an afterlife, predicated by most archaic societies. The simplest state seems to be that of ancestral spirits, as among the Nandi of Africa, who announce their presence by the otherwise unexplained little creakings and whisperings about every dwelling; such spirits devote their entire existence to no more than an occasional trivial prank or a sip of unattended beer. From here we branch in two directions, either to more and more profound involvement by spirits of the dead in the affairs of the living or to increasingly complex allocation of the dead to realms of eternal reward and punishment. The sense of omnipresent ancestral spirits eventuates in the Chinese ancestor worship, the oldest and most persistent feature of Chinese religion. Designating eternal residence for deceased spirits will build up to the awesomely complete system of Dante in the Divine Comedy with elaborately appropriate handling discriminated to the exact drop of earthly virtue or sin.

"Last" things for the earth, even the entire cosmos, fall into two categories: catastrophe or death-and-resurrection. If etiology ushers in this world gloriously, eschatology uniformly insists upon ending this world disastrously. The macabre imagination of mythologizing man seemed to exhaust every possibility of destruction: fire or ice, bang or whimper, monstrous eruptions from the depths, scourges on the surface, invasions from outer space. Our era produces its own variants in ecological exhaustion and pollution, nuclear explosion, even robot insurrection. Archaic man frequently denied any "natural" death, ascribing all extinction to violence, and as the individual life is violently terminated so is the entire cosmos. Perhaps all of these destructions are possibilities, but mankind seems rather morbid, rather suicidal, in its intense preoccupation with multifold obliteration. A more encouraging, though perhaps less likely scenario, is the pattern of death-and-resurrection. As the individual is conceived of as dying from this imperfect state to assume (possibly) a state of perfection, so the entire earth or cosmos can similarly perish in its present form only to emerge in a different and ecstatically radiant perfection. Note that eschatology never imagines a new cosmos emerging from the shards of this stricken universe to be a carbon copy of this world or a worse world. Apparently St. John wrote the Apocalypse during a

26

period of Christian persecution. Millions of readers have been exalted by his stupendous revelation of William Blake-like conflict and devastation from whence "a new heaven and a new earth" majestically rise like the Russian national anthem out of the Napoleonic turmoil of Tschaikowsky's 1812 Overture. Similarly elevating is the Götterdämmerung or Ragnarok of Northern mythology which brutally wipes out all the living gods as well as villains only to announce triumphantly a whole new age and whole new cosmos emerging in scintillating glory, keynoted by the revivified Balder, the shining Apollo of the North. The grandeur of this death-and-resurrection theme still grips men even when shorn of its supernatural lustre. The Marxian dialectic is a secularization of this noble theme, postulating the inevitable bloody revolution and subsequently the anarchic reign of perfection beyond.[43]

Much time and ink have been lavished by learned folk on whether specific myths originated at one point in the world and spread from there to the antipodes or whether specific myths arose independently in many areas of the globe.

The first theory is the Diffusion (or Migration) theory. The 17th century proponents of this idea, Bochart, Kircher, Marsham, and John Spencer, their eyes and hearts fixed irrevocably upon the Judeo-Christian scriptures, avowed that all myth everywhere was simply a corruption and misunderstanding of the ancient Hebrew scriptures. Belatedly Jacob Bryant in a six-volume New System (1807) tried to reassert this antiquated theory. It is Bryant whom George Eliot had in mind when in Middlemarch she portrayed the utter futility of Casaubon in assembling a universal mythological study centered on the Jewish origin of all myth.

Diffusionists in the 19th century took a different tack as Western knowledge of other cultures sizably increased. Theodor Benfey, awed by the fertile literature of India, suggested the spread of tales from India throughout the world. William Perry and G. Elliot Schmidt were Pan-Egyptionists, declaring that from the Nile came the world's great stock of stories.

Diametrically opposed to the Diffusionist theory is the concept of Polygenesis, i.e. independent origin. Adolf Bastian in the 19th century was the chief advocate of this theory. Arguing from a Darwinian viewpoint, Bastian asserted that the psychic as well as physical unity of mankind meant the production in every society of "elementary ideas" (Elementargedanken). Since the human organism everywhere is uniform, so uniform will be the broad myths of all humanity.[44] Edward Tylor and Sir James Frazer concurred, and more recently Claude Lévi-Strauss has suggested that all myths "can be reduced to a small number of simple types," a few elementary functions.[45]

A sort of compromise is offered by postulating an independent origin for a myth in several scattered parts of the world and then the diffusion of the myth. The "Culture Circle School" (Kulturkreislehre) with Wilhelm Schmidt as its leading figure attempted to trace the diffusion of myth from clusters or complexes of basic cultural elements at separate points of origin thence to other areas over space and time. This school has not been very active since the 1930's, but the "Historical-Geographic School" or "Finnish School" continues active study and publication. Kaarle Krohn, C.W. von Sydow, and Axel Obrik seek to locate the birthplace of a myth and then carefully trace the routes of diffusion and the stages of modification.

Unquestionably some diffusion can be proved. The Amerindian had no knowledge of horses until the coming of Europeans, but some Amerindians have now incorporated the horse into their creation myths. Asmodeus, from the Book of Tobit, is a standard Christian demon derived from Aeshmadaeva of ancient Iran. The tale of "Barlaam and Josaphat" c. 700 from St. Johannes Damascenus (or Chrysorrhoas) is rather obviously the account of Gautama Buddha, the very name Josaphat a corruption of Bodhisattva. The Greek Orthodox Church on 27 November still venerates Josaphat, the Indian Buddha, as a Christian worthy. Some Indologists even claim that Christianity is altogether a westernized version of Buddhism.[46] West may also influence East, as Indologists suggest the possibility of the Indian Shri-Lakshmi cult resulting from the introduction of Pallas Athene by Indo-Greek kings from early 2nd century B.C.[47]

We are now certainly in the arena of keen dispute, as note these myths:

The Meru of Kenya state that their culture hero Mugive led the Meru people out of bondage across a sea that parted for them and eventually brought them to a promised land. Mugive possessed a magic staff and transmitted to the Meru seven commandments vouchsafed to him by god.

Tahiti myth states that Ta'aroa, the creator-god, put the first man to sleep and then extracted from his body a bone (ivi) from which Ta'aroa formed the first woman.

Most Jews and Christians would immediately leap to the conclusion that these myths are borrowings from the Hebrew scriptures, but there is really no clear-cut evidence for either diffusion or polygenesis.

Less likely to involve any prejudice are the extraordinary statues of Easter Island, long the subject of puzzled discussion. There are two other places in the world that have produced similar statues--the former Kafiristan (called Nuristan since Islamization) in Afghanistan and some remote scattered parts of the Sumatra jungle. These three locales are so separated (Central Asia, Indonesia, and the lonely Pacific west of Chile) that no one has proposed diffusion to explain these similarities. Here as generally in the diffusion vs. polygenesis debate there is infinitely more discussion than conclusive evidence.

Dante explicitly states that there are four levels (literal, allegorical, moral, and anagogical) of interpretation to be applied to the Divine Comedy, and Dante determinedly incorporated all four in every line of the poem. One would like to believe that certainly in Myth I there is no such supersubtle Italianizing, but we may underestimate archaic societies. Among the Piaroa of southern Venezuela the mythical narratives make scanty sense even to most native listeners, who, however, display utmost respect for the myths, resolutely affirm that the myths are true and extremely important, and sincerely praise the religious leader for his excellent presentation. Initiates into the secret religious cult of the Piaroa assert their understanding of the myths, but there are still mythical accounts genuinely understood only by the narrator himself.[48] Perhaps this is customary obfuscation by religious specialists to enhance their mystery and prestige, but it is also possible that archaic societies, dwelling for generations upon sacred myth with intelligence every whit as high as any normal human, might eventually rival Dante in complex interpretation.

The Vedas of India probably represent the oldest mythological material of the Indo-European peoples, dating from 1500-1000 B.C. One would expect relative simplicity here, but actually the Vedas presuppose a three-tiered audience like that of the Piaroa Amerindians. Consider in the Rigveda the mythological figure of Aditi ("not limited"). To the humble plebeian Aditi means the divine mother, the sacred fecundity of womanhood. To the educated, Aditi means freedom from the bondage of the material world and its incessant suffering or emblemizes, as the name of the goddess indicates, infinity. To the spiritually minded few, the esoteric minority, Aditi means the unity of the human soul with total undifferentiated reality.[49]

Actually, most Myth I, at least, has the interpretation problem not so much of varying levels as of varying stances of observation. The multitude of theories in subsequent chapters will indeed indicate many ways of viewing and thereby interpreting a specific myth. We are really groping in trying to explain archaic myth. One might expect the commentators of classic antiquity to know what their living myth was truly about, but they were almost always dealing with narratives extensively modified from archaic sources. Besides, they insisted on a rational approach to material often opaque to mere reason, and they frequently made their "interpretation" actually an extraneous philosophical or other propaganda piece.

Consider the Egyptian myth of the brutal struggle between Horus and Set (uncle of Horus on his father's side by some accounts and on his mother's side by other accounts). The ghost of his slain father Osiris appeared in a dream to Horus and urged him to drive Set out of the kingdom. After back-and-forth conflict Horus routed Set, mutilating his uncle and losing an eye to Set in the melee. The god Thoth miraculously healed both Horus and Set. The latter appeared before the divine council to claim the throne of Egypt, but the gods awarded the kingdom to Horus as the rightful ruler. We can never know exactly how an Egyptian of the time of Rameses V interpreted this myth, but we can conjecture (roughly in order of complexity):

Humor, even to the point of coarseness. This interpretation is not obvious from the summary above, but the embellishments of the original version permit the passage of arms to evoke raucous soldier laughter. Especially, the complete healing of both Horus and Set can reduce the whole tale to a caper with a happy ending.

Overpowering of wicked usurper uncle by valiant young hero. This was a familiar folk theme long before Hamlet.

Historic joining of northern Egypt (Lower Egypt under Horus) and southern Egypt (Upper Egypt under Set).

Patrilineal succession supersedes matrilineal succession (if Set is the maternal uncle). In matrilineal succession a brother logically succeeds a brother (as both are offspring of the queen), while in a patrilineal succession son succeeds father. The myth implies such a change in the ruling of the divine council for Horus.

Sacred revelation in dream. Horus would have difficulty in justifying his attack on Set, especially if his cause were traditionally deemed wrong. In vision, however, he receives sanction that arguments and persuasions could not affect.

Ritual struggle of good vs. evil, day vs. night, New Year vs. Old Year, and other pairs of opposites. The Middle East seems routinely to have had an acting out of such a conflict ritualistically. The myth may arise as an explanation or concretization of the ritual.

Homosexuality. Psychoanalysts perceive in the relishing of contact and especially mutilation of each other (again more extensive in original account) a homosexual propensity with strong sadism-masochism tendencies.

Structuralist analysis of opposites in age, geography, and, most of all, culture (legitimacy) vs. nature (brute strength).[50]

Perhaps an ancient Egyptian favored an interpretation not listed above, or possibly he accepted more than one of the interpretations above, for these interpretations are generally complementary, not conflicting. Most likely, he undertook no conscious probing of the myth but accepted the narrative with reverential awe and acknowledged it as divine truth, leaving the zealous search for the meaning of the myth to the later Greeks and ultimately to our inquiring age.

Have Myth I and Myth II died? Are they a closed book, opened only occasionally when, for instance, this space age wants names of fire gods for volcanoes on Jupiter's satellite Io: Amirani (Russian Georgia), Marduk (Mesopotamia), Masubi (Japan), Pele (Hawaii), Prometheus (Greece)? One may happily report that in India, the most prolific of all myth originators, the process of mythmaking actively continues apace today. Charles P. Mountford reports a myth involving a bloodwood tree that was very much alive in 1978 at Piltadi in central Australia. Area aborigines say that a wanambi (mythical serpent) had a human wife who was digging for food with her sharpened digging stick. Startled by the sudden appearance of her reptile husband, she hurled the digging stick at him and ran. With the stick projecting from his flank, the wanambi pursued and swallowed her. The serpent was transformed into the tree which photographs show grotesquely distended in its lower trunk with a protruding dead branch resembling a spear thrust into the tree.[51] An existing myth might have been applied to the extraordinary tree, but the singular appropriateness suggests specific creation to fit this recent object. Updating occurs even in archaic myth. The Lacandon Maya of Central America now assert that their supreme deity, Kyantho, is the creator of automobiles and airplanes.[52]

32

Chapter II
The Beginnings to the Nineteenth Century

Early Manifestations

Man is a mythmaking creature. Regardless of the
millions of years now ascribed to hominids, our
species cannot be regarded as truly human before
articulate speech. Ernst Cassirer points out that
language and myth have a common source and are
subject to constant interplay.[1] Until man could
produce significant pictorial representation (as
distinguished from early squiggles), which is
inconceivable without articulate speech, we must make
deductions from often cryptic remains. Cautious
archeologists and pre-historians such as Stuart
Piggott and Sir Mortimer Wheeler refuse to make any
deductions from meager artefacts. Some speculative
anthropologists such as Johannes Maringer believe
that early man lived an intensely mythico-religious
life. Raymond Dart, examining the bones in a humanid
midden dating c. 600,000 B.C., finds remarkable
parallels to the cult of cave-bear skulls in later
Alpine caves.[2] Man is the only creature to bury his
dead, and we interpret burial as indicating belief in
some form of life after death, a genuinely mythical
concept. The oldest known human burials belong to
the middle Paleolithic Age, c. 100,000 B.C. Placements of bear skulls from approximately the same era
suggest either sacrifice to some deity or a means of
resurrecting the animal through "skeleton magic" (or
"bone magic").[3]

The cave paintings of the upper Paleolithic
period, c. 30,000 B.C., notably in Spain and southern
France, awesomely reveal an extensive mythical
atmosphere. Theorists have regularly suggested that
the animal representations, some of superb artistry,
are for magical purposes, to plead to the Lord or
Lady of the Beasts for more game animals or to
represent some religious cult of man's hunting-
nomadic culture. Almost certainly Isador H. Coriat
was correct in conjecturing that early man regarded
the cave as the womb of the Earth Mother; the animal
paintings hopefully implant in her capacious womb the
animals that men want the Earth Mother to produce in
abundance for human hunters.[4]

Less frequently depicted are humans. If
ithyphallic they are certainly representative of a
fertility cult. Often the humans have animal
attributes, are half-man half-beast, or wear animal

masks. Especially intriguing is the startling figure
of "The Sorcerer of Lourdes," apparently a man
disguised as a deer. Probably the figure is a hunter
in a deer dance preparatory to a hunt, much as the
Mandan Amerindians and others wore buffalo horns and
hides in a ritual before the hunt. Possibly the
figure represents a shaman ceremonially summoning the
prey, or even the Lord of the Beasts himself, the
deer-god who will provide ample prey for his true
devotees. The man-beasts such as centaurs and satyrs
of much later myth obviously have a very long ancestry.

Perhaps the most bizarre of the cave paintings
present figures combining two animals, e.g. a bear
with a wolf head. These are clearly the prototypes
of much later mythological mixtures such as the
hippogriff. "Outlandish" we would label such
mythical beings, for in analytical fashion we rigidly
distinguish between the natural and the supernatural,
between the waking and dreaming, between the factual
and the imaginary. Early man probably was more the
synthesist who put everything together, merging
natural and supernatural, waking and dreaming, the
factual and the imaginary. Note that the masked
figures of archaic dances and mummers did not
represent gods but to the awestruck audience were the
actual gods.

The earliest human society was certainly food-
gathering. Armed only with hands and teeth, and
dependent upon his legs for mobility, man was no
match for the speed and strength of many other
animals. Fruits, nuts, berries, vegetables upon
plants or in roots, honey, and grubs could be
supplemented by mussels and other seacoast pickings,
with eggs, a lucky kill of some small animal, and
scavenging when larger animals had gorged from a
slain prey. The deities of such a society were
almost certainly female, the source of all fertility.
The male role in procreation was apparently
unrecognized. In primitive societies a girl usually
engages in sexual intercourse well before puberty, as
early as six or seven years. A woman's fertility
will end in her mid-30's under arduous conditions,
though intercourse will continue. Consequently, for
quite some years of a primitive woman's life there
will be no conception. Since the gestation period of
humans is nine months, primitive man long failed to
realize that an event three-quarters of a year before
is responsible for the childbirth occurring today.

Growing self-consciousness, strongly nurtured by maturing language, realized that only the years of menstruation permitted conception and led to acknowledgement of the male function in fertilization. The great impetus to male deities first arose from the prestigious position of the male in the hunting period when his weapons made him, at least collectively, a match for saber-toothed tigers and woolly rhinoceri. Now come the Lord of the Beasts and a host of male-gods. Such male dominance was further enhanced in the nomadic cultures where males tended the flocks of cattle, sheep, reindeer. The myths of the hunting-herding age stressed in the hero the individual prowess and personal achievement of the male.

An agricultural society strongly reinforced the basic earth mother, the generatrix of all life. The archaic Mediterranean society before the invasion of the Indo-Europeans was almost devoid of male gods, but has bequeathed multitudes of female statuettes.[5] The aboriginal Dravidian population of India was devoted to the Earth Mother under numerous names. Scholars have sought to find male gods in the Indus River Valley civilization, but certainly the female divinities were overwhelmingly predominant. The myths of such a society demand conformity to a fixed social, economic, and political system. In an agricultural civilization the individualistic hero of the hunting society must be modified to an instrument of social service; the labors of Heracles are consequently portrayed as largely for the benefit of the community.[6]

A great division, therefore, within myth is chronological, between the earlier preeminence of the matriarchal goddess and the later emergence of the patriarchal god. Further, a notable distinction separates the mythical visions of East and West. Joseph Campbell, in terms of analytical psychology, reports the human ego scorned by India as delusion, properly obliterated; the West, however, exalts the conscious ego over the unconscious, even pre-human, id.[7] Géza Róheim proffers a psychoanalytic explanation of this dichotomy by suggesting that India has genitalized the entire body and seeks in contemplation to establish union with the Infinite (to Róheim the libido or total life force), while the West directs its libido upon outer objects and powerfully espouses materialism.[8] In conventional terminology one may venture that the Indian myth[9] searches inner depths, while the Western myth looks to outward events and objects. Of course this is a very rough generalization, but it definitely indicates that, while there are numerous points of similarity, the myths of East and West cannot be measured by the same yardstick.

Karl Jaspers labels as the Axial Period of history the 8th to 9th centuries B.C. In all the higher civilizations he diagnoses the passing of the Mythical Period into the modern consciousness and self-consciousness of rational man.[10] The all-important point here is that mythical thinking has been the standard pattern of humanity universally for all the countless millenia up until the 8th century B.C.[11] Since the 8th century B.C. non-mythical thinking has become highly significant and to many greatly beneficial, but it is relatively recent in the long history of mankind and is still very far from total triumph.[12]

Thales (c. 640-596 B.C.) is generally designated as the world's first philosopher in the modern sense.[13] No works of his have survived, and we must depend upon later ascriptions. Reputedly he proclaimed water as the first and universal principle. It is tempting but dangerous to assert that herein first appears the break from older mythical thinking to modern rationalism. The concept of Thales would now be totally dismissed if he had stated that Oceanus and his kingdom were primal and basic. Actually his theory seems a restatement of the creation myth that the primordial waters preceded all else. Thales is uttering the mythical plea for unity (monism) and the mythical start with the amniotic fluid where every human organism begins life. Aristotle actually looks like the first genuine rationalist in our modern vein, while all the previous Greek philosophers from Thales and his fellow Milesians through Plato are still thinking mythically, still, as Jean Piaget states, mining the childhood mind. Thales and his fellows did, however, make notable strides:

First, semantically they break away from the mythological language and the personalized forces of nature. Their mind-set and expression truly facilitate philosophy and science by freeing ideas from alleged deities and from the aition.

36

Second, they break the cake of custom of archaic society. Myth for traditional societies has been a consistently powerful force to freeze everything as it was in alcheringa (Dreamtime of Australian aborigines) or, when change cannot be withstood, to trumpet that the innovation is really not new at all but implicit since the beginning--and unobtrusively revise the myth. The Milesian philosophers dramatically opened the way to a dynamic intellectual life, a wide-ranging questioning transforming the world of man.

For two millenia readers have delighted in just such explorations in the Platonic dialogues; nonetheless, it is necessary to realize that Plato was not really the first modern philosopher but the crowning glory of archaic and mythic thought. His most famous passages are mythical: Atlantis, the cave, Er. Above all his assertion of reality as existing solely in the spirit realm, while the material world is illusion, stems directly from the primitive mythical mind. The Platonic idea seems obviously rooted in the Divine Goanna behind all the individual flesh-and-blood goannas.[14] Plato was still so dependent upon mythical concepts that he could not break through to a linear theory of history but espoused the archaic cyclic theory.[15]

NATURE ALLEGORY (celebration of external nature). Thales is credited with the first theory about mythology, interpreting myths as allegories of natural phenomena, and mythical beings as the personification of natural events or mythopoeic labels for elements of nature. Thus, the myth of Demeter and Persephone depicts the regular recurrence of winter and summer. The crashing of thunderbolts seems the bravado display of some colossal being, Zeus the thunderer. The dawn is personified as Eo, the winds as Aeolus. Grain deities abound in every mythology. Americans are fond of vestiges of this practice, elaborately designating an attractive nubile young lady "Miss Idaho Potato" or "Miss Cucumber of 1983."

The outwardly directed mind of the Westerner shines in Thales and his approach to myth. For more than two millenia thereafter theorizers of Western society will continue to ponder the meaning of mythology with the easy Thales assumption that all myth arises from man's observation of the outward world. So convincing proved the Thales concept that

37

other Greek thinkers such as Epicharmus, Theagenes of Rhegion, and Pythagoras agreed with the nature allegory concept. Socrates is quoted in the _Phaedrus_ as derogating the notion,[16] but in the questioning of Meletus in the _Apology_[17] Socrates strongly implies that he accepts Helios as the sun-god and Selene as the moon-goddess. Anaxagoras of Clazomenae, to whom Socrates ascribes the accusations of Meletus, had been earlier banished from Athens for averring that the sun was a burning stone and the moon a chunk of earth.

The nature allegory theory has had advocates ever since Thales. In the 19th century the solar myth,[18] especially with the support of Max Müller, reached a crescendo. Ingenious analyzers saw every mythical conflict as the sun against the demons of darkness and every heroic myth as the sun rising to its zenith and then tragically falling to its nadir. Émile Senart suggested that the entire account of Buddha, especially the "turning of the wheel of the Law," was another solar myth.[19] In this century Leo Frobenius has strongly advocated the sun as the chief source of African and other mythologies. _The Epic of Gilgamesh_, although seemingly a collection of tales, has been suggested as the journey of the sun through the zodiac. Myth of the solar disc has been the major emphasis, but the rays of the sun have been suggested as the hair of Samson. James C. Moloney claims that this and many other biblical references refer to the sun's rays.[20] Certainly the Greek account of Zeus visiting Danaë in a shower of gold sounds like sunlight impregnating the earth mother. The arrows of Apollo are frequently deemed the rays of the sun. It is hard to deny considerable validity to the solar myth, but exaggerated claims have caused most scholars today to shy away.[21]

Apparently early man employed a lunar calendar earlier than the less obvious solar calendar, and thus may have focussed upon the moon. Lunar myth is unquestionably extensive, but only since the 19th century has the moon been made preeminent. The Society for the Comparative Study of Myth, founded in Berlin in 1900 with a host of impressive members, ascribed most myth to the moon. The many indistinct features on the moon and its rapidly succeeding phases offer elaborate material for myth. It has been suggested that in the nursery rhyme Jack is the waxing moon and Jill the waning moon, "tumbling after" is the successive disappearance of moon spots with waning, and the water they went to fetch is dependence of rainfall on phases of the moon.[22] The love story of Artemis and Endymion is one of the most romantic of moon myths. Probably the overwhelming majority of myths involving twelve are indebted to the moon. Oriental scholars see the lunar theme as powerful in Asiatic mythology. John Tu Er-Wei asserts, "All of Buddhism and Taoism is based on the moon-mythology systems."[23]

Cloud formations, wind, and sky colors have had their advocates as major celestial sources of myth. The struggle of Indra against Shushna ("the witherer") indeed looks like the desperately sought thunderstorm with fertilizing rains overcoming the searing dry season of India. Many other myths are susceptible to the nature-allegory theory. In Teutonic myth Frey woos Gerda, who promises to wed him in nine days. Gerda is a frost giantess wooed by Spring. The nine days probably correspond to the nine chilly months of the north. Her union with Frey is the surrender of frost to the fertilizing and blossoming warmth of springtime.

MORAL ALLEGORY (ethical admonition and conventional "wisdom"). Those who apply the moral-allegory theory postulate a conscious intent in mythmakers to use a narrative to inculcate social and personal moral precepts. Obviously didactic is heroic myth to persuade impressionable youths to emulate the valorous men of the past. Most archaic myth (Myth I), however, does not clearly offer a specific moral premise. Of course, it is clear from Chapter 17 of the Book of the Dead that the ancient Egyptians were employing a moral-allegorical interpretation at least from the middle of the second millenium B.C., but the Nile civilization of that era was some distance beyond archaic societies.

A growing self-conscious and inquisitive mind-set will probe for veiled meanings even if they really are not there. By the 5th century B.C. the Greeks were interpreting Homer's works as moral allegory. This tradition, since Hellenistic culture dominated the eastern Mediterranean, induced Jewish scholars to the moral-allegory treatment of such themes as the serpent tempting Eve and the Tower of Babel. Philo Judaeus of Alexandria, about the start of the Christian era, zealously applied this theory. Christian scholars followed this Greco-Hebrew practice with St. Paul setting the example, and

39

Clement, Origen and others continuing. St. Bernard's interpretation of the Song of Songs as the wedding of Christ to his church is probably the most noted example.

The major stream of moral-allegory treatment of myth begins with the Stoic philosophers headed by Zeno of Citium who in the late 4th century B.C. strongly espoused the moral interpretation. Urban Greece of this period was at least as civilized as the 18th century of our era, which also employed human slavery. Perhaps it was more civilized than our era, for while we suspend the Olympic games because of war, the ancient Greeks suspended war to permit the scheduled Olympic games. Zeno and refined Greeks like him were appalled at the savagery and the bestiality extensive in archaic myth. They simply could not literally accept the bloody butchery, the cannibalism, and the incest rampant in archaic myth. Consider the story of Kronos swallowing each of his own children as Rhea bore them (Goya in 1817 painted a nightmarish canvas of the ghoulish deity ravenously devouring his children). Aha, shouted the Stoics, Kronos is close to the Greek word Chronos which means "time" (as in chronology, chronometer, etc.). Therefore, they stated exultantly, the myth is not at all about a demoniacal being gulping down his own offspring. It is the strongest possible statement that "time devours all things." Supporters of this theory argue that the original concocters of myth realized that unadorned moral admonition would be shrugged off, but that narratives with potent shock effect would long be transmitted and would insure the constant inculcation of a wise moral. A high percentage of sensitive and thoughtful ancients accepted this theory. It was applied in mounting quantity and supersubtlety, climaxing in the fantastically elaborate allegory developed by Orphism.[24] A rather simple Orphic interpretation is to see the death and resurrection of Dionysus as initial overpowering of the soul by sensual and material compulsions (Titans) and then the rebirth to a nobler and more spiritual life through the intervention of divine power (Zeus).

Allegory may possibly be applicable to a work like the Ramayana. Its supposed poet is the 3rd century B.C. Valmiki who seems more flesh-and-blood than the legendary Homer[25] and who lived in an India more culturally advanced and self-conscious than the world of Homer. Conceivably Valmiki may have thought of Rāma as the human soul successfully traversing delusion (the forest) and slaying passion and hatred (Rāvana and Vālin) finally to be united with peace and beauty (Sīta). Still another interpretation proposes Rāma as god (an avatar of Vishnu) and his brother Lakshmana as the human soul seeking god and thereby attaining true grace.[26]

When we come to a relatively sophisticated state of culture, wherein Myth II dominates, an interpretation of moral allegory is quite feasible. The Eros-Psyche myth is late in classic Greece and clearly points the moral of true union of love and the human soul. The Baucis and Philemon account is obviously a morality lesson in hospitality and faithfulness. Thor, the mighty god of the north, was thrown to one knee by the old nurse Elli; i.e. age weakens and overpowers all. Zoroaster in Iran assigned as companions of Ahura Mazda the Amesha Spentas: Vohu Manah ("good mind"), Arta ("good order"), Xshathra ("dominion"), Ārmaiti ("devotion"), Haurvatāt ("welfare"), Ameratāt ("immortality"). It sounds like the cast of characters for a rather stuffy medieval morality play.

The theory of moral allegory salved the sensibilities of ancient man, medieval man, and modern man until recently. Thomas Bulfinch gave prominent place to this theory in his famous Age of Fable (1855).[27] Today we might confidently declare that moral allegory appears frequently in Myth II but seldom in Myth I.

INTELLECTUAL ALLEGORY (scientific or pseudo-scientific knowledge, profound esoteric truths). The mystagogues among the Piaroa Amerindians heighten their prestige by suggesting wondrous revelations behind their mythical accounts. Proponents of the intellectual-allegory theory seriously accept such a claim. The intellectual-allegory thesis appeals particularly to proponents of the degeneration theory (and most ancients postulated such a decline from earlier heights of wisdom); they wanted to believe in profound, hidden truths imparted by our forefathers. Magazine advertisements today frequently proclaim books and cult groups that assert their penetration of "occult knowledge of the ancients," i.e. maintaining in our times this theory of intellectual allegory applied to works of the distant past.

41

Among the ancient Greeks the Orphic cult was flourishing at least as early as the 6th century B.C., and more than any other group this cult fostered the interpretation of myth as intellectual allegory. Orphic doctrine perceived Vulcan as the eternal creative and formative power (cf. Brahma), Venus as the eternal preserver (Vishnu), and Mars as the ceaseless destroyer (Shiva); all three cosmic forces are indispensable and ceaselessly operating. As far as Myth I is concerned, this theory looks wholly untenable, and Myth II from Greco-Roman antiquity scarcely justifies any such approach. The Orphic cult appeared to its devotees as revealing many profound truths, and perhaps it did, but the truths were of the cult's own devising and are not genuinely ascribable to archaic myth.

Not myth but hermetic writings of considerably advanced societies are the proper subject matter for the intellectual-allegory theory. Alchemical writings of the middle ages, for example, made frequent reference to the eagle and the serpent. This theme is familiar in myth, where the eagle clearly suggests the etherial, the heavenly, and the serpent represents the earthbound, the chthonic. Alchemical literature, however, intends the eagle to represent mercury and the serpent, sulphur. Such is a valid interpretation of alchemy as intellectual allegory, but this approach is not valid for archaic myth.

Many late stories are genuine allegory, not properly designated as myth. For example, Sambandha (c. 639), an Indian Shaivite saint, accompanied by Appar, a musician of the untouchable class, found securely locked the door to the shrine of Vedaraniam. Tradition said that the Vedas (the early sacred writings in Sanskrit) had slammed the door shut after worshipping Shiva's image. Sambandha prayed and in Tamil language Appar sang. Miraculously the door swung open to admit all. Like virtually all accounts conceived as intellectual allegories, this story obviously betrays itself. In the classic tongue of Sanskrit, the Vedas had barred most of India from divine knowledge. Sambandha and Appar open divine revelation to all peoples.

Heraclitus in the 6th century B.C. interpreted myth as intellectual allegory, e.g. the account of Zeus binding Hera means that the ether is the limit of the air. Since Zeno, founder of the Stoic School, had advocated the theory of moral allegory, logically Chrysippus (3rd century B.C.), major formulator of stoicism for antiquity, supported the concept of intellectual allegory, reducing the Greek gods to physical and chemical reactions. This intellectual-allegory principle was invoked by the Greeks for other mythologies. In the 1st century A.D. Plutarch interpreted the myth of the Egyptian Isis to harmonize with the mystical Platonism of his day. Such tendencies were widespread in the early centuries of the Christian era. Julian ("the Apostate") in the 4th century declared that the castration of the Asiatic Attis represented the cosmic checking of the unlimited. Henceforth a creative and symmetrical Providence would restrict all generation to definite and consistent forms.

Allegory was extensively utilized by medieval and Renaissance writers; Renaissance Humanists frequently assumed, therefore, that ancient myth was equally allegorical. Natale Conti in Mythologiae sive Explicationum Fabularum[28] (1551) asserted that the Greek myths were simply the noted classic philosophies attired in allegorical costume. We may extol Francis Bacon as an innovator in science, but in myth interpretation he continnes the hoary intellectual-allegory tradition. De Sapientia Veterum[29] (1609) by Bacon deems the claws of the Sphinx the axioms and arguments of science grasping and holding the mind. Bacon considers Perseus the emblem of war, and his attack upon the only mortal amongst the Gorgons is shrewd council to undertake only wars that offer likely prospects of victory. The sober Bacon thus showed himself as imaginative as any of the poets.[30] Though wrongly conceived, this theory of intellectual allegory assured many Renaissance and subsequent thinkers that myth was not to be dismissed as fantasy but warranted sober, meticulous study.

RATIONAL DISMISSAL OR IGNORING OF MYTH. In brushing aside myth and deities or in straight-forwardly denying their validity, rationalists are definitely interpreting mythical thought and deeming it profitless fantasy. Perhaps the earliest public avowal of philosophical materialism is the Indian Cārvāka School (c. 600 B.C.), one of the three "heterodox" Hindu doctrines.[31] Though long a philosophic ferment, Cārvāka was rather inimical to standard Indian thought and can be reconstructed solely from subsequent writings. Far more influential has been the Chinese Confucius (6th century B.C.). Blandly he shrugged off myth and the entire supernatural in favor of this world exclusively. His emphasis is upon humanity, reverence for the ancient sages, and government by personal integrity. Certainly he was in tune with basic Chinese pragmatism, but his immense reputation effectively directed Chinese intellectuals away from interest in and speculation about myth, leaving Taoism and Buddhism to commonality and reducing the official religion (often mislabeled Confucianism) to a pro forma ritual. Ironically in the official Chinese religion Confucius was accorded the veneration appropriate to a deity.

Greek rationality about some myth appears as early as Homer (c. 800 B.C.?). The Sirens, frequently depicted as bird-women in antiquity, are normal young women in Homer's account; and the centaurs of Homer are normal human males, not fabulous men-beasts.

More explicit and more the philosophical critic, Xenophanes of Colophon, about the same era as Confucius, denied any divine gifts to man and considered all the knowledge and technology of man a product of human thought and experiment. He scorned the anthropomorphic concepts of gods and in a famous passage suggested that horses would conceive of equine gods and oxen would worship divine cattle.[32]

Protagoras of Abdera (5th century B.C.) similarly perceived human institutions as purely human in origin, the interaction of man and his environment. Confucius would have nodded in polite agreement to the agnosticism of Protagoras: gods may or may not exist, and there is no way to be sure.

The chorus of Sophocles' Antigone (mid 5th century B.C.) in its paean to the glory of man agrees with Xenophanes that man has devised his language, his technology, his society.[33] All subsequent rationalists in the vein of Xenophanes have thus implicitly dismissed myth as vain fancy.

Epicurean philosophers were especially severe, belittling the myths as fabrications designed to bolster the authority of priests and kings. Rational 18th century philosophers like Voltaire concurred, and H.L. Mencken in this century has most vociferously attributed all religion to the power drives of crafty priests.

NON-THEISTIC RELIGION. Atheism is distinctly a recent Western phenomenon, associated with solid materialism and anti-religious fervor. With its essentially outward-directed mind the West generally assumes that religion is impossible without gods.[34] In India the inward-directed mind has often proved intensely religious, while dispensing with deities. The Buddha was himself non-theistic, though ironically he is a virtual deity in Mahayana Buddhism, the largest wing of the faith today. Theravada Buddhism is still non-theistic. Jainism, totally separate from Buddhism, is strongly non-theistic. Samkhya, one of the six "orthodox" Hindu philosophies, originated as non-theistic. Elitist Indian spiritual and intellectual thought has not dissected myth as has the West, but by its inward concentration and especially with a strong non-theistic tendency has subordinated myth, deeming it maya ("illusion"). Of course, in the popular mind of India myth flourishes as probably nowhere else.

EUHEMERISM. The theory that gods are deifications of actual human beings is named for Euhemerus (c. 300 B.C.) of Messene, but the concept had been long brewing in Greek thought. Prodicus (5th century B.C.) of Ceos suggested that the discoverers of useful arts had been elevated to divinity. Demeter, he declared, was the woman who had invented agriculture and thus became the goddess of grain, while Dionysus developed viniculture and hence was similarly deified.

"The father of history," Herodotus (5th century B.C.), might properly be credited with the first full-scale application of Euhemerism.[35] He asserted that Zalmoxis, a chthonic god of Thrace, had originally been a slave of the Greek philosopher Pythagoras. Returning to his homeland, Zalmoxis proclaimed himself a deity able to assure devotees of a happy afterlife. He convinced the credulous by spending three years in an underground chamber and then reappearing as a reborn god. Herodotus furthermore scrutinized the mythical account of Cyrus of Persia, reportedly suckled by a bitch. Herodotus explains this mythical passage as referring to the upbringing of Cyrus by a woman named or nicknamed Spako ("bitch"). In late Roman times euhemerism suggested that Romulus and Remus were actually nursed by a woman nicknamed Lupa ("she-wolf").

45

Sacred Writing by Euhemerus irrevocably fixed his name upon this theory. In a highly imaginative voyage to islands somewhere beyond Arabia, Euhemerus claimed to find Uranus, Kronos, and Zeus all buried in graves, for human beings and no more had they been. Euhemerism condescendingly smiles on human weakness which often exaggerates the exploits of the dead until they have been exalted to the stature of gods. Euhemerus saw the gods of Homer as confused memory or the imaginative transfiguration of deeds of primitive heroes.[36] The Latin poet Ennius (3rd-2nd century B.C.) produced a derivative work entitled Euhemerus, applying the concept especially to Roman deities.

Diodorus Siculus in the 1st century B.C. euhemerized the Cybele-Attis myth. Cybele was supposedly the mother and carnal lover of Attis. Learning of Cybele's pregnancy, her father slew Attis and the child of incest. Cybele roamed the world in desperate grief. Phrygia in Asia Minor, suffering from a devastating plague, was commanded to give ceremonial burial to the body of Attis and to worship Cybele as a goddess.

Actually, all the alleged examples of Euhemerism above seem erroneous to us today. Like many other theories, Euhemerism sprang from practices then current and unwisely was applied universally, especially to archaic myth. In classic Greek times Heracles, Ganymede, and Psyche were characters of myth specifically depicted as human beings who were deified. Among genuinely historic personages Euhemerism was a classic reality. Imhotep, chief minister of a pharaoh c. 2670 B.C. and builder of the first step pyramid of Egypt, was worshipped as a god and identified with Asclepius, the Greek god of medicine. Amenophis (c. 1400 B.C.) was also a high-ranking government official. Statues dedicated to Amenophis or a mortuary temple erected to him by a grateful pharaoh may have induced his deification. Especially during the Greco-Roman period his cult developed appreciably.

Gods and men were much closer in ancient days than in modern Judaism, Christianity, and Islam. Homeric kings claimed lineal descent from the gods. The deities constantly roamed the world in human guise. Properly awed today by a magnificent person, we will label him "god-like" or her "a veritable goddess." It is not a giant step beyond to name so

46

astounding a figure as Alexander the Great the son of
Amon-Re. Romulus was deified as Quirinus. Under the
Roman empire the Senate dutifully proclaimed each
emperor a god, though most intelligent persons
regarded this action as merely a device to aid
imperial solidarity.

Around the start of the Christian era Gnosti-
cism, various Mystery Cults, and even some early
Christians employed the idea of deification of humans
in the metaphoric sense of assimilation into the
deity or immediate communion with divinity. An impressive regiment of the early Church Fathers--
including Clement of Alexandria, Commodian,
Lactantius, Arnobius, Firmicus Maternus, and others--
vociferously supported standard Euhemerism because it
denied any godhood to the pagan deities. As late as
the 7th century Ioannes Malalas euhemeristically
explained the abduction of Europa by Zeus as a naval
raid upon Tyre by a King Taurus ("bull") of Crete who
carried off Europa, daughter of King Agenor.
Especially in the light of Cretan bull culture, abduction by a bull totem seems rather likely.

Saxo Grammaticus (c. 1200) applied Euhemerism to
the gods of the north, deeming Odin an apotheosized
king and explaining the weapon that slew Balder as a
sword called Mistletoe. Dādū (1544-1603), founder of
the Hindu reforming sect called Dādūpanthīs, offered
a Euhemeristic explanation for Brahma, Vishnu, and
Shiva. Late in the 17th century Sir Isaac Newton was
a staunch Euhemerist, believing that all deities, except his Christian god, were apotheosized humans.

The gods of China probably originated as did
most archaic deities, but for the past two millenia
the orthodox Chinese viewpoint has been Euhemeristic.
Taoists, Chinese Buddhists, and proponents of the
official religion (mistakenly labeled Confucianism)
agree that all the present gods were at one time
human beings. Important Chinese deities have spent
several human existences before achieving their
present eminence. Lesser gods have been human beings
for only one existence. Paralleling the Roman
practice, the Chinese emperor by decree would confer
divine rank upon noted heroes and worthies. Kuan Yü
was a general murdered in 220, honored widely as a
cult figure in the (7th century, and by the 19th
century elevated to "Grand Emperor Who Subdues the
Demons"; his divinity was revered in countless
temples and chapels. God of the harbor bar of

Chekiang is Wu Tsî-sü, an ancient minister of a local prince; unjustly executed, Wu Tsî-sü attempts each year to destroy the area and its capital Hangchow by hurling waves against it. There was even a goddess of the privy, a girl assassinated and flung into the privy. Judges of the Chinese underworld were ancient officials of integrity whose dates of death were carefully recorded.

Euhemerism may be applied to myths of many cultures.[37] In Japan the emperor Ojin was worshipped in his divine manifestation as Hachiman Sai-Bosatsu; many other notables were regarded as kami ("gods"), some even adored as gods in their lifetime. Tangiia of the Pacific island of Raratonga is generally accepted as a dead chief now deified. The Avá-Chiripá of Paraguay regularly deified their powerful shamans. In west Africa all of the orisha ("gods") of the Yoruba people were admittedly humans, notably Shango, a king whose memory was reviled and whose spirit retorted with devastating storms. The process continues, for Isaiah Shombe (1867-1935), originally an African Baptist cleric, founded his own sect, the Church of the Nazarites, among the Zulus of South Africa; he is now revered as a god under the designation of uMvelingQangi.[38]

Unquestionably, some gods are fully explained by Euhemerism, especially the Chinese and Japanese mortals frankly proclaimed deities. Often, however, as with Euhemerus himself, the theory is applied in conscious and rational eras to gods whose actual origin is probably quite different. The theory still has potency, and William Ridgeway early in this century was apparently the last theorizer to attribute all gods to Euhemerism.

ASTROMYTHOLOGY.[39] It is impossible to ascribe all myth to star observation,[40] for some sizable bodies of mythology such as the Japanese are virtually devoid of astromythology. Probably the earliest myths developed from the immediate earth-bound problems of man, before he could devote time and speculation upon the starry skies beyond the far more obvious sun and moon.

Astrology and astronomy probably originated in ancient Mesopotamia where many months of cloudless skies during the dry season encouraged careful scrutiny of the night sky. The perfect regularity and predictability of the starry dome overhead in

contrast to the variability and uncertainty of
terrestrial things certainly implied order and plan,
always sought in deities. In Assyrian and Mazdean
belief the planets were deemed evil since they did
not follow the regular pattern of the "fixed stars"
and could mislead a night traveler. During the 19th
century extensive archeological discoveries in
Mesopotamia stimulated the astromythological school.
The Panbabylonians (mostly German) saw all religion
originating in Mesopotamia, chiefly in star lore, and
from thence diffused worldwide. Socrates in the
Cratylus obviously regarded astromythology as non-
Greek. Star worship among the Greeks from the 9th
century B.C. onwards was evidently an importation and
a sign of growing cosmopolitanism. Aristotle's
theology evolved, but in De Philosophia, an early
work, he suggested that the gods had originally been
stars. Writings composed in Alexandria c. 150 B.C.
and ascribed to a fictitious king Nechepso and a
priest Petosiris especially fostered astromythology
in late antiquity. De Astronomia[41] attributed to
Gaius Julius Hyginus (died 17 A.D.) is a potpourri of
astronomy text and star myths. Arthur Drewes in this
century has claimed that there was no human individual Jesus and that the entire Christian concept
was based on oriental astrology.[42] The most vigorous
supporter in this century of astromythology has been
Alfred Jeremias who believed that solar zodiacal
astronomy was the key to early Near Eastern religions
and far beyond.[43]

Probably the greatest impression upon early man
by astromythology was the material and rational sense
of immortality, i.e. an endless continuation of life
as it is known. Hence numerous myths that carry
earth creatures into the heavens as stars are asserting immortality. Thus the Karadjeri of Australia say
that the slain Bagadjimbiri brothers have gone to the
sky to become the Magellanic Clouds. Onondaga
Amerindian myth says that children in dancing whirled
aloft to form the Pleiades. In fighting the Lernian
Hydra, Heracles summarily despatched the attacking
crab. Greek myth states that Hera, an enemy of
Heracles, rewarded the crab by placing it in the
heavens as a constellation, Cancer. In the Egyptian
Pyramid texts immortality was achieved by joining the
circumpolar stars.

As immortal (or constantly resurrected) beings
the gods are logically identified with stars. In the
Near East the most prominent star is the planet

Venus, anciently designated as Asshur, the Semitic war-god. Perhaps the association arose from the significance of brilliant Venus in the sudden desert raids. With the Babylonians the five planets are five deities: Ishtar (Venus), Nabu (Mercury), Nergal (Mars), Marduk (Jupiter), and Ninib (Saturn). The Babylonians recognized in the pole star Anshar the god of the upper world. In India the star Canopus is the divine rishi Agastya. The Pyramid Texts of Egypt identify Isis with Sirius.

Dipping below the horizon means descent into the underworld. The Abipon of South America identified their major deity with the Pleiades and greatly feared for the welfare of Queevet during the months his constellation could not be seen. A Semitic myth about Orion calls the star Kesil ("fool"). Trying to reach heaven, Kesil was seized and bound by God, and fixed in the sky as a sign to other rebels. Because he must also serve his time in Sheol, in autumn Kesil disappears below the horizon. This Semitic account, more than most astromyths, seems clearly to have originated solely from observation of the star itself.

Diffusionists point confidently to the widespread similarity of some constellation names. "Snake" is the meaning whether the Babylonians named it for the ocean-dragon Tiamat, the Greeks called it Draco for the dragon slain by Cadmus, or the Norse labeled it the Midgard serpent hurled into outer darkness by Odin. "Fish" (Pisces) is the meaning For Arabians, Babylonians, Phoenicians, Greeks; to the Romans the constellation represented the two fish into which Venus and Cupid were transformed as they fled Typhon; Christians interpreted the "fish" as Jesus' feeding of the multitude or the fish symbol identified with Christianity; the Chinese, perhaps from Jesuit influence, call it the Two Fishes.

Ursa major has monopolized more astromythology than any other constellation. The familiar Greek story tells of Callisto, seduced by Zeus, then changed into a bear by Hera. To the ancient Hebrews it was "Bear," and to the Arabs it was "The Greater Bear." The ancient Cretans identified the Greater Bear and the Lesser Bear as two bears that fostered the infant Zeus. Iroquois Amerindians explain Ursa major as three brothers and a dog chasing a rogue bear; the four stars in the bowl of the dipper constitute the bear, the three stars of the handle are the pursuing brothers, and the Iroquois see a little dog following them. The arch of Corona Borealis shows the mouth of the cave into which the bear crawled to rest. Amerindians of the Pacific northwest see the constellation as the orphaned children of slain Bear Woman: little brother is the pole star, next is little sister, and five younger brothers follow. Other ascriptions are of various animals: The Wild Boar (Syrians), Camel (Berbers of North Africa), Wild Reindeer Buck (Koryaks of Siberia). In Hindu myth the seven rishi, the mind-born sons of Brahma, are the seven stars of Ursa major. The Buriats of eastern Siberia call the same constellation "The Seven Old Men." For the Chinese it is "The Emperor's Chariot." In Norse myth the original designation was "Odin's Wain," changed after Christianization to "Charles' Wain" (Charlemagne).

Most of the astromythological ascriptions look like long-established myths of earth belatedly transferred to the heavens, e.g. the Hindu identification of the three bright stars of Aquila with the three huge footsteps of Vishnu across the cosmos, and Argo as the ship in which Jason and the Argonauts sought the Golden Fleece.

Myths about the Milky Way range from the awesome to the quaintly amusing. The Celestial Ganges appears as the Milky Way in the heavens, issuing from the left foot of Vishnu; the river flows onto the head of Shiva and thence, as the terrestrial Ganges, through India. Egyptians said that the Milky Way became the Nile at the First Cataract. Many peoples from the Akkadians to the Chinese termed the Milky Way a river, while others called it a road or path, e.g. Odin's Way to the Teutons, the Way of the White Elephant to the Thais, the path followed by the Wild Hunt of northern European myth. To the Magyars it is the Way of War, for the Milky Way guided their migration from Asia. Finno-Ugric and Amerindian myth frequently interpret the Milky Way as the road traversed by souls from this world to the next. In contrast the Armenian myth of the war god Vahagn claims that one cold night he stole straw from Barshamina and in escaping dropped straw which now forms the Milky Way.

An impressive stellar myth suggests stars as the eyes of god. Ancient Mexican codices stud the heavens with eyes, and other Amerindians concur. The Maasai of Africa interpret the stars at night as the watchful eyes of their god Ngai.[44] Polynesian myth

51

believes the morning and evening stars are the eyes of Maui's sons. Perhaps the mysterious Eye Deity in images from Brak, Mari, Lagash, and elsewhere in Mesopotamia is stellar (or sun and moon) in origin. So also could be an early Bronze Age drum-shaped image from Folkton, Yorkshire. Multiple eyes upon statues of gods and on priestly raiment probably represent the all-seeing stars.

Under the Han dynasty of China (206 B.C.-221 A.D.) the capital was designed upon the pattern of Ursa major and Ursa minor with the palace in the position of the pole star. Most star-struck of all peoples, the Mesopotamians saw objects of earth as modeled after stellar counterparts. The Tigris river had its model in the star Anunit, and the Euphrates in the star of the Swallow. Cities had constellations as prototypes: Sippara in Cancer, Ninevah in Ursa major, Assur in Arcturus, Babylon in a combination of Aries and Cetus.

From Patristic Writers through the Renaissance

PAGAN DEITIES AS DEVILS. Beset on every hand by worshippers of other gods, the ancient Hebrews resolutely branded all but Yahweh as devils. We may shrug off Marduk and Osiris, Dagon and Zeus as imaginary, but in the days of their fervent believers and virtual omnipresence such gods seemed very real even to the Hebrews. As an offshoot of Judaism, Christianity understandably espoused this position, keynoted by St. Paul in branding pagan deities as devils (I Corinthians 10:20). Justin Martyr, Tertullian, Cyprian, and other early Fathers of the Church vigorously concurred. Milton in Paradise Lost (1667) superbly portrays the demons of hell because to him they are genuinely supernatural beings, not abstract fancies. Until recent times Christians have conceived of the cloven-hoofed devil as the ancient Pan or Satyr, and the goat in a witches' coven is the same demoted god of old. Medieval Christians usually pointedly avoided any fair study of Islam; for long they accused Islam of worshipping Apollyon (the classic Apollo).

CONDESCENSION. Almost all Christians of the Roman empire were children of pagans or had immediate pagan ancestors and loved ones. Many sincere Christians would find it quite distasteful to denounce their parents and families as deluded devil-worshippers. St. Irenaeus enunciated the more palatable doctrine of Condescension. Condescension stated that god had provided early man with limited divine truths tailored to his capabilities. As man collectively matured, god then granted ampler revelation. Thus during the era of paganism it was right and proper to revere the pagan gods, but with the revelation of Christianity, the final divine truth should be universally accepted and the pagan deities wholly discarded. Dante in the Divine Comedy (1321) professed this doctrine, assiduously punishing equally pagans for impiety to the old gods and Christians for impiety to the Christian deity. The famous passage, "Lo, the poor Indian"[45] by Alexander Pope in 1733-34, applied Condescension to aborigines of the New World. Subscribing to the doctrine of Condescension, John Spencer in De legibus Hebraeorum ritualibus[46] (1686) was able to establish the modern study of comparative literature.[47]

ENCYCLOPEDIC APPROACH. The chaotic centuries following the fall of Rome almost obliterated learning in western Europe, and one might assume that Christian fanaticism would have administered the final coup de grace to classical mythology. Actually the gods and goddesses of old were never forgotten,[48] largely because the precious learning that survived was Latinitas and the skein of classic writings is liberally threaded with ancient myth. To us the break with antiquity seems sharp and violent, but to the Middle Ages the classic culture was deemed a living, unbroken continuum. The most significant medieval treatment of classic literature was the desacralization of ancient myth, which the Patristic Fathers even in their most virulent hostility had recognized as religion. Numerous compendia recounted (or distorted) classical mythology but never as religious material, simply as society's notable storehouse of fascinating narrative. Persisting to the present from this medieval attitude is the still-widespread notion: "Our myth is pure religion; all other myth is pure fancy." The compilers of medieval collections of mythology, even the most devout clerics, usually interpreted ancient myth by one or more of these pagan theories: nature allegory, moral allegory, euhemerism. Perhaps the strengths and the shortcomings of such encyclopedic labors are best focussed in Boccaccio's De Genealogiis Deorum Gentilium[49] (1351-60). Boccaccio employed one of these interpretations for some myths, another or even all three for other myths. Above all he wrung from most pagan myths highly edifying morals compatible with Christianity, effectively defending himself against any imputations of frivolity or impiety. The encyclopedic approach certainly got beyond the idea of one key to explain all mythology, but in its interminable and usually strained explanations it really has not influenced modern interpretation.

MYTH AS CONSCIOUS ART. The word Renaissance means "rebirth," and there can be no rebirth unless first there is a death. Historians are tinting with increasing grey the distinctions between the Middle Ages and the Renaissance that appeared so black and white to 19th century thinkers.[50] The distinction that seems almost paramonnt and ungreyable is the Renaissance recognition that classic antiquity was truly a dead past, a dream world deliciously imagined and hopefully to be emulated, above all a repository of beauty unsullied by pragmatism. Illustrative of the Renaissance treatment of mythology is Lorenzo Cartari's Imagini degli dei degli antichi (1556),[51] a vast cataloging of classic myth as fit subject for painting, sculpture, and literary art with elaborate details on costuming, pose, landscaping, and decorative accessories. The standard Renaissance view considered ancient myth as the conscious creation of highly skilled and intellectual poets and artists, or, we might say, as an Elizabethan masque gorgeous with sumptuous garments, glittering gems and metals, eloquent verse. Shakespeare's treatment of the wedding of Theseus and Hippolyta in Midsummer Night's Dream sparkles with the Renaissance fresh relish and imaginative handling of Greek myth as superb story material. Venus and Adonis by Shakespeare shows Renaissance sensual appreciation of classic subject matter: sexy, yes; sacred, absolutely not. This approach is utterly remote from Myth I.

In our century myth has been so pre-empted by anthropologists, sociologists, religionists, and psychologists that we may erroneonsly have downgraded the concept of myth as the product of art. Perhaps Richard Chase is returning to fundamentals when he declares that "myth is literature and must be considered as an aesthetic creation of the human imagination."[52] Other scholars of our era agree that myth is primarily a literary creation.[53] Because the creators of myth deem their subject momentous, they speak with elevated diction, impressive imagery, highly symbolic figures of speech, emotional power, and supple imagination. The ancient Greeks ascribed the conscious poet's skill to the inspiration of

Mnemosyne, mother of the Muses. The name Mnemosyne means "memory." The memory drawn upon by the poet is not simply that of the poet's own experience but the mythical inheritance of the society, as themes from myth dominate classical literature. Sometimes a narrative is so blatantly a literary creation that it is difficult to consider it myth at all. The elephant-headed Indian god Ganesha, patron of the literati, has but one tusk. One explanation asserts that when Vyasa, the author of the Mahābhārata, was declaiming his great epic to the god, Ganesha was so determined to record the masterpiece that he tore out one of his tusks to use as a stylus.[54] A sizable area of modern literary criticism is "myth criticism," finding in the most sophisticated and highly conscious belles-lettres the basic themes of immemorial myth.[55]

Condescending Rationalists of Age of Reason

Modernity sweeps over us in the Age of Reason from approximately the mid-17th century to the closing years of the 18th century. The modern quality is not mere rationalism, for Francis Bacon, a noted rationalist of the Renaissance, in myth theory remained mustily medieval, opining that Dionysus was allegorical for "desire" and Cassandra for "plainness of speech." The thinkers of the Enlightenment were modern theorists of myth in refusing to follow traditional concepts and insisting upon thinking independently and freshly.[56] In myth theory this is not yet contemporaneity, for while the Age of Reason dearly loved speculation, it was painfully lean on field work and painfully limited in basic materials. Bits and pieces of Amerindian myth in this period provided the first genuine Myth I available to Western civilization; much Teutonic myth studied during this age displays appreciable thought and art, and the Old Norse poem Voluspá can properly be called profound. Remarkably, the Enlightenment theorizers, with incomplete materials, produced some astonishingly penetrating and valid concepts. These rationalists (until we touch Vico) were patronizing, rather amused at the bizarre maunderings of simple folk. They generally took the position: what would one of our moderately bright peasants concoct if he lacked the clothing, gadgetry, and a modicum of our culture's accumulated knowledge?

MYTH AS PSEUDO-SCIENCE. Bernard Fontenelle (1657-1757) was among the first and the greatest of the French philosophes, the most exciting brain-trust of the Enlightenment. His deceptively brief essay, De l'origine des fables[57] (1724)[58] probably has more new and significant discussion of myth than any previous writings. As never before, Fontenelle sought to understand the mind of the primitive from whom myth would emerge. Even today we still have things to learn about archaic societies and their mindsets. Fontenelle had no personal contact with primitives or any important anthropological information; he extrapolated from children, rude peasants, and scattered reports about savages by European travelers. Myth theory is set upon a firmer basis than ever before as Fontenelle argues that the human mind is essentially the same everywhere and at all time, and that similar conditions will evoke the mythic response from all peoples worldwide. Primitives, said Fontenelle, operate exactly as a modern thinker, seeking to understand the unknown by proceeding from what is already known. The only difference between the mental processes of today's nuclear scientist and those of a primitive is the superior range of factual knowledge now available. Purely as a hypothetical example, Fontenelle suggests that primitives trying to explain running water would from their own pouring of water out of a pitcher produce the myth of a god pouring from a pitcher. Ancient Mexicans actually asserted that the chacs or rain-gods made thunder by breaking clay pots up in the clouds, and the rain accompanying thunder had poured from the broken pots. The Yuchi Amerindians declare that there is a big water vessel in the sky; when this vessel is jostled, water spills over the edges, falling to the earth as rain. Even closer to the Fontenelle pattern is the Chinese Master of the Rain who is portrayed as a warrior in yellow armor clutching a gigantic water-filled vase.

Had Fontenelle elaborated a bit upon some of the proposals he quickly tossed out, he could be credited with the evolutionary pattern associated with Edward Tylor and the linguistic theory attributed to Max Müller.

PRIMEVAL MONOTHEISM. The Age of Reason bred a Religion of Reason--Deism. Seeking a universal religious impulse, these rational religionists assumed that monotheism was the highest form of religion and that primitive man (a hypothetical creature of innate nobility and rationality) had therefore believed originally in only one god. Why then the rash of polytheism over much of the world? Chicanery of the priests, state the deists. Wily ecclesiastics figured that more gods meant more sacerdotal employment and much more in emoluments. Shrewd clerics maintained a two-tier system: their own intelligent religious concept restricted wholly to the priesthood, and also a public worship of multitudinous deities adroitly exploiting the credulity of the superstitious mob. John Toland in Christianity not Mysterious (1696) was an early proponent of this deistic notion, widely enunciated in the 18th century.

The wholly unsubstantiated deistic claim of original monotheism long seemed quite inconsequential. Especially when the evolutionist theory reigned in the 19th century, the idea of primeval monotheism seemed hopelessly dead. Then quite surprisingly the idea resurfaced in Andrew Lang's The Making of Religion (1898). Lang marshalled an impressive list of "high gods" throughout the world among archaic cultures; high gods are usually creator-gods who subsequently retreat, often to be virtually ignored in favor of a covey of younger, later deities. Extraordinarily, Varuna, the most important of the deities in the Rigveda subsequently disappeared in later Hinduism. Probably his name is cognate with the Greek Ouranos, another high god who fell on hard times. Paul Radin, a specialist in archaic religions, applauds Lang's proposals but suggests that the high gods probably represented the speculation of elitists rather than general tribal worship.[59] Early in this century heavier artillery was unlimbered in support of primeval monotheism. Wilhelm Schmidt studied the African Pygmies as perhaps the most primitive form of extant mankind and proceeded from the Pygmies to other archaic societies, formulating a theory of Ur-monotheism ("primeval monotheism"). Schmidt's multivolume study[60] amasses vast evidence with Germanic indefatigability and cannot be ignored, though its supporters today are meager.

What about sacerdotal charlatanry? Certainly it has_ always been a possibility. In the Indian Rāmāyaṇa (no later than 2nd century A.D.) Jabali lengthily complains to Rāma that the accounts fostered by religion are mere ruses by self-seeking priests to bilk the credulous. Lucian of Samosata reports from the 2nd century A.D. one Alexander of Abonutichos who claimed to be a prophet of

Aesculapius and, as his major prop, manipulated a
pseudo-snake with a human head. The cult established
by Alexander actually survived the hoaxer's death.[61]
Such an example, however, comes from a period
culturally rather similar to our own. It is rather
unlikely that archaic religious figures acted like
the pious frauds known to Lucian or to us. Such
religious specialists of old were very likely to
believe fully in current religious traditions.
Probably when priests spoke from behind or within
statues of deities or priestesses ceremonially went
into trances or oracular effusions, by auto-
suggestion they were themselves convinced of the
authentic presence of the deity. Even when clerics
conceal facts from laity, it is not necessarily the
hypocrisy roundly condemned by anticlerics. Common
folk of Zimbabwe hear voices resonating from deep
caves of the Matopo Hills and believe them the actual
voice of the god Mwari. Priests know, however, that
the sounds come from mediums possessed by Mwari.
Many sincere and intelligent Christians of today
would refuse literal belief in all the miracles
chronicled in hagiographies, but they would balk at
calling these saints' miracles hoaxes, preferring to
say: "Understandable exaggeration," "metaphoric
heightening of a profound religious experience,"
"edifying and conducive to piety in many people,"
"truly symbolic of a spiritual reality." We should
recognize exactly similar reactions by religious
specialists of archaic faiths.

What about a two-tier religious system?
Certainly no one would ever say that what religion
meant to Savonarola and Krishnamurti it also meant to
the average man of the same time and place. Those of
great spiritual depth will always have an infinitely
more profound brand of religion than commonality
whether in the Grand Mosque of Mecca or in the snow
hut of an Eskimo shaman. Knud Rasmussen found in the
angakok (shaman) of the polar circle some awesome
perceptions of the divine that any saint would
respect.[62]

MONOMYTH[63] seeks one controlling system or
scheme into which the vast welter of global myth as
narrative will fit. Can all the multifarious
accounts form one stupendous theme, each brief, even
enigmatic, tale part of one grand overview?
Admittedly, the scope of myth available to Andrew
Ramsay in The Travels of Cyrus (1728) was quite
limited, and his orientation was strongly Christian,

58

but he offered four elements which he proposed as the sum of all the world's myths:

(1) Original paradise, a supposititious primal period of innocence and perfection. This is the classic Golden Age, the Judeo-Christian Garden of Eden, the Australian Dreamtime, the Amerindian Mythological Age.

(2) Paradise lost, the descent into the present world of complexity and confusion, suffering and injustice. Here range the myths of the fall of man or the withdrawal of god, the coming of death, the burden of labor, the reign of autocrats, the ravages of war and pestilence. The heroic accounts belong here, the glory of the greatest men irretrievably dimmed by the inevitable tragedy of this fallen world.

(3) Paradise regained, the future era of a new perfection and grandeur. Such euphoria ahead may be predicated of an afterlife or of the society of the future. Here repose such strange bedfellows as Ezekiel and Karl Marx.

(4) A savior, a soteriological figure, to aid the suffering in this fallen world and eventually to inaugurate the paradisical future. No amount of failure and disillusionment can eradicate humanity's desperate yearning in every age for this needed savior. When the millenium refuses to occur, mankind casts about hopefully for another wonder-worker or recalls the former days of the lost savior as sparkling with mythic luster.[64]

Joseph Campbell with a 20th century Jungian approach has viewed the myth of the hero as the all-encompassing monomyth.[65] All myths involving humans or anthropomorphic deities are segments of the over-all heroic account. All myths not obviously involving mankind are considered projections from the inner psyche and equally part of the heroic cycle.

The flip side of this theory is the claim that the primordial Earth Mother and her service by the male underlie all myth. Robert Graves, the English poet, has eloquently pled the case[66] but has enlisted relatively few supporters, although present scholarly opinion recognizes the pre-historic dominance of the goddess.

More recently Northrup Frye has proposed a rather updated and amplified revision of the Andrew Ramsay scheme. Frye posits:

(1) Spring (dawn, birth). Creation, beginning, promise.

(2) Summer (noon, marriage or triumph). Success in love, war, and life generally.

(3) Fall (twilight, death). Tragic descent and defeat.

(4) Winter (night, dissolving into formlessness). Reign of the inchoate and malevolent.[67]

Ultrasonic imaging now permits observation of the shape and movement of the fetus in the womb. The fetus has been seen to move in apparent pleasure and apparent displeasure. From this information neo-Freudian psychoanalysis[68] theorizes that in the fetal struggle within the womb and the subsequent birth trauma originate all myth and ritual: conflict and resolution, the heroic quest, death and resurrection, creation and eschatology, and the rest.[69]

These searches for a monomyth as a foundation garment to provide one trim figure for all myth are stimulating and helpful, but many critics see such attempts as strainings for a strait-jacket. Deceptively similar myths among different peoples may have quite disparate meanings, and symbolism can be distressingly slippery and variable.

MYTH AS PSYCHOLOGICAL PROP. David Hume, purely in speculation, without any anthropological backing, rather anticipated the Functionalist theory of this century. In The Natural History of Religion (1757) this arch rationalist could doubt reason itself, as his Enlightenment contemporaries could not, and could understand that early man was not a naked 18th century philosophe but a scared naked animal in a hostile world. Myth is not intellectual explanation but psychological reassurance; any bizarrerie will be applauded if it can mitigate human panic and render adversity more tolerable. To give form to nameless terrors, to personalize the painfully impersonal, to have a formula for facing all vicissitudes, to be able to say "as it was, so shall it be" - these are the irrational assurances by which the primitive created and clung to myth. In the Phaedo when the arguments against immortality of the soul seemed overwhelming, even the intellectual companions of Socrates urged refuge in mythical thought. Hume could drily remark that the same practice will happen in this very age. In Freudian terms the Pleasure Principle in man will almost always sweep aside the Reality Principle in intense crisis.

The Romantic Counterattack

IMAGINATIVE PRIMAL WISDOM IN POETRY. Giambattista Vico in Scienza Nuova[70] (1725) offers Euhemerism to account for much of the origin of myth, but his transcendent importance, meagerly appreciated in his own day but increasingly respected ever since, is to applaud myth qua myth and myth as an essential stage in human culture. Previous theorists may in their hearts have relished myth qua myth, but they had to justify it as something other than it appears (especially as allegory) or condescendingly try to understand it as a fastidious Victorian dowager might explain harlotry. Vico with revolutionary fervor trumpeted that myth is the sensitive intuitive perception by primitive man of a cosmos of power and passion. Best known today for his cyclic theory of history, Vico saw the mythic proclivities of early man as essential to starting the entire wheel or spiral of human destiny. Myth was man's response to the basic forces of life, and it was poetry to enunciate and celebrate the fundamental rhythms of man and the world. To classic theorists Homer was an "ancient"; Vico for the first time had a vision of myth that saw Homer as a late polished poet, the primal mythmakers extending far back before him. Vico elevated early myth among the "gentiles" to poetic truths serving them as Yahweh had guided the Hebrew people. Vico's very title, "the new science" is to exalt myth from a bedraggled bypath study to a worthy full-fledged discipline of research. Modern respect and enthusiasm for myth found expression first in Vico.

SPIRITUAL VISION OF THE PEOPLE. At the end of the 18th century and into the 19th century a throng of vocal Romantics waxed enthusiastic about myth and folklore, ensuring their modern and continued fascination for millions and pedestaling them high in the ranks of human culture. All these Romantics shared a delight in myth as the art of the anonymous "folk," sure proof that creativity and imaginative splendor were not exclusive prerogatives of the refined intellectual but poured forth with spontaneous power from the people, the humble and the unlettered. For millenia art had been the sole province of the elite. First the ballad literature of Bishop Percy's Reliques of Ancient English Poetry (1765), then the widening collections of folklore and myth, extolled the unsung populace as the true repository of poetry, art and vision.

French, English, and, belatedly, American Romantics lauded the people's art, but early and consistently the German Romantics were the great champions of myth. Johann Herder, August and Friedrich Schlegel, F.W.J. Schelling, Friedrich Hölderlin and Novalis, chiefly as artists and critics, eventually Joseph Görres and Friedrich Creuzer in vast scholarly tomes, provided a special Germanic twist. Nationalism was surging forth amidst contemporary Germans. In no other modern country has the national mythology carried the weight of national destiny ascribed to it by the Germans. Remarkably, the Nibelungenlied was first published in full in 1782; during the Napoleonic period many German soldiers reportedly carried the work in their knapsacks. No other recent artist has exploited myth as assiduously as Wagner and made it such a national mystique. German Romantics celebrated myth as the truest expression of the national spirit, as deep wisdom of the folk beyond the superficial intellec-tualizings of the rationalists, and as an autonomous form of human art to be judged solely within itself and not by any other criteria.[71]

19th Century and the Specialists

THE SCIENTIFIC APPROACH. The most important innovation of 19th century myth theory was the decline to extinction of the talented amateurs, speculative savants, and exuberant artists; hence-forth the professionals will arise to dominate the study of mythology. Karl Otfried Müller, an eminent scholar of the classics, epitomizes the new age in Prolegomena zu einer wissenschaftlichen Mythologie[72] (1825). George Eliot in Middlemarch compounds the irony as her dry-as-dust mythologist Casaubon still labors at the hopelessly outdated idea of all myth derived from the Bible after Müller's volume had already instituted a new era; ignorant of German, Casaubon plods on futilely. The difficult but essential task set by Müller is interpreting myth only through total knowledge of the society producing that myth. The true scholar will not come with pre-

conceived notions and will not apply the criteria of
his culture, but seeks the understanding of myth in
the terms of its own culture. Let the facts speak
for themselves and speak in full. Like many other
concepts that may seem eternally true to our times,
the scientific approach to mythology is recent in its
enunciation.

THE LINGUISTIC APPROACH. Herder and the
Romantics generally had seen language as "faded
mythology." Friedrich Max Müller asserted the
diametrically opposite view that myth is "diseased
language" in Comparative Mythology (1856). A native
German, F.M. Müller was not related to K.O. Müller;
in his youth he became an Oxford don, writing
extensively and impressively in English. Until his
death in 1900 he was probably the leading Sanskrit
expert in the West, and his arsenal of philological
and linguistic knowledge overawed the Victorians.
His position was based on a supposed Aryan language
underlying all Indo-European tongues (in practice
F.M. Müller depended largely upon Sanskrit).
According to F.M. Müller, the original Aryan language
was incapable of abstractions. Hence, he suggested
that it was impossible in that tongue to say that the
sun was setting; Aryan speakers could merely report
the sun as dying, eaten by some black monster, or
pulled into a cavern. Presumably, as the Indo-
European peoples scattered afar, the original meaning
of the metaphors was lost and mythical narratives,
taking the figurative language as literal, then
elaborately explained what had started as a simple
statement. Distressingly, all the erudition of F.M.
Müller reduced the entire body of myth to a
startlingly narrow band: solar phenomena. Apollo's
pursuit of Daphne is ingeniously manipulated to mean
that the sun is embracing dawn. The death of
Hercules from a shirt poisoned by the blood of Nessus
is neatly if monotonously interpreted as the sun
setting amidst red clouds.

Today agreement is general that F.M. Müller
considerably overdid the solar mythology, and the
concept of myth as "diseased language" is similarly
moribund. There still may be some genuine truth in
the linguistic theory, though much less than the 19th
century thought. While the story is complex, the
Vedic god Rudra was apparently deemed ferocious and
destructive; to propitiate so dreadful a deity he was
politely called "auspicious" (Shiva). Rudra-Shiva
gradually became Shiva altogether, and by the 2nd

century B.C. Shiva had attributed to him aspects of considerable benevolence. In myth as in human life every example has a contrary. The Greeks termed the Furies the Eumenides ("Kindly") without abating their wild destructiveness. In explaining the Egyptian Coronation Drama, Theodor H. Gaster points out that the trampling of grain on the threshing floor is mythified as trampling of Osiris by the henchmen of Set, who are then beset by Horus for striking his father; in Egyptian the words for "grain" and "father" are identical.[73] The royal corselet is placed upon the mummy of Osiris, because "corselet" and "embrace" are almost identical words in Egyptian.[74]

Chapter III Myth and Religion:
Personal Experience and Piety

Part One - Personal Religion

The substantive or inward aspect of religion is an altered or heightened state of awareness experienced by an individual.[1] Here glows the very essence of myth and its sacral nature. Most of the rational theorists of myth from Thales onwards have totally missed the point in interpreting myth as allegory, theology, nonsense, or whatever. The fundamental purpose of all true archaic myth is the communication of that heightened state of awareness.[2] A myth can never hold to the mundane world of everyday fact, for it must soar, it must evoke the marvelous, the fantastic, the uncanny. Only thus can it achieve for the listener the lifting to another and different plane of consciousness and perceptivity, a vaulting to the religious sphere.

The periods of heightening are relatively small portions of even the most saintly lives. When we are told of the completely changed nature of the Buddha after his Enlightenment, we must acknowledge an altered personality; but, even so, only a meager percentage of his 24 hours daily could be spent at a spiritual peak. Otherwise the peaks become commonplace little hillocks. Ordinary people may rarely experience the heightened states. Even for archaic societies religion is often relegated to crises, and exactly like their sophisticated, urban counterparts, when life is easy and troublefree, they blithefully ignore religion. Archaic peoples tend, however, to find life most chancy and danger-laden; therefore they frequently pursue the heightened state with far more assiduity than relatively protected modern city dwellers.

Dionysian religion

Altered states of awareness through strong impress upon the body[3] are Dionysian. In psychological terms such experience is dissociational, i.e. the customary relationships of the psyche are broken, usually with the submergence of the conscious self and the emergence of subconscious or unconscious impulses.[4] No primitive ever used such terms, but he profoundly sensed an awesome alteration within him. Dionysian heightenings run an astounding gamut:

65

ENTHEOGENS. Literally, the word entheogen means "inducing a god within."[5] Alcohol, fermented from a wide variety of plant materials, may be among the most anciently employed entheogens as it still remains widely consumed. In all cultures wine and beer are gifts of the gods. On the Damascus Chalice, Christ is enthroned amidst tendrils of the vine like Dionysus, the Greek god credited with viniculture. Mayuel, the Central American goddess, discovered the agave from whence pulque is made. The goddess is represented with 400 breasts (cf. Diana of Ephesus) and is seated before or upon the plant. The Nahua regarded the agave as the tree of life; its milk, from the breasts of Mayuel, was used by Xolotl to nurse the first man and woman created by the Aztec gods. In ancient Peru chicha was a maize beer brewed exclusively by the Mamakona, a sort of Vestal Virgin group, for extensive consumption in religious ceremonies. The Papago of Arizona today ferment nawait (wine) from cactus; in rain-making rituals participants consume the nawait until vomiting, which is regarded as the showering of rainwater upon the earth.[6] Mead fermented from honey was the heavenly drink of the ancient Teutonic gods and was supplied by Odin's goat Heidrun, who fed on the cosmic tree Yggdrasil. Beer, according to the Prose Edda, originated from the spit of the gods; probably humans first prepared the beverage from mouthfuls of liquid mixed with the yeast in the mouth, then regurgitated. Initiates in the Eleusinian Mysteries drank kykeon, possibly a mixture of wine with grain and cheese. Islam forbids intoxicants, but Judaism and much of Christianity still employ alcohol in religious ritual. For most in Western civilization today the consumption of wine and beer will be treated with ceremony not accorded other food or drink items; this secular ritualizing is the remnant of the once universal religious quality ascribed to alcoholic beverage.

Tobacco smoking seems totally devoid of spirituality to Western man, but among the Warao of the Orinoco delta tobacco is the sole psychoactive agent employed by shamans embarking upon a spirit journey. Amerindians consume tobacco by smoking, sniffing or having tobacco blown into the nostrils, sucking, chewing, drinking, even eating a paste-like mixture of tobacco boil and casava starch. The Tukano of the Bolivian Andes consider powdered tobacco a magic repellant against demons and disease spirits. The Yanoama of Guyana place a final roll of tobacco under the lower lip of the dying so that thunder and spirits of the Other World will gladly receive them. Many Amerindians assume that gods and spirits crave tobacco smoke and cannot resist it; hence offerings of tobacco and solemn smoking when summoning supernaturals. Smoke from nostrils and mouth meant visible breath, merging of air and fire, an incense of the gods. The Mundurucú Amerindians claimed that the Mother of Tobacco created tobacco smoke and carried it in a calabash from which she periodically sucked this breath of life. When the calabash was emptied, she died.[7] Mother of Tobacco may be a wholly appropriate label, for psychoanalysts interpret sucking from cigar, cigarette, or pipe as a nursing habit, the infant sucking upon its mother. Inhalations from other entheogenic sources include the smoking of sumac leaves by Tewa and Jicarilla Apache Amerindians and the breathing by the oracle of Delphi of sulphurous fumes from the deep chasm under her tripod seat.

Approximately 150 plants[8] worldwide are mind-altering. Several societies report learning of hallucinogenic plants from deer, reindeer, wild boar. Perhaps this is ascription to totem or animal deities, but there seems some evidence that animals may seek out psychotropic experiences. Archeological evidence indicates use of cannabis in Northeast Asia in neolithic times, 6000 years ago.[9] The areas of most extensive use of hallucinogenic plants are Central and South America with about 130 entheogens. Use of such psychoactive plants is especially frequent in food-gathering and hunting societies, far more prevalent in the Western Hemisphere than elsewhere.

In every society these entheogens are used sparingly, but adult males in archaic societies usually have access to the psychoactive materials several times a year. Societies of greater stratification and complexity witness monopolizing of entheogens by elitists, especially priests. Whatever the plant drug--peyote,[10] fly agaric, jimson-weed, psilocybe mushroom, coca, or the multitudes of others--archaic societies consistently report a profound religious experience. Consumers of entheogens experience a sense of floating or flying through the air, perhaps because of increased pulse rate and tachycardia. Visions of ancestors, gods, paradise, wondrous places and beings are shot through with psychedelic color and action. Hallucinations suggest the transformation of the participants into animals or birds, objects such as rocks or trees and even into gods themselves.[11]

A common theme is animation of the plants as humanoid deities, most famous with the ancient Indian _soma_. In all early Vedic rituals _soma_ was the basic libation to the gods, who dearly love _soma_, and a welcome draught to the officiating priests. Soma was a deity in his own right, and an enormous literature surrounded the substance with bewildering clouds of myth. Over the centuries a host of possibilities has been canvassed, but J.M. Allegro[12] and B.G. Wasson[13] seem to have established the fly agaric mushroom as the ancient _soma_; the same mushroom is still used as an entheogen by many other Asiatic people. In Iran the cognate _haoma_ became incarnate in the mighty hero Duraosha. Frequently the deified plant is seen as a very tiny, elf-like creature or a vast towering colossus. Perhaps drug alteration of the pupillary activity may be the cause.[14] Geometric designs of stunning brilliance and scintillating color are an awesome depiction of form and structure. Somehow, apparently, the rods, cones, lattices, and cylinders in the human visual system are magnified and illuminated from within. Time as normally perceived is completely overthrown, a moment drawn out seemingly to eternity, a long passage of time telescoped into an instant.

Barbara G. Myerhoff summarizes the religious experience credited by the Huichol Amerindians to the eating of dried peyote: an awesome sense of the inexpressible and ineffable, an obliteration of any time perception, a feeling of intense intimacy and love of others, a profound realization of complete unity with all humanity, all life, all the cosmos.[15] The hallucinogenic substances so affecting the mind may have developed within plants as a defense against animals, or their active chemicals which, except in marihuana, contain nitrogen atoms, may simply be part of the plant's excretory system. Neither explanation has general acceptance. Perhaps the effects upon the mind by the psychoactive drugs result from their chemical similarity to neurotransmitters in the brain. When "almost the right" chemicals seep in, the neural connections are possibly disrupted with the attendant visions.[16]

Undoubtedly many of the world's dramatic and wondrous myths have resulted from archaic man experiencing the mind-boggling impact of entheogens and with perfervid intensity and awe sharing the encounter with his fellows in the form of narrative. The manifestations mentioned in the previous paragraph will appear especially in the discussion of shamans in the next chapter. R. W. Masson now suggests that possibly the kykeon of Eleusis was identical with soma, the fly agaric.[17] We know that the Oracle at Delphi chewed laurel leaves which contain a modicum of cyanide and are psychoactive. Since laurel was sacred to Apollo and the famous myth about Daphne has Apollo apparently confusing a tree with a girl, can his divine illumination arise from entheogens? Various preparations have been suggested for the Lotus-eaters in the Odyssey, perhaps hashish or again the mushroom. Especially in the Americas archaic societies frequently represented realistically or stylistically a number of the psychodynamic plants. There was apparently worldwide allusion in bygone eras, and only now may we realize the tremendous impact of these substances upon archaic man and his myth.[18]

Bioprocessing adds to the entheogenic substances affecting humans. Certain animals--ducks, cañanes lizards of Peru, Siberian reindeer, the pink pigeon of Mauritius, the borracho ("drunken") fish off the coast of Peru--feed upon psychotropic plants or poisonous flora and fauna, process the ingested chemicals and store up resultant hallucinogenic compounds. Humans eating such animals may sicken, may become intoxicated, may experience entheogenic visions.[19]

To the natural entheogens of immemorial usage, modern chemistry has added artificial chemical relatives such as LSD (lysergic acid),[20] DMT (dimethyl tryptamine) and DET (diethyl tryptamine). Western man has sampled the old and the new quite extensively, and often he has not found all the wonders (in some cases none at all) reported by archaic man.[21] Remember that ours is a determinedly secular age, but, most especially, note that we do not regularly condition the takers of entheogens as do archaic societies, where the participants are carefully told in advance exactly what they are to see. So conditioned, the percentage of true believers will be extremely high. Also conducive to the religious experience of entheogens is their complete social acceptance by archaic society. With sophisticated ideas of what religion is expected to be and realizing that much of our society frowns upon hallucinogens, today's subjects have a built-in mental block.

A modern Amerindian, John Rave, rather acculturated to modern Western society, nonetheless reports that after eating peyote he was stunningly awed by an overwhelming vision of god.[22] He also reported the powerful sensation: "a living object seemed to have entered me."[23] Such a report certainly sounds like spiritual possession, frequently associated with religionists. An impressive roll of modern experimenters from the noted author Aldous Huxley[24] through scientific researchers reports that the natural and man-made drugs do indeed generate intensely religious experiences.[25] Investigators report powerful experiences of the death-and-resurrection theme in LSD intake. Masters and Houston note that many entheogen experiences remarkably parallel the forms of consciousness reported by mystics.[26] There is growing conviction that the origins of myth and religion may be inseparable from early man's employment of the entheogens.[27]

DEPRIVATION.[28] A changed state of consciousness can certainly be induced by refusing the body its normal intake of sustenance, including breath.[29] The gaunt, drained faces of starving refugees hardly seem spiritual, but their eyes are haunted, withdrawn, elsewhere. Apparently it is this condition that ascetics of both East and West have long sought in advocating fasting as a means of heightened spirituality.[30] A Westerner seldom finds as edifying as do Asiatics the statue of the fasting Buddha, a living skeleton with unfleshed skin tight drawn over every protruding bone. Such self-abuse is motivated by a despising of the body, regarding it as a polluting prison of the soul. Deprivation is the triumph of the will over bodily appetites, the victory of the soul over the body. Hinduism saw the power of asceticism (tapas) as conferring magic capabilities even surpassing divine potency. The Sufis in Islam have exalted asceticism, but Indian asceticism has always exceeded that of Islam. In the native tradition of China and Japan, as well as Greco-Roman culture, such practices were meager, almost nonexistent. Jesus in calling for self-denial in Mark 8:34 was propounding a distinctly south Asian concept, but he seemed not to argue for later Christian rigid austerities in some medieval monasticism and extreme sects such as Montanists, Albigensians, and Waldensians.

Persuasive is the psychoanalytic suggestion of nourishment from the deified parent. The hungry infant is fed by the god-parent, so primitive logic would insist that the hungrier the child, the more likely is the visitation of the divine parent. Of course, a starving person is especially subject to visions and dreams.[31]

Perhaps the basic rationale for deprivation has been effectively stated by archaic societies. The Mescallero Apache of Mexico tell of a tribesman half dead from hunger and thirst. When granted peyote, he felt a holy spirit enter him and conduct him to heavenly regions where a powerful spirit explained that his sufferings were to make him prepared for and deeply appreciative of spiritual visions. Far to the north the Eskimo shaman Igjugarjuk told Knud Rasmussen: "The only true wisdom lives far from mankind, out in the great loneliness, and it can be reached only through suffering. Privation and suffering alone can open the mind of a man to all that is hidden to others."[32] Could any ascetic saint say it better?[33]

Hyperventilation and purposeful holding of breath are less frequent techniques but are employed especially by South American shamans. A form of deprivation is self-hypnosis, depriving oneself of the normal range of perception and even inducing trance. In the Sufi fraternities of Islam dhikr ("remembrance") is endless repetition of a pious phrase such as "God is most great," "Praise be to God," or simply "Allah," chanted monotonously, to produce ecstasy. In Hinduism the term is namakirtana for the incessant repetition of a god's name, again to attain an ecstatic state. The corresponding Christian practice, the "Jesus-prayer," was advocated by Diadochus of Photice (5th century) and John Climacus (7th century); early Christian ascetics paralleled yoga in endless repetition, "Jesus, Jesus, Jesus," with controlled breathing and fixed contemplative posture. Self-hypnosis can be achieved by undeviating concentration upon an image, a mirror or glinting light, and other objects.

MORTIFICATION. A further twist of the screw is purposeful injuring of the body in the search for spiritual vision. In ancient Central American representations Quetzalcoatl frequently appears with instruments of mortification such as a bone dagger and abrasive thorns. Perhaps this tradition underlies the celebrated Penitentes of the southwest of the USA, where devotees were ritually and voluntarily crucified to hang like Christ upon the cross. Flagellation was one of the notable mortifications of medieval Europe. In 1259 in Perugia, Italy, public whippings to spur spiritual vision became common, spreading throughout Europe; the practice probably sprang from general psychological tensions of the era. The greatest outbreak of flagellation accompanied the Black Death (bubonic plague) in the mid-14th century. The Brotherhood of the Flagellants in Germany arose in 1349 and stimulated comparable mortification throughout all the West. To the present day Roman Catholicism deems a notable sign of spirituality the appearance of scourge marks upon the back and stigmata upon the hands in correspondence to the mortification of Christ.

Less dramatic but continuously irritating were horse-hair shirts worn next to the skin by medieval ascetics. The flesh was incessantly scratched and irritated to effect permanent discomfort. Thomas à Becket, the archbishop of Canterbury martyred in 1170, had seemed more engrossed in the church temporalities than in its spiritualities, but his private saintliness capped his public martyrdom when the monks undressing the battered corpse were astounded to find horse-hair cloth enclosing his trunk and so festering the flesh, reported the awed monks, that it "boiled over" with vermin "like a simmering cauldron."[34]

Everyone is familiar with the multitudinous varieties of mortification practiced by Indian fakirs, but even the pragmatic Chinese have developed the Lin-chi sect of Zen (the corresponding Japanese sect is Rinzai) which claims that regular beatings help induce enlightenment.

Early man set the example for such mortification. In the Paleolithic caves c. 30,000 B.C. many handprints appear upon the walls, and the number of handprints with missing phalanxes is far too high to be explained as normal accidents. Apparently joints of the fingers were chopped off as mortification for spiritual perception. Such a practice was widespread among Amerindians of the Great Plains of North America well through the last century. One version of the Oedipus story has him gnaw off one of his own fingers to placate the avenging Furies. Whatever the form of mortification, it is difficult for modern man not to interpret it as masochism and any resultant reaction as more hysterical than spiritual.

PHYSICAL STIMULUS. Dissociation can be realized in the intense concentration accompanying a heavy loading of the sensorium. In its active form the participant exercises his muscles vigorously, often to total exhaustion. In the passive form the participant may be physically immobile but is surrounded with overpowering sense impressions. Active forms are:

Dancing.[35] Apparently all primitive dancing possessed a religious or magical quality. From Paleolithic times the "Dancing Sorcerer" is still gyrating upon the wall of Trois Frères Cave. The rhythms of the world and the cosmos were epitomized in the dance. The Pelasgian creation myth states that Eurynome, goddess of all things, initiated the entire process of creation by dancing. Most elaborate of all dance mythologies surrounds Shiva, who, as Nataraja ("king of the dance") dances all of creation, all of the constant rhythmic movements of earth and life and time, and eventually all of destruction and dissolution. Ananda Coomaraswamy considered the awesome Dance of Shiva the "clearest image of the activity of God which any art or religion can boast of."[36] The Indian mystic Jñānadeva made direct contact with the deity and found him in joyous dance.[37] Especially spectacular and impressive are sacred dances of Amerindians of the Great Plains: the Sun Dance of the Dakota, the New Life Lodge of the Cheyenne, and the Mystery Dance of the Ponca. Each dance was to insure the renewal of fertility and well-being of the earth, and no dance was complete without a great accompanying vision.

W.O.E. Oesterley finds eight types of sacred dance among the ancient Hebrews, ranging from the sober marching procession (II Samuel 6:5) to the ecstatic movements of a dancer "possessed " by the divine (I Samuel 10:5 ff).[38] The apocryphal Acts of St. John (94-102) presents Christ and his disciples in a "Round Dance of the Cross." In spite of its rich dance heritage in Judaism, Christianity from the outset eschewed the dance because of its orgiastic aspects in the ancient Eastern world. The Dance of the Seven Veils by Ishtar was considered a religious dance in Mesopotamia, but it most certainly represented an erotic projection of a great fertility goddess. The priests of Baal performed a "limping dance" around the altar of their god (I Kings 18:26),[39] and frenzied religious dancing was prevalent throughout the Levant. Perhaps the most violent dancers were the priests of Mâ, the Anatolian fertility goddess, who celebrated Mâ in wild ecstatic dancing that included wounding themselves in her honor. Perhaps, especially with the worship of Dionysus, the Greeks may have imported the frenetic dancing of Asia Minor. Greek religion of antiquity was danced through by a host of Terpsicore devotees: Maenads, Thyiads, Bacchantes, Kouretes, Korybantes. The maniacal transport of the dancers of Dionysus is demonstrated in the rending asunder of Orpheus, whose exquisite song would normally charm even the most savage aspects of nature. It is chilling in The Bacchae by Euripides to witness such mad possession of the Dionysian dancers that a mother, Agave, joins in the murder and dismemberment of her own son, King Pentheus; such seems the ultimate dissociation. The mainline Olympian deities were never celebrated with such frenzied dancing.[40] Aristotle states that the entire drama of ancient Greece developed from the dithyramb, originally a rather formless mimetic dance upon Dionysus, forever after the patron god of the theater.

The Sarume (musicians and dancers) represented from early times a respected priestly class of Japanese Shintoism, and temple dancers were once widespread across all Asia and at least as far as ancient Egypt. Islam in the Mevlevi dervishes,[41] founded by Julāl al-Dīn Rūmī in the 13th century (Mevlevi is derived from Mawlānā, "our master," a title given to Rūmī) has perpetuated one of the most engrossing of sacred dances in a "higher religion." The dancers begin in long black coats which emblemize the dark earthly plight. When the full contagion of the dance seizes the dervishes, the coats are cast away, and the dancers whirl ecstatically in white robes, "the garments of resurrection," the spiritual body. Dramatically this performance displays the dissociational achievement of the dance. In the 19th century the Shakers of the USA (now extinct) earned their designation from their religious dancing. Sacred dance is central to the contemporary Hare Krishna, which is Indian-inspired but far more Western in origin than it admits. As recently as 1947 a Japanese sect, Tenshō Kōtai Jingūkyō, was founded by a woman Kitamura Sayo; it is popularly known as "the dancing religion" because of ecstatic dancing at its worship sessions.

Sex.[42] A psychoanalyst can declare that to the unconscious "'to worship' and 'to copulate' are virtually equivalent."[43] Before man had any comprehension of the generative power of sexual intercourse and thus came to regard copulation as sacred fertilizing, he experienced the eerie gripping possession in coitus by a force infinitely stronger than his conscious will and utterly irresistible. The Orphic creation myth that Eros (love) set the entire universe in motion is admittedly metaphoric; perhaps it indeed means that the primal sense of the divine was first aroused in the orgiastic sexual act. Assuming such an origin, religion has branched in two directions. The essentially masculine desire for the will to control the flesh has emphasized the Apollonian and Mystic qualities and has dominated so-called "higher religions." The basically feminine (or so male psychologists have thought) has exalted the flesh and its sexuality. To complicate the problem, psychologists suggest that religious males sense their own souls as feminine. Origen early in the 3rd century established the Christian interpretation of the Song of Songs as the marriage of Christ and his church. Mystical union is regularly symbolized as sexual union, even to the point of rape, as Bernard of Clairvaux (12th century) suggests to indicate the violent overpowering of the self by the divine might.

From the general direction taken by Western society, the depiction of sexual intercourse in religious association is condemned as pornographic and the shockingest antithesis to religion. The Conquistadores were righteously indignant to find in Mayan temples depictions of various goddesses copulating with the sky-god Itzamna. Westerners may still shake their heads at the numerous representations of copulation upon Hindu temples. In the immense religious ferment that is India there can be the most austere chastity and also the strongest proclaiming of the power of sexual intercourse as spiritual exaltation. Long viewed askance because of its emphasis on sex, Indian Tantrism still needs more adequate study. It seems to have a very ancient origin in pre-Aryan India. Mithuna can be interpreted symbolically (just as Christianity insists upon viewing the eroticism of the Song of Songs), but in modern Bengal there is a quite literal interpretation of mithuna as a divinization of sexual intercourse. Sacred Tantric coitus is credited with producing the highest religious ecstasy.[44]

Games and sports. Primitive men may have conducted informal matches of strength and skill, but it
requires rather moderately advanced social structure
and social discipline to invent and sustain games by
rules and organized athletic competition. Because in
early societies any recognized organization was
sacred, all games apparently were religious rituals
in origin. The sacred ballcourts of Central America
were among the most ambitious constructions of pre-
Columbian America. Psychologists see all games
involving the movement of balls or similar objects as
fertility rites. Any pitting of one against one or
team against team is the ritual battle of good vs.
evil (as the fans will clearly demonstrate at most
football games today). Participants in the games of
early man probably felt decided spirituality in the
intense concentration and exertion coupled with the
sacred in ritual games. In classic times the sports
such as racing, wrestling, javelin hurling, and so on
were under the auspices of the gods as were the
Olympic Games. The playing of the games was a sacred
event, suspending wars, and by divine edict summoning
the youth to compete for the sacred wreath conferred
upon the victor. Funeral games (as in the Iliad and
the Aeneid) celebrate the life force in the departed
and the ongoing energy and life-impulse in the
mourners. Except for Plato who abjured his youthful
athleticism when lured to philosophy by Socrates, we
have few athletes among the ancient authors and none
who report how the games affected them psychically.
Perhaps behind I Corinthians 9:24-27 lurks the
religious sensibility in athletic sport which the
Hellenized St. Paul writing to Greeks wanted to
relate to and then appropriate for the new faith.[45]
In recent days the Perfect Liberty Organization
founded in Japan in 1912 by Kanada Tokumitsu calls
for vigorous exercise to achieve true Buddhahood.
Today numerous athletes "pumping iron" report that
after incessant pumping they feel a genuinely
religious experience. Exertion that constantly
varies in amount and intensity kindles far less sense
of the sacred than a hypnotizing, unbroken rhythm.

Individual fighting. Long before homanids
appeared, the larger mammals knew the shock of
individual combat, as predator or victim, as a male
vying for a female, as a mother defending her young.
Fighting for one's own life or for a desperately
needed meal is guaranteed to stimulate the adrenalin
flow. Supercharged with sudden glandular secretion,
a man is astounded at his incredible surge of power

and speed, i.e. the transformation sensations associated with the strange and supernatural. Homer could attribute this suddenly erupting strength of a fighting man to a visitation from a god. Warriors indeed seemed "god-like" in the towering frenzy of combat.

War and battle. Soldier ants, soldier termites and ratpacks fight an all-out war with the ferocity and ruthlessness of Homo sapiens. Among large mammals, however, true warfare seems restricted to humans. Mammal predators in groups such as the dreaded wolfpack will stalk herds of ungulates, but war is not the purpose, and few enemies will ever charge the horns and stomping forelegs of a massive bull. All the predator wants is to cut off the weak and the slow and make a meal upon them. How, therefore, could mankind have devised warfare?

With no mammalian heritage to account for human warfare, some peculiarly human trait must explain the origin of war; the standard theory today advances religion as the cause. Even if religion is attributed to animals,[46] mankind alone has a conscious religion and only humanity has extensively developed religion. Archaic man still considers any social organization sacred and any sort of act in concert as sacral. Perhaps warfare began in neolithic times as a religious ritual of creation, a struggle ostensibly between the forces of order and the forces of chaos.[47]

Certainly the ritual warfare seems to be a contest of good vs. evil. From time immemorial the Egyptians at Abydos enacted a ritual conflict between the supporters of the slain Osiris (led by his son Horus) and the troops of Set (who killed Osiris). Ritualists (see Chap. VIII) assert that the ritual battle long predated the Egyptians and Osiris. Many Egyptians testified to the spirituality and exaltation gripping them in witnessing the Abydos ritual. Psychologically they had experienced the channeling and exorcising of hostility; the victory of Horus triumphantly assured the defeat of evil and the optimistic era ahead.

Our so-called "civilized" warfare is infinitely less civilized than the ritual battles still performed in New Guinea between fighting men of hill tribes. After lavish display of strength and threatening armament, accompanied by vociferous boasts of heroism, the resultant clash of fury and pyrotechnics may produce only one fatality, seldom more than a handful. The dead are apparently regarded as sacrificial scapegoats. So-called "advanced" societies, turning the ritual battle into a secular donnybrook, exact hecatombs of corpses instead of the very few slain as a sacred token in New Guinea.

Archaic peoples appear universally to consider war a sacred activity in which the gods of the respective combatants are ranged against each other. The pharaoh Narmer (c. 3000 B.C.) swaggers upon carvings as the indomitable slayer of the enemies of Egypt with divine assistance of the god Horus. In the Iliad the gods are constantly attending on either side and tipping the scale of battle, for uncanny indeed was the savage stour of combat and then the sudden break of one line and the forward surge of the other. Virtually every people or nation even to the present has seen its wars as the wars of god, and soldiers in smiting the enemy merely fulfil divine commands. Mars to the Romans was a majestic deity rivaling imperial Jupiter. More even than in rigorous sports, warriors will experience "scrimmage blackout" in which intense concentration, exertion, and resolute purpose will induce superhuman strength to leap from common mortals and rash heroism from otherwise hesitant mediocrity. Battle can be wild intoxication as appropriately designated in the Irish goddess Medb ("intoxication") who waded into battle, weapons in hands. Until recent generations the standard propaganda on war shouted almost unqualified exaltation at the battle clash and the ecstatic triumph of the sacred cause. Never seeing a battle, Stephen Crane in the Red Badge of Courage (1895) nonetheless superbly sensed the awe-inspiring, sacred experience that battle can represent to the humble ranker.

Emotive music.[48] Sacred to early man were man-made sounds in imitation of animals or of birds deemed messengers, spirit vessels, totem representatives, and the like. Another type of sacred sound would be the "abnormal" noises made by adapting natural objects to produce sounds (bull-roarer, drum, ram's horn) and by employing the human voice outside its familiar gamut of speaking. Hence singing, chanting, intoning have always been associated with religion; it is often deflating to observe the banality of the words accompanying celebrated oratorios and other sacred music. Oracles and shamans

regularly project a rhythmic voice that is disturb-
ingly unusual. Ghosts and spirits are frequently
characterized by high-pitched squeekings or deep
sepulchral tones. Each Amerindian of the Great
Plains was supposed to receive a unique "spirit song"
from his guardian spirit. Musical instruments with
the marvelous facility of providing more than one
note, even if no more than a didgerydoo, are
obviously of divine origin, as Hermes invented the
lyre and Pan invented the syrinx. Most especially,
highly rhythmic music is peculiarly emotive. Intensive and repetitive cadences help achieve trance and
spirit possession as in modern "Holy Rollers."
Shamans have long used drumbeating to contact the
spirit world. Some shamans report that specific
musical patterns evoke specific visions or types of
visions. Temple musicians have been commonplace from
Japan through the Near East and ancient Egypt. The
Olympian worship made meager use of music, but the
Greek mystery cults emphasized ecstatic music; conservative critics especially objected to the inflam-
matory effect of the aulos (a reed instrument) in
such cults as the Dionysian. In general the emphasis
in classic times seems not upon the aesthetic
qualities of music but upon the ability of music to
stir the listener to action, as the Dorian mode
supposedly induced martial valor and the Lydian mode
lured to the pursuit of love.[49]

In the passive forms of physical stimulus the
recipient of religious impulses does not employ his
own muscularity, but has his senses powerfully
assailed to arouse feelings of altered awareness.

Ritual and its surroundings.[50] Participating in
ritual even as a spectator, ancient man undoubtedly
experienced the religious impulse from the rites
themselves and especially from the atmosphere of mass
concentration and rapture. Certainly the ecclesiastic rationale of recent times is to affirm ritual for
the same reasons as the ancients, but saintly figures
do not always concur. Hadewych, a 13th century
Flemish woman mystic, found that the eucharist precipitated the mystic experience for her, and Ignatius
Loyola sensed the living presence of god in the
Christian liturgy. On the other hand Meister Eckhart
among medieval Christian mystics, the 10th century
Moslem mystic al-Halladj, and the 16th century
Alumbrados ("enlightened") or Spanish ecstatics
denied any inner religious awareness from ritual.

Early man was a food-gatherer, nibbling constantly on whatever provender he could scrounge. Quite likely, the first full-scale communal meals were truly sacred meals, as pious people today utter prayers to accompany meals and to secure divine blessing for the food and for the diners. Ritualistic eating of the flesh of the god (or of surrogate, animal or human), as in the Christian mass, is certainly deemed a spiritual experience. Macarius, the 4th century Egyptian monk, and numerous other mystics have likened their transcendent experience to that of a banquet hosted by god with the soul as a guest.

Not merely the ritual qua ritual, but the entire ambience surrounding the performance may enhance dissociation for participants. Westerners are astounded by the extraordinary masks and decoration of New Guinea ritualists. Probably these aborigines would find the elaborate raiment of Christian ecclesiastics just as bizarre. Both are intended to establish ritual on a completely different level from the mundane and thereby to induce a changed state of awareness. Banners, candles, mosaics, statuary, paintings, and the rest of the visual trappings of modern cathedrals probably descend from earlier versions in the Paleolithic caves. Incense proved especially significant in most countries of antiquity, apparently on the assumption that its invisible fragrance is the veritable essence of the divine.

Romantics of the 18th and 19th centuries waxed eloquent on the "temples of nature," "the cathedrals of the Alps," and so on as inspiring natural religiosity in the primitive. The key point is the sense of difference from the routine and worldly. Lifelong residents of the most glorious mountains or splendid prospects accept the surrounding landscape as familiar, normal terrain. Prehistoric cave worship in Crete and elsewhere was facilitated by its very unconventional locale. Until the Industrial Revolution ecclesiastical structures such as Karnak in Egypt, Heliopolis (Baalbec) in modern Lebanon, Borobudur in Java, and the cathedrals of medieval Europe represented in size and workmanship the epitomes of their eras, and they were indeed truly imposing because there was nothing then in the secular realm to rival them. Awesomely they overpowered audiences with the sense of divine spaciousness and amplitude. Reportedly a Russian delegation to Constantinople was so overawed by Hagia Sophia, "the Great Church," largest and most magnificent in the entire world of medieval times, as to commit Russia to the Greek Orthodox Church.

Drama.[51] Religious ritual is inherently dramatic, and universally the drama has developed from religious ritual. Actions are performed by persons who are always symbolic of some other beings (to primitives the actors are taken as the actual beings of the drama), and even in our cynical age the drama is always a transport to another place (often another time and even another world). These certainly were religious experiences to the viewers of the past. As imitation, the drama probably originated in mimicry of animals, a wholly sacred act under totemism and in a hunting society. The masked dancers on the walls of Paleolithic caves were probably engaged in miming animals to induce quarry by sympathetic magic--"like to produce like."

The Abydos Passion Play, depicting the dismemberment and reassembly of the body of Osiris, may date as far back as the third millenium B.C.[52] It is impossible conclusively to ascertain Egyptian influence upon the ancient Greek drama, but the rites of Dionysus were the putative origin of Greek drama, and his death-and-resurrection theme certainly parallels that of Osiris. In Hellenistic times the Greeks frequently identified Dionysus with Osiris. The statue of Dionysus was brought to the amphitheater in ancient Greece and throughout the performance occupied the seat of highest honor. The presence of the god rendered drama a sacred performance throughout Greek antiquity and effectively prevented the enacting of violence on the stage as a desecration. Tragedy possibly arose from the ritual of the seasons; before modern food preservation the end of the harvest season seemed a horrible death of living things. The scapegoat theme is also strong in tragedy, springing from a religious ceremony like the scapegoat account in Leviticus 16:20-22. Comedy apparently began in fertility rites associated with the springtime rebirth of all life.

PILGRIMAGE (JOURNEY, QUEST THEME, WITHDRAWAL AND RETURN).[53] Modern man offers lame secular excuses for travel presumably for its own sake: "variety," "escaping the old routine," "getting away from it all," "change of scene." Dramatic breaking from the familiar and the mundane actually permits dissociation, as ignored and submerged elements of the personality can be aroused in situations and surroundings unlike the repressive, confining world of everyday.

Amerindians recognized the spiritual transformation that the wilderness journey could induce in youths or in anyone. When a recent migrant from Czechoslovakia undertook a solitary quest in the wilds of northern Canada, an old Amerindian advised him: "Don't hurry like a white man. There will come many things that you won't understand, but be patient. You still need to feel the country. When you return you'll be a new man."[54]

Agricultural societies, forced to static residence and much routine labor, sense more acutely than nomads the need to venture forth and seek an altered state of consciousness. The compulsory structuring of agricultural societies compels a specific goal, instead of the earlier nomadic wandering. Hence the pilgrimage worldwide and especially in medieval Western culture proved the only acceptable non-economic justification for travel. After the Black Death of the mid 14th century many ostensible pilgrims (and the overwhelming majority of Chaucer's pilgrims) realize that the journey itself rather than the alleged goal is their purpose.

In truth, the all-important reason for the journey is the significant alteration within the psyche of the traveler. The three major stages of the quest theme are:

(1) Separation or departure. The quester must break away from the familiar and launch into the strange and different. Abandon the known and venture into the unknown. The most exciting and definitely the best part of The Good Companions (1929) by J.B. Priestley is the initial tearing away from the commonplace and commitment to the journey theme by each character.

(2) Discarding of customary perspective and the alteration of state of consciousness. Away from the conventional, the quester must first slough off non-essentials and misconceptions (voluntarily, by force of circumstance, or from guidance of mentor), and fully open the psyche. Novel and extraordinary experiences elicit new responses and compel learning and revised viewpoints. Perils must be met and overcome. People, often vastly different from the

traveler's previous acquaintanceship, must be dealt with effectively; and new, hitherto inconceivable, personal relationships must be established. Above all shines the exhilarating realization by the quester that he is himself a different person from the being who embarked upon these travels. Every noted traveler from the mythical Gilgamesh and the real, persistent Herodotus to the present has recapitulated this path.

(3) Return and reintegration into original society. The returned pilgrim or quester has a new spiritual vision. Frequently the returnee is pictured with precious and exotic treasures, like the scintillating gems sewn into the garments of the Polos, but actually all the hoards of riches symbolize the priceless jewel of a transformed nature.

Travelers whose journeys have swung far out of the ordinary circuit may experience grave problems in readjustment. The mind-boggling adventures of Gulliver amidst the Houyhnhnms unfit him even for prompt reunion with his own family. Coleridge fully appreciated that the fantastic voyage of the Ancient Mariner would permanently mark him and transform him wholly beyond any possible absorption into conventional society.

DREAMS AND VISIONS.[55] While we are awake or semi-awake, any of the previously discussed Dionysian effects might possibly produce visions, projections from the unconscious; but in sleep dreams are the universal experience of all mankind; and in their intensity, freakishness, and violent overthrow of everyday conscious experience, dreams may be the primal religious encounter of humanity, the most basic of altered states of awareness.[56] As dreams vividly portrayed the known dead, man may thus have first conceived of an afterlife. The frequent dream experience of leaving the body, flying through the air, and visiting a totally different world suggests the shaman's familiar pattern, the quite widespread belief in soul not coterminous with the body, and the myths of paradisical and demoniacal realms. If we are honest with ourselves, even we moderns are not always sure whether we consciously saw certain dramatic events or whether we dreamt them. Primitives and even more recent men may recognize no clear-cut boundary. The appearance of god to Balaam (Numbers 22:8-13) is treated as a palpable visitation, but since it is at night and the passage ends with the rising of Balaam in the morning, it certainly appears to be a dream, even preprogramed by the prophet. Probably the night journey (the Mi'raj) of Mohammed upon the steed Buraq up to heaven is best interpreted as a dream. Sura 39:42 of the Koran is the Islamic basis for accepting as veritable the witnessing of souls and spirits during sleep.

In the 11th century the Chinese Emperor Shên-tsung reported extensive visitations of the gods in his dreams. An apparently worldwide practice is the purposeful seeking of a god in a dream vision. In India this custom is called dharna, sleeping at night in the temple of the deity (his or her residence, of course) with the expectation of the appearance of the god in a dream. Thothmes IV slept beneath the Sphinx and in a dream was told by the sun-god to clear the image of the Sphinx from encroaching sand. Gudea of Lagash by sleeping in the god's temple received directly from the god Ningirsu specifications for a new temple, even down to a list of materials. The Greeks extensively followed the same practice, designating it by the confusing term incubation. Bellerophon was visited by the goddess in Athene's temple and received from her a heavenly bridle that was beside him when he awoke. Down to the present the Kiwai Papuans practice dharna by sleeping at Augaromuba, an area controlled by the god Sivagu, who regularly visits sleepers there.

Men have always recognized dreams as symbolic, and undoubtedly, dreams have powerfully influenced all conscious manifestations of figurative and symbolic expression. Where we see dreams as generated from within, earlier man regarded dreams as visitations from some outside "other" world. Where we believe that the contents of dreams are all from the dreamer's previous experience, earlier man considered dreams as prophetic. Obviously, then, an expert at interpreting dreams was a prophet himself, a gifted seer. According to Genesis 41:39-44 the Egyptian pharaoh made Joseph a prime minister or vizier solely on the basis of dream analysis. Rationalists might hypothecate that Joseph was an alien who rose in the echelons of administration. Astute rulers of old, conscious of sectionalism and possible revolt from native nobles, often chose competent aliens as officials, but most especially they felt that alien subordinates were more likely than natives to be personally loyal to the monarch. Perhaps the far less sophisticated Hebrews of the era, puzzled at this alien in high Egyptian office, proposed expertise in dream interpretation as the cause for Joseph's rank. However one examines the account, it greatly exalts the interpreter of dreams. Gudea, the king of Lagash, had an even more eminent interpreter, for the goddess Nanshe specifically analyzed the monarch's dreams.

Dreams come in two opposing categories. Men have generally assigned to benevolent spirits the pleasant and prophetic dreams, while terrifying dreams come from malevolent demons of hell. In puritanic societies obviously sexual dreams are ascribed to devils. The Greeks asserted that there were two gates to the cave of dreams: the gate of ivory to release false dreams and the gate of horn to emit true dreams. The Skidi Pawnee Amerindians have a similar myth: dreams from the brown eagle above are holy and valid, while dreams from the white eagle are secular and often false.

AFFLICTIONS. Archaic peoples often feel that the naturally deformed or physically abnormal are under divine protection, but there is no evidence, except in epilepsy and possibly in blindness, that the afflicted themselves thereby felt religious impulses. Since the blind (non-congenital) could visualize from their past and have visual dreams, they were often credited with "second sight," notably Tiresias. Perhaps the blind perceived these qualities as religious, or found survival value in encouraging the notion. Unquestionably epilepsy is associated by many shamans with intense religious awareness, and St. Paul probably experienced an epileptic seizure on the road to Damascus, profoundly altering his spiritual life. In classic times epilepsy was honored as "oracular possession."

Total dissociation, madness, is generally deemed intolerably aberrant in Western minds[57] (and also in China), acceptable within a religious context in the ancient Near and Middle East, and most advocated in India. The ancient Greeks were a bit embarrassed by Dionysian frenzy and ascribed it to the wild orgiastic bacchanals of Asia. Since the Renaissance, classical scholars have conducted a long-standing love affair with ancient Greece, have nonetheless been rather disconcerted by Dionysian madness, and similarly have agreed that it was an alien import from the Middle East. W. F. Otto is rare as a scholar who claims the Dionysian cult indigenous to

Greece.[58]   It would be a relief if all Dionysian
wildness could be explained as purely metaphoric (and
most poets of recent centuries have so treated
Dionysian revels), but the evidence is entirely too
convincing that such extravagant excesses actually
occurred.[59]   The celebrants of Dionysus, goaded to a
towering frenzy, threw themselves upon animals, tame
or wild, with superhuman strength, tore them to
pieces and gnawed with mad delight on the raw flesh;
humans might suffer a similar fate from the
impassioned Maenads (whose name seems etymologically
related to mania), as did Orpheus and Pentheus.[60]
Though not exclusively, women were the chief devotees
of the Dionysian cult.   It would be ungallant to
suggest that the rites precipitated a very primitive
female ferocity glimpsed today only in a stupendous
bargain sale.   Women of classic Greece were
psychically and sexually repressed, and the insane
revels of Dionysus could be the explosion of pent-up
emotions.   However, such overcompensation still
remains hard to stomach.   As W.K.C. Guthrie says with
a puzzled shake of the head, "The worship of Dionysus
is something which can never be wholly explained."[61]
As we push toward ultimate Dionysian dissociation,
rationality is baffled.   The pattern of Euripides'
Bacchae, repeated elsewhere, suggests the male
repugnance to the Dionysian madness but the
inevitable and gory triumph of the mad rites.   The
Greeks attributed the Dionysian excesses to the
lascivious and insanely ecstatic East.   Perhaps the
entire account simply symbolizes reason opposing
madness but being overwhelmed by divine frenzy.

One of the most engrossing passages in Frazer's
Golden Bough is his dramatic recreation of the Day of
Blood when male novices in sacred hysteria emascul-
ated themselves for Cybele, the Great Mother of
Phrygia.[62]   Their genitals were carefully buried in
earth, for to be richly fertile the goddess demanded
the deposit of her priests' virility.   Astarte and
Diana of the Ephesians were similarly imperious.   In
this Asiatic area genuinely flourished the ancient
madness erupting in Dionysian excesses.   Possibly the
rites of Dionysus, largely practiced by women, arose
from the primitive dominance of the Earth Mother, and
Dionysus, frequently represented as an effeminate
male, was her priest.

India proffers some of the most rational of all
human contemplation of the divine, and it also displays the extreme of religious experience in madness.

The primary incentive to this attitude is a Hindu impulse to go beyond any other religion in freeing gods from anthropomorphism. In the three major traditions of Hinduism--Shiva, Vishnu, and Shakti (the Great Goddess)--"the gods and goddesses are often called mad or are described or portrayed as acting as if mad."[63] Shiva[64] and Kali are most obviously the exemplars of divine madness, but to some degree all the deities are mad because:

(1) The gods are the antithesis of all human regulations and restraints. Their behavior ignores all earthly motivation and model. Unpredictable, they are wholly free from the normal and the conventional. The gods are especially awesome as they stun and bewilder mankind.

(2) The gods affirm their transcendence in boggling the pitiful reason of humanity. Madness is divine assertion of a totally different realm, a dimension incomprehensible to mortals.

(3) The gods are aloof from the world and indifferent to it. Creation and destruction are mad capricious whims, since the world is totally inadequate for divine interest.

(4) Man desperately desires stability, rationality, predictability. The gods are totally otherwise, randomly throwing out a world that is ephemeral, illogical, unstable, mad as they are.

Amidst such divine madness, logically (if logic applies in such a universe) the profoundest religious states of man will likewise reside in madness.[65] The mad saints are imitating the deities (Krishna[66] maddens with the insanity of love and life; Shiva and Kali madden with the crashing insanity of the cosmic void). Madness in the saints means their complete absorption into the divine. The mad saints have wholly opted out of this world; their madness is indifference, freedom, transcendence. In Bengal the Baul ("crazy") cult rejoices in total, rapturous divine madness.[67]

Dying is or might be the ultimate "peak experience" of religious madness.[68] For all such devotees there is an appropriate deity, the Indian Chinnamasta ("beheaded"), a Tantric form of the goddess Durga. Perhaps the most appalling upsurge from the deep well of the divine, Chinnamasta is depicted as holding a blood-dripping sword in her right hand and her own severed head in her left hand. Three jets of blood spurt from her headless neck: two jets fountain into the mouths of her devotees and the third arches into her own mouth. The symbolism certainly suggests that her self-slaughter reinvigorates others and is a life-renewing force for herself. This twofold purpose apparently lies behind the ultimate religious dissociation that seeks and demands self-destruction in many tribes of Amerindians of the Great Plains, in berserkers among the Teutons, and in Christian martyrs and crusaders. The first purpose is amenable to rationality, as "the Church is built upon the blood of the martyrs." Participants in "holy wars" rapturously contemplate their own deaths as furthering their sacred cause. The second purpose, of self-rejuvenation, is darkly mythological and magic. Indian myth frequently presents humans who eagerly seek death as the means of another incarnation. Westerners in similar mood probably apply a concept of sacrifice: the destruction of the physical body supposedly releases the non-material spiritual essence, presumably for heavenly reward. But there is a deeply magical concept even beyond this. Apparently many suicides, especially the young, cannot really believe that self-slaying is obliteration of the being and of any further terrestrial existence for them. The pulsating unconscious seems to assure them that suicide is not an end but a means to an end, an acquisition of heightened powers and purity, actually a rebirth. Thus the widespread death-and-resurrection theme is religiously re-enacted by the suicide.[69]

Apollonian religion

Probably the overwhelming majority of intelligent religious moderns would claim that their altered state of awareness, constituting the personal religious experience, is Apollonian. Archaic societies are uniformly Dionysian, and it is doubtful that any appreciable Apollonian religion precedes Ikhnaton, the pharaoh reigning c. 1375 B.C.[70] Psychological association would support and affirm the Apollonian power of the human mind, seeking the fullest balance and harmony of all faculties within the individual. In religion the Dionysian impulse climaxes in emotional raptures, whereas the Apollonian approach finds a quiet, even contemplation, a sense of well-being and spiritual elevation.

Aesthetics.[71] Probably all human art began as religious,[72] communicating an altered state of consciousness within the artist or producing such a change within the observer. Illuminating indeed is the comment of an Indian painter, Jagdish Swaminathan, upon the impact of religious art: "It is like a man chancing on a fragment of mirror in the night and it lights up."[73] To archaic man art is the means whereby human creation can reflect the divine creation. The artist is the vehicle for divine communication to humanity, and the works of art bear coded messages from god to man. In medieval Christianity the avowed role of painting, sculpture, mosaics, and stained glass windows was doctrinal. In the Renaissance much appreciation of religious art became, as is frequent today, aestheticism divorced from religious impulses. Japan from the 8th to the 12th century is the choice example of aesthetics, when, as G.B. Sansom says, "religion became an art and art a religion."[74]

Emotive religious music is Dionysian. Apollonian music is either aesthetic or conceptual. Probably the most consistent wedding of aesthetics and religious awareness in Western society has been in church music, reaching elaborate apogees in polyphonic music, anthems, oratorios, masses, requiems. Conceptual religious music is doctrinal, notably in Protestant hymnology.

Education and learning. Formal education seems universally to have originated in religion and until quite recent generations resisted transfer to purely secular groups. Well into the 19th century Oxford and Cambridge dons, regardless of their academic subjects, were required to hold clerical orders. St. Thomas Aquinas perceived all learning as leading to and summarizable in the deity.

Theology. Perhaps the pinnacle of Apollonian religion is assembling the mass of myth and the heated controversy of ecclesiastics and codifying all into a system agreeable to rationality as well as to the feelings. Reading Bishop Headlam on Christian theology[75] is, for an intellectual, a heady and exhilarating experience--masterful marshalling, weighing, comparing, superb organizing and presenting. Understandably, academic types could well experience from such theology the heightened state of religious awareness, much as Sir James Jeans from physics and astronomy felt an awesome sense of God the Mathematician.

Mysticism

Avoiding psychological terminology, mysticism is transcendence.[76] The mystic ignores, so he says, both mind and body in favor of pure soul, which soars beyond all temporal and spatial limitations. Traditionally all mystic experience has been deemed religious, the ultimate sacral condition attainable by man. In recent generations we are encountering, apparently for the first time, some "secular mysticism," as in Virginia Woolf, which manifests many of the traditional features of mysticism without asserting any religiosity.[77]

In this century the time-honored glory of mysticism has for the first time perhaps suffered some real tarnishing from intellectual sources. Archaic societies encourage mysticism, while modern societies tend to disparage living mystics (like St. Francis of Assisi) but venerate them in retrospect. Today the secular spirit is particularly critical of mysticism even in the area of its greatest survival, India. Depth psychologists refuse to accept the mystic's assertion of total divorce from body and mind. Freudians regard mysticism as a desire to return to the womb,[78] while Jungians interpret mysticism as ouroboric incest, an unwillingness to mature and accept adult realities and responsibilities. Both schools deem mysticism as regression, an aching desire for the sense of total unity in the pre-natal state. In scrutinizing mysticism since the 12th century, Herbert Moller[79] labels much of it hysterical, libidinous, and sado-masochistic. The experimental psychologist J.M. Charcot also associated mysticism with hysteria. Richard Sterba sees mysticism as the human need "to sugar the bitter pill of life with illusions."[80] Other unflattering suggestions are the resemblance of some mysticism to a manic-depressive state[81] or to schizophrenia.[82] Philosophical doubts are also being expressed, denying that the mystic can produce anything beyond his own experience and psychology.[83]

The extensive testimonials from mystics and most non-psychological discussions have otherwise been favorable, even reverential. Archaic societies tend to emphasize Dionysian religion for the general individual and mysticism for their religious leaders. Some archaic societies demand minimal but always some religiosity in the average man, while others demand a great deal, as Amerindians of the Great Plains expected every adult male to experience a profound spiritual vision; but among all archaic societies only the shamans and religious leaders (including chieftains) demonstrated the union, the oneness, with the divine which is the distinctive hallmark of mysticism. The Oglala Sioux named Black Elk recounted to John Neihardt[84] a magnificent and wondrous mystic experience that would honor any saint.

In spite of the multitude of mystics through time and the globe, there seems a remarkable consistent pattern, five stages in the mystic path:

(1) The Awakening. Some jolting experience compels a person otherwise normal and worldly to deep realization of the inadequacy of mundane living and the far greater desirability of the spirit realm. While mankind may generally sense the "other" (the "numinous," as Rudolf Otto terms it)[85] the mystic from the outset is different in his intense desire for union with the numinous. Protected from the harsh sufferings of the world, Gautama was eventually shaken from all conventionality by the sight of hideous human ailments and mutilation and impelled to seek the "other."[86]

(2) The Self-Imposed Exile. In search of union with the "other," the would-be mystic flees from the contagion of the world to practice rigid austerities in isolation, seeking to nullify mind and body so that soul may dwell unsullied in the spirit realm. John the Baptist sought the lunar bleakness east of the Jordan, holy men of the East have sought the mountain fastnesses of the Himalayas, and Christian monasticism was a purposeful retreat altogether from the world.

(3) The Opening of the Door. Cynics will sneer that anyone in dire isolation, long denying even essential food and drink, will begin to hallucinate. Mystics uniformly insist, however, that the fruit of their lonely asceticism is the powerful emergence of the spiritual vision, closed to the worldly, now clearly discernible to the conscientious mystic. Nearby he senses the glory and loveliness of the spirit, and he is joyous with delight surpassing any earthly pleasure.

(4) The Dark Night of the Soul. Having experienced this grandeur, the mystic is distraught to be redeposited in this world of shabby materialism, when

he would yearn for eternal repose in the spirit. The mystic feels himself the most inadequate of beings, the most sinful and despicable of mortals to be lowered from his soul's desire. The phrase, "dark night of the soul" is taken from a classic mystical writing by the Spanish St. John of the Cross.[87] Perhaps the most harrowing depiction of this spiritual agony appears in "Song of Myself" by Walt Whitman. Many would-be mystics never go further. They are presumably edified by their partial traversing of the mystic path although their lives henceforth are lived in the world. The monstrous horrors of hell described by various faiths are certainly indebted to thwarted mystics who seek some personal consolation in imposing upon other people their own sense of guilt and weakness.

(5) The Holy of Holies. The genuine mystic will persistently renew his austerities and can be granted the ultimate rapture. Now he is not nearby but is part of the glory. Warmth and love envelop him; he is one with eternal and infinite truth, and absolutely nothing of the world can match the supernal bliss of this spiritual encompassment. William James suggests[88] that the exalted visionary encounter lasts for about half an hour, perhaps an hour at most. Presumably true mystics may, virtually at will, precipitate these experiences for themselves.

The great power of the mystic among archaic societies is his intense conviction. Moderns skeptically challenge the sanity of such dogmatism, but under archaic conditions the burning sincerity of the mystic is overpowering. Hence the mystic's sense of beatific joy and his absolute certitude that he has gazed upon ultimate truth and eternal wisdom have substantiated (possibly instituted) all the paradisical concepts of man. The well-nigh universal assurance of the mystic postulates goodness and benevolence as the basic cosmic reality. Alistair Crowley of this century has been termed a genuine mystic by his devotees, but when Crowley penetrated through the veil of illusion which is this world to the mystics, he found the ultimate nature of the cosmos to be evil. If truly mystical, Crowley was an extraordinary and recent exception to the usual mystic position.

Further, the mystic recognizes the ineffable nature of his experience. There is no human vocabu-

lary to convey what he underwent. The mystic in
trying to communicate with common mortals must therefore employ figurative language. Some examples from
the wealth of Indian mysticism: god is described as
sounding like the beating of cymbals or the sweet
notes of an invisible stringed instrument; divine
light is that of countless shining jewels and without
visible fuel source, blinding illumination everywhere, like billions of suns; pervading the presence
of the deity is the fragrance of celestial glory.[89]
Possibly all religious poetry is finally mystic in
origin, and the acknowledged symbolism of mysticism
has probably colored and conditioned artistic expression from early times. The concepts of eternity
and infinity almost certainly owe a great deal to the
mystic's rapture.

But the massive and monumental achievement of
mysticism has been the transcendent conviction of
unity, oneness, absolute totality, displaying itself
in:

Unity within the self. R.C. Zaehner designates
this as "monistic mysticism."[90] Such an experience
is an intense interior realization of completely
undifferentiated oneness, not of the divided being
that most humans are. This encounter is the goal of
standard Buddhist mysticism and in Theravada Buddhism
can be non-theïstic.[91] The purpose of such mysticism
is never for the glorification of the ego; mystics
tell constantly of the loss of conventional selfhood.
What is unified and profoundly experienced is the
Cosmic Self (paramātman).[92] Such was the mystical
experience of the Buddha himself.

Unity with all life and nature, what Zaehner
terms "panenhenic mysticism."[93] Such mysticism
experiences total unity and rapport with all mankind,
all life, all nature, all things. Wordsworth in The
Prelude is frequently interpreted as this type of
nature mystic. He conceives of his experience as
focusing upon a god, though he is careful to avoid
the label itself in his early version. Here is a
reaction (not necessarily theistic) from Ramakrishna:
"One day it was suddenly revealed to me that everything is Pure Spirit. The utensils of worship, the
altar, the door frame--all Pure Spirit. Then like a
madman I began to shower flowers in all directions.
Whatever I saw I worshiped."[94] Zen satori cultivates
this type of mystic unity, and drug-induced states
are reported as producing it. Westerners find this

type of mysticism most acceptable as the intensified feeling of brotherhood and camaraderie in Walt Whitman and in Albert Schweitzer's "reverence for life."

Unity with God, the "theistic mysticism" of R. C. Zaehner.[95] This is the most celebrated type in the West, for it is the goal of Christian, Jewish, and Moslem mysticism. Such mystic experience generates a profound sense of identity with the deity, absorption into the godhead. All contradictions and opposites are fully reconciled in the One. All Becoming has been superseded by the One Being. The mystic has reached the Full Stop of life and death, universe and void. Most mystics of this type in the West are highly metaphoric and symbolic, but the 13th century Persian mystic Julāl al-Dīn Rūmī asserts explicitly: "The man who says 'I am the servant of God' asserts that two exist, one himself and the other God. But he who says 'I am God' has naughted himself and cast himself to the winds. He says, 'I am God': that is, 'I am not, He is all, nothing has existence but God, I am pure nonentity, I am nothing.' In this the humility is greater."[96] For Hindu mysticism such a statement, "I am God," similarly is accepted as total unity with the deity.

Impressive as the examples may be from advanced societies, the impact of mystic personalities upon archaic societies has been far greater. Of course, every man has the potentials for these religious experiences, and the mystic can act hypnotically upon his fellows to make them accept much of his revelation, even if they never follow the mystic path as far as he has. Probably mysticism such as that of Ramakrishna, when it would occur among primitives, would institute or substantiate the veneration of many objects as sacred, as living. The common man of the remote past was probably as religiously vague as many humans today,[97] but his half-sensed dreads or hopes would be given definite form and meaning by the inspired mystic. Unquestionably, the mightiest influence of the mystic upon early man consisted of the concept of unity. Some of the possible mythic implications are:

Conceiving of the one animal or totem creature behind the multitude of individual animals; hence the Great Bear, the Great Wallaby, the Great Crocodile.

Conceiving of the one anthropomorphic figure who rules and supervises one type of food animal or all food animals as Lord or Lady of the Beasts.

Conceiving of the High God. The rational deistic view, though wrong in explaining an early monotheism as produced by the logical human mind, could be right in claiming an aboriginal single deity apprehended mystically.

Conceiving of deity incarnate in humans. Rūmī in sophisticated fashion expresses what mystics for millenia have been realizing. Modern man altogether scoffs at recent claims of living persons as incarnations of god, but the concept is widespread in traditional societies and will explain not only religious specialists but also rulers as divine incarnations.

Conceiving of monotheism. Although increased sophistication may account for some monotheism, the origin of belief in a lone deity probably arises from the mystics. To the common man all things are various, and a contest of opposites (good vs. evil, etc.) seems undeniable. To sum up all spirit in One and to penetrate "beyond good and evil" to find all reconciled in the One is the herculean accomplishment of mysticism. Polytheism may properly be applied only to the less thinking and really less religious mob of any society. The mystic compulsion is always towards monotheism. Aeschylus (not necessarily himself a mystic) has a concept of Zeus that strongly resembles the monotheistic Yahweh before the Babylonian captivity. Throughout Indian religious history, the truly spiritual drive has ever been in the direction of monotheism.

Conceiving of the whole idea of unity and oneness in human life with ramifications eventually extending perhaps as far as the resolute quest of today's scientists for a Unified Field Theory. For archaic societies it may well have been the effect of the mystic to enforce a oneness of tribe or clan, a oneness of ruler. The persistence of mysticism into the contemporary world, even though it might appear anachronistic and inappropriate, may well suggest that in early times mysticism was immensely potent and influential far beyond its acknowledged domain in our era.

Part Two - Piety

Personal religion is undergoing a changed state of awareness. Many people who term themselves "religious" seldom if ever actually experience appreciable religious alteration of consciousness. Instead, they are pious, respecting, venerating, worshipping the manifestations of the spirit in other persons and other things. The common man deems most of his world profane, the routine, familiar places and rounds of life. The intrusion of the different, the unusual, arouses in him that combination of admiring and dreading that he terms the sacred and towards which he displays piety. In this age the individual labors under considerable circumscriptions upon arousing the sacred within himself (though bursts of emotive religion will occasionally astound us); piety, perceiving the sacred in something outside, still has remarkable staying powers, as a visit to Russia's holiest shrine, the tomb of Lenin, will demonstrate.

Émile Durkheim as a sociologist proposed this discrimination between the sacred and the profane as the major religious impress upon the common man (mystics see differently, but they are very uncommon persons and statistically negligible). Mircea Eliade has developed this thesis more fully and more recently.[98] Only because almost everything is profane do the sacred things stand out awesomely. In ancient Greece any spot struck by lightning henceforth was sacred to Zeus. Among the ancient Incas anything out of the ordinary was <u>huaca</u> ("sacred")-- twins, an albino, even an egg with two yolks. The inexplicable objects introduced by the Spaniards (e.g. things made of glass or sealing wax) were <u>huaca</u>. Looking outward, piety carefully discriminates the sacred in places, objects, actions, and beings.[99]

Sacred places.[100] Springs, wells, lakes, and rivers of water are perhaps the most obviously sacred spots in many a terrain. Thirst must be quenched at more frequent intervals than hunger must be assuaged, and life-giving water to a desperate man is miraculous and sacred. Christianity took over many pagan practices; hence, York Minster is built over a well, holy long before the coming of the Anglo-Saxons to Britain. The Zande of Africa attribute birth and resurrection to their holy springs. Among the Romans the goddess of springs was Juturna,[101] honored by a

96

fountain in the Roman Forum. In Bandeshwar, Bengal,
is a pond called Poati Bil. A woman, disconsolate at
her failure to become pregnant, tried to drown herself in the pool but was rescued by the water spirit
who promised her pregnancy; because the promise was
fulfilled, barren women ever since have flocked to
bathe in the holy pool of Poati Bil. The Venda of
Africa declare that Lake Fundudzi is the primal womb
from whence all creation started. The Muisca of the
Andes report that mankind first arose from a sacred
lake in the Iquaque region. The same people, living
amidst five sacred lakes, regularly perform baptism,
ritual purification, and lustral rites in these
lakes, sacred especially for "rebirth." In Tibet
prophetic visions from the sacred lake Chokhorgyal
have been instrumental in ascertaining what male
child is the reincarnation of the Dalai Luma.

Moving and especially sounding water is most
marvelous of all. When the early Hebrew scriptures
speak of "living waters," they refer to the sacred
stream in an arid land; originally they meant
"living" quite literally. Early myth seems uniformly
to associate rivers with femininity, the emblem of
fertility and nourishment. The section of the Niger
flowing through Bambara territory is considered the
body of Faro, the goddess of all proliferation. In
the vast mythology of rivers perhaps India is outstanding from the charmingly "cute" to breath-taking
majesty. The holy river Kaaveri is named for the
lovely daughter of Brahma who married the sage
Agasthya on condition that he never leave her alone.
Going on an errand, Agasthya deposited Kaaveri in a
vase entrusted to a disciple. Piqued, Kaaveri caused
the disciple to stumble, the vase fell and shattered,
and Kaaveri flowed off as the river. The sacred
Ganges is really three rivers--celestial, earthly,
and subterranean. The Ganges originates from the
foot of Vishnu from whence it flows across the
heavens as the Milky Way. It descends to earth from
the locks of Shiva's hair and so emerges through the
Himalayas (abodes of gods) into the plains far below.
Benares is especially a holy city at the intersection
of all three Ganges. The river Ganges is personified
as a goddess of abundance and health. Only three
places in the world exhibit spouting geysers and
eerie thermal areas. For the Scandinavian settlers
in Iceland, for the Amerindians of the Yellowstone
area, and the Maoris about Rotorua in the North
Island of New Zealand, these wondrous regions conferred awe and generated extensive myth. The Council

of Tours in 561 A.D. forbade water worship as idolatry, but a century later St. Cummin was still fulminating against the practice.

As rivers are sacred, "crossing over" is momentous and the specific place of crossing is especially holy, notably in the days before bridges. The ford, the river crossing, the tirtha of India, has been a place of devotion and pilgrimage probably long before the origin of any myth attached to it. Deities frequent fords, as Hera in the guise of an aged crone at a ford accosted Jason, who carried the goddess across on his shoulders. The most awesome river crossings proceed from the land of the living to the land of the dead. Thus Greek souls crossed the Styx to Hades, and Indian dead cross the Vaitaranī to the realm of Yama. The map of England is dotted with the names of fords (Oxford, Thetford, Crawford, etc.). We generally assume that the designations arose solely from transportation needs, but it is likely that in far-distant times these fords were profoundly sacred.

The Kogis of the Andes affirm that caves are openings into the body of the Universal Mother. The "Cave of Eileithyia" in the Odyssey (XIX, 188) near Knossos was a shrine for the Goddess of Childbirth. Since the Early Stone Age the cave has apparently been a symbol for the womb. What amount to artificial caves, such as prehistoric dolmens and more recent mausoleums, are equated with the womb. Complications arise with limestone caverns displaying stalagtites and stalagmites; these caves are associated with the lingam of the male and also suggest the vagina dentata ("toothed vagina"). Caves were apparently the only shrines of prehistoric Crete. At Ajanta near Bombay is an ancient Buddhist monastery consisting of caves cut into the rock hillside. Probably this ancient symbol explains why many religious edifices are constructed as dark caverns.

A sacred stone is a baetylus, and most obviously of divine origin is a meteorite, hurled from heaven. The sacred black stone (Hajaru 'l-Aswad) in the Kaaba at Mecca is a meteorite holy long before Mohammed. The Great Phrygian Mother Cybele was transported to Rome in the shape of the sky-fallen stone of Pessinus. At Tekekekiör, Turkey, stands a shrine for a meteorite supposedly airlifted from Khorassan a millenium ago. Zeus Kappotas was a huge Grecian rock

struck by lightning and thereafter charged with the
dread power of the Thunderer. Pausanias reported (I,
43, 2) that the women of Megara performed rites at a
nearby stone to which Demeter supposedly summoned her
ravished daughter Persephone from the underworld.
Stones heated by volcanic or thermal energy are
obviously touched by the divine. So concluded the
natives of Tanna Island in the New Hebrides about
rocks in a steaming spring at Port Resolution.
Cook's crew gathered these stones ostensibly for
ballast, but, knowing better, the Tannese assert that
the Westerners sought those sacred stones of wisdom
to gain their present knowledge and power.

The Mosaic commandment witheringly denounces
"graven images" and "likenesses" (and Yahweh was
angered by the Golden Calf), which are properly
termed iconic, but there is absolutely no prohibition
on aniconic (i.e. unshaped stones) surrogates of the
god. The stone worshipfully selected by Jacob
(Genesis 28:18) and anointed with oil looks like just
such an aniconic "god-stone." This same anointing
with oil of an aniconic surrogate is still practiced
in Indian village worship. In very early Greek religion aniconic idols preceded statues. In archaic
Arcadia a square block represented Zeus, and at
Thespiae a crude stone was the earliest representation of Eros. Ordinary appearing stones are
profane, but stones in unusual shapes from natural
forces are commonly regarded as sacred. The standard
practice, as widely demonstrated today in India, is
to interpret strangely formed stones as female
deities, especially stones with hollows, holes, or
swelling curves. Stones with resemblances to balls,
the lingam, or a bull are attributed to male gods.
Stones piled up in small heaps generally represent a
local deity in India. The ancient Incas followed the
same practice, as did the early Greeks. Hermes
literally means "he of the stone heap," apparently a
deification of such cairns marking travel routes.

Aniconic representations of male deities frequently take the form of pillars. Still a bit enigmatic is the Djed-column, ritually raised to an erect
position in the annual ceremony celebrating the
resurrection of the Egyptian Osiris; the column may
have consisted of a tree trunk with branches stripped
off, or perhaps a human backbone. The Baalim (a
plural) were Canaanite and Syrian male deities
symbolized by a pillar. In Greece pillars represented the Heavenly Twins (Dioscori) among the Spar-

tans and symbolized Zeus of Mount Lykaios on the mountain peak. Such pillars are usually considered phallic symbols, as are the prehistoric monoliths, menhirs, and the traditional maypole. Frankly phallic is the lingam, strongly associated with the worship of Shiva. Millions of the lingam are displayed in India from the innermost section of the deity's shrines to the amulets given by husbands to wives on their wedding day. The Westerner usually reacts to the prevalent representation with shock or with lascivious jest. Most Indologists protest that the lingam has no such crudely sexual meaning to Indians. The Christian cross (which some have labeled as a phallic symbol) meant shame and degradation to pagan Rome but means glorious salvation and heavenly hope to a Christian. Indians should be given credit for as much change in symbolism as Christians. Even among ancient Greeks and Romans the phallus did not signify mere copulation but bore the wider connotation of fertility and nutrition (psychoanalysts claim that eating and sexual intercourse are interchangeable to the unconscious). Indians insist that the lingam symbolizes the creative energy of Shiva and the generative drive of the universe.

In South India a sacred site is often an anthill (actually a hill of termites). In spite of its dramatic upward extrusion, the anthill does not appear phallic; actually it is frequently associated with the goddess Bhavani whose representation shows her as an anthill topped by a divine head hooded by an overarching snake. The anthill is interpreted as entry to the lower world, as treasure trove, as residence of subterranean serpents. The uplifted portion of the anthill suggests the primordial mound, the hill of creation.[102]

Trees as well as pillars and mountains have also been identified as phallic symbols. Perhaps our unconscious is quite monotonously repetitive, but there are other possibilities. The tree is the largest and most omnipresent of living things to most humans and is logically an arch symbol for life and divinity. Many myths associate females rather than male deities with trees. In ancient Chinese myth the giant mulberry tree Fu Sang was the Mother God. Early inhabitants of Cyprus worshipped the cypress (a tree giving its name to the entire island) as manifestation of the goddess Beroth. Teutonic myth states that an elm tree given soul by Odin, senses by Hoenir, blood and warmth by Lodur, became the first woman, Embla. The dryads and hamadryads (tree nymphs) of ancient Greece were female. The Daedala festival in Boeotia was based on a myth of Hera quarreling with Zeus and hiding in pique; Zeus then artfully dressed an oak trunk as a bride and circulated rumors of his remarriage. The enraged Hera swept in to rip the clothes from the tree trunk. This episode looks like a very ancient rite of male marriage to a tree bride. Such a rite is still performed in village India, and in India many trees are residences of goddesses: Durga in the jujube tree, Banni Mahankali in the banni tree, the wife of Vishnu in the tulashi tree.[103] There appear too many, and too archaic, ascriptions of the female to trees to accept phallicism solely.

Many tree references, at least consciously, are less phallic than metaphoric of life, luxuriance, and productivity, as Krishna says in the Bhagavad-Gita, "among all trees I am the ashvattha" (ficus religiosa), and Christ says (John 15:1), "I am the true vine." Trees to archaic societies suggest intermediaries between earth-bound man and deities of the sky. The messengers of the gods, birds, perch extensively in trees. Fires, usually from firewood, shoot flames and sparks skywards; and any sizable object lifting skywards can be interpreted as an axis mundi (cosmic axis). Sacred groves are an extension of the sacred tree concept. Once prevalent in pagan Europe, they are still widespread through Africa and Asia, in many areas representing the only surviving wooded tracts. An especially majestic tree may be the focal point of the sacred grove, or some aniconic representation may be at the center. Vedic literature considered heaven a sacred grove (Nandana) of Indra. In effect, such sacred groves often acted as game preserves, as animals taking refuge there are obviously under divine protection. Agamemnon, hunting near unfamiliar Aulis, apparently slew a deer from a sacred grove of Artemis and further multiplied the horrors of the House of Atreus.

Sacred trees may originally have been trees growing from the graves of ancestors. Trees would logically seed an area of turned soil. The Aeneid (Book III) reports a bush growing from the grave of Polydorus, a son of Priam murdered in Thrace; blood drips from the broken branches, and the voice of the slain Trojan groans from his disturbed rest. In many parts of the world a tree is ritually planted upon the grave of the deceased. Wordsworth suggests in

Laodamia that the souls of the dead lovers have entered the trees sprung up from their graves; the concept is ages old.

Psychoanalysts suggest that a mountain may stand for the _mons veneris_, and the Venusberg ("mountain of Venus") of Tannhäuser legend literally states it. "Sleeping woman" or "Supine goddess" is the meaning of many names for mountains suggesting female breasts. Even more frequent seems the practice of naming the largest of mountains in an area as "Mother" and considering smaller mountains as her children. Such is the practice on Tsushima Island, between Japan and Korea, and among the Kogis and Ijcas of the Andes. Most, however, of the "sexed" mountains are conceived of as males, like Mt. Parwatararaja in early Java and the five sacred mountains (Wi Yo) representing the center and compass points of China. Early agricultural societies regard mountains as sacred because vivifying waters pour downward from the heights to the cultivated fields below. Preponderantly, mountains are holy or sacred because they suggest nearness to celestial beings. As an erect biped, man's inherent symbolism suggests that the upper, the higher, is nobler, more divine. While Fujiyama is a Shinto deity, the chief purpose of ascending the mountain is to approach the celestial. In Greece and Greek-cultured lands of antiquity many mountains and ridges still show the remnants of thrones cut into the stone for the gods. Among the Kogis of the Andes everything above 2000 meters is sacred. In India, Vishnu dwells atop Mount Meru, and Shiva upon Mount Kailāsa as Zeus resided upon Mt. Olympus. As recently as 1913 Nhlangakazi became a holy mountain of the Nazaretha Church, founded amongst the South African Zulus by Isaiah Shombe.

If one lacks mountains, then build one's own sacred mount, as did the Mesopotamians in a flat countryside. The Babylonians demonstrated that their ziggurat was an _axis mundi_ by designating temples as "House of the Mount of All Lands," "Mount of Tempests," or "Link between Heaven and Earth." Even with surrounding hills, Buddhists erected a magnificent mountain at Borobudur in Java; the devotee would ascend the successive terraces which promised ever-ascending levels of spiritual heightening. The most zealous construction of artificial mountains was in Central America. Hundreds are already known from the huge pyramid at Teotihuacan near Mexico City to little jungle-smothered ziggurat-type structures; out in the dense tropical forest are probably hundreds more, constituting the world's most ambitious attempt to construct mountains reaching toward god above.

The pious from time immemorial have worshipped at sites where the sacred has occurred in the past. Hermopolis (Greek for the Egyptian Chmunu), according to its priests, had been the spot where the primal cosmic egg had been deposited; and, apparently, awed pilgrims of antiquity were permitted to gaze upon fragments of this cosmic egg. Heliopolis (Greek for Egyptian Junu), a sacerdotal rival, countered with the boast that the temple of Atum bestrode the primeval hill where all creation began. The sacred area of Nippur, Mesopotamia, encompassed the very spot where the god Enlil had split the crust of earth with his pickaxe so that mankind could emerge from the depths to populate the world's surface. A sanctuary of the Kabre of Togo is a rock marked with resemblances to human footprints, made by the first pair of humans on earth. A bit macabre is the Shaivite shrine at Silda in West Bengal; as Shiva was whirling about in despair with his dead wife Sati on his shoulders, part of her decomposed body fell off here. Representative of the original creation of shrines and temples are the three types of Buddhist reliquaries (stupas):

(1) Body relics of Buddha. A magnificent temple in Rangoon, Burma, houses some hairs of Buddha, while his left eye-tooth constitutes the great treasure of Kandy, Sri Lanka.

(2) Objects associated with his life. Various temples enshrine the begging bowl, staff, water pot, and fragments of his robe.

(3) Events in the career of Buddha. The "Four Great Miracles" are celebrated at: birthplace of Buddha, scene of his Enlightenment under the bodhi-tree, site of his first sermon, place of Buddha's death. The Sikh faith erected at Gurdwara a temple to house the original text of the sacred scriptures of Sikhism, known as Ādi Granth or Guru Granth (i.e. surpassing any human teacher). Islam has tried vigorously to prevent the cult of relics, but the tomb of the Prophet at Medina receives extensive veneration from pilgrims.

In historic times religious structures have regularly been erected basically because a local population needs a nearby worship site. Under such circumstances the concept of the sacred must be generated by: visions of the holy reported on this site, the clergy elaborately consecrating as hallowed ground, or sacral omens or compass point directions rendering religiously symbolic. Early worship places during the adoration of the Great Mother apparently heightened their symbolism by resemblance to the womb. Religious edifices of late patriarchal origin often seek to represent the Macrocosm in the Microcosm; angels and heavenly vistas on church ceilings are part of the symbol of the entire universe.

The nomadic life was standard for early man. When taking up residence in a new area, tribes or clans would bring their traditional myths with them and often apply these myths to the surrounding landscape. The Maui myth is shared by all the Polynesian peoples from Hawaii to New Zealand; the original homeland for these far-roamers and for the Maui account probably was Tahiti or some similar central Pacific island. On each of the major islands of the Hawaiian group (Hawaii, Maui, Kauai, and Oahu) residents have identified specific locales with objects, characters, and sacred places of the Maui myth.[104]

Jerusalem is a holy city for three religions: Judaism, Christianity, Islam. Benares in India is sacred to two great faiths--to Hinduism because here the celestial, the earthly, and the underground of the goddess river Ganga converge; to Buddhism because Buddha preached his first sermon at suburban Sarnath. Ancient Cuzco was so sacred a city that the roads thereto had special shrines at the point where the Peruvian capital first came in sight. Whatever the mythical explanation, the sacredness of capital cities usually arises from the awesome concentration of power and population in the major metropolis.

Sacred actions. Obviously the god has spoken when bumper crops and ample hunting animals reveal a beneficent and contented deity. The wrath of an angry god is more manifest and more fearsome by far when flood, drought, pestilence, earthquakes, and similar catastrophes blast a humanity ignoring its obligations to the deity. Such is sacred overt action by deities, and the divine mood is all too clear; but what is the reason for divine disfavor and how rectify our impious derelictions? A diviner is needed to ascertain the ways of god, unfathomable to common mortals but revealed to this religious specialist. Mantic art is especially needed to interpret divine predictions of the future, again cryptic to most people but analyzable by trained specialists in the flights of crook-clawed birds or a soaring eagle on the right flank of an advancing army.[105]

Independent sacred objects. All the following sacred objects are highly symbolic and supposedly endowed with supernatural power:

Fetish[106] is some object into which supernatural force has entered to charge it with the strength of the spirit world. Men have never merely worshipped "stocks and stones" as we might derisingly sneer. They have made fetishes of relics from saints and martyrs, because obvious divine power is located there. Formal Christianity and formal Buddhism both insist that the relics are simply to aid reverence and meditation, but, in fact, many pious members of both faiths have made fetishes of such remains. Back in the 18th century K.A. Böttiger suggested that the trident of Poseidon and the caduceus of Hermes began as fetishes and were deified or had local deities attached to them. Japanese Shintoism especially venerates shintai ("divine substance"), fetishes of little intrinsic value, but a repository of the divine: stones, sacred texts, ancient swords, and such. The shintai at the great imperial shrine of Ise, reverently enveloped in numerous clothes and caskets, is a mirror (a sun-symbol or magic with its image-reflecting power). Auguste Comte muddied the waters by extending the concept of fetishism so far that it really meant complete nature worship. The term fetish should better be confined to an object such as the omphalos rock at Delphi in ancient Greece.[107]

Palladium is some object which is a guarantee of tribal or group security as long as it is carefully retained and protected; the loss or destruction of the palladium means the destruction of the group. The classic example is the statue of Pallas Athene, guarded assiduously by the Trojans and stolen by Odysseus and Diomedes to doom Ilium. The equivalent for an individual is known as a life-token, an object which contains the core of a person's life. A famous example of a life-token is the firebrand inextricably tied with the fortunes of Meleager. His mother,

Althea, advised that Meleager would live only until the brand was consumed, snatched the firebrand from the flames at the child's birth; enraged when he killed her brothers, she hurled the brand into the flames, and as the brand was consumed, Meleager expired. A Kashmiri story ascribes to Panj Phul a necklace which similarly was her life-token.

A talisman[108] is an object that actively creates good fortune, attracting welfare and greatly aiding the person wearing it, for a talisman is normally small and light. One of the most impressive of talismans is the "medicine bundle" of the Amerindians of the Great Plains. The Skidi Pawnee also call their bundle "wrapped-up rainstorm" from its ability to induce rainfall or "mother" from the dried corn in the bundle, symbolically the progenitor of the tribe. Aladdin's lamp, Aaron's rod, the magician's wand, and cloaks of invisibility are among the numerous talismans.

An amulet[109] is also normally a small object carried or worn, but it is a passive device, warding off evil and suffering from its possessor. Possibly all decorative jewellery originated as amulets. The Iroquois Amerindians wear a miniature canoe to prevent drowning. Jade bracelets are protection from harm according to the Chinese. In the Punjab rings or earrings of copper fend off sciatica. As an infant, Krishna (an avatar of Vishnu) received from his foster-mother Yashoda an amulet that thereafter effectively guarded him against all malevolent forces.

Chapter IV Religious Specialists

"It is highly probable, indeed, that the first priest appeared in the world simultaneously with the first religion; nay, that he actually invented it."[1] This squib, snorted out of anti-clerical scorn by H. L. Mencken, probably seemed to him and to his readers hyperbolic satire, but it must be partially true. As the myths about culture-bringers indicate, humanity realizes that its culture results from the creative experience and communication of a very few individuals.[2] The few members of a primitive society who were deeply stirred by religious impulses and had the faculty of imparting their heightened state of awareness first promulgated myth. Subsequent creative and religious persons added new and more profound perceptions.[3]

Almost certainly the religion of both Greece and India before the Indo-European invasions was worship of the mother goddess, emphasizing fertility. The works of Homer and the Vedic literature countered with the warrior gods of patriarchal war bands. For most of classic Greek antiquity the Homeric deities were the nominal, though growingly inappropriate, gods for a society vastly different from Homer's era. Perhaps one of the reasons for the growth of Greek philosophy was the quelling of fruitful spiritual expansion because of the dominance of Homeric myth. The spell of Homer's mythmaking belatedly gave way to the yearnings for individual spirituality and individual immortality, catered to by the mystery cults. In India the Vedic grip was loosened at one end by the resurgence of the Great Mother in Shaktism and at the other by the remarkable thrust of Buddhism. The recurrent pattern consists of a mythical system, assignable to an individual or an elitist group, that persists with amazing strength well beyond its full usefulness, yielding grudgingly but eventually to a new visionary, a new myth creator. Buddhism was classified as an "unorthodox" form of Hinduism and apparently could not supersede the entrenched Hinduism that now has virtually excluded it from India.

Although right in ascribing the origin of religion to religious specialists, Mencken was wrong in crediting the invention to the priest, a relatively recent professional. Long before priests there were religious specialists of unknown antiquity. The following list, therefore, cannot claim chronological order, although we have evidence suggesting the shaman before the other religions specialists and we know of the late appearance of the priest. A multitude of labels has been applied to these specialists in religion,[4] but all should be subsumed under the few categories below. Understandably, there are numerous examples of mingling several elements in a single religious specialist, and there are countless shadings and gradations, but the listing below still should give reasonable structure to a complex worldwide manifestation.

Figures of dissociation

The basic personal religious impulse discussed in the previous chapter under Dionysian, certainly the oldest state of altered awareness, is dissociational. The earliest religious specialists were thus moved to a usurpation by the unconscious. While their fellows might display kindred symptoms, the specialists regularly and intensely dwelt upon dissociational tendencies rare or even unknown personally by many members of their society. To be a religious specialist under archaic conditions and to maintain prestige with one's society it was essential continually to display these unusual dissociational qualities.

Shaman. The distinctive characteristic of the primitive shaman is the dissociational faculty[6] of ekstasis,[7] literally "standing outside oneself." Such ekstasis involves bilocation, i.e. presence simultaneously at two totally different points. The shaman often states that he can stand at some distance from his body and gaze upon himself as he is devoured or pulverized by supernatural forces. He is also capable in the presence of others of leaving his body while he is making a journey to the spirit realm. We would interpret this experience as employing the metaphor of an outer, geographic journey for what is an inner, psychic quest. Dreams have certainly contributed, but the idea of a soul separate and distinct from the body must have gained its major conviction from the fervid narration of an intense vatic personality, the shaman. T'ie-kuai Lo, one of the Eight Immortals of Taoism, could project his soul out of his body for days at a time. Once he instructed a disciple to burn his body on the seventh day if his soul had not returned. Hearing of a problem at his home, the disciple cremated the body on the sixth day and hastened home. Returning, the soul of T'ie-kuai Lo had to settle for the body of an aged beggar just dead from the cold. Hermotimus of ancient Greek Clazomenae reputedly could leave his body and return months later. Bilocation has been claimed for Pythagoras, Aristeas, Apollonius of Tyana in antiquity and St. Anthony of Padua and Francis Xavier of Christian times. Luke 24:33-36 suggests bilocation for the risen Christ. Other aspects[8] generally associated with the shaman are:

(1) Call to shamanism. The hallmark of shamanism is an intensely individual galvanizing, an imperious summons to the religious life. Properly, no one is a shaman by birth or by a planned career. Often the shaman begins as a very commonplace, even disreputable, character like Nāmadeva of India who had robbed and killed in his youth before the call. Young people are often reluctant to obey the call to shamanism, for it is a difficult and lonely existence (cf. the initial reluctance of many Christian saints). Some grave climax turns a life completely around: serious illness or injury, a shattering emotional experience, a deeply moving visitation of the spirit. Frequently, among many peoples, shamans are said to be recognizable in youth: shy, moody, introverted young males who are better dreamers than hunters. Mohave Amerindians declare that masturbating and effeminate young males are likely to become shamans. There is, consequently, a difference of opinion among psychological authorities, some deeming the shaman normal but sensitive and gifted,[9] while others look upon the shaman as hysterical, himself undergoing severe regression and inducing regression in his society.[10] Because of his position as mediator between mankind and the mysterious supernatural world, the shaman usually dwells apart from his fellows and often seems to be depressed, highly eccentric, unsocial. Mircea Eliade sees the shaman[11] undergoing a self-triggered initiation instead of the traditional and formal group-sponsored initiation. Such an experience effectively channels the shaman's neurosis into personal and group benefits. The dramatic conversion of a mundane secular person to the awesome religious vocation of the shaman is an immemorial practice still operative today. If we assume that personal religion basically arises from individual crisis, then the shaman is the archetypal religious personality and the model for many humans in their spiritual quest.

(2) Induction into shamanism. The would-be shaman usually is a disciple to an established shaman, but his chief instruction is from spirits. First he must undergo a death of the old self and the rebirth of a new self, the full-fledged shaman. The

term shaman[12] is taken from the Tungu people of Siberia who insist that the ghosts of dead shamans skeletonize the new candidate, eating his flesh and drinking his blood before covering his bones with new flesh. Similarly the nearby Buriats aver that the spirits of deceased shamans conduct the initiate into the heavenly realm, cut him into pieces, consume all the edible portions, then reassemble the bones and cover them with flesh, all the while giving him instruction. Samoyeds of Siberia say that a smith from the underworld hacks the shaman's body to pieces, then boils the flesh as food for the spirits. The smith clamps the shaman's head upon the anvil as he instructs the novice how to cure disease and save souls; then the smith reconnects the bones with iron wire and covers them with flesh. In Tibet one Tantric rite calls upon the celebrant to summon the terrifying, cannibalistic spirits to come and eat of his flesh. Reputedly the Buddha gave his own flesh to starving animals. Three angels or perhaps just St. Gabriel opened the body of Mohammed and washed away all doubt, paganism, and error. The transformation of the inner nature is graphically depicted as physical death-and-resurrection. The prevalence of this concept in tropical areas untouched by seasonal cycles of vegetation certainly suggests that the basic origin of the death-and-resurrection theme is psychological, not arising from mere observation of plant decline and regrowth. The refleshing of the bones is a theme powerful among primitive hunters, fostering bone and skeleton preservation in expectation of rebirth. The spirit eating of the candidate's flesh encourages ritual cannibalism (i.e. taking literally what had developed as an effective symbol).

Many cultures report that the spirits in reconstructing the shaman implant some magic substance within him; such concretization symbolizes the new element in the shaman's psyche. A quartz crystal (a superb image in its transparency and glitter) is suggested among many Australian aborigines and other peoples, paralleling the "diamond" (vajra) of an Indian yogi. The Siona in South America consider the magic additive intangible and dispersed throughout the shaman's body. This dau may be fused together and removed by the shaman himself for high-powered invocation of spirits. Dau is double-edged, waxing in potency as it grows but also becoming more susceptible to injury, again vividly portraying the glory and the peril of the psychic realm.

(3) The shaman's journey. Ekstasis,[13] central
to shamanism, is regularly represented as a journey
to the spirit realm. The shaman leaves his body to
fly to another world, often as a bird or flying
insect. This bird-flight of the shaman possibly explains the mythical attitude toward birds. To many
peoples a bird is a shaman's spirit. Hence the
talking birds, creatures of great knowledge like the
birds who informed Siegfried of Regin's villainous
designs. Many gods, like Egyptian Horus and Grecian
Athene, look like birds deified, perhaps originally
as shaman spirits. Hermes, angels, and similar
supernatural beings are winged humans, intermediaries
like the shaman between earth and heaven. A carved
bird on a post has been the shaman insignia for millenia, the proud badge of the specialist in flights
of the spirit.

   Psychoanalysts interpret as a symbol of sexual
intercourse the universal human dream of flying; they
further suggest that for the shaman the sense of
flying represents incest with the Earth Mother. The
shaman himself interprets this ekstasis as transcendence, and certainly we might accept his flight as an
emblem of escape from the routine world and the
conscious to the other-worldlike unconscious. Much
of the myth of the South American Siona centers upon
this flight to the spirit realm. The outstanding
characteristic of the 84 Great Grubchen of Tibet was
their ability to fly by innate ability or with aids
such as magical shoes. Abaris, a Hyperborean priest
of Apollo according to the ancient Greeks, flew on an
arrow. The flying carpet of Arabian Nights fame is a
parallel. Among central Asiatics the shaman often
undertakes his journey upon a wondrous horse, similar
to Pegasus. Mohammed flew to heaven astride Burāq, a
fabulous beast resembling a horse. The shaman may be
accompanied by a humanoid guide, a psychopomp
("spirit escort") guiding souls from this world to
another, or the shaman himself acts as psychopomp to
another soul. Hermes looks more and more shamanic as
we note the god's role as a psychopomp in antiquity.
The Sybil of Cumae is a shamaness psychopomp who
conducts Virgil to the underworld. Many shamans
worldwide venture upon the spirit journey whenever
any group member dies, in order properly to conduct
the soul to the realms of the dead.[14] St. Christopher
("Christbearer") may be the alteration of the
Egyptian psychopomp Anubis, now made the bearer of
Christ across the waters of life to the eternal.[15]

   Most awesome of the shaman's ekstasis is his

momentous and eerie encounter with the other-world. The euphoric delights of heaven and the loathsome stenches of hell are in everyman's dreams, but, unquestionably, the specialist in visits to these areas, the shaman, has colored all our myths and all our ideas about these eldritch habitations. Some island or coastal people launch shamanic voyages to the bottom of the sea, like the Thongas of Africa whose religious specialists claim long stays in the ocean depths. The extraordinary journey of the shaman has largely created the concepts about the judgment of souls and the extremely hazardous bridge that must be traversed to heaven, the unskillful plunging into hell. More than any other human, the shaman has from primeval times actually reveled in the rapturous state of the celestial realm and trembled amidst the abysmal horrors of the infernal regions. The later discussion of psychology-and-myth will explore this otherworldly geography that, above all others, the shaman has bequeathed to mankind.

(4) The shaman and animals. Already noted is the frequent appearance of the shaman as a bird. Herodotus (4.14) reports that Aristeas of Proconnesus would appear in the form of a crow. The first Buriat (Northern Asia) shaman was the son of an eagle. Kiowa Amerindians say that at death a shaman's soul enters an owl. The idea of the soul departing the body in dove form probably owes much to shamanism. Especially in a hunting society, the culture stage in which the shaman apparently originated, the shaman was of extreme importance in his ability to assume animal shape by sending his soul into the body of an animal. A Malaysian shaman can assume tiger form, while among some Amerindians the shaman may appear as a jaguar. Among the Desana of South America the same word means either "jaguar" or "shaman." Tupari (South America) shamans communicate with dead shamans who reappear as man-beasts. The shaman of many areas will don an animal mask, indicating the creature he has become. The host of bizarre Egyptian half-man half-beast gods (e.g. hawk-headed Horus, jackal-headed Anubis) certainly look like shamans. All the world's mythology is replete with this extraordinary mixture of human and animal, and the shaman is behind many of these weird combinations. The centaurs may have originated as horse-masked shamans, the satyrs as goat-masked shamans. Especially, many Amerindians have a remarkable figure combining sly trickster, creator, and culture bringer: Coyote (Great Plains), Great Hare (Eastern Woodlands), Raven (NW Pacific coast). All of these beings are labeled as animals

but they behave exactly like human beings, i.e. exactly like the masked shaman--half-man half-beast.

The shaman regularly possesses an animal spirit helper as companion. Birds are favorites, to soar along with shamans in their flights. Dogs often accompany shamans, for dogs seem to perceive spirits that normal humans cannot. Cats always have an aloof air of detachment, as though they really belong in some other realm and are rather bored here. Many animals may be spirit guardians, but especially relished are creatures that are mixed, to indicate participation in two worlds. Grasshoppers are insects that hop rather than fly. Ducks are birds but swim like a fish. Vultures, crows, ravens, and cranes display unusual feeding habits for birds; vultures, crows, and ravens act as scavengers while cranes eat frogs and snakes. Even common folks may learn the language of birds and animals when serpents tongue their ears just as snakes treated Melampus, but shamans simply by being shamans can understand the speech of birds and beasts. Everyman's dream-world, certainly among primitives living closely with the animal world, contains the beasts that speak and the uncanny mixtures of man and other species; but powerful impetus certainly came from shamanic practices.

(5) Shaman and sexuality. We have no trace of the shaman before the hunting period and therein the shaman is a male. Among the Yagé of South America the Jaguar Mother is the mother of shamans, suckling them at her breasts. The death-and-resurrection theme here is interpreted as dying to this world and being reborn as a child of the Jaguar Woman. The representation of pharaoh sucking on the teats of the cow goddess Hathor therefore suggests the shaman origin of the sacred king. Many peoples, such as the Tajiks and Uzbeks of central Asia, believe that the shaman has sexual intercourse with the goddess. For the Fon of Dahomey, the great demigods are vodu (cf. voodoo of Haiti); the male religious specialists are vodusi ("mates of the god"). In ancient Babylonia in the ritual marriage of Tammuz and the goddess Ishtar, the king took the role of Tammuz. Central to the Middle East is this myth of the generally mortal male (Tammuz, Adonis, Attis, Eshmun) in liaison with the goddess. All of this sounds like the male shaman and the Great Mother. In addition to his spirit spouse, a shaman might be married to a mortal woman, but far more frequently than most adult males, the shaman was likely to be celibate, anticipating the practice of

113

many later clerics. The shaman was rendered less attractive to women because of his moody, introspective nature, because his frequent forays to the other world would disconcert many wives and force hermitage upon him,[16] and also because of the shaman's frequent sexual ambiguity.

Transvestism[17] is still the practice of many male shamans and probably is one of the reasons for the female apparel of many Middle Eastern priests in antiquity and a robed priesthood even to the present. The shaman and his society interpreted this transvestism as another representation of the mediating and unifying function of the shaman. As he brought this world and the other world together in his person, he also united both sexes within himself. Psychologists would state this in other terms: a shaman is an androgynous personality with strong elements of feminine sensitivity joined with the male. French explorers of North America applied the term berdache to transvestite Amerindian shamans. Tiresias has the appearance of a transvestite shaman; the transvestism of Hercules and Achilles, while less obvious, still suggests shamanic origin. Possibly the shaman was the idolized figure of Palasgian (pre-Greek) society or of early Indo-European hunting culture. Homer and his age obviously preferred the warrior-band hero as their central male figure, but some features of the remote societies may have survived from the primitive shamanic Hercules and Achilles. In these later portraits the transvestism of Hercules is treated as a punishment and that of Achilles as a game.[18] Shiva reputedly cursed any intruder of a sacred grove, so that when the male Ila inadvertently entered this forest, he was transformed into a woman subsequently known as Sudyumna. Eventually Sudyumna altered: a woman one month and a male the next month. Certainly this account has the earmarks of ritual transvestism, suggesting that at religious ceremonies in the sacred grove Ila was a transvestite. Frequently the berdache was homosexual, and the Mohave Amerindians still assert that a homosexual shaman, taking the passive or feminine role of a catamite, proves far more powerful than a heterosexual shaman. Again the shaman is perceived as a male-female combination.

The female shaman seems a later religious specialist than the male shaman. The shift from a hunting to an agricultural economy with the attendant elevation of the Great Mother tended to shift shamanic roles to women, especially as the priest now emerges in this culture as the male religious specialist. In many societies with priests today the shamanic role frequently is deemed inferior and is generally associated with women. The shamaness dominates among the Samoyed people of N. Asia, modern Korea and the Philippines, the Araucanian and Guajiro Amerindians of S. America. The female performs the same functions as a male shaman and often has a divine male spouse. Possibly Greek myths of women copulating with gods had an origin in the shamaness. In ancient Peru the chief female religious specialist was regarded as the wife of the Sun. Among the Yoruba of W. Africa the priestess is a wife of the god Oko. In Bahia, Brazil, a female initiate into the African-derived cults is considered the spouse of the deity. In Japan the priestess of the Sun was termed the wife of the Sun as early as the 5th century A.D.; possibly she is the origin of Amaterasu (sun-goddess ancestress of the present mikado), who was apparently established in her present role in the 7th century. A Christian nun is still called a "bride of Christ."

The entire process suggests a repetitive pattern in myth and religion: an initially symbolic statement is later taken literally and still later is once again viewed as a metaphor. The shamaness is far less likely than the male shaman to be a transvestite or homosexual. With the shamaness the male role tends to be conceptual rather than perceptual. Among the Abkhazians on the NW coast of the Black Sea the shamaness in her sacred role (not otherwise) is addressed as a man. The Abkhazians explain this practice by insisting that in the shaman role the shamaness is really representing Achi Zoschan, the primal male shaman of the people. The change of sex is wholly ritualistic and temporary. Queen Hatshetsup of ancient Egypt wore the ceremonial beard of a pharaoh and required foreign emissaries to address her as a male; in assuming the role of the sacred king she was ceremonially masculine. The same logic caused Queen Elizabeth II in 1949 on a visit to the patriarchal Arab areas to be designated as a male for ceremonial purposes. Some shamaness vestiges cling to the above examples, but probably the practice of the African Nuer is conceptual sex change without appreciable religious overtones. A barren Nuer woman may ritually "marry" another woman who will bear children for her. The female "husband" is designated as a man and exercises full fatherly authority over the offspring. Smacking of such conceptual change of sex is the male chauvinistic

Buddhist insistence that there are no females in heaven. Eminently religious women, capable of Enlightenment, will be transformed into males for heavenly residence. The Lotus of the Good Lew (Chap. 11) is quite explicit: the daughter of Sagara, king of the Nagas, was spiritually meritorious and therefore suppressed the female elements within her, fully developed the male organs, and now could become a Bodhisattva.

(6) Stimulating the shamanic journey. The evidence is strong throughout the world that a typical shaman (less likely with the shamaness) will consume some type of entheogen. Nonetheless, Mircea Eliade considers all such dissociational agents as vulgar substitutes for a "pure" trance.[19] Others argue that rhythm and music are sufficient to induce the shamanic trance.[20] The Baiga of tribal India relate how the first shaman attained his powers by sniffing the steam from a pot cooking the dismembered body of Nanga Baiga, apparently a dema deity. This myth suggests the physical tearing apart of the shamanic initiation and may hint at an entheogen or the earth vapors inhaled by the Delphic oracle.

The drum is the standard musical instrument among shamans, but tamborines, cymbals, bells, and other percussion instruments may be employed. Pipes or any instruments producing tones are quite rare, suggesting the remote origin of shamanism. The rhythmic beating of the drum is hypnotic, momentously summoning from the routine world. Shiva is associated with the drum and also with Lord of the Beasts, suggesting a shamanic origin of the god. The Indian mystic Namadeva in telling of the divine presence likened it to the loud beating of drums. Altaic shamans will sprinkle the shell of the drum with beer to "bring it to life." Much of the public appearance of the shaman will be at night when darkness will add mystery and intensity to the drumbeat. The pulsing thump of the drum stimulates the shaman's audience, but primarily it is to induce his ecstatic journey, flying through the air and soaring to communion with the spirits.

The costume of the shaman, certainly for his professional appearances, is strongly symbolic. Traditionally it has often contained feathers, and the shaman may don a bird mask, for flight is perhaps the oldest symbol of man for transcendence. Any number of animals may be represented by fur, head, claws, etc., for the shaman establishes contact with

numerous animal spirits, communing with them as a
fellow member of the spirit world. Numerous additional symbolic extras may be affixed to set the
shaman apart and proclaim his spiritual prowess:
fragments of mirrors or quartz crystals, semi-
precious or precious stones, stars, eyes, wings, and
the like.

Perhaps, as Eliade indicates, the "pure" trance
of the shaman is a self-induced dissociational
experience requiring no outward stimuli. Shamans
frequently work themselves into a frenzy of intense
sweating. Walt Whitman in "Song of Myself" emerges
"sweaty" from a mystic experience. The most famous
demonstration of "sweating it out" is the tapas
("heat") of Hindu and Jain practice. Through
asceticism the true yogi generates magical heat that
is tremendously creative and destructive. By centuries of tapas Matanga received from Indra the power
to fly like a bird and change shape at will; certainly these are shamanic capabilities. According to
the Rigveda Prajapati actually creates the world
through potent tapas. Hindu myth is replete with
accounts of powerful ascetics solely through tapas
burning up their opponents. Tapas can produce god-
like force. World-shattering as all this sounds, it
seems like the self-induced trance of the shaman.

Essential equipment for most shamans is some
form of axis mundi, a bridge to the spirit realm.
Korean myths uniformly associate shamans with
mountains. Frequently the shaman climbs a tree, a
pole, a hanging rope, or a ladder as a symbol of his
lift to spiritual heights. Polyaenus (Strategemata
7.22) tells of Cosingas, a Thracian king and also
high priest of Hera. When his subjects proved
recalcitrant, Cosingas effectively threatened to
climb up a wooden ladder to complain directly to Hera
about their unseemly conduct. In The Clouds Aristophanes depicts Socrates as suspended in a basket from
the roof of the thinkery; in spoof the satirist
suggests the physical lift as symbol of spiritual
heightening, the concept of the shaman. The Baiga of
tribal India declare that in the olden times the
shaman could simply sit upon a pole and fly through
the air to heavenly realms.

Observers have likened the public performance of
the shaman to a ballet act combining dance, music,
poetry, and drama.[21] The shaman will enact his
journey to the spirit world or his own death and
resurrection. A predisposed audience is enraptured

117

and vastly edified by such a performance. Perhaps dance, music, poetry, and the drama owe a tremendous debt to the first professional in all these fields, the shaman.

(7) "Illumination" of the shaman. The Eskimo angakok reports the suffusing of his person with "lightning," a blazing radiance completely filling him and granting him total vision. He has sight of things past, present, and future, even with closed eyes, even in the midst of stygian darkness. The shaman possesses clairvoyance and extra-sensory perception. The Australian shaman is supposed to be filled with solidified light in the form of rock crystals.

The light image is general to visionaries both East and West, ancient and modern.[22] The German medieval mystic Hildegarde of Bingen characteristically termed god Lux vivens ("living light"). The metaphor of light indicates a profound sense of revelation and a powerful transcendence of the mundane world.

(8) Purposes and achievements of the shaman. Under a hunting and later a cattle-breeding culture, the shaman fulfils a key role in communicating with animal spirits and the Lord or Lady of the Beasts to insure ample food supplies and healthy herds. Illness often seems eerie and quite unnatural to us; archaic societies ascribe illness to evil spirits. The shaman sends his soul on that far quest to the spirit realm where he enlists beneficent spirits against the disease demons; you can see him in trance writhing and contorted as his soul battles the monstrous demons for the safety and welfare of his society. The shaman is also called upon to launch spiritual assaults against human enemies because of his power with spirits. Among archaic peoples every human battle is therefore accompanied by a parallel struggle in the spirit world, and the shamans on both sides summon and deploy spiritual contingents whose conflict will determine the outcome.

With his enormous and unearthly powers the shaman may exercise extraordinary social functions. Among the Avá-Chiripá of South America the shaman conducts all the rites of passage (birth, initiation of young males, marriage, funeral), acts as community counselor and arbitrator (reconciling enemies, placating family enmities, even treating with aliens), administering justice often by finding the culprit in his dreams, generally exercising social regulation and control by threatening to unleash his redoubtable spirit allies upon transgressors, even determining the time and place for crops.

But the monumental achievement of the shaman, guarantee of his survival in many societies today and often in clandestine form even in highly civilized cities, is his treatment of human ailments. The standard shaman assistance to the sick, injured, and mentally disturbed consists of:

(a) Prayer, direct appeal to the spirits allied with the shaman to quell the disease demons.

(b) Breathing upon and touching the patient, thereby conveying to the ailing some of the potency of the spirit-powered shaman in the struggle.

(c) Medicaments, generally medicinal herbs but on occasion preparations from animals, even humans (usually some blood). The shaman explains this dosage as the spirits of the preparations summoned to battle the spirits of disease. He explains all events and all objects as fundamentally spiritual, though with material manifestation. The shaman conducts his treatment in the primary arena of the spiritual.

(d) Sucking, generally upon the afflicted area or presumed focus of the ailment. The shaman takes into his own mouth the cause of the pain and suffering. He will often produce the sliver of wood, stone or other concrete substance which he triumphantly announces as the source of the whole illness.[23] Liquid poison is usually spat out. In some cases the foreign matter is so noxious that the shaman must step away and vomit out the noisome mess. The routine explanation is hostile implantation within the patient by an animal spirit rather than by an enemy shaman. If the infection is attributed to an opposing shaman, then no other struggle in fury and vehemence can approach the battle of two shamans, hurling against each other titanic and puissant forces in bitter physical and spiritual conflict.

(e) Sending his soul to another world on a desperate quest. Though he frequently undertakes this remote journey, the shaman always realizes its colossal perils. Modern psychology would say that he is descending into the darkest well of the unconscious at grave risk, for failure to return means hopeless psychosis. The shaman interprets it as a dangerous trip afar, ventured upon only because of severe need. The worst ailments, causing unconsciousness, fever ravings, and madness are explained with superb symbolism as "lost souls." In sleep, stupor, or coma the soul apparently leaves the body and, because the layman has no real grasp of the awesome spirit realm, his poor soul is trapped and beleaguered. Perhaps even worse: the soul has been snatched away by evil spirits or by witchcraft and now suffers in durance vile and hellish. The shaman resolutely sends out his own strong and daring soul to locate the lost soul, to obtain it through spirit aid or spirit struggle, then to shepherd the rescued soul back across the vast and terrifying outer realms to secure haven in the flesh once more. It is the shaman's mournful task at the death of one of the group to send his soul way out there to act as psychopomp, conducting the soul of the deceased to the land of the dead. The Puget Sound Amerindian shamans annually staged a spectacular quest to the land of the souls and herded back en masse the souls of all living persons found there, thus rejuvenating a good portion of the tribe.

Cartoonists relish a sketch of a grotesquely masked shaman in bizarre regalia displaying his M.D. diploma from The Johns Hopkins Medical School or solemnly diagnosing his native patient as suffering from schizophrenia or "sublimation of an oral fixation." Truth to tell, the shaman looks like the oldest professional healer, the proto-physician and the proto-psychiatrist.[24]

Both the shaman and the much later physician share a surprising number of characteristics: search for cause of onset of ailment, collecting full case history, examining the patient's body, establishing a bedside manner of confidence and charisma--in fact, the whole panoply of consultation, diagnosis, prescription, treatment, prognosis, perhaps even a second opinion. Shamans were specializing long before physicians were even general practitioners. Some shamans specialize in rattlesnake bites, others in injuries and ailments of limbs, still others in fevers and chills, and so on. The essential difference between the shaman and the physician is the shaman's orientation wholly to the spirit realm and the supernatural, while the physician claims total engagement solely with the natural physical world. Religious and pious folk today must call upon two professionals: the physician and the priest. Probably this present-day combination, often jarringly opposite, can hardly carry the conviction that rode upon the spirit-weighted shoulders of the shaman. The shaman's patient believes heart and soul, and he is sure that the whole cosmic order has been activated in his behalf.

Perhaps the shaman should rather be called the first psychiatrist, practicing psychosomatic medicine eons before the term was invented. Like a psychiatrist the shaman offers to his patient suggestion, suppression, confession, and reassurance. He realizes the basic human need to believe, to keep the faith, to hope in the midst of bleakest despair. Much of the symbolism of the shaman is that of integration. He, the mediator between worlds, between sexes, between all the bewildering dualities of life, offers wholeness. It is extremely reassuring that someone in the community can actually perceive what is invisible to the rest of us and can bring back direct and reliable information from the supernatural realms. We are not alone and helpless, for we have a great champion and savior. The Navaho shaman, who never heard of Freud, diagnoses many ailments as essentially Freudian: father or mother fixation, childhood trauma, etc.[25] The shaman may have exceeded the modern "head-shrinker," who receives some degree of resistance from the total present society, while the archaic shaman was quite successful in sociotherapy, giving confidence and reassurance to the entire community.

On the walls of the Paleolithic cave at Lascaux, France, appears a shaman-like figure with a bird on a pole, still the badge of the shaman in many societies. S. M. Shirokogorov and some anthropologists of the so-called Vienna School of anthropology suggest an agrarian origin for shamanism, but Eliade and most authorities believe shamanism started during the hunting economy,[26] when it seemed to be worldwide. In recent society the most thoroughgoing employment of shamanism has centered about the circumpolar area at the far north of the world. Shamanism has consequently been explained as arctic hysteria induced by the extremely rigorous life of the frigid north.[27] The shaman has apparently become extinct in China and Western Europe but otherwise is still active through much of Eurasia, Australia, and islands of the Pacific. The Amerindians of both continents still look to the shaman.[28] Africa is the one area where shamanism has not been dominant, though perhaps shamanism in Africa was once rampant and has declined.

121

Whatever the deprecations of the past, we now recognize the profound religious and other implications of the shaman, but what sort of religion is shamanism? Is it:

(a) A special kind of religion peculiar to the hunting period and vestigial now only in quite altered form, or

(b) A worldwide religion which at one time was standard for all mankind, or

(c) An evolutionary stage in the development of religion, indispensable at an early era, but inevitably superseded?

Weston La Barre states the case perhaps most emphatically: "There were shamans before there were gods,"[29] and "It is not so much that shamanism is the root of all religion as that all religion is in sober essence shamanism."[30] Bon, the pre-Buddhist religion of Tibet and still a potent force, is best described as shamanism. The name Vishnu may mean "flyer" or "assuming various forms"; he seems pre-Indo-European in origin and resembles a shaman. Perseus with his marvelous flight, cap of darkness, and Gorgon-slaying by mirror, also his guardian spirits, looks very much like a shaman. The underworld journeys of Odysseus, Theseus, Heracles, Orpheus, and Aeneas appear shamanistic. Odin's journey to Hel in search of wisdom suggests a strong shaman element in Teutonic myth. Indian myth repeats the shaman characteristics constantly, and shamanism is very much alive in tribal India. In recent years the writings of Carlos Castañeda about the self-styled "sorcerer," Don Juan Matus, have sold extensively and have enjoyed almost a cult status with many. Actually the instruction of Castañeda seems shamanic. Don Juan initiates Castañeda into three entheogenic plants: peyote, Jimson weed, the psilocybe mushroom. The ekstasis experiences and Castañeda's flight as a crow are right out of stone age shamanism. The "allies" of Castañeda sound like shamanic guardian spirits.

Witch.[31] Intellectuals of the 19th century generally agreed that witchcraft never truly existed, but was the fantastic and hysterical panic reaction of the 16th and 17th centuries[32] to some toothless and repulsive old hags, falsely branded as witches. Margaret Murray early in this century argued that witchcraft was a real and active pagan fertility cult mistaken for a satanic anti-Christian conspiracy.[33]

There have been slightly eccentric theories, one, for instance, claiming that witchcraft of western Europe originated in Indian Tantrism.[34] A moderate and widely accepted view recently has proposed that the concept of witchcraft is basically an obscene travesty upon Christianity and was essentially imagined by the Inquisition on the slender evidence of folklore "wise women" and "cunning folk"; sensing hostility to orthodoxy, the Inquisitors tortured the naive until they got the answers to fit the inquisitors' horrified imagination.[35]

The inescapable fact is that archaic cultures of Asia, Africa, and the Americas extensively portray witches, who have obviously been around (or have been thought to be around) for a long time. Let us start with two salient features of witchcraft--witches are female (warlocks, male witches, are insignificant and scarcely mentioned until recently), and all the implements of witchcraft must be bronze. These facts suggest that the witch is the continuation of the female shaman. As an archaic institution loses prestige, it tends to move from men to women. By the bronze age even the shamaness was antiquated and submerged, remaining clandestinely in that fossilized condition ever since. Note the many characteristics held in common by shaman(ess) and witch: preternatural strength, shape changer or transformer of others, ability to fly through the air, power to become invisible, ability to materialize and dematerialize objects, knowledge of drugs to produce extraordinary effects, power over others through charms and spells, animal familiars, mating with supernatural beings, dealings with the dead. The overwhelming difference between the shaman of old and the witch of recent centuries is that the shaman was the admired figure of archaic societies, but the witch is always contrary to the conventional society of more recent culture and hence is derided and downgraded. Thus the accusations of incest, bestiality, cannibalism, profanities, and obscenities leveled against witches. Many tribal societies of India conceive of the witch as the most miserable of all human conditions--a barren widow. Some of the extravagant accusations against witches probably arise from the infant male's memory and resentment of the "terrible mother," also the sneaky suspicion that the weak possess hidden powers of resentment and hatred.

Oracle. The distinctive quality of the oracle is _enthusiasmos_ ("state of god within").[36] Divine

123

possession of an oracle means that the god is speaking directly through the oracle. The shaman sends his soul through the invisible to the remote spirit world, but the oracle never leaves his or her locale; a god descends to take over the body of the oracle. We might say that the shaman mediates from man to god, while the oracle mediates from god to man. Both experiences are dissociational, but the shaman retains a portion of his psyche intact, even though it separates from the rest of his inner nature. With the oracle there is a complete submergence of the conscious psyche and a complete takeover by the unconscious, an experience which seems to the oracle to be possession by a supernatural being.

Modern man tends to be incredulous about this entire religious encounter, deeming it an intentional fraud. Under genuinely archaic conditions the human mind is not so dominated by conscious pragmatism as is mankind today; in distant times the unconscious could far more often surge up to overwhelm the conscious psyche. In origin this divine possession of an oracle was wholly genuine, amazing to the oracle and to the surrounding group. In time this experience was professionalized so that the oracle carefully worked himself or herself into the possession trance and emerged from the trance in reasonable time to resume normal personality. Even among quite archaic societies still extant, the oracle has displayed this professionalism, demonstrating his or her ability to control the personality shift and not totally lose governance of the psyche. Still later the oracle's unusual religious experience is institutionalized, as it appeared in classic Greece. Since the oracle had professional competence and control, he or she would be acceptable in the era of priesthood. The modern mind would be right, of course, in suspecting a great deal of chicanery among oracles of a quite self-conscious era. By the 1st century B.C. the official state religion of Greco-Roman society was spiritually bankrupt, its practitioners frequently cynical and time-serving. The fraudulent conduct of many oracles in such an age should not negate the complete authenticity of the religious experience of earlier oracles.

The potential for the personality shift within the oracle is present in all humans, but it is rare today to have the oracle chosen from a group of devotees by lot as is still done among the Nairs of

India. The man upon whom the lot falls is then cleanshaven, transvestite, long-haired. The spirit of the earth goddess enters him, driving him to frenzy in which he will wound himself, drawing blood. In such a condition he is believed to have magic healing powers and mental telepathy, and of course, the goddess speaks directly from his mouth.[37] Here today is a demonstration of primitive oraclehood. Obviously a highly susceptible personality is conditioned to accept the dissociational concept and let the unconscious take over in a rush.

The oracle while possessed always speaks in an abnormal manner, indicating, of course, the god as the real speaker. It may be no more than a high-pitched tone from a male oracle and a deep resonant voice from a female oracle, but it is preferably an eerie, awesome, powerfully rhythmic chant, the extreme antithesis to commonplace speech. Since a god is speaking through the oracle, the language may be the sacred tongue rather than the current vernacular. Indian oracles spoke in Sanskrit or Pali long after these languages had fallen out of popular speech. Oracular utterance in the current tongue may be full of archaisms, obsolete and otherwise forgotten words. The oracular speech may go so far as an incomprehensible jargon. This phenomenon, glossolalia, may simply awe a baffled audience with the presence of the unfathomable divine, or it requires some trained religious specialist hearing glossolalia to interpret it to the untrained.[38] Whatever the divine utterance through the oracle, it was considered as either an order from the deity to human beings or a prophecy of things to come.

We have rather extensive material on the oracles of ancient Greece, constituting a quite formalized and institutionalized oracle corps.[39] The most famous was the oracle of Apollo at Delphi. Seated on a tripod athwart a great fissure in the earth, the female oracle breathed in the fumes from great depths and, possessed by the god, spoke oracularly. Probably her technique was hyperventilation, a sensory overloading that triggered dissociation in the oracle. The Mwari cult of the Matopo Hills of present-day Zimbabwe bears remarkable resemblance to the Delphic oracle of antiquity. Until the recent conquest by Communist China, the Näch'un was a highly respected and highly placed functionary as the official oracle of Tibet.[40] In 1838 the Japanese woman oracle Miki established the Tenri-kyo sect (about 5 million followers today) on the basis of

125

revelations as the Lord of Heaven possessed her.

Such oracular possession is the ostensible basis for much of the world's religious writings. Many orthodox Christians believe that god dictated the Hebrew and Christian scriptures through inspired figures. Likewise the Koran arose from the possession of Mohammed by Allah. The phenomenon is oft repeated, though in recent centuries most of these possession writings have been ignored altogether or have generated only small cult groups. The practice may be accelerating today as modern anxiety causes many to desire a new religions revelation. One of the most extraordinary of such contemporary manifestations is A Course in Miracles, purportedly a dictation from Jesus Christ to an atheist medical psychologist at Columbia University, Dr. Helen Schucman, Jewish in upbringing. First published in 1976, the three-volume work had sold over 60,000 sets by 1980.[41]

Oraclehood is not without its perils. Prince Peter of Greece and Denmark relates how a Tibetan oracle, Lhag-po Thöndrup, abandoned his profession because while possessed by the deity Dorje Chung-den he was almost suffocated by a scarf. When in human form, the god had been thus assassinated.[42] All possessing spirits can be dangerous. Note also that quite frequently the oracle is reënacting a role while being possessed. Perhaps the oracle as well as the shaman contributed to the world drama the acting out of divine doings. Frequently modern cinema advertisements blare: Rod Steiger IS Napoleon. Future archeologists of our era may well conclude that oracular possession was still popularly accepted in the 20th century. The spiritualistic medium of today, through whom speak voices purportedly from another world, is the most prevalent contemporary manifestation of the oracle.

Greek drama employed masks, possibly from the oracle speaking through a mask. In archaic times the oracle was not a human holding a mask before his face; here was the actual god impressively present and awesomely orating. At the Mysteries of Demeter at Pheneos the officiating religious specialist donned the mask of Demeter Kidaria, and the voice from the mask was that of the goddess. Masks were ubiquitous in ancient times until the late Roman empire. We find them extensively depicted on vases and other pottery, in murals and reliefs and mosaic floors. Apparently they were a sort of poor man's

126

statue of the god. The deity was felt to reside in this representation, and when employed by an oracle, one heard the veritable god speak.[43] In effect, many ancient statues were body-masks, hollow or backless, admitting the oracle so that awed listeners would hear the god's statue addressing them.

The Yukaghir of Siberia remove the head of a dead oracle and mount it upon a trunk of wood; henceforth this skull is consulted for advice on war, hunting, and so forth. If the living oracle was the vehicle of the dead, so equally or even more should be the skull of an oracle. This custom must one time have been widespread throughout Eurasia. It will explain the oracular head of the dismembered Orpheus and the Teutonic myth of Mimir's oracular head. The cult of the severed head is in fact the best attested symbol of Celtic faith.

In addition to the divine possession of the oracle, enthusiasmos may appear randomly among non-professionals. Within historic times and even among archaic societies there is a certain wariness about this enthusiasmos. A clear distinction is made between "good" possession which is presumably by a benevolent god and "bad" possession which is ascribed to a demon. With the professional oracle there is confidence in the god's real presence, but there are understandable reservations about enthusiasmos sprouting amidst the laity, and there is a grey area of uncertainty. Consider the approval today in so-called Charismatic churches of possession trances by the laity, producing glossolalia. These experiences are uniformly interpreted within the church congregation as authentic visitations of the Holy Spirit, true enthusiasmos. This is an intense state of popular dissociation, apparently granted religious approval because such hyperaroused experience is followed by a delicious relaxation, a sensation of considerable euphoria. The recently instituted Pocomania and Revival Zion Cults of Jamaica are largely based upon possession experienced by congregation members. Under crisis situations, generally in the background of the possessed, this dissociation seems a viable mechanism of adjustment. In a sort of border area is Mohammed's objection to poets because the pre-Islamic poets of Arabia were supposedly possessed by a familiar spirit; the Prophet said that only God was a proper possessor.

"Bad" possession varies from the disagreeable to the heinous. Widespread through much of Eastern Asia is the belief that a snake spirit will possess, usually, an aged woman (note the witch parallel here). The Ainus, aboriginal inhabitants of Japan, call this condition imu. Possessed by the snake spirit, the old woman will inexplicably rail and curse; such conduct is utterly forbidden under normal circumstances, but is ruefully tolerated in the old crones. We would say that it is understandable outbursts from the frustrated senile. In China foxes are supposed to possess humans, and such possession produces nasty, vindictive people of all ages. Having fever is widely accepted as possession by evil spirits. Demonic possession has long been the explanation for monstrous appearance and behavior of any human being. Down to the present we attribute our silly and our incredible actions to devils taking us over: "Something got in me." All the "bad" possession requires another religious specialist, the exorcist.

Of 488 societies worldwide 360 or 74 percent believe in spirit possession. The lowest percentage of belief (52 percent) is in aboriginal North America, and the highest percentage of belief (88 percent) is in the insular Pacific.[44]

Magico-religious figures

Sir James Frazer contended that religion originated in magic.[45] Chronology is impossible to determine, but human dissociational experiences certainly seem anterior to the magic phase. As Frazer points out, magic theory presupposes order and regularity within the natural and supernatural worlds; such conviction seems far more consciously and intelligentially advanced than the dissociational tendencies. Further, the magic concept imputes to its specialists their own profound knowledge of cosmic operations and of the formulae to control these operations. The professional shaman and the oracle will control their own dissociational experiences, and they will have supernatural friends and helpers, but they do not control the supernatural forces. The shaman possesses considerable knowledge about the supernatural, but the specialists in magic claim not mere knowledge but effective control over the supernatural. Psychologists suggest that the earliest period of our life, infancy, is dominated by the unconscious and therefore has strong correspondence to the shaman-oracle stage in religion. The magic stage is a subsequent period of childhood when growing self-consciousness produces the salient features of magic: confusing symbol with event and believing that to imagine is to accomplish. Magic therefore seems an intermediate religious condition between the earlier dissociational phase and the later ritual-rationalistic pattern.

Mankind was probably induced to practice magic because many symbolic acts demonstrably produced benefits. It has been suggested that ploughing began as a purely symbolic act, emblemizing the entry of the phallus into the female earth, as Chinese emperors until recent generations ceremonially performed the first ploughing of the season; ploughing genuinely increased the yield of crops, convincing men of the efficacy of magic. Another such symbolic act was scattering fish fragments in a field of crops, for fish are singularly fertile with their multitudes of eggs. Once again the undeniable pragmatic success of this symbolic fertilizing would fuel man's belief in magic.

"Wishing will make it so." Humanity has amazing powers of self-delusion. If someone is earnestly, desperately eager for a miracle, the slightest hint will suffice to convince that person that the miracle has really happened. Faith-healing still has remarkable success with those who yearningly believe. Mass hysteria can sweep a large group, carrying along with it all susceptible persons and thereby producing a host of witnesses frenetically asserting the authentic miracle. Memory plays tricks with us also, as we know from hearing family members report some past event as far more dramatic and amazing than sober recall would have it. The "Vailala Madness" early in this century in New Guinea was conclusively unmasked by natives themselves as a crude hoax. Nonetheless, decades later an astounding number of natives recalled that fraud as producing many miraculous events and objects.[46] Such is the nature of man that he will fanatically believe in magic.

The shaman and the oracle specialize in unconscious symbols found mostly within. Practitioners of magic specialize in more conscious symbols, for the most part outward and for the most part learned from an established specialist and then transmitted to a follower. The sociological theory of magic sees the practice as ritual actions, social products carefully handed down from generation to generation.[47] It is likely that in Paleolithic times the shaman was the only professional of any sort. Other professionals, such as the smith and the potter, were probably emerging in the era of the magic practitioner and among archaic people still retain some of their magical qualities, mysteriously manipulating secret spells and formulae carefully hidden from the populace. Basic to the practitioner of magic is an arsenal of techniques to compel the supernatural by word, gesture, act, all meticulously programmed. Note the famous "Sorcerer's Apprentice" by Dukas, demonstrating the absolute rigidity of the rules of magic. Secrecy is essential, for the correct ritual will compel the supernatural, whoever performs it. Ignorance of the full panoply of magic will result in the disasters of the bungling apprentice. Magic must be left to the thoroughly skilled professionals.

Magician.[48] This practitioner employs positive magic for the benefit of mankind. The bases for the magician's compulsion of the supernatural rest upon premises we would seldom accept:

Physical contact transmits health and power. Long before the physician employed auscultation and stethoscope, the magician touched and listened to a patient with hands or with wand or tube. The correct verbal ritual, proper gyrations and other motions, and contact all have magic effects. Egyptian deities are represented as touching the mouth and nostrils of devotees, thus magically imparting life. Probably the laying of hands upon a newly consecrated bishop by an established bishop and a British policeman's touching of a prisoner's shoulder originated in this magic contact, the first to convey sacerdotal power and the latter to signify the manifest weight of the royal law. Psychologically, anyone who touches another holds, or assumes, higher status and greater power than the person touched.

Resemblance indicates identity (like produces like). The Amerindian rain dance is performed by repeated leaps in the air to descend in the fashion of rain, thus compelling the rain gods above to shower down moisture in similar fashion. The ancient Teutons induced rain by the magic rite of pouring water over a naked woman representing the earth. The wonder-working Apollonius of Tyana in the 1st century A.D. rid Antioch of scorpions by burying a bronze image of a scorpion.

Metaphoric association. Much magic seems ridiculous or meaningless to us because we fail to understand the figurative language and thought. Germans of Hesse and blacks of the southern USA shared the belief that a bat's heart worn on the sleeve would make one a sure winner at cards. At first glance this practice may seem merely preposterous, but note that bats are popularly associated with supernatural forces because of their nocturnal habits and remarkable ability by a sort of organic radar to sense objects in total darkness. In folk belief the devil is linked with card playing. The bat's heart will consequently confer magic power upon the card-playing hand, enabling it to triumph over the demon.

Mythical accounts may themselves be employed as magic. Among many archaic peoples rests the belief that exact knowledge of origins will give control over present circumstances. Magicians in many societies as a vital part of the healing magic will chant the myths about how death and disease entered the world. Babylonian religious specialists regularly repeated the divine myth of creation, Enuma Elish, to summon the gods to give benison to man.

While the shaman has been all-important in most of the world, in black Africa the magician has been more significant, at least in known times. In black Africa he has worked in daylight as a conscientious helper of his fellowmen, an expert professional religious specialist. Morton Smith has recently claimed that Jesus was really a magician from a Galilean strain of Semitic magicians who offended the establishment with his remarkable feats of magic (miracles),[49] but sober scholars have not been impressed.

Fang Shih is the Chinese designation for the Taoist practitioner skilled in the arts of preparing medicines and effecting healing. Many have considered the Fang Shih as a magician possessing supernatural powers. The pharmacist, the physician, and especially the alchemist have the magician in their genealogy.

Exorcist. Defensive magic is practiced by exorcists who aid men by detecting and eliminating witches, sorcerers, and their evil doings. Men cherish and applaud this religious functionary because of his helpfulness to humanity, but he is not the positive magician. In Africa the exorcist[50] has a constant task of identifying sorcery. An evil sorcerer can be the cause of illness, crop failure, and all sorts of blight. The malefactor must be hunted out and precisely pinpointed. The specific objects by which the sorcerer has brought misfortnne are found and exactly designated by the exorcist. In black Africa the offending objects pounced upon by the exorcist are flawed articles of household use, images of harmful beasts and spirits, symbols of the householder and his family with mutilation or other evil spell.[51]

The crowning task of the exorcist is to negate the malevolent workings of sorcerers, wizards, and evil spirits. By his magic powers he finds and destroys the concrete objects by which evil has been inflicted. By proper magical acts of word and movement in solemn ritual the exorcist ejects the evil spells, repulses the evildoer, and bars the ill-wishers and their foul machinations from wreaking further damage henceforth. He casts out the evil spirits possessing the unfortunate; today we would see these afflictions as mental disturbance. The exorcist employs the same premises as the magician but turns them against the wicked.[52]

Wizard.[53] Especially in Africa where the magico-religious specialists are most numerous and most employed, the distinction is important: the wizard is an unconscious evil worker of magic, while the sorcerer is consciously evil. The BaVende and the BaThonga of Africa typically conceive of the wizard as an ordinary woman by day who at night leaves her body and in company with her peers works monstrous ills.[54] Here again is ascription of the witchcraft pattern. Except for unconsciousness, the wizard is otherwise like the sorcerer.

Sorcerer.[55] The sorcerer is the magico-religious specialist who malevolently injures mankind.[56] His or her techniques follow the premises of the magician but are employed to compel supernatural forces to injure or destroy humans. Of course, the major technique of sorcery is to inform the victim of the malevolent intent towards him; thus the victim is himself the guarantee of successful sorcery.

Contact magic. Widespread in Africa and among Amerindians is the belief that sorcerers sneak into a residence during the night, make invisible incisions in the bodies of sleepers, and insert "doctored" stones, metal, splinters, and other objects. Even more adept, sorcerers in parts of New Guinea can project disease-producing slivers (labuni) of bone, stone, or coral as much as 60 meters to lodge in a victim's flesh. The skilled exorcist frequently extracts these objects from the suffering patient as the shaman does and will display the concrete cause of the ailment. In some cultures the sorcerer can project the injurious object for kilometers; among Australian aborigines the "pointing of the bone" is far-ranging sorcery. Men in apparently robust health have withered and died when knowing that the bone is pointed at them.

Resemblance is identity. Sorcerers worldwide are notorious for making dolls or images resembling the party to be harassed, then mutilating or destroying the resemblance to injure and even kill the original party. Injury to nail parings, hair combings, or even excrement of a victim is believed to injure the person himself.

Metaphoric association. In Indian acts of sorcery to inflict evil, the rites are performed while circling counterclockwise. This is exactly the widdershins pattern of medieval European sorcery. In the Icelandic Gisla Saga, Audbiorg encircles a house counterclockwise and brings a crippling snowstorm upon a neighbor's dwelling. An old north-of-England folk theme claimed that circling a church three times widdershins would summon the devil. This concept posits the counterclockwise movement as diametrically opposite to the course of the sun and hence advancing the powers of darkness and sin.

The most momentous and horrifying sorcery is the curse, summoning the whole grisly legion of demons and hurling their annihilating terrors upon the victim. We may assert, "Words will never hurt me," but even the most rational will wince or cringe under a monstrously denunciatory curse, and in archaic societies the word was deemed to be the thing itself. In Africa today a sorcerer's curse can actually kill. In ancient Greece the curse uttered by the dying had a sorcerer's power. Iphigenia at Aulis was purposely gagged to prevent her from uttering a curse, and the dying curse of Eriphyle against her matricidal son Alcmaeon had frightful consequences. The curse of Ernulphus in Tristram Shandy topples the anathema (an ecclesiastical curse) into laughable absurdity, but behind it still looms the fearsome sorcerer.

Sorcery is all too common in a narrow, isolated, repressed society from which there is no real escape. Milaraspa is the most famous Tibetan sorcerer. By his magic spells and incantations he caused the deaths of 35 members of his uncle's family who had cheated him out of his inheritance. Later he destroyed the crops of his native village by conjuring up a devastating hailstorm. Medea must be the world's most notorious sorceress, with Circe not far behind. The sorcerer is a dire creature of night, as the helpful magician is a being of daylight. Many folk say that a sorcerer can gain powers only by slaying one or more of his own relatives. Some N. Amerindians believe that a sorcerer's magic bundle contains flesh of a close family member. All such beliefs are powerful metaphors of the destructive effect of a malevolent person upon his own family. Similarly metaphoric is the accusation of cannibalism against the sorcerer. Also figurative is the claim, as in the original Faust theme, that the sorcerer to obtain his horrendous powers has sold his soul to the devil. Especially interesting is the belief among Africans such as the Azande that a woman exposing her genitals to a man is an act of sorcery; psycho-analytic thought considers the concept of the petri-fying Medusa as based on such vagina sorcery.

The medieval Christian priesthood, perhaps in professional rivalry, hounded magico-religious prac-titioners so that sorcerers took refuge in hiding and found patronage only from the most ignorant and credulous: magicians were reduced to secular enter-tainers. Nonetheless, in spite of priestly avowals, magic persists vigorously within modern religion. Many of the devout still believe that church rituals and prayers can, for example, actually send the soul of the deceased to heaven or at least speed its passage through purgatory.[57] As Claude Lévi-Strauss avers: "There is no religion without magic any more than there is magic without at least a trace of religion."[58]

Searchers for divine purpose

Diviner.[59] The practitioners of magic and the diviners all believe in a systematic cosmic order, but diviners make no claims to govern supernatural forces. Eagerly, man desires certainty in this quite uncertain world. The diviner is a trained specialist in the cryptic signals of this cosmos that supposedly proclaim divine will and that only the diviner's skill can penetrate. The bewildering ways of god can be fathomed, though, of course, not controlled, by the diviner. There are three major divisions of divination:

(1) Automatic, assuming that future events are faithfully foreshadowed in observable phenomena. Most famous and most durable of this form of divina-

tion is astrology[60] which assumes that specific heavenly bodies by their position and movement actually influence individual human lives. Ancient Mesopotamian observers of their night sky (cloudless and hazeless for much of the year) were fascinated with the precision of celestial movement in vivid contrast to the vagaries of earth. Understandably, they linked those starry heavens with divine plan and assumed that the clockwork precision above precisely regulated the mundane world below, thus launching astrology. The medieval Christian church vigorously opposed astrology and thereby actually encouraged the emergence of astronomy (the scientific study of celestial phenomena as distinguished from astrology, which is divination). Although ecclesiastics and scientists, for different reasons, concur in condemning astrology, it remains, as it has for millenia, the most prevalent and culturally acceptable form of divination.[61]

Among the ancient Romans the outstanding form of divination was augury. Augurs, forming a venerable and prestigious college, scrupulously observed the daytime sky for auspices (omens). Clouds with attendant light and shadow, lightning most dramatically, but bird flights and behavior above all were the omens interpreted by augurs. Reputedly Romulus had been an augur, and the college included many illustrious Romans: Sulla, Pompey, Cicero, Marc Antony, Julius Caesar. Favorable omens were necessary before the Roman army could be committed to battle; the sceptical Julius Caesar would drily inform his augurs that he sincerely hoped that the omens would be found favorable. Celtic augurs especially emphasized bird flights, for birds are the messengers of the gods, and mysteriously purposeful are the sudden coordinated shifts of flocks of flying birds. The vast migrations of birds are still only partially explained by science and remain awesome.

(2) Interrogatory, requiring that expert diviners ask for divine purpose by probe. The diviner for this technique needs some object or collection of objects which will offer multitudinous different combinations. One method employs objects of natural origin but with countless variations. Ancient Shinto diviners of Japan minutely studied the shoulder blades of deer and tortoise shells. The main feature of the ancient Etruscan religion was haruspy, i.e. examination of the entrails of sacrificed animals. As any veterinarian will quickly inform you, no two animals have identical entrails,

and the learned Etruscan diviners could elaborately ascertain divine intent from the size, position, color of animal interior organs. Abnormalities such as swollen, streaked, noduled organs were notably portentous. The Romans inherited this practice but tended to concentrate upon animal livers, which are especially variable organs. In celebrating the gifts of Prometheus in Prometheus Bound, Aeschylus lists haruspy as one of the many estimable sciences conferred upon man. Second only to Delphi in ancient Greece for revealing divine will was Dodona in Epirus. The divination here consisted of careful observations of oak trees sacred to Zeus; diviners were expert in interpreting the slightest quiver of the leaves and the numberless intricate patterns of light and shade. Bells were affixed to branches further to create opportunity for scrutinizing the god's intent. King David was instructed by "the sound of a going in the tops of the mulberry trees" (II Samuel 5:24) to attack the Philistines; it seems parallel divination.

The other technique of interrogatory divination is to set up artifically a collection and distribution of objects that will permit numerous different combinations. The ingenuity of diviners is almost endless. In ancient Mesopotamia oil was dropped in water, forming colorful kaleidoscopic patterns. Popular in tropical coastal areas and Pacific islands is divination by cowries, sea shells. Through much of central and South Africa the winnowing basket is a diviner's favorite. As many as 200 varied objects of wood, bone, pebbles, seeds, and other natural objects are shaken in the basket and the pattern at the top of the basket is analyzed. Man-made objects offer limitless possibilities; the Tarot cards and modern playing cards are best known to moderns as such divination. All of this practice probably arose in what seemd a logical extension from shrewd nature-watchers who see animal and plant behavior as presaging heat, cold, and other phenomena.

(3) Intercessory, in which the diviner actually employs magic powers to summon up supernatural beings to provide information. Probably this is a primitive form of divination and a transition from magic practice toward divination. African diviners call upon spirits dwelling in trees or rivers out in the bush; outside observers have often designated these spirits as fairies.[62] The most frequent form of this type of divination is necromancy, in which the diviner consults the dead on the assumption that they

know the future. Gilgamesh consults with the dead Enkidu in The Epic of Gilgamesh (Tab. xii). The so-called "Witch of Endor" summons up the dead Samuel (I Samuel 28:7-20). Odysseus seeks the dead Tiresias in the underworld (Odyssey XI), and Aeneas receives prophecy from his deceased father Anchises in the Elysian Fields (Aeneid, VI). Though of remote origin this necromancy is still very active, as spiritual mediums today regularly call up spirits of the dead, sometimes as specifically sought by clients, but generally as "familiar," spirits of the dead who habitually assist an individual medium in necromancy.

Ritual artificers

Astrology and astronomy were long bound together, emerging separately only in recent centuries. Many other activities of early man were simultaneously religious and utilitarian. In such combinations probably originated priesthood, practical and sacred equally. Each ritual artificer accompanied his prescribed pragmatic service with ritualistic observances and divine sanction. As professional specialists developed in archaic society, probably every one of them, at least initially, exuded a sacred aura as did the shaman, possibly the earliest of all professionals. Here only three representative figures are considered, the first exclusively masculine, the second either male or female, and the third wholly feminine.

Smith.[63] The early blacksmith seems to have exercised a priestly function because his working with red iron ore suggested the blood of life, and his forging paralleled the bringing to birth of red flesh from the uterus. His molding, hammering, and shaping awesomely displayed the divine creation of structure and pattern from chaos and shapelessness. The Rigveda (10.7.2) asserts that "Brahmanaspati has forged this [world] like a smith." Ilmarinen in the Finnish Kalevala is the eternal smith who forged the sky, the sun, the moon, the famous Sampo (mill?), and even a golden wife for himself. Slavic myth states that the great smith Svarogu forged the sun; Lithuanian myth attributes the making of the sun to the heavenly smith Telvelik. The Greeks regarded the Dactyls as fabulous smiths. Weyland Smith is the magical smith of the English. A blacksmith god is standard in many cultures, e.g.: Ogun (Yoruba, West Africa), Girru (Babylonia), Hephaestos (Greek), Vulcan (Roman), Goibniu (Irish), K'daai Maqsin (Yakut, Siberia), Kalvaitas (Baltic area). Vedic

137

myth appears frankly euhemeristic in stating that Hibhu, Vibhu, and Vaja were smiths whose skills in divine service caused their elevation to godhood.

Frequently, as with Hephaestos and Weyland Smith, the blacksmith is a cripple. This deformity may have been natural, causing crippled males to become relatively sedentary forge workers. It is also possible that cruel rulers of the long ago purposely maimed skilled smiths to prevent them from taking their talents elsewhere. Perhaps we are simply dealing with a folk theme emphasizing the marvel of a deformed smith producing objects of perfect form. In many areas the smith was itinerant and could encounter hostility. An ancient Middle Eastern practice distinguished smiths and tinkers (Hebrew Qayin, Cain) by a mark on their brows to indicate divine protection; this is a likely explanation for the famous Brand of Cain.

The smith is generally associated by archaic peoples with the shaman. The Samoyeds of Siberia say that the initiated shaman is cut to bits by an underworld smith who then reassembles the shaman, meanwhile indoctrinating him into shamanhood. In Borneo, Celebes, and Bali the forging of the human soul is associated with the smith; as master of processing, shaping, and changing matter the smith is also the artificer of spiritual salvation.[64] "We could almost say that the forge is the church of the African village."[65] Shoes must be shed before entering an African forge to avoid impurity. No quarreling or bawdy is permitted within the forge. Sterile women call upon the blacksmith to pronounce spells insuring fertility. The smithy is a sanctuary for refugees. Remember that the famous Gretna Green in Scotland until recent generations had marriage vows solemnized by a smith.

Potter. Psychoanalysts tell us that all pots, vases, and similar containers are symbols of the uterus.[66] Moist clay suggests birth creation, and the name Adam means "red clay" in Hebrew; especially, then, red clay would seem the stuff of life itself. A sculptured representation of the divine birth of King Amenhotep III (1405-1370 B.C.) at Luxor shows the god Khnum shaping the infant monarch and his ka (soul) upon the potter's wheel at the moment of conception. In India today the potter is a sort of village priest. Frequently the local deity is represented by a god-pot from the potter who will also make iconic representations of the god. The potter's wheel is the symbol of fertility. In the public celebrations of the village god the potter is usually the officiating ritualist.

Sacred prostitute. The Hebrews indignantly denounced temple prostitution (Deuteronomy 23:17-18) and the Moslem rulers of India in similar scorn made concubines out of the devadāsi ("slaves of the god," i.e. Shiva), temple prostitutes of Hinduism.[67] In ancient times the practice of sacred prostitution was widespread from Southeast Asia all the way to Greece. Especially in the Middle East a host of fertility goddesses--Ishtar, Astarte, Mâ, Anaitis, Anahita-- were served by temple prostitutes. In classic times Aphrodite was served by temple prostitutes at Corinth, Greece. The practice was sacred, not pornographic as the leering puritan of today might chortle. Its origin was also more complex and less overtly erotic than we might assume.

In Saturnalia and similar ancient festivals the rites of reversal completely violated normal mores and permitted any man to copulate with any woman. An early society wanted all women pregnant, especially those of impotent husbands. As the ascription to Saturn indicates, this unbridled copulation is a sacred ritual, perhaps institutionalized as "sacred prostitution." As the many fertility goddesses were notoriously lavish in offering themselves to the male, the sacred prostitute was a logical surrogate and priestess of the generous goddess; or every woman in the society would be required to give herself just once at the temple of the deity. The offering of a woman to a stranger (a practice still followed in some archaic societies) arose from the association of strangers with fertility; besides, as any ancient Greek could inform you, a stranger might be a god in disguise. Children born from this sacred prostitution were children with divine parentage. Possibly Aeneas was the son of Anchises by a priestess of Aphrodite. Rhea Silvia was mythically assigned to some sort of sacred female group, possibly the very reverse of the later Vestal Virgins. Romulus and Remus are termed offspring of Mars because of their later warlike prowess. Possibly Rhea Silvia was impregnated in ritual prostitution by a stranger who could have been the god in disguise. Many of the fatherings of Zeus might similarly be explained. Alexander the Great even disowned his father and claimed to be a son of Amun-Re. Some psychologists today seriously suggest temporary sexual liaisons for therapeutic purposes. Possibly such an unconscious purpose also motivated sacred prostitution.

Institutionalized ritualist

Priest.[68] Perhaps the contrasts between the first professional religious functionary and the now dominant religious specialist can best be appraised by parallel columns:

Shaman	Priest
maker of myth	steward and rationalizer of myth
product of loosely organized food-gathering societies	product of well-organized food-producing agricultural societies
medium for dissociational experience	specialist in ritual
ecstatic alteration of consciousness	detailed pedagogical indoctrination, ritual elaboration and heightening, theological structuring
individual vision	institutional conformity
called by supernatural agencies	often hereditary, designated by family, consciously choosing clerical career

Our interest in the priest is his relationship to myth. Under shamanism myth tends to develop a growing and changing revelation, capable of immense alteration and power with the additional visions of new shamans. The whole course of priesthood is to freeze and rationalize myth. Perhaps this is a benison to myth in certain respects. European voyagers early in the 19th century found a religious seminary at Opoa in Polynesia. Here priests elevated Ta'aroa to the supremacy of the Polynesian pantheon and created the Ariori Society of literary artists to celebrate the god. Possibly priesthood has performed similar roles for ancient Greek and other mythology, producing symmetry and good sense and beauty within the myth corpus. However, the ancient priests of Greece may be the chief culprits in the fossilizing of myth so that it was ineffectual by the 1st century B.C.

The individualistic religious experience of the

shaman will constantly erupt, opposing the staid, conservative, entrenched priesthood. Judaism was sufficiently strong internally to withstand the assault of the disruptive Christian sect, but another great shaman-type figure, St. Paul, shrewdly transformed Christianity into a gentile religion and started the eventual overpowering of the moribund Greco-Roman religion. Mohammed was the shamanistic figure again, successful in overwhelming the old priesthood of Arabia. Buddha's shaman-like eruption was withstood by Hinduism and eventually virtually excluded from India.

The path of the shaman becomes increasingly rocky as archaic societies are vanishing or are being transformed. The Jicarilla Apaches of the SW USA are an interesting test case. Originally a hunting people with only the shaman as a religious specialist, these Apaches started a pueblo maize-growing culture in the 19th century. The solid, stabilizing priesthood has completely triumphed over the dangerous and unpredictable flurries of individual shamanistic vision. An agricultural village society must emphasize social unity and conformity. Religion that apparently started as one person's lonely journey far beyond human bounds must yield to a systematically organized religion of community.

Chapter V Community Religion:
Animatism to Lord of the Beasts

Many Westerners equate religion with church attendance; they are thereby asserting that religion is not basically a personal experience but a community unification through an institution. A. R. Radcliffe-Brown asserts that the primary function of religion is to bind society together by stressing non-rational cohesive elements and by perpetuating these elements through tradition.[1] Etymologically religio (Latin, "religion") may mean "to bind together"; certainly in late antiquity the official state religion of Rome was regarded chiefly as a force to unify society.

The major relationship between gods and men was initially collective rather than individual. Supplication to and propitiation of the deities were on the basis of "Help us" rather than "Help me." Proper sacrifice, rituals, and observance of tabu assure the favor of the gods, while individual morality is quite late in divine concern. Of course, it is necessary to note that even in its origin community religion was complex and has since branched into four different divisions:

Materially oriented religion. Primitive man demanded that religion produce concrete results, generally in fertility. Ample food supplies and plenty of offspring were indisputable evidence of benevolent deities and competent religious specialists. Although very few are honest enough to admit it, many people of our day show religious concerns only when their material condition suffers or is threatened.

Spiritually oriented religion, the type considered in the two previous chapters. This religion probably began with shamanic visions and has burgeoned into the great universal churches of our era. Many today assert that this is the sole meaning of the term religion.

Civil religion, early centered about the priest-king, the sacred king of old. For most elitist Romans of classic times their actual god was mighty Rome, divine as Virgil reveals in the Aeneid. Nationalism has in recent centuries similarly occupied this place in many Western hearts. In this century Marxism-Leninism and Maoism have proved potent civil religions.

142

Folk religion, which has never claimed formal congregations as have the above religions. It is a mélange everywhere of popular beliefs about the supernatural, rather secret rites, non-establishment myths, and vestiges of superseded religions. Astrology and divination still have sizable followings in this era, proof of the sustained power of folk religion even in face of intense scorn, even persecution, from spiritual and civil religion.[2]

The discussion below follows an evolutionary pattern, made familiar by the English anthropologist, Edward Tylor. The scheme should be interpreted as convenient rather than certain, for contemporary anthropologists shy away from espousing an evolutionary thesis. Probably the major changes (advances, if one prefers) are not evolutionary but revolutionary, the product of dynamic personalities or dramatic alterations of community life. Contrary to the idea that a noble concept of a monotheistic god is peculiar to an advanced civilization, the extremely primitive tribes of Tierra del Fuego are reported as having a remarkably, almost unaccountably, high theistic level.[3] The powerful One is conceived as an omniscient, all-powerful invisible being without any material needs, who lives in the sky beyond the stars, presiding alone over the universe. Prayers of thanksgiving and supplication and simple token offerings are the only rites of his worship.

From Animatism to Anthropomorphism

Animatism.[4] T. K. Preuss predicated pre-animism as an impersonal magical power (Zauberkraft) present in everything, animate and inanimate, within the sensual range of the earliest primitive.[5] Perhaps a similar meaning was true of kami (now "god"), employed in ancient Japan to refer to the magical quality in anything.[6] Animatism is ascribing consciousness and purpose to inanimate objects, to trees and bushes, and, of course, to animals. Animatism is certainly indicated in the Indian adhidaivata explanation of the universe which attributes all manifestations of energy to conscious beings, both visible and invisible.

Animals apparently consider as living beings anything in motion, such as leaves whirled by an eddy of wind. Psychoanalysis would see the entire religious impulse of humanity as originating in "infantile anxiety,"[7] the concern that anything and everything in the environment has designs upon the infant--and, not unlikely, hostile designs. Children regularly ascribe elaborate actions and speeches to rag dolls and wooden toys.

Rivers and streams certainly seem animated, with Sarasvati and the Ganges deemed female deities by Indian adults today. The Ainus, aborigines of Japan, similarly regard rivers as female, applying to the river mouth the Ainu word for the vagina. The Ainu look upon rivers as beings who sleep at night and lose weight in the summer. Two rivers that meet are viewed as copulating to produce a child river.

Ancient Athens had a vestige of animatism in the special court in the Prytaneion to try inanimate objects responsible for death. If the object was found guilty, it was cast beyond the state boundaries. Plato in _Laws_ (IX, 873d) himself calls for such legal treatment. A popular Amerindian myth smacks of animatism when trickster gives his blanket to a boulder to warm it. Later trickster snatches the blanket away, and the offended rock rolls after him. The rock pursues trickster some distance before that clever rogue escapes. Thus any moving object-- water, wind, fire, avalanche--is logically animated; but any object, even wholly stationary, may have consciousness attributed to it. Mountains from size and height induce animatism, generally as males.

Animatism has a variety of possibilities:

(1) Objects may contain an inseparable consciousness.

(2) Objects may contain a consciousness that comes and goes.

(3) Objects may be possessed by an alien but permanently resident spirit.

(4) Objects may be possessed by an outside spirit that comes and goes.

(5) Objects are pervaded by a separate soul-stuff that can be devoured by malevolent spirits or can go to the land of the dead.[8]

The mind-set of animatism arises not from a search for knowledge but from a pragmatic need to deal with the world. Animatism offers a consistent

144

and unified concept of the world and the opportunity for subsequent religious structure. Animatism has left its legacy in what we now term personification, as ships are each named and called "she" (probably as containers, wombs). In myth one of the notable manifestations is the named weapons: the swords Durandal (Roland), Gram (Siegfried), Excalibur (Arthur). Mirganka in Indian tales is a magic sword whose possessor can conquer the world. Brahmashiras is the puissant spear of Shiva with which he will eventually destroy the universe. Shastradevatā is a weapon actually deified.

Mana. R.H. Codrington[9] popularized the word mana from Melanesia and Polynesia, but the term has generally lost currency with today's anthropologists. It may have some value if defined as power or magic possessed by a living being or, later, by images of gods, a quality physically transferrable to another. High-ranking men and heroes possess especially potent mana. In New Caledonia stones are regularly kept in the cemetery to be saturated with the mighty mana of ancestors; from the cemetery these stones are taken to the fields to strengthen taro roots with the ancestral mana. The Munda of India declare that their first shaman Dananteri ordered his body to be burnt and thrown into the river; drinkers of this water absorbed much of the shaman's wisdom. Aleuts similarly would place the bodies of successful hunters in streams and drink of the water; dried bodies of celebrated hunters were sometimes cut into pieces and rubbed over the heads of whale spears. Cannibalism in part developed from eating the flesh of the wise and powerful to obtain some of their mana. Meat-eating still maintains some of this mystique. The Miris of Assam assert that tiger meat will impart strength and courage to males but would make women into viragoes. Many Amerindians of the Amazon and the Gran Chaco puncture their skin with bone awls: jaguar bone for ferocity, deer bone for swiftness, and so on. A late practice, still of the mana type, is to drink water poured over a statue, as in Bengal a sufferer from smallpox will drink the water that had bathed the image of Sitala, the smallpox goddess. Today many Westerners still shun articles associated with the dead, for the mana concept still abides. Even the most trivial objects used by the great or notable are dearly prized, solely for the mana power they carry from their distinguished possessors. The Roman numen from whence our etherial word numinous has derived apparently in distant days meant just about what mana means.

Orthodox Buddhism claims that holy relics benefit a devotee by generating inward grace through contemplation. Actually laymen have quite generally (especially in Mahayana Buddhism) treated the sacred objects as charged with mana power. Reportedly King Gopāli won a war by having relics of the Buddha ostentatiously carried into battle. Relics of Christian saints have radiated this same mana potency to many of the pious. A Winnebago Amerindian myth starkly depicts mana in the slaying of the uncle of the Children of the Sun: the Sun sadly explains to his offspring that their uncle's slayer by dangling the severed head from his belt thereby possesses not only his own power but also that of the slain.

Animal deities.[10] The first deities were almost certainly animals. The strength and speed of many creatures, the dread power of predators, the animal fears of childhood, and the always mysterious and stealthy behavior of many animals in human presence awed men especially when they lacked weapons and domestic animals. In ancient China and Egypt the earliest gods represented are animal in form. At Sinai the Hebrews turned to the worship of a golden bullock (Exodus 3:2), and similar animal deities were honored by Jeroboam, king of Israel, at Dan and Bethel (I Kings 12:28-29). At present many groups in India worship tiger gods. The avatars of Vishnu as a fish, a wild boar, and tortoise suggest animal origins of the Indian god.

Indo-Europeans apparently worshipped horses. In Ireland as late as the 12th century a king pantomimed copulation with a mare, which subsequently was killed and cooked, the broth swallowed by the king. In the immensely elaborate horse sacrifice of India a queen mimicked coitus with a dead stallion. Poseidon Hippios probably was a horse; as a stallion Poseidon pursued Demeter in mare form. The Vedic Ashvins probably were horse gods later anthropomorphized. Since the Paleolithic era the strength, ferocity, and virility of the bull have insured his deity. A bull cult was practiced at Çatal Hüyük in the 7th millenium B.C., and the Minotaur of Crete sounds like a bull god. The Apis Bull was worshipped at Memphis, Egypt, from early times; a dead bull was mummified, and priests immediately searched for his reincarnation as a bull calf bearing special marks. The cults

of both Baal and Cybele included a divine bull, and
the sacrifice of the cosmic bull was the supreme
cultic act in Mithraism. Worshippers addressed
Dionysus as a bull, also as a kid. Egyptian Hathor
was frankly a cow goddess, and probably Pasiphaë, Io,
and Europa among the Greeks and Aditi in Vedic tradition were originally cow goddesses. The devotees
of Dionysus, the Bassarides who tore Orpheus to
pieces, bore a name meaning "fox." The young priestesses of Brauronian Artemis in Attica called themselves "bears" and referred to the goddess as "The
Great She Bear." Zeus Lykaios, Apollo Lykeios, and
the hero Lykos all refer to wolf and probably arose
from a wolf god. The slaying of Adonis by a wild
boar may mean that Astarte was a sow goddess, and
Adonis, a pig, was killed in a battle for the female
pig.

Hunting has apparently always generated a
mystique in males. The tribal encampment or settlement is the mundane world of feminine security, of
commonplace domesticity. The masculine hunting party
ranges afar into the forest or jungle, the prairies
or the savannahs or the veldt, up into mountain
fastnesses, eventually in boats upon lakes and the
great deep--into another and different world. "The
Bear" by William Faulkner superbly captures the
exalted realm of the hunters even in a very recent
era. In archaic times this "other" experience could
certainly evoke the religious emotion in primitive
hunters. Further, the exhiliration and excitement of
the hunt, climaxed by the victory of man over
immensely powerful animal adversaries like the saber-
toothed tiger, the mastodon, and the whale (successfully hunted by Eskimos with stone age weapons)
elevated the male to heroic and superhuman dimensions. Nimrod was the Mighty Hunter of Genesis,
forever immortalized; inconceivable is a Mighty
Nut-Gatherer or Mighty Kohlrabi Digger. Without the
hunting epoch the myth of the hero would be far less
imaginable. Perhaps above all, the best of hunters
with modern high-powered weapons realize how chancy
and fickle is the possibility of hunting success. To
the archaic mind the abundance or scarcity of
animals, the seeming ease or the tantalizing difficulty of making a kill suggested supernatural agency
and meant that the Great Antelope behind all individual antelopes and later the Lord or Lady of the
Beasts had to be evoked and propitiated.

The sheer difficulties of stalking and finally slaying sizable animals must have been appalling to the earliest human hunters; the rare resultant meat supply alone could not really have justified the fantastically elaborate effort. Almost certainly hunting began as a religious ritual sacrifice, and the flesh of the slain was eaten to absorb the mana power of strong and agile beasts. Perhaps myths of original female monopoly of religious rites followed by male usurpation really mean that the female religious foraging for vegetable food was supplanted by the far more dramatic hunting by males, awesomely consecrated by blood. The laborious fertility rites of food-gathering give way to the Dionysian ecstasies of the hunt.

Sacral hunting demands supplications to super-natural agents before the hunt begins. African Bushmen before setting out on a hunt plead with the animal king to provide them with quarry. George Catlin, in the early 19th century faithfully painting the Amerindian before acculturation, impressively depicted the Buffalo Dance of the Mandan of the upper Great Plains. The savage rapture of the perfervid dance ceaselessly whirled night and day until the sought-for herds of buffalo would pour over the nearby prairies.[11]

Animal ceremonialism is the ritual treatment of slain animals to prevent animal spirits from ven-geance against the human killers, to placate the Great Bear or Great Impala, and to ensure ample food animals later. The Mescalero Apaches of SW USA and Northern Mexico believed that the hostile powers of the great carnivores even after death could penetrate a man's body, causing illness or death. Most Amer-indians apologized to the dead animals. Eskimos held mourning rites for the souls of slain seals; the animal souls were expected to migrate to the remote realm of the seals and return in new bodies. The Labrador Amerindians observed elaborate ceremonies and tabus in the eating of bear meat to avoid offense to the animal spirit and to guarantee more bears for future feasts.

Man-beasts.[12] Worldwide stalk the transitional figures between animal deity and anthropomorphized deity. People in all eras have ascribed human features and behavior to pets and animals gen-erally.[13] The practice should be clear to us in many "animal" stories such as those of Albert Payson

Terhune where the central figure of the narrative is an animal best characterized as a mute human. Amerindians have extensive accounts of their "Mythological Age" in which Coyote, Raven or another animal talks, wears clothes, fabricates objects, uses tools, and consistently resembles a human. Hindu myth symmetrically demonstrates the combinations: Kimpurushas boasting horse bodies and human heads, Kinnaras equipped with human bodies and horse heads. Human bodies and animal heads are represented by: ox-headed Niu-t'on (China), jackal-headed Anubis (Egypt), elephant-headed Ganesha[14] (India), the alligator-headed god of Chiriqui of Panama. The Greeks preferred human heads plus trunks and animal extremities, as with centaurs and satyrs.

Both of these combinations strongly suggest the shaman with animal mask or with pelt, tail, and so forth on lower extremities. Hawk-headed Horus bears a striking resemblance to a shaman with a bird mask. Totemic decoration and behavior could also explain the man-beast. Members of the bear totem would wear the bearskin or portions of the bear anatomy, might wear tattoos suggesting bear appearance, and could imitate the bear in behavior. The myth of ass-eared Midas and the Golden Ass of Apuleius possibly originate in the totemic ass-men. Possibly the strange Scorpion Men of the Epic of Gilgamesh may refer to the constellation Scorpio. Empedocles speculated that in the throes of creation various body parts were scattered in space, randomly combining. Thus he would account for minotaurs, sphinxes, centaurs, and sirens of Greek myth as genuine biological freaks. Presumably, only the truly functional combinations survived to become the present species of animals and men. Of course, the monstrous mixtures could be dream products from eras when the animal world was much closer to man than now and deeply entered into his dreamlife. Perhaps as an almost universal phenomenon the man-beast is best described as the union of animal and human natures with both discernible in the patchwork amalgamation.[15] The 14,000-year-old cave sanctuary of El Juyo, Spain, has yielded a sculpted head with human features on the right side and features of a lion or leopard on the left side. The archeologists discovering this head interpret it as "the synthesis of a dual nature, animal and human, into a harmonious whole."[16] The man-beast has never deserted folklore, still flourishing as a werewolf or a mermaid.

149

Perhaps the most famous man-beast is the Greek centaur--half-man, half-horse. Some possibilities:

(1) Wild horses either spottily observed or imaginatively seen as partly human.

(2) Horsemen, perhaps the cowboys of the era, the Thessaly horse-riders. The Amerindians of Central America at first interpreted Spanish Conquistador and steed as one being. Palaiphatos in antiquity suggested that "centaur" meant "pricker of bulls" from archers who on horseback shot wild cattle.[18] American Plains Indians employed exactly this technique to kill bison.

(3) Members of a horse totem wearing horsehides, perhaps arranging hair to resemble manes, with sounds and actions suggesting horses.

(4) Dream visions with amalgamation of human and horse elements.

(5) As horse is power symbol (horsepower, horseradish, etc.) for man, it may be a symbol for natural forces. If etymology of "centaur" is "waterwhipper," the word could refer to violent water spirits, probably of tumultuous mountain torrents.[19]

(6) Perhaps the centaur is a symbol of the symbiotic relationship between horse and human rider. Man has become the horse's brains, and the horse provides man with four-legged strength and speed.[20]

In the East, gods are frequently accorded mounts, animals that may represent the actual origin of the gods; for example, from India: elephant (Indra), rat (Genesha), owl (Lakshmi), bull (Shiva), ass (Sitala). The Chinese Woman in the Moon (Ch'ang-o) rides a three-legged toad, while Madame Wind (Fêng p'o-p'o) rides a tiger. In Japanese art the mounts of the deities have usually become wholly human except for animal heads. Greek myth tends to have various animals drawing a god's chariot, doves for Aphrodite, leopards for Dionysus, dogs for Ares, possibly all indicating the animal deity origin of the anthropomorphized deity. Athene is represented with an owl perched on her shoulder; the goddess could well have originated in an owl goddess or owl totem. Hera is regularly termed "ox-eyed" or "ox-faced," hinting at a basic cow goddess. The earlier man-beast concept attempted unification and balancing of the animal and the human within each individual. This later concept separates the animal and the human, elevating the human as master over the animal.

Bestiality. Ancient Semitic myth seems to envisage a primordial state, apparently before the creation of woman, when human males lived with wild animals, copulating with them as did the wild man Enkidu in the Epic of Gilgamesh. Behind Genesis 2:18-24 may lurk a similar notion, since Eve is formed from Adam because animals are insufficient "helpers." Such concepts, of course, ascribe to primal man "natural" and "animal" conduct in contrast to the supposedly more cultured times of the myth-maker. Furthermore, such bestiality seems a mythical attempt to explain the extraordinary man-beasts. The Minotaur may represent the supposed mixed offspring from the sacred wedding of the queen Pasiphaë to the Minoan Bull deity. A similar idea is probably behind Baal's liaison with a bull to produce a bull-calf, and Zeus as a bull mating with Europa to produce three human males. Appropriately the first Buriat (Siberia) shaman was the son of an eagle and a Buriat woman. The Indian Urvasi as a swan mates with Pururavas just as Zeus in swan form coupled with Leda; both accounts seem the product of feminine dreams.

Many cultures depict humans with animal lovers or spouses, as Eskimos report a woman married to a dog, and in many parts of the Pacific women are said to have crocodile lovers. Perhaps actual sodomy is the basis here, or it may be human mates of an animal totem, or it could be the nightmare fears that folk-lore still perpetuates in whispering that a pregnant woman scared by a pig will have a child with a pig's snout. Many Amerindian myths depict a human married to a bear or a deer. The gamut can run from the bawdy jest to a "lost mermaid" idyl. The Iroquois laugh jocosely about a confirmed bachelor tricked into marrying a frog. A popular Plains Amerindian narrative reports a man marrying a buffalo. Offended by an insult from her husband's sister, the buffalo wife flees, taking their child to join the buffalo herd. The distraught husband desperately seeks his wife and child, one of the buffalo calves secretly signalling that he is the missing son.

A shapechanging pattern calls for alternate human-animal form. A frequent Amerindian tale reports a girl with an unknown lover who is a dog by day and a man at night; she gives birth to puppies and is deserted by her tribe. Jamaica legend tells of King Henry, bull by day, man at night. A variation of this shapechanging is the frog that a princess changes into a prince by a kiss or the Pacific Toyo-Tame-bime who bans her husband from her in childbirth, but his spying reveals her as a shark. If one seeks morals in myth, such accounts suggest that we must philosophically accept a modicum of animality in humanity.

Shapechanging (shapeshifting). The explanations above of man-beast and bestiality may explain shapechanging, but the fundamental element must be a sense of personality alteration. The entire concept of shapechanging seems literalizing a metaphor. We speak of a man displaying dashing courage as a "lion," and a cozy, obliging female as a "pussy-cat." Shapechanging is describing these people as actually undergoing physical alteration in order to intensify our symbol. The Teutonic berserker was so kindled to demonic battle fury that it was easy to conceive of him as transformed into a raging beast. Just so obvious is the Malaysian tale of the boy who, "given many stripes" by his harsh teacher, fled into the jungle to become the first tiger. In South China the tiger is a notorious shifter into human form, while in North China the fox takes this role. Proteus proved so adept at shapechanging that protean is our standard term for shapechanging. Ishtar and Circe both change men into beasts. Literary people will interpret this alteration as animalizing by lust and sensuality. In folklore such transformation is a euphemism for death.

Totem.[21] A socio-religious organization of a group designated usually by an animal, occasionally by a plant, and rarely by some other object is called totem from the practice of the Ojibwa Amerindians. Early in this century totemism loomed vast in the discussion of religion as Robertson Smith, Émile Durkheim, and Sigmund Freud all asserted that religion began in totemism. Today anthropologists and ethnologists have considerably soft-pedaled totemism largely because of its immense variety worldwide without a clear-cut common denominator. Much of the early theory was based upon Australian aborigines, but even here are wide variations. In India a surprising number of "totems" are trees, and perhaps tree cult is a more accurate label. In the

Bombay area the <u>devak</u> is a guardian spirit, a deity, an animal, a tree, even a trade implement, considered the ancestor or head of the household. Usually people with the same <u>devak</u> are forbidden marriage, as in a totem group. Perhaps some order may be imposed upon this vastness by classifying:

Matrilineal totem with social emphasis and generally forbidding the eating of the totemic animal.

Patrilineal totem with ritual emphasis and eating of the totem animal, usually at carefully specified times.

The extensive discussion of totemism in past decades has offered three major theories to explain the practice:

(1) Nominalist. Andrew Lang proposed that the totem designation arose from using animal names for men. Thus the clansmen of a man named Wolf would eventually form a wolf totem. Actually it seems more likely that the totem would arise directly from the animals themselves, as the troops of Peleus and Achilles are the Myrmidons (ants). The reverse of Lang's conjecture may be the case. Caleb, meaning "dog" in Hebrew, may be a totem that gave its name to a man.

(2) Sociological. Émile Durkheim considered the totem as the visible representation of primitive social organization and religion. To non-literates the totem is a unifying, rallying symbol that assures protection and identity. The totemic insignia will warn enemies to keep hands off ("you slay one of us wolves and a pack of wolves with blow-guns will kill you") and will clearly display acceptable and unacceptable marriage groups. Probably this remains the most credible theory. Theorists of today, however, strongly question Durkheim's claim that all religion originated from totemism.

Our own literate era perpetuates totemistic practices in the labels of the Detroit "Lions," Philadelphia "Eagles," and Miami "Dolphins" for athletic teams. As archaic totem members donned garb suggestive of the totem animal, players of the Los Angeles "Rams" wear helmets painted with ram horns and supporters of the U. of Arkansas ("Razorbacks") sport headgear in the shape of a hog's head, somewhat resembling the boar's head helmets of ancient Teutonic warriors. Paralleling the social structure of totem groups are today's gangs of young men. Barrio gangs in Los Angeles will answer to such designations as "Wolves" or "Kinkajous." Motorcycle gangs such as "Hell's Angels" display the cohesiveness and the hostility to outsiders characteristic of totem groups.

(3) Psychological. James Frazer noted that among many archaic peoples the totem is actually referred to as "father," and killing of the totem animal is symbolic slaying of the father. Freud insisted that the childish fear of the father causes the displacing of the emotion upon animals. Thus when primitives call the totem "father" or "ancestor," they are admitting that it is the father symbol. The Oedipal complex insists that the totem (father) may not be slain, and women of the totemic group (collectively "the mothers") may not be married. The killing and eating of the totem animal, Freud claimed, is ritual reenactment of the primal slaying of the father by the band of brothers, and the eating of the totem animal is ritual absorption of the power of the father (god) in reëactment of the first cannibalistic feast.[22]

Totemism is still a reality. The Torres Straits Islanders see men as displaying the attributes of their totem animal: Crocodile men are strong and pitiless; Cassowary men are belligerent and boast of their thin legs and speed in running; Dog men are fierce but can become friendly; members of the shovel-nosed skate totem are taciturn and peaceful until goaded.

Clearly, many myths of talking animals and men-beasts could refer to totemic men. The recurrent struggles of the Lapiths against the Centaurs suggest that these Thessalians were probably in frequent contest with members of a horse totem. The animals behind many of the gods may be totem figures. Perhaps Apollo Smintheus ("mouse god") is a remnant of totemism. The competing Egyptian gods from various provinces (nomes) probably originated as totemic animals. A frequent pattern in totemic myths is the birth of twins, one of the pair representing the totemic animal, the other the tribal ancestor. The Dogrib N. Amerindians report a woman bearing six puppies; three remained dogs (the tribal totem), and the other three were the ancestors of the Dogribs.

Perhaps the totemic meaning is clearest in this passage about the African Dinkas: "When I asked what I myself should invoke as my clan-divinity, it was half-jokingly suggested that I should invoke Typewriter, Paper, and Lorry, for were these not the things which had always helped my people, and which were passed on to Europeans by their ancestors?[23]

Tabu.[24] The Tongan word <u>tabu</u> means "sacred,"[25] expressing the ambiguity of this term, simultaneously meaning "I want" and "I must not," holy and consecrated on one hand but dangerous, forbidden, unclean on the other. Freud believed early childhood to be under severe parental repression; the commands of adults force down or restrain desires, producing tabu. Simultaneously, the tabu is trying to obey the parental commands and also silence the sense of guilt from forbidden desires. Freud considered tabu originating in the sacral and prohibited nature of the totem animal.[26]

Most tabus say: DO NOT TOUCH! The most awesome of such touch tabus is visited upon Uzzah who is struck dead for touching the Ark of the Covenant, even though Uzzah simply meant to steady the holy object on a bumpy road (II Samuel 6:7). Possibly the good man's horror at his unintentional impiety precipitated a heart attack. In our society allergies and nervous disorders often result from violation of a moral or psychological tabu. Tabu is metaphorically extended in "You must not get in touch with..." and "Untouchables." In bygone days the food of a Brahmin upon which fell the shadow of an "Untouchable" had to be discarded, and any contact with such pariahs demanded elaborate ritual purification. Metaphorically, the eyes may not gaze upon the holy of holies, and lips must not utter the name of the sacred. Freudians see tabu as essentially a compulsion neurosis.

Probably the tabu basically serves an important function as a social regulator, implementing social unity and behavior. Most of the mythology of the Andaman Islands is concerned with ritual offenses and the dire consequences of violating tabus. Community religion is made firm by fear and dread of the imperious deity, while a good natured, easy-going god receives scant consideration from archaic peoples. The trouble, however, with any symbolic system is that it can get out of hand, proving ridiculously complex and burdensome, resulting in silly and meaningless restrictions. Pythagoras vigorously forbade the eating of beans supposedly from their resemblance to testicles. Beans are associated with fertility and divination; perhaps opposition to a primitive fertility cult and to magic motivated the philosopher. The Ndembu (Africa) magician cannot eat zebra, for its dark coat could cast a shadow on his clairvoyance; fish with sharp bones are also forbidden, since the bones could prick his organ of divination, the liver.

Complicated explanations surround the Hebrew and Moslem prohibition against eating pork. The origin could be:

(1) Sanitary, because pork in a warm climate can easily transmit trichinosis. Enforcing a religious tabu would prove infinitely more effective than trying to explain to and enforce a sanitation code upon archaic peoples.

(2) Unclean in label, because the pig was worshipped by enemies. The sow goddess seems general in the early Middle East as a fertility symbol. Eating pork could therefore be considered a religious ceremony forbidden to true Hebrews. Note how in Reformation England a man proudly asserted his Protestantism by refusing to eat fish, associated with Roman Catholicism.

(3) Sacred animal now reversed. Whenever one finds a strong tabu upon some food, it is not unlikely that at one time this was a most sacred food, and the forbidding in time develops into a conviction that the food is loathsome.

Modern food tabus continue to be potent even if shorn of religious prohibitions. The English-speaking world generally abhors the eating of horse flesh, although such food is commonplace in other cultures. The horses cut into the chalk hills of England may indicate a horse worship of great antiquity. The legendary leaders of the Anglo-Saxon invasion, Hengest and Horsa, have suspicious names, both meaning "horse," and strongly suggesting horse totems. The horse has been man's co-worker and still implies "noble steed." Like the dog, whose flesh is also unacceptable to the English, the horse is closely associated with man, is deemed quasi-human. Oxen, though draft animals for many generations, have no such esteem. These food tabus are still difficult to understand, for the French have a distinguished cavalry tradition but nonchalantly chew on horse steaks.

Developing Anthropomorphism

Soul.[27] Myth is strangely meager in relating the origin of the soul. A 3rd century A.D. sarcophagus now in the Museo Capitoline, Rome, depicts Prometheus fashioning men and Minerva inserting the soul in butterfly form. Modern theologians are hesitant to expound definitively on the soul in light of recent psychological theory. Perhaps the concept of soul originated in the early body consciousness stage of individual life. The child realizes with wonder the miracle of wanting candy and seeing his arm snake out, grasp the sweet, and convey it to his mouth. I seem to be a separate will that desires and then impels the body to obey my wishes. I am the soul; the body is just the body. Many neurotics and especially psychotics accept pleasurable body sensations as indeed their very own but reproach aching organs as if they were complete aliens. In dreams and visions one seems to range free of the body, as the soul expatiates far from its normal clay residence. Reflections in water or mirror suggest a separate self or soul away from the immediate flesh. Many Gypsies and archaic people object to pictures or photographs which seem to capture and carry off this soul. Sickness and the religious experiences treated in the two previous chapters also suggest an apparent separation from the body that can therefore be considered the soul. Perhaps all these experiences may originally provoke the soul concept, but thereafter man has made the concept fantastically complex.

The 'Alawis, a Moslem Shi'a sect in Syria, somewhat simplify the problem by declaring that women have no souls, though they make one exception in the case of Fatima, daughter of the Prophet. The ancient Hebrews, at least before the Babylonian Captivity, associated the soul with breath (nephesh) and wind with "the breath of God." When breathing stopped, the soul was no longer in the body. The medieval Zohar considered the nephesh as the vitalizing soul and the neshamah as the super-soul, conferring a holy character upon a man; the ruach is the intermediary between the nephesh, which remains with the body, and the neshamah, which ascends to heaven. The Homeric concept posited thymos as the conscious self and

157

psyche as the animating principle of life which alone survived death as an unconscious wraith. By the 6th century B.C. Orphism, Pythagoreanism, and Platonism regarded the psyche as the only soul, the inner conscious self that is pre-existent and will survive the body. The single soul concept appears in Christianity and Jainism as separable from the body, while Zoroastrianism and the official Chinese religion postulate one soul inseparable from the body.

Two souls are claimed by the ancient Egyptians: the life principle (ka) and the idea or blueprint of physical form and bodily nature (ba). The Finno-Ugric and standard N. Amerindian belief predicated two souls: the free-soul that might leave the body in trance or dream and the life-soul that leaves the body only after death. Guarani of S. America say that each person has two souls, a gentle human soul, and also a savage animal soul. The Nairs of India note one soul that undergoes rebirth and another which is a malevolent ghost to haunt the living. Manicheism carried its dualism everywhere, asserting that man had a good soul replete with all virtues and also an evil soul harboring all vices. A variation posits a single soul during life that splits in two at death. The Kilaman of the Philippines declare that the right half of the soul goes to the sky, while the left half goes to the underworld.

A three soul system is asserted by the Balahis of India: a vital principle which may leave the body during sleep, an inner self which is immortal and on death is reborn into the same family or caste, and the thinking conscious mind. The Samoyeds of Siberia possess three souls: an intellectual soul, a physical soul, and a shadow soul. The Surára of NW Brazil posit a physical soul located in the bones, a positive soul that may roam in sleep, and a shadow or negative soul. An interesting variation is a single soul split three ways at death. In NE Arnhem Land of Australia one part of the divided soul returns to the totemic center to await rebirth, the second is bound to the locality and the third part goes to the land of the dead. The Nagas of India offer this three-way split at death: one part to the land of the dead, a second part remaining attached to the skull, and the third part wandering about the earth.

Four souls are claimed by some West Africans. The Dakota Amerindians believe in these four: physical soul that dies with the body, local soul that remains with or near the dead, soul that goes to the spirit world and accounts for earthly deeds, and a soul that lingers in a small hank of the deceased's hair and can be hurled into an enemy's territory to become a hostile demon. The Purums of Manipur go even farther in ascribing five souls to each person.

The soul is frequently represented as a bird in Central Australia and in New Zealand. In ancient Babylonia bats were deemed flitting souls. In some areas of Japan dragonflies represent the soul. The most familiar symbol is the butterfly, probably because of its transformation from apparent death in the chrysalis stage. The butterfly soul appears in early Minoan and Mycenean art and in Greek art from the 5th century B.C. In Finland, Burma, and Mexico the butterfly symbolizes the soul. Nagualism is the belief in an external soul: a man and an animal are born at the same time and shall both die at the same time. Nagualism is widespread in Central America and in some Pacific islands.

Most Amerindians believe that the soul is lost by sneezing, and apparently the well-wishing to sneezers of Western society is a polite hope today that the soul has not been lost. Contrariwise the Koita of New Guinea believe that a sneeze signals a return to the body; someone who fails to sneeze for an extended period has a lost soul voyaging afar off. Yawns may cause a soul to escape; hence the politic covering of the mouth, surviving today as politeness. Obviously the mouth is a danger zone, requiring lip ornaments and even the strange lip plugs of Central Amerindians to retain the soul and frighten away evil spirits. Nose rings and bones through the septum serve the same function for many peoples. In the Marquesa Islands both mouth and nose are shut at the moment of death to prevent the escape of the soul.

Elard Hugo Meyer (1837-1908) asserted that all mythic thought was based on the concepts of soul in Seelenkult ("soul cult"). The Meyer theory has some justification in the widespread and remarkably extensive speculation about the soul.

Ghost.[28] After death a human soul may inhabit an animal. As the snake is a fertility and life symbol, Greek heroes frequently reappeared after death as serpents. The Roman genius seems originally to have been a snake.

The conventional concept of ghost involves two mythic concepts: the soul identical in appearance to the human from whence it came, and the local soul haunting a place associated with its possessor when alive. The first concept seems to stem from the original primitive notion of the soul as an exact duplication of the body. Perhaps most intelligent Occidentals would consider ghosts metaphoric for states of mind in the living. If the ghost concept is accepted literally, it presents a problem to those who doctrinally would subscribe to the single soul idea. A ghost making an occasional appearance, like Banquo's ghost in Macbeth or the ghost of Hamlet's father, can be interpreted as on brief furlough from the land of the dead; properly such a ghost is termed a revenant. A permanently resident ghost is a local soul, implying the two-soul system.

Beneficent ghosts watch over the living, promoting the welfare of the surviving family or clan and fending off evil spirits. The Ganda of E. Africa believe that the ghosts of outstanding men may become incarnate in an animal and therein act as guardians of a clan segment or a locality. Disembodied ghosts (balubaale) are responsible for all actions of the invisible world. Balubaale are the ghosts of exceptional men--noblemen, warriors, magicians--who continue after death to exercise their powers. Kindly ghosts are generally ancestors, as the later Roman regarded the Lares, enshrined in every household.

Malevolent ghosts more engross human attention, as their depredations can be appalling. An enemy during life will continue as a ghost to attack surviving opponents. Many people propitiate the souls of slain enemies or executed persons to forestall such assaults. "Speaking good of the dead" today is not just letting bygones be bygones; it is a fossil practice from the days when hostile ghosts were truly formidable. Some archaic peoples will actually change their names to delude the ghosts of adversaries. Souls of the kinless dead reputedly wax spiteful and injurious from their loneliness. Such hostile ghosts were the lemures of ancient Rome who were ritually appeased and dismissed at the Lemuria in May. Actually one has most to fear from the ghosts of family and clan members, for they are considered tremendously vindictive towards living relatives just because they survive while the dead are denied the boon of life. Eskimo shamans maintain constant vigil and, observing a hostile ghost prowling the village, shoo everyone indoors until the shaman with the aid of good spirits can drive off the malignancy. The African G/wai[29] realize that the ghosts of those dying young are the most resentful toward the living and will strive to propel the living toward death. Ghosts of the elderly are more resigned to the cold solitude of the grave. G/wai ghosts are provoked to monstrous rage by violations of sacred tabus; the excruciating fear of ghastly vengeance is paramount in compelling social conformity. The Cambodians and many other peoples claim as the most vicious of all ghosts those of women dead in childbirth and of stillborn children. Such ghosts are toweringly infuriated because of their sharply abridged lives and will wreak havoc. Fears of malicious ghosts have prompted numerous stratagems: taking a corpse through a hole (quickly closed) in the house to prevent a ghost from finding the way back, the conciliatory funeral ceremony itself, ostentatious mourning and fasting to show ghosts that we are suffering, shrouds and coffins to pinion and confine the ghost, tying the limbs of the dead or even breaking the legs of a corpse (found in Stone Age interments) to prevent return, memorial services of propitiation, "ghost-shooters" (straws filled with gunpowder) to ward off ghosts.

Ancestor worship.[30] The cult of the dead involves all deceased, not just ancestors. This section will consider only divinized ancestors. Herbert Spencer late in the last century asserted that ancestor worship was the root of all religion.[31] The earth goddess is, of course, our Great Mother. Freud in his theory of the primal horde of one dominant male and a throng of women and children postulated this "father of all" as the prototype of god. Patriarchal deities are obvious father figures: Jupiter means "father Jove" and Odin was All-Father to the Teutonic North. Christians generally feel that God the Father is basically a symbolic term, but it is not unlikely that all divine mothers and all father gods originated in very human mothers and fathers.

Burial of some cadavers beneath domestic hearths in Paleolithic times may indicate ancestor worship. Portrait skulls from Jericho and Çatal Hüyük c. 7000 B.C. suggest ancestor worship. Ancestor worship is the most ancient and persistent element in China. As in Dahomey, Chinese gods are all former human beings, dead now and deified. The introduction of Confucianism into Japan during the 5th century A.D.

strengthened, perhaps even created, Japanese ancestor worship. In Egypt the father-son relationship was divinized in Osiris and Horus, with the god Osiris as the dead father. The pitrs ("fathers") of the Rigveda and the fravashi of ancient Iran are apparently at least semi-divine ancestors. The ancient Hebrew teraphim (Genesis 31:19) probably indicate horsehold deities formed from patriarchal ancestors. When Jacob swore an oath with Laban (Genesis 31:42 ff), Jacob swore by the Kinsman of Isaac while Laban swore by the God of Nahor, his father. Although the swearers were then in Mesopotamia, which seemed to have no ancestor worship, both ignore the standard Mesopotamian deities to swear by what look like ancestor gods. The famous painted sarcophagus of Hagia Triada may depict a Minoan ancestor cult. The Hero cult of antiquity was probably Cretan before it was Hellenic, and both may stem ultimately from ancestor worship. An inscription by the river Numicus near Rome to Lar Aeneas deems Aeneas as the deified ancestor of all Romans. The Romans used the formal term Di Indigites ("native gods") to refer to all deceased Romans since Aeneas and presumably descended from Aeneas.

Ancestor worship is still widespread. In East and South Africa ancestor cults occupy most of the religious energy. Ancestor worship is rife among tribal Indians and Amerindians. Despite the introduction of Christianity, Easter Islanders still practice aku-aku, ancestor worship. It seems entirely too much to assert that ancestor worship is the sole root of community religion, but Spencer was right to consider it a major source.

Terrestrial Spirits. This discussion considers terrestrial spirits as supernatural beings, thereby distinguished from the vague "power" of a talisman or amulet. These beings are specifically localized to a limited geographical sphere or to objects (e.g. the spirit in rice). The power of all such spirits is restricted to a small area; though potent, even deadly, in this narrow compass, these spirits are definitely minor supernaturals, no match for the eminent deities and not even qualifying as "godlings." All of these spirits are closely tied to earth and concrete objects. Carl Jung interprets the entire spirit world as the realm of the unconscious; the awesome spirit ranges of imaginative cosmography will be found in the discussion of psychology ahead, while here are considered terrestrial spirits that invisibly populate the visible world of everyday.

Mankind has tended to assign animal spirits to animals that are: causing considerable fear, dwelling in special intimacy with humans, slain at rituals such as sacrifices or funerals, or forming important prey for a hunting tribe. Forests and jungles are inhabited by the dread spirits of predatory animals-- tigers, jaguars, wolves. Field spirits tend to be grazing animals. Cave spirits are usually snakes.

Most terrestrial spirits are anthropomorphic. Such ascription of human appearance to a multitude of objects is normal; children in playing "cloudies" generally report human faces and figures in cloud formations. The Roman peasant of antiquity found spirits crowding the landscape, a spirit of human form in each stream, wood, hill, hollow, tree. Amerindians envisaged the spirits of plants in human form but usually manifesting some element or symbol of the original plant, something like the tobac- conist's wooden Amerindian clutching tobacco leaves. When the natural surroundings are dangerous, spirits like Scylla and Charybdis develop. Estonia has no such perilous features, so the waterspirit Nakk is a charming pixie-like creature whose singing beguiles. In the Guianas of South America there is an especial tendency to conceive of the terrestrial spirits as distorted humanoids: grotesquely hairy, bulging eyes, jointless limbs, huge mouths, enormous feet or hands.

Guardian spirits. Ruth Benedict[32] coined this term for the concept (not limited to Amerindians but apparently most developed in the New World) that every human being has a companion spirit closely accompanying and protecting him for a lifetime. Unlike the relatively impersonal terrestrial spirits, the guardian spirits are intensely personal, assuring deep religious consolation and individual signi- ficance to each person. The Amerindians of the Great Plains often demanded that as part of initiation into manhood each young male should experience a vision of his own guardian spirit, generally receiving specific messages and assurances from the guardian spirit, often a unique "spirit song" which would always be cherished just between a man and his guardian spirit.[33] After the death of Genghis Khan many Mongols believed that his guardian spirit still resided in his black banner.

House spirits. All the outdoors can suggest the alien, but one's own household is a safe haven, a friendly, homey place. The spirits inhabiting one's

house tend to be wholly friendly and remarkably
similar in behavior to the human residents. According to Belorussian tradition a male house spirit is
monogamously married, with sons that become house
spirits of new homes and daughters married off to
house spirits, some remaining spinsters. Thrifty as
all good peasants, the house spirits conduct the
weddings of their children at the same time as the
marriages of human children of the house.

Lady and Lord of the Beasts.[34] Approaching the
standard god figure, the Lady or Lord of Animals is
largely or wholly anthropomorphic, beyond the Great
She Bear and the King of the Elk, and has wide-
ranging power, not the circumscribed and local impact
of a terrestrial spirit. The Lady or Lord of Beasts
seems the product of a hunting society, while the
more familiar deities are generally the later concepts of an agricultural and urban society. The Lady
or Lord of Animals is the leader, "owner," governor
of one type of beast in a hunting society relying
upon one major food animal, and extending control
over all hunted creatures in a hunting society
diversifying its quarry. This ruler of the animals
governs the number and distribution of animals to be
hunted; he or she will respond to prayers and
entreaties, but will deny prey to those violating
tabus and slighting the Lady or Lord of the Beasts.

The idea of such a ruler of the hunted creatures
seems quite an advance over the preceding concepts.
It recognizes the reality of human leadership and the
necessity of group loyalty to that leader; it
reflects the observation that herd animals clearly
have leaders and other animals display leadership,
and it assumes animal fidelity to its leaders. The
Lady or Lord of the Beasts is conceived as the
guardian of collective animals, while simultaneously
acknowledging human needs. The net effect is sacral
ecology, divinized conservation.[35] Both Lady and
Lord of Animals represent fertility; hence ithyphallic Lords of Beasts and Ladies of the Animals
with exaggerated hips and breasts.

The so-called "Dancing Sorcerer" of the Trois
Frères Old Stone Age cave, in the midst of animal
representations, may be a Lord of the Animals; the
figure is a hybrid man-beast. The presence of such
Paleolithic animal paintings in caves suggests that
they are placements in the womb of the earth mother,
who even at that early date may have been viewed as

Lady of the Animals. At Çatal Hüyük in Anatolia appears a fertility goddess c. 6000 B.C. in the role of Mistress of the Animals. At Mohenjo-Daro from the 3rd millenium B.C. is the image of an antlered Lord of Animals. Some scholars feel that this figure may depict Shiva, who is probably a pre-Indo-European concept, one of whose titles is Pashupati ("lord of animals"). Ancient Japanese hunting tribes 2000 years ago apparently believed in the Divine Mother of the Mountain, who controlled the animals; she frequently accosted hunters as a young mother seeking food for herself and her infant.

Primitive societies are symbiotic, establishing a reciprocal balance with Nature. As societies become increasingly self-conscious and proud of their accomplishments, men become more self-centered, concerned solely with exploiting Nature. In this changeover, the Lady or Lord of Beasts is transformed from leader of the animals to the mighty hunter. Such a shift is clearly demonstrated with Artemis. The statue of Artemis of Ephesus with incredible rows of breasts clearly represents the original earth mother, the Lady of the Beasts as fantastically fertile. Homer specifically calls her "Mistress of Wild Animals" (Iliad, XXI) and apparently conceives of her very much like an athletic young lady today, expert in archery. The great mother has been transmogrified into the sports-loving virgin, as notably with Britomartis ("sweet virgin"), apparently a Cretan divine huntress identified with Artemis. Circe looks like another Lady of the Beasts with sorceress powers. Often a culture would have both Lady of the Beasts (the Irish Flidhais), and the Lord of the Beasts (the Irish Cernunnos, antlered like the ancient figure of Mohenjo-Daro). The Eskimos revere a Lord of Land Animals in Aningakh and a Lady of Sea Animals in Sedna. Ukupanipo is the Hawaiian Lord of Fishes who supplies food for the people by herding schools of fish toward shore and denies food by shepherding fish far from shore.

Surviving archaic societies often still retain the Lord or Lady of the Beasts. One pattern is the Master of All Animals like Vaí-mahsë of the Colombian Tukano. Vaí-mahsë frequently appears as a red dwarf (red means blood and life; a small man is considered phallic). This Master of All Animals withholds animals and inflicts disease if hunting tabus are violated. Altar Woman is the Lady of All Beasts for the Hopi of SW USA. The "owner" of animals may be confined to the major hunting creature of a group, as the eastern Lapps consider Luot-chozjik the Lady of the Reindeer. Each animal deemed vital to a society may have an individual governor. The Piaroa of Venezuela have separate Lord of the Peccaries, Lord of Monkey, Lord of Wild Bees, Lord of Jaguars, and so on. Cambodians assert that every animal species has a ruler: kings of large animals and birds dwell high in the mountains, while the kings of each variety of fish dwell in the concentric seas around the mythical Mount Meru.

Man early observed that flesh is quickly stripped from the bones, but the bones long endure, especially if they are saved from dogs and similar creatures. Hunting societies worldwide have therefore presumed that intact bones are the very essence of life, the repository of the soul.[36] The Arapaho Amerindians believed that originally the buffalo had consisted solely of bone; flesh had been subsequently attached to assure food for the Arapaho. To ensure new animals, fleshed upon the bones, early man stacked piles of bones in caves, covered bones in middens, or otherwise buried bones in the womb of mother earth so that more creatures would be gestated from the mother of all life. The Huichol of N. Mexico bury the roots (they call them "bones") of peyote to cause the rebirth of the entheogenic plant. It is possible that all agriculture developed from the practice of burying "bones." Burying plant "bones" demonstrably produced crops, genuine rebirth of the plants.

The Lord of the Beasts was the great re-creator of animals, the clothier of flesh upon the bare bones. Apparently Thor originated as a Lord of the Animals. The Teutonic god, his chariot drawn by goats, visited with Egil and declared that it was perfectly all right to eat the goats providing the bones were preserved intact. Thialfi, Egil's son, was persuaded by the mischief maker Loki to crack one of the bones for its sweet marrow. Thor struck the goat bones with his magic hammer Mjollnir, refleshing and reanimating the goats--except for one goat with a badly lamed leg from the cracked bone. For this violation Thialfi and his sister Hoskova were given by Egil to Thor as bond servants; evidently the tabu against damaging animal bones was quite severe. The Irish god Manannán seems also to have been a Lord of Beasts, for at feasts pig meat was eaten entire, but the god brought the pigs back alive from bones to provide more pork repasts. In Odin's vast hall

Valhalla the warriors gorge upon the flesh of the magic boar Saehrimnir, whose flesh is constantly renewed.

Quetzalcoatl may have an origin as Lord of Animals, but his re-creating powers are extended to humans. Descending to Mictlan, the underworld, the god brought to the surface the bones of people of previous worlds and, sprinkling his own blood upon them, transformed the bones of the dead into the living people of today. This myth obviously imposes the sacred duty of burying the dead, and perhaps human burial arose from the idea of thereby granting reincarnation to the dead as skeletons would be re-fleshed. Blood, as will appear in the subsequent discussion of psychology, is also a basic symbol of life. This Quetzalcoatl myth declares that modern mankind has the bony framework of the dead and the living blood of a god. Among numerous hunting people the dead must await the disappearance of the flesh for permanent burial or will be interred upon a platform (many Amerindians) or in trees (many Australian aborigines). The Parsee practice of exposing corpses upon the tops of funeral towers probably has this origin. The Baniwa of S. America say that the first human, Inapirikuri, was wholly made of bones and therefore was immortal. Algonquian and Ojibwa N. Amerindians say that Paguk was a hunter who starved to death in the bush. Before normal death he prayed that his life and the strength of his flesh should be transferred to his bones. His flesh then fell away and he was a true living skeleton. Anyone seeing Paguk or hearing his bones clattering in the forest knows with dread that his own death is nigh. Probably the long tradition of moving, dancing, living skeletons has its beginning in this concept of bones as the life essence.

Chapter VI   Anthropomorphic Gods to Present-Day
            Religious View of Myth

Conceiving of Gods and Kindred Supernatural Beings

From ancient times through the 18th century
theorists consistently assumed that gods such as
Vishnu of India, Zeus of Greece, and Odin of the
Teutons sprang from the primal religious impulses of
mankind. We are now confident that such gods are
older by many more centuries than previous theorists
believed and younger by many more millenia than they
could imagine. Even with a healthy scepticism about
the evolutionary pattern outlined in the previous
chapter, it seems indisputable that the familiar
anthropomorphic deities were preceded for many
thousands of years by the range of belief from
animatism through Lords and Ladies of Animals.[1]
Vastly oversimplified, the development, as archeological finds and surviving archaic peoples suggest,
appears to be:

Lady or Lord of Beasts - Paleolithic (Old Stone
Age) as early as 60,000 B.C. Statuettes of the Earth
Mother date from Upper Paleolithic.

Tribal god - Mesolithic (Middle Stone Age) as
early as 25,000 B.C., in well-defined hunting groups.

Village god - Neolithic (New Stone Age) as early
as 8,000 B.C. The Stone Age labels are cultural, not
chronological, and some societies found by modern
explorers have retained Paleolithic (Tasmanian man)
or other Stone Age levels.

Community religion presupposes a strong conscious sense of community apparently generated by a
male-dominated hunting society. The worship of the
Great Mother is deeply buried in the infancy of the
species and in the individual unconscious, rever-
encing fertility and nourishment long before any
community spirit consciously emerged in mankind.
Ibofanga of the Creek Amerindians, Obassi of the
Niger Delta Ekoi, Pathen of the Indian Thadou Kuki
tribesmen are male tribal gods whose sole purpose is
to provide for a specific tribe, not for anyone else.
Such tribal gods expect due propitiation and rigorous
tabu observance, but they have little or no concern
about private morality. Tribal societies are small
and, in the long course of prehistory and history,
have often been annihilated or absorbed. Allah

probably originated as a Bedouin tribal deity, but it required the vastly amplified vision of Mohammed to make Allah a worldwide god. Unless such a powerful religious leader transforms the tribal deity, that god will remain significant only to his tribesmen, an anthropological datum rather than a great spiritual force in mankind.

Most of the gods of history[2] apparently descend from village gods, beginning with Neolithic settlements approximately 10,000 years ago. The village god is the protector of the collective community, responsible for fertility in fields, animals, and wives. The village god shields the community from flood, drought, fire, hurricane, and other natural catastrophes. This deity requires regular offerings and due observances, and virtually no one ever expects such a god to provide spiritual vistas of Eternal, Absolute Truth. No inscrutable deity is this village god. Villagers will mistreat the god's images, even lashing the statue, jeering and cursing a god obviously remiss in his wonted tasks. From such origins have developed the great gods, amplified by the cultural expansion of an entire society, but magnified especially by a profound reinterpretation from an elite of heightened spiritual perceptivity.

General characteristics of mythic gods. The number of gods is as boundless as the human imagination. Hindus often state that there are 33 crores of gods and goddesses (a crore is ten million). Swami Vivekananda declares that every human is a god.[3] Regardless of their number, all gods of myth are basically homanids with diverse modifications to set them apart from mere humans.

The life span of gods is always far greater than that of mortal men and women. The Greek gods were born in time but thereafter were immortal. The Teutonic gods were born in time and in time will die, but their lifespan far exceeds that of humans. The Judeo-Christian concept predicates a god born before time began and surviving the end of time. The Indian concept, held also about dead-and-resurrected gods everywhere, claims that immortality truly means repeated rejuvenation or rebirth. If a god is to be born, it should be an extraordinary birth like Aphrodite's from the genitals of Uranos fallen into the sea near Cyprus. Or the birth must be attended by such awesome circumstances as to evoke holy dread. No one can forget the swallowing of his own children by Kronos at their birth. If gods are to die, it should be with the cosmic catastrophes of the Teutonic Götterdämmerung. The dead-and-resurrected deities achieve a miraculous rebirth while simultaneously exalting all devotees with the etherial themes of rebirth and immortality. Gods are certainly non-human in coming to birth full-grown. The Aztec war god Huitzilopochtli sprang into the world completely armed from the womb of Coatlicue, while Pallas Athene in full armament leaped from the brain of Zeus. Zeus himself was born a babe but reached full maturity in one year; he sounds here like a year-god, still depicted in our infant New Year and aged Old Year. Precocity is typical of gods, whether Hermes and Heracles of Greece or Wol Fat in Polynesia. Many shrewd and richly metaphoric interpretations have been made of the above myths, but these ingenious explications may miss the basic point: before all else, something or many things about a god must be absolutely extraordinary.

Our word divinity probably comes from an Indo-European root div ("to shine," "to be resplendent"). Sun-gods worldwide obviously shine brilliantly, hence the flaming Apollo. The same resplendence is attributed to other gods, notably Zeus. Contemporary motion-pictures depicting Christ usually represent him at a climactic point, e.g. resurrected, as radiant with light.

To many cultures the hallmark of the supernatural is an elaboration or multiplication of anatomical elements far above the animal or the human.[4] The dark archaic monsters of Greek myth--Chimera, Sphinx, Cerberus, Scylla, the Lernean Hydra--seem such modifications of animals from the animal-deity stage. The maam or mamandi of Australian aborigines have extra arms and legs as the badge of the supernatural. The most remarkable of such extra-appendaged deities are those of India and Tibet. Brahma is assigned four faces and Vishnu six arms. But Lamaism goes further: Avalokitesvara has 11 heads arranged pyramidally, while Yamantaka with but nine heads nonetheless has 16 feet and 34 hands. Azrael, the archangel of death in Jewish and Moslem myth, is described as having as many eyes as there are men in the world, an eye closing whenever a human dies. The purpose of such fantastic imaginings is to inspire religious awe in the worshipper, but there can be a shadowy area between the awesome and the repulsive. Humbaba, a nature god in the Epic of

Gilgamesh, has a face built up of intestines, while Tlaloc, the Aztec rain-god, has a face composed of two serpents (his head corresponds to the caduceus of Hermes). Demonic supernatural beings appear with appalling features such as Medusa or disgusting behavior such as Azhi-Dahāka from the Iranian Avesta; this demon's three heads, six eyes, and three mouths might resemble the appearance of beneficent gods, but Azhi-Dahāka has serpents darting out of each shoulder and he feeds constantly on human brains.[5]

Bilocation, characteristic of shamans, is, of couse, a divine characteristic. Every churinga (ceremonial object) of the Australian Arunta has the god within it. In Vedic times the fire god Agni was present in every flame. The ancient Greeks believed that a specific god was a regular visitant in his temples every night, attended every ceremonial in his honor, and was a regular indweller within his statue images.

Sky gods and astral gods, day and night above us, suggested visual omniscience. Heimdal among the Teutonic deities saw all things below Asgard; he could even hear the growing of grass and the growing of wool. The standard mythic viewpoint, that of Greco-Roman and Teutonic societies, deemed the inner world of man a privacy inaccessible to the gods; as long as anyone displayed the outward signs of reverence or devotion, the gods could only consider him pious. An interesting but very thin scattering about the globe consists of older cultures that ascribed total omniscience (complete knowledge of each human heart and mind) to their deities: Babylonia, Jews, Kachin (Burma), Haida (N. America), Ona-Selknam (S. America).

The behavior of the gods is usually all too human. Older societies think of supernatural beings as clothed like aristocratic contemporaries. Zeus in garb resembled an early king of a Greek city-state, and Thor looked like a massive Teutonic warrior. Religion is reluctant to follow the rapid changes of a dynamic society. Christian visionaries still report god in the flowing garments of the ancient Middle East. Interestingly, Christians can accept the devil dressed like a contemporary maitre d'. Gods reside in structures which are human dwellings giganticized like Valhalla. The food and drink of deities resemble but quite surpass those of humans. Amirta is the Vedic beverage of the gods, etymo-

logically related to the ambrosia eaten by Greek
gods, who drank nectar. The gods of the north
relished the magic apples of Idun.

Achilles eloquently complains to Priam about the
fickleness of the gods (Iliad, XXIV). Modern
religions polarize supernatural beings into good and
evil, but the Judeo-Christian concept of the devils
as fallen angels suggests the earlier ambiguity of
the supernatural. The same deity can be radiantly
beatific and viciously cruel, as archaic man pragma-
tically observed woe and weal inextricably mixed in
his world. Apollo still has a superb reputation as
the scintillating god of light and art, but he
savagely abetted his sister Artemis in slaying all 14
children of Niobe; hubris is one thing but the harm-
less maternal boasting of Niobe is another, and the
gods should have rebuked the vain woman instead of
massacring her offspring. Artemis is simultaneously
the chaste young sportswoman and the dread Hecate,
foul goddess of the dark of the moon. Health deities
are especially ambiguous, like the smallpox god
Sopanna of the W. African Yoruba or Gula, the ancient
Babylonian disease goddess. Both may annihilate with
horrible disease or grant miraculous healing. The
painful ambiguity is highlighted in the closely
related cultures of Aryan Iran and Aryan India. Both
societies shared the common word deva and the cognate
ahura (Iranian) and asura (Sanskrit). In India deva
was associated with benevolent gods, but in Iran deva
was applied to demons. Ahura in Iran is a label of
the beneficent deities, while in India asura (in
post-Vedic times) has meant devils.

Gods frequently appear in human guise, but
usually their divinity displays some distinctive
badge. The Indian Mahabharata explains how to detect
gods who appear as humans. Unlike mortals the gods
are non-sweating, unblinking of eye, with feet never
quite touching the ground, and bedecked with flowery
ornaments that never fade.

Human as the gods frequently seem, they are the
"other." Semitic peoples especially felt the incredibly strange nature of the divine, too often beyond
human grasp. The earliest known religious impulses
of the Indo-European people appear in the Rigveda,
which declares that Daksha was born from Aditi and
Aditi born from Daksha (10.72.4). Daksha seems a
male sky god and Aditi an earth goddess in origin.
Such a paradoxical assertion is common in religion as

an attempt to exceed mere rational limitations in contemplation of the supernatural. The Rigveda postulates "two-in-one," a duality forming a unity (cf. Christian "three-in-one," a trinity forming a unity). Such Vedic thought is behind the "two-backed beast," the copulating and generating human pair that is one. Eastern religion, especially Hindu Shaktism, frequently regards copulation as a sacred act, symbolically reuniting into primal unity.

High gods. Andrew Lang and Wilhelm Schmidt dealt extensively with "high gods," what seem to be early primitive monotheistic gods, usually sky-gods, often considered Father-of-all. High gods have therefore been suggested as the basic monotheism from whence polytheism was a descent. Generally the high god is reported as creator of the world or the world's primal deity who in course of time has simply drifted away or retired to a haven, ignoring the world and mankind; such is a deus otiosus[6] ("superfluous god"). The high god appears in numerous cultures, perhaps most often in Africa, but also in Australia and the Americas. Uranos looks like a Greek high god, and probably Tyr in northern myth is another high god. Viracocha of ancient Peru created the world but soon delegated authority to his many deputies and never had any temples of his own. Similarly Shingrawa among the Kachins of Burma lost interest after creating mankind and has no present worshippers. Shoshone Amerindians say that Pakrokitat the creator became annoyed because the trouble-maker Kukitat kept demanding changes in the make-up of man (eyes in back of head, webbed feet, etc.), so in annoyance Pakrokitat simply abandoned the earth. African Bushmen state that the high god Kang who created all things became infuriated by the perpetual criticism of his creation (too much rain or too little rain, too hot or too cold, and so on upon any subject); Kang therefore retreated in disgust. The Mundurucú of Brazil say that Karusakaibe did everything for humanity, but quit altogether because of man's ingratitude. The Yao of Mozambique declare that the sky-god Mulungu fled from the world, appalled at the wickedness of mankind.

Perhaps Lang and Schmidt[7] are right in postulating the high god as primal monotheism. Such a view is tempting when we contemplate the high gods of the Nuer, Dinka, Lugbara, and Igbo tribes of Africa. In each case when a society has experienced severe cultural stress, a deus otiosus has once again risen to the fore, re-elevated from obscurity to preeminence. Could monotheism today simply mean the re-emergence of a high god of immense antiquity? Perhaps the high god is less mankind's primal deity than everyman's infantile god, springing from prenatal oneness. The high god as Father-of-all may simply be the child's deification of its father in a brutal society dependent upon the single dominant male. Radin suggests that the high god was a philosophical concept espoused only by the intellectual elite of an archaic society.[8] Polytheism looks like the world of the growing and grown-up person, multifarious, splintered, fragmented. The withdrawal of the high god to become <u>deus otiosus</u> seems the childhood euphemism for death. To a child the dead have simply gone away and wilfully refuse to reappear. Just as the male parent declines in the eyes of adolescents while numerous other interests and forces seize the growing youth, so does the high god diminish, shouldered aside by a host of superseding deities.[9] High gods among archaic peoples probably represent receding deities, outmoded and anachronistic gods rather than genuine monotheism. Any true monotheism presents a god with deep-seated convictions about moral and immoral behavior. Generally, though not universally, the high god is morally indifferent.[10] The paucity of narrative myth about high gods may mean that they are very old deities, that they are simply hypothetical prime movers whose function is solely to start things and then step aside, or that they may be the nebulous infantile gods of little interest to the adult framer of myth. Among many peoples the high god after starting everything has retired; but, eventually the high god will destroy the world he made, as the Apapocuva-Guarani of S. America assert about Nanderuvuçu ("our great father"). Such may be an adult dismissal of the childhood god in disillusionment or an acknowledgement of blind cosmic forces: "The Lord giveth and the Lord taketh away."

Polytheism. Marcus Aurelius employed both the singular and the plural of <u>theos</u> ("god") as synonyms within the same sentence. His conception of divinity implies that categories of polytheism and monotheism are irrelevant. Much Indian thought would concur. Most Occidentals, however, insist that the two terms are very different in meaning. Polytheism in the Western mind reflects human experience of the universe and life as displaying diverse and often irreconcilable manifestations of supernatural agency. Monotheism denies the adult apprehension of the world to insist that behind the multifaceted phenomena is an unsplit divine oneness.

Polytheism seems to imply a staggering multiplicity, but the full panoply of gods in one society will often in careful classification show remarkable parallels to other and even remote systems.[11] Emphases will vary considerably, and the categories below are intended to suggest patterns, not rigid structures. If we have meager information on a god, it is easy to classify him; the more we learn about a deity and his worshippers, the more complex and exception-ridden is his classification. The gods of a long isolated society such as the Australian aborigines are reasonably classifiable, but the many streams and tributaries, the currents and cross-currents of Indian and Greek myth make for very muddied waters. A difficult problem occurs in scrutinizing the gods of a dynamic society. Many Amazonian tribes probably have maintained much the same concept of their gods over millenia, while Shiva has apparently risen from Lord of the Beasts to be governor of the universe. Some bodies of myth almost elude classification. The gods of Central America sweep from upper to lower regions in unseemly haste, display bewilderingly varied functions, and change shape disconcertingly. Ancient Irish myth contains many beings of magical energy--kings, heroes, magicians--but hardly any gods.

(1) Terrestrial deities.[12] The world about us is the center for terrestrial gods, and those who conceive of such deities appraise all things from an immediate earthly viewpoint. The original Romans had a pantheon of gods of woods, fields, rivers, hills, and other eminently practical and observable objects. To the peasant of old Latium the landscape seemed jammed with supernatural personages: every brook had a water nymph, and the tree spirit had to be propitiated before any tree was chopped down.

Before there were any gods there must have been the goddess of earth, the Great Mother.[13] As all humans are born of woman and all fertility is hers, so the earth itself is feminine and maternal. For a people dominated by terrestrial deities like the N. American Zuñi the sun is not the progenitor of life; the earth mother is the real animating principle of the universe. The archaic vision is cherished today by the Desana of Colombia who regard the earth in most literal sexual terms. The earth below is the uterus of the Great Mother. She bore us and to her we shall return: the grave is also her womb, and from her is rebirth. Human burial probably started for this reason, and human burial for expected rebirth may be the earliest formulated religious concept. The Cágaba of Colombia proceed even further--all life is part of the Great Mother and all life is within her, never to be sundered. The Votyaks of N. Asia similarly imagine the whole earth to be an animated female, Muziem-mumi.[14] The concept of the Earth Goddess seems to have preceded any intellectual groping for first causes and supreme rule. Consequently, it is rare to have a creator-goddess, as do the Paressi Amerindians of the Matto Grosso who assert that the stone woman Maisö created the world. Indian Shaktism today is the major proclamation of the supreme female goddess, but Shaktism is a relatively recent development, and supreme deities are generally males.

Masculinity powerfully asserted its fertility power in the hunting stage, but agriculture vigorously reasserted the Earth Mother. Cultivation of crops probably arose from ritual burial of plant "bones" or "bodies" and the resultant growth. Harvest represents a worldwide symbol for birth. The stalks are severed from the roots as the new-born child is cut loose from the umbilical cord that rooted it in the "ground" or "garden." The Garden of Eden, paradise, and all gardens are emblems of the fertile Earth Mother. The bundles of grain are carried in the arms as an infant would be carried. In every bit of food that sustains us we are nourishing at the breast of the Great Mother. In India alone the innumerable names for the Earth Mother are staggering, but worldwide they are overpowering from Atargatis of Syria to Zlotababa of the Ugrians. Probably no female deity has ever existed without origin in the Great Mother. Greek myth frankly offers her in many guises: Gaia, Rhea, Demeter, Hestia, Hera. Artemis of Ephesus demonstrates the Earth Mother origin of Diana. Vital to the nature of Aphrodite is her character as Venus Genetrix ("child-bearing"). Frequently the Great Mother is associated with water because of the amniotic fluid. Anahita, the Iranian Great Mother, was the goddess of all fertilizing waters, and Aphrodite was born of sea foam. Patriarchal religions have tried to ignore the Great Mother, but only Judaism and Sikhism have been completely successful. Christianity has embraced her in the Virgin Mary, and much of Islam venerates her as Fatima, daughter of the Prophet.[15]

Each harvest time Mother Earth lavishes her colossal fertility, but next year produces a brand new cycle, commencing all over again. This immemorial pattern suggests the renewal of virginity by the Great Mother, as Hera annually renewed her virginity. The many female deities of S. India are almost always simultaneously the Great Mother and the eternal Virgin. Another viewing of the same cycle interprets the Old Year goddess as a mother and the New Year goddess as her daughter. Hence Demeter (Mother) and Persephone (Daughter or Kore). Among archaic peoples no pubescent girl escaped defloration. Virgin meant fresh fertility, not an intact hymen. Morals are a male creation, a legal formulation of a patriarchal society. The Great Mother accepts no moral restrictions: her only obligation is fecundity. Kunapipi, the Great Mother in Arnhem Land, N. Australia, was perpetually pregnant in the Dream Time and bore all mankind.

The daughter of the Earth Mother would logically succeed her mother, but in the temperate zone of the world winter always separates one summer from its predecessor. The maiden goddess is abducted to explain the gap between periods of the earth's fertility. Persephone's kidnapping by Hades looks like winter seizing the nubile spring and effectively delaying its arrival upon the earth's surface. Guinevere is probably such a spring maiden (gwen, "white," and hwyvar, "fairy" or "spirit") who is abducted by Melvas or Meleagant and must be rescued to insure the new season of fertility. Possibly a number of the mythical abductions and imprisonments of young women from Andromeda to the kidnapped maidens of medieval romance stem from the winter-preventing-spring theme.

While the daughter of the Great Mother is a nubile young woman, the male child of the Great Mother is often an infant. The female role is thus considered as producing offspring, while the male role is being offspring. The seasonal decline of Nature was interpreted as the loss of a child (usually a male like Attis or Adonis, but Persephone is the lost daughter of the Earth Mother, Demeter). Isis the Great Mother of Egypt with her son Horus in her arms was mistaken by early Christians for Mary and Jesus. Among the Ibo of W. Africa, Ala and her child are the madonna and infant son. At the mouth of the Ob until recent generations the Ugrian, Vogul and other tribes worshipped the statue of Zlotababa

177

and her child. Walt Whitman said, "Or I guess the grass is itself a child, the produced babe of the vegetation."[16] Millenia ago archaic man drew the same parallel to build an elaborate mythical structure.[17] Tubers are interpreted as the child in a mother's womb; in tropical areas some tubers grow to gigantic size, suggesting a human body. In Occidental countries, the mandrake, shaped somewhat like a human, was supposed to cry out in protest when wrenched from Mother Earth. Fruits and nuts fallen to the earth are like babes "dropped" by a mother. Fruits and nuts plucked from the bough are like infants ("fruit of the womb") drawn from a mother by a primitive midwife.

The Witoto of S. America state that their god Moma ("father") dies each year and is reborn annually in the new fruits. The eating of Nature's food is therefore a sacral event, eating the son of Mother Earth. Everyone has experienced the miraculous lift that eating provides for the lethargic, weary, hungry person. Food energizes and reinvigorates, bestowing life again--and the life force is divine. The eating of the god has consequently been practiced throughout the world. Archaic societies, recognizing the profane effect of everyday living, will devise elaborate ceremonies for, say, the first fruits or bread from the last sheaf. To make the symbol eminently clear, Aztec priests fashioned statues of Huitzilopochtli and Xiuhtecutli out of toasted amaranth seeds glued together with the blood of human sacrifice; these images were worshipped, broken into pieces, then eaten by the communicants. A kid was the surrogate for the god in the Orphic cult. Sacral cannibalism occurs when a human is substituted for the deity. In Christian communities the eucharist is frequently the central ritual, interpreted by Roman Catholicism in the immemorial concept of the actual body of the god consumed in the ceremony.[18] For secular men today meals probably constitute their most ceremonial occasions, a heritage from the sacred meal, eating the body of the god.

The grain-god[19] becomes a momentous figure in an agricultural society. Cultivated fields are so commonplace and ubiquitous to our age as to seem "natural." To early agricultural societies the cultivated plot (tiny in comparison to the vast wilderness surrounding) was sacred, uniquely crammed with the life-giving divine seed, miraculous growth of the son of the Great Mother. Survivals from the

sacred fields of old are the separately named fields
of England. The ancient Egyptians identified grain
with Osiris, weeping and wailing at the first mowing.
Reputedly Isis collected the scattered limbs of
Osiris in a winnowing basket, and throughout the
Roman Empire the winnowing basket was ritually
carried in the procession of the Isis cult. Widespread is the theme of the dead and dismembered god
whose fragments are eaten (as above) or buried to
fertilize the earth. The distribution of the shattered Osiris over Egypt almost certainly mythicizes
the use of plant segments to fertilize the soil.
Generally the dismemberment and fertilization mean
sundering of a male in sacrifice as Indian tribes
such as the Khonds and Meriahs strangled or impaled a
male victim until the British stopped the practice.
The flesh of the sacrificed male was distributed
among the festival participants who buried it in the
fields or burned it and scattered ashes over the
countryside to fertilize the soil. Every part of the
victim (hair, spittle, etc.) had miraculous potency.
Consecrated, he ceased to be a mere man and became
the incarnate spirit of male fertility. Indian myth
also reports a female similarly treated. Inconsol-
able at the death of his wife Sita, Shiva wandered
aimlessly about the world carrying her corpse on his
shoulders. To cure Shiva's obsession, Vishnu cut up
the body of Sita and scattered the pieces. Any spot
where a fragment fell was henceforth sacred.

Threshing furthers the image of the dismembered
deity, limbs torn asunder for the life-sustaining
seed. Milling represents still more dismemberment.
Apparently the millstone was standard among the
Indo-Europeans; the quern, a primitive hand mill, was
widespread in Neolithic times. Psychoanalysts suggest the mill as representing an infantile fantasy of
birth from the assembly of scattered parts: male is
miller, female is the mill, the meal is the embryonic
child.[20] Bread is then the reborn god, the miracle
of new life from the sundered and reassembled deity.
"Give us this day our daily bread" is celebrating not
only a food staple but also the divine son reborn, as
the Christian mass posits the bread as the body of
Christ.

The innermost temple sanctuary in India, en-
shrining the major deity, is regarded as a container
of the "seed." As the Earth was the female germinal
plot, the male provided the seed and was himself the
seed. Ploughing the soil in readiness for the seed

179

was a sacred act, as the emperor of China until recent generations ritually ploughed the first furrow. In Vedic myth Sita ("furrow") was the goddess of agriculture. Sowing the seed was a sacred act of burying the dead in Mother Earth, as the ancient Egyptians mourned their sowing as the burial of Osiris.[21] The new crop then was the resurrected lord.

The _femme fatale_ is infinitely older than 20th century "vamps." Perhaps the first profound feeling of life's tragedy was the necessity of the god's death in order to be reborn. Especially in the Middle East, the hosts of handsome young gods like Tammuz (Mesopotamia), Adonis (Syria), Attis (Phrygia), Telipinu (Hittite) must serve the Great Mother and they must die. Gilgamesh protests against this maddening destruction of her lovers by Ishtar, but he complains in vain. When the male is a mere stripling, a nubile youth, he lives only to serve the Great Mother's fertility, then dies for rebirth. The mother-son incest theme, as with Oedipus, may simply symbolize this very ancient agricultural myth. Possibly the biblical Eve (Hebrew _Hawwah_, "life" or life-giving"), responsible for Adam's downfall and the bringing of death into the world, is one of those _femmes fatales_. Since the male power of impregnation, his "seed," lies in his genitals, he is symbolically dead by castration. The priests of Cybele castrated themselves and buried their severed genitals in the earth, thus performing a ritual fertility sacrifice to the Great Mother.

The sampo in the Finnish _Kalevala_ has been variously interpreted, but it probably is a mill, the symbol of the fertile womb. The Danish king Frodi reportedly had a huge mill that ground out gold and peace and prosperity for him until he became so greedy that the giant maids who turned the stones changed their spell and instead ground out disaster and war. A similar womb symbol is the cauldron in India, in Teutonic myth as Odhroerir, and perhaps most daringly as Brian's cauldron of regeneration in the _Mabinogion_. A variation is the cornucopia named for the horn of the goat Amalthea that suckled the infant Zeus. Prevalent among Amerindians of the Great Lakes area is a myth about a wondrous pipe that, smoked by the hero, produces clouds of turkeys and pigeons. When a thief steals the pipe, his smoking produces dung, beetles, and flies. Psychoanalysts suggest that the dragging upon cigarettes and pipes is the infantile suckling at the mother's breast.

Dema deities[22] are gigantic beings, generally slain though occasionally self-immolating, whose bodies become the earth and whose innate vitality then exudes to produce plants and animals, especially food items. The myth apparently dates back to the period of animal deities and the dominant female goddess. In the Amerindian Nahuatl myth Cipactli is the huge crocodile whose gnarled and spiny body forms the crust of the earth. Mesopotamian myth portrays Marduk slaying the sea dragon Tiamat and from her body fashioning heaven and earth. Aztec myth states that from the body of the goddess Atlatentli the gods Tezcatlipoca and Quetzalcoatl made all the earth: trees from her hair, rivers and caverns from her mouth, mountains and valleys from her nose and shoulders. Among the Eskimos, Sedna is the Lady of the Sea Beasts whose panicking father threw her overboard in a storm and chopped off her fingers as she clung to the gunwale. Her fingers became all the sea creatures--seals, walruses, whales. Japanese myth says that the God of the Moon killed the Goddess of Food, whose limbs turned into the seeds of all useful plants. Probably of later patriarchal origin is the male dema deity. Virtra, the primal Indian male serpent or dragon, was slain by Indra; the power and strength of Virtra then became trees and plants. The gigantic Ymir was slain by Odin and his body made into the earth. Pachacámac, god of the central coast of Peru, tore the body of his "brother" apart, forming maize from the teeth, tubers from ribs and bones, cucumbers from the flesh. P'an-ku is a similar figure from South China; his breath became the wind, his voice the thunder, his hair the vegetation of earth.

Fire remains have been found in Swiss caves inhabited by Neanderthal man (75,000 B.C. or earlier), but Neanderthal man apparently did not cook his food. Fire may have been cherished as a blazing emblem of the divine for millenia before it was actually put to utility by man. The theft-of-fire motif is worldwide, often from animals hiding fire inside themselves, according to Australian, African, and American myths. Part of the sacred nature of trees arose from their supposed containing of fire, released by divine force in lightning. Amerindians declare that fire was originally thrown into trees and the rubbing of two sticks together releases the innate fire. The rarity of fire in nature and its sudden fury in forest fires made fire awesomely sacred. Fuji, the ancient fire goddess of the Ainu of Japan, and Pele, the Hawaiian fire goddess, suggest the hazardous snatching of fire from volcanoes. The theft notion may have been enhanced by the secrecy of early priests in husbanding divine fire. In India the fire drill, the twirling of the fire stick upon a wooden slab with tinder, probably was a priestly secret for a long time. The fire drill suggested the lingam in the yoni. Psychoanalysis states that the burning pressure of urine during sleep is turned into dreams of fire and from pressure in genital areas is sexual.

Most fire gods such as Nusku (Mesopotamia), Hephaestos (Greek), and Vulcan (Roman) never achieved the eminence of Agni, the Vedic fire god. To the Indians Agni was the priest of the gods and the god of the priests. Agni's crucial role arose from the essential need of fire in sacrifice. Agni was therefore the mediator between gods and men, the all-pervading power in the universe. With each kindling of the flame Agni was reborn. Eternally young and bounding with vitality and sexuality, he bestowed life, placing seed in woman. His chariot was drawn by red horses who left a blackened trail.

(2) Humanoid deities. Gods recapitulating human experience are especially characteristic of the Teutonic North. The gods and dead heroes in Valhalla are almost exact copies of the mead hall revellers on earth. Most of the myths about Thor sound like the roistering swaggering career of the brawny Germanic warrior.[23]

Local Bengal myth makes Shiva not the towering deity of destruction dear to mythological texts but a poor man sweatily working rice fields to feed himself, his peasant-shrewd wife Parvati, two sons and two daughters. Shiva dallies with pretty girls, and his annoyed spouse disguises herself to make love with him. Poor Shiva can pay with no more than a simple brass ring, and when he sneaks home, Parvati confronts him with the evidence as Tamar confronted Judah.

Among Vedic deities the boastful, heavy-drinking Indra is a counterpart of the contemporary Aryan warrior. The war-like Romans exalted Mars, but the less bellicose Greeks had no great respect for Ares, with the possible exception of a local cult at Thebes. Heracles (Hercules to the Romans) was mutually applauded, proving the first foreign cult introduced into Rome. The whole tenor of the head-knocking, bashing Heracles suggests a popular bruiser elevated in rank the way sports figures can now become knights in England.

More esteemed by far among the Greeks was the goddess of war, Pallas Athene, the mistress of strat-agem against the headlong battle plunge of Ares. Bellona, the Roman war goddess, received scanty attention. Perhaps war goddesses were suggested by camp followers who often killed wounded enemies on the battlefield, or more likely, from the sexual itch of soldiers that terms female numerous things from weapons to the infantry itself, "The Queen of Battles."

Meager in myth but mighty in ancient Greek hearts loomed Hestia of the Hearth, the deification of each household's focal point of food and warmth and love. The eminently practical Chinese even had a Goddess of the Privy, K'êng-san-ku, who as a second-wife in the 8th century had been killed by the dis-gruntled first wife and pitched into the privy. Every trade and craft of China had its own deity with careful specialization: a red goddess as patroness of workers in red lac and a black goddess as patroness of workers in black lac. Aesculapius seems hope-lessly old-fashioned in comparison with the elabor-ately bureaucratic Chinese celestial ministry of medicine with neat subdivisions: diagnostics, sur-gery, dermatology, anatomy, yin-yang and the diges-tive system, medical properties of plants and minerals, veterinary science, the nervous system.

(3) Psychological gods. All deities offer a strong flavoring of human psychology, but this category refers to gods who are specifically symbols of the interior world of mankind. The Kalevala of Finland provides such deities, but the ancient Greek mythology here seems pre-eminent. Indian attitudes reveal a position strange to the Occident: the intense spiritual power of the rishis (seers) can overpower the gods themselves, clearly indicating that the gods are within man.

Apollo may have originated as some wild Asiatic spirit or even wilder Hyperborean fanatic, but classic Greece glorified Apollo as the epitome of human inspiration and illumination. Athene may have started as an owl goddess or a Mycenean household deity but was elevated to be the exemplar of calm wisdom.[24] Even if Aphrodite began as some sort of fertility goddess, as Uranian Venus she meant for the ancients all sorts of noble and etherial love. In Hippolytus Euripides asserts that Aphrodite is no deity perched on Mt. Olympus but a powerful universal force surging through every human being.

(4) Celestial deities. The ancient Egyptians especially looked to the heavens above because their world on either side of the Nile was stripped and barren. Celestial gods rule the sky, the sun and the moon, the starry nights.

As yet we have no proof that Paleolithic man honored the sky-god, but among peoples from very ancient times to the present, almost everybody except the Egyptians has conceived of a male "father" deity above the female earth. Knaritja is the emu-footed Great Father sky-god of the Western Arunta of Australia, Algaloa was the Hawaiian sky god, Anu was the Sumerian sky-god, Shang-ti (or T'ien) was the Chinese sky-god, Sin ("day") was the sky-god of the Haida Amerindians, Yahweh was the Hebrew sky-god. The early patriarchal Indo-European peoples universally worshipped the Father Sky-God: Dyaus (Vedic), Dievas (Lithuanian), Zeus (Greek), Jupiter (Roman). In India Varuna succeeded Dyaus; probably Varuna and the Greek Uranos are etymologically related.

When the Great Mother rules humanity, heedless of any male god, rain is equated with milk, and clouds are seen as women's breasts or, from early Indian myth, as cows or cows' udders. When in a patriarchal society the sky-god becomes prominent, he is seen as fertilizing the female earth with his semen (rain).

From the era of animal deities, Amerindians of the Pacific NW say that lightning is the flash of Thunderbird's eyes. Probably Jove originated as a god of lightning, for his name seems to mean "light," and a very archaic representation of Jupiter is aniconic, a great flint stone. Thor is reported as having a flint in his forehead. To archaic man the life energy of humans and the blasting energy of lightning were both awesome life forces. Ancient Babylonian cylinders depict Adad with a boomerang (thunderbolt) in one hand and a spear (lightning) in the other. The Skidi Pawnee Amerindians hear the voice of Paruxti in thunder; Paruxti showers the land with rain, then returns to his lodge to enjoy smoking with his fellow deities and receive the praise of grateful mankind. The lightning bolt hurled by the god Paruxti reputedly had a stone head (arrowhead, spearhead, axhead) with divine fire hidden within. The Yoruba of W. Africa refer to their storm-god Shango by the epithet Jacuta ("stone thrower"), for they think of lightning as a spear thrust with a stone tip. Shamans dearly prize thunderstones, and the Ka'aba was probably regarded as a thunderstone.

In temperate zones dawn is so long drawn out that it might well be considered separate from the sun. The exquisite delicacy and beauty of daybreak apparently explain the personification of dawn as a female deity. Once having conceived of Eos, the ancient Greeks characterized her chiefly as an aggressive goddess who staged torrid love affairs with Tithonus, Cephalus, and Orion; by either the wind god Aeolus or the Titan Astraeus she was the mother of winds and stars. Vedic myth perhaps more appropriately imagines Ushas, the bright daughter of heaven (Dyaus) and bride of the sun (Sūrya). She opens the gates of the sky, scatters the evil spirits that burden the night, and drives through the sky in a car drawn by red cows. Ushas is the prime link of the divine between this mundane world and the celestial realm above.

Myth provides a very few examples, probably of extreme antiquity, of sun and moon both feminine. So say the Ainu, aborigines of Japan. The Lodhas of W. Bengal assert that sun and moon are sisters, both of whom had numerous children, crowding the skies. The deceiving moon told the sun that she was devouring her children to reduce the population, but she actually hid her progeny. In good faith the sun ate her children, thus leaving the sky wholly to the moon and her offspring. The indignant sun hates to see the successful moon and therefore pouts by night, showing herself only during the day when the moon and her star children have retired.

The standard pattern worldwide proclaims a male sun god[25] and a female moon deity.[26] The Kharias of India say that the sun (Bero) and the moon (Lerang) are husband and wife, while the stars are their children. The Bunas of Bengal aver that sun and moon are brother and sister; once the female moon was brighter than the sun, but in a sibling hassle the sun hurled mud upon his sister's face, making the moon spotty and relatively dim ever since. Unusual is the Eskimo concept of the sun as female and the moon as her brother. At night the moon would creep into his sister's bed. She smeared ashes on her hands to mark the culprit, and ever since the sun has heatedly pursued the marked moon through the sky. In far northern latitudes, of course, the sun lacks the fierce masculine intensity of warmer climes.

The Yuchi of SE USA consider the sun feminine and themselves her offspring from the menstrual blood of the reddened sun. Even though an Indo-European people of patriarchal origin, the ancient Hittites worshipped a sun goddess. Amaterasu, the Japanese sun goddess, is thought to be a lineal ancestor of the mikado.

Most peoples, however, deem the sun to be male. The ancient Peruvians regarded the sun as the ancestor and principal god of the Inca dynasty. The Natchez Amerindians built temples to the sun and addressed their chief as a divinity, "The Sun." In the almost eternally cloudless skies of Egypt Re shone as the midday sun, Atum as the setting sun, and Horus as the newborn sun. The Aztecs similarly revered a sun triumvirate: Tonatiuh, the sun face; Tezcatlipoca, sun of night and the underworld; chief-reigning Huitzilopochtli, radiant sun of day. The pyramids of Cheops (Egypt) and Teotihuacan (Mexico) are gigantic demonstrations of solar worship. The rays of the sun suggest, as with Apollo, that the sun is an archer or spearman. Vishnu, derived from a solar deity, notably employed the sun-shaped discus (cakra) of the ancient Indian warrior; twirled and flung, this emblem of the sun proved a formidable weapon.[27]

The ancient Greeks specifically named the sun for two titans, Hyperion and Helios, but except for a cult of Helios on Rhodes the mythology is meager and the worship even less. In Iran, Zoroaster elevated Ahura Mazda, the sun god, to cosmic and essentially monotheistic heights, and from Iran the worship of the sun was introduced to the Romans in the 1st century B.C. eastern campaigns of Pompey. The adoration of Sol Invictus ("the unconquerable sun") swept through the legions of Rome, who erected temples of Mithraism as far west as Morocco and along the Great

Wall separating England from Scotland. Such solar worship competed with Christianity and bequeathed the celebration day of Sol Invictus[28] to be observed henceforth as Christmas. The male sun god has been a major deity from Beiwe of the northern Lapps to Hiro of the tropical Polynesians.

Max Müller and other 19th century mythologists certainly overdid their ascriptions of all myth to the solar disc, but quite possibly a number of heroic myths may be linked to the sun. The Celtic Gawain looks like a sun god in his diadem of golden hair and with strength waxing until midday and waning thereafter. Cuchullainn is similarly associated with the sun. Any pattern of rise to apogee, then fall to death or darkness may have some background in the sun's daily and annual jaunt through the heavens. Light is often seen in myth as the crucial act of creation, and light itself is mythically impregnating. Indonesian myths portray the sun as sexually fertilizing the earth to produce all life. The Indian Brahmanas[29] equate sunlight with semen. An ancestor of Genghis Khan reputedly was conceived by sunlight falling upon his mother, and the same origin is claimed for Shenrab, the founder of the Tibetan Bon religion. Zeus appeared to Danaë in a shower of gold (sunlight) and conceived Perseus.[30] A Tibetan concept claims that originally the sexual instinct was satisfied solely by sight. The light from the male penetrated and impregnated the female. Degeneration has produced the vulgarization of physical contact.[31]

The Surára of NW Brazil consider the moon as bisexual; believing in reincarnation, the Surára think the moon the paradise of the dead and the soul reservoir where the male Poré inserts souls into the female Perimbó for rebirth. A sizable and significant minority of world myths says that the moon is masculine. The Abor of India state that the sun and moon are brothers, at one time providing 24 hours of brilliant light between them. Distressed at the ceaseless heat, the frog shot the scintillating moon so that it died and now is without warmth. Both the sun (sun-stroke) and moon (moon-stroke) in anger now shoot their arrows at the earth, and the recreant frog hides in the water. Chandra ("bright one") is the male moon in Sanskrit. When the moon laughed at the antics of the elephant-headed Ganesha, the angered deity tore off one of his tusks and hurled it at the moon with the consequences noted in its waning and its spotted appearance. As the Japanese sun is feminine, so Tsuki-yomi, the Japanese moon, is male. Egypt had two notable lunar deities, both male. Khonsu of Thebes was a handsome young man with the crescent moon upon his head. Thoth of Hermopolis was the "recorder of time," "the measurer," the scribe of the gods, the inventor of the exact sciences, an adult moon god; apparently Thoth dates from the lunar calendar period. Perhaps the pre-eminent lunar god was Sin of Mesopotamia, the father of Ishtar and of the sun god Shamash. Until the 6th century A.D. the worhip of Sin persisted at Harran in NW Mesopotamia.

The Society for the Comparative Study of Myth founded in Berlin in 1906, including notable German scholars, regarded the moon as the source of most myth, especially because of the primacy of the lunar calendar, preceding the solar calendar in most soc- ieties. As the moon would herald rain it could be considered masculine, but the major employment of the lunar calendar was in planting and harvesting, the fertility occupations that would suggest femininity. The phases of the moon have generally been associated with the menstrual periods of women, and the lesser light of the moon has to many archaic societies suggested the female in contrast to the flaming male sun. The majority of pantheons offer a moon goddess: Hina (Polynesian), Ch'ang-o (Chinese), Ilumquh (Arabian), Astoreth (Canaanite), Selene (Greek), Luna (Roman). Perhaps the most melodramatic moon myth is Aztec: in fighting his enemies the great god Tezcat- lipoca unintentionally slew his beloved sister Coyolxauhqui ("Golden Bells"); he severed her head and hurled it into the sky to float as the moon.

Eclipses of sun or moon are almost always attri- buted to demons. The Buna of Bengal shrewdly suggest that the swallowing demon has a big hole in his throat through which the sun or moon emerges. The Birhors of Chotanagpur believe that the sun and moon stand security for the debts of poor men. Eclipses occur when creditors despatch bailiffs to seize the sun and moon for debts.

(5) Chthonic beings. Supernatural beings of subterranean origin, of darkness, and of death are chthonian. Homeric literature generally deemphasizes these often sinister and terror-laden beings, and classic culture as a whole minimizes the chthonic element, but the popular mind and the peasant mind of the era seem grievously concerned about these dan- gerous spirits.

Night and darkness were subjects of dread to
early man, and their dire aspects survived in man's
mind until recent times of abundant nocturnal illumination. Darkness and night seem to cling to the
soil at sunrise and then steal upwards from earth at
sunset; hence their association with chthonic ("of
the soil"). Early Greek myths portray Night and
Darkness as the primal elements of Nature (cf. primordial darkness of Hebraic account). Nyx ("night")
was so formidable that she might subdue even Zeus
himself. The Orphic creation myth stated that before
all else Nyx was courted by the Wind and thereby laid
a silver egg (the moon) from whence Eros (love) was
hatched. In addition Nyx was the mother of the Fates
(Clotho, Lachesis, Atropos), of Death (Thanatos), of
Sleep (Somnus), of Mockery (Momus), of Dreams, of
Cares, of Revenge (Nemesis), of the Hesperides, even
of Light. The Walpurgis-Night scene in Goethe's
Faust and "A Night on Bald Mountain" by Mussorgsky
indicate the horror-packed concept of night even to
recent generations.

Foundation sacrifice is the sacrifice of a life
in erecting a new building. Human remains, often
infant skeletons, have been found in walls or under
floors of early Middle East structures. Probably
this practice means the propitiation of chthonic
spirits whose domain has been invaded by the construction. Wol Fat, the sly trickster of Polynesia,
cleverly evaded being such a sacrifice. Portrait
skulls found under floors at ancient Jericho probably
represented foundation sacrifice. In Mesopotamia
human images found beneath buildings look like surrogates for human victims. The Votyaks of Siberia
believe that "House Ruler" is a spirit dwelling
immediately underneath the floor. Generally beneficent, the "House Ruler" may maliciously substitute
a changeling for a small child left alone in the
house. When offended, the "House Ruler" must be
appeased by the sacrifice of a black sheep (note that
white animals are sacrificed to the terrestrial and
celestial gods, while black animals are sacrificed to
chthonic beings). A hole is dug in the floor and the
sheep's blood drained into it (cf. Odysseus slaugh-
tering black sheep and pouring their blood into a
trench for the dead in the Odyssey, XI).

The subterranean world is almost universally
split into two areas, upper and lower. The upper
area is ambiguous. It can be highly favorable as the
source of agricultural riches (Pluto means "wealth")

189

or mineral treasures (Kubera of India is in charge of minerals and precious stones). Persephone probably was the original chthonic deity responsible for pushing upwards the vegetable life; her rape by Hades (euphemistically "the hidden one") indicates a male takeover from the earlier female domination. The great and supposedly beneficent dead can dwell in the shallow underground in their tombs. The early Cretan and Mycenean tombs were provided with special conduits to convey offerings and libations to the illustrious dead below. Probably the hero cults of archaic Greece followed this localized concept rather than the Homeric idea of one subterranean residence for all souls of the dead.[32] Burial places today are still popularly thought to be dwellings of the spirits of the departed. The underworld could be eminently attractive as in the Elysian fields where Anchises, father of Aeneas, enjoyed an idyllic existence. A utopian work by a Dane, Ludwig von Holberg, in 1761 imagined a perfect realm inside the earth, a paradise fascinating to the young Wordsworth.[33] The benevolent god of healing, Aesculapius, might be of chthonic origin as suggested by the snake coiled about his staff.

The snake is the messenger of the underworld as the birds are messengers of the celestial deities. Hence the dramatic struggle between the eagle and the serpent (the conflict reportedly determined the location of the Mexican capital and the present-day flag insignia of Mexico). The serpent of Genesis is cursed to crawl on its belly and eat dust; serpents do not eat dust, but such a diet is regularly attributed to the spirits of the dead in the Babylonian-Assyrian underworld. Greek heroes were often expected to reappear as serpents, especially in the vicinity of their tombs. Medea in part displayed her chthonic nature by her magical power over the sacred serpent guarding the Golden Fleece. Slithering from heaps of rocks and crevices, snakes have been scary creatures to multitudes of humans for eons, unpleasant intruders from the dubious underground.

In recent Chinese mythology the kuei are spirits dwelling below the earth, and the kuei are uniformly demonic. Many people in Africa and the Americas similarly interpret all subterranean spirits as evil or easily incitable to vicious acts.

Among those who assign all their dead to a spirit life underworld,[34] the ruler of this area is a dread but not demonic figure, like Nergal of Mesopotamian myth and Hades of Greek myth. The ministers of death are also greatly feared, but, of course, they are simply doing a job, even the emissaries of Yama, Indian god of the dead, who bind a dying man's spirit with a noose and drag him off to the realm of death. The judges of the dead, whether the Canaanite Yam on the banks of the river separating the living from the dead or the Greek triumvirate (Minos, Aeacus, Rhadamanthus), are awesomely forbidding, but not evil. Similar are the solemn recorders of man's deeds, like the Indian Chitragupta, and also the weighers of souls like the Egyptian Maat. Of course, it has generally been acknowledged that any actual slayer, like the Babylonian Mu-u-tu, was a devilish killer. The Greeks originally thought of Orcus as a deity who punished perjurers in the underworld. The Romans made him the slayer of the dying, and a man garbed as Orcus carried the dead gladiators from the arena. Orcus has survived as a horrible man-eating ogre.

There is no ambiguity about the lower infernal regions. Here is the abode of heinous demons. Zoroastrianism, Manicheism, Judaism, Christianity, and Islam regard these vicious beings as minions of the devil, one quintessential embodiment of all evil. Taoism, Hinduism, Buddhism, and the Mesopotamian religions regard the evil spirits as independent evildoers without any true central command. Certainly these monstrous fiends are man's personification of the most depraved and most diabolical elements deep in the psyche, for the deeper the yawning abyss of the underworld, the more demoniacal and repulsive the denizens. Although living in secure isolation for many centuries, the ancient Egyptians morbidly dwelt upon the gross monsters of the depths: Am-mut (ghoulish eater of the dead), Apophis (giant serpent daily threatening the sun god Re), Bebon (mind-boggling demon of darkness). Mesopotamian myth, with more justification in an oft-troubled land, was hag-ridden with demons. The Greeks had their quota of demonic beings: Alastor (avenging demon), Eurynomous (corpse-eating demon), Sphinx, Harpies (death angels), Erinyes (personified conscience), Sirens.

Supernatural beings dwelling below in the great waters are properly chthonic, like Sedna among the Eskimos and, off the coast of San Christobal, Ngorieru who makes passing canoe crews fall silent

191

and dip their paddles quietly. The Olympian emphasis in classic Greece tended to conceal the chthonic origin of some mythical figures. The rather mysterious Zagreus, associated with Dionysus, may derive from an ancient Cretan chthonic god. Amphiaraos seems a normal human hero in the Seven Against Thebes account, but he apparently was a local Boeotian chthonic god as he departs this world dramatically by descending in his chariot into a suddenly opened chasm. Vulcan by residing under Mt. Etna is obviously chthonic; his combined attributes of fire, volcanoes, metal-working, and magic artistry reflect a complex of cultural-religious interests at an early level of culture. Fire and sexuality are associated, as the Roman Caeculus was born from a spark from Vulcan's anvil.

To consult the oracle of Trophonios at Lebadeia a suppliant was required to descend into the dark underground. That inveterate tourist of antiquity, Pausanias (IX, 39), himself made the descent into this chthonic realm and clearly indicated the parallelism to the ancient mystery cults that gripped many hearts in the declining years of classic Greco-Roman society.

The chthonic supernaturals do not accept extinction quickly. Agricola was a Renaissance graduate of Leipzig University with postgraduate studies in Italy. A physician in a German mining area, he became the authority on contemporary mining. His Bermannus (1530) attributed the abandoning of the Annaberg silver mine to the slaying of twelve miners by demons lurking underground. Agricola labeled black pitch as stercus daemonum, the excrement of subterranean devils.[35]

(6) Spiritual deities. Other gods and goddesses are essentially products of quite earth-bound humans, but the spiritual deities brush aside all worldly concerns to assert that another, totally spiritual, realm represents the "real" and meaningful existence. Notable examples of such spiritual quests are: mystery cults of Asia Minor, Syria, and Greece; the Osiris cult of Egypt; Mazdaism of Zoroaster, Mithraism and Manicheism; many aspects of Hinduism, Jainism, Buddhism, Christianity and Islam. All these groups (admittedly dulled and diluted by pragmatic religionists) strongly emphasize the afterlife and regard this life as mere preparation, advocate transcendental aims rather than worldly, espouse a pessi-

mistic outlook upon natural life but an optimistic appraisal of the spirit realm. The profound eschatological preoccupations of such devotees jettison the rational and the material in favor of heady intuitions and gripping revelations.

Freud and other rationalists postulate the inevitable rise from superstition and belief in supernatural beings to a triumph of rationality and the reality principle. The adherence to spiritual deities seems quite to violate this evolutionary pattern, for these deities are products of relatively far advanced civilizations and never, so far as we can ascertain, emerge from early subsistence societies. Even if the names of primitive gods like Osiris and Allah are retained, the transmogrification to spiritual deities demonstrates a vast alteration. Psychologists suggest that the spiritual deities are generated by social crisis, but social crisis is the norm not the aberration of human life, and the stupendous vitality and grip of these spiritual deities seem too potent to be thus derogated.[36] Apparently they fulfill widespread need even if their consolations are only psychic projections.

Indian speculation beyond all others has centered upon spiritual deities, and even the earliest Upanishads (perhaps 700 B.C.) are deeply insistent upon the escape of the human spirit from this physical world to the glorious realm of the spiritual deities.

(7) Ceremonial and allegorical deities. This is a rather miscellaneous category, bounded only by the limits of human ingenuity. A good example of a purely ceremonial deity was the Roman goddess Furrina who had her own priest, the flamen Furrinalis, and her festival, the Furrinalia, celebrated on 25 July, although her nature and function had been totally forgotten.[37] Iacchus seems just such a ceremonial god, for there are no myths about him separate from the Eleusinian mysteries, and the initiates remained silent about him.[38] In India multitudes of local gods are perfunctorily labeled as avatars of Vishnu or other aspects of Shiva. In ancient Greece a local designation could be tied to a famous deity such as Zeus Acraeus ("of the summit"), Zeus Averter of Flies, or Zeus Picus ("woodpecker").[39]

God creation has proceeded even to momentary gods[40] who exist only for a specific purpose at a special place and time. Such in ancient Arcadia and Elis was the god Myiagros who chased away the flies during the sacrifices to Zeus and Athene, and had no other existence.

Any object may be personified and deified. Originally _adri_ represented the stones used by Indians to extract the soma juice; the stones were divinized as Adri and invoked to drive away calamity and give fertility. The throne of the pharaoh was deified as the goddess Isis, so that the ruler of Egypt, when seated on the throne, was in the embrace of the goddess. The Sumerian god Ig-galla is "the great doorleaf," i.e. personification of the temple door. Carried into Late Assyrian, this deity had a son Hedu ("lintel" or "arch"). Cardea was the Roman goddess of the door hinges (from her name comes _cardinal_ with its multitude of meanings). Janus started as the numen of _ianua_ ("entrance gate") which, of course, looks both ways; hence the two-faced god looking in opposite directions. Shrewd Hindu priests probably exalted _dakshina_ (the voluntary gift given to a priest at a sacrifice), which as the goddess Dakshina was identified with Mother Nature, giver of all life. Mahayana Buddhism has been incredibly prolific, deifying the compass points, religious musical instruments, each gesture and position in prayer. The Yurok of California even conceived of trails as deities.

Personification and deification of abstractions can have no limit. As a droll concept, Ocnus in Greek myth was the personification of delay; in the underworld he continually twines a rope of straw that is eaten by his ass as fast as he weaves it. Bushyasta in Zoroastrian myth is the demon of lethargy who causes men to oversleep and neglect their religious duties. Phobos was the Greek personification of fear; Alexander the Great celebrated rites to Phobos at night while his army slept. The Hindu god of fear Bhaya was the grandson of Adharma ("vice") and Himsha ("violence"); Bhaya's son was Mirtyu ("death"). Hinduism even has an unknown god Ka, a deification of the interrogative pronoun.

The "unknown god" in Acts 17:23 probably resulted from increasing syncretism and the attendant fear that some deity might inadvertently be neglected. In view of its monotheistic implications, its authenticity has been debated. Perhaps it was erected by a cult group, for "hidden god," "veiled deity," etc. were terms frequent in ancient mysticism. Greek Orphism, for example, developed elaborate divinized abstractions such as Eon ("life"), personified as a son of Chronos ("time"). Eon was adopted as the tutelary deity of Alexandria and his birth was celebrated annually on the night of 5-6 January. Later Gnostics made Eon creator of the world (cosmos) and time (chronos). The Romans personified Eternitas as an heroic male with wings of an eagle, clasping a globe encircled by a snake; Eternitas was associated with the imperial destiny of Rome. Possibly St. Agnes, Christian martyr, may have originated as personification of chastity (Greek hagné means "chastity").

Personification of a deity may arise accidentally. In the Jewish scriptures belial apparently means no more than "scamp," "rogue" as in "son of belial" (Judges 19:22). By the time of Christian scriptures Belial is a designation for the Devil (II Corinthians 6:15). Just plain misunderstanding made Moloch a foul demon. The term melech or moloch is employed eight times in the Hebrew scriptures, always in conjunction with child-sacrifice. Older scholarship associated the term with melekh ("king") or the Phoenician god Melgart, but recent research indicates that moloch was a technical term for child-sacrifice.[41] In the Rigveda Indra is termed Sacipati ("lord of the power"). This epithet was misconstrued as Sacipati ("husband of Saci") and thus was generated a goddess Saci as wife of Indra. Plutarch's famous anecdote of a voyager hearing the cry "Pan is dead" was long celebrated as the formal demise of pagan gods at the coming of Christ, but now the cry is regarded as misinterpretation of a ritual lament for Tammuz.[42]

In the supreme Taoist deity Yü Huang we may have a god created by order of a Sung Emperor.[43] Abraxas was apparently devised by Basilides early in the 2nd century A.D., composed of the Greek letters which, according to the numerical system then in use, stood for 365; it is doubtful that anyone in ancient times ever worshipped Abraxas as a deity. Originally the phrase vishva-karman ("fashioner of the universe") was an epithet of Indra, but later Vishvakarman was regarded as a god in his own right, the Indian God above all gods. Parallel is the course of the word prajāpati ("lord of living beings"), a label applied to the Aryan sun-god; in time the deity Prajāpati was predicated as the great creator. In many mythologies a god is provided with a wife purely for symmetry. The Chinese goddess Si-wang-mu offers the reverse. By the 1st century A.D. she was regularly depicted at the western end of the ridge-beam of every home. With the feminine yin principle to the west, the male yang principle was logically placed to the east as balance. Hence the Lord-king of the East, Tung-wang-kung.

Incarnate Gods

Possession of a human by a deity, as in the case of an oracle, is momentary, and with the god's departure, the human is again but a normal person. A special type of possession was that of pharaoh by Amun so that the god in coitus with the queen would produce a divine heir to the Egyptian throne. This possession of the pharaoh was customary and was constantly repeated. Greek myth had no such practice and consequently hedged about the father of Heracles. Probably the appearance of Zeus in the likeness of Amphitryon imitated the Egyptian account; frequently Heracles was called Alcides as a descendant of Alcaeus, Amphitryon's father.

Frequently mystics (e.g. Catherine of Siena, St. Theresa, and Jacob Böhme) report that they have been possessed by god and write or speak automatically at the dictation of the divine will, even without understanding their own utterances. Psychologically this experience would be termed dissociation. Such is the rationale for numerous religious works (e.g. Bible, Koran) reputedly dictated by god through a prophet or visionary.

Incarnation of a god in a human means that god and human are coterminus and permanently united until the death (or translation) of the human. Orthodox Christianity posits such incarnation for Jesus, although the concept is repugnant to the Hebrew background of Christianity, much of the Greek world of early gentile Christianity no longer supported the idea, and for at least a millenium and a half the Western mind has scorned any new claim of such incarnation. Convinced of absolute union with the divine, mystics will say, "I am God." Sunnite Islam (the orthodox majority) has proved as intolerant of the incarnation concept as Judaism and consequently executed the mystic Hallāj in 922 for stating that he was god. In India the statement, "I am god," is wholly acceptable, merely asserting that the deepest focal point of man, <u>atman</u>, is simultaneously the deepest focus of the universe, <u>Brahman</u>. Alan Watts calls this attitude the "mode of inclusive consciousness" in which the center of the mystic is the center of the entire cosmos and of all time.[44] Of all gods undoubtedly Vishnu has had the largest number of reincarnations (avatars). Vishnu has regularly reappeared in mortal flesh for the express purpose of restoring divine law (<u>dharma</u>) on earth.

Shamanistic incarnation. Non-institutionalized reincarnations are the assertions by or about individuals of their divinity, evidenced solely by their actions (and reputed actions).

Basava (1106-1168), a major figure in the Virashaiva ("heroic Shaivism") movement, was proclaimed by contemporaries and later supporters as Shiva incarnate on earth. Madhva (1197-1276), chief proponent of dualistic Vedanta, was regarded by his followers as an incarnation of the god Vāyu ("breath"), mediator between god and man. Caitanya (b. 1485), founder of one of the four principal Vaishnava sects, was considered an incarnation of Krishna, or of Krishna combined with his divine beloved Radha, or simply of Radha (sometimes dressed in female garb, Caitanya believed himself to be Krishna's female companion).

Most Moslems view Adī ibn Musāfir (d. 1162) as an admirable Sufī, but the Yazīdis around Mosul insist that he was indeed god in human flesh. Various divisions of Shī'ite Islam (Ismailians, Druses, 'Alawis) believe the twelve <u>imams</u> (Alī and his successors through Muhammed al-Mahdī) are incarnations of god. Elijah Muhammed of 20th century Black Muslims in the USA taught that his predecessor, W.D. Fard, was Allah in human guise before his disappearance and apparent translation in 1934.

In the West, Christ has been the only significant incarnation of a deity in human flesh. Mirza Ghulām Ahmad (1835-1908) founded the Ahmadiyya Movement; the Qadian wing sees him as the Jewish Messiah, the Christian god, the Mahdī (Islamic savior), and Krishna all united in one incarnation. In W. Zaire the BaKongo, recent offshoots of Christianity, have proclaimed as incarnate gods both Mpadi Simon and Mbumba Philippe.

Priestly incarnations. Some ecclesiastical institutions are especially reinforced by a priesthood consisting of an unbroken line of incarnated deities. The priestesses of Pele were the goddess herself and lived in solemn isolation on the Hawaiian volcanoes where the fire goddess was manifested. Many Japanese high priests were incarnations of the gods (kami).

Until the Communist Chinese takeover in Tibet that area had the most extensive and systematic priestly incarnations. The Grand Lama of Lhasa was the incarnation of the god Avalokitesvara, the Grand Lama of Tashi-Ihunpo was the incarnation of the god Kālachakra, the State Oracle of Netchung was an incarnation of the divine Pehar, and the Abbess of the convent of Semding was an incarnation of the goddess Marīchī.

Among European religious groups perhaps the outstanding example of priestly incarnation was among the Russian Dukhabors whose leaders from 1755 to 1864 all claimed to be reincarnations of Christ.

Divine king. Mixtures occur, of course, but properly there is a careful discrimination between the divine king and the sacred king.[45] The divine king is god incarnate on earth, like the Egyptian pharaoh and the Japanese mikado. The God-Emperor of ancient Rome was titular, a device to induce loyalty throughout a polyglot empire. The old Shinto motif in Japan displays the true divine king in the cosmic renewal specifically instituted by the deity himself in the annual rituals of the mikado. It is easy under this pattern to relegate the divine king to an aloof functionary merely performing the prescribed sacred rituals while astute ministers do the actual ruling or unruly warlords struggle for earthly domain.

The theory of the divine king, though not so verbalized by believers, postulated the king's possession of the divine essence temporally and temporarily. At the royal death the temporal returns to the eternal and the actual to the ideal for reincarnation in the next monarch. Such seemed the theorizing about the ancient pharaoh, and much the same aura apparently clings to many African tribal rulers of today (e.g. Loango, Ganda, Ruanda).[46] Labels may be misleading, but throughout the world one finds archaic god-kings: Cambodia, Tibet, various Indian tribes, various Amerindians.

The sacred king is not considered a god, but is rated as the greatest of all men, blessed by unique communication with the gods. The murder or deposing of the sacred king is not therefore the abysmal horror that assassination of a divine king represents; obviously, such slaughter is the will of the gods, and the successor, however Macbethian, is the proper new sacred king. Apparently, the sacred king was often ritually slain. Such a monarch shades into a socio-political figure, best treated under sociology.

The Mystery Cults

Community religion primarily unites a society and secondarily provides for the religious needs of the individual. A society sorely beset from without tends to cling to a unifying religion, the individual subordinating his personal needs or wishes to the imperative necessity of the group. The supposed unanimity of archaic societies can be questioned, for careful anthropological study reveals the sceptic and the apathetic even in ostensibly tight-knit "primitive" social groups. The larger a society, the less willing is the individual to submerge himself in the group religion. When a society minimizes outside pressure and maximizes individualism, many are dissatisfied and seek religious consolation beyond the standard community faith.

By the 3rd century B.C. the orthodox community religion of classic Mediterranean culture was spiritually very attenuated. The majority of folk went along with the standard religion from traditional habits and the inertia of custom. Intellectuals leaned towards philosophy, and artists after Aeschylus usually treated the old myths as aesthetic and dramatic rather than religious. Those with spiritual cravings generally turned to the mystery cults.[47]

The word _mystery_ in its Greek origin means "secret ceremony." The basic nature of all mystery cults is their separation from general public worship and limitation to presumed elitists. The existence of mystery cults, even when they flaunt no overt hostility to the public religion, highlights the inadequacy of orthodoxy to fulfill spiritual yearnings. The secrecy of the mystery cults is intended to treasure esoteric spiritual revelations not supplied by orthodoxy and presumably beyond the spiritual capacity of the majority. The mystery cults of classic times uniformly chose would-be initiates carefully, exacted a vow of secrecy, performed somewhat elaborate initiations and rituals barred to the public, enacted highly symbolic (often cryptic) ceremonies and teachings. Above all, they claimed to impart to the participant life-meaning and life-significance not provided by orthodox public religion.[48] No matter how complex or how profound these mystery cults seemed to be or claimed to be, they actually represented recidivism to the fundamental and archaic religious search for psychic security. The search for basic religious assurance apparently takes two forms: either the infantile demand for the unqualified love of mother, or the later childhood reliance upon the law-enforcing father.

The mystery cults focusing upon the Great Mother originate in the infancy of every human and in the remote infancy of our species; conceivably, the worship of the Great Mother may be pre-human. Certainly her worship was indigenous to Europe and the Middle East long before the introduction of male gods. The patriarchal Semitic and Indo-European cultures tried to overpower the Great Goddess, but she always remained potent, even though submerged. As "Queen of Heaven" she was powerful among the ancient Hebrews.[49] She was dominant throughout the Middle East and she was never eliminated by the Greeks. All the cults of the Great Mother involved fertility, death, and rebirth. The initiates (both male and female) descended into subterranean darkness (or possibly a sunless chamber), made some sort of passage usually through an aperture, were suddenly dazzled by brilliant illumination. Life triumphing over death, and the promise of immortality and/or a splendid afterlife were the climactic revelations to the initiates. Ethics and morality were minor or ignored, while joyously exalted was the supernal love of the Great Goddess.[50]

Probably the most "primitive" of the mysteries indigenous to Greece were those of the Cabiri, chiefly on the island of Samothrace.[51] For initiates the cult recreated the primeval earth goddess and the eternal rhythms of birth, death, and new life. Similar rites in the Arcadian Pheneos involved a male priest who wore the mask of Demeter Kidaria, a terrifying Gorgon-like visage emphasizing the "terrible mother," for the Great Goddess brings to death even as she brings to life.

The most famous of all Greek mysteries were those of Eleusis only a few kilometers from Athens and the especial pride of Athenians.[52] The great and the humble of antiquity reverentially sought initiation, even Roman emperors walking the sacred way barefoot from Athens to Eleusis. Those participating in the Eleusinian mysteries, men as well as women, "became one with Demeter." The mythical basis for the rites was the rape of Persephone by Hades, leaving her mother Demeter in bleak despair until the reunion with her daughter. The obvious symbol is the miraculous renewal of life. Only since Persephone has been Queen of the Underworld has there been sowing and harvesting (as in the biblical account, procreation, birth, and agriculture have existed only since death came into the world). Archaic intuition perceives that generation and fertility, especially in grain, are inextricably bound up with death. We lament with Demeter the apparent loss of the life she bore, and then we rejoice that Persephone indeed lives with glorious vitality and bountiful fertility. It is not really essential to pinpoint Persephone as the grain on the stalk, the threshed grain, the seed grain, or ground grain.[53] The Christian bishop Hippolytus stated that the climax of the ceremony was holding up to the initiates a shaft of sprouting wheat. We might disparage this act as too trivial a climax and thereby dismiss the entire mystery as puerile, but we would miss the point of religion. Theologians may spin supersubtleties, but the glory of ritual and religion is to find an epiphany in what all men see with fleshly eyes but can truly perceive in spiritual rapture only by the sudden flash of the sacral.[54] Writing to the citizens of Corinth, about 50 kilometers west of Eleusis, St. Paul may have the mysteries of Demeter and Persephone in mind when he says, "That which thou sowest is not quickened, except it die" (I Corinthians 15:36).

Many of the mystery cults imported into Greco-Roman civilization are still centered upon the Great Goddess but make the life-symbol, the resurrected figure, not the female like Persephone but a male. The theme is the female as bearer of life and the male as the child born to her. The first mystery cult brought to Rome was that of Cybele, the Earth Mother of Phrygia, in 205-204 B.C. Her spring festival chiefly commemorated the death and resurrection of her young lover Attis. Widespread also in the Greco-Roman world was the cult of Isis from Egypt. Isis reassembled and revivified the dismembered body of her husband Osiris and bore his post-humous son Horus. Apuleius in The Golden Ass (XI) portrays a Lucius who by magic has been transformed into an ass but is restored to human form by Isis, who brings to true life and to true humanity. This 2nd century A.D. novel movingly depicts the real presence of the goddess and her profound impact upon her devotees.

The shift towards the male is even more pronounced in the Greek celebration of the Adonis-Aphrodite myth. The emphasis in this mystery is upon the handsome shepherd lad, his untimely death, and the heartfelt rejoicing in his resurrection. His return to the earth's surface in the classical version is by the judgment of mighty Zeus, while Persephone and Aphrodite resemble spoiled society girls squabbling over a matinee idol. The rites of Adonis were generally celebrated by women. Also the Dionysian cult was mostly though not exclusively practiced by female devotees, and the standard mythic theme portrays male distaste for the cult and male resistance that is wildly ripped asunder. Central to the mysteries of Dionysus was the tearing to pieces of a young living bull, probably a surrogate for an earlier human male infant. Note that the potent feminine cult of Shaktism in India today demands the extensive slaughter at Kalighat-Calcutta of male animals only. Powerful as the death-and-resurrection theme is for such mystery cults, the central male figure is neither hero nor father figure.

The mystery cults definitely arraigned against the Great Mother focused upon the male mystique and often excluded women altogether. There seem to be three major types of such masculine mysteries:

(1) Heroic, originating in the secret male initiations starting in a hunting culture. This ritual, more discussed in the next chapter, emphasizes courage, resolution, duty. In pre-Zoroastrian Iran, Mithra was probably the god of sacred contract (mithra), binding men to feudal loyalty and heroic career. The cult of Mithra spread westward, absorbing Babylonian astralism en route and in the eastern campaigns of Pompey sweeping through the Roman legions to become a vigorous mystery religion confined exclusively to males. The focus of the initiation was the slaying by Mithras (the western name of Mithra) of the Cosmic Bull. As in Spain today the bullfight symbolically exalts human skill

and mind and determination in overcoming the brute natural menace of the world about us. Furthermore, in representations of the bull slain by Mithras all sorts of plants and vegetation life sprout forth, proffering the theme of new life and fertility. Every Mithras confraternity comprised seven grades, each severely testing a man's courage and devotion.

(2) Intellectual, originating in secret male groupings in primitive agricultural societies where women are the economic pillar. Apparently women instituted plant gathering and the subsequent plant cultivation. These secret male societies create intellectual and symbolic structures of vast complexity in a drive to retrieve what they lack in economic and social status. Probably dating from the Middle Stone Age, such male secret groups are still widespread in Africa and Melanesia. These cult groups may indeed probe into deep esoteric truths, but they may also multiply mystification to enhance their own prestige and elevate themselves above the less comprehending populace. Orphism[55] in antiquity proffers more conjectures than certainties. Supposedly the Orpheus of the Eurydice myth is the founder of the cult, but it could be another man of the same name (with only one name, many Greeks in antiquity are easily confused), or, perhaps more likely, it is a label to suggest magic power and divine harmony. The dismemberment of Orpheus may suggest identification with Zagreus-Dionysus. Apparently new initiates into the Orphic mysteries first were presented the account of the divine Dionysus torn to pieces and devoured by the brutal Titans. The angered Zeus struck the Titans with thunderbolts that burnt them to ashes, and from these ashes man was formed. Man is therefore a duality of Dionysian elements (the psyche) and Titanic elements (physical body). Notice the Orphic spiritualization of Dionysus instead of the popular, sensual, emotional image.

A chthonic Dionysus[56] origin from Thrace has been suggested for the cult emphasis upon immortality. Orphism believed in transmigration of the soul, purification and atonement, strict accountancy in the afterworld for moral virtue and defects. Above all, Orphism interpreted all traditional myths and the entire pantheon of gods in elaborate symbolic fashion.[57] Such incredibly extensive moral allegory has conditioned much of subsequent thinking about mythology. There were no cult centers for Orphism;

any residence could be used for initiation and indoctrination, and Orphics were the first travelling clerics. These practices may have been communicated to Christianity by Orphism,[58] and possibly many Christian rituals and symbols are adopted from Orphism.[57] Early Christian iconography sometimes depicted Christ as the new Orpheus and surrounded him with other obvious Orphic symbols.

(3) Syncretism, consciously creating a god and a mystery religion. Apparently the cult of Serapis in Alexandria was founded by the first Ptolemaic king of Egypt c. 300 B.C.[59] The name of the deity was taken from Oserapis, the title of the dead Apis-bull at Memphis, identified with Osiris. Serapis was conceived as the universal god and, in the syncretic manner of late classic times and the cosmopolitanism of Alexandria, was identified with all major deities. His images resembled those of Zeus-Jupiter, but his attributes were those of Osiris. He was a savior god of healing and fertility, granted all the pomp of classic deities. As chief god of Alexandria he was honored by one of the grandest structures of that flourishing metropolis, the Serapeion, so carefully oriented that at a certain hour sunlight fell upon the lips of the magnificent statue of Serapis. Although, by the time of Christ, Alexandria had outstripped Athens as the cultural center of ancient civilization, the cult of Serapis had meager impact outside the city.

Myth and Religion Today

Western civilization now displays many of the religious characteristics of the late Greco-Roman culture of antiquity. The majority of the world's intellectuals seem unorthodox, perhaps non-religious (at least in conventional terms). Much of the populace appears apathetic or only nominally religious. New sects and cults, many indebted to the East, attract especially the young who are stirred by religious impulses but are dissatisfied with traditional outlets. We seem to manifest all those tendencies of two millenia ago and, especially from spokesmen for religion, generate perhaps some new reactions towards myth.

God is dead (or, trying to change myth). Newspapers in the 1950's publicized the statement by some liberal theologians that "god is dead." A few literalists bristled, but the general populace must be sophisticated indeed, for no witch hunt was ever mounted against "dirty atheists." Apparently the current society nonchalantly or sadly recognized the striking slogan as dramatizing the contemporary loss of religious orientation and traditional faith. The main positions of the "god is dead" theologians are:

(1) Familiar language about god is passé, i.e. the myth from the past is no longer viable. National and scientific culture has made the traditional ideas about deity untenable to modern man.[60]

(2) God is no longer a living reality for modern man. God is not experienced as a personal presence and is almost impossible to sustain as a supernatural agent in a universe of consistent physico-chemical forces.[61]

(3) An anthropomorphic deity is discredited. For some time an animal deity has been unacceptable to cultured people. Now a god constructed from man is proving equally unsatisfactory. Especially, the traditional god has been a deification of conventional culture, and contemporary man has lost confidence in much of his society.[62]

(4) God has purposely withdrawn so that man can be free and responsible.[63]

(5) While the traditional deity does not exist, god should be perceived as a dynamic spirit creatively permeating reality.[64]

(6) "God is dead" means the end of monotheism and the opportunity for a new polytheism.[65] If gods are "value-centers,"[66] a pluralistic and fragmented society such as ours will logically produce a plurality of deities.

(7) Man is moving from a parochial terrestrial viewpoint to a cosmic viewpoint and is therefore preparing for a vastly altered religious stance. Contact with extraterrestrial sentience will compel a new vision of god, junking almost all that is earthbound and forging an amplified and expanded concept.[67]

By the late 1960's the "death of god" slogan had largely been dropped from intellectual discussion, but the concerns expressed in the furor still engage liberal theologians.[68]

Demythologizing religion (or, trying to extirpate myth).[69] Less dramatic than the "god is dead" assertion is the attempt to remove from Christianity the mythology that may no longer seem convincing to modern man. Rudolf K. Bultmann, the major figure in this movement, believes that concealed within Christian myth is the kerygma, the essential word of god addressed to man. The extraction of kerygma from myth will present the vital content of divine message in a form fully meaningful to humanity today.[70] Such a proposal may sound quite commendable, but it ignores the continuing potency of myth within modern man and leaves unanswered the question to what degree religion can be freed of myth and still remain religion.[71] Some demurrers have suggested that what Bultmann creates is another myth (i.e. Myth IV to replace Myth I or Myth II). Already some groups have attempted just such demythologizing (viz. Ethical Culture, humanistic Unitarianism); such groups have often been labeled religion-substitutes instead of religion, and their appeal to modern man has been quite limited.

The reputation of myth today with scholars of religion. For all his good labors for mythology Andrew Lang could not shake off the 19th century equation of myth with "fiction" and "fable"; therefore he termed religion what impressed him as noble and exalted, while he relegated to myth all that he believed to fall short of his standard of solemnity and sublimity. Mircea Eliade, an eminent historian of religion in our time, asserts:

> Myths are the most general and effective means of awakening and maintaining consciousness of another world, a beyond whether it be the divine world or the world of the Ancestors. This "other world" represents a superhuman, "transcendent" plane, the plane of absolute realities.[72]

It has become the practice to entitle a book, The Religion of the Kwakiutl Indians[73] where past generations would label, The Myths of.... Students of religion now acknowledge myth as the vehicle and very body of religion.

Walter F. Otto sees myth as the truest way to convey the infinite and eternal to mankind, to suggest to even the simplest of mortals the ineffable divine.[74] Joachim Wach considers myth the "theoretical expression of religious experience."[75] The keynote of today's strong approval of myth by religionists is Peter Slater's definition of myth as "the portrayal of transcendent reality in story form.[76]

Chapter VII Myth as a Mirror of Society[1]

Ibn Khaldûn (1332-1406) of Tunis in The Muqad-dimah asserted that religion is society transfigured, that myth and religion are symbols of the social system.[2] Émile Durkheim in 1912 proved the notable modern proponent of this concept.[3] The power of religion, Durkheim stated, rests upon the sustained worship of one's own society.[4] Participating in collective worship or group recitals of myth, the primitive deeply senses something vastly superior to any lone individual, something that precedes him and survives him, something that gives assurance and purpose to the individual, something worthy of his allegiance and zealous contribution. The actual object of worship is this compelling force of society.

The upsurge in recent centuries of nationalism and secularism has blunted for Western civilization any clear perception of religion as the transfigura-tion of society. To a medieval resident of Western Europe the concept of Christendom and his membership in that community bulked far larger than his affili-ation with a local political unit (Burgundy, Bavaria, Bologna, Britain, etc.). Much of the vast futility of the Holy Roman Empire was an attempt to realize the "true" and universal Christian state in flesh and geography. Present orthodox Islamic society still verbally upholds a position similar to that of medi-eval Western Christianity. The term Islam is inter-preted as "sincere surrender to the will of God." The truth (haqq) of Islam means law and customs ordained by the deity. Such law and customs simply are not open to debate or persuasion, but must be observed undeviatingly throughout the Islamic world.

Indignant religionists have retorted to Durkheim that religion is not a social phenomenon; instead, "society is a religious phenomenon,"[5] or, "God is not a symbol for society, but rather society is a symbol for God."[6] Social scientists, however, have general-ly sided with Durkheim as observing both religion and myth arising to satisfy a basic need of society. The religious impulse is always present in mankind, but an individual's religiosity will perish with him or soon afterwards unless society finds it eminently beneficial. In the last century upper New York state witnessed a dozen or more eruptions of new religions for which we can give no fully adequate explanation. All of these once energetic, even fanatical, sects have vanished except Mormonism, which has flourished remarkably, even though no disinterested scholar has ever deemed its sacred writings authentic. Religions persist because societies deem the faiths worth preserving, but even elaborate theories like those of Arnold J. Toynbee cannot fully explain the mysterious decline to extinction of once mighty religions like Zoroastrianism and the even more astounding eruption of Islam from a thinly populated and relatively obscure area to the status of a major global religion.

As Durkheim and social scientists appraise it, religion and myth to survive and to grip human hearts must preserve the family and clan structure,[7] providing cement for essential relationships and tabus for injurious relationships, insuring the fullest strength and continuation of the foundations of that society and its harmonious and productive life.[8] A key to the success of Mormonism has been its ability to offer its members such provisions. No explanations satisfactorily account for the course of Buddhism in India. One of the world's great religions, Buddhism in the early centuries of the Christian era seemed on the verge of dominating the land of its birth; but, while extending through much of eastern Asia, it has receded from India almost to extinction. We can only venture that the basic Hinduism of India has offered that society a more adequate religious vision than Buddhism.

As the challenges of a society change, its religion must alter to meet those challenges or be superseded by a more viable religious vision. Change is always difficult in religion and myth, the most conservative elements in any society, since the very existence of society is symbolized in its myth. The shrewdest ploy with myth in a changing world is to effect the inescapable change but solemnly to insist that society and faith are totally unaltered. The Aztecs were late invaders of the great valley of Mexico, long controlled by the Toltecs; in 1376 the Aztecs chose their first emperor and proclaimed that the new dynasty actually descended from the Toltec kings whose ancestry boasted unbroken descent from the divine Quetzalcoatl. A neat amalgamation, demonstrating socio-political realities in mythical terms, was Babylon's treatment of Sumerian myth when that city took over the quite ancient provinces of Sumer and Akkad under King Hammurabi c. 1728 B.C. Babylon accepted the chronological primacy of Sumerian deities but made the Babylonian god Marduk supreme by ascribing his parentage to the primal god Ea and by having the older deities appeal to Marduk for protection against the rampaging monster Tiamat. In gratitude and in recognition of his complete authority the other gods built Esaglia, the illustrious temple of Marduk at Babylon. Instead of such diplomacy, force majeure, the ultimate imposition of new myth, may be employed in a coherent, rather advanced, and rather docile society. The Japanese Emperor Temmu (reigned 673-686) commanded a codification of national mythology with the central dogma of the sovereign as "the manifest kami" (divinity). The extremely stylized Japanese court rituals were justified as earthly reproductions of heavenly rituals.[9]

A society may develop culturally until it wholly outstrips its mythology. Such an attendant internal weakening of the mythic structure invites a supplanting faith as happened to the classic Greco-Roman society. The causes for the triumph of Christianity are numerous and complex, but consider the sociopolitical appropriateness of Christianity at the time. Constantine and his successors who gave Christianity its social respectability and eventually its temporal triumph behaved exactly like unscrupulous pagan rulers and seemed Christian not from personal spirituality but apparently because they sensed the bankruptcy of the pagan myth and the superior mass appeal of the Christian mythos. Christianity offered a living myth to replace a moribund myth. The old paganism had never grown spiritually with the empire but still reflected essentially a city-state culture. Christianity offered a monotheism and universalism either modeled upon the empire or far more fitted to the empire than the old faith.[10] The Christian ecclesiastic structure was modeled upon the civil service of the Roman Empire, and the Pope in the West and the Patriarch of Constantinople in the East maintained the vision of the empire in their sectaries long after the political empire had crumbled. In England the church was administratively unified while the seven Anglo-Saxon kingdoms of the Heptarchy still bristled at each other.

An even more painful situation occurs when a previously sustaining myth is overridden by a powerful outside society. Probably numerous Christian converts from alien cultures believe that conversion is admittance to a higher social, political, economic, cultural status. In black Africa today Islam is succeeding well beyond Christianity on the basis of absolute racial equality in Islamic society, i.e. an ostensible spiritual struggle is really a social conflict. Catastrophic is the situation of archaic societies that cannot accept the social myths of overwhelming civilizations and have lost confidence in their own myth. Too many Amerindians and Australian aborigines have truly become lost souls, finding little solace save in alcohol.

Accepting the contention of the social scientists that myth and religion are a transfiguration of the society, to what stage of the society does myth relate? Early Mesopotamia operated upon rough-and-ready democracy with a council of elders. Two thousand years after monarchy had completely superseded this early council, the gods of Mesopotamia continued to act as a council of elders.

In mirroring society the mythical image may be astoundingly accurate as in Japanese and Chinese myth. Heaven is a faithful transcript in Japanese myth for the mikado's court (though it may ignore the incessant struggles of shogun and samurai). The celestial bureaucracy of the Chinese official religion was identical to the imperial civil service. On the other hand, "political science" in medieval Europe consisted of ideal depictions of government in the true Christian state, representations fantastically remote from the actual society of the time. Machiavelli was deemed an agent of the devil when he described politics as really practiced. Mythological symbolism may faithfully reproduce reality or it may contrast clashingly with actuality.

The most vexatious problem in the interpretation of myth as society transfigured is our total inability to establish principles for the including or excluding of specific cultural elements and for emphases. Ulithi Islanders (Pacific) have a number of references to suicide in their myths, although suicide on Ulithi is unknown in this century and its previous incidence and social status cannot be ascertained.[11] As in folklore, historical events that we consider monumental to a society may be totally ignored, while obscure personages and minor episodes can receive grandiose treatment in myth. Scholars tend to believe now that behind Arthur was some historical figure, but that figure is shadowy at best and most certainly infinitely less colossal than the mythical Arthur.

Myth may take puzzlingly opposite ethical posi-

tions. Many Amerindian myths are intensely moralistic to reaffirm social standards; violators of
cultural tabus are summarily punished, while dutiful
conformists are rewarded with plentiful maize and
stalwart offspring. Contrariwise, a favorite Amerindian myth cycle deals with the Sly Trickster whose
scandalous violations of accepted mores are often
relished (though in stories addressed to the young
these derelictions are properly chastised). What we
are faced with here is a psychological tension, with
the need for social solidarity assailed by the desire
for individual autonomy and self-fulfilment. The
religious impulse in man seems by nature aberrant,
abnormal. A shaman is honored among hunting peoples
but is usually committed to a mental hospital in
advanced societies. Ironically, the more powerful an
ecclesiastical establishment, the more it represses
the individual vision of myth and the more it
actually promotes civil religion through the myth of
stability and conformity.

The mirroring of society in myth seems most
obvious in the early preoccupations of archaic myth
with the basic survival compulsions of primitive
social units: food and offspring. Both these needs
can be summed up in the word fertility. Perhaps con-
tributing powerfully to the early concentration upon
the female was the deep-seated desire to be a fetus
once more and know the complete protection and
nourishment of the womb.[12] While the meaning (other
than decoration or play) of man's earliest scratch-
ings upon stone is still highly debatable, Paleolithic symbols suggest womb, vulva, clitoris rather
than phallus. Possibly these female symbols represented not merely the exit into life but also the
re-entry into the fetal condition.

Kinship

No matter how metaphoric the interpretation,
"God our Father" is clearly anthropomorphic myth,
building the most cosmic religious structure upon
family relationships. Kinship myth may rival
fertility myth in age, and in its origins was apparently focused solely upon females, not males.

"The Mothers." A possible evolutionary scenario
for the goddess may read:

Mother Earth[13] who bore without being born and
who bore without impregnation from any male. This
primitive myth appears among quite archaic peoples

such as the Ifalik Islanders (Carolines), the Navaho Amerindians, the Ainu of Japan. At least 30 virgin births of notable religious figures range from Adonis to Zoroaster.

Goddess with her son as consort. He is a subordinate mortal to her immortality. The multitude of Middle Eastern goddesses like Ishtar with human lovers like Tammuz are probably rooted in this myth as, almost certainly, is the Oedipus-Jocasta liaison.

Goddess with god of equal stature. Apollo and Artemis, brother and sister, are relatively coequals. The numerical balancing of god and goddess among the Olympians suggests a compromise between an earlier goddess dominance and the masculine power of Homeric gods.

Triumph of male deity. Before Mohammed the Meccans had worshipped goddesses, and they sought from the Prophet a compromise by which their goddesses could be retained as mediators with Allah. The Koran vehemently insists, however, that God had no sons (denying Christian myth) and no daughters (denying Meccan myth).

Resurgence of the Great Goddess. The Aryan invaders of India brought with them a patriarchal culture which attempted to overwhelm the Mother Goddess, but her worship has always endured and today as Shaktism is the world's most impressive manifestation within major religions of the immemorial Mother. Tibetan Tantrism posits the familiar patriarchal mythic pattern in depicting the radiant male Shiva as the active, life-inciting force who stirs his consort Shakti to fertility and creation. Conversely, Hindu Tantrism extols Shakti as the vivifying female energy who kindles to life the static, passive, detached male Shiva. The Indian version must certainly be pre-Aryan, possibly dating from a distant period of seasonal human rut, still vestigial in June as a marriage month in the northern hemisphere. As athletic males today often expend sexual energy in exertion, the gross physical demands upon early males, coupled with frequent dietary deficiency, may indeed have rendered the early human female the initiator and inciter to sex and life. Even more likely to elevate the female role is the desperate infantile dependence upon the all-providing mother, and in archaic thought such childhood patterns are still quite powerful into adulthood.

The patriarchism of the Hebrews long contended with the numerous versions of the Near Eastern Mother Goddess, especially Asherah, a Canaanite fertility deity. Apparently the Jewish worship of Asherah was not finally stamped out until the Deuteronomic reforms.[14] Of all the major religions today, only Judaism has struggled with the Great Mother and completely eliminated her. Sikhism, another wholly masculine faith, is the only major religion never assailed by the Mother Goddess.

Mariolatry was a heresy in the early Christian church because of the patriarchal traditions of both Judaism and the Indo-Europeans, and probably in reaction to the many cults of the Mother Goddess in the Mediterranean area. The medieval adoration of the Virgin gradually engrossed the popular mind; a man of the people, like Robin Hood, would be celebrated for his devotion to Mary, but no mention would usually be made of his worship of Christ. By the end of the 19th century the Roman Catholic Church had dogmatically asserted the immaculate conception of the Virgin and her translation.

Perhaps a more deep-seated challenge to Christian patriarchism lies in the attitude of Julian of Norwich, a 14th century Englishwoman mystic who proclaimed the threefold Motherhood of god: motherhood of creation, motherhood in the flesh, motherhood at work. The femininity of god, asserted by Julian, has usually been dismissed in the past as metaphoric, but recent women scholars of religion are suggesting that Julian be taken at face value.[15]

Contending that all the major religions (Judaism, Christianity, and Islam) impacting Western society are distressingly and obtusely dominated by male imagery, Naomi Goldenberg advocates a new religion reinstituting the loving, nurturing Mother Goddess.[16] Apparently only one significant religious group, the Japanese Tenrikyo (founded in 1838), has completely eliminated the sexist element by neutrally terming God our Parent (Tenrikyo denies an androgynous interpretation).

The Matriarchy. Herodotus reported that the Lycians of Asia Minor named their children after their mothers instead of after their fathers and inherited through the female line. The ancients deemed this a bizarre eccentricity and a rather unusual exception to conventional practices. J.J. Bachofen from this clue proceeded to enunciate Das

Mutterrecht[17] (1861) and the concept of an original matriarchy which, presumably in all societies, preceded patriarchy. Myth offers some substantiation of a matriarchal society (i.e. early female monarchs).[18] Ainu (aborigines of Japan) myth postulates Princess Chikisani as the first deity to rule the earth. Perhaps the nearest suggestion to an actual ancient female dynasty appears in a 3rd century A.D. Chinese chronicle where a female shamanic ruler Pimiku (in Japanese, Himiko, "sun princess") reigned over a Japanese kingdom and, dying without issue, was succeeded by a young female relative Iyo (or Ichiyo). We must always be suspicious, however; the myth of primal female rulers may simply represent the dominance of the very young by the mother.

It is unlikely that, in days when muscle literally ruled the world, there ever was tribal or political matriarchy, although domestically there have always been matriarchs. Hatshepsut (15th century B.C. Egypt) wore the ceremonial beard of pharaohs and expected foreign emissaries to address her as king. The legendary Semiramis, queen of Assyria, looks like the historical Sammu-ramat who briefly acted as queen regent for her son (811-808 B.C.). Matrilineal and matrilocal practices are unquestionable and still operative among many peoples, but matriarchal monarchy probably never existed. Actually, in the 20th century female line of the Netherlands House of Orange we are almost certainly experiencing a truer matriarchy than mythic times ever knew.

What about female warriors? Greek myth refers extensively to the Amazons,[19] purportedly an all-female war-band on the north coast of Asia Minor who reputedly invaded or raided Greece, Syria, Arabia, Egypt, and Libya. Supposedly each Amazon had her right breast amputated to permit freer play by the sword arm, but all classic art represents the Amazons as full-breasted.[20] Theseus, king of Athens, wed the queen of the Amazons, Hippolyta (or Antiope). Ancient Athens had a structure, the Amazoneion, and Amazon graves were somewhat liberally scattered over classic Greece. It is possible that societies without adult males (such as the Argonauts encountered on the island of Lemnos) have really existed. Hiuen-Tsang reported to China about an island of women near the Byzantine Empire, the Mahabharata of India also mentioned a woman's island, and Marco Polo ascribed such an island to the Indian Ocean. The Makurap of the upper Guaporé River in Brazil believed

215

that not far off was a village of warrior women who killed encroaching males. Many tribes (like the ancient Teutons) are shrilly encouraged to fight by their womenfolk who, in dire need, may even plunge into battle. Belligerent peoples often had war-priestesses (perhaps an origin of Pallas Athene) to exhort fighting men. Women camp followers (Valkyries?) would remove friendly dead and savagely despatch enemy wounded. All these might be factual hints upon which to construct the Amazonian and Lemnian accounts.

Perhaps the women warriors were not females at all but men in attire which opponents would associate with women. In World War I the Germans nicknamed the kilted Scotsmen "The Ladies from Hell." The so-called Amazon graves may indicate a chthonic origin; infernal forces are frequently female and frequently deadly, hence women warriors. Perhaps behind the Greek myth rumble genuine struggles with Asiatic people who, like the historic Lycians, were strongly matrilineal and matrilocal. It may be that the Amazonian theme represents role reversal, the "world turned upside down"; ritual reversal of sex roles is often "unwinding" or the rite of chaos before the reëstablishing of conventional order.[21]

Individual female warriors are even more prevalent in myth. When Amaterasu, the Japanese sun goddess, had her domain invaded by her destructive younger brother Susa-no-wo, she confronted him in the full regalia and armament of a male warrior and challenged him with the traditional battle-cry. Durgā in India was a notable warrior goddess. The Rigveda reports a female warrior, Vishpalā, who lost a leg in battle; considerate gods supplied her with an iron leg to fight again. The Irish Cuchulainn on the island of Skye received his military training from the renowned woman warrior Scathac. Boadicea, the Warrior Queen of the ancient Britons, committed suicide when the Roman legions quelled her rebellion. The Eskimos of Kodiak Island relate a series of myths about women warriors. Greek legend claims that Harpalyce was trained in manly arts by her father Harpalycus, and that after his death she turned brigand and was eventually trapped in a snare by shepherds and killed. This narrative has a rather genuine ring about it. There are fully authenticated women warriors like Joan of Arc (1412-1431) and Caterina Sforza (1462-1509), "the warrior-countess of Forli," who wore soldier's armor, proved dextrous with the sword, and led troops into battle on horseback.

The mythological explanation may rest, however, in the recurrent theme of man-hating warrior women like the Princess Malayavatī of India. If the Amazonian theme originated with women, the warrior women could represent the venting of envious rage by repressed females. Today women can be soldiers; in an era of submerged womanhood, they could only imagine Amazons matching men at their strongest and most audacious. If the Amazonian concept sprang from males, childhood memory of vigorously chastising women or an adult male's encounter with a virago would suffice. The assignment of Amazons to the East in Asia (cf. Dionysus) embodies the Greek mythical East as violent and aberrant. Or the concept of Amazons may simply lie in masculine masochism (which could explain Heracles being relegated to women's tasks by Omphale while she wore his lion's pelt).[22] Many mythical female warriors may simply result from a male desire to be sexually dominated by a woman, and a warrior is the arch symbol of a forceful, aggressive personality.[23]

While matriarchy and Amazons may largely be myth, matrilineality still governs many archaic peoples by making the family descent, membership in totem or clan, and succession of rulers wholly dependent on the female line. Especially important in such a society is the mother's brother[24] (maternal uncle); because they come from the same womb, brother and sister will be closer than any other blood relationship. Even behind dogmatically patriarchal Judaism may lurk an earlier period of feminine dominance. Rabbinical tradition says that Adam and Lilith were made from dust at the same time, and Lilith would not acknowledge Adam as her superior since she was created at the same time.[25] Greek myth has numerous examples of matrilineal influence. Antigone renounces marriage to her beloved Haemon in order to bury her brother Polynices. Eriphyle sacrifices her husband Amphiaraos to the interests of her brother Adrastos. Althaea precipitates the destruction of her son Meleager because he killed her brother. Especially interesting is the conduct of Penelope's suitors, whom no one would characterize as delicate or scrupulous. Why don't they simply poignard the ineffectual Telemachus and take over Ithaca? Their protracted pursuit of Penelope's hand certainly suggests that to claim legitimacy the king of Ithaca must be married to the queen. Perhaps the same practice lies behind the marriage of Jocasta to the newly arrived hero Oedipus. The remaining of Aethra at Troezen, and her eventual bearing of Theseus there, while Aegeus goes on to his kingdom of Athens, probably means matrilocality. Another matrilocal case is suggested in the ancient Burmese kingdom of Tagaung which ran out of male rulers. A noble Indian prince Dhajaraja, venturing by, was married to a princess of Tagaung and became king. Probably a dashing young adventurer was thus mythically provided with aristocratic credentials. An early king of Ceylon, Vijaya, could not be inaugurated without a queen-consort, but a delegation to Southern Madhura in India obtained a princess for him. This episode suggests that a bachelor king is no king at all. The crowning of a Yoruba king in W. Africa was always performed by a Queen Mother (theoretically the king had no natural mother), and the royal mother in charge of monarchical insignia could prevent the coronation if she disapproved of the candidate.

A patriarchal society elevates the ties of husband, wife, and children as the most important of blood relationships; but a matrilineal society emphasizes sibling loyalty above all others (closest blood ties are among the offspring of the same womb). Herodotus (III) found surprising the decision of Intapherne's wife. When all her relatives were seized by Darius, the Persian emperor, she was offered the life of one person. She chose her brother and let her husband and children go to execution. She reasoned that since her parents were dead, she could never have another brother, while she could remarry and have more children. The most persistent of these matrilineal ties has been the maternal uncle and nephew. Gawain, the original hero of the Arthurian cycle, was the nephew of Arthur. Beowulf was the nephew of Hygelac. Among the Paladins of Charlemagne were four of his nephews: Roland, Baudoin, Anseîs, Gui. Other heroes with strong ties to their maternal uncles were: Cuchullainn, Perceval le Gallois, Bertrand, Bernaldo del Carpio, Ogier, Vivien, Raoul de Cambrai, Foucon, Gascelin, Aiol, Galien. The father of the hero is frequently ignored or portrayed as cruel and brutal. The Oedipal hatred of the father supposedly reinforces the uncle-nephew relationship, turning the young man from the father to a close adult male. Note that in most myths the persecuting uncle is the paternal uncle: Peleus vs. Jason and Claudius vs. Hamlet. The paternal uncle is identified with the father and can be branded as evil with less guilt feeling than is experienced in stigmatizing the father.

Marriage by capture conjures up in our minds the vision of a young male, aided by his male friends, snatching an unhappy girl as his bride from some alien tribe. This pattern, of course, fits a patriarchal society. Early matrilineal groups, with their cores composed of women, may have captured males from other tribes to secure husbands. The Tupinamba and Urubu of S. America and the Garos of Assam have consistently followed this matriarchal practice. The kidnapping of Hylas by amorous nymphs at Cyzicus may refer to such male captivity for mating purposes.

"The Fathers."[26] Patriarchal practices have not yet dominated all societies. Many African tribes, for example, still follow matrilineality and even deem paternity irrelevant.[27] For the few food-gathering tribes still extant, as during the millenia when all mankind survived by simple food-gathering, women are extremely important in foraging for vegetables, nuts, berries, tubers and also for ready milk in their breasts, probably for most of female adulthood. By the hunting period the male role in procreation was apparently acknowledged, and the male hunter gained immeasurable masculine esteem. Nonetheless, hunting is a very chancy means of nourishment, especially with no technique for food preservation until relatively recent drying of meat. The middens of the hunting era are packed with animal bones, but for extended periods every hunting society finds game sparse, and the female food-gatherers still remain the major and constant source of nourishment.

The triumph of the male and the reign of patriarchy[28] depended upon the era of herding and cattle-breeding. Now the male could claim to be the great provider of consistent food. The ancient Semitic society was patriarchal on the basis of herds, as the early fathers of the Hebrew people demonstrate. The patriarchal Indo-European people similarly developed such a male-dominated society on the same basis, as the Aryans of India indicate resoundingly in the Vedic literature. Vegetation as food had earlier exalted "the mothers," and the development of agriculture often re-elevated the Great Goddess, as notably in Indian village culture. In an agricultural society the patriarchy frequently asserted its continued dominance in the fashion suggested by Egyptian myth. The goddess Isis had searched in the wilds for vegetable food. Her husband, the god Osiris, was honored as the first cultivator of crops and as the instructor of mankind in ploughing,

219

sowing, and harvesting. Such an account claims the masculine monopoly of conscious cultivation in contrast to random feminine foragings. Woman, declares this myth, is the unconscious, unplanning food supplier, but the male is the thinker who deliberately plans and thereby vastly increases the supply and availability of food. It is also possible that in many communities conscious agriculture may have been developed by women, and the patriarchy peremptorily usurped a female achievement in order to maintain male supremacy.

Feminists may assert that this assumption of the father as the fertility symbol means that the male was deeply envious of pregnancy and thereby tried to supersede the female as genitor.[29] Multitudes of myths suggest a desperate masculine desire to gain superiority by ascribing primal parturition to males. The reported forming of Eve from Adam's rib looks like male chauvinism. In Greek myth Zeus bore Dionysus, and Pallas Athene leaped fully armed from the brain of Zeus. Defiled by a visit to the underworld, the Japanese deity Izanagi stripped off his clothes and hurled them away, twelve deities springing from the twelve separate pieces of his attire. Plunging into the bath, Izanagi spawned other gods, notably the God of the Deep Sea. Washing his right eye produced the Goddess of the Moon and washing his left eye produced the Goddess of the Sun. In all the world the Indian male especially doth seem to protest entirely too much. Brahmā, we are told, sprang from a lotus growing from the navel of Vishnu (here the male produces an umbilical cord). The entire warrior class of ancient India was termed "arm-born," for it was generated by the arm of Brahmā. Balarāma was formed from a white hair from Vishnu's head, while Krishna was formed from a black hair of Vishnu's. Because Darika proved cruel and treacherous, Shiva blinked his eyes to give birth thereby to two vengeful goddesses who destroyed Darika. Because Yuvanāsha wanted a son, sages placed a vessel of consecrated water on the altar. Thirsty during the night, Yuvanāsha drank the liquid and bore a son through his right side.

An even more naive tactic in the male campaign to usurp the female fertility role may have been the custom called couvade. Still practiced among many archaic peoples, couvade is the custom of a prospective father taking to bed, complaining of birth-pangs, and generally diverting attention from the pregnant woman. Couvade might be viewed as a rather childish pout to demand recognition, but it could, as Tylor thought, represent a transition from female dominance to the patriarchal rule.

The tabu shift from sacred to unclean seems clearly exploited by patriarchy in reversing the position of women. Woman had been the awesome sustainer of life in "matriarchal" society, but rigidly orthodox patriarchal Judaism brands woman as basically "unclean." In primitive societies the bloody discharges of women are mysterious demonstrations of the feminine life-force. Rivulets cascading downward from Mt. Kamakhya in Assam are reddened with haematites; the native Khasias recognize this discharge as the menstruation of Mother Earth. Before sowing, the Bhil tribes of India scatter vermilion (which they interpret as menses) over the fields to promote fertility. However, a patriarchal system stigmatizes menses as disgusting pollution.[30] The Ainus of Japan aver that the smell of menstrual and parturient blood is terribly offensive to the deities and that it does not disappear even with meticulous washing. Consequently, women are wholly excluded from Ainu religious rituals. The Zulus of Africa regard all secretions (sap, rubber, etc.) from trees as menses and hence tabu. In many parts of the world menstruating women are barred from holy places by a patriarchal society.

Widespread is a mythic account of males acknowledging an earlier feminine predominance and then snatching it from the women. Perhaps the most violent version comes from the Yahgan of Tierra del Fuego. At an earlier epoch, the myth states, the women were sovereigns of the tribe, possessors of the sacred objects, and sole performers of the holy rituals. Wearing masks, the women impersonated ghosts and terrorized the men. Eventually the Sun discovered the hoax and alerted the men. In a brutal battle of the sexes, all adult women were slain, leaving only small girls too young to know the grown-up mysteries. Now the men are in total control, and the Yahgan women know nothing about the male rites. The Soromaja of West Irian say that originally the culthouse belonged to the women, and the women possessed the magic flutes, excluding men altogether from the sacred rituals. With the help of supernatural powers the Soromaja men stole the flutes from the women and forcefully occupied the culthouse. The men claim that the women can grow sago only because the men play the "life-giving" flutes. In much of Australia and Melanesia, myth tells of original possession of the bullroarer and other sacred objects by the women, with men later seizing the sacral objects and rituals from the women.[31] Possibly the male takeover from female dominance required violence, but it is even more likely that the basis of this entire theme is the masculine recognition of women as the original givers of life and the rulers of all children. The myth of male usurpation may simply represent adult masculinity asserting its freedom from mother's overlordship and asserting the preëminence of adult manhood. The frequent reference to sacred objects suggests that a fertility cult practiced by women in early times was preëmpted and probably altered by males.

Incest.[32] The overwhelming majority of mankind soberly denounces incest[33] and has always considered it quite rare. Nonetheless, myth extensively alludes to incest and often treats the subject as snickering humor or even acceptable practice under certain circumstances. Modern social studies suggest that incest is much more prevalent than the 19th century admitted, and modern psychology ventures that the vehemence usually expressed against incest arises because of an innate desire that man wishes to curb. It is entirely too glib to take the stance of some nature mythologists that incest is entirely metaphoric. The sun is interpreted as father, brother, son, while the moon is mother, sister, daughter; interrelationships between sun and moon are then alleged to generate all myths of incest.[34]

It is far easier to condemn incest than to define it. For myth, incest may be defined as violation of the social tabu against copulation with members of the opposite sex in specified kinship categories. Since the mythic mind equates sexuality with fertility, myth ignores incestuous homosexuality and conduct (passionate caressing, fondling, and general eroticism) with close relatives that psychology deems incestuous. For example, Noah's naked exposure to his children (Genesis 9:21-24) could be considered incestuous, but the biblical treatment suggests no more than gross indignity.[35]

The revulsion against incest may be genetic, for it is virtually inconceivable that early man could reason that inbreeding would produce deterioration and eventual extinction.[36] The widespread cross-fertilization of plants suggests that living matter basically repudiates incest.[37] Careful studies of certain mammals reveal their scrupulous avoidance of matings with blood relatives: prairie dogs,[38] lions,[39] macaque monkeys.[40] Craig Packer and Anne Pusey offer a persuasive explanation for the absence of incest in a pride of lions. The male lions exercise "risk-benefit analysis," realizing how counterproductive is ceaseless struggle against males of their immediate group. The strength and harmony of the group are vastly increased by mutual coopera- tion among the male lions. The males will, of course, savagely duel with outside males for the favors of outside females. For different reasons, then, Packer and Pusey agree with Lévi-Strauss that the ban on incest is social rather than genetic.

Bewildering among humanity are the varied, even contradictory, concepts of forbidden kinship rela- tions. Most Westerners disapprove of first cousins marrying, but cross-cousin marriage with the daughter of a man's maternal uncle (i.e. first cousin on the maternal side) is widespread among Australian aborig- ines today and in Melanesia, Indonesia, and India. Isaac commanded Jacob to marry the daughters of Laban (his mother's brother) in Genesis 28:2. Gotama, the Buddha, married the daughter of his mother's brother.[41] This cross-cousin marriage stems from a matrilineal society, while in a patrilineal society the parallel pattern would be a man marrying the daughter of his father's sister. Possibly this cross-cousin marriage is a modification of or sub- stitution for brother-sister marriage. Whatever might be the genetic compulsion, incest for most human communities is fundamentally a social practice.

The Penare of Venezuela condemn incest, stig- matizing it as "to have sex like monkeys." Such a view regards incest as natural, while man must live by culture. Here may be the crux of the incest problem: incest is all too natural, and it is imperative to avoid incest in order strongly to assert man's humanity and difference from the brute. As with other tabus, ultra-sophisticated modern man is so far from confusion with the natural that he can view incest far less vehemently than did the savage, cheek-by-jowl with nature. Malinowski indicates that organized family life is quite impossible unless incest within the family is suppressed.[42] For much of mankind the family is indispensable, and the structured human family system simply does not exist even among monogamous birds and beasts. Incest would destroy the human family: hence man's social detest- ation of incest.

One may go further and suggest with Lévi-Strauss that the essence of culture is exchange, and for all societies the basic irreducible exchange is the exchange of women.[43] A primitive social group retaining all females for inbreeding has absolutely no means of exchange.[44] Early explorers of Africa and Australia were constantly proffered women from archaic societies. Such practices do not indicate immorality but the necessity of outbreeding women to give a society exchange potential. One could even go so far as to agree with Layard that the incest tabu compels the external fulfilment of the mating instinct in order to enlarge the social and experiential world of each human.[45] The mythic mind portrays incest as purely physical, but the modern mind would emphasize psychic and cultural benefits as major in pairings and quite minimal in any incestuous relationship. Even early man in tabuing incest may subconsciously have sought a mating more likely to expand the horizons of both partners.

When we find such a practice as incest generally excoriated but frequently accepted or even approved in myth, we can be sure that society has consciously imposed the tabu upon the lawless flesh and equally lawless unconscious. Picturing the Dreamtime or the immemorial past, myth recognizes that in very early times the present law did not apply and therefore the present incest tabu did not hold sway. The perspective of distance and time makes tolerable then what is intolerable now. Respectable matrons of today will chuckle over the escapades of distant ancestors who were pirates and cattle-thieves, while the dear ladies are shocked beyond measure at black sheep in the family today. Some incest myths of the Creation may arise from archaic folk with a mind like Pierre Bayle's contemplating where Cain and Abel got their wives: they must have been their own sisters! After all, even archaic man could reason, where else could the young men have found nubile young women?

Incest among deities bears no opprobrium, for the gods are never to be bound by the laws and customs of men. Myth records multitudes of divine incest. Zeus was the father of Persephone by his sister Demeter and, of course, was married to his sister Hera. Orphic myth states that, by his own daughter Persephone, Zeus had a son Zagreus. Obviously here is allegory, perhaps indicating that, as culture advanced, the literal incest even of the gods is changed to pretty metaphor. A great deal of divine incest seems no more than metaphoric, as the daughter of Zeus and Hera, Hebe (Juventas, "youth," in Latin), is the personification of eternal youth.[46] As incest among deities is wholly outside human criticism, incest by divine kings is beyond question. Hence the brother-sister marriages of the Incas or the Egyptian pharoahs.[47]

Perhaps the most appalling incest pattern to Westerners is mother-son, the Oedipal theme, so abhorrent to the Greek mind that all participants in the Oedipus-Jocasta account are presented as ignorant of the true situations as they occur. "The Theogony of Dunnu" from Babylonia straightforwardly proffers the same theme, as Lahar quite intentionally kills his father Amakandu and marries his mother (The Sea). Typical of the Western view is the portrayal in the Zoroastrian Avesta of the incest of the devilish Azhi Dahāka with his demon mother Artak. In some mythologies the allegory is clearly the metaphor of the male phallus generated from the earth and in turn fertilizing the earth: Finnish myth states that Sämpsä Pellervo, the vegetation god, had his mother as wife; Sumerian myth claims that all living things arose from the union of the air god Enlil and his mother Ki, the earth. The Middle Eastern pattern of Ishtar-Tammuz and Cybele-Attis suggests that in each case the Great Mother bore the son parthenogenically and later mated with him. Supposedly Semiramis lusted for her own son and seduced him.

In contrast to this strongly condemnatory attitude, there is a parallel story of acceptable mother-son incest in a great arc through Indonesia, the Philippines and up through Taiwan. Typical is the version of the Li tribe of Hainan Island where catastrophe kills off everyone except a mother and her son. She leaves him, advising him to marry any strange woman he finds. In the bush she changes her tattoo marks (seen as the true means of identification) and returns to marry her son and replenish the world. The excuse for the many versions of this myth is stark compulsion upon the only surviving couple, incestuous as they are.

The Zuñi Amerindians tell of a grandmother sleeping with her grandson to give him sexual instruction. The Shawnee Amerindians say that in former times such was their regular practice. A very rare mating is aunt-nephew. Jimmu Tennô, reputedly the first emperor of Japan, was brought up by his aunt, Tama-yori-bime, who eventually married him. Psychologists say that mother-in-law jokes and

225

hostility to one's mother-in-law mask a son-in-law's actual attraction to his wife's mother. Myth treats as humorous any son-in-law yearning for his mother-in-law. The Shoshone Amerindians say that Coyote, an amoral trickster, seduced his mother-in-law. The Khasias of the Himalayas say that the moon fell in love with his mother-in-law who threw ashes in his face, producing the markings on the moon.

Perhaps the different attitudes towards mother-son incest arise from different meanings of the word mother. Among early peoples all the mature women are collectively "the mothers." Perhaps many of these "mother-son" incest accounts mean no more than a young man marrying an older woman ("old enough to be his mother"). Semiramis apparently shared with Catherine the Great of Russia a sexual appetite for younger men; her own son could be added to the list by scandal-mongering enemies. In vulgar circles a male may constantly be accused of coupling with his mother.[48] Behind the repeated obscenities may be a germ of truth. Probably most mother-son incest myths arise from the Oedipal complex in males rather than from overt actions.

Similarly, the myths of father-daughter incest may essentially spring from the Elektra complex in women. Asia Minor myth depicts Myrrha as lusting for her father, who made her pregnant with Adonis. Or, in a society where all older men are "the fathers," the theme may merely mean marriage of a mature man to a much younger woman. Perhaps many myths of father-daughter incest misinterpret a practice like the Indian putrikā-putra ("daughter's son"). A man without male offspring could adopt his daughter's son as his own; no incest is involved here, but those unfamiliar with the custom could easily misinterpret it. We are accustomed to older men addressing any young man as "son"; subjects, loyal retainers, all young males can be so bracketed without any incest involved. In a matrilineal society a widower monarch might of necessity espouse his daughter in order to retain the throne. Perhaps the origin of many so-called incest myths is demonstrated in the account of the Desana of Colombia who say that Father Sun committed incest with his daughter, precipitating a period of horrible chaos, a period in which savage animals and demons endangered the very life of the world. The creator reëstablished order by prohibiting incest. To enforce the stability of society and law, myth throws up shocking pictures of anarchy (triggered by violation of sacred tabu as in incest)

226

to force the "uncivilized" into the "civilized."
Psychoanalysts will nonetheless insist that father-
daughter incest is concealed in some myths. Claiming
that the bull is a father symbol, such a view would
interpret the Zeus-Europa and Zeus-Io myths as
father-daughter incest.

Some myths are euphemistic but transparent. A
South Slav myth tells of a king with a beautiful
daughter whom he treats as his wife. Through a charm
he renders her pregnant (a not-very-subtle cover-up
of incest). Hindu legend assigns five heads originally to Brahmā. Because he lusted for his daughter,
one of his heads was lopped off by Shiva. The
Rigveda account of Brahmā's incest with his daughter
may be allegorizing of heaven and dawn. The Indians
even have a special hell, Mahājvāla, reserved for men
committing incest with a daughter or daughter-in-law.
Father-daughter incest is universally condemned,
though in the Amerindian trickster cycles Coyote, or
whatever name is given him, is thought a clever
scoundrel in his disguising of himself to seduce his
own daughters.

Brother-sister incest is the most common in myth
and the least excoriated. Much of the problem lies
in defining sibling relationship. In a totemic
society, all young females of a young man's totem are
his "sisters." In any society all males of the same
age may be labeled "brothers." In many societies
parallel cousins on father's side, mother's side, or
both sides are "brothers" and "sisters." So-called
"brother-sister" incest may be endogamy but not
pairing of blood kin. In a polygamous patrilineal
society, such as that of the early Hebrews, children
of the same father but different mother (and
separately brought up) were perfectly proper marriage
partners, as were Abraham and his half-sister Sarah.
Leviticus 20:17 later prohibits the practice but it
apparently was acceptable in the days of David, whose
son Ammon sought to ravish his half-sister Tamar (II
Samuel 13:13). His half-sister urges Ammon to get
David to betroth her to Ammon. She resents rape but
accepts marriage with her half-brother. Note here
how obvious is the primitive concept of sexual
contact as attack; hence, perhaps, much of the
revulsion from brother-sister coupling.

Probably the brother-sister incest of primal
gods arose from splitting an original hermaphrodite
into male and female. Vedic literature gives Yama,
god of the underworld, his sister Yami as wife. In

227

Iranian myth, Yima, the king of men during the Golden Age, is married to his sister Yimaha. In Babylonian myth Lachmu and his sister-wife Lachamu were twins. In the Jewish Kabbala the divine King and his sister-spouse the Matronit were Siamese twins born attached back to back. In Plato's Symposium the same concept is ascribed to Aristophanes; it must stem from very old myth. Many archaic peoples perceive brother and sister as one soul in two bodies, as Edgar Allen Poe does in "The House of Usher." Possibly this concept is behind the many pairings in Egypt of divine sisters and brothers (Shu and Tefnet, Nut and Geb, Isis and Osiris) and of pharaohs with their sisters.

Sometimes the mating of brother and sister is coyly symbolized as in the account of struggle (clearly sexual) between the Japanese sun-goddess Amaterasu and her brother Susa-no-wo. She chewed up his sword and spat out the pieces as children, considered his. He masticated her jewels and likewise spat out children, considered hers and the ancestors of the present imperial family. During the historical reign of the Emperor Ingyo the Crown Prince Karu mated with his full sister. Although one or both were exiled, the Japanese chroniclers are sympathetic with what they deem true love. Aristocracy as well as royalty in Persia, Siam, Sri Lanka, Wales, Burma, Hawaii, Uganda, Egypt, and Peru contracted brother-sister marriages. In ancient India an inferior queen of Okkaka by intrigue secured the throne for her son. The four disinherited royal princes founded Kapilavastu along with their five sisters. To keep the line "pure" (Sakhya) the eldest sister was designated Queen Mother and the princes married their sisters. The Sakhya dynasty also founded royal lines in Burma and Sri Lanka. Probably a great deal of this royal brother-sister mating stems from a matrilineal society where a man could be king only by marriage to the queen, his own sister.

Of course, the brother-sister pairings of gods and of archaic nobility are not for us commoners. In myths about general humanity, typical is the Philippine account of brother and sister as the sole survivors of mankind, compelled to mate for the species to continue. And in Dreamtime such matings were acceptable: Arnhem aborigines in Australia say that Djangawwul landed there with his two sisters and kept them perpetually pregnant, thus providing ancestors for all the aborigines. Generally, however, brother-sister incest for the populace is repugnant. Kullervo of the Kalevala is pictured as quite a wicked fellow, but even he is so horrified to learn of his inadvertent seduction of his own sister that he commits suicide. The downfall of Arthur and his goodly Round Table is attributed to his incestuous begetting of Mordred upon his own sister.[49] Widespread among Eskimos and Amerindians is a myth of a girl mysteriously copulated with by a night visitor. Painting her hands or smearing them with soot, she finds to her horror that the intruder was her own brother. He flees as the moon, while she pursues as the sun. A neat touch by the Caddo of SW USA is spotting the culprit brother in the moon markings. The Sanpoil Amerindians have an especially poignant and monitory version: the parents apprehend the incestuous pair and slay them. For the first time, therefore, death comes into the world. From the Trobriand Islands comes the myth of a youth preparing an aphrodisiac for a girl.[50] By accident his sister inhaled it and, mad with passion, pursued him and seduced him on a lonely beach. Guilt-ridden, they perished of starvation in a grotto. From their interlaced skeletons grew an aromatic herb which is reputedly the most potent aphrodisiac today. Thus the frightening outrageous produces the terrifying success.

Social creations and conflicts

Verbally we proclaim as our ideal the person of lofty morals and noble principles. Early man was too preoccupied with the problem of sheer survival to afford such luxury. Obviously the primitive greatly admired brute strength and would actually deify the strong man, as Oorpazhassi is a god in Kolathnad, India. Like Heracles, another gross brute elevated to godhood, Oorpazhassi slew his tutor when he was beaten and thereafter killed anyone opposing him or in any fashion irking him. When a society matures, it tends, like Hellenistic Greece, to consider a Heracles coarse and stupid. Hou Yi, the Chinese Heracles, similarly slew dreadful monsters and similarly became despicable in conduct, inducing his own servants to cudgel him to death. Interpreting the labors of Heracles as beneficial to humanity is an attempt in an advanced society to make respectable what originally were the self-willed acts of destruction by a muscular brute.[51]

Sly trickster.[52] The High God looks like the spiritual vision of the early shaman. The Sly Trickster looks like the anti-spiritual viewpoint of the early common man. In the myths of many Amer-

229

indians the Trickster and the High God are in direct
and bitter opposition. To some degree Trickster vs.
High God is individuality vs. conformity, unconven-
tionality vs. conventionality, disorder vs. order,
destruction vs. creation, chaos vs. cosmos. Since
man apparently asked "How did the world become its
present self?" before asking "How did the world first
begin?", the trickster-transformer may have preceded
the High God and may be one of the oldest figures of
all mythology. Jung describes the Trickster as "a
faithful copy of an absolutely undifferentiated human
consciousness, corresponding to a psyche that has
hardly left the animal level."[53] The Trickster is a
completely amoral character who lives by his wits and
enjoys perpetrating coarse and cruel jokes against
anyone. In many African and Amerindian myths the Sly
Trickster is an animal; perhaps the idea originated
from seeing animals steal food or otherwise succeed
by stealth.

No chicanery is beyond the Trickster and his
cleverness is unbounded, but there seem two basic
feats of the Trickster: theft of valuable objects and
defeat of a "cannibal monster" by wits and duplicity.
The stealing may be of fire, water, sun, fish, game
animals, cereal grains, human or divine property,
maidenheads, and anything else within his knavish
grasp. Autolycus is an obvious example in Greek
myth. Odin in the Norse mythology stole mead from
the dwarfs and giants and triumphantly bore it to the
gods. The "cannibal monster" seems metaphoric for
famine, disease, enemies, and other dire perils.
Heracles would overpower such obstacles by brute
strength, but the Trickster conquers by duplicity, as
Odysseus outwits Polyphemus. Amerindians of NW USA
often depict Trickster luring animals by stratagem to
a precipice and then tricking them or forcing them to
leap to death; unknown among Amerindians of this area
in historic times, the practice suggests primitive
driving of animals over cliffs.

Though apparently the product of a vulgar and
earthy populace, Trickster is far from a simple
character. He seems to fulfil the following human
needs:

(1) Sheer entertainment. All men need escape
from the mundane world. The shaman's escape is an
eerie and perilous flight out of this world. Perhaps
the Trickster tales were the very early release of
the common man, tickling him with the deucedly clever
and the outrageously ludicrous in this world.

(2) Satire. Much of the Trickster material seems parody or travesty of the shaman. The self-dismemberment of Trickster is a laughable parallel to the shaman's solemn dissection. The "excrement advisors" of Trickster burlesque the shaman's spirit guides. Trickster is himself outwitted on occasion by birds and animals, again looking like a sneer at the shaman's power over the animal world.

The shaman certainly is a prestige figure in archaic societies. How, then, could he become so ridiculed by the sly trickster? People of an archaic society are people like ourselves. Pressures of their environment force upon them a more rigid outward conformity than Western society demands, but they grumble and grouse just as soldiers do in the best disciplined army. For example, the Korekore of Africa unanimously agree that the spirit mediums always communicate truths from the otherworld and always must be obeyed; nonetheless, in practice the Korekore often evade or ignore the spirit mediums.[54] Beneath the facade of apparent unanimity archaic man's undercurrent of scepticism and hostility can produce the sly trickster.

(3) Blowing off steam. Like the medieval Feast of Fools, Boy Bishop, and similar escape valves, the Trickster accounts represent a "ritualized rebellion." Society is an unnatural imposition, and a provident society must offer means to get hostilities and frustrations out of one's system effectively, while not breaching the actual citadels of that society. Trickster lets the audience purge itself of its anarchistic and socially undesirable drives.

(4) Psychological satisfaction. Trickster institutes one of the surefire successes of all storytelling: the cheeky little chap who bests giant adversaries. Trickster offers ambivalent effects. One may enjoy one's own noble virtue by scornful disapproval of that immoral Trickster. Or one may revel deliciously in vicarious enjoyment of tabued acts.[55] The Navaho Amerindians are most unusual in carefully discriminating between the two responses to Trickster. Navaho Coyote tales to children are very moralistic, always ending in exemplary punishment meted out to Coyote in exact proportion to his degree of tabu violations. Navaho Coyote tales to adults evoke guffaws and thigh-slapping pleasure at the wild, clever antics of that wonderful rascal.

(5) Re-evaluation. For many archaic cultures

the strongest, most penetrating undercutting of society is the Trickster cycle with its madcap ridicule of sacred social practices: tribal rituals, male and female roles, sexual and religious tabus, social structure and customs, even behavior in eating and excreting. The enormity of the criticism demonstrates the rigidity of archaic societies, where change is rare and usually minute. Only the clout of the Trickster myth has much chance to effect internal change in a static society.

(6) Unification of society. Strange but psychologically true is the statement that this apparently disruptive element in society actually works as a catalyst to greater social solidarity. The regular rituals and customs of a society tend to accentuate class and role distinctions and enforce inflexible status and behavior. When social structure is bent or broken by the Trickster myth, there is actually a powerful reinforcement of the sense of community in the ungusseting and fellow merriment.

(7) Individual development. The picaresque novel from the Spanish Renaissance onwards proffers a rogue who, very much like the Trickster, lives by his wits through a series of dramatic encounters. Actually, in the individual myths about the trickster there seems little maturing of the character. Nonetheless, the emergence of Creator and Transformer from the Trickster and the ennobling of the trickster to Promethean stature suggest that the trickster cycle is the Bildungsroman or developmental novel in embryo.[56]

(8) Spiritual enhancement. Paradoxically, the agent of disorder and caprice may actually compel the spiritually lackadaisical to turn to the gods. Legba is the sly trickster among the Fon of Dahomey, W. Africa, who as a disruptive and destructive force causes mankind to seek divine order and harmony. Probably the sly trickster lurks behind Goethe's Mephistopheles, whose machinations and nihilism will eventuate in the greater glory of god and the firmer achievement of divine symmetry.

The earliest manifestation of Trickster seems the basically egotistical, amoral, wholly self-motivated personality, only incidentally benefitting mankind. Apparently the Amerindians gradually developed this selfish rascal into an elaborate Trickster-Creator-Transformer and Culture-Bringer (or various combinations).[57] Amerindians usually designate Trickster as an animal--Coyote, Wolf, Fox, Raven, Crow, Raccoon, Badger, Bat, Mink, Bluejay, Hare--but Trickster is not described as an animal, and his actions and speech are altogether human. Reynard the fox in medieval beast accounts is similar, but in Europe is distinctly described as an animal. Sometimes Amerindians frankly make Trickster fully human, as Wisakedjak (Whiskey Jack) is the Creator-Trickster of the Cree Amerindians. Among Dakota and Arapaho Amerindians the Trickster is Spider, as is also true of many African accounts. Legba is the humanized Trickster of Dahomey who , maliciously will stir up trouble, forcing men to turn to the gods; at other times he will free men from the stern edicts of the gods. Legba has been introduced into Brazil, Trinidad, Cuba. 'Ti Malice is another African Trickster transshipped to Haiti, Martinique, and other West Indies. The Br'er Rabbit of American folklore is basically an African Trickster with perhaps an Amerindian admixture. Trickster may change sex but is basically male. Afrekete from W. Africa is a rare female Trickster. Miss Nancy of Sea Island (S. Carolina) and Aunt Nancy (Gullah of S. Carolina) are Anglicizings of Anansi ("spider") of W. Africa.[58]

Just as the gods themselves seem to have originated in animal deities and from such a humble source rose to the heights of Ahura Mazda and Allah, so Trickster from amoral animal beginnings moves upwards towards the esteemed Prometheus. Vishnu behaved exactly like the Amerindian Trickster in transforming himself into the lovely Mohini who seduced Shiva and bore a child, Hari-Hara, a combination of Vishnu and Shiva, an attempt to produce an essentially monotheistic god. Loki in early Teutonic myth resembles the wily Odysseus and is often most helpful to the rather slow-witted gods of the north, but apparently Christian influence prevented Loki from rising in reputation. Increasingly Loki is depicted as demonic. In Christian tradition Trickster becomes Mephistopheles.

Prometheus the Fire Bearer[59] is the supreme success story of the Trickster.[60] Probably this notable figure began as a thieving animal. Archaic reasoning holds that all things belong to the deities: animals to the Lady or Lord of Beasts, fruits and surface edibles to Mother Earth, tubers and roots to chthonic deities. Natural forces such as fire are the jealously guarded possession of Nature's gods. Around the world archaic myth portrays the dog, kingfisher, dove, jaguar, chameleon, rat, tortoise or other animal as stealing the divine fire and giving it to man.[61] Punishment from wrathful gods is usually visited upon the thief: the rat is reduced to scavenger, the tortoise is slowed from earlier agility, and so on. The liver of Prometheus was pecked at by a vulture as punishment because the liver was regarded as the seat of the passions.[62]

Consider the effrontery of mankind, even in the very pious Aeschylus, ennobling a thief, and above all, a thief stealing from the gods. A theft by the Trickster has benefitted mankind; so now we laud the Trickster as a Christ figure suffering agonies for his benevolent theft, and (especially from 19th century Romantics) the defender of our species from the tyranny of the gods. The rebellious, amoral Trickster apparently appeals to all mankind and we excuse his theft and glorify his character. The basis for the myth is the widespread conviction that the gods permit only limited power and happiness to mankind, and castigate humans for getting more than the gods ordain. Deities traditionally consecrate the old conservative society, and man feels that change and progress may produce significant benefits but certainly will generate pains of adjustment for all and perhaps severe hostility from reactionaries.

In the manner of many Amerindian Tricksters, Prometheus is also Creator and Culture Bringer. Again, these aspects have been considerably elevated in Prometheus from the rather disreputable origin of Trickster. The account of Prometheus in Hesiod still displays the shady, unscrupulous trickery of the basic figure.

Culture-Bringer.[63] Mohave Amerindian myth about Coyote probably explains the origin of the Culture-Bringer. In some far-off land Coyote ate watermelon, then wandered to the Mohave area and defecated the seeds from whence the vines grew. Early man observed how animals and birds carried seeds, and thus the first Culture-Bringer unintentionally conveyed valuable cultural benefits to man. Mohave myth also relates how Mastamho at his father's death needed fire for the cremation pit. Fly made fire by rubbing sticks (note the ceaseless rubbing of forelegs by a fly. Thus fire (like watermelon) came to man not from purposeful benefaction but accidentally, fortuitously. Gluskabe (or Glooscap) of NE America is unusual among N. Amerindian culture-bringers because he is wholly human and wholly altruistic. Probably

234

the worldwide figure of the Culture-Bringer was initially an animal (like Coyote, or any other of the birds and animals recognized as Culture-Bringer by Amerindians), then a man-beast (like the fearsome Oannes, half-man half-fish, who taught the arts of civilization to archaic Babylonians), then probably a supernatural being or deity (like Prometheus or Quetzalcoatl), and finally a full-fledged human (like Yima, who showed early Iranians to mold bricks, lay foundations, and erect buildings).

S. Amerindians and most of the world have conceived of the Culture-Bringer as an intentional benefactor to man, the revered introducer of what makes and sustains human culture. Even the most backward and rigid society recognizes the contrast between animals in nature and the culture of men. Someone must have started human culture, and that one must be the Culture-Bringer. The effective technology introduced by the Culture-Bringer renders possible a degree of social coherence and individual well being setting the human condition above that of animals. The separation of man from Nature by the Culture-Bringer is sensed, however, as a violation and often has the Trickster's taint of theft. The Culture-Bringer has advanced human society at the cost of our lost innocence. Huang Ti (China) taught government, crafts, manners, and proper sacrifices. Tahmūrath (Iran) taught domestication of animals and the spinning of wool. Uazale (Paressi S. Amerindians) discovered manioc, cured tobacco, and planted his own hair to produce cotton. Taruma S. Amerindians report that their Culture-Bringer fished the first woman from a lagoon. Chaco S. Amerindians say that their Culture-Bringer noted that the mysterious thieves stealing the hunters' food were women who descended from the sky by a rope. Cutting the rope, the Culture-Bringer insured mates for the hunters. Myths through much of the Pacific and western N. America state that humans were instructed in the use of genitalia by the Culture-Bringer; in some myths the genitalia are congenitally totally misplaced and have to be rearranged by the Culture-Bringer and fixed in their present sites. All such accounts suggest the rise of conscious sexuality and the realization of the male procreative role.

Generally the conscious technology and instruction from the Culture-Bringer are associated with the male. The Irish Brigit and the Taoist Nü-kua are among the very rare female Culture-Bringers. The Australian Murngin myth indicates the Djunkgao sisters as Culture-Bringers, but they were captured by males and thereafter were ordinary women. Perhaps wiser than they realize, the Malekulans (New Hebrides) have five Culture-Bringers, the Kabat brothers, whose names are also used for the five fingers of the hand, the major instrument in human technology.[64] Ingeniously, many myths in the Amazonian Basin posit twin brothers: a "bad" Trickster brother and a "good" Culture-Bringer brother. Thus the Culture-Bringer is separated from and contrasted with his Trickster origin.

Sacred king. The divine king is a living deity like the Egyptian pharaoh or the Japanese mikado. The sacred king is recognizable as a human ruler, but (like many of the aristocrats as well) he boasts descent from a divine ancestor and from his eminent position he presumably possesses direct communication with the gods. The ancient king Mehabub-uddaula of Hyderabad was notable for his success in persuading the deities to bring rain. Especially, the fertility of the soil and of herds is directly linked to the virility of the sacred king. Hence the aging king must die in order to prevent sterility from blighting the tribe or chiefdom.

There seems no doubt that when pressures were severe enough, groups throughout the world would sacrifice their leaders. Snorri Sturluson tells the grim story of famine in Sweden during the reign of King Dómaldi. In the first year the Swedes sacrificed oxen. In the second year they sacrificed men. In the third year, with unremitting famine, they sacrificed the king, reddening the holy altars with royal blood.

No one denies such slayings of the king because of adversity. There is considerable controversy, however, about an established practice of king slaying. Frazer's Golden Bough starts, ends, and rather consistently focuses upon widespread sacrifices of kings at regular intervals. The inevitable reaction to Frazer's enormously influential work has sometimes sought to deny any such ritual altogether. An accurate statement seems to be that ritual slayings of the king certainly occurred in much of central Africa and in parts of the Middle East, India, and Java.[65] Elsewhere, if such ritual ever prevailed, it is suggested by myth but not stated forthrightly.

Many customs worldwide seem to be remnants of

king slaying: temporary kings of the Saturnalia, Lord of Misrule, mock-kings, and so on. The ancient Aztecs treated a prisoner as though he were a king, then slew him. The somewhat mysterious Heb-sed Festival of the Egyptian pharoah, ritually restoring his vigor and magically transferring it to the earth, may symbolize a ritual king slaying.

The chilling drama of ritual sacrifice of a king has induced many to apply it to ancient Greece, but there actually is no clear-cut evidence. All the mythical kings of Greece die violent deaths, which may be later revisions of sacred king slayings; but in a barbaric warrior society such violent death was normal expectancy. Some Greek myths, however, seem likely examples of ritual king slaying. The elaborate story of Aegeus throwing himself into the sea in lamentation for a son he had known for only a very few days may cover up the killing of an old monarch so that the vigorous young Theseus may be the new king. The strange Phrixus episode may recall the ritual slaying of a sacred king in ram costume.[66] The death of Peleus, ascribed to a wicked witch (Medea) from the East, may be another distant echo of sacred king slaying. The Fisher King myth behind the Grail Quest and behind T.S. Eliot's <u>Wasteland</u> looks like a softening of the original slaying by suggesting a magic restorative potion for the declining monarch.

The flesh of the slain sacred king may be eaten in communion by the populace to absorb his sacred mana. The sacred king of Quilacare in W. India immolated himself by cutting off portions of his anatomy and hurling them over the throng; to be touched by even a droplet of the royal blood was to obtain superlative blessing. Among the Yoruba the expression <u>je oba</u>, translated as "to become a king," literally means "to eat a king." A new monarch actually became the legitimate ruler only by eating a dish prepared from the heart of the previous king. Discontinued, the practice is still treasured, and grumblers snort that recent kings are not authentic since they have not eaten the flesh of their predecessors. Another possibility is the dismemberment of the body of the sacred king and the deposit of the fragments in the earth for fertilization. Almost certainly the placing of portions of the body of Osiris in each of the nomes or provinces of Egypt commemorates such a fertility ritual.

Stratified society. Mesopotamian society,

arising from patriarchism, early developed a make-shift democracy, a council of elders (clan heads) like that in the Book of Job. When outside threats demanded prompt, authoritarian leadership, the council would appeal to a capable fighting man to assume dictatorial powers. Exactly this pattern appears in the myth of the gods, dismayed by the chaotic destruction of Tiamat, pleading with Marduk to take control. The monarchy became a fixed institution in a growing, maturing society; the mythical account, however, retained the ancient pattern of the council of elders.

Waxing indignant, Jeremiah (9:23) denounces wisdom, might, and riches, probably deemed alien notions by the prophet. Georges Dumézil[67] conjectures that this alien ideology is the encroaching social system of the Indo-Europeans, penetrating Palestine perhaps as early as 2300 B.C. Peculiar to the Indo-Europeans, Dumézil claims, was a social system of three classes: priests, warriors, cultivators.[68] Each of these classes, according to Dumézil, maintained its own gods and its own myths. The sacred myths, often of religious and artistic profundity, would come from the priestly, administrative class, such as the Brahmins of India. The heroic tales and romantic legends spring largely from the fighting men. Folklore and myths of fertility and homeyness are produced by the class of agriculture workers and craftsmen. Here are examples of the tripartite division as they seem to appear in early Indo-European society:

	God of Priests	God of Warriors	Goddess of Cultivators
Indian (Vedic)	Mithra	Indra	Sarasvati
Early Roman	Jupiter	Mars	Ops[69]
Scandinavian	Odin	Thor	Freyja

This threefold division of society, according to Dumézil, affects many aspects of Indo-European thought and behavior, e.g. threefold division of universe, with heaven assigned to priests, the surface to warriors, and the soil to workers. In the judgment of Paris the bribes offered to the beauty contest judge follow the tripartite scheme: administrative power (Hera), military power (Athene), and physical delights (Aphrodite). Even the patterns of inflicting sacrificial death in early Indo-

European society seem to fall into the scheme: hanging (relished by Odin), slaying by weapons (Mars) or burning in great wicker baskets (sacrifice to god Taranis of Gaul and other northern warrior deities), and drowning or burying alive (offerings to chthonic and fertility deities).[70] Though critics are inevitable, the Dumézil concept has gained wide credence.[71]

Myth as History.[72] The Grimm brothers in the first half of the 19th century believed that folklore material could be used to establish historical facts, but this theory has been generally discarded. At the end of the 19th century Victor Bérard led the movement to accept about 75 percent of Greek myth as depicting actual Greek history. The Historical School of myth study in this century, spearheaded by W.R. Rivers,[73] while recognizing that myth is not history per se, asserts that it genuinely encapsules the historical struggles of a society, the crisis situations that are the truly meaningful events of any group. This cautious statement must be conditioned by still more cautions. There is ample evidence that much of African myth has been regularly manipulated to bestow prestige upon rulers and lineages; events and characters of myth are radically altered for political and ideological purposes.[74] Much of the mythical history of China and Japan has similarly been molded for dynastic reasons. The coming of Aeneas to Italy may remotely indicate an Asiatic origin for the Etruscans, but the British myth of Aeneas' great-grandson Brutus as the founder of the British race seems utterly without historical foundation, and even more bizarre is the Irish myth of Noah's granddaughter Cessair coming to Ireland because the ark was crowded. The Siegfried story crams in three historical personages of completely different centuries: Ermanarick, Ostogoth king of the 4th century; the Merovingian Wolfdietrich of the 5th century; and Theodoric, emperor of the Goths in the 6th century. The Song of Roland changes the adversaries of Roland from the historical Christian Basques to Islamic Moors. We must remember Malinowski's warning that "myth, taken as a whole, cannot be sober dispassionate history, since it is always made ad hoc to fulfil a certain sociological function, to glorify a certain group, or to justify an anomalous status."[75] We might also add imagination, syncretism, and downright confusion. History qua history is quite dubious in myth, but myth is certainly revelatory of major social concerns.[76]

The ancient Vedic god Mitra possesses a superb name, for mitra seems the Indo-European word for "compact," the personification of a social institution and the social agreement that alone permits community life. The social compact is well stated in a myth of the Yoruba (W. Africa). The good god Oko returned from hunting to find his wife being seduced by Ogun, a coarse war god. Oko admitted that there was no law against Ogun's actions, and Ogun was consequently free of punishment and reprisals. Oko decreed, however, that henceforth there would be a stringent law against seduction of a man's wife, and the ravisher henceforth would be slain. Observe how ex post facto law is denied and how a previous anarchic period is superseded by the era of stipulated laws.

But myth is almost wholly concerned in human relations with the failures to get along together, the conflicts of life and society. Some of these conflicts are actually projections of conflicts within the psyche, others are quarrels within the group, while many are accounts of alien invaders. Myth as inner struggle will be discussed under psychology. Conflicts within the group produce the agonies of the fated House of Atreus. Less obviously, war in heaven probably is mythicizing of internecine struggles

How is a society to accommodate misfits? The Sumerian myth of human creation offers an almost puckish treatment of a serious social problem. After human creation Enki, male god, and Ninmah, goddess, in bibulous playfulness experiment with human flesh. Ninmah fashions a barren woman and a eunuch, and Enki rises to the challenge by inserting the barren woman into society as a spinster and the eunuch as a harem guard.

Most of all, myth dwells upon conflicts with outsiders. When history finally emerged from myth, it still dwelt for many centuries upon dynastic quarrels and warfare with other groups. One's enemies are equated with demonic forces. In Vedic Hinduism the pishācas ("raw flesh eaters") and dasyus ("barbarians"), disgusting devils, undoubtedly were peoples against whom the Aryans fought in the conquest of North India. The Rjonga of Mozambique are almost paranoic about their enemies. They have been decisively vanquished in battle by the neighboring Nguni and Ndjao peoples. The Rjonga blame flood, drought, crop failure, all disasters and unpleasantries upon those vindictive unrelenting Nguni and Ndjao gods. A whole series of conflicts between ancient Semites (Abel vs. Cain, Jacob vs. Esau, Gilgamesh vs. Enkidu) look like our vaunted civilized compatriots against the uncivilized brutes out in the bush. As often in myth, a man-to-man struggle may be simplifying a complex group vs. group conflict, e.g. Abel as nomadic herdsmen vs. Cain as agriculturists, Jacob as the Israelites vs. the nearby Edomites.

Myth is psychologically and culturally advantageous when it can resolve conflict. The generations of the Greek deities certainly appear, as Keats argued in Hyperion, to struggle from bestial savagery to Olympian heights in the succession of Uranos, Kronos, and Zeus. This series could be interpreted as waves of conquerors pouring into Greece, as successive cultural periods from food gathering to urban society, as layer upon layer from Pelasgian to late Greek society, or as unvarnished Oedipal complex. Whatever reading, it resolves the conflict and ends with the firm and unchallengeable regime of almighty Zeus. Also achieving resolution is the tale of the wars between Nordic Aesir and Vanir, who certainly look like the warrior Indo-Europeans and the agricultural aborigines (or, possibly, a class struggle between an aristocratic caste and the workers). By the marriage of Odin (Aesir) to Freyja (Vanir) the groups are united and peace reigns. From time immemorial warring tribes have settled wars in this fashion, usually marrying royal children of the opposite sides, this widening the kinship area and the area of peaceful activity.

Expulsion from Eden. Judeo-Christian tradition interprets the loss of the Garden of Eden as the loss of innocence, the maturing of a human from childish naiveté to adult recognition of carnality, sin, and evil. The mythical theme of the lost paradise is worldwide, but over much of the globe no sin or guilt is attributed to mankind, and the loss is deemed an accident, divine caprice, or unwarranted enmity against humanity. Psychoanalysts perceive as the universal basis for this myth a yearning for the paradise of the womb and a bleak disappointment at being thrust into a hostile world.

Possibly the loss of paradise refers to the loss of an attractive way of life such as the transition from a food-gathering society to the drudgery of agriculture.[7] C.P. Snow theorized that the sensitive members of early human society may have been pro-

foundly distressed at the loss of variety and surprise encountered by the nomad, may have lamented
sadly the routine and regularized life of the farmer.
The loss of paradise may represent the protest of the
early artist at the loss of a challenging and
rewarding existence.

An especially intriguing interpretation involves
the early technique of swidden farming, i.e. clearing
land for cultivation for a few years, permitting the
reversion to jungle, then clearing again. The knotty
problem in swidden farming concerns fruit and nut
trees after reversion to jungle. Perhaps the entire
concept of property ownership originated with the
first planters of nut and fruit trees; they insisted
on exclusive rights to these productive trees regardless of who was cultivating the surrounding land. In
the Philippines today the Hanunoo of Mindoro are
swidden farmers. "Theft of fruit and damage to other
people's fruit-trees seem to be virtually the only
crimes recognized by Hanunoo society. The theft of
fruit is indeed the original sin."[78]

Cargo cults.[79] The reaction of an archaic
society to an overwhelming intruder may be an intense
and pathetic desire to share in the material prosperity of the prestigious culture. Extraordinary
have been the cargo cults developing in Pacific
islands since World War II.[80] In all the century or
more that European presence has been strong in these
islands, it was always on a small scale until the
struggle with Japan. To the astonishment of natives,
vast flotillas of vessels streamed to many far isles
of the Pacific with immense cargos of jeeps, radios,
clothing, food, and countless other equipment items.
Clearly, as natives opined, all this treasure trove
must have been intended for the legitimate, long-term
inhabitants, but somehow it was misaddressed and
misdirected. Since the Second World War cargo cults
of the Pacific have preached that the gods, ancestors, or a new messiah will be bringing great ship-
ments of wondrous goods to produce instant utopia.
Even as late as 1971 a new cult was organized at
Yangoru to prevent Americans from erecting geodetic
survey markers on a mountain island; infuriated,
natives were convinced that the markers would enrage
the gods and prevent the promised cargos from
arriving.[81]

Pacific islands and Indonesia have a background
of dema deities as a predecessor of cargo cults. The
long-standing West Ceram story of Hainuwele ("coconut

242

girl") reports this vegetation semi-goddess as
excreting all sorts of valuable objects such as
Chinese dishes, gongs, gold earrings, and many other
import items. The Japanese awaiting of the boat of
Maitreya (the future Buddha) is a counterpart of the
cargo cult. Culture-bringer and messiah myths also
contribute to the cargo cult concept.

"We shall overcome."[82] The cargo cults naively
want to garner all the gadgets and goods of the
advanced impinging civilization. There is none of
the Japanese shrewdness that absorbs the alien technology and outdoes the alien. There is none of the
wisdom of the shamans who realize the doom of their
own society and the even greater indignity of puppy-
like nibblings at the alien civilization. Archaic
myth can protest and can humble the arrogant intruders from an advanced civilization. The Eskimos of
northern Canada assert that the Creator experimented
first with Kadluna ("white man") but recognized the
botched job; although wealthy and powerful, Kadluna
totally lacked true character and spirit. The
Creator corrected his errors by his second and
infinitely superior creation of the Eskimo.

There is still another reaction, a widespread
terror among archaics, knowing that they are trapped
and desperately seeking a miracle that will dissipate
the oppressive white man. Unable to assimilate an
alien miasma of ideas, confused as the old ways are
shrugged off, socially disintegrating, feeling
inferior and hating the feeling, archaic societies
lash out in panic with myths that promise the expulsion of white civilization and paradisical return to
the time-honored way of community life. There are
two tactics employed. One method is to assert that
the ancient gods, the spirits of the ancestors, the
legendary culture-bringer, or inspired elders of the
tribe will properly reassert their rightful power,
cast out the aliens, and establish the future paradise (which, like most utopias, is an idealization of
the supposed past). The other technique is to employ
the obviously potent spirit figures of the successful
society and turn that spirit or those spirits against
white civilization; now supporting the natives,
these spirits will give the truly deserving people
their new and glorious era. All of these movements
present themselves outwardly as social regeneration
sparked by perfervid charismatic leaders. Actually
the underlying concern and the chief arousal of
followers are the dazzling hopes of liberation and
relief for the outcast, the outsider, the lower

class, underprivileged ethnic groups.[83]

A sampling of such movements using native materials:

Antonism arose in 18th century W. Zaire with a woman leader, Beatrice. Blacks, according to Beatrice, sprang from the fig tree n'sanda (down to the present a solemn symbol of the village elders), while whites came from fuma, a soft white clay or stone in streambeds and deprecated as ghosts and spirit wraiths.

Wovoka (or Jack Wilson) about 1889 among the Paiute of Nevada began the ghost dance from visions he received during a fever and during solar eclipse. He foretold the purging of the white man from the continent, and Amerindians henceforth would escape all disease and suffering; the earth would be regenerated, and spirits would joyously walk with men.[84]

Among the Nanai of Siberia from 1870 well into this century the cult of Heri Mapa preached that the old spirits were bitterly assailed by the new spirits, but the mighty power of Heri Mapa would defeat all others and elevate the Nanai people.

The Molonga cult of Australian aborigines at the turn of this century declared that Ka'nini, the spirit of the "Great Mother from the Water" would swallow and destroy all the whites.

A sampling of such movements exploiting Christian symbols and references:

The recent Worgaia cult of Australian aborigines claims that Jinimin (Jesus) in a vision promised that the entire country would once again belong wholly to the aborigines. Jinimin shall provide a stone boat[85] with immense riches (as in the cargo cults) to save the aborigines while all the whites shall drown in a vast flood.

In Peru the Taqui Ongoy movement against the Spaniards began as early as 1564; the two women in high leadership positions called themselves Holy Mary and Mary Magdalen.

The Cult of the Holy Cross in Quintana Roo, Mexico, in 1850 started a rebellion against the Mexican government that was not really concluded until a peace treaty of 1915. Originally a small cross claiming to be the true cross reputedly spoke directly to the Mayan peasants, urging them to oust the Mexican government. Destroyed by government troops in 1850, the cross miraculously reappeared as three daughter crosses to exhort to rebellion. Still extant is a sermon supposedly spoken by the Holy Cross itself.

Some interesting variations:

While fishing alone in 1941 a Tukuna Amerindian boy Nora'ne received an unexpected vision from Dyei ("our father," creator of mankind), who, although white himself, promised the complete expulsion of all whites if the Tukuna would erect a temple in his honor and inaugurate certain rituals. Even though the Tukuna complied, the white man did not budge. In a subsequent revelation Dyei explained to Nara'ne that the contemplated actions had been thwarted by the violation of a marriage tabu. The whiteness of Dyei was associated by the Tukuna with white men, but remember that Quetzalcoatl was white and so were gods of the New Zealand Maoris. Such whiteness can mean moon deities or ghosts.

Generally the visionaries launching these movements are intensely sincere, but the "Vailala Madness" of 1919-1921 in the former German colony of Papua seems to have been largely a hoax perpetrated by Evara, the founder, and other leaders. A spirit vessel, thought of as a steamer, was expected to bring back the souls of the dead who would effect a religious, social, and political revolution for the natives.[86] The chief feature of the cult was mass hysteria fanned by glossolalia, claimed by the leaders to be the spirit tongue of Djaman (German). Special food magazines, intended for the returning spirits, were actually opportunities for gorging by the leaders. Many natives confidently asserted that they had seen the Phantom Ship. One night numerous Papuans saw the spirit vessel on the Vailala River and heard all the sounds of a steamer. One morning at Orokolo and Arihava smoke obscured much of the oncoming vessel, but ecstatic viewers were certain that they observed it. In full daylight at Karaita many witnessed the wash of the Phantom Ship and heard all the sounds of a docking vessel. Even though natives themselves unmasked the hoaxers, in retrospect many who had closely experienced the "Vailala Madness" did not recall it as a fraud, but pleasurably recalled that period as a time of remarkable

245

visitations, exhilirating signs and portents, amplified and intensified living.[87]

The Mayo of Sonora, Mexico, have a long history of visionaries. Up to 1885 the standard message was incendiary, urging violence to throw off the Mexican government. Countering with troops, the Mexican government as late as 1892 banished the major living "saint" of the Mayo, Santa Teresa de Cabora. Since 1885, however, the visionaries have abandoned the cry to physical rebellion and have urged spiritual devotion because of impending global catastrophe and the imminent end of the world. This latter mythical theme is widespread through mankind and probably arises from a situation like that of the Mayo: if unable to effect a desired physical change in the social atmosphere, a society opts for spirit alteration in a doomed universe.

The intense pressures of contemporary civilization frequently precipitate religious revivals. Among the deprived and suffering there is often a powerful emotional avowal of orthodox faith. More alienated and venturesome souls will flock to exotic movements; hence the enthusiasm among middle-class youth of Western society for Zen Buddhism and other oriental cults. When a substratum of archaic myth still survives, there can be a surprising resurgence of very old beliefs amidst industrialized societies. It is claimed that the Umbanda cult of Brazil, African in origin and worshipping the African god Iemanjá, now numbers 30 million people. Resurgent in oil-rich Venezuela is the cult of María Leonza, reputedly an Indian maid who fled from the Spanish conquerers to maintain the old religion in jungle fastnesses. The newspaper El Diario de Caracas comments, "While the country advances, . . . millions of Venezuelans find spiritual guidance in the myths and legends of the past."[88]

Myth in a flourishing high culture. The social concerns of a relatively primitive community are defense against external adversaries. Therefore, the myths of this stage of society emphasize group solidarity and loyalty, maintenance of kinship and ruler authority. Most of the surviving Greco-Roman mythology comes from an era considerably advanced beyond these early basics. The Myth II of classic Greece decidedly modifies the materials and attitudes of Myth I in order to defend the city-state (polis).

Whatever the sanguinary fates of members of the

House of Atreus may have meant to archaic Greeks, Aeschylus in the Oresteia makes their savage feuding the epitome of rural anarchy of the benighted past. The ringing conclusion of the dramatic trilogy is the triumph of urban law in the divine judgment of Pallas Athene. Romantics of the 18th and 19th centuries, fed up with cities, would chorus with William Cowper: "God made the country, and man made the town."[89] Athenians of the Periclean Age claimed the reverse, exalting the city as divinely ordained order and true humanity. The mythical history of Athens from Cecrops to Theseus consists of spectacular individual figures, but its cumulative power is a celebration of the polis. Remember that the story of Dick Whittington and his cat would be forgotten if centered about Norton-in-the-Marsh. The whole point of the Whittington tale is to glorify London and Londoners.

The sophisticated urban culture of ancient Greece certainly developed internal hostilities just as the sly trickster seems an anti-establishment figure of early society. The pattern of rebellion in classic Greek cities produced opposite reactions:

Transcendence, trying to rise above the mundane urbanite. Pythagoreanism is a bit hazy, reported altogether at second hand, but it clearly was a revolt against the mercantile materialism of commercial Greece. Pythagoras sought to liberate the soul from the bondage of materialism by careful study of nature and by asceticism. Orphism proved remarkably extensive among classical idealists and produced enormous interpretations of myth as elevated moral allegory; it also added considerable mythology of its own to this transcendent search. Orphism demonstrates the vast, complex structure that the intellectual can erect upon the rather shifty sands of myth.

Descendence, seeking in things "natural" a welcome relief from the artificialities and stifling banalities of urban life. The Dionysian revels are opposed by the city establishment, as with Pentheus, but the apparently staid city-dweller is swept up in the wild frenzy, participating or being destroyed. Although Dionysus was worshipped in prehistoric Greece, his great and disturbing power became most manifest in classic Greece as the rebellion against reason, order, conformity. Dionysus was not necessarily un-Greek; his orgiastic rites represented an essential psychic safety valve. Classical Cynicism in its early stage (Antisthenes, Crates) exalted

247

virtue, despising learning. Later Cynics such as Demetrius and Demonax seemed to earn the label cynic ("dog") because of totally brutish behavior, flaunting their scorn of so-called "civilization." The earlier Cynics long preceded the 18th and 19th century intellectuals who flee from reason and intellectuality; the later Cynics anticipated by millenia the present-day disillusioned, amoral denizens of the ghetto.

Perhaps the ultimate tragedy of classical myth was its total inability to provide the mythic structure for a world state. Greek myth never got beyond the polis. Roman myth, in the hands of some of the world's all-time great administrators, tried the tactics of syncretism (putting together all the gods of all the empire) and divine emperor; but neither of these techniques succeeded in creating a true world myth. Christianity provided the much needed myth and through the vicissitudes of medieval times unified Western man with the mighty concept of Christendom.

Chapter VIII   Social Scientists Theorize about Myth

Rationalists, scientists, and intellectuals generally have been especially impressed by the 20th century theories about myth from social scientists, for these theories hardheadedly confront myth with its actual use by social groups.[1] Various labels and combinations have been suggested,[2] but the major contributions of the social scientists fall into these three divisions:

Functionalism

Functionalism says that myth is created and perpetuated primarily because it actually works in social stability and integration of a group. The French sociologist Émile Durkheim is credited with propounding this theory in 1912.[3] Durkheim declared that myth basically fulfills the function of establishing, maintaining, and expressing social solidarity. Myth gives identity to a social group, binds together the members of a community, and carefully sets each group apart from others. Within myth are the fundamental structures[4] and organization of society, and within myth are the cherished values of a society.

Myth as a projection of society takes these major forms:

(1) Political. The official religion of China before the upheavals of this century was the most thoroughgoing demonstration of the deified state. Heaven maintained precisely the same system as the imperial court and the civil service. Designations for the divine functionaries were not for specific beings but, as in China, for bureaucratic positions. Even the Jade Emperor (Yü-Huang) had a predecessor as supreme deity and will in time have a successor. The holders of divine office were uniformly dead humans whose earthly service to Chinese society warranted their assignment to celestial posts. The rare religious persecutions in China and the constant derogation of unorthodox religion sprang not from any theological questions of truth or falsity but from concern that heresy was highly injurious to the social and political stability of the empire. The Confucian tradition quite frankly employs religion largely for the salvation of society, the assurance of a wholesome and effective social system.

(2) Social. Myth works extra hard in India to

insure socially acceptable conduct. Although conversation with infidels was expressly forbidden, the good-natured king Shatadhanu politely talked to a Jain, a friend of the king's war minister. Dying shortly thereafter, Shatadhanu because of his violation of tabu was successively reborn as a dog, a jackal, a wolf, a vulture, a crow, and a peacock. The righteous queen Shaibyā ignored the Jain altogether and consequently remained undefiled. Dutifully she ascended her husband's funeral pyre to die and was properly reborn as a royal princess. Her royal father wished to marry her off, but she demurred, hoping that Shatadhanu would eventually be reincarnated in an acceptable husband-form. Largely because of her exemplary behavior, the gods graciously caused Shatadhanu to be reborn as a noble prince, at last reunited with the flawless Shaibyā. In double-barreled manner this myth shows the horrible consequences of what seems mere innocent politeness to an infidel and also tells every woman precisely how she should behave.

(3) Moral. The pattern among the Sisala of N. Ghana is repeated by many groups worldwide. The ancestral spirits of the Sisala labor unceasingly to whip the living into line, inflicting all sorts of punishments from the loss of small personal items to hideous death upon any tribe member violating the moral code. Failure to propitiate ancestors by proper conduct can grievously injure oneself, the whole family, even the entire clan. Among the negroes of Dutch Guiana the supernatural force Kunu deals severely with all transgressions of the social code. For heinous offenses such as incest or murder, Kunu can exterminate the entire family of the offender. Moses proclaimed his moral law dictated by the powerful god Yahweh. Generations before, Hammurabi had attributed his legal strictures to Marduk. Thus man invokes the most awesome of mythic concepts to enforce social morality.

(4) Psychological. Myth will urge the individual to contribute to society and assure him of society's appreciation of his service. Certainly a nasty problem in archaic societies is that of the maimed, all too frequent in ancient warfare. Life is hard enough without the gross disabilities of maiming. Tyr among the Teutonic gods lost his hand to the Fenris wolf so that the gods might bind that monster. Henceforth he became the Germanic god of loyalty, law, and faithful contract. Odin gained wisdom and prophetic power to aid gods and men only

by sacrificing an eye to draw knowledge from the well of Mimir. Roman legend reports a one-handed hero Mucius Scaevola, and a one-eyed hero, Horatius Cocles, who saved the Roman army in its struggle against the Etruscans. Nuada among the Irish and Surya among the Indians are other examples of one-handed gods. Modern patriotism has extolled the sacrifice of maimed veterans as pledges of liberty, badges of glory, and so on. Such epithets are mere paraphrases of the Germanic and Roman myths.

Anthropologists have been especially attracted to functionalism after extensive scrutiny of archaic societies in the field, and anthropologists have often emphasized one or another of the four areas of functionalism above. A.R. Radcliffe-Brown refused the label of functionalist, but he seemed the major scrutinizer of "structure," "process," and "function" in primitive society.[5] He insisted that in a non-literate society facing formidable hostility from nature and other humans there is absolutely no room for the superfluous. Every feature in archaic social life, Radcliffe-Brown asserted, must serve a quite useful function.[6] Under such conditions myth and religion prove eminently functional; otherwise they must be altered or discarded in favor of what will demonstrably be useful. Myth I generally fulfills this purpose, but classical Greek myth is Myth II and therefore quite often minimal or even negative in actual function.

Bronislaw Malinowski was the great unfurler of the banner of Functionalism, but his emphases were essentially upon the social, moral, and psychological functions of myth rather than upon the structure that interested A.R. Radcliffe-Brown. Malinowski nails his flag to the mast of functionalism in ringing fashion:

Studied alive, myth, as we shall see, is

not symbolic, but a direct expression of

its subject matter; it is not an ex-

planation in satisfaction of a scien-

tific interest, but a narrative resur-

rection of a primitive reality, told in

satisfaction of deep religious wants, moral cravings, social submissions, assertions, even practical requirements. Myth fulfils in primitive culture an indispensable function: it expresses, enhances, and codifies belief; it safeguards and enforces morality; it vouches for the efficiency of ritual and contains practical rules for the guidance of man. Myth is thus a vital ingredient of human civilization; it is not an idle tale, but a hard-worked active force; it is not an intellectual explanation or an artistic imagery, but a pragmatic charter of primitive faith and moral wisdom.[7]

Malinowski spent some years with the Trobriand Islanders, off the coast of New Guinea. Pragmatic himself, Malinowski found the Trobriand Islanders basically a pragmatic people, right down to the root of their mythology. The Creation Myth of these islanders seems primarily to substantiate present class structure and power base. Men emerged from underground (i.e. born from Mother Earth) near the village of Laba'i. The four main clans (iguana, dog, pig, crocodile) issued forth, with the pig ridiculing the dog as vulgar and ill-bred. Ever since, the Malasi clan, whose totem is the pig, has produced the chiefs, while members of the Lakuba clan, whose totem is the dog, are deemed lower-class and rather trashy. Mythic claims of life beyond the grave calm some of human terrors and scares; they also contribute to social conformity, as individuals follow the do's and don't's of the group to insure a desirable afterlife. Malinowski found Trobriand Islanders about as sceptical as advanced societies in contemplating alleged miracles today and as reverentially acceptant of past miracles as the pious of advanced societies. Mythic miracles sustain faith in any society.

An archaic society is a traditional society, and myth is the great buttress of tradition. Myth bestows upon tradition elevated prestige and enhanced value by ascribing moral and social practices to a higher, more ideal, supernatural level. The distance of time totally removes myth from doubt and from comparison with the mundane present world. Malinowski terms myth the charter of primitive society, "the dogmatic backbone of primitive civilization."[8] It must be noted that subsequent observers of the Trobriand Islanders have found these natives less pragmatic and more imaginative than Malinowski found them. Other anthropologists essentially of the functionalist position suggest that myths codify the points of conflict within a society and then resolve the problems to make society efficient as a whole and satisfying to each member of the group,[9] and that myth works upon the gaps in the social system, smoothing, tying together, strengthening and reëstablishing the frayed cords that bind the social structure.[10]

While Malinowski and most functionalists emphasize the social function of myth, Clyde Kluckhohn emphasizes the function of myth in providing personal satisfactions for all the individuals in a society. From extensive field work with the Navaho Amerindians, Kluckhohn concluded that most of the Navaho myths functioned as assurance and consolation for the individual. Navahos are often worried about their health; consequently, numerous myths celebrate the successful cures of the medicine man. For every society numerous myths from those of the divine origin of an individual's lineage to the heavenly paradise for the faithful reconcile a member of the society to his position in life and to his experiences, no matter how deprived.

Functionalism states some important truths about myth, but the functionalism of the early 20th century has generally fallen out of fashion. Trends in 20th century myth interpretation outside of the social sciences have given increasing weight to the effect of personal religion and notably to psychological influence, both frequently extraneous to functionalism. Still very much alive is Neofunctionalism, which broadens its consideration to all social and practical benefits attributable to myth in archaic societies.[11] However, within the social sciences the interest in myth has shifted for the most part to the following approaches.

Ritualism[12]

Ceremony is secular; ritual is religious. Both ceremony and ritual mean an established pattern of actions and possibly words solemnly and repetitiously performed to mark a specific occasion. Ritual is believed by archaic man to have transcendent power. Magical ritual compels supernatural agencies to effect a desired action, while petitionary ritual is thought to gain the attention of supernatural forces which are thereby placed in a favorable attitude likely to grant requests. Sociologically, the intended achievements of ritual are:

(1) To channel emotions in the individual and the group. Shapeless emotion leaves everyone perturbed and confused, but the directing of emotion can carry it to complete form and expression, thence to resolution and resignation, as in funeral ritual.

(2) To minimize feelings of chaos and uncertainty. Individual ritual can occupy otherwise amorphous and disturbing time, but especially it gives individual reassurance of divine order and concern. Some Christian athletes therefore routinely cross themselves before a contest.

(3) To communicate and instruct. Notoriously, adolescents today believe their sexual longings and general groping for maturity are unique and terrifying experiences. Perhaps the distressing suicide rate among the young and the widespread malaise in this age group would be lessened if modern society reinstituted the formal rituals of the past. All the verbiage addressed to the young fails to attain the effectiveness of group ritual, where the participant senses the eternal systole and diastole of which he is part and feels that he truly belongs and understands.

(4) To create group unity. The loneliness gripping many moderns stems in part from today's virtual lack of community ritual, notably in the urban concentrations. Much of the success of Nazism was its cultivation of group rituals, hypnotizing and unifying. To an outsider many community rituals seem quaintly irrational or unnecessarily esoteric, but

ritual has well served the community if it minimizes group and personal fears, if it resolves or subordinates conflicts within the group, and if it succeeds in social bonding. Ritual in its origins supported group survival and only in late self-conscious and individualistic eras is considered as bestowing a desirable mindset upon the individual.[13]

(5) "Ritual represents the creation of a controlled environment."[14] Ritual to be truly effective must deal with simple concepts (which, of course, become heavily loaded with symbolic weight) presented with grace, dignity, relative precision. The haphazard everyday world can never match the neat, adroit, even aesthetically impressive realm of ritual. Not merely the members of an archaic society, but the religious devotees of a highly sophisticated modern society, can experience in ritual a sense of rightness and truth quite elevated above the mundane world. Probably ritual, the nearest thing to perfection ever experienced by a worshipper in this imperfect world, has been the mightiest force in collective mankind to sustain religious power and prestige, to convey the sense of ideals and aspiration in humanity, and to inculcate strong belief in divinity and heavenly glory.[15]

(6) The supposed efficacy of ritual strengthens individual and community morale and confidence. Much ritual is mimetic, hoping to achieve the desired effect by imitation of an action. The ancient Egyptians could be sure that their deceased loved ones were enjoying immortality because the ritual for the dead carefully recapitulated the ritual actions that effected the resurrection of Osiris. Even moderns, who will strongly assert that ritual is purely symbolic, seem elevated and exalted by ritual, sensing atavistic comforts and assurances in ritual. For most of archaic societies and even for multitudes in advanced cultures, ritual is the major art form to stimulate and amplify the feeling of intense and satisfactory living.[16]

Ritual long preceded humanity, as we all know from frequent television programs on animal life. The courtship ritual of animals can be laughable in the case of walruses, dramatic and ominous in mountain goats and elks, awesomely aesthetic in the lyre bird. Many archaic societies still ritualize a pretended flight by the bride, her pursuit, capture, and subjection; all the phases of this ritual abduction correspond to the love play of some animals before mating. Ritual among animals was symbolic long before mankind existed. Herring gulls disputing a territory will vigorously pluck grass with their beaks instead of attacking each other. This ritual clearly resembles that of a sorcerer mutilating the image of an enemy or of kings ritualistically symbolizing the destruction of an adversary. Upon such bases the ritualists assert that with humanity ritual was conventional long before man became articulate and that myth arose from ritual to accompany and explain ritual.

Almost beyond the comprehension of modern man, archaic societies are ritualistic societies, to such an extent that Eliade asserts that "every responsible activity in pursuit of a definite end, is, for the archaic world, a ritual."[17] It is impossible, of course, to perform every activity at the same high serious pitch; so archaic societies have three basic treatments of ritual:

(1) Low intensity. Routine acknowledgement of supernatural forces and casual but constant ritual performance is just keeping up, properly but not excitedly according recognition. The ancient Greeks rather automatically slopped a drop or two from the wine cup as sacrifice to the gods. Such practice becomes perfunctory, but it is regularly performed.

(2) High intensity. Obviously, high intensity can be reached and maintained only briefly at discreet intervals. If we still employed the early lunar calendar, would we celebrate a person's birthday every month? Obviously such frequent ritual would be boring and quickly just nominal, while a birthday celebration once in 365 days is significant and memorable. Seasonal rituals and infrequent rituals for the joys and worries of individuals and groups can peak with emotional and psychic intensity.

(3) Escape valve. To encompass human emotions and channelize them, ritual must offer not merely solemn majesty but also laughter, criticism, emotional release, even rebellion. Such periodic rituals will prevent pent-up feelings swelling up to antisocial explosions. Hence medieval Boy Bishops and Feasts of Fools, strange to the modern mind but invaluable devices of social expression and control. Rites of reversal such as the ancient Saturnalia (servant and master roles exchanged, transvestism, and similar role reversals) let off steam and unwind the social structure in preparation for a rewinding

into the fixity that follows.[18]

Primitives cannot conceive of any automatic law of nature, any inevitable progression from birth to death. Archaic societies believe that no one is a man or a woman automatically; a boy is transformed into a man and a girl into a woman by ritual. Similarly, the growth of nature and the celestial events don't just happen; they must be induced by human ritual.

Rites of passage. This label is a literal translation of Les rites de passage (1908) by Arnold van Gennep, one of the relatively few book titles to be imbedded in the language as an essential technical term. Rites of passage are the rituals by which society celebrates the successive stages of each person's life: birth, naming, admittance to family or clan, social or physiological puberty, marriage, parenthood, occupational acceptance, death. Movement of a person from one prescribed territory to another, adoption of an adult into a family, admitting an adult into another tribe, and numerous other individual rituals are also observed by archaic peoples worldwide. According to van Gennep, rituals involve three elements: separation of the individual from his previous condition, transition to prepare the individual for his new status, and incorporation into the new group. Myth may refer to all parts of rites of passage, but Victor Turner associates myth most with the transitional or liminal elements.[19] The rites of passage are fascinating insights into the archaic mind, but we must here concentrate upon just one consummately important ritual, the initiation into adulthood. Probably no other rites have contributed so much to mythology as well as to human culture generally.[20]

Emphasis will be placed upon the male initiation ritual[21] because archaic societies apply this emphasis; in most archaic societies the female initiation ritual is private or considerably less extensive than the male ritual. The scope of the male initiation[22] has caused scholarly examination in a variety of directions:

(1) Purely sociological.[23] The initiation is interpreted as emphasizing sexual identity and social role. Youthful male energy must be directed into socially accepted channels as husband, hunter, warrior. The ritual might be considered an attempt by tribal elders to assert and maintain power.

(2) psychological. In many archaic societies all children until puberty are brought up in the women's quarters or under maternal control. A boy must be startlingly awakened to his removal from feminine security and sweet nurture to the masculine world of forceful action amidst peril.[24] Freud[25] and Reik[26] suggest that the male initiation rites arise from the hostility of the older generation. Note the sadistic glee traditionally associated with sophomores in their hazing of freshmen. The infliction of pain and mutilation is seen as an outlet for the older men's envy of youth; furthermore the elders have brutally asserted their command over the young. Bettelheim[27] shares the Freudian view but shifts emphasis to the male envy of the female.

(3) Symbolic and religious. Frazer[28] interpreted ritual as exchanging one's individual soul for the soul of the totem. Frobenius[29] thought that the participants believed that they were transformed into spirits with power beyond mere humanity. Eliade[30] emphasizes the death-and-rebirth imagery to symbolize transformation to a new nature, a new being.

(4) Cultural patterning. It is possible to see the male initiation ritual and all rites as the collective expression of mankind, separating the human from the natural and developing extensive cultural systems. Johan Huizinga[31] would see all ritual as play, as purposeful pretense.

(5) Ritual and myth. For a male in archaic society, his initiation probably remained always as the most dramatic and climactic experience of his life.[32] The male initiation ritual seems the basis for subsequent initiation into secret and religious cults. It is impossible to say how much the shaman's vision and the male initiation ritual mutually influenced each other. This ritual, secretive of course, probably impacts numerous myths, often cryptically.

Any ritual as universal as the male initiation[33] ritual has countless variations, but the following seem to be the fundamental units:

(1) Separation of the male from "the mothers." Many Australian and Amerindian initiations suggest that the ritual and its sacred objects had once been in the hands of the women but were all forcefully wrested away by the males. Since this is a male initiation ritual, such a ploy is probably meta-

phoric, really asserting to the boys that they are to shake off petticoat rule and as males dominate women henceforward. Among the Ona of Tierra del Fuego the initiation is a pretext for men to domineer over women; masked dancers try vigorously to frighten the women and convince them that powerful, dangerous spirits now control the boys. Among the Chamacoco S. Amerindians the women must scatter into hiding during the male initiation; it is feared that if the women should discover that the awesome spirit beings were just familiar men in masks, the entire tribe would perish.

(2) Symbolic death and resurrection. All humanity would agree that death effects a tremendous transformation. Logically, then, symbolic death is the strongest possible image to an archaic society to proclaim the complete destruction of the former boy and the creation of a new creature, the full-fledged adult man. Depending upon the tribe, the boys may be painted white to represent death, be immured in caves or pits, may lie in graves or trenches. A recurrent pattern is the swallowing of the novice and the regurgitation by a giant or monster. Every continent offers this pattern, with an especial frequency in Indian myth.[34] Often the swallowing is by a giant fish, dragon, or sea serpent (note Jonah); psychoanalysts would hasten to point out that the fetus is an aquatic creature inside the mother.

The cave, pit, or other letting into the earth is a womb symbol; any enforced seclusion there will be symbolic of return to the prenatal condition. Among the Gikuyu of E. Africa a boy must crouch at his mother's feet as she pretends to be in labor. Upon "birth" the lad must cry like a newborn infant and for several days must live solely upon milk. Of course, this is a new birth, indicating access now to an elevated, heightened mode of existence. Among Indians an upperclass boy when initiated is termed "twice born" (dvija). While the Hindu ritual is wholly for males, the Parsis initiate both sexes in the ritual termed "new birth" (navajota). Several Congo tribes officially call the male initiation ritual "resurrection."

(3) Ordeal. If a tribe has a reasonably peaceful situation, like the natives of remote Pacific isles, young males will be subjected to minimal pain and suffering. If a tribe, as was true for most archaic societies, has harsh nature and hostile humans to contend with, the boys will undergo serious

ordeals often to the point of an occasional fatality. Heat, cold, hunger, and thirst must be endured stolidly without childish complaints. Amerindians often required the boys to spend extended periods in the wilds with no weapons, and with only their skill and agility to permit survival. Often sleep is denied, as sleep is equated with restful death and with the absence of full knowledge. Remaining awake is proof not only of physical strength but of spiritual strength. "You're not mama's little boys any longer," the candidates are told. "You're men who gut it out and don't whimper for the easy, safe life. You must live like heroes."[35] A hunting society with low calibre hunters and warriors is a doomed society. Living reality forces the creation of tough fighting men from downy cheeked boys.

(4) Vision. All youths are expected to gain a vision of their adult behavior and responsibility. In a hunting society the lonely vigil in the wilderness is not simply to demonstrate the courage and resourcefulness of the novice. He is expected to get a spirit vision of the totem beast (Great Bear, King of Emu, etc.) or the Master of Animals. His relationship to his quarry is sacramental. He is granted an animal life to give life to himself, but he must kill reverently, only after perceptive contact with the spirit that governs animals. Often an entheogenic substance is administered to the boys and they are carefully instructed about what vision they will encounter. With such a briefing most of the young men experience the vision they are expected to see.[36] Note in hallucinogens and visions how the boys' initiation parallels that of the shaman. Even further, the Urabunna of central Australia tell all outsiders that the bullroarer is the voice of a spirit who takes the lads far away, rips out all their insides, and replaces with totally new material before returning the young men. The physical transformation is, of course, a symbol for spiritual transformation.

(5) Indoctrination. Most learning until comparatively recent times was observing and imitating. Apparently the first formal instruction began in the male initiation ritual. Of course, formal lecturing to a non-literate group is wholly ineffectual; so the tribal elders conveyed their instruction by a much more colorful and impactful technique: the drama. The content of the indoctrination was the mythology of the group, especially the legends of heroes whom the boys were expected to emulate.

Flesh and blood people moving through roles have always been the most effective way to convey a story and point a moral. More than that, the drama had an especially momentous impact upon impressionable young men who in many tribes had never before witnessed the drama (it was solely for the initiates).[37] The actors in elaborate regalia and masks seemed awesome beings from another time and place. The tribal myths were thus depicted not as chitter-chatter but as living experiences far more real and exciting than mundane life. The drama in all the world had a major origin in the male initiation ritual, and the classic Greek drama with its mythical cycles looks like the lineal descendent. Schools for boys (long preceding formal education for girls) seem likewise to have originated in the male initiation ritual.

Some archaic initiations have a deflating effect like telling youngsters there is no Santa Claus. Initiates among the Hopi Amerindians have the Kachinas built up as wondrous supernatural visitors, but at the climactic point see them unmasked as neighbors. Youngsters and women are told by the Wiradthuri of Australia that Dhuramoolan is a terrifying spirit, but the male initiates learn that the eerie sound of the monster came from a bullroarer. Apparently these are intentional shocks to wipe out juvenile naïveté and compel an adult viewpoint. The coarse, low-calibre mind can thereby shrug off religion as a silly hoax, but the truly perceptive mind realizes that the outward show is a symbol for a non-corporeal reality.[38]

(6) Physical marking. The ingenuity of man knows no limit in carving upon the male anatomy distinctive markings that will forever identify a man as a Sioux warrior or a Watusi fighting man. In part the hacking is an ordeal, but it always concludes initiation, certifying successful completion of initiation. It was a boy who left the women's quarters; it is a man who returns to the men's quarters, and the markings are certification of his manhood. Nez Percé means just that, "pierced nose" to identify this male Amerindian. The South Pacific boasted the most elaborate markings, fantastic tattooing covering most of a warrior's body. The Hsiung-nu (Huns) inflicted one of the most brutal markings, as a boy's cheeks were virtually ripped off, ever thereafter leaving a hideously scarred face to appall enemies. Probably the Cyclopes, with only one eye in the forehead, were quite archaic tribesmen on an isolated island, a backwash at the time of Odysseus; sailors

261

from Ithaca must have been astounded at that tattoo of an eye in the center of the forehead. The third eye upon the forehead of Indian deities may have the same origin, but it is treated so symbolically that the eye seems a metaphor.

As made clear by the Bible, the mark of Cain is a protective insignia, indicating to any viewer that the marked man is protected by his clan. An unmarked man is fair prey for anyone, but many a stray hunter owed his life to his clan mark. The anatomical mutilation also demonstrated what man was eligible and what man was prohibited as a marriage partner. The most controversial of the initiation mutilations is circumcision. The practice, known to tribes through much of the world, is so ancient that no one has a definitive explanation. Perhaps the clue appears in the Australian aboriginal declaration that no one is a man by nature, but must be "made" a man by circumcision. Apparently primitive reasoning is that the male prepuce is at least a symbolic uterus, certainly a sheath masking the penis. Stripping away the prepuce suggests a permanently alert penis, fertile sexuality, and greater assurance of the group continuance.[39] The Damara of Africa reckon a man's age from the date of his circumcision.

Generally, mating is considered later and separate from the male initiation ritual, but Reik interprets sexual intercourse as a conclusion to the initiation when he suggests that the biblical story of Eve's creation from Adam's rib stems from this ritual. The removal of a rib is symbolic of ritual mutilation. The ecstatic sleep and final possession of a woman indicate proof of success in initiation to manhood.[40]

While the male initiation ritual is worldwide in archaic society, puberty rites for females vary considerably.[41] Some groups simply have a mother or adult female relative take a girl aside at her first menstruation and privately instruct her in the privileges and responsibilities of womanhood. Frequent is isolation in a dark hut or cave (symbolic of "the mothers"). Perhaps the Sleeping Beauty is a fossil from such early puberty rites for girls,[42] also Snow White.[43] In the hut the girl is prohibited from touching the earth (mother) or letting the sun (father) fall upon her. The visit of Zeus to the imprisoned Danaë in the form of a shower of gold (sunlight) looks like an item from girls' puberty rites. The girl is also prohibited from touching her own body, apparently as a prohibition of clitoral masturbation. In some puberty rites for girls the clitoris is snipped off in analogy to male circumcision; the clitoris removal is freeing her from a symbolic phallus and "making" her a woman. If female initiation rites are formally celebrated, they will contain symbols of death and resurrection to indicate the end of sexless life and the inauguration of fertile womanhood. The female rites generally include magical spells to cast out the demon of menstruation and invoke the spirit of fertility.

Tribal rituals. The rites of passage are performed for specific individuals at times appropriate to his or her movement through life. Tribal rituals involve the entire community in wholly public rites independent of the individual (except, of course the monarch, who is the palladium of the group). Though highly secularized, our society perpetuates these tribal rituals in celebration of New Year's Day, Christmas, national independence, and so forth. Our celebrations are properly ceremonies, commemorating and symbolizing but hardly anything more. A genuine religious ritual does all this and more. It is an escape from the profane world to the sacred world, where conventional rules are abrogated. Especially, ritual is eschewing profane time to live now the wondrous past and eternity. Greek Orthodox ritual for Easter notably emphasizes, "Christ arises"; this is not an event of the past or of time as we experience it in the world--the arising of Christ is in the eternal now. The ritual evokes the divine presence, whether Marduk, Apollo, or Christ. Ritual is magical: the proper performance by accredited personnel will inevitably produce the desired result. Ex opere operato has been Roman Catholic doctrine since the 13th century. The validity of Christian ritual is dependent solely upon the authority of the celebrant and his meticulous performance. If these criteria are met, the miracle of the mass, for example, is certain to transform the bread and wine into the flesh and blood of Christ even if the celebrant himself doubts the efficacy and even if he is morally and spiritually reprehensible.

Myth provides ample indications of dire disasters if ritual is not fully carried out as prescribed. The Japanese god Izanagi and the goddess Izanami circled the pillar of their home and, face to face, the goddess spoke first, a serious breach of ritual. As a result they had two abortive births. Oracles ascertained the reason for their misfortune and the two recircled the pillar with the god speaking first. Because of this exemplary ritual they subsequently gave birth to the principal islands of Japan. Some major narratives of Greek myth are precipitated by failure to follow the proper ritual. The Calydonian Boar Hunt occurred because Oeneus neglected to include Artemis in his annual sacrifices to the Olympian gods; the slighted goddess incited the monstrous boar to attack the cattle and laborers of Oeneus, generating the memorable events. The troubles of Minos stemmed from his failure to sacrifice the Cretan Bull to Poseidon, and all the woes of Hippolytus sprang from his ignoring due sacrifice to Aphrodite. A clever reversal appears in the myth of Sisyphus who shrewdly advised his wife to omit the obligatory ritual for the dead. Taken before Hades in the underworld, the wily Sisyphus persuaded the god that his wife deserved punishment for her omission; therefore, Hades sent Sisyphus back to earth to compel his wife to perform the necessary ritual. Once back home, Sisyphus shrugged off the orders of Hades about the ritual.

Myth and ritual display significant patterns of relationship:

Ritual preceding myth and resulting in inaccurate myth. The tale of Lady Godiva's naked ride through Coventry probably attempts to explain a quite archaic fertility rite in which nude women rode through a community to bring plenty to the land. Such ritual nudity for fertility persisted in parts of Europe until recent generations. Regularly, in ancient Greek sacrifice the humans ate the flesh of sacrificed animals. In Hesiod the myth of Prometheus making a dupe of Zeus and diverting sacrificial meat to mankind looks like a trumped-up explanation for the practice. In late antiquity the Greeks averred that Zeus had actually seen through the hoax.

Myth preceding ritual and causing ritual. The Pyramid Texts of Egypt indicate that the standard mortuary ritual consisted of verbally treating a mummy as Osiris. The myth of Osiris appears much older than the embalming art, and certainly the application of the ritual to non-royalty is relatively late in dynastic times. The embalming technique caused the representation of Osiris in mummy wrappings.

Ritual remaining while the myth alters. The celebration of Sol Invictus, the unconquerable sun, the newly born luminary, was taken up by Christianity to commemorate the birth of Jesus. The ritual goes on, though the myth changes.

Myth remaining while the ritual alters. Dragon-slaying George has been long celebrated. Perhaps the Perseus legend looms behind the familiar story. Apparently he was worshipped as the god Kresnik among the Slovenes and as Zeus Georgios (probably from an earlier local deity) in Asia Minor.[44] His dragon-killing myth has consistently survived, but he has been demoted to a Christian saint, albeit a highly celebrated saint.

Ritual, but very loosely structured, retelling of myth. The Piaroa of Venezuela disclose a rather primitive bonding of myth and ritual. Their culture bringer Wahari upon death became a tapir. To avoid being forgotten by the people, Wahari created ill-nesses carried by animals and transmitted to the Piaroa should they neglect Wahari's memory. Since the Piaroa depend largely upon meat, they frequently (though not at exact intervals) recount the story of their culture bringer to ward off disease.

Ritual and myth tied together and complementing each other. This combination seems the standard pattern in societies with established priesthoods. Christians witness this bonding in the Easter ritual which always retells the story of Christ's resur-rection and in medieval times accompanied ritual and myth with dramatization.

Etiological myth accompanying ritual. General among many archaic societies i⌐ the belief that to establish the origin of something will mean control. Hence in Mesopotamia the ritual for treating tooth-ache started with the recital of the myth about the origin of the worm supposed to inflict toothache. In larger fashion in ancient Mesopotamia was the solemn recitation of the creation myth Enuma Elish by priests to precede rites of the New Year. The telling of the creation story reproduced the beginn-ing, just as the New Year meant a fresh beginning.

Myth as metaphor in ritual. The ancient Semitic poem, The Marriage of the Moon-god, describing his nuptials with the goddess Nikkal, was regularly sung by professional women singers at human weddings. The mortal bride and groom were not interpreted as themselves divine, but here certainly were richly appropriate mood music and narrative.

265

Ritual as metaphor of myth. In the spring festival of Xipe Totec among the Aztecs a man was slain, his skin flayed and donned by a priest to symbolize earth's renewal. The traditional stone head of Xipe Totec represents the god with a cowl of human skin, in emulation of a snake sloughing off old skin and putting on new skin. Such is an archaic concept of taking a metaphoric statement quite literally.

Myth and ritual tied to age groups. We are quite familiar with myth-and-ritual conducted by and for adults, and with myth-and-ritual conducted or supervised by adults for children. Children may have their own myth-and-ritual divorced from adults. In parts of Bengal children from 5 to 12 years of age venerate Jamburi with no adults participating or watching. Each day a crude clay figure is molded with a hint of mouth and eyes but without limbs. The tale of Jamburi concerns a girl without hands or feet who nevertheless accomplishes many things because she wills to achieve. The lesson is that we must endure the inescapable.

Myth and ritual persist together though reduced to folklore and are no longer understood. The children's game of London Bridge probably derives from the ancient sacrificial rites in conjunction with bridge foundation.

Scrutinizers of myth from the ancients onward have always recognized the parallelism of myth and ritual[45] as in the Eleusinian Mysteries, centered in the Demeter-Persephone account, but the great majority of myths have generally appeared separate from specific rituals. Before the end of the 19th century, however, D.G. Brinton[46] was asserting that myth, long germinating in human minds and stories, eventually produced the tribal rituals. The moderating position was stated by Wilhelm Wundt[47] in 1900; he enunciated the firm linkage of myth and ritual without committing himself to the hen-or-the-egg problem of which takes precedent. Wundt insisted that the close relationship of myth-and-ritual meant an identity or the constant play of one upon the other. Probably no student of the subject today would fundamentally object to the Wundt position, and myth-and-ritual can no longer be treated as wholly separate categories. More recently Leach has suggested that myth and ritual are different forms of communication conveying the same message; both he feels are symbolic, cryptic assertions about the social structure.[48]

While the close tie-in of myth-and-ritual is generally recognized, there are puzzling variations. A scrutiny of A.B. Cook's exhaustive _Zeus_ will reveal the ritual commemoration of virtually the whole range of myths about Zeus, but there were extremely few Greek rituals involving Ares, although Ares is often mentioned in ancient myth. The central Eskimos and many tribes of Africa and Australia have ritual analogues for virtually every detail of their myth. The Mohave Amerindians, however, have an extremely extensive and complex mythology and almost no ritual whatsoever. Myth-and-ritual proponents explain such gaps as resulting from cultural change separating myth from its earlier bond with ritual. The situation seems best summarized: Myth I is by consensus linked to ritual, but Myth II, III, IV have almost altogether split from ritual.

The most extensive controversy in the discussion of ritual and myth has arisen from the contentions of the so-called Cambridge School, composed for the most part of anthropologists, classicists, and Middle East specialists at Cambridge University. As early as 1889 William Robertson Smith[49] had declared that myth is an offshoot or projection of ritual. Subsequent Cantab dons like Frazer leaned towards Smith's position, but it remained for Jane Harrison in _Themis_ (1912) to establish firmly the theory of ritual origin of myth. Harrison pointed out, for example, the ritual for the dismemberment of the sacred child and his subsequent reassembly; the ritual persists whether the sacred child is Zagreus, Zeus, or Dionysus. Myth, she declared, consisted of the narrative accompanying the ritual action. First was the act, then came the word.

Harrison based her theory chiefly upon Greek myth. Samuel H. Hooke, perhaps the best balanced and best known of the Ritualists, worked with the mythology of the Middle East. In discussing myth Hooke places ritual myth first and suggests that it probably was the earliest kind of myth,[50] but he recognizes other divisions of mythology and the possibility of myth developing independently of ritual. In the Middle East, Hooke found these basic myths-and-rituals: death and resurrection of the god, myth of creation, ritual combat with the victory of the god over enemies, sacred marriage, triumphal procession.[51]

The following discussion considers basic myths-and-rituals according to Ritualists. Consult the index for treatment elsewhere of death-and-resurrection and other themes.

The union of a god and goddess was believed to assure or restore the fertility of earth, herds, and humans. The Murray Islanders off New Guinea say that the marriage of their culture bringer Sido to Pekai produced all the plants. Royalty quite logically was paired with divinity to insure tribal prosperity. Early Hindu kings were married to Lakshmi (in addition to their mortal wives, for polygamy was accepted), thus espousing fertility and fortune. In the early monarchical period of Athens the queen was annually married to Dionysus, the fertility god. The lower orders of all societies celebrated the betrothal ritual to formalize matings, while the solemn marriage ritual was apparently reserved only for royalty at the outset. Graciously and shrewdly monarchs began to honor generals and high-ranking officials by letting them share in the sacred marriage rite, and Alexander the Great included many of his soldiers in weddings to Persian women when the world-conqueror married the Persian princess, Barsine. When the professional women singers sang The Marriage of the Moon-god at private Semitic weddings the ritual and its metaphor of sacred marriage had been extended to the general public.

One of the origins of the drama is the ritual enactment of the contest of the tribal god (or pharaoh, the living god of Egypt) with the enemies of the tribe. A very old form of this ritual portrays Indra slaying the primal dragon; this reënactment was the main mythic event of early Vedic society. Later the ritual depicts a conflict with military opponents. Probably team sports have also started from this ritual. Here shines the theme of countless myths, endless stories and movies: after heart-stopping vicissitudes our god conclusively overwhelms our enemies, the good vanquishes the evil. The early Yahweh of the Hebrews was a powerful war god who quite literally smote the enemies of Israel hip and thigh. Egyptian monuments monotonously depict a colossal-sized pharaoh uniformly inflicting ignominious defeat upon the foes of Egypt.

Perhaps the earliest form of the procession was conducting a sacred animal, especially the tribal totem, through the tribal settlement and to each residence. This is social communion and affirmation of communal solidarity centered about a sacred object. Most of all, every procession, every parade, is a vibrant symbol of life and movement; by its organization and ritual progress it especially emblemizes the order and meaning of life. Even the most blasé of modern sophisticates can be interested, even excited, by the implicit symbolism of the parade. How much more gripping when the statue of the god or the monarch himself moved triumphantly in the procession. Even a funeral procession is not the exception it appears, for its discipline and structure are negations of death's shapelessness and anarchy. The great procession for Osiris in ancient Egypt is somber mourning, but it turns to joyful assurance in recognizing the god's resurrection in grain and in the Nile. Military manuals worldwide prescribe slow march and funereal music; with the conclusion of proper obsequies, the troops are everywhere to be marched out at normal pace with a lively air. The basic assertion of the procession is the vigorous forward thrust of life.

Lord Raglan[52] was the most extreme Ritualist, asserting categorically that myth is "simply a narrative associated with a rite."[53] Lord Raglan was unwilling to consider any myth as separate from ritual. In The Origins of Religion (1949) he predicated these basic tribal rituals: symbolic destruction of the old world by catastrophe, killing of the sacred king (or surrogate), dismemberment of victim and communion or fertilization of the earth, forming of images from combination of earth with blood or other moistener, vivification of images, sacred marriage.[54]

Baron Cuvier in the 18th century seemed the epitome of scientific rationalism in his theory of successive catastrophes to account for the different eras of geology. Actually, he was enunciating a mythic concept of immemorial antiquity. Many myths of universal flood or other general annihilation may not refer to any physical event at all; instead they may be impressive symbols for the end of one era and the start of another. The catastrophe is conceived as the means of wiping the slate clean for a fresh start. Numerous S. Amerindian myths frequently display this pattern. The human experience of life indicates that the world is a continuum, but the myth of man must dramatize an end as sensed by the mind of man and a new beginning as man believes it.

The prophets of doom have long predicted that

the end of the world is imminent,[55] and eventually the gloomy eschatologists may hit the target. Nonetheless there seems something almost pathological about the countless mythical prophesies of universal destruction, when the world somehow continues its diurnal rounds and somehow imperiled humanity survives. As every human life inevitably has its sharp cut-off, man must assert the same of the cosmos. Fire, ice, flood, and earthquake were the traditional catastrophe myths; contemporary myth predicts even more horrendous disaster in nuclear explosion, oxygen exhaustion, "greenhouse" effect, suicidal population increase, fatal pollution of air or soil or water, and so on.

To modern man a painting or statue is artistic, commemorative, or (under religious auspices) a help to devotion. Undoubtedly the original purpose of representation was magical, and magic suggests that the likeness of an object or action will merge with reality or even be reality. Probably the "Dancing Sorcerer" of Trois Frères cave is an attempt to freeze and hold permanently an especially potent dance. The archaic mind will recognize the picture as the act, the picture embodying the power of the action. While some remarkable rock formations resembling animal or human features may have inspired images, it is more likely that images arose from the hands of men. Frazer suggests that images arose from animal skins or pelts stretched upon a frame or stuffed to represent an animal deity.[56] Human handicraft may be an origin, as in S. India today the village potter fashions plain pots acknowledged as symbolic images, aniconic representations of the goddess; a quick swipe of fingers upon the pot to suggest eyes, nose, and mouth then produces an iconic image of the deity. Starting as an aniconic representation, tree trunks have been adorned and worshipped by numerous archaic peoples. Baucis, Philemon, Cyparissus, Daphne, Dryope, Myrrha, Phyllis, as well as the Heliades and Dryads were humans in tree form, according to the Greeks. Scandinavian and other mythologies claim that men and women were first formed from trees. When the Arikena of Brazil state that their god Purá carved human figures from wood and then animated them, it certainly sounds like the process of iconic images from the sculptor's hands. Siberian tribes often affixed the skull of a noted shaman to a wooden trunk.[57] The ancient Taino of the West Indies created <u>zemi</u>, idols of wood or cotton fabric, frequently containing skulls and bones of revered ancestors.[58]

270

Whatever the origin of divine images, the belief is widespread that the god is within his statue. The image of Dionysus was placed in the choicest seat of the Greek amphitheatre to witness the drama, and Greeks believed that thus the god himself was a spectator.[59] In India the appropriate rites will cause the god to take up residence in his statue. As bilocation is a godly privilege, the deity may be elsewhere at the same time that he inhabits the statue. In old-fashioned Chinese popular religion, most worshippers believed in continuous residence by the god in his statue. Others felt that the divinity roamed about freely but entered his statue when he was worshipped; ringing of bells or other ritual would summon the god to inhabit his statue. Proper ritual was also thought to infuse the gods into Egyptian temple statues. The animation of Galatea by Aphrodite, the vivification of statues of Christ or the Virgin or saints in medieval times, and the coming to life of statues in Gothic novels all spring from a very old tradition. Demons may also leap to life in their representations. The Tibetan lama expressly forbade the image of the devilish Pehar in a fresco at the temple of Tshel-tung Th'ang, but the demoniacal Pehar transformed himself into a young assistant to the painter and inserted into the fresco the picture of a monkey with a torch. The monkey came to life as Pehar and set fire to the religious edifice.

The image of the god is therefore treated as the god himself. Indian myth says that, presented to the statue of Vishnu in marriage, Andal was absorbed into the statue! Mirabai, a 16th century Rajput female saint, had a lifelong love affair with Krishna and similarly disappeared into the statue of Krishna. Woe betide the god who, receiving ample attention and offerings, fails to deliver expected benefits! During droughts the statue of the Chinese God of Walls and Moats, responsible for local community welfare, was brought from his temple and fully exposed to the scorching sun until needed rains appeared. Frazer reports extensive manhandling and violence to saints' images in Sicily in 1893 when the Christian saints failed to break a long dry spell.[60]

Some sociologists do not care whether myth or ritual was first, but note, like Lévi-Strauss, that myth is the "conceptual level" and ritual the "level of action."[61] Gaster insists that, contrary to the Ritualists, myth and ritual serve separate functions. The ritual is performed by humans in profane time;

the myth is the idealized performance by the supernaturals in sacred time.[62] Always, of course, there
must be recognition of the close relationship of
ritual and myth. In the Heian period of Japan all of
life, so far as possible, became ritualized; and
myth, and much else, was wholly integrated with
ritual. Imperial China was a manifestation of the
state as a liturgical community, myth and ritual
inextricably tied together. Archaic societies
generally are myth-and-ritual oriented beyond the ken
of modern man. Conversely, there is the all too
frequent ascription of "obscure ritual" to anything
that anthropologists or archeologists cannot explain.[63]

Structuralism

Ritualism has not died, but like an old soldier
it has faded. Many classicists still find virtues in
ritualism, but recent social scientists have tended
to espouse structuralism. The lineal ancestor of the
structural analysis of myth seems to be the Prague
School of Linguistics organized in 1926 with initial
impetus from Nicholas S. Troubetzkoy. Structuralism
in myth study may be attributed to Vladimir J. Propp
in 1928.[64] The Russian group of Vladimir Propp,
Dmitry Segal, and E.M. Meletinskij has consistently
exemplified the basic approach of all structuralism:
attempting to decipher the fundamental meaning and
structure of myth and folklore. In examination of
Russian folktales, the Russian scholars have ascertained a remarkably narrow range of actual plotting
(Propp listed 31 basic events), even though there is
a bewildering variety of names, descriptions,
locales, and so on. From the Prague School developed
structural linguistics, enunciated by Roman Jakobson
in 1956.[65] In turn the most prestigious wing of
structuralism in Western society emerged in 1958 with
"La Geste d' Asdiwal,"[66] an intensive scrutiny by
Lévi-Strauss of a myth from the Tsimshian Amerindians
of the Pacific NW.

Fundamental in all structural approaches to
narrative is the ascertaining of "a chain of relations, a succession of concepts, a system of signi-
fying oppositions distributed on different planes, at
various semantic levels."[67] The "oppositions distributed on different planes" fall into three groups:

Material. With the omnipresent problems of
survival, archaic peoples are concerned with the
concrete and the physical. Obvious contrasts are the

familiar vs. the alien, the good food provider vs. the bad denier of food, security vs. peril.

Mental. Myths of a more sophisticated and self-conscious society will contrast abstractions, concepts, ideas. We certainly encounter classic Greece in Hesiod, for his opposites are dike (justice) and hubris (excess). While archaic society might possibly register such a mental contrast in its intellectually and aesthetically oriented elite, this type of opposites is more likely as Myth II.

Spiritual. An ancient shaman could propose this contrast, but its logical seedbed is a rather advanced society with ample time for contemplation and meditation. India is the prime example for such opposites, positing the eternal and the infinite of the spirit realm against the temporal and limited world of the flesh.

The structuralism of Lévi-Strauss[68] is built upon these four principles:

(1) Remarkable parallelism of mythic plots is worldwide. Functionalism emphasized the differences of one culture from another, while structuralism emphasizes the similarities. As Propp demonstrated, beneath a bewildering variety of details stands a remarkably stark pattern of a relatively few basic conflicts. Whatever the genesis of individual myths, time has apparently hammered almost all down to the fundamental concern of every archaic society.

(2) Myths must be interpreted serially to understand any specific social group. Meaning is not revealed fully in any single story, and the total meaning will exceed the sum of individual myths. Humanists, especially, pick and choose carefully, concentrating upon the myths that appeal to them.[69] Structuralists insist upon a complete examination of the entire mythical corpus of any people without selection for literary or moral value. Structuralism also insists upon examination of every version of the myth. Quite frequently past theorists about mythology would search to find the earliest version, or, most often, the version that supported their viewpoints.

(3) Myths can be analyzed into pairs of opposites. The electrical circuitry of the human brain, like radar, operates on opposites. While ultraconscious man may in story creation today be able to minimize or possibly even eliminate these natural op-
273

posites, Myth I will always be structured in opposites. Structuralism rests its basic case upon the
presence of such opposites in every myth, either:

(a) Wholly contrasted opposites such as: night-
day, pure-polluted, order-chaos.

(b) Opposite positions about one object or idea:
overstressing of kinship vs. minimizing of kinship,
overvaluing of conformity vs. devaluing of conformity. The structural analysis can prove discon-
certing. When Lévi-Strauss tots up the opposites on
the Oedipus myth, he finds the meaning of the myth to
be the failure of a society that considers humanity
autochthonous to accept birth from male-female
union.[70]

(4) Conflict or tension is resolved or mediated
in a reconciliation of the opposites (of course, a
stubborn contradiction can hardly be reconciled).
Lévi-Strauss therefore interprets all myth as a try
at problem-solving. Faced with the baffling and
frequently ambiguous choices of life, man attempts in
myth to obtain adjustment to the world, his fellows,
and himself.[71] Lévi-Strauss thus explains the
problem disturbing some anthropologists: why are
archaic societies often quite realistic in reporting
current events but bizarrely mythical in reporting
events of the past? The present is individually
pragmatic; the past (or future) is collectively
appraised by archaic peoples for the solutions to
general and universal questions. Myth, as the structuralists study it, is the great repository of man's
philosophical and speculative thought, his would-be
answers to the great riddles of life.

Structuralism interprets god as necessary in the
scheme of opposites; god, the anti-man, is posited in
the mind as the antithesis of man. As society
becomes increasingly self-conscious and sophisticated, anti-man, god, becomes more complex and enigmatic. While intellectually logical, god, as the
complete antithesis of man, proves unsatisfying
emotionally. Structuralists are understandably
preoccupied with the in-between figures, the intermediaries such as deities in human flesh, for such
are notably sought by mankind as reconcilers. Often
an intermediary may become a major worship figure; in
practice, as distinguished from theological theory,
the Virgin Mary engrosses millions of Roman Catholics
beyond any other Christian figure. Monstrous beings,
mixtures of various animals like the Sphinx, and the

multitudes of man-beasts are particularly fascinating intermediaries. All of this middle ground is non-natural, abnormal, scary, holy: traversed by the shaman and visionaries, riddled with tabu, cajoled with ritual, viewed with awe and fear. A key personality of this intermediate area is the sly trickster, apparently a man-beast in origin and certainly an outsider, an anti-establishment figure. As a mediator he departs from order toward chaos, but he permits (and among Amerindians as Creator-Transformer-Culture bringer he forms) a revised, different order to emerge.

Of the four volumes of Introduction to a Science of Mythology by Lévi-Strauss, the most impressive still seems Le Cru et le Cuit (1964).[72] From almost 200 S. Amerindian myths the structuralist examination finds the powerful opposites of the "raw" and the "cooked," the contrast of Nature and human culture. Lévi-Strauss derogates the interpretations of Nature references in myth as allegory, moral instruction, and so forth. The total body of myth of a society he interprets as symbolizing the human mind, establishing categories, parallels, relationships, contrasts; the sum of all is the structure of the mind in its apprehension of the world and life. Man strives for unity and therefore offers a very few basic themes ("raw" vs. "cooked" is such a major theme), constantly repeated, but the extensive replication explores many levels of meaning from the most pragmatic to the most abstract. Analysts of the archaic mind have often deemed it another sort of mind from that of modern man, notably in Lucien Lévy-Bruhl's Les fonctions mentales dans les sociétés inférieures (1910).[73] Lévi-Strauss finds the archaic mind the same as the human mind anywhere today; archaic societies simply use different materials. Just as Durkheim stated early in this century, structuralism finds in myth the basis of science and the substance of philosophy and psychology.[74]

Social scientists and scientists in general have rallied to structuralism, as have many intellectuals. No other approach to myth analysis has seemed so scientific and (perhaps thereby) no other study of myth has proved so adaptable to the modern computer. The structuralist analysis has been applied to multitudes of myths, folklore, even the comic strips.[75] Humanists have occasionally demurred, chiefly on the basis of how the pairs of opposites are perhaps arbitrarily deduced.[76] Perhaps the most telling objection to structuralism comes from the

students of religion. Admitting that all myth involving social and cosmic order (or purported order)
is validly analyzed by structuralism religionists may
nonetheless object that a large amount of "myth in
the context of ecstatic poetry is a revelation of
God,"[77] and hence not measurable by the tools of
structuralism.

Middleton suggests the over-all sociological
view when he states that "society itself is given
meaning and validity by myth,"[78] but structuralism
goes further in seeing myth as the arch revelation of
human mentality.

Chapter IX   Psychology Grapples with Myth
          and Some Mythic Concepts

        Frazer was accused of being a "library anthro-
pologist" rather than a "field anthropologist."
Psychologists have tended to haunt the library to
encounter Myth I. Psychoanalysts have found many
interesting parallels between the dreams plus unconscious life of their patients and Myth II as recorded
in books. Twentieth century emphasis has strongly
shifted from the earlier view of myth as based on
outward objects to a concept of myth as fundamentally
a projection from the mind, and from the earlier
attribution of myth to conscious creativity towards
the contemporary idea of myth as chiefly arising from
the subconscious or unconscious of man. With so
widespread a viewpoint many students of mythology are
now advancing essentially psychological interpretations.[1]

        Myth satisfies psychological needs. Freud
wanted mankind to arrive at 100% reality principle,
facing the facts bluntly and without evasion; but
even he had to admit that no human organism can
achieve that goal. Bald fact and scientific objec-
tivity simply cannot satisfy the diverse requirements
of the psyche, cannot inspire confidence in troubled
or perplexed hearts, and cannot curb fear in the face
of the uncertain and unknown. Science must be supplemented with myth[2] or, as our age remarkably demon-·
strates, science is itself mythologized. Psychology
and mythology are interchangeable.[3]

        Aristotle ascribed a therapeutic value to tragic
drama. Actually, all myth serves the cause of mental
health in communities and in individuals by objec-
tivizing the universal fears and desires of mankind
and working these drives to solution.[4] Myth exhibits
numerous examples of human failure to achieve social
and inner harmony, but almost invariably myth shapes
toward community and personal balance and resolution
(as in the fated house of Atreus). Myth unites the
members of a group, and it unites the disparate and
conflicting elements within the individual.[5]

        Simultaneously, the myth of a community recog-
nizes the multiplicity within each human. The mythic
power of Shelley's Prometheus Unbound in part arises
from the concept of the drama, frankly stated by
Shelley, as taking place within each human; all the
"characters" in this play and all "characters" in

myth are facets of every human psyche.[6] Myth would be less than thorough if its characters failed to range to the extremes of the human psyche--the all-provident, all-loving mother and the blood-chilling voracious monsters of the savage galaxies on the edge of the cosmos. Man is physically and psychically struggling to maintain a steady state, but such a state is actually homeostasis, a median drawn between his oscillations.[7] Man will not measure his own boundaries or delimit his psyche unless in myth he explores the far reaches of the omnibenevolent gods and the foulest demons.[8]

Archaic peoples wisely permit myth-telling only on rare occasions, for myth must surprise and startle. The awareness of mystery, the breathless sense of the sacral, the realization of awesome other possibilities of living and perceiving are conveyed by myth, thus amplifying and diversifying experience. The bizarre, the unexpected, force an "inverse effect," making the listener suddenly cognizant of a world apart from the routine and monotonous. Thus "myth destroys the oppressive finiteness of man."[9]

Notably in heroic myth, but also with many other personalities of myth, listeners gain vicarious satisfaction, working out aggressions and frustrations, finding a solution to personal problems by identification with the figures in mythical narratives.[10] In each culture the totality of the myth corpus should try to provide outlets for all the stresses generated within that culture or normally inflicted upon that culture.[11] The Tangu of Melanesia demonstrated how a culture's myth can provide what its members need when they revised a traditional myth about older and younger brother to proclaim that the difference in status between the native and the white man is unfair and in divine eyes certainly must be rectified.

Etiological myth is no mere end in itself but represents part of mythology's highly significant bestowing of structure and organization upon the world and life. The human mind without such controlling framework would be bewildered and dismayed by the shards and fragments of experience. Myth confers form and meaning for the reassurance and stabilizing of each psyche.[12] Such benefits of myth become apparent only when the entire body of a society's mythology is grasped. Modern man has a quite different Weltanschauung from that of archaic

societies; this is just another way of saying that
our mythology is not the same as that of Amazonian
Amerindians or Papuans.

Perhaps the ultimate psychological basis of myth
is the humanization of the world and the cosmos. Man
does not want to be an alien in a wholly unconscious
world running solely by impersonal laws of physics
and chemistry. Mythology implants human-like characteristics throughout the cosmos, placing conscious
spirits in every nook and crevice of the landscape,
in totemism and animal deities ascribing human-like
nature to the world of life about us, and emblazoning
upon the earth and the heavens the majestic conscious
power of deities. To drop the mythic attitude is to
render modern man a lonely outcast in a puzzling
machine. Hence in "The World Is Too Much with Us"
Wordsworth prefers the confidence, the solidarity,
and the humanized universe of the mythic past. In
our own day the incessant expression of hope for
sentient life elsewhere in the multiverse maintains
the basic mythic urge of mankind.

Myth in specific operation. All the above may
sound impressive to library psychologists, but the
real meaning of myth in human experience becomes
apparent only as we contemplate the actual impact of
myth upon archaic societies. Kluckhohn witnessed
myth recitals in Navaho Amerindian society and
reported their memorable quality to both narrator and
listener. The teller of myth is highly conscious of
his importance and his accomplishment. He gains
considerable social prestige by his memory of the
sacred tales and by his effective performance. Our
storytelling seems pale and withered in comparison.
The reciter of archaic myth is dignified (even in the
occasional descent to jocosity) and formal, setting
himself and his myths quite apart from the routine
world. He displays considerable histrionic ability,
gesticulating and moving about, varying voice
effects, often dramatically. For the narrator his
respected social position and his sense of effective
performance are immensely sustaining to his psyche.

Listeners to myth in archaic society tend far
more than their counterparts in a sophisticated
audience to be energetic, enjoying vigorous participation mystique. Their familiarity with the myth
encourages virtually a choral effect--nodding,
gesturing, sighing, chuckling, groaning, and so
forth. The entire audience is absorbed in one group

reaction, and the whole group psychically follows the rhythm, the rise and fall, of the tale. Myth, perhaps more than any other form of expression in archaic society, is an excellent outlet for emotions, a superb vehicle for the acting out of feelings.[13] The comforting sense of group solidarity and group faith caused one Navaho to say: "Knowing a good story will protect your home and children and property. A myth is just like a big stone foundation--it lasts a long time."[14]

Plumbing the wellsprings of myth. Perhaps perception and imagination are rooted in a common faculty in the human nervous system and were originally identical, as suggested by Hernz Werner.[15] Just consider how motion-picture montage handles a purported automobile crash. Flashed on the screen are unconnected shots: careening vehicles, horrified motorists, screeching brakes, a vertiginous blur wildly swinging around, sickening crash of metal upon metal with after-tinkling of glass. These disparate flashes are conceived of as one event, and, except for the most sophisticated, viewers would claim that they have actually witnessed an automobile collision. The myth-making activity in man, by which imagination organizes and fleshes perception, may therefore be as basic as his powers of observation.

The creativity of the human mind is emphasized by neo-Kantian philosophers, notably Cassirer.[16] The long-potent doctrine of Locke and the powerful behavioristic psychology of our day would treat man as an organism responding to stimuli, but the neo-Kantians, like Kant himself, would construe the human mind as a molding and creative force which forms symbols to interpret sense data. Early man did not merely perceive animals as we might; his mind charged the image of an animal with emotional and magical powers, producing the totem animals, animal deities, and the man-beasts. Mythical thinking is not a quaint aberration but the basic imaginative faculty of humanity in grasping the world and experience. All the cherished feats of the human mind in science, philosophy, and religion are built upon the fundamental symbol-making ability of imaginative, mythical thinking. Cassirer suggests that philosophy and science are concerned with the perception of outward things, but myth is the perception of human expression itself. Science and philosophy try to see things as independent of man, but myth sees the world solely through the human mind.

Adrenalin enables a human physically to surpass himself. Myth is the faculty that enables a human to surpass himself psychically. Eliade[17] points out that myth compels mankind to rise above his normal limitations. Anatomically man has not altered for many, many millenia. Culturally man has immensely changed, and responsible in large part for this change are the self-stimulus and challenge that man has devised for his species through myth.

The play theory of Huizinga[18] suggests that myth, like most human culture, has developed from play. Play, myth, and religion[19] all proffer a symbolic meaning beneath the superficial; all set up a pretended system and then carefully live by its rules. Play is set apart from the mundane by absorption in make-believe or mimicry. All mammals play, and humans are far and away the most play-centered, as an afternoon at the world soccer matches will conclusively reveal. Almost certainly the epitome of mythic play is the lila (sport or play) of Shiva who dances spontaneously, without purpose, with great joy, simply expressing his own instinctive vitality. Thus he maintains the existence of the cosmos and grants rapturous release to his devotees. The 9th century Tamil poet Mānikkavācakar ecstatically celebrated the play of Shiva, play free from all accountability, free from all necessity or compulsion, free from all constraint, free to be limitlessly vivacious and creative. Sober scholars in the Judeo-Christian tradition have always minimized myth and religion as sheer enjoyable entertainment, but any observer of colorful religious festivals and processions cannot ignore the play delight therein.

The myth theory with the greatest number of supporters among psychologists and theorists generally considers myth as wish-fulfilment. Myth and folktales are replete with powerful gods like Zeus and Marduk, puissant heroes like Beowulf or Rama, exquisite beauties like Helen and Lakshmi, sparklingly clever adventurers like the Amerindian Coyote and Odysseus. All these beings display the power and success we earnestly yearn for in ourselves. And the events in myth sparkle with drama and thrills and chills that we would like to experience in our own drab lives. It is possible to deprecate this psychological benefit, defining myth as Larsen does, as "adolescent wish-fulfillment fantasies of the species."[20] More generously one might say with Barthes: "Mythology is in accord with the world not as it is, but as it wants to be."[21]

Psychoanalysis states: a dream is a private myth; a myth is a public dream. Freud considered The Interpretation of Dreams[22] his major work and made the analysis of patients' dreams a central concern of psychoanalysis. Freud deemed the symbol a means by which the forbidden wishes of the unconscious (id) are disguised in order to get by the moral censor (superego). The disguise takes several forms:

Condensation. A number of images or concepts are incorporated into one symbol.

Displacement. Some figure or action unacceptable to the censor is shifted to another figure or action, while still symbolizing the original.

Splitting. An object may be divided into two parts, one part given favorable characteristics, the other unfavorable.

To complicate matters, secondary elaboration when we are awake causes us to give a connected, rather orderly, organization to our frequently chaotic dreams. All these concepts from psychoanalysis suggest the formulation of myth,[23] which among primitives presents somewhat structured narratives of raw violence, sexuality, incest, cannibalism, and similar topics;[24] as civilization increasingly generates restraint, dreams and myths increasingly mask the crudities of the dark unconscious, and the waking mind concocts deceptively plausible and logical plotting.

Freudian theorists claim that the symbols and actions of both dream and myth spring from the early stages of life. As the fetus recapitulates biological evolution, the individual supposedly recapitulates the cultural development of the species.[25] Here is the hypothetical libido dream-and-myth evolution:

(1) Prenatal. Some Freudians push dream-and-myth symbolism to the ultimate. The mystic state which Meister Eckhart, the 13th century German mystic, described as the emptiness preceding existence has been identified with ovum memory. The dream of floating or bobbing on the water has been referred as far back as the ovum between ovulation and fertilization (other theorists would suggest the fetus in the amniotic fluid). The hero's dragon fight has been linked with the struggle of the sper-

matozoon to unite with the ovum, for hormonal resistance must be overpowered. The mother may very well be associated with the resisting "dragon," which often is female. If the dragon (or kindred monster) is male, then frequently the dragon's mother as well as the dragon must be slain, as Grendel and Grendel's dam are both destroyed by Beowulf, and the dragon Virtra and his mother Danu are both killed by Indra in Vedic literature.[26] Psychoanalysts attribute many other mythic themes to the fetus in the womb (such as paradise and unity) and to the birth trauma (night journey, tunnel passage).

(2) Oral stage. More acceptable to most people is the postulation of an initial condition in infancy of demanding nourishment. An infant takes everything into its mouth. From such a stage comes the human metaphor of eating for consumption of any kind: the earth "sucks up" moisture and the flames "devour" the forest. In myth Charybdis, a whirlpool, is treated as a voracious female imbibing anything caught in its swirl. In folktale even a residence is edible, as in the gingerbread cottage of the Hansel and Gretel tale.

(3) Anal state. The infant seems to find pleasure both in retention and in excretion of the feces. The infant apparently feels that in return for mother's milk it gives fecal material. Hainuwele in the myth of Ceram (Moluccas) excretes numerous valuable import objects such as Chinese bowls and boxes. Myth I has a far larger preoccupation with excrement (notably among Amerindians) than the more sanitized Myth II.

(4) Latency period. Freud postulated a period from about 4 or 5 to about 12 years of age during which sexual interest is sublimated. Anthropological observation indicates that this stage is not necessarily universal and varies considerably among different cultures. Freud proposed this period from his experience in European society. Of course, there is ample evidence from many societies of myths about remarkable conceptions without sexual contact, males giving birth, organisms created from earth or wood or other substances asexually. The enormous amount of such accounts certainly seems to limit much myth creation to the concepts of early childhood.

(5) Genital phase. This term does not necessarily mean an obsession with phallus, pudendum, and

coitus. Rather, it means a fully mature affection for one's sexual partner. Myth can celebrate such a phase in the loves of Shiva and Sita, but overall myth is too often immature, as in the casual promiscuities of the Greek gods. We must come to late Myth II, perhaps even beyond proper myth itself, to find depiction of deep affection as applauded by our day. The Greek accounts of Protesilaus-Laodamia and Ceyx-Alcyone form an engaging diptych. In both cases a young husband against his wife's pleadings takes a sea journey to his death, and visions of the dead husband appear in the dreams of each widow. Obviously the ghost of Protesilaus is the sexual dream of Laodamia, and she is condemned to death for mere physical love. Morpheus in the guise of Ceyx appears to Alcyone, and pains are taken to signify that both are gripped by spiritual love, not pure libido. For their permanent and spiritual love Ceyx and Alcyone are transformed into birds, winged angelic creatures free of earth's bondage in comparison to the transient physical bond of Laodamia and Protesilaus.

Mythic thinking

For decades Lucien Lévy-Bruhl through his influential Les fonctions mentales dans les sociétés inférieures (1910) caused Westerners to apply his label of "prelogical" to the thinking of archaic man, the maker of Myth I. The archaic mind, we were to believe, is a different mind altogether from that of historic man. Distinguished as he was, Lévy-Bruhl was strictly an armchair ethnologist, never studying the aborigine out in the field. Anthropologists working extensively with archaic societies in the field report that aborigines have essentially the same mental processes as highly civilized man. Such observations are notable in Franz Boas, The Mind of Primitive Man (1911) and Paul Radin, Primitive Man as Philosopher (1927). We may rightfully assume that in any ethnic group of sufficient numbers there will be about the same amount of human potentialities.[27] Remember that in the age we brand as altogether mythic, mankind effected momentous practical and technological achievements: domesticating animals and plants, harnessing fire, devising numerous specialized tools, shaping pottery, establishing towns and cities, and so forth. Bear in mind also that even to the archaic mind there are many aspects of life beyond the sacred and the mythical. In any group the realm of the conscious will approximate what is culturally known or allowed. Usually the pressure is implicit, unstated; but when Galileo incautiously spoke against his society's cosmogonic myth, he was silenced summarily. What a group culturally disallows or simply does not know will either be absent from group members or will be found in their unconscious. All this means that the archaic mind is not one whit inferior to the civilized mind and that the archaic mind actually contains all the possibilities of the civilized mind. However, cultural conditions compel the manifestations which make the archaic mind appear strange to us[28] and which produce myth:

(1) Unity. Analysis is familiar to us, but the archaic mind seeks to synthesize, forming the world into an organic whole. James Lovelock, Gaia (1979) sees all earth and all upon this planet as one; he must use the name of the ancient earth goddess, for millenia ago archaic man so conceived of this unity.[29]

(2) Association. Resemblance or any sort of analogy means relationship, even identity, to the archaic mind. This association is cultural and will produce extraordinary, even unique, pairings. The Egyptian sun-god Re is represented with a falcon head probably because in that cloudless hot land the falcon tended to be airborne at sunrise and sunset. Amerindians associated the eagle with thunder (thunderbird), and the Crow tribe had the interesting association of tobacco with the stars. Ancient Mexican women wore shells of the sea-snail so that their children might glide forth from the womb as easily as the snail from its shell.

(3) Part for the whole (pars pro toto). Moderns are as guilty of this practice as archaic people ("The French are highly volatile; I knew a Frenchman once"). Frequently diviners ascertain that drought, flood, and other disasters have afflicted an entire people because one tribe member violated a tabu. The sin of one is visited upon the entire group. Conversely, as a scapegoat one member of the group bears the sins of the entire group.

Another aspect of this same concept means the substitution of a part of an object or person for the whole. Human sacrifice seems widespread in prehistoric times. A substitution seems likely in the ritual cutting of the hair of Achilles for Patroclus, the hair being appropriate as the head is seat of the soul. The self-castration by the priests of Cybele is such a _pars pro toto_, since destroying the powers of generation was symbolic of giving up one's life altogether. The self-blinding of Oedipus may carry the same weight.

(4) Touch, even sight, will transfer potency and power as evidenced in the concept of mana. The laying-on of hands is necessary in consecration of a bishop, and an English policeman must touch the shoulder to make arrest formal. Healing and cursing are accomplishments of touch. The evil-eye can affect likewise, notably with the Medusa's head.

(5) Wearing garb or mask means an actual transformation. _The Book of the Dead_ of ancient Egypt depicts human figures with animal or bird heads, probably masked priests who to early viewers were indeed the actual supernatural beings. To Australian aborigines the bull-roarer is truly the god himself.

(6) The deed can be substituted for the thought. We would call this acting out a figure of speech, strikingly revealed in the Japanese account of the ruffian god Susa-no-wo. A divine council compelled him to present objects emblemizing his misdeeds. These objects were hurled into the sea, thus carrying off all the sins of Susa-no-wo. Similar practices have been worldwide and may be Hebraic in "all our sins will be cast into the depths of the sea" (Micah 7:19).

(7) The world is viewed as static or cyclic. All the meaningful changes supposedly occurred in the Dreamtime, in the Age of the Gods, in the days of the culture bringer. Then were established all things, and ever shall it be. There is nothing new. All supposed or apparent change is simply renewal of the original condition _in illo tempere_. Any inescapable innovation is treated as merely making explicit what has been implicit from the very beginning. The circular theory of history is still dominant in Plato.

Of course, the archaic mind was all too sadly familiar with mortality, for death was omnipresent; but the archaic mind could not conceive of Nothing, Non-existence. The archaic mind recognized the change of form as seeds sprout into stalks of trees and plants; hence it felt deeply the cyclic pattern in life and Nature. Many peoples worldwide assume a limited supply of human souls, ceaselessly moving

from the dead to the newly born. There is no beginning nor ending. Death and birth are simply the passing back and forth of life through a curtain or veil.
Such a view puts a brake upon recognition of full
human sexuality, since the major consideration in
birth is the transmission of an ancestral soul.

(8) Nothing works automatically. Infants are
not by nature part of the family or tribe, but must
by proper rites be incorporated. Boys are made men,
and girls must be transformed into women by tribal
action. It even requires proper tribal ceremonies to
install the dead in the tribe eternal. All the
phenomena of Nature follow the caprice of wilful
spirits who must be aroused, attuned, cajoled, propitiated, stimulated and directed constantly and
regularly. Mistakenly, we often sigh for the sim-
plicities of archaic peoples, when they might envy
our simplicity, uncomplicated by the countless tabus,
rituals, and required observances of traditional
societies.

(9) Reality to the archaic mind is not the
sensate world about us but the repetition or imitation of some primal example. Traditional societies
thereby cherish a certainty and security of mind no
longer possible to modern man. It is infuriating and
incredible to a modern agronomist to demonstrate
scientific agricultural techniques to an archaic
society, conclusively proving that higher, better
yields will result. The natives will be polite, may
even perform as taught, for they are as intelligent
as anyone; then they return to the old, woefully
inefficient but time-honored ways, ordained by culture-bringers and the immemorial gods. Actually it
is really something of a miracle that our open,
unbounded society came into existence, defying the
treasured pattern of archaic man.

(10) Archaic man is a being who lives by symbol.
Perhaps it is more accurate to say that man is fundamentally a creature of symbol. Piaget sees children
as developing symbology as early as 18 months and
employing symbols in play even before socializing in
play.[30] Multitudes of myths are metaphors, as the
story of Phaëthon is a narration of the statement,
"high-flying youth gets his wings singed." Munz
defines myth as extended metaphor.[31]

Consciously chosen figurative language and thought are "emblems" according to Ernest Jones, while the term "symbol," he asserts, should be reserved exclusively for unconscious analogy. Such terminology has not been universally accepted. Jones also indicates that the total number of unconscious ideas is relatively small.[32]

In psychoanalysis and analytical psychology there is agreement that the symbols of dream and myth come from the unconscious, but there are two opposing schools. The Freudian approach interprets the symbol as a generalization from a particular: e.g., pits, caves, apertures, hollows in Nature and man-made boxes, pots, bottles, valises, rooms all symbolize the womb. Jungian interpretation takes the opposite tack, regarding the symbol as the particularization of a general concept. The womb is the womb of the Great Mother, the symbol of eternal fertility and nourishing care. Any woman in dream and myth is the symbol of Woman, of womanhood, womankind. The Freudian concept of symbols is therefore tied to outward stimuli, the specific impact of the sensual world upon the human mind, and there is a point-to-point analogy consistently sought. Thus any erect or pointed object such as tree, pillar, spear, sword, needle, pin is equated with the phallus. The Jungian viewpoint finds the ultimate basis of symbols within the psyche, and a symbol is representing not a thing but an attitude. Hence any symbolizing of the male represents law and authority (both protective and repressive), the assurance of stable rule and protection, all in the Father image. This chapter will consider the essentially Freudian position about symbols, while Chapter X will consider symbols from the Jungian stance, although, of course, total separation is impossible.

Examples of Freudian symbols for specific body parts. The theory behind head-hunting seems pars pro toto. As the head is the seat of much sensation, especially eyesight, it is deemed the seat of the soul. Heads or skulls displayed in a village or about a residence will chase off hostile spirits and also assure more births as the souls of the dead enter females in order to be reborn.[33] Freudians also interpret the head, tongue, and teeth as phallic. The Pelasgians, pre-Hellenic peoples of Greece, explained their origin from the teeth of

Ophion, the great world-serpent. The dragon's teeth sown by Cadmus produced armed men. Archaic necklaces and bracelets were strings of teeth, supposedly laden with life and vitality. Losing a tooth symbolizes the loss of a relative.[34] The knocking out of a tooth at male initiation rites is deemed the adult man's hostility towards the virile young male. Among some peoples a tooth is removed from a boy's left side to make him a man, and a tooth is taken from the right side of a girl's mouth to remove male qualities from her.[35] The Kenyahs of Borneo assert that old stone axes found in their fields are the fallen teeth of their thunder-god Balingo. The hair of Samson has been equated with the sun's rays especially by interpreting Samson as Shamish, a Semitic sun-god. Hair is certainly equated with sexuality as beauty queens prove with a proud sweep of their manes. In general folk belief hair signifies strength and vitality. Shaving of harlots' heads is to negate their sexuality, and the shaving of witches' heads to remove their malevolent power. Nisus, king of Megara, owed his strength to a purple or golden hair in the middle of his forehead. Scylla, daughter of Nisus fell in love with Minos of Crete and pulled the magic hair from her father's head to betray him to Minos. Mourning practices reveal our feeling of guilt that we live when worthy folk die. The assaults by mourners upon their hair, disheveled (Leviticus 10:6), tearing (Ezra 9:3), or complete cutting off (Amos 8:10) are to torture a symbol of our vitality; Freudians see it as a castration complex.[36]

Female breasts have always been a symbol of fertility and nutriment. Undulating landscape has always been associated with the fertile Mother Earth, and numerous hills worldwide have been named Sleeping Woman Mountain or have simply been deemed feminine. The Neolithic sanctuary at Çatal Hüyük was adorned with a frieze of plaster breasts suggestive of the classic Diana of Ephesus, a multi-breasted female. The breast was a symbol of Isis, and Egyptian pharaohs are pictorially represented as suckled by goddesses. A statue of Astarte in Spain instead of nipples had holes through which liquid might flow into a bowl held by the goddess. Figurines of Mesopotamian, Canaanite, Hittite, and Aegean goddesses show them offering their breasts. Luke 11:27 contains a blessing upon the breasts of the Virgin Mary.

Psychoanalysts believe the male semen is symbolized in all fluids bestowing life and restoring youth. Rain is obvious, and many myths deem precipitation the semen of a rain-god to fertilize Mother Earth. The magical fluids of man's making--soma, mead, nectar, alcoholic beverages generally--are considered symbols of semen. Further, all forms of treasure, gold, silver, coins, jewels, riches generally, are termed symbols of semen. By such an interpretation it was semen that was responsible for the entire bloody cycle of the treasure of the Nibelungs.

Note how the psychoanalytic emphasis is largely sexual, causing moralistic folk to brand Freud as a "dirty old man." His insistence was that the major human drives were self-preservation and continuance of the species. The first drive, he felt, is relatively above board almost everywhere, but sexuality, he believed, was so hedged with tabus and guilts and misconceptions that it was the major source of symbolizing, overt sexuality being repressed only to flower in the potent dream-and-myth symbols of the unconscious. Societies, however, vary greatly, and Freud's patients almost entirely came from European society, one of the most sexually restrictive of all human societies. It would be unwise to insist that all of these symbols are identical in all cultures.

If the Freudian belief is correct, dream-and-myth symbolism is almost painfully monotonous.[37] In addition to the womb symbols above, ships, houses, shoes, gardens, villages are also suggested as symbolizing the pudendum; besides the phallic symbols above, the penis is supposedly symbolized as snake, rat, lizard (even hat, hood, cloak stand for the prepuce and by pars pro toto for the entire penis). Ernest Jones declared that there were relatively few basic objects behind all the symbols. Such repetitious symbolizing portends a relatively poverty-stricken human unconscious.

The upsurge of the id. Freud offers extensive myth material in the dramatic form and theme of unconscious impulses. Freud divided every human psyche into three parts: ego (Latin=I), the conscious element; superego (Latin=upon the self), the censor built into each human to enforce social conformity; and id (Latin=it), the unconscious. Róheim denies the older theory that culture is generated by ideals (i.e. the superego) and also contradicts the

Marxian contention that culture is produced by economic conditions (i.e. the ego); he insists that culture arises from the unconscious (i.e. the id). From
the id emerge the great basic themes by which men
live and act, and as the cultural condition alters,
from the id arise impulses that permit man adaptation
to a changed world.[38]

Freud placed enormous emphasis upon the Oedipal
complex, the desire of the young male to slay the
father and marry the mother. Freud declared that
"the beginnings of religion, morals, society and art
converge in the Oedipus complex."[39] Late in the last
century the noted psychoanalyst discovered in his
neurotic patients a considerable hostility to the
parent of the same sex and incestuous cravings toward
the parent of the opposite sex (the Elektra complex
is the female desire to slay the mother and wed the
father). Freud enunciated the concept of the Oedipal
complex in 1900;[40] Róheim, a widely experienced field
anthropologist, declared in 1950 that every culture
known to us displays the Oedipus complex.[41] Malinowski suggested that mother-son and father-daughter
incest is distinctly characteristic of a patrilineal
society, while brother-sister incest is more true of
a matrilineal society.[42]

Freud postulated an original human social
pattern quite different from the present family. One
alpha male dominated a host of women and children.
In the "old man" of this group, Freud suggests,
originated the idea of god. A boy reaching puberty
had to fight the "old man" for access to the women,
or much more likely, he fled to the wilderness to
gain strength and cunning. A bunch of young men
finally ganged up on the "old man," killed, and ate
him. The women were now theirs, but the youths
realized that ceaseless internecine violence would
result from their rivalry for women of the group; so
they agreed to take spouses from outside the group.
The imprint of this episode is bequeathed to all
subsequent humanity.[43]

The Oedipal complex is thus accounted for, plus
perhaps too much else. The first cannibal feast is
explained as well as the origins of god and exogamy.
Freud's theorizing is quite challengeable. While
some of the primates have social patterns such as
Freud hypothecated, others, like gorillas, follow the
modern human pattern of couple plus offspring. Freud
realizes that the women of the primal group are

collectively the "mothers," but he altogether assumes a patriarchal society and ignores all possibilities of the matrilineal and the matrilocal. The entire episode is first dominated by instinctual thought and behavior but ends surprizing in a rational conclave. Other and quite cogent conjectures have been proposed for the origin of gods, cannibalism, and exogamy. Perhaps the shakiest part of the concept is the "imprint." Freud ascribed to this episode a persistent guilt complex haunting humanity down to the present. But orthodox psychology since John Locke has denied such inherited psychological bents to the mind, opposing the whole concept of innate ideas. More recent theorists such as Karen Horney, Ian Suttie, and Alfred Adler have hypothecated that the Oedipal complex is indeed universal but not from any inherited imprint. Every child receives unwitting sexual stimulation from parents and also unintentionally is aroused to hostility towards parents (frequently one parent purposely or unintentionally encourages a child's antipathy towards the other parent).

Nature mythologists of the 19th century could charmingly explain Oedipus as the solar hero who slew his father, darkness, and lay with his mother, the dawn. Just like the setting sun he dies blinded. Unfortunately, worldwide myth offers the Oedipal story without any such celestial beauties but with frightening agony of the spirit. Christian legend has interestingly employed the theme unfavorably in the case of Judas Iscariot and favorably in the case of Gregory the Great who, according to Hartmann von Aue, was the child of incest, was exposed with his mother in a box at sea (cf. Perseus and Danaë), was saved to become a Christian knight, unknowingly received his mother's hand for his prowess, did penance for 17 years on a rocky shoal, and finally by divine command was made pope.

Hatred instead of love may be directed at the parent of the opposite sex. Myth is replete with young women who betray their fathers, as did Medea; however, the usual explanation posits not hostility to the father but affection for a young male stranger. Young men slay their own mothers as Orestes killed Clytemnestra and Alcmaeon killed Eriphyle. In both cases the youths are supposedly compelled to destroy "sinful" mothers, only to suffer terrible torments of conscience. Perhaps the vicious hate in the young men's hearts is attributed by them to their mothers, whom they then in attempted self-exculpation brand as sinners.

Freud first advanced the term Narcissism in 1914 to refer then only to the concept of sexual self-love. The label comes from the Greek youth who fell in love with his own image (and, of course, with his own body), thereafter pointedly ignoring any female. Recent psychoanalysts find Narcissism more complex and displaying elements not necessarily self-erotic. Children are reported as normally Narcissistic before reaching out for love from those their own age. Before one can love another or be loved, one must have a strong perception of oneself as truly lovable.[44] Only when an adult is unable to shake off Narcissism is the tendency malign. Nature mythologists like Friedrich Wieseler[45] of the 19th century claimed that the myth merely describes the plant: the narcissus grows along pools and springs, often bending over the water like the youth peering at his own image; the plant has both sexual and asexual reproduction, the Greeks familiar with only its bulb method; the plant is poisonous (Pliny thought the name related to narcotic); and the narcissus looks good to the eye but has an unattractive smell. As frequently in myth, there are convincing cases for both outward and inward explanation.

Psychoanalysts suggest that the inner desire for one's own omnipotence produces the heroic myth. If our unconscious cannot shake off the fact that we are lesser beings, then we summon forth, from within, the Father or authority figure as an omnipotent and benevolent deity to provide the security and prosperity we non-heroic creatures cannot win for ourselves. Our dread of failure and punishment summons from within the wrathful deities and demoniacal tempters or torturers; there is, of course, some relief in blaming outside and independent agents for our own shortcomings. Accounts of monumental disasters and destruction such as The Great Flood and the obliteration of Sodom and Gomorrah may be wholly imaginary products of the psyche's fears. The specific fears of starvation and sterility generate the death-and-resurrection theme. The childish query, "Where do babies come from?" is deemed the cause of all etiological myths. Such is not genuine intellectual curiosity but the demand of the unconscious to support the life impulse. Towards all myth Freudianism is fundamentally condemnatory, for Freud wants mankind to accept the Reality Principle instead of fleeing to the Pleasure Principle, thus evading unpleasant truth. Freudians perceive the classic example in the Oedipus story. Oedipus is earnestly pushing and prodding to find the full facts (Reality Principle), but Jocasta, sensing the dark horrors ahead, urges him to ignore his search and simply enjoy his good fortune in Thebes (i.e. accept the Pleasure Principle). "Grow up" is the Freudian imperative. "Get over this infantile imagining, jettison myth in favor of reality, and be adults."

Psychology of some mythic concepts

The Word. "In the beginning was the Word, and the Word was with God, and the Word was God" (John 1:1) has generated extensive philosophizing from ancient Greek and subsequent philosophers, but its origin is immemorial myth. For example, the Dogon of Mali and the Witoto S. Amerindians state the same concept, apparently without any influence from Christianity. The archaic mind believes that the word is an integral part of identity. The archaic mind conceives of the object when it is named, and by projection into the outer world sees the name and the thing as the same. Egyptian myth has Thoth, self-created and existing in chaos, speak; every word then becomes the thing it signifies, thus starting creation. A Yoruba proverb states: "Whatever we have a word for, that is."[46] All men can be terrified of the unknown and are better able to face the named and the described even in its abysmal horror, but the Yoruba viewpoint, shared by other archaic peoples, denies the very existence of the nameless. A possible meaning of Brahmā is "word" or "speech" and therefore anything manifest, created, existent. From such a concept could develop the idea of Brahmā as transcendental reality. In the Rigveda Vak is sacred speech, the Word; she is the shaper of all forms to be. Ptah, Ea, Yahweh could all create simply by power of the word.

Uttering a name, according to ancient belief, has the force of a summons. Hence the refusal to name the dead or the demonic except in euphemism, for naming would summon the spirits. By ritually conferring the name of a dead man upon his statue, that statue henceforth was the residence of his soul, according to Egyptians. The same concept makes the statue of a god the residence of the god. Supernatural beings are invoked by name, and such direct address (by qualified invokers) has the magical power of compelling the spirits to appear and perform.

The immense potency of the Word is indicated by the ability of Ea of Mesopotamia to slay Apsu solely "with his word," apparently a powerful spell. The Babylonian gods tested Marduk by depositing a garment in front of him. By the mere power of his words Marduk caused the garment to disintegrate and then recalled it to existence. Magic is rare in Homer, but when Odysseus was gored by a wild boar, incantation caused healing (Odyssey, XIX, 457).[47] Amerindians of Oregon believe that "talking doctors" cure ailments by smoking tobacco, then reciting the myth of creation to dismiss the illness.[48]

Since all men sense the excruciating drama in human execution, the last words from someone dying violently are deemed momentous. Men by projection then assume that the gods must accept and implement a dying curse. Iphigenia was thus gagged to prevent any words from her as she was sacrificed on the altar at Aulis. Both Clytemnestra and Eriphyle in dying cursed their matricidal sons with profound consequences. Cursing may seem only an emotional escape valve to us, but, with his identification of word and thing, archaic man believed that the words would actually effect the desired actions. Egyptians believed that cursing a man by name might destroy his soul. Cairbre, an ancient Irish poet, cursed Bres for niggardly hospitality; thereafter, Bres "decayed" pathetically.

Obviously the process of initial naming of a person must be absolutely precise, since a person is incomplete and imperiled if naming is flawed. Note the archaic reasoning: weak naming, weak life. As the Polynesian Maui was being named, Tangaroa accidentally left out one of the names of Maui. This omission was the loophole by which enemy deities eventually destroyed Maui.

Control of a name means control of the being. This archaic concept lies behind the concealment of a deity's name, although ancient Hebrews claimed that the tabu was to prevent irreverence. Among the Narrinyeri of SE Australia hunters lift weapons skyward to symbolize allegiance to Biambun, but the god's name is never uttered except at the solemn ceremonies involving only initiated devotees. Thus, unauthorized and hostile folk cannot invoke Biambun when they do not know his name. Similarly, to know a man's name is to have power over him. This practice is familiar in the romance of Lohengrin and in the folktale of Rumpelstiltskin; in both, the name of the central character is zealously concealed. Hence many archaic groups and the ancient Egyptians and Brahmans have a pair of names, a public name and a secret "true" name known only to the immediate family. Some societies will reveal no name to an outsider. When an Araucanian S. Amerindian is asked his name by a stranger, he answers, "I have none." Perhaps this pattern was behind Odysseus' shouting to Polyphemus that his name was "No-man."

Punning to us is an attempt at wit, intended today as humorous. Term it paranomasia, however, and you refer to a literary embellishment divorced from humor. John Milton had extremely little sense of humor, but he soberly employed paranomasia. Still further back lies the mythic identification when by coincidence two quite different objects bore designations that were homonyms. Buried too far back in Egyptian language and myth to reveal origins and indebtedness, the words for "father" and "grain" were the same in sound (like English to, too, and two). In the Osiris rites Horus pleads, "Thrash my sire (grain) no more."[49] Such punning may indeed have made Max Müller's linguistic theory valid for some mythic creations.

Cannibalism. Examples of cannibalism occur among insects, but among other animals it is rare, even in times of extreme food scarcity. Primates are not known to be cannibalistic, though some classes of monkeys will occasionally devour other monkey species. The remains of Peking man, c. 400,000 B.C., indicate cannibalism with human skulls and bones treated in the same fashion as other edible animals. Today cannibalism is known only among agrarian peoples, not in food-gathering or hunting societies.[50] Mankind overwhelmingly claims to find cannibalism repulsive, but sophisticated society snickeringly jokes and jests rather extensively about the eating of human flesh. Apparently man has practiced cannibalism not from any natural proclivity but from psychological urgings toward the forbidden and the exceptional. Many accounts of cannibalism in myth are probably of psychological origin and do not refer to actual eating of human flesh. The tangled web of cannibalism seems thus:

(1) Food cannibalism. In historic times the most extensive eating of human flesh occurred in pre-Columbian Central America. This area had a

minimum of protein-supplying animals (few domestic animals until the Conquistadores, while the buffalo and other food animals were far to the north in the Great Plains). The eating of human flesh was apparently to supply a dietary insufficiency. As with the Greeks and many other peoples, the slain victims were primarily regarded as sacrifices to the gods although among the Aztecs only the heart, ripped from the chest, was directly offered to the sun-god. Any possible compunctions were allayed: the god is the real recipient, and we are privileged to eat consecrated flesh. Accusations of gourmet cannibalism most likely follow the tendency of Swift's "Modest Proposal": to stigmatize as cannibalistic connoisseurs is the most vehement denunciation of inhuman exploiters. Psychoanalysis declares that cannibalism is the infantile desire to subsist upon the mother. Such desire is retardation experienced because humans have a greatly extended period of immaturity, while other animals quickly pass beyond such wishes.[51]

(2) Cannibalism for revenge and aggression. The 20th century has displayed enough savagery to make plausible the serving by Atreus of the flesh of Thyestes' children to their own father. It is also possible that the accusation of inducing cannibalism is the most emphatic way for the archaic mind to delineate monstrous hatred and the inhuman extremes of vengeance. Almost worldwide, witches are accused of cannibalism because of their bitterness toward all mankind. To scare children mothers warn them that wicked witches will eat them up; in the oral stage of development a child's entire concern is with eating (and being eaten). Cannibalism is therefore the only understandable allusion to destruction at this early age.

(3) Cannibalism for magical purposes, to gain capabilities of the eaten. If an enemy has been strong and valorous, eating his flesh will presumably communicate some of his mana to you. The Baiga of central India say that Nanga Baiga, father of mankind, at his death instructed his sons to cut up his body, cook and eat it, thereby absorbing his power and magic. By the intervention of Bhagavan, the creator, only a tiny portion of flesh was actually eaten. We are the subordinate beings that we are because man got to eat very little of Nanga Baiga. The Surára of NW Brazil cremate their dead and drink the bone ash mixed with banana soup. Similar practices hold among certain Melanesian, Australian, and

other S. Amerindian peoples. In the past the new king of the Yoruba ate a portion of the heart of the deceased ruler. The Munda of India say that their first shaman directed his pupils to eat of his corpse. Obeying, they too became powerful shamans. Remnants of this cannibalism appear in the potent unguent that Alaskan Aleuts concoct from the tissues of dead bodies and in the Mexican practice of eating sugar or candy skulls.

(4) Cannibalism as a religious practice. Kronos was a very archaic Greek god of vegetation and animal life, the likely recipient of sacrificed children. From this sacrifice probably developed the myth of his swallowing his own offspring (aren't we all offspring of the god of life?). Omphagia (Greek, "eating of raw flesh") was the culminating rite of Dionysian ecstasy, the tearing to pieces of a live animal and the gnawing of its flesh. Greek myth accords this same fate to Orpheus and Pentheus, suggesting human victims originally. Such a practice was a eucharist, the sacramental presence of the god in the flesh rapturously dismembered and eaten by devotees.[52] Parallel practices are reported from Morocco and British Columbia. Orphic doctrine reports Zeus as devouring Phanes and the heart of Dionysus-Zagreus, then begetting Dionysus-Lyseus upon Semele. Orphism interpreted this account as the doctrine of flux between the many and the one, the formless and the formed, the chaotic and the ordered; supposedly it also embodied the Orphic concept of transmigration as the soul passes through different corporeal forms until, purified and spiritualized, it regains its divine home. Tylor infuriated Victorian clerics by tracing the communion ritual to a cannibal feast. Possibly nutritional cannibalism is a debased form of ritual, sacred cannibalism.[53]

(5) Cannibalism associated with social and political practices. Most people practicing cannibalism require exocannibalism, i.e. eating of humans outside the social group (slaves, captives, and criminals are within the accepted categories). Endocannibalism, i.e. eating members of the community, will destroy a group unless rigorously circumscribed, as endocannibalistic Tierra del Fuegans ate only the aging and maimed members of their society. Certain tribes of the Eastern highlands of New Guinea practice endocannibalism and thus incur kuru, a rapidly progressive degenerative disease of the nervous system. Natives explain kuru as a pro-

duct of sorcery, but outside observers are confident that only by eating human flesh can anyone contract kuru.[54]

(6) Cannibalism as a symbol of incorporation. Perhaps much reference in myth to cannibalism is actually a metaphor for becoming part of a social group. Many initiation rituals and tales of heroes involve the swallowing of humans and their subsequent regurgitation intact. The children of Kronos undergo this process to emerge as a united generation, subsequent rulers of heaven, earth, and underworld.

(7) Cannibalism as a symbol of peril and destruction. The Buddhist Pali canon refer to yakkha as "flesh devourers." Possibilities are: demonic spirits haunting desert places and eating travellers, wild beasts of prey, actual cannibalistic tribes of early India, disease, any power to destroy humans. A host of cannibalistic vampirish creature Lilith, Lamia, Yogini, Baba Yaga, Ghoul, Pisacha, Rakshasa-- may be metaphors like sarcophagus (Greek, "eater of flesh") or a personification of death.

(8) Cannibalism as a symbolic stigmatizing of anyone not in our group or at our cultural level. Most archaic peoples today abhor cannibalism and are righteously disgusted at their supposed cannibalistic neighbors or the man-eating savages on the other side of the mountain range. Explorers then get the same story from the neighbors themselves and from the tribes across the range. The label of cannibalism may mean no more than recognition of inferior manners in the past, as the Lacandon Maya say that U Djum K'ash ("Lord of the Jungle") formerly ate people but is no longer cannibalistic. Anyone not our sort may be branded a cannibal, as the Lugbara of the Sudan affirm that all Europeans are cannibals. Algonquian Amerindians believe that a hunter lost in the bush may revert to animal behavior and end up eating human flesh; this man-eater becomes a windigo.[55]

Sacred sacrifice.[56] Some discriminations first:

Offering--presentation of gifts to a supernatural being. Metaphorically contributions of flowers, fruits, vegetables, incense, money, precious stones and metal have been termed sacrifices, but properly all these are offerings.

Killing rituals--slayings without intent of presentation to supernatural beings. The rites may invoke deities and the killings may even be termed sacramental, but the slayings do not mean presentation to the gods. These rituals may involve only one person, as to this day we encounter fanatics who maniacally insist, "God told me to kill him."

Secular sacrifice--slayings more typically social than religious. In Eastern Indonesia some quite elaborate sacrifices are fundamentally community sociability. Probably such was the case with the later Athenian sacrifices preceding the drama of the Greater Dionysia.

Self-sacrifice--total self-immolation, as Buddhist monks have incinerated themselves or as Hindu widows used to commit suttee. Otherwise self-sacrifice is token sacrifice, a median between offering and sacrifice. Flagellation for religious purposes or crucifixion (non-fatal) as with the Penitentes is token sacrifice; there is a loss of blood but otherwise almost always a full recovery. The nine nights that Odin hung upon a tree (Yggdrasil?) as a sacrifice "myself to myself" in the Hávamál invite varied interpretations, but most likely meant token self-sacrifice in order to gain superior wisdom and capability. Actual mutilation and self-deprivation offer portions of the body to supernatural beings. Amerindians of the Great Plains frequently severed joints of the fingers as gifts to the gods, and apparently Stone Age men did the same. Freud predicates guilt from the desire for incest with the mother, or abject submission to the father, as the reasons for self-castration. In the case of Cybele's priests their ostensible reason was pious sacrifice of the genitals to the goddess. Circumcision or any mutilation inflicted upon a person by another does not constitute self-sacrifice. Perhaps the most important self-sacrifice features the voluntary death of a dema deity to provide the body of the earth and all the life thereupon. Central American myth tells of four previous suns, all perishing prematurely in darkness. To form the present Fifth Sun, two gods, Tecciztecatl and Nanautzin, both leaped into the colossal sacred brazier and therein were forged into the mighty sun.

Sacred sacrifice--presentation to a supernatural being or to the supernatural world of some person or animal ritually slain. All subsequent discussion is solely about sacred sacrifice.

The etymology of <u>sacrifice</u> establishes its meaning: <u>sacer-facere</u> (Latin, "to make holy"). The basic element of sacrifice is the transformation of something from the profane world to the spiritual world. Death is the most obvious and dramatic of transformations as a living, breathing creature is suddenly a cadaver. Offering of fruits and vegetables is despised by archaic deities as Cain learnt when Yahweh rejected his gifts but truly relished the blood sacrifice of Abel (Genesis 4:2-5). Burnt sacrifice is especially a transformation as the smoke visibly wafts upwards, presumably to celestial beings. Archaic peoples see the reduction to ashes as a spiritual transformation; substance has been refined to pure primal essence. In India the sacred ash of sacrifice was Bhasman, the semen of Shiva. The ash altar of Ge at Olympia was believed charged with the numinous presence of the goddess. Agni, the Vedic fire-deity, was the revered god of the priests and priest of the gods, ritually recreated with the flame of every sacrifice. For chthonic deities blood from the sacrifice must flow to the ground, especially into trenches as in <u>Odyssey</u> XI. Aquatic deities receive sacrifice pitched into the water or floated on the waters for the gods to swamp and take unto themselves.

The major theories to account for the origin of sacrifice are:

Gifts to supernatural beings to secure their favor and minimize their hostility. In time this practice develops into homage and ascetic renunciation (E.B. Tylor).

Initially providing food and drink for dead at their graves. As ancestors rose to godhood, the provisions for the dead evolved into sacrifices (Herbert Spencer).

Sacramental communion between worshipper and the worshipped. The eating of flesh of sacrificed beings was participation of man in divine life (Robertson Smith).

As with humans, gifts obligate recipients to respond with favors (<u>do ut des</u>, Latin, "I give that you may give")[57] and fulfill requests (James Frazer).

Gods have human appetites and wants which are fulfilled by sacrifice of what humans relish (Edward Westermarck).

Probably sacrifice originated in the killing of other humans. In battle a warrior's adrenalin glands supercharge him with giant strength and divine rage, so that the slaying of an enemy is a sacred act. Apparently, in very remote times all killing was sacramental, including human slaughter. Slaying an enemy has been a divine command up to the present. Archbishop Turpin in the Song of Roland urged as Christian penance the killing of Mohammedans. In World War II Josef Stalin branded the Germans as rapists of the "sacred soil" of Russia, again a divine abjuration to kill the rapists of our mother.

The stories clustered about Jason probably arose from a deep layer of Greek experience predating the Trojan War and revealing interesting possibilities about human sacrifice. The Jason accounts seem to catch the start of the historical and at least semi-civilized world when human slayings are no longer sacramental but profane, even despicable, acts. When Phrixus and Helle are to be sacrificed, no one appears distressed except their mother. When the Argonauts are at Pegae, the nymph Dryope affection-ately draws to herself young Hylas as he fills his pitcher at a spring; maybe an accidental drowning is recorded, but it could well be a sacrifice by ritual drowning. The deaths of King Cyzicus and King Amycus, as well as the later death of King Pelias, may be profane acts or sacred slayings; especially the killing of Pelias looks like an attempt to resume the slaying of the sacred king, now met with violent distaste. Most of all, the killing and dismemberment of Apsyrtus look like sacred slaying and distribution of parts for fertility; nonetheless, even though this action by Medea saves the Argonauts, it stigmatizes Medea as a monstrous creature. With the early Greeks thus sounds the modern cry against murder, indig-nantly condemning archaic man's practice of sacral slaying.

Human sacrifice, presumably the first type of sacrifice, was a long time dying. Possibly human sacrifice arose from cannibalism; deeming human flesh the most valuable and desirable, men perhaps for millenia sacrificed human beings for divine feasts.[58] Sacrifice of the firstborn children to propitiate deities, especially when danger threatened, is pro-bably behind the intended sacrifice of Isaac (Genesis 22), and possibly the deaths of the Egyptian first-born (Exodus 12:29-30). The sacrifice of children to Moloch is denounced in Leviticus 18:21 and 20:2, but the slaying of children in foundation sacrifice is mentioned without condemnation in I Kings 17:34. Participants in ancient human sacrifice did not necessarily tremble in terror and detestation; typically among the Aztecs--

for the victim was the certainty of immediate transport to the gods in heaven,

for the priests and theologians it was a gift of life to the gods from whom came all life, and

for the congregation it was an exciting opportunity to absorb some of the divine power by a nibble upon the corpse blessed by the god's presence.

Sacrifice of humans seemed justified to archaic peoples for the following purposes:

(1) To assure fertility of the soil. The Khonds of India conducted human sacrifice for this reason until stopped by the British. The Khonds believed that turmeric would never get its proper deep color unless human blood primed it.

(2) To feed the gods or promote their vitality and fertility. The Aztecs so justified their hecatombs of slaughter.

(3) In funerary rituals to provide the dead with companions or servants in an afterlife. The Shang Dynasty of China and kings of ancient Ur of the Chaldees followed this practice. The frugal Egyptians even in early tombs provided pictures, replicas, and images as substitutes for human slayings.

(4) To regain contact with mythical ancestors or recently dead relatives. Much human sacrifice in black Africa was so justified.

(5) To despatch a messenger to the gods. The ancient Thracians thus killed a man to communicate with Zalmoxis. This action is motivated by the desire to reëstablish the primordial situation when men could communicate directly with the gods. It also bears striking comparison with the flight of the shaman to deities of the otherworld.

(6) To replicate the primal sacrifice reported in myth, hence assuring full continuity of life and

society. The Indonesian myth of Hainuwele suggests a ritual human sacrifice long practiced there. Human sacrifice (<u>Purushamedha</u>) in old India was considered a re-enactment of the original creation and a renewal of creation.

(7) As a foundation sacrifice to animate a building by transferring the life and still un-realized potentialities of the victim into another "body." Ancient Polynesia as well as the ancient Middle East regularly sacrificed a human in the post holes, walls, or flooring of new construction. Even in this century peasants of Bulgaria, Greece, Romania, and Yugoslavia have sacrificed animals upon erection of a new building.

(8) Of war captives "devoted" to a god. Saul went through considerable perturbations of the spirit but ended up by slaying Agag, king of the Amalekites as a sacrifice to Yahweh (I Samuel 15). Germanic chieftains would hurl a spear over enemy ranks to de-dicate all of them as sacrifices to Wotan.

(9) Of aging kings to sustain the fertility of land, herds, and tribe. This sacrifice is the ritual slaying of the sacred king, a widespread practice in the Middle East, also in parts of Africa and India.

(10) As a scapegoat to carry off the sins and guilt of the entire group, as in the case of Christ.

(11) Propitiation of supernatural beings. Agamemnon to appease Artemis slew his daughter Iphigenia on the altar at Aulis. Sacrifice may be rendered to demons as thus the Hadjerai of Chad attempted to persuade the devils to abstain from evildoing against the tribe. Amidst peril men fre-quently made vows of gifts to the deities in return for succor. Jephthah made such a vow contingent upon victory in battle. The first creature coming forth to meet him when he returned home would be sacrificed to Yahweh. The first to greet him was his only child, his virgin daughter (Judges 11:30-40).

(12) Blood sacrifice may have originated as an offering to Mother Earth. Blood is associated with womanhood by archaic peoples because of menstruation, defloration, and childbirth. Deposit of the severed bloody genitalia of Cybele's priests looks like such a sacrifice, and to this day the goddess Kali in Calcutta demands the killing of numerous male

animals. Yahweh's insistence upon blood sacrifice may be the usurpation by the male of the former female prerogatives.

Gradually most human societies substituted animal sacrifice for human sacrifice, but devotees of the archaic religion yielded grudgingly. Even into historic times human sacrifices formed part of the cult of Zeus on Mt. Lykaion. Durga in one of her aspects exacted human sacrifice at her Assam temple until 1832. The transition period is dramatically portrayed in the aborted sacrifice of Isaac and an animal surrogate (Genesis 22). The Vedic story of Harishchandra tells of his vow to give his son to Varuna if he would be blessed with a son, but, once so blessed, Harishchandra kept postponing the sacrifice of his son. With lavish bribes the second son of a brahmin was secured as a substitute, but prayers to Varuna by the intended victim spared him, and henceforth Varuna required no more human sacrifices. The gift of dolls at the Roman Saturnalia seems a remnant of human sacrifice. The ram in the Phrixus-Helle story looks also like an animal substitute for human sacrifice. The animal surrogate was almost always a domestic beast with characteristics resembling those of humans. Animal sacrifice instead of human sacrifice, therefore, could hardly have become standard before the era of the herdsmen.

Apparently through most of Eurasia the boar or pig was the first substitute sacrifice, followed by cattle and horses, sheep and goats. Perhaps the sacrificial practice reinforced the respect for animals and produced such concepts as the Minotaur, for animals tagged for sacrifice were tended and treated virtually as humans, and as scapegoats they carried off in death the full human burden of sin and guilt. Even into our present century Balkan peasants continue the sacrifice of domestic animals: sheep to St. George, a pig at Christmas, a bull (in Greece) for St. Helena.

The following justifications for sacrifice apply specifically to animal slaughter:

(13) Food for the gods who are not at all deemed cannibalistic. This practice was followed extensively in Mesopotamia.

(14) Food for the dead. In south Africa mourners would assegai scores of cattle upon the

graves of mighty chiefs to provide nourishment in the next life.

(15) Divination of entrails. Haruspy was emphasized in Mesopotamia, Etruria, and Rome.

(16) Confirmation of covenant. Moses made quite a point of blood sacrifice in Exodus 24:4-8 to indicate the Hebrew covenant with Yahweh.

(17) To ward off evil. The Passover ritual with the blood of sacrificed lambs is apotropaic. Greek temples and altars were often decorated with the skulls of sacrificed oxen, later represented in sculpture, chiefly to fend off possible evil.

Perhaps the summation of all sacrifice is man's desire to convert a situation of death into a situation of life, whether expressed as health, happy household, children, wealth, social stature, afterlife. The wish in all sacrifice is: for the life we give, grant us more and more abundant life. The archaic mind, starkly realistic, knew that anything worthwhile had a price, and if it is life you want, you pay the highest price possible. In Vedic India sacrifice became so exalted that it was claimed to be the sustaining of the universe and the attuning of each individual to the harmony of the cosmos.

Death comes to mankind.[59] Archaic societies lived amidst omnipresent death but relished personal extinction no more than do humans of any time. Myth has perhaps its most challenging task in trying to reconcile man to the heart-rending inevitable. With psychological adroitness myth has met the challenge with almost every method of attempting to molify man's anguished protest:

I. Put the blame on man, for only he is responsible for the entry of death into the world.

A. Man has been cursed with death because of his immorality. The familiar Judeo Christian tradition attributes death to the violation of divine commands by Adam and Eve. The African Kongo say that Nzambi, the creator, told the first parents not to bury a dead child but place the dead infant in a corner for resurrection in three days. When the parents disobeyed and buried the dead child, Nzambi commanded that for their disobedience all humans henceforth would die. The African Ba Songe say that the creator sentenced all mankind to death because of constant human falsehoods. In the Loyalty Islands humanity in digging yams stole the property of chthonic deities and hence has been cursed with death as a thief. Perhaps this explanation is the formulation of a primitive philosopher, his voice rueful with the irony that in gaining our livelihood we are irrevocably condemning ourselves to death. A gross sin according to the Australian Murngin, the early incest of the Wauwalak sisters, brought death as a punishment.

B. Man brought death on himself by ignorance and carelessness. The first man, say the Nias Islanders, had the choice of bananas or crabs as food. Taking the easier course, he ate bananas and thereby condemned all humanity to death. Had he known enough to choose crabs, which shed their skins, man would never know death. The Ye'kuana of Venezuela tell of the first man at birth cutting his own navel cord and burying it simply as easy disposal. From the rotted cord arose the evil Kahu who in sheer devilment brought death into the world. In the Caroline Islands a myth indicates that a superb magician once had a formula that brought the dead back to life. Relatives toyed with the practice and with the magician. He died, they could not recall the formula, and now no one returns from the dead. The Huchnom of California report that the creator brought back to life a man who had died the day before, but people complained that the resurrected man stank badly. The creator therefore let all future dead remain dead. The Tamanak of Guiana take the easy route of blaming a woman. Their culturebringer before departing from earth said that men could avoid death by shedding their skin regularly. One woman vociferously and scornfully ridiculed the whole idea; irritated by her harangue, the culture bringer departed after proclaiming that henceforth mankind should know death. The Bassa of Africa state that the creator formed man as an immortal just so long as he would stay awake. Man tried to avoid sleep but eventually yielded to sleep and thus to death.

C. Man voluntarily chose death. Once from the village of Bwadela in the Trobriand Islands an old grandmother and her little granddaughter went to bathe. The grandmother stepped into a side creek, sloughed off her skin (which snagged on a bush), and reappeared to her granddaughter as a vigorous and beautiful young woman. The small girl cried in terror that she wanted her real, true grandmother. To sooth the distraught child the grandmother reclaimed the sloughed-off skin and returned as her wrinkled, arthritic self. Since then men no longer have the renewal power now confined to the "animals of the below"--snakes, crabs, iguana, lizards. The pay-a-price theme has many versions. The Abor of India declare that their tribesmen were immortal until the sun pouted and hid; to reappear the sun demanded the life of an Abor maiden, and ever since then death has been the lot of the Abor. A Nupe myth from Africa insists that the creator originally made all species immortal but without offspring. The tortoise first begged for descendants and man concurred. Henceforth mankind and all other species have children and also know death. In apocryphal Christian writings Jesus reputedly answers Salome's question about how long death would prevail: "As long as women bear children."[60] The Muria of central India use the Tithonus motif. In the old days, they claim, the Muria were immortal but with the passing years became hopelessly senile--blind, helpless, toothless, wasted, racked with pain. In desperation they appealed to Mahapurab, the maker, and mercifully received the boon of death.

II. Blame outside sentience for inflicting death upon mankind.

A. Benevolent divine intent. The Mahabharata (VII, 54,48) of India reports the gross overcrowding of a world that knew no death. The gods mercifully instituted death to provide enough wherewithal for man and beasts. Death in the form of a beautiful girl was loath to undertake the dreadful task of destruction, but divine will cannot be thwarted. The despairing tears of Death became the diseases and ailments to slay humanity. Teeming India has many versions of this myth, but the same theme is widely reported, e.g. Shoshone Amerindians, Eskimos, Vogul of northern Asia. The Shoshone account is bitter irony: Wolf (creator) regularly brought the dead back to life, but Coyote (sly trickster) persuaded Wolf to let men die to prevent overcrowding; Wolf caused the son of Coyote to die and Coyote pleaded for the lad's resurrection, but Wolf calmly reminded Coyote of Coyote's own argument.

B. Malevolent or merely carping supernatural intent. God acts in pique to inflict death according to many African myths. The Sever say that immortal men lamented the death of a dog, thus irritating god who commanded that if men did all that for a dog, they should have better justification in lamenting human death. The Korongo relate the mock funerals of immortal man; an annoyed god ordered death to give men just cause for funeral rites. The Chams of Annam and Cambodia believe that the goddess of good luck once restored dead humans to life immediately, but the sky-god tired of her constant interference with the laws of Nature and transferred the goddess to the moon; ever since, men like other creatures experience the finality of death. In the Epic of Gilgamesh the title character is told that the jealous gods meant eternal life solely for themselves and made death one of the signs of man's inferiority to the gods. But the cruelest sport of any deity is that of the god Ea in the Ninevah myth as the human Adapa approached the gate of heaven. Ea cautioned Adapa against accepting a drink of water, for it would be the water of death. Carefully following Ea's advice, Adapa refused what actually was the water of life, thus forfeiting immortality for all mankind.

C. Malevolent intent of animals or human sorcerers. Many Australians and Africans as well as other peoples attribute all deaths (with the possible exception of infants and aged) to sorcery; diviners and oracles meticulously study each death to ascertain the human evil-doer responsible. Sometimes petulant animals are blamed. The Bahnars of SE Asia report that lizards, out of sorts from humans stepping on their tails, therefore caused all humans in time to die. The Yurok of California state that locusts from sheer viciousness wished death into the world.

D. Unintentional divine cause of death. Widespread is the myth of primordial closeness of god and man, for various reasons ending in a sundering. The Arunta of central Australia believe that death entered the world only upon a breakdown of communications between man and god. Many variations are played upon the "failed message" or "perverted message" theme. God intended immortal life for humanity, but god's messenger botched the mission. A pattern frequent in Pacific islands and in Africa has two messengers, one with assurance of immortality and the other with proclamation of death. The animal (usually) with the message of death beats the other

to mankind. Perhaps the messenger wrongfully presents the message. A Hottentot myth has the moon
charge the hare with the message of immortal life to
man, but the muddled hare states the message as death
for man. Angered, the moon hurled a stick at the
hare, splitting his lip; the hare clawed the moon's
face to leave permanent marks upon the moon. Other
versions have the messenger entrusted with a token of
immortality which is lost or stolen, as a snake eats
the fruit of immortality in the <u>Epic</u> <u>of</u> <u>Gilgamesh</u>.
From the Ryukyu islands comes the account of the
messenger sent with a yoke of two buckets on his
shoulder. He was ordered by the sun and moon to pour
the waters of life upon man and the waters of death
upon snakes. The messenger set down the yoke as he
relieved himself. A big serpent appeared and poured
the waters of life over himself. The messenger then
had only the waters of death to pour upon man.

      E. Quarrels in the supernatural realm.
Perhaps the most humbling of all myths make man a
pawn subjected to death simply because colossal
supernatural beings fight among themselves. An
Assamese myth claims that Yama had rule over Jampur,
the City of Death, but, since men were immortal, he
had no subjects. Eventually he physically thrashed
Brahma until the great deity promised to kill man off
in order to populate Jampur. From the Ivory Coast
comes the explanation of man's physical form from
Gela-from-Below and his life force from Gela-from-
Above. Men were immortal until the co-creators quar-
reled. Ever since in petty fashion Gela-from-Above
keeps snatching back the gift of life which he had
injected into the beings molded by Gela-from-Below.
A Madagascar myth states that Earth, daughter of god,
in play molded clay men. Her father, humoring her,
bestowed life upon the little clay figures. Much
later god from a high mountain gazed on the world,
astonished at the prosperity men had brought to the
earth. He demanded half of the men from his
daughter, but Earth protested that he had granted
life without conditions. In divine pique god commanded death for all mankind.

      The psyche contemplates death. The conscious
rational mind may face the reality of death even to
accepting or rejoicing in total oblivion like
Lucretius, but the life-impulse in the unconscious
will not accept death as annihilation. Piaget indicates that children normally cannot conceive of
extinction.[61] With children and with myth there is

no death but only appearance, disappearance, reap-
pearance. The archaic mind cannot think of life and
death as being and nothingness; life and death are
simply different states of being. The death of
another person is deemed removal or absence, as
children constantly expect the dead to return in
living form. Certainly this expectation of the very
young is strongly contributory to the death-and-
resurrection theme.

For oneself final death is inconceivable. Death
may be regarded by the unconscious as a severe injury
(e.g. castration) from which recovery will occur.
The Fisher King myth, the myths of health-restoring
beverages and food, the eager beliefs in magicians
and wondrous cure-alls stem from this refusal to
believe in one's own demise. Another tack of the
psyche is to interpret death as merely a loss of
consciousness. Hence the theme of buried alive, so
dear to Poe and other 19th century Romantics. The
sleeping beauty theme and the multitude of sleeping
saviors (Arthur, Barbarossa, etc.) spring from this
concept. The frequent remark about the dead as
sleeping is not necessarily a conscious euphemism but
a genuine vision by the unconscious.

Freudians have made a great deal of Thanatos,
the death impulse. Probably it would be best with
Jung[62] to predicate only one drive, the compulsion to
life. Except for the hopelessly deranged, no human
ever deems his life potential fully realized. The
psyche, denying extinction, regards death as no more
than a slight interruption, a sort of entr'acte, with
the psyche continuing thereafter upon its destined
course of life. This life impulse ironically pushes
the ambitious and the thwarted towards self-destruction with the deep unconscious confidence of enhanced
life beyond.[63] This life-impulse generates the
belief in an afterlife. With many peoples this
life-after-life is free, unsullied by the moral or
other deficiencies of this life. Universally this
afterlife is considered fair, not sullied with the
manifest injustices of this world; and even so calmly
logical a person as Socrates stakes all upon a magnificently euphoric hereafter. Heaven is our destination and the destination of those we deem worthy.
Hell is the fate of those we dislike and disapprove
of.

Or, death can be regarded by the unconscious as
a reversal of the birth act, a return to the prenatal

311

condition inside the womb. With both Jews and Moslems, the Angel of Death is the Angel of Birth. The aperture to the underworld at Avernus, the hole to Trobriand Islanders at Tuma, and the widespread magical practice of drawing someone through an opening all symbolize the re-entry through the maternal portal into the fostering womb. The fetal position of burial in Stone Age tombs; the placing of the dead in graves, caverns, vaults, or in a necropolis; the carrying of the dead to mountain tops; the ferrying of corpses to islands of the dead, the floating of the dead in boats or burial ships, burial at sea or scattering of ashes at sea--all indicate the unconscious conviction that we leave life by the same route we traversed into life.

If attention is concentrated upon mortal remains and their preservation, whether the bones of early hunters or the elaborate mummies of Egypt, the next life is interpreted as simply another round of this physical existence. If transference of the individual life is supposedly possible to another object or body, a less materialistic view is conceivable. But under any circumstances rebirth, reincarnation, transmigration, afterlife in any of their multitudinous variations are conceived in analogy to man's earthly experience, however idealized.

Chapter X Times and Places of the Mind

The life experiences of mankind will vary enormously, but the life-drive of all humans will share much in common. This chapter will consider geography and chronology as conceived by the mythic mind.

Mythical terrestrial geography

Center of the world.[1] For each person the world is a circular disc with himself at the center. The ancient Greeks saw Delphi as the center of the world, but Cuaco, Delhi, and many other cities have also been the putative center. The Chinese proclaimed their country as set in the center of the world, with the capital of the sovereign at dead center. To the Southern Paiute Amerindians the Kaibab Plateau was the world's center, and the Zuñi insist that their pueblos are the center of the world. For Christians Golgotha is the world's center; for Moslems it is the Ka'aba. Men feel no inconsistency in a moveable center for religious rites. In ancient India the site of every horse sacrifice (Ashvamedha) was regarded as the world's center, and every fire-altar of Agni was also at the center of the world.

The symbolism is carried further by terming this center an Omphalos or "navel." The Buddhist anchorite contemplating his own navel observes in himself a symbol of the world's center and the means of spiritually comprehending the centrality of the entire universe. At the temple of Apollo in Delphi the Greeks honored a holy navel stone guarded by golden eagles. Homer terms Ogygia, the island of Calypso, "the navel of the sea." Navel is apparently a symbol for a womb, since frequently the myth to accompany the navel of the world makes it the start of creation. The Egyptians universally agreed that creation began with the emergence from chaos of a mound, an omphalos, and that the creator extended creation from that spot. Various Egyptian cities each claimed to be built upon that original navel, but Atum and Ptah proved the most successful claimants. Mesopotamian myth declared that man was initially fashioned at the "navel of the earth," of course in Mesopotamia. Ohrmazd of Iranian myth created Gajomard, primordial man, at the center of the earth. Judeo-Christian tradition designates the Garden of Eden, where Adam was created, as the center of the primal world.

313

Archaic societies generally sever the umbilical cord at birth and let time cause absorption into the body. Probably this protuberance helps suggest a mountain as an omphalos: Mt. Meru (India), Haraberezaiti (Iran), Himingbjör (Norway). Mt. Gerizim in Palestine was the "navel" (tabbur) of the world,[2] and Mt. Tabor may also mean "navel."[3] Mt. Mandara in India was termed "Indra's peg" as the world's center so specified by the god. The ziggurats of Mesopotamia were man-made navels as were the temple pyramids of Central America. Temples were supposedly located at the juncture points of Heaven, Earth, and Underworld as the Mishna indicates for the Temple of Jerusalem. Babylon ("door of the gods") as a city stood athwart such a cosmic crossroads.

Sacred directions.[4] From the center of the world, wherever we stand, the created earth radiates out in all directions. We still say "to orient" (i.e. face east) when we talk about getting our bearings. The east, for almost all archaic societies, is the reference point as the place of the rising sun. The east is therefore the symbol of springtime, resurrection, and life. The star announcing the birth of Christ was appropriately to the east. Stonehenge is aligned eastwards as were Greek and Roman temples and Christian cathedrals. Ancient Greek and Roman cartographers as well as medieval Christian mapmakers regularly placed the east at the top of the map. Literally the Hebrew word for east means "front," while the term for west means "the back." West is the direction of death ("going west") because of the setting sun. Autumn and advanced age are also associated with the west.[5]

North and south automatically produce different associations in the northern and southern hemisphere. Even in the northern hemisphere the symbolism is contradictory. The north appears evil to Hebrews, Zoroastrians, modern Parsees. The north is associated with death and sterility by the Aztecs and the Chinese. Medieval Christianity saw the north as the realm of Lucifer and barbarians; the gospel read from the northern end of the altar symbolizes the Church's efforts to convert the heathen. In Masonic symbolism the north is darkness and the profane. On the other hand both Egyptian and Hindu societies interpreted the north as masculine (crisp winds and weather from the north) and eminently favorable. Gnostics, Manichees, and Mandaeans recognized the north as the top of the world and therefore noble, while the south was considered lower and inferior. Jung found in his patients (usually central and northern Europeans) a high regard for the north and a derogation of the south. In most myths the south is viewed favorably, as the Chinese considered the south more godly. Shinto altars of Japan face south, and to the Aztecs the south represented riches and food. Among Egyptians and Hebrews, however, the south means darkness and death.

In number symbolism four is obvious from front, back, and both extended arms. Many archaic societies, such as the Zuñi Amerindians, add three more--point of standing, above and below--to total seven.[6]

Imaginary land features. Preoccupation with the number seven caused the Indian division of the world into seven continents. The central continent, of course, is Jambudvīpa, India itself, surrounded by salt water. The other six continents are surrounded respectively by sugar-cane juice, wine, clarified butter, curds, milk, and fresh water. The obviously nutritional settings of these continents suggest Mother Earth, the nourishing female, to psychogeographers.[7] Imaginary continents and islands, including Atlantis and Mu, are explained under psychogeography as yearnings for maternal care and security amidst a sea of troubles. Imaginary island groups in a pair or sets of pairs are interpreted as unconscious renditions of breasts.[8]

Cambodians indulged in mythical giganticism when considering the diameter of the flat disc we inhabit as over 16,000,000 kilometers. A great circle of mountains more than 800,000 kilometers high supposedly rings this enormous world. In Indian myth the circling mountain range, not quite so colossal in dimensions, is called Lokaloka, dividing the visible world from the region of perpetual darkness (cf. Cimmeria of ancient Greek myth). Kaf (Qaf, Caf) is the mountain chain of emerald that according to Arabic myth encircles the world beyond the farthest ring of ocean. All these imaginary outer mountains, like the Atlas myth of the Greeks, are attempts to hold up the sky.

Long before Swift conceived of Laputa, Indian myth provided aerial cities suspended above the earth. Hiranyapura ("golden city") was built by Vishvakarman (also attributed to other deities).

315

Grief and suffering are unknown in this golden city floating in the sky beyond the visible ocean. Another Indian account tells of king Harishchandra who beggared himself to provide elaborate sacrifices for the gods who thereby lifted the entire community to the heavenly realm. Harishchandra started to boast, and down plummeted the city towards earth. The king's repentance caught the city in midair where it still remains suspended and occasionally may be descried. Such aerial cities may be suggested by the refulgence of sunrise or sunset upon clouds hinting towers and structures, but it may also be man's hope to rise from earth towards the divine realm while realizing his inadequacy in getting there.

Accepting the world as a flat disc, Myth I felt constrained to explain its stability (and occasionally its earthquaking instability). Standard is the myth of layers with various numbers of sub-worlds beneath the earth's surface and super-worlds atop this earth. The Yurok Amerindians imagined the earth floating on water, but most myths postulate an under-pinning. Because the archaic mind always tends to interpret any agency as animate, the earth is supposedly propped up by living beings. The Lacandon Maya say that the world is supported by 100 pillars guarded by deities. Various superhuman beings resembling humans are stated as holding up the world: Amala by a long pole (Tsimshian Amerindian); Drebkhuls (Latvia), Atlas (Greek) and Chibchachum (Chibcha of Colombia) upon their shoulders; Homophore (Manichean faith); The Old Woman Underneath Us (Tlingit and Athapascan Amerindians); four brothers at compass points (Mayab Amerindians). Overwhelmingly, however, the usual mythic supporter of the earth is some animal: turtle or tortoise (Hindu, Amerindian - Iroquois, Delaware, Algonquian), hog (Celebes), crab (Iran), serpent (Sumatra and Moluccas) or seven serpents in shifts (Hindu), white cow (Indian folktale), buffalo (Malaya, Bali, Borneo, Constantinople, Bulgaria), frog (Mongolia). Spectacular is the Indian concept of up to 16 white, four-tusked elephants as supporters at the cardinal and intermediate points. Since this support comes from "below," animals are most logical, while humanoid and bird-like creatures are generally believed "above."

Axis mundi (cosmic axis). Because he is an erect biped, man symbolizes as "lower," "baser," what is beneath his feet and as "higher," "nobler," what is upper, as his head is upward. He will himself yearn to be higher for close contact with the etherial deities; therefore, he seeks a connection between earth and heaven. The axis mundi is the mythic linchpin of the cosmos, the long, normally straight axis extending from the lowest point in the universe to the highest.

Perhaps the most awesome concept of the axis mundi is the vast world tree, Yggdrasill, of Germanic myth. The mighty ash tree has three roots: in the fountain of Urd constantly watered by the Norns, in icy Niflheim, and in the well of Mimir (its waters so precious that Odin bartered an eye to drink of it). The world of man is Midgard upon the middle of the colossal tree trunk. Up in the branches gleams Asgard, the realm of the gods, and there nests the giant eagle who wheels far above on tireless pinion and scrutinizes with sharp eyes all the cosmos below.[9] Tibetan myth cites a "king willow" very much like Yggdrasill. Many other mythologies depict this world tree: Aztec, Mayan, Mbocobi (Paraguay), Japanese and Russian (metal trees in both cases), ancient Baltic, Akkadian, Egyptian, Mithraism. A Solomon Islands myth reports a magic areca palm growing at fantastic speed and carrying a man into the skies like Jack upon the Bean Stalk. Vainamoinen in the Kalevala causes a fir tree to shoot up to touch the sky. Stretching trees likewise reaching heaven are reported from Indonesia, Congo, Cape Verde Islands. In Amiradhapura, Sri Lanka, grows a tree, a slip from the sacred bo tree of Buddha, connecting all parts of the universe, visible and invisible; its vertical branches represent man's striving for perfection.

Mountains are logical axes mundi, for it is customary among men to expect ever increasing spirituality as one ascends. For the Kogis of S. America's Sierra Nevada everything above 2000 meters is sacred area, and the snow-covered peaks at the highest altitudes are the dwelling place of gods and the noble dead. The mighty Enlil, a Sumerian deity, was termed "The Great Mountain." As Mt. Meru was the axis mundi for Hindus they believed that the sun and moon revolved about it.

Pillars are axes mundi for Malays (the pillar Batu Herem stands in Kedah, center of the world) and for the Lapps (pillar sprinkled with the blood of the god Varalden-Olmai). St. Simeon Stylites and other pillar saints sat atop columns in order to be lifted

to heaven. Pole-climbing stunts, the Maypole, flag-
pole sitting, and similar practices are attributable
to the pole as an _axis_ _mundi_. An ambitious,
Yggdrasill-like account comes from the Haida Amerindians who report Sacred-One-Standing-and-Moving
with a great pole resting on his chest and extending
from the underworld through the surface world to the
heavens above. Sacred poles among Australian aborigines and Siberian shamans (often in treeless areas)
are _axes_ _mundi_. The Arunta of Australia say that
Numbakulla ("always existing") planted a pole,
anointed it with his own blood, then climbed it to
disappear above.

During the Vailala Madness in Papua (1919-1921)
leaders supposedly received messages from the spirit
realm through flagpoles; listening at the base, a
leader heard the enunciation in Djarman (German),
actually nonsense syllables. A Fiji Island tale
reports that the son of the sky-god stuck his walking
stick into the ground before sleeping. Waking in the
morning, he rejoined his father by climbing the now
sky-touching stick. Arunta myth states that the two
Ntjikantja brothers jammed a spear into the earth and
climbed it to the sky, then pulled up the spear with
a death curse upon mankind.

In S and E Australia the _axis_ _mundi_ is created
by rapid and successive spear throws to form a path
to heaven. An arrow chain as the _axis_ _mundi_ appears
widespread in Oceania, NE Siberia, and America. A
sky rope or liana rope appears among Indonesians and
S. Amerindians. N. Amerindians and some Siberians
report a basket drawn up and let down from heaven.
Jacob's ladder is famous from Genesis 28:12. A
legend of old Poland has a pilgrim to the Holy
Sepulchre ascend a ladder made of bird feathers. Wol
Fat, a sly trickster of Pacific islands, ascends to
heaven upon a column of smoke from burning coconut
shells. The Surára of NW Brazil believe that the
souls of the deceased rise toward heaven on the smoke
from the funeral pyre. Probably this concept explains many cremation practices.

Psychoanalysts perceive the phallus in the _axis_
mundi, but there are numerous other possibilities.[10]
An interesting proposal is the human spine within the
embryo and within the human.[11] Buddhist mysticism
definitely likens the spine of the Buddha to the _axis_
mundi. The _djed_ pillar of Egypt was equated with the
backbone of Osiris. This spine symbolism seems to be

borne out by water, filth, or "lower" elements such as the snake at the base[12] and by associations of spirit, wisdom, nobility at the upper end. Another cogent conjecture is the umbilical cord.[13] This theory looks attractice, as it would make a mountain, for instance, quite consistent in mythic thinking as both omphalos and axis mundi. As the navel cord connects with Mother Earth, it could extend to the heavens linking man with both below and above. The axis mundi is invisible as the extension of the umbilical cord--material in its tie to earth, spiritual in its unseen link to heaven.

Under the patriarchy the axis mundi may well be a phallic symbol, but under the earlier Great Mother the umbilical cord, conceived of as tree-like, could well have been the model. Numerous myths worldwide report humans born from trees. A seal from ancient Harappa depicts a woman upside down with a tree growing from her womb. The biblical Tree of Life and Tree of Death may both have been umbilical in origin.

Other worlds in this world.[14] Psychologists of virtually every persuasion will inform you that the optimism or pessimism within humans is externalized. Earthly paradises, fountains of youth, golden cities, lands of boundless treasures, Shangri-Las, happy valleys, and the rest have always proved mythical projections of human hopes and wishes--heaven on earth. Everyone has heard some exhausted or distraught person blurt out, "I've just been through hell." Such a statement seems metaphoric to us, but to our ancestors it was very real. Until only a few generations ago dark, rocky glens were thought inhabited by demons, as were sterile and perilous places, veritably hell on earth

Initiation rites, the general rituals for young males and the specialized rites for many religious groups, follow the pattern of terror and pain (the tortures of hell) with the eventual outcome of heavenly rejoicing. The normal folklore pattern (not so true of myth and legend) and that of popular fiction generally employ this same structure. Sometimes the symbol of three worlds (underworld, this world, heaven) is employed, as in the quest of the hero of the Gesar Epic of Mongolia or in the Danish version of the Siegfried tale. Upon sacred Japanese mountains worshippers must traverse areas specified as jigoku (hell) and gokuraku (paradise) to follow the Buddhist perpendicular cosmology of underworld, earth, and heaven.

Men and especially priests are anxious to aver that heaven has touched earth at their spots. Egyptians declared that the nomes or administrative divisions of the country were divinely ordained with a specific deity ruling over each. In Sumerian legend a celestial Nippur preceded the terrestrial Nippur and served as a model for its later, earthly counterpart. Jerusalem is several times (Galatians 4:26; Hebrews 12:22; Revelations 3:12 and 21:10) perceived as a divine city in heaven and a material city on Mt. Sion. Tollan, an Aztec city near the present-day Tula, was consciously constructed as a reproduction of the cosmic order in the heavenly city of the deities. Many villages of archaic society, notably in Africa and America, are precisely laid out to symbolize divine organization.[15] Much treasured by mankind are buildings, usually ecclesiastical, which are earthly replicas of divine structures in heaven. Esaglia, the temple of Marduk in Babylon, was an exact copy of an edifice of the gods above. While atop Mt. Sinai, Moses received from Yahweh the plan of the Tabernacle even to its furniture (Exodus 25:9, 40). The Ka'aba at Mecca is an earthly facsimile of the palace of Allah above. Gothic and Renaissance architects regularly regarded cathedrals and other sizable churches as images of the "Heavenly Jerusalem."[16]

Any visitor to a European cathedral today may feel overwhelmed by the docent's detailing of the symbolism from the massive eastern portals to the magnificent rose-window at the western extremity, but the visitor will generally perceive that all the symbolism sums up the cathedral as a microcosm of the spiritual universe. Quite literally it was deemed "the house of god," the macrocosm in miniature. Temples of ancient times and of the modern era often depict deities and angels or the starry heavens upon the ceiling to show that the entire universe is encompassed within the sacred walls. Archaic societies long anticipated this concept. The Ainu of Japan regard the hearth of each household as a miniature universe. Sioux Amerindians consider each tepee as an image of the cosmos with the central fire representing Wakan-Tanka, the deity, as the focal point of the universe. The huge temple of Luxor was specifically dedicated to the teaching of man as microcosm.[17]

Since man tends to make all things in his own image, the most familiar of all macrocosm-microcosm concepts perceives the entire universe as a super-colossal human and individual humans as point-to-point reproductions of the whole cosmos. Archaic man designated stars as the eyes of god, the wind as the divine breath, and bequeathed to us the familiar terminology: mouth of the river, foot of the hill, shoulder of the mountain. The _Rigveda_ terms the Cosmic Man _purusa_, comprising the entire universe. The Baul cult of Bengal today posits as one of its fundamental concepts the human body as the microcosm of the cosmos. The later Tantric doctrine of India is largely inspired by the parallelism between man the microcosm and the whole cosmos. Mahā-Vairochana Buddha (the Japanese Dainichi) in body, speech, and thought comprises the entire universe. Taoism states that the human body is the image of a country with the anatomy of man corresponding to mountains, woods, lakes, and so forth; the human mind parallels the sovereign ruler and our bodily organs represent subordinate officials. In western society two 16th century worthies, Cornelius Agrippa and Paracelsus, belabored the microcosm-macrocosm parallel most of all and bequeathed to subsequent generations the most elaborate of such systematizings.

Horizontal Hereafter. Island and coastal peoples frequently site the abode of the dead[18] on the same plane as the earth's surface, usually on islands somewhere to the west (the direction of sunset and death). Probably from the fetus in the amniotic fluid arises this symbol of another existence amidst the surrounding waters, or it may be a symbol of safe haven in the midst of the eternal flux or some saving grace of selfhood surrounded by the waters of the unconscious. Variously this isle of the blessed is: Pulotu (Polynesians), Niraikanai (Japanese islanders of Panari and Ishigakijima), Kur'an'up (northern Australians), Tir nan Og (ancient Irish). Avalon of the Arthurian legend is such a happy island, and Atlantis may be also. The traditional Greek underworld was hardly hospitable, but the distant western Isles of the Blessed were deemed paradisical by the Hellenes. Although an inland folk, N. Amerindians of the Great Basin also located the abode of the dead upon the plane of man's world, either west or south. This afterworld possessed the features most sought after by tribesmen: green grass for the Washo, pine nuts for Owen Valley Paiute, and buffalo aplenty for the Shoshone.

321

All such horizontal Hereafters omit the unpleasant aspects of man's existence; otherwise, this
horizontal heaven displays a life-style scrupulously
the same as on familiar earth. Dante's Purgatory is
located on the earth's surface, but the whole idea of
Purgatory was a post-classical Christian idea arising
from the delay of parousia (second coming of Christ);
the concept was intellectually derived with no appreciable mythic predecessor.[19] The Melanesians have a
remarkable spectrum of possibilities for the dead.
Souls of the deceased go to surface residence:
islands for many tribes, rocks (Aneitum Islanders),
woods (Jabim and other clans), ravines (Usiari),
lagoons (Rossel Islanders). New Ireland dead enter
caves, i.e. underworld. Dead of the New Guinea
Mafulu settle on mountain tops, i.e. heaven. Permanent residence on volcanoes awaits the deceased of
Vao, Buka, and other tribes.[20]

Geography of Underworld

The standard and obvious cosmogony among most
peoples, ranging from the early Japanese through the
Greek and Judeo-Christian concepts to many S. Amerindians, calls for a three-tiered universe: heavens
above, surface of the earth, the underworld. The
schemes that postulate a number of layers are modifications of the basic three-tiered system. The
Dogon of W. Africa designate the surface as highest
of the lower worlds, with six levels of the lower
world below and seven levels of heaven above,
totalling 14 stories. Seven heavens in cosmological
systems possibly originate with the seven planets.
At Lagash during the reign of King Gudea (c.
2600 B.C.) stood the temple of Heaven, "temple of the
seven zones," referring to planetary spheres. In the
classical Hindu scheme the earth's surface is the
lowest of the seven heavens, with seven levels of
Patala immediately below. Patala is a region of
riches and pleasure, according to the sage Narada who
toured Patala extensively. Down at the lower depths
are seven layers of hellish Naraka, but later ingenuity or the growing iniquity of mankind increased the
levels of Naraka to as many as 28, each with 144
sub-sections. This entire universe is Brahmanda
("Brahma's egg") suspended in space. The Aztecs
similarly assigned the majority of tiers to the
underworld, nine out of a total of 13 levels. The
entire cosmos, according to the Aztecs, was Anahuac
("between the waters"), held in the palm of the god
Ometecuhli. The Campa of Peru suggest eight tiers

322

with five above the earth and two below the earth. Perhaps more balanced is the cosmos of the Witoto S. Amerindians with the earth level in the center and two heavenly tiers above and two underworlds below.

The Greeks reserved the heavens altogether for the gods and expected most dead souls to descend underground. From the primal myth of the Great Earth Mother and from the practice of burial, most souls everywhere were destined for the subterranean world. Any approach to the realm of the dead is fearsome, for we venture into the deep pit of the unconscious and the darkest dreams. Heracles wrestled Alcestis from death and returned her to Admetus; this episode looks like the flight of the shaman to grapple for lost souls in the afterworld. Even for the shaman it is a terrifying experience. The Orpheus myth, with striking versions in Japan and among Amerindians, underlines the profound difference between the land of the living and the eerie realm of death. In dreams we are tantalized by the sight of those we dearly loved and have lost, but we reach for them and grasp--empty air. Odysseus encountered the same thwarting when in the underworld he tried in vain to embrace his dead mother. We feel repulsed, as though "the living offend the dead by the fact that they are living."[21] At the same time we feel deep revulsion against the spirits of the dead. In the Japanese version of the Orpheus myth Izanami in the land of the dead ordered Izanagi, her husband-brother, not to look at her. Disobeying, he was horrified to gaze upon the deathly corruption of her body and fled in terror. Medusa bore the countenance of the dead and the damned; the living who gaze upon that other-worldly face are petrified.

Perhaps the most dramatic opposition of other worlds to this one appears in the food tabus. World-wide is the prohibition against eating the food of the dead or the food of fairyland. The most famous mythical account of violating this tabu relates the eating of pomegranate seeds by Persephone. Although the point is not made explicit in the Epic of Gilgamesh, this prohibition seems clear in the care-ful provisioning of Gilgamesh before he enters the underworld. Vainamoinen in Tuonela knew better than to accept a tankard of beer from the dead. The Maori version of the Orpheus myth tells of a young man whose loved one died and went to Reinga, the under-world; granted permission to visit her, the youth was cautioned to eat nothing in Reinga. Celtic myth tells of Conle biting the apple thrown to him by a fairy woman; he was irresistably and permanently drawn to the otherworld.[22] The tabu apparently arises from a basic association of food with life. Nursing at the mother's breast, the infant is preoccupied with food; it is life altogether to him. Early society commonly witnessed hunger and starvation. The miracle of recovered energy and vitality after eating would reinforce the formula: food equals life. The archaic mind therefore sees our food as our existence, while the food of the dead sustains their type of existence. To eat the food of the otherworld means to be wrenched wholly from this life and condemned thereafter to experience the otherworldly existence solely.

The nearest anyone can come to rendering death a rubberstamped routine was achieved in the official Chinese religion, just as anxious as Leibnitz to remove all mysteries and rationalize the most irrational. Reputedly a soul is taken away to the Temple of Walls and Moats for the first 49 days after death. The celestial bureaucracy has seven weeks to assemble and study all the records. If death is untimely by accident or suicide, entry into the underworld is deferred until the appointed date. If celestial records are correct, the dead soul is duly processed and assigned a slot in the underworld for 28 months. Promptly at the termination of this subterranean residence, the soul is inserted into the body of a newborn child. Perhaps death under such a scheme is no less appalling; the Chinese system is simply excruciatingly bureaucratic.

The Chinese Cult of the Bereaved Spirits considers character and morality immaterial, and apparently in early human conception of an afterlife there was no concern with earthly virtue or vice. Rather primitive societies like the G/wai Bushmen[23] or a relatively easy life as on Bali considers an afterlife wholly irrelevant to morality. Selection for assignment to Valhalla demanded courage in death but had no other moral consideration. Vedic India and ancient Sumeria believed that one's status in the other world was determined by the magnitude of offerings and sacrifices made in life. The Marquesas Islanders believe that one's favorable quartering in the afterlife depends upon how many pigs have been sacrificed in a person's name. Apparently a harsh nomadic life emphasizes moral and spiritual values since the sensual is relatively unobtainable, and man must establish terms with his existence, making a virtue of necessity. The Maasai of Africa are nomads of high ethical standards, demanding virtue for any rewards hereafter. Jacob spells out the hardships of Jewish nomadic life in Genesis 31:40; Hebrews and their fellow nomads of Islam have a puritanical moral code and severe moral criteria for bliss in the afterworld. Many Christians feel that masses by the living can hasten the transit of a soul through Purgatory. Thus, the ticket to the underworld, if any is needed, may be a moral life for some but for others mere ritual observance or physical prowess.

To the portals of the afterworld. The entry into the unconscious, the dream realm, is hazardous and terrifying as so worldly wise a poet as Virgil solemnly notes. The Ojibwa Amerindians kept a fire burning upon a new grave for four days and nights, the length of the difficult journey to the land of the dead. It is highly desirable to have a psychopomp (Hermes for Greeks, Cumaean Sybil in Aeneid, Virgil himself in Divine Comedy). Amerindians suggested a star or a dog (from dogs or similar beasts in burial areas, and from dogs barking supposedly at spirit visitors). The aged and dying may be instructed, as in the New Hebrides, about the toilsome route they must traverse and, for the Malekulans, about the Female Destructive Ghost in the form of a giant devouring crab. The knowledgeable shaman of the Caingangs of Brazil crouches beside the newly dead and tells them of the route to take, avoiding the giant spider, the boiling pot, and the slippery path past a swamp.

The ancient Celts suggested many possibilities of travel to the underworld: inside burial mounds or hills, at the bottom of a well, on an island across the western sea, through a cave like the sinister Cave of Cruachan in Ireland, across a river or ocean. The Celts also suggested the numerous means of access to the underworld: death, making love to an immortal and earning entry to the lover's territory, being seduced by an immortal, assisting a deity who fights on earth, honoring the request of gods to battle divine foes anywhere, even by trickery (for the gods were tricksters and appreciated a really cunning person).

Virtually all myths of the journey to the otherworld include crossing water or a great morass. The frequent bridge[24] to be traversed spans a frightening abyss, and those who fall off plunge into filth and torments. Clearly implied is a pleasant abode in the underworld near the surface and dire horrors at the depths. The fear of falling certainly contributes; lower is "baser" or "more vile" in human metaphor, and perhaps the pit represents the human bowels and excrement. Bogs, marshes, swamps bear this latter stigma for they certainly are nasty physical impediments and are nonproductive; psychologically they are in-between areas, confusing and distressing. The Todas of India must flounder through a viscous, almost impenetrable, swamp, Puvurkin; the virtuous eventually reach the underworld, but immoral souls are blanched white and stung brutally by leeches. The simplest form of the bridge is the slippery log of the Cherokee and Iroquois Amerindians. Many religions interpret this bridge as the final test of moral or ritual fitness of the deceased for post-mortem rewards: Zoroastrianism (Chinvat Bridge), Islam (Shirat), Scandinavian (Gjallarbru), medieval N. England ("Brig o' Death" or "Brig o' Dread"). The Menek Kaien of Malaysia envisage the bridge Balan Bacham as spanning the whole sea to the afterworld. The Hindu concept (Shatapatha Brahmana) and the Christian (Matthew 7:14) suggest a very narrow path, perhaps a causeway through a great morass.

The Roman priest was pontifex (from whence comes "pontifical"), a "bridge maker." Possibly the origin is shamanic, as the shaman was the archaic link between this world and other worlds. Of course, rivers and streams are still logical separators; the other side is another realm, "across the Jordan," even if the Jordan itself is no sizable river. The funerary symbol is clear in the transportation of the dead across the Nile to a necropolis. Vaitaraṇi in Hindu myth is the river between the land of the living and the kingdom of Yama (land of the dead). This river, like the abyss of many myths, is filled with blood, hair, and filth. Styx is the divider for the Greeks, so momentous a river that the gods themselves swore oaths upon it and Thetis made Achilles immune to weapons wherever the waters of the Styx had bathed him. The Anglo-Saxon and Norse ship burials indicate that to these seafarers not rivers but the open sea had to be crossed to the other world.

The Underworld.[25] Understandably, many Pacific Islanders conceive of an undersea afterworld. The Hawaiians believed that the souls of the dead descended to the kingdom of Milu beneath the ocean

floor. The Wagawaga located the underwater land of
the dead, Hiyoyoa, near Maivara down on the ocean
bottom at Milne Bay, New Guinea. Most peoples,
however, who posit an afterlife below the earth's
surface consider it subterranean.

The guardian of the portals to the underworld is
usually an animal, a lion in Egypt and Crete. Greek
myth posts a three-headed dog, Cerberus, and Teutonic
myth reports a blood-stained canine, Garm (or Garmr).
Possibly the canine guard of the underworld originated from dogs or jackals eating corpses; the
barking of dogs when humans observe no justification
suggested that dogs sensed the spirit world. Some
myths have a humanoid guard. Trobriand Islanders say
that Topileta, the guardian, demands a valuable gift
from would-be entrants. As Charon likewise demanded
a fee, archaic burials often included a gift for such
underworld functionaries, eventually coins in an
advanced society.

Advanced societies develop for the afterlife an
extensive and legalistic judgment of entering souls.
Probably the original criterion of judgment was that
still recognized by many Australian aborigines: the
great judge in the afterworld wants to know whether
you were properly initiated into the tribe; the
uninitiated adults are annihilated or reborn as
verminous animals. The fullest treatment of antiquity was in Egypt. The Book of the Dead (c.
1400 B.C.) details an elaborate weighing of the heart
of the deceased against Maat (Truth) in the presence
of Osiris. The judgment here is twofold, morality
and proper fulfilment of all ritual requirements.
The concept of psychostasia (Greek, "weighing of
souls") installs three solemn judges in Hades--
Rhadamanthus, Minos and Aeacus--though their earthly
careers suggested power and piety rather than juris-
prudence. Psychostasia on the basis of faith and
morals is a prominent image in many "higher" religions: Christian (especially in the medieval Doom),
Moslem, Zoroastrian, Hindu, Buddhism. Central
Asiatic Buddhism offers ten judges, each with
separate court and separate functions. The ancient
Egyptians claimed 42 judges.

There are three major choices. The souls may be
assigned to a pleasant abode in the underworld,
corresponding to the Elysian Fields (suggesting
return to the mother's womb, say psychoanalysts).
The Kharias of India commit all dead to a happy under-

world, except those dying "unnaturally" and those who copulated with forbidden castes and tribes. The Bagobo of the Philippines provide in this underground haven a giant female with numerous nipples (cf. Diana of Ephesus). Shipap is the underground home of the Corn Mother of the Pueblo Amerindians, and return to her security is preparation for rebirth. Souls of the Arunta of Australia join "the hidden ones" in the deep caves where existence is euphoric until rebirth. The subterranean paradise Virgil depicts for Anchises is really a heaven below the surface.

Perhaps the earliest of man's myths about the afterlife is depicted in the primitive concept of souls of the dead as resentful of the living. Existence in such an afterlife is a shadowy, unsatisfactory vagueness presaging the Greek Fields of Asphodel. The Gallas of Ethiopia see all the afterlife as such a shadow-like existence, as did the Hawaiians. Such a nondescript afterlife really looks like mythmakers attempting to depict annihilation, non-being, non-existence, so far as the powerful life-force in the unconscious will permit.

The third possibility is a realm of torments, a realm immensely dwelt upon in world myth except in Confucianism and Shintoism. Bahai faith interprets hell as a symbol of annihilation, and the liberal Ahmadiyya movement in modern Islam sees Hell as allegorical. Probably most liberals in Western society, if they believe in an afterlife, would agree with the Hengma Nagas of India that in the land of the dead the wicked are tortured solely by memories of their perfidy.[26] Sheol, the trash and garbage dump of ancient Jerusalem, dreadful with stench and constant fires, is translated as "Hell," the Teutonic realm of death. Mythical places of torments tend to be hot in warm areas and icy cold in climes like those of the Scandinavians and Eskimos. Psycho-analysts suggest hot or cold womb in contrast to the happy underground womb, or oral and anal sadistic cauldron (cf. "Jaws of Hell" and the medieval Hell-mouth). The Old English word hell means "coverer-up" or "hider." Perhaps this label is eminently appropriate, as it is a catch-all for everything that conscience or the superego wants concealed in community and individual living.

All of the Sumerian land of the dead, Aralû, was a veritable hell. The best that a soul could expect was to eat dust,[27] agonize from hunger and thirst, shiver from cold and darkness--with all lost except a pitiful yearning for life and light. Those condemned by the virago goddess Allat wasted away with the unspeakable disfigurement and numbness of leprosy. Tuonela, the afterworld of the Finnish Kalevala, similarly seems without truly redeeming features. Most mythical hells have been more carefully measured, applying the principle of punishment fitting the crime long before Gilbert and Sullivan. The Rigveda describes adulterers compelled to embrace red hot metal statues of the opposite sex. The hell of the Iranian Avesta portrays adulterous women with bodies loathsome from the bites and tunnelings of vermin. The Koran reports that the inmates of hell must wear fiery garments while being drenched with scalding hot water; when their skins are burnt off, Allah will restore their epidermis so that they can writhe again in torture. The fiendish ingenuity of the torturing gods in the Greek Tartarus still supplies us with essential terms like tantalize and unforgettable myths such as that of Sisyphus. The most carefully discriminated of all hells, far surpassing even that of Dante, is the Hindu Naraka, offering perhaps as many as 4032 separate compartments with Avīci as the very lowest and most hideous hell. With so many choices we can assuredly find a place for every social offender and every one of our enemies.

Some of the presiding deities of hell are vicious beings like the Sumerian Allat, but most, like Hades, are administrators and judges rather than torturers.[28] Yama, king and judge of the Hindu dead, superintends warders who inflict punishment upon the sinner in Naraka (hell); these wardens are man-beasts with faces of owls, vultures, cats, jackals, etc. All traditional devils are distorted, misshapen, grotesque parodies of the human. We apparently conceive of demons at a very early age when any thwarting of any sort is attributed to hideous heinous monsters, fit torturers of the deepest, foulest hell. A most interesting pattern, suggestive not of the infantile demon concept but of adult thinking, appears in the Norok (hell) of Cambodian myth. The tormentors of the sinners of Norok are themselves the damned who thus must expiate their own sins and themselves experience the stabbing pains they inflict upon their victims.

Man gags at an irrevocable decision. Even the unchangeable edicts of the Olympian gods could always

be evaded somehow. In the Harrowing of Hell Christ
extracted the Jewish prophets and patriarchs from the
infernal regions. In Chinese Buddhism, Ti-tsang,
designated by the Jade Emperor as Instructor of the
Regions of Darkness, ceaselessly patrols the underworld in search of souls to redeem. Only the Dvaita
sect among Hindus believes that eternal damnation is
the fate of some souls. The almost universal Hindu
doctrine considers Hell as purgatorial, with all
souls from Hell returning to the great cycle of
rebirth. Conventional Moslems believe that all
atheists and polytheists are doomed to eternal punishment, but monotheists will eventually go to paradise, with good Moslems far ahead in the van.

Mercifully, souls released from the otherworld
for rebirth in human flesh generally have previous
existences blotted from memory,[29] though Empedocles
claimed that "in former times I was already a boy and
a girl, a bush and a bird, a mute fish in the sea"
(Purifications, 117). The Greeks postulated the
Lethe River in the underworld; souls returning to
earthly life would drink of its waters of forgetfulness and start another round of life with memory
extinguished. More thoroughgoing in detail is the
Chinese Buddhist myth stating that Lady Meng prepares
the Broth of Oblivion at the exit from the underworld, and demons force souls to swallow the broth
before rebirth. Souls are then conducted to the
Bridge of Pain which spans a river of crimson. Souls
are pitched by demons into the reddened river which
will conduct the souls to a new birth. It is almost
literally an account of the career of the human
fetus.

The Realm of Heaven

The myths of mankind herald a paradise at the
start of things and a paradise at the end. Psychoanalysis hazards that each end is womb security and
nourishment. Probably the most sophisticated believers in heaven would agree with the Bahai faith that
heaven is a symbol for the journey to god. Mystics
contemplate heaven as union with the divine. As long
as a matriarchal focus prevailed, the beatific afterlife was underground in Mother Earth.[30] The emphases
are clear in the New Hebrides, which is divided
between matrilineal and patrilineal moieties. The
matrilineal portion sees the home of the dead as a
cave, while the patrilineal portion assigns the dead
to a volcano top. The patriarchal Angami Nagas of

India send the good souls to the sky, while the rest
are destined for the underworld. Cremation, superseding the earlier burial, generally (though not in
ancient Greece) meant sending the spiritual essence
upwards to heaven in a column of smoke.

The longed-for paradise ahead is often thought
of as the paradise of creation tantalizingly snatched
upwards from mankind at that primordial time of the
sundering of earth and heaven, once cozily nestled
together. Hence Dante sites the earthly paradise at
the top of Mt. Purgatory, just as many medieval
travellers' accounts ascribed paradise to some mountain peak. The Glass Mountain of European folklore
seems a land of the dead. The Maidu of California
say that the dead go to the Marysville Buttes, which
are within view. In ancient Assyria the regular
expression for dying was "to clutch the mountain,"
i.e. to go up into the mountain habitat of the dead.
Amarāvatī ("abode of the immortals"), the capital of
Indra's paradise on the eastern slope of Mt. Meru,
boasted of a hundred palaces and a thousand gates;
"to enter Amarāvatī" was a Vedic euphemism for dying.

When the dead are ranked, the higher the heaven,
the more virtuous or exalted the spirits and the
longer their sojourn. Taoism establishes three
categories: good spirits atop mountains, notably
virtuous spirits in a higher heaven, the saints in
the very highest heaven. Cambodians predicate a
paradise of 26 tiers above the earth, each tier more
elevated and spiritual than the tier immediately
below. Above the top heaven is Nirvana, eternal
absorption into the divine.

Instead of ascent to heaven in funeral smoke,
the Egyptians provided a ritual ladder (Book of the
Dead). Some Asiatic peoples, like the Lolos and the
Karens, as part of mortuary rites set up actual
ladders to permit souls to climb to heaven. The
Wiradthuri of Australia climb hand over hand up a
cord or rope let down from the heavens. Always the
myths of the underworld are vivid with concrete
detail and homey allusion, while the myths of heaven
are rather vague and poetic and spiritualized, rather
like Dante's "Paradiso." The Kulin of Australia
lyrically celebrate the souls of their dead ascending
to the sky on the bright rays of the setting sun. In
NE Queensland the dead souls follow the road of the
Milky Way; Finno-Ugrian and much Amerindian myth
concur. The Kamilaroi of Australia believe that

their dead soar to the Magellanic Clouds, i.e. to galaxies beyond our Milky Way. Early Chinese literature, before the triumph of Confucianism, assigned deified rulers to the region of the Pole Star.

In contrast to the pyrotechnics of hell, heaven seems anticlimactic. Simpler societies such as Indian hill tribes and Amerindians report a paradisical existence exactly reproducing earthly life except for the omission of pains and problems. The Islamic paradise still manifests many symptoms of such sensual heavens. The Hindu heaven is the realm of contemplation, a noble spiritual concept but about as exciting as watching a yogi in motionless trance. The Christian idea of heaven with its eschewing of marriage seems attempting a similar disembodied preoccupation with religious contemplation. The heavenly city portrayed in Revelations 21:18-21 is obviously metaphoric but a bit too redolent of earthly riches. The outstanding elements of this realm are order and peace, eventuating in the <u>City</u> of <u>God</u> of St. Augustine. Buildings and cities as images of eternity have sought to reproduce on earth the perfection that men know is non-existent here but predicate as existing above. Hell has the gripping intensity of a powerful realistic drama; heaven has the frozen symmetry and perfect proportions of an exquisite oriental tapestry.

Mythic Time[31]

Modern man seems so much the slave of the clock that he believes the reality of time is an endless series of cucumber slices, each precisely the same by computerization. For humans the actuality of time is subjective, sometimes slower than clocktime, sometimes faster, and trailing off vaguely at both ends of life. This is mythic time, the time indicated in Joshua 10:12-13 when "the sun stayed in the midst of heaven." In the intense battle with the Amorites an enormous amount of action was crammed into moments, so that truly time seemed to stand still.[32] Most societies recount tales about members venturing to fairyland, land of the dead, or other worlds; returning after what in their mind seems a brief visit, the far-voyagers discover to their astonishment that friends and relatives have deemed them absent for a very long time. Here is mythic time, subjective time as humans truly perceive it. The shaman or other traveller to the beyond feels that his trance is very brief, but to those interested in him or concerned about him, his distant quest seems vastly extended. Myths also use extended (and exaggerated) time references to impress the listener. The Trojan War, we are told, was ten years in length and the subsequent wanderings of Odysseus another decade. The round numbers are suspicious, and the total of 20 years in a world of quite short life-expectancy looks unlikely. The narrators do not literally mean 365 days x 10 anymore than we mean 365 days x 1 when we say, "It must be a year since I last saw you." These alleged time spans merely mean a long time, a very long time by man's inner calendar.

In the Beginning. Quite a few archaic societies, food-gatherers and hunters, lack extensive creation myths and may even have no myth of the cosmic start. Apparently the important questions in primitive minds were: "How were things before the present era? How did today's world get its present form?" Myth tries to answer these questions by dwelling upon what really is the world of early childhood as contemplated by adults. Probably the world's best autobiography of childhood is Years of Childhood by Sergei Aksakov.[33] His first chapter is "Scattered Recollections" followed by "Consecutive Recollections." What Aksakov handles realistically, myth treats impressionistically. Perhaps the most interesting and revealing mythical cycles about the supposed primordial times are the Dreamtime myths of Australian aborigines and the Amerindian tales of the so-called Mythical Age. Both accounts are actually describing the formative mind of earliest childhood.

The major feature of the Australian Dreamtime is the transformation of the vague and the formless into sharp, clear form. The original landscape is featureless, unshapen. The living creatures are potentials, not yet fixed into mold as any specific species. This is the time of "scattered recollections," when the emergent mind of a very young child is coming to form itself and bringing to form the world outside. To the developing consciousness of the child the giants of this Dreamtime are surrounding adults; these heroes-formers-transformers make the landmarks and shape the plastic earth, they mold the various living creatures into specific animals and humans, they establish the practices and customs of the tribe. Most aborigines are loath to move out of the familiar "formed" area, for the amorphous "unshaped" world beyond is dangerous, treacherous.[34] All of this time is the distant, shaping time of the mind coming to consciousness and fashioning its world.

Most Amerindians (Eskimos not included) offer numerous accounts of the Mythical Age, again that remote and different time preceding the present era. Outstanding about this period is undifferentiated uniformity. There was no distinction between animal and human forms, and all creatures spoke the same language. Like Dreamtime the Mythical Age represents the groping mentality of the very young, but the Amerindians emphasize the Sly Trickster, an amoral figure of unconscious desire, not subject to the full conscious restraints of a mature society. The metamorphosis of the proto-animals into the present sharply differentiated animals is variously explained by Amerindians:

(1) Freezing of status quo. Tlingit myth indicates that the imprisoned sun caused primordial beings to cover themselves with any available wrappings against the cold. When Raven released the sun, each creature became what he was wearing at the moment: wearers of furs became the fur-bearing animals, wearers of scales became fish, wearers of feathers became birds.

(2) Agreement. Californian Amerindian myths offer extensive details about proto-animals learning of the human era ahead and agreeing to accept specific animal roles. The animals-to-be elaborately spell out where they will live, what food they will live upon, what practices of life they will follow.

(3) Punishment, chagrin, or guilt. The Sanumá of N. Brazil have a version of the Prometheus story with the theft of fire from alligator-man, who secreted fire in his mouth. Bird-man defecated in the face of alligator-man, who laughed and thus permitted fire to be snatched from his open mouth. The Sanumá urinate casually but are disgusted by defecation or the sight of feces. In shamed confusion alligator-man hid in the water and has remained an aquatic animal ever since. The concept resembles the delusions of some psychotics who from deep guilt feelings consider themselves animals.[35] Possum-man killed a bee-girl and in return was slain by the bee-men. The killers desecrated the body of possum-man, smearing themselves with his blood, brains, viscera, and so on. Immediately the killers were transformed into animals with fur, plumage,

coloration, etc. similar to their body-painting. Here is another in the human vs. nature dichotomy of myth. Because they behaved in such bestial fashion, they are doomed to be animals and not men.

The Tower of Babel account (Genesis 11: 1-9) that postulates an original "one language" for all mankind (highly unlikely in light of the radically different linguistic structures) suggests an Hebraic concept of a primeval uniformity without differentiation. The confusion of languages inflicted by Yahweh has often been interpreted as punishment for man's hubris, but it can also from this passage be considered the action of a jealous god intent upon circumscribing human activities.

Cosmic times and cycles. The Indians conceive of a pulsating universe, the Breath of Brahma; at the end of each day or age (kalpa) of Brahma, the world is dissolved (pralaya) and recreated. The Babylonian Berossus in the 3rd century B.C. popularized the Chaldean doctrine of the "Great Year." Although eternal, the universe is periodically reduced to chaos and reorganized at every "Great Year."[36] Supposedly the assembly of all seven planets in Cancer would signal destruction by flood, and their congregation in Capricorn would trigger consumption by fire. The Amerindians of the Chaco and of Tierra del Fuego grimly predict four successive cataclysms: fire, prolonged darkness, deluge, freezing cold. The Judeo-Christian theory assumes a linear universe inexorably moving toward final annihilation. Such a concept of absolute nullity is late and sophisticated, for the unconscious utterly refuses to conceive of nothingness.

Refusal to accept nullity is not optimism. Most of these mythic theories about time seem the product of masculine consciousness, and the almost invariable pattern of successive cycles is a decline, a spiral downwards. Occasionally an archaic myth permits interpretation of cultural progress upwards, as in the Nahua (Central Amerindian) myth of Five Suns. The traditional contrast of cultured man with uncultured nature is the only progressive idea of archaic society, and as the Promethean myth it is the only really significant progressive idea of classic Greek society.[37] Much more influential and prevalent was the Greek concept of the Gold, Silver, Bronze (sometimes an Heroic Age only momentarily improving), and Iron Ages, each plummeting downwards from its predecessor. Hindu myth roughly corresponds to the Greek series: Krita, Tretā, Dvāpara, and Kali; the names of these ages or cycles are the Sanskrit names for the numbers upon dice in descending order: 4, 3, 2, 1. As the pessimistic males of the Australian Unambal observe, with shaking heads, the future will reverse the social order completely, ousting the men from their present power and putting the women in charge. Similar wise heads have been predicting disaster from the earliest mythic times to the present. The aged, until recent generations the unquestioned repository of wisdom and truth, have always insisted that the former days were the good old days and that now the world is deteriorating horribly. Within ourselves is the idea of security and protection far behind (in childhood) in contrast to the uncertainty and peril of the world in which we now live and the even more disturbing dubiety of the era ahead, promising little but debility and decrepitude for every aging member of an archaic society.

The end of things. Myth is silent about the present except to note with distress that we are condemned to a late and degenerate age on the skids towards catastrophe. Confucianism and Shintoism omit eschatology, but almost everyone else has something to say about the future--and it looks horrible. Optimism about the future is not fashionable these days anyway, and in science fiction, our imaginative projection of things to come, the picture of the future ranges from bleak to appalling. Often, as in myth, total destruction lies ahead. Freudians, who regard much of myth as neurotic-psychotic, explain the consistent mythical portrayal of horrendous future catastrophe as the individual's inner collapse projected upon the cosmos.[38] Of course this theory is possible, especially as the dramatic and sensational reported with fervent intensity will always fascinate mankind. The shrewd primitive who suggested that the human situation would be pretty much the same even in a world without saber-toothed tigers or with an ice age has been ignored by myth-tellers. Bear in mind that death lurks down the path for every human and makes obliteration a painful reality not for the neurotic-psychotic alone but for all humanity. It is impossible to imagine a primitive adult who in a normal lifespan had not witnessed violent death and destruction.

The standard patterns of mythical "end of the world" are:

336

(1) Natural catastrophe. Primitives long ago proposed the destruction of the world by fire or ice, deluge or darkness. The end can be interpreted as casual or accidental, simply the cyclic running down, or the savage crushing by irked deities. Starting with errant comets, modern man has suggested many more such disasters: erosion, population explosion, oxygen depletion, "hot house" effect of carbon dioxide, pollution of air and water and soil, nuclear explosion, and so on. Note that the older myth predicted destruction wholly independent of man, though often justified by his wickedness, while modern myth blames the environmental havoc solely upon man. Especially, the myth of destruction inculcates a sense of sin and guilt; its ultimate purpose may be moral, social, and ecological admonition like a parent's warning of dire consequences to erring children.

(2) End of task. Personalizing natural phenomena, archaic peoples frequently ascribe the end of the cosmos to the completion of a job. The Iroquois of eastern USA report that a woman was unhappy because she did not know when the world would end. She was transported to the moon and set to weaving a forehead strap (to hold a carrying bag upon the back). Once a month she interrupts weaving to stir a kettle of boiling hominy. The cat beside her (all the objects named were identified by the Iroquois upon the moon's surface) then unravels the weaving and she must start over. When the strap is actually completed, the world will end. The parallel Shawnee Amerindian myth states that the female creator each day weaves a basket or a net which is unraveled at night (like the shroud woven by Penelope); when she finally completes her weaving, the world will end. The Haida of the North American NW say that Sacred-One-Standing-and-Moving holds the end of a pole, an axis mundi, in a shell upon his chest. This pole, extending from the underworld to the heavens above, constantly turns within the duck grease lubricating the shell. When the lubricant is exhausted, the entire cosmos will collapse. Behind these myths is an archaic predication of entropy on a cosmic scale.

(3) Mutually annihilating battle. Apparently entire tribes of ancient Teutons were actually exterminated in battle, and among warlike peoples such destruction may have been witnessed worldwide. In distant days tribal existence was at least as important as individual survival, certainly far more

than modern man can imagine. Tribal annihilation thereby seemed an ultimate destruction. Armageddon (Revelations 16:16) is the famous last battle of the world according to the Bible. The Ragnarök of Scandinavia is the most devastating of all myths as the forces of good and the forces of evil obliterate each other in the last awesome conflict. Perhaps all this colossal struggle symbolizes the total dissipation of all natural forces, all good, all evil. If one accepts the Freudian idea of Eros (life) and Thanatos (death) ceaselessly warring within each psyche then perhaps this rending Armageddon is the eternal inner struggle, eventuating within each psyche in obliteration.

(4) Monster as destroyer.[39] The monstrous creature precipitating global catastrophe can be an animal, from the huge savage dogs of the Abakan Tartars to the one-eyed dajjāl of Islamic tradition and the seven-headed beast of Revelations.[40] Or the monster may be humanoid like the giant Dakhkal of the Caucasus mountains or the Antichrist of Christian tradition. In any case, this monster is primal chaos reasserting itself. Archaic man senses the frightening fragility of the world. Chaos is the natural condition and the imminent threat. All order, whether of god or of man, is artificially maintained only with agonizing difficulty and always in peril of overthrow for the triumph again of anarchy. Under primitive conditions such fears are not neurotic-psychotic but all too real in a hostile world.

(5) Divine will. The Judeo-Christian tradition posits a masterplan of the deity that will arbitrarily terminate clock time and the present world. The Hindu concept surpasses even the stupendous vastnesses of the astronomers. The world of Brahmā is supposed to endure for 2,160,000,000 years (one day and one night of Brahmā) after which the world will be incinerated to be recreated by the god. After a hundred of such divine days have passed (216,000,000,000 Years), the entire universe and the deities themselves will be resolved into primeval substance.

The Hindu account defers the ultimate conclusion almost to infinity and concludes not with nullity but with something like the astronomers' concept of a dark universe of equally distributed random atoms (i.e. an order of absolutely basic simplicity instead of an order of immense complexity). Of course, the psyche refuses to recognize nothingness as the end. Perhaps the most powerful enunciation of the death-and-resurrection myth operates on a cosmic scale. The myth of eschatological destruction really means the wiping of the slate clear in order to start a new configuration. The mammoth catastrophes of ancient myth may not refer to any physical destruction at all, but are symbols of cleansing and renovating, the fresh start, the new beginning. The Christian account proclaims: "Then I saw a new heaven and a new earth; for the first heaven and the first earth had passed away, and the sea was no more" (Revelations 21:1). Along with Jewish and Zoroastrian tradition, Christianity foresees a totally new dispensation, the old order wholly abolished and an evil-free new reign of perfection (i.e. incomplete order superseded by perfect order). This renaissance following the destruction of the present scheme of things is the standard pattern of eschatology; it is an end only to recommence in far better fashion. The Götterdämmerung of the Germanic peoples results in the renovated universe wherein Balder is the shining deity. The hecatombs of slaughter and the vertiginous terrors of chaos seem essentially contrasts to the glorious era ahead.

Most of this chapter largely follows the concepts of Carl Gustav Jung,[1] his associates, and his
disciples.[2] No one can deny the significant insights
into mythology offered by Freudianism, but those
interested in literature and mythology have tended to
sidle towards the Jungian school. Freud and his
followers regard myth as infantile, neurotic-
psychotic, and always escapist. Jung and his supporters have deemed myth vital to man's creativity
and maturation. Freud's emphasis upon the libido
concentrated considerably upon sexuality, although
the later Freud broadened his view of the libido.
Jung and the Jungians have looked rather to the
assertion of life and growth which, of course, includes sexuality but considers far more in the
psyche.
Jung attributes two layers to the unconscious.
The first and upper layer is the personal unconscious, encompassing repressed or forgotten material
from the specific life experience of the individual.
When this material surfaces, it is private, a "personal myth," not the subject of public myth. The
second and lower layer is the impersonal or trans-
personal unconscious. This is best known as the
"collective unconscious"[3]; such collective unconscious is not as with Georg Groddeck a mass unconscious, but every individual's copy of the shared and
inherited experience of mankind. This collective unconscious is a foundation or substratum that makes
all men one, as the personal unconscious makes us
separate and distinct. Jung views this collective
unconscious as the repository of myth. The similarity of many myths in plot and characters, the
immense attraction and persistence of myth, arise
from the common store in the unconscious of all men.
The master story tellers of all eras create truly
memorable narratives by tapping the collective unconscious[4] and thus gaining a universal appeal.
Such a theory reaffirms the concept of innate
ideas which John Locke seemed to sweep away late in
the 17th century. Unquestionably some animals respond in a uniform fashion to stimuli they have never
encountered before and without any assistance from
adult and experienced animals. Newborn chicks will
dive for cover when a hawk or a fake model hawk
appears overhead, but will continue calmly to peck
for food when any other type of bird soars over.

Since the old-fashioned word <u>instinct</u> is no longer stylish, the present term "innate releasing mechanism" (IRM) indicates an hereditary structure in the nervous system triggering automatic response to a stimulus never before encountered by the individual organism. Jungians see IRM as justifying belief in the collective unconscious and its inherited store of characters and plots common to humanity.

"Archetype" is Jung's term for the inherited patterns of events and characters in the collective unconscious.[5] The archetype in the human psyche is like the image of the chicken hawk in the freshly hatched chicken, a sort of inborn Platonic idea of the hawk, a permanent imprint that presumably all men share in common. Filtered through the personal unconscious, this archetype will in dreams and myths take the form of persons and actions experienced by the individual. For example, the archetypal father is the older, authoritative male. For members of a matrilineal society the maternal uncle could fulfil the father's role. Stepfathers and any older men could be the father figure. Further, monarchs and gods can represent the paternal image. Thus, the imprint figure of the father is a universal archetype with countless individual imagings. "Archetypal ideas" or "archetypal themes" may be the proper label for concepts that the personal unconscious symbolizes in vivid pictures. Suppose that the deep unconscious feels that all control has been lost and the psyche is thrashing about blindly. In bygone days the personal unconscious reproduced this "archetypal idea" as a runaway horse, eyes wide-staring, nostrils aquiver, reins trailing uselessly. In the last century the runaway locomotive or railway train frequently proved the up-to-date image. Today the runaway automobile[6] seems the general symbol in Western society for this feeling of lost control. For the future the conventional depiction could be the colossal robot running amok, an image already popularized by science fiction. Beneath all of these transient representations is the primal and permanent "archetypal idea" of lost governance.

Major Jungian Archetypes

The four functions. From observation of his patients Jung postulated four basic characteristics in each psyche--reason, inspiration, body, emotion. Each of these functions, he asserted, is assigned to a compass point in every person's internal map and is personified in dreams and myths as a human figure. From the outside world, theorists would suggest the front, back, left, and right as producing these four,

341

or perhaps the four limbs. Jung, however, interprets the entire process as inward, imposing its inner fourness upon the outer world. Why four? In a conscious number system five and ten are logical bases from the fingers and toes of every human. Unconscious numbering must result from some basic building blocks of the organism. Jung offers a chemical foundation in the quadrivalence of carbon, perhaps the most indispensable element in living things. These four "hooks" of carbon may explain the inner four of the psyche.[7] Kerényi proposes a biological explanation, the four-cell division of the zygote, ceaselessly replicated, perhaps like a relentless template stamping four into the protoplasm and psyche of mankind.[8]

Central to Jung's analysis of the psyche is the mandala (Sanskrit, "essence seizing"), a symbol notably employed in the orient[9] and appearing frequently among Jung's occidental patients.[10] The mandala is a circle circumscribing a square which is divided into four triangles.[11] Frequently a deity or divine symbol appears at the very center of the mandala. The square Vedic fire-altar apparently took its shape from the mandala square. The huge Buddhist temple of Borobudur in Java is a three-dimensional mandala in stone. Jungians would see the square (not present in nature) as a projection from the four in the psyche.

The fourfold pattern is certainly quite extensive in myth.[12] The Aztecs especially observed four-in-one in deities. Tezcatlipoca, one of the creator deities, comprised four male gods in one. Tlazolteotl was a four-in-one goddess. The Indian Brahmā is a fourheaded god, as is the Tibetan and Nepalese Tantric deity Trailokyavijaya, simply another way of saying four-in-one. The Roman god Janus, two-headed in early representations, appears as four-headed in later depictions. The Gnostic Barbelo may be translated as "fourness is God."[13] The Potawatomi Amerindians see their culture-bringer Nanabozho as the eldest of male quadruplets. The Kurichiyas of Kerala, India, revere the Four Mothers or Four Mother Goddesses who bring to life and take to death. Many Buddhist stupas are adorned with sets of four divinities.

Jung theorizes that reason and inspiration receive heavy emphasis in the male, while emotions and the body are more central to women.[14] In a patriarchal society the tendency is strong towards a central pantheon of four deities with a male head (reason), female consort (usually body), son (inspiration), daughter (emotions). Such is the ancient Canaanite set of four at Ugarit (4th century B.C.): El (father), Athirat or Asherah (mother), Baal or Hadad (son), Anath (daughter). The Zohar, most important book (c. 1286) of the Jewish Kabbala, proffers a similar foursome: Divine Father, Supernal Mother, Son the king, daughter Matronit. The Kabbalists insist that all four are attributes or aspects of one god. On Panari Island, Japan, and elsewhere a similar pattern of four is repeated

It seems easy, if we wish, to assign hosts of gods and goddesses to the four functions of Jung. The female Greek psyche would supply: Hera (authority, reason), Athene (inspiration), Demeter and other earth goddesses (body), Aphrodite (emotions). Both Hera and Athene seem mannish on many occasions, while Aphrodite and the earth goddesses are the supposed epitome of femininity. Greek males in dreams and myths would personify the four functions as: Zeus (ruler, reason), Apollo (shining inspiration), Dionysus (the body) and Eros (emotions). Zeus is eternally the commanding male figure, and the statue of Apollo Belvidere is often deemed the ideal male. Dionysus (the body) is frequently represented as soft, plump, effeminate. Eros in earlier times blazed as the flaming god of love, but in the late Hellenistic form of Cupid he seems a pretty actress in the role of Peter Pan. The considerable ancient interest in hermaphrodites (who statistically are inconsequential) may spring from the inner world where a man sees one of his functions as womanish or a woman perceives one of her functions as male-like.

Threefold. Freudians frequently propose the male genitals as source of the important number three.[15] Another Freudian suggestion is the threefold body apertures--mouth, anus, urinogenital area--that seem to be the sole preoccupations of the infant.[16] The three-aperture theory may explain the hellish female threes of Greek myth. The very young infant knows only the mother, even feels still part of her. The emergence of the "terrible mother" theme in any infantile thwarting and the later repression of the devastating concentration on the alimentary system and especially upon excretion may account for the chthonic triads of terrifying or loathsome females: Fates, Furies, Gorgons, Graeae.[17] The three Fates of the Greeks are paralleled by the Parcae (Roman), the Norns (Scandinavia), Wyrdes (Anglo-Saxon), and the three Fates of the old Balts.

Jung explains the three as four less one. In each human psyche, he hypothecates, one of the four functions is dominant. In dreams and myths the individual assumes the position and person of the dominant function and looks out to perceive the three other functions personified as three humans. The three-in-one concept recognizes that basically there is but one deity who appears in three separate manifestations. At Çatal Hüyük from the 7th millenium B.C. the chief deity was a goddess in three guises: young woman, mother in childbirth, old woman. The Stymphalians in Arcadia and other Greeks apprehended Hera as threefold--maid, wife, widow. Perhaps best known is the triple goddess: Luna, the moon in the sky; Diana, the huntress on earth; Hecate, queen of darkness in the underworld--three fold but the same goddess. The male deity may also be a triune god, as Trinath, folk deity of Bengal, is recognized as three naths in one, a single deity but also threefold. The Trikaya doctrine of Buddhism affirms three separate existences of the unitary Buddha. A three-faced deity, a three-in-one god, was worshipped under various labels in pre-Aryan India.

Three separate goddesses can form a sacred trio like the Deae Matres, worshipped extensively in the ancient Roman provinces of Gaul, Britain, and southern Germany, but rarely in Spain or Italy. Apparently they were associated with fertility, but it is still debated whether they originated in pre-Indo-European culture, or among Germans or Celts (this latter appears most likely). An Indian female triad is composed of Durgā, Lakshmī, and Sarasvatī. The Eleusinian trio of Demeter (mother), Kore (daughter), and Iacchos (son) is probably a remnant of the era of the Great Mother as sole deity, the male not perceived as a parent. In Rome the parallel triad consisted of Ceres (identified with Demeter), Libera (identified with Persephone), and Liber (identified with Dionysus).

Male trios are more numerous, probably superseding earlier triads of females. Many California tribes of Amerindians predicate a triple creator team. The Araucanians of S. America have three male deities: a god of good, a god of evil, and a god overall. Taoism relishes trios of masculine gods, from the three supreme rulers to the three divinities governing each man's life. The most awesome concept of the threefold godhead is the Indian Trimūrti (Brahmā, Shiva, Vishnu), not a popular notion but a highly advanced theological concept. The three gods represent the ceaseless systole and diastole of the universe. Brahmā eternally creates by divine compulsion, and with equal fervor Shiva must incessantly destroy. Shiva is no villain; he simply must destroy so that Brahmā may create. The apparent continuity we frequently observe in this variable world is caused by Vishnu, the preserver. Dumézil's three-tiered pattern of gods resulting from social classes produces trios such as Jupiter (magic god of the priests), Mars (warrior god), Quirinus (god of fertility).[18]

Another form of the divine trio in a patriarchal society is the familiar nuclear family--father, mother, and son (when patriarchism posits only one child, it is male). This pattern is widespread among Australian aborigines and among patrilineal tribes of Africa. Mohammed interpreted the Christian trinity as Father, Mother (Holy Ghost), and Son. The Jamaa sect in the Congo, an offshoot of Roman Catholicism, agrees with Islam apparently, for it proclaims the trinity as Mungu (god the father), Bikira Maria (Virgin Mary), and Bwana Jezu Kristo (Christ).

And what is the meaning of the mysterious trinity? In the Gnostic Secret Book of John, the brother of James, John, experiences a mystical vision of the trinity after the crucifixion and asks god, "How can a unity have three forms?" He was answered: "I am the one who is with you always. I am the Father. I am the Mother. I am the Son."[19] A Jungian approach ventures that the dominant function gazes upon the other three functions; veritably there are three but they are all part of the one psyche.

Twofold.[20] The dominant theme in all the world's narratives is conflict between two persons of the same sex, usually two males, since men are generally deemed more aggressive than women. Many narrative struggles between contending groups, especially in myth portrayal, are treated as one-on-one contests; the Cain vs. Abel conflict certainly looks like the fight between agriculturists and nomadic herdsmen.

Jung considers as distinctly masculine two of the four functions: reason and inspiration. These opposites within each male psyche war with each other constantly. A busines man, dominated by reason, condemns artists as wild-eyed, irresponsible, utterly impractical. Artists, conversely, will accuse rationalists of inhuman callousness and cruelty; with a shudder Wordsworth shrinks from the scientist, who, the poet says, would "botanize upon his mother's grave."[21] In both cases the condemnors are not talking about real people in the outside world; they are repelled by the spectacle within themselves of the function opposite their dominant function. Jung applies the term "shadow" to the way a function appears to its opposite. To the dominant function the opposite function appears misshapen, ugly, depraved. The classic example is The Strange Case of Dr. Jekyll and Mr. Hyde (1886) by Robert Louis Stevenson. We are carefully informed that the story deals with one man who manifests two aspects; the favorably portrayed rationalist is Dr. Jekyll the dominant function, and to him Mr. Hyde is the "shadow," a being of evil and villainy. Freudians suggest that the concept of two derives from the mother's breasts, but myth says little about the comforts of two or about paired females. Myth says a great deal about antagonisms between paired males, and folklore extensively exploits the theme of good sister vs. bad sister (usually the elder or step-sister).

The pair of contesting males can be viewed as a sort of Brahma-Shiva pair, creating vs. destroying, the anabolism and catabolism of life and the cosmos. Shintoism asserts that all souls, of both gods and men, are inevitably composed of two parts: nigi-mitama (refined, mild, good) and ara-mitama (rough, brutal, evil). Refinement and mildness are the prized virtues of an advanced, secure, populous society; the opposite characteristics are therefore stigmatized as evil. In a hunting society toughness, brute strength, relentless will are esteemed virtues; mildness and refinement are sneeringly despised. Hinduism, Platonism, and Orphism see evil as ignorance of the true nature of the self. Taoist thinkers such as Lao-tze and Chuang-tzu considered good and evil purely as relative. Buddhism views evil as the lesser, the inferior. Perhaps evil may best be defined as the way the dominant function regards its opposite.

Quetzalcoatl, the feathered serpent god and deity of light, ceaselessly battles with Tezcatlipoca, the god of night. Perhaps this contest represents the struggle of the Aztecs against the preceding Toltecs; even such an ascription looks like an identification of our enemies with the function opposite the dominant one. In all wars each side customarily associates itself with noble ideals and rational truth, relegating its opponent to brutal, irrational debasement. The Winnebago Amerindians postulated two supernatural forces in eternal battle: Earthmaker, the affirmative principle vs. Hereshgunina, the negating principle. The G/wai of the

Kalahari say that N!odima created the world and continues creation by quickening the fetus in the womb, while G//awama[22] destroys life and spreads evil.

The standard pattern is an implacable feud between brothers. Possibly a pre-Aryan dualism is the basis for the Jainist myth of the bright savior Parshvanatha vs. his dark devilish brother Kamatha. Hindu myth assigns to Shiva two sons, Ganesha, who brings prosperity and well-being, and Kartikeyta, a satanic thief and seducer. The Serrano Amerindians of S. California state that Pakrokitat, creator of mankind and the constructive spirit of the world, is bitterly countered by his younger brother Kukitat, who scatters death and destruction throughout the world.

Younger brothers, however, are altogether favored over their elder brothers in countless folktales and in recurrent sets of biblical brothers. In the pairs of Cain-Abel, Ishmael-Isaac, Esau-Jacob, Reuben-Joseph, Menasseh-Ephraim, the elder brother is rejected and defeated, while the younger brother is preferred and victorious. The favorite younger son may be the traditional preference of mothers for their last child. Back in the distant matrilineal society of the Near East apparently the first son was sacrificed, if we accept the repeated patterns of mother and ritually slain son (Ishtar-Tammuz, Cybele-Attis, Astarte-Eshmun). The occasional practice in a later patriarchal society of sacrificing the first born son may have been adopted from the matriarchal period. The first born son may have been deemed the son of a deity rather than the son of a human father. Such a practice might explain the multitudes of early Greek heroes (a good percentage of the Argonauts) who are sons of Poseidon or Apollo or another male deity; Alexander the Great, first born, was called a son of Zeus while a younger brother was admittedly of human parentage solely. In Western folktales a contributory element to the disfavor of the elder son may have been the <u>droit de seigneur</u>. Many peasants apparently reckoned their elder son as the child of the Seigneur. In a strongly patriarchal society the elder son as the inheritor of possessions and power often suffers the envy and enmity of all others. Besides, everyone sentimentally favors the underdog, here the younger son.[23]

With the majority of Amerindians[24] and peoples worldwide, a frequent pattern involves twin brothers, with the first twin usually considered the good brother and his younger twin brother deemed the "shadow" or evil-doer. Some African tribes such as the Ibo of W. Africa used to kill the younger twin, presuming him to be demonic. To prevent twins, pregnant Hopi Amerindian women have the medicine man by spells and incantations cause the two fetuses to be twisted into one; of course, the dual nature of most humans is an inevitable result. Women elsewhere scrupulously avoid "twin" fruits, nuts, vegetables, eggs to prevent conceiving twins. Many peoples such as the Miskito of Nicaragua assume that a man can father only a single child, and twins are therefore proof of a faithless wife. Frequently twins are believed to have different fathers. Heracles was the elder twin, son of Zeus (in the guise of Amphitryon); his younger twin Iphicles was the son of the mortal Amphitryon and inconsequential in comparison to his twin brother of divine parentage. The Guarani of Paraguay predicated three primal deities, two males and a female. Both males inseminated the female who bore twins, the sun and the moon, each the child of one of the male gods.

Multitudinous versions of the good-twin-and-bad-twin appear among Amerindians. The most momentous of such pairs appears in Iranian myth. The oldest writings of Iran, the Gathas, announce two primal deities, Life and Not-Life, Good and Evil in constant opposition. This concept and the Indo-Iranian sky-god Varuna, who combined life and death, light and dark, probably underlie Zoroaster's twin deities: Ahura Mazda, fair and sweet-smelling, and his younger twin brother Ahriman, black and foul-smelling. Probably the Iranian influence made Satan the puissant adversary of Yahweh. Orthodox Christianity posits Satan as a creation of the deity and a rebel against his maker, but to recognize Satan as Prince of This World comes perilously close to the Iranian dualism. For a millenium at least, from Manicheism (which long appealed to St. Augustine) through the Cathari and Bogomiles to the 12th century Albigensians, dualism was a division into two in a Christian society striving for monotheism.

The One. If anything is truly alone, single, unitary, it would be a random hydrogen atom in interstellar space; but even such an atom is part of the total universe. Every organism has a unicellular stage, but the cell itself is a tremendous complex of various elements and specialized parts. No material object is a lone unit, but in the aggregations of stars and mankind and much else there is a drive towards unity, unifying even the most disparate. Scientists seek a unified field theory that would put together all the energy manifestations of the cosmos. Science is trying to achieve the awesome mythical concept of the Taittiriya Upanishad (III,1, 1): Brahman (not the masculine agent Brahma) is the neuter "all-pervading, self-existent power," the cosmic unity. There is nought but Brahman, the material and efficient cause and being of the universe. All comes from Brahman, all exists in Brahman, and all is part of Brahman. Religious spokesmen explain the yearning for unity as man's desire to live in communion with god. Eliade regards this urge as man's "nostalgia for paradise."[25]

Freudians believe that the long and anxious childhood of man establishes his need for dependence upon the parent and thereby generates goddesses and gods. The female deity offers unity through return to the undifferentiated state in the womb. A single all-powerful male deity is interpreted as the superego.[26] Agreeing with the "unity of being" of the mystic Meister Eckhart, Jung asserts the desire of the psyche to assemble all its components, each fully developed and creative, into one powerful, fully functioning inner being.[27] At the center of the mandala, the focal point of the all-embracing circle, stands the one god.

The physical process of man is from one cell to many cells, but he is always at his physical best when operating as one co-ordinated organism. Likewise the psyche seems to have a unitary beginning, followed by a vast proliferation of parts, of beings within beings. The best health and achievement of the psyche are possible only by its integration (or reintegration) into one. An evolutionary pattern, ontogeny recapitulating phylogeny, suggests a very archaic sort of Platonism, conceiving of the Great Bear, Great Antelope, Great Wallaby, of whom specific bears, antelopes and wallabies are copies or representatives. The process of syncretism can successively generate man-beast combinations, fully anthropomorphosed deities, an amalgamation of deities from different cultures, a merging of deities towards monotheism. Perhaps Lang and Schmidt were basically correct in positing original monotheistic "high gods." Possibly even in the food-gathering stage mankind might have adored the Mother Goddess as the sole deity. Arthur Evans appraised the Minoan Goddess as the basis of an essentially monotheistic cult in ancient Crete.[28]

Domestic syncretism appears early in both Egypt and India. Egypt originated in a host of small self-governing communities each jealous of its local prerogatives and local deities. When united into Upper Egypt and Lower Egypt, and eventually into one nation, the communities tried to give truly national dimensions to their deities by absorbing hosts of divine attributes into each. Anyone consulting the index of an extensive book on Egyptian mythology is a bit nonplussed by the Osiris entries: "as tree spirit," "as moon child," "introduces agriculture," "solar deity," "river god," "corn god," "Judge of dead," "as son of hippopotamus," and then Osiris-Apis, Osiris-Re, Osiris-Sokar, Osiris-Seb, Osiris-Serapis.[29] Similar accretions about a Vedic storm-god Rudra and his propitiatory epithet Shiva ("auspicious") have eventually built up to the Lord of the Universe, the maker, sustainer, and destroyer of the entire cosmos (Shiva has, for most Hindus, absorbed all the roles formerly distributed among several deities. The Indian cult of Vishnu is replete with avatars, thus insisting that an apparent multitude of gods really means a series of incarnations of one deity.

International, intercultural syncretism seems Greek in its inspiration. In the 5th century B.C. Herodotus claimed the identity of Egyptian and Greek deities: Amon=Zeus, Isis=Demeter, Horus=Apollo, Osiris=Dionysus. Herodotus explained the parallels as a common origin and transmission by diffusion. In the 9th century B.C. in the era of Alexander the Great and his conquest of enormous and varied areas this syncretism became rampant. Subsequent Bactrian rulers of Greek background, neighbors of Hindu India, identified Greek gods with Brahmā, Shiva, and Vishnu. Among the somewhat extraordinary modifications was Teshub, a Hittite-Hurrite storm-god retained as Jupiter Dolichenus. Such syncretism became general in late classic antiquity. The Romans had a meager and rather uninspiring mythology of their own but insisted: Jupiter=Zeus, Juno=Hera, Minerva=Pallas Athene, Diana=Artemis. As brazen conquerors of Greece, the Romans pre-empted the rich treasury of Greek myths and recorded most accounts in Latin, causing many generations of Westerners to assume Roman originality. The Romans termed such syncretism interpretatio romana and calmly lumped together all the deities of their polyglot empire into one pantheon. When the ancient Jewish synagogue at Dura-Europas was excavated, the mosaics demonstrated astounding utilization of pagan art motifs for Jewish themes. David is represented as Orpheus, the Egyptian princess rescuing Moses from the bullrushes is Anahita (Iranian version of Aphrodite), and Moses instead of the traditional staff is equipped with the club of Heracles. Orthodox Christian art has depicted Christ as Pan or Apollo, and many of the designations of the Virgin Mary stem from Mother Goddesses such as Isis. In the mission field Christ and the saints are often identified with local deities. In India the attempt goes on to identify Christ with Krishna. Indologists suggest that if there is any connection, Christ is indebted to Krishna.[30]

From the Nile Valley comes the earliest known proclamation of concepts basic to advanced monotheism. Early in the 15th century B.C. Thutmose III in 20 years of conquest carved out an Egyptian empire from the Fourth Cataract of the Nile in the south to Greek islands and the Mesopotamian highlands to the north. He elevated Amon to the position of supreme god and ruler of the entire world, an honor never before achieved by any deity. Perhaps this assertion by Thutmose III is less a new spiritual vision than shrewd imperialism by a great empire-builder. Late in the 14th century B.C. Amenhotep IV changed his name to Ikhnaton and proclaimed one and only one god, Aton. The monotheistic "High Gods" are disputable; this is the first indisputable assertion of total monotheism anywhere. Ikhnaton clearly envisaged a world religion wholly transcending national or imperial boundaries.[30] Depth psychologists suggest that Ikhnaton was obsessed with an Oedipal complex. He discarded his name Amenhotep presumably because of his hate for his father, Amenhotep III, and even expunged from the records so far as possible the very name of his father, a very strong and forceful personality. Aton, his mother's deity, was consequently exalted because of his affection for his mother.[31] Under Ikhnaton the supreme and sole god, Aton, was shorn of anthropomorphic features and was represented solely by the solar disc. Possibly the priests of Aton instituted this image as less subject to hostility than a bald replacement of Amon by Aton's statue; perhaps the Oedipal antipathy of Ikhnaton denied any sort of father figure in favor of a neutral insignia. Statues of Ikhnaton, puzzlingly bereft of all genitals, have caused some scholars to dismiss Ikhnaton as a "degenerate," while psychologists suggest self-castration from fear of or resentment toward the father, or desire for an androgynous[33] (appropriate to one sexless god) instead of monosexual condition. More neutrally it may be suggested that the idea of one ruler for the Egyptian world-empire led logically to the notion of one spiritual ruler.[34]

It is impossible to pinpoint the century of Moses, but the name is Egyptian rather than Jewish. Hebrew tradition ascribes circumcision as a fixed practice to Moses, and evidently it was adopted from the Egyptians who long practiced it. Moses certainly encountered Hebrew relapses into polytheism, while he supported a rigid monotheism. Moses may have been an Egyptian courtier (the reed raft looks suspiciously like an attempt to concoct an Israelite origin for him) imbued with the monotheism of Ikhnaton and, in the tumultuous resurgence of Amon and polytheism following Ikhnaton's death, throwing in his lot with a dissident people and indoctrinating them with monotheism.

Independently, for purely rational reasons, Xenophanes of Colophon in the 6th century B.C. was arguing for one supreme eternal god. In the 1st century A.D. Dion Chrysostomos was reporting a wide-spread attitude of late classic antiquity: "Some tell us that Apollo, Helios, and Dionysos are one and the same...and generally reduce all the gods to a single force or power" (Orationes, XXX, ii).

Archaic peoples exhibit decided tendencies towards monotheism, even excluding consideration of the "High Gods." Back in 1867 Friedrich Max Müller coined the word henotheism[35] (Greek, "one god") to mean the concentration upon one major deity while not denying the existence of other gods. Possibly the ancient Hebrews followed this route as demonstrated by their word for god, Elohim, a plural actually meaning "the gods."[36] Australian aborigines fre-quently conceive of their earth serpent or other deity as a unity but also a totality of numerous spirits. Similar is the concept of "diffused monotheism" in African traditional religions.[37] In ancient Mesopotamia each city-state had its own original deity. Babylonia exalted Marduk above all others but retained the lesser gods. These minor deities held a status much like that of angels in the Judeo-Christian system. In a fourfold pattern such as the Osiris myth of ancient Egypt or in a threefold pattern accepted by the early Koreans or the present-day Zinza of Tanzania, there is a strong tendency for one of the deities to be foremost. Twofold systems resemble the "good" and "bad" qualities of Dr. Jekyll. Zoroastrianism laments the ceaseless con-flict of the opposites in the present world but foresees an apocalyptic triumph and eternal reign of righteousness; it is a dualism in process towards monotheism,[38] an eventual uniting of the Jungian adversaries into one victorious entity.

India has always been the most prolific breeder of gods and, paradoxically, the greatest seeker of the One behind the many. In elitist Indian thought there has not been the Western quest for the highest and most powerful of the gods but a constant search for the common divine nature behind all the names and labels. From early India sounds the contention: "The great divinity of the gods is One" (Rigveda, III, 55). This early Vedic period produces a syncretism of now-superseded gods--Indragni (Indra-Agni), Indra-Soma, Indra-Varuna. In more recent times the tendency continues undiminished. Hari-Hara is a combination of Shiva and Vishnu in one person. In images the left side (Hari) represents Vishnu, and the right side (Hara) represents Shiva. Supposedly Iyenar is a corruption of the name Hari-Hara; Iyenar is the only major male village deity in India, where village deities are almost exclusively female. In the 14th century a temple was erected to Shiva-Buddha, trying to absorb Buddhism back into Hinduism. The Indian probing for the divinity beyond the label produces a Visvakarman ("all-creator"), originally an epithet of Indra but eventually proclaimed a god in his own right. Likewise Prajāpati ("lord of living beings") was first an epithet applied to a Vedic god like Savitr (the sun); in time the separate god Prajāpati was regarded as the pre-eminent deity. A very old element in Indian thought, Tantrism, has persisted in both Hindu and Buddhist versions. Both strains recognize a bipolarity of the cosmos and the inner self; this sundering or fragmentation must be eliminated by a reunion of all opposing components into one.

India has itself produced one of the world's important monotheistic faiths, Sikhism. The first Sikh guru, Nānak Chand (1469-1538), was transported by angels to the presence of god, who ordered him to proclaim one and only one god. Islam and perhaps Christianity have probably influenced a variety of monotheistic movements in Hinduism of recent centuries. Interestingly Brahmo Samāj, founded in 1828, insists on monotheism and considers contemporary Hinduism a degeneration from earlier true monotheism.

Animus and anima. There is no such creature as a 100 percent male or a 100 percent female. Genetically all our species have far more similarities than differences, sex nonetheless playing interesting and necessary variations upon the fundamental leitmotif of humanity. Physiologically each sex bears components linked to the other sex, as men have nipples on their chests, and the clitoris corresponds to the

penis. Psychically there is a femininity in every
male which Jung terms the anima (Latin, "Breath of
life," fem.) and a masculinity in every woman which
Jung calls animus (masc.). The presence of the
opposite in each sex encourages the drawing together
of male and female, but the purpose is not simply
physical union. Notoriously, marriages based solely
upon physical attraction are doomed. Jung insists
that marriage is not merely physical but also
psychic. For the proper balance of each human psyche
there must be the complement of the other sex, the
body and emotional functions of the woman correcting
this functional deficiency in man, and the reason and
inspiration functions in man providing a needed
harmony in woman.³⁹ Old maids often prove strident
and cantankerous because there is no male to provide
them with the proper complement, and old bachelors
frequently are fussy and somewhat womanish since they
lack the female needed to balance their inner nature.
     Christian nuns are regularly spoken of as
"brides of Christ." Certainly this concept looks
like the feminine ego seeking union with the animus,
personified as Christ. Male mystics refer to their
own supernal experience of union with the divine as a
Marriage.⁴⁰ The male identifies his soul with the
anima and treats it as feminine. The "spiritual
hero" differs radically in psychology from the physical hero who satisfies his anima by wedding the
beautiful princess. The "spiritual hero" is wed to
the male deity through union with his anima. Hence
the physical hero like Roland or Oliver admires a
warrior cleric like Bishop Turpin but doubts the
masculinity of highly "spiritual" clerics ("There are
three sexes: men, women, and priests"). The powerful
anima in religious males probably accounts in part
for celibacy and for feminization of clerics from
laced and skirted garments to castration.
     Jung suggests an overarching anima in every man
and a separate anima joined to each of the personified four functions in each male.⁴¹ The system is
best illustrated in the relatively complete inner
life of the poet William Blake. To the total anima
in the private mythology of his prophetic books Blake
gives the name Jerusalem (city and woman symbolically
identified), and to each of his personified male
functions (Los, Urizen, Luvah, Tharmas) he assigns a
complementary female (Enitharmon, Ahania, Vala,
Enion, respectively). The Indian mythology approxi-
mates the Jungian scheme in the Shiva-Shakti union.
Mahadevi ("great goddess") looks like the all-inclu-
sive anima, while shakti is the female consort of a

specific personified function. Thus, the shakti for Brahma is Sarasvati, for Vishnu is Lakshmi, and for Shiva is Uma.[42] The cult of Krishna and Radha as a divine pair remains unique today within major religions. Krishna, an avatar of Vishnu, is coupled with Radha, a gopi or cowherdess. There is no marriage involved and no intent of offspring. This mating is celebrated as sacred sexuality, psychic harmony, and spiritual rapture.[43]

The animus in women seems especially evident in the lovers of the Middle Eastern great goddesses. Tammuz, Eshmun, Attis, Adonis, and the rest are perceived from the feminine viewpoint. Completely dominant is the great goddess Ishtar and her numerous parallel goddesses, the male displaying the same relation to the goddess as, in the masculine psyche, the female bears to the god. An Oberon is elevated to importance as king of fairyland in a patriarchal society, but originally Titania as queen was undisputed ruler of fairyland, and the male was for her pleasure as her animus. Eros looks like the animus in the Eros and Psyche myth, even to his invisible night visitations, like a dream figure. Although Eros extends assistance, Psyche is the active female straining at the tasks whose completion will let her obtain her animus.

The anima is woman, not any specific female. A very young male puts his mother in the anima image, and some males never appreciably alter this image, seeking the Mother Goddess in every woman. Most males shift in adolescence to the "girl friend" or "goddess of love and beauty," i.e. to an Andromeda or an Aphrodite. In later years they envisage the anima as the comforting Hestia of the Hearth. The father is the animus figure to young girls, and many women want a husband in his image. The normal adolescent shift of the animus in a woman is to the matinee idol, the Knight in Shining Armor, the Adonis or Balder. The older woman will settle for a Philemon.

There is a dark side of the animus/anima, perhaps a notable deterrent to brother-sister incest. Generally the anima/animus is projected upon an outer figure like God or Clark Gable, Helen of Troy or the girl next door. When the anima is felt to be the twin sister, the animus the twin brother, disturbing erotic and guilt feelings are aroused. A life-long struggle must be sustained against the evil twin of the opposite sex: karineh in many Semitic areas, bori among the Hausa of Africa, elose to the S. African Zulus, badi among Malays. Interestingly the Malays also use the word badi for the active ingredient in poisons. Among the Trobriand Islanders a boy at puberty must never play with or even look at his sister; an adult male must exercise absolute separation from his other self, his sister-half.

Gender archetypes. Jungians have greatly multiplied the supposed sub-archetypes of the animus and anima, casting some doubts upon the validity of these numerous imprints. Certain, however, is the freezing tendency strong in human minds. Even if we realize the passage of the years, we tend to fix some male in our mind as the dashing youth or some woman as the vigorous mother and feel shocked when incontrovertibly they have outgrown these images. Often individuals get trapped in an image and insist upon emulating their Cary Grant or Marilyn Monroe youth even when grown double-chinned and paunchy.

The following seem the most viable suggestions for archetypes of the male:

Puer aeternus (Lat., "eternal child"). The eastern Arunta in central Australia offer the divine trinity of a gigantic man with emu feet, his woman, and their son, a child who remains forever a child. Such is the eternal child, the infant Horus or the infant Jesus. Even parents-to-be who, influenced by women's rights, say that the sex of the first child is immaterial, really subconsciously want a male. A boy sustains the husband's ego, and in a woman lurks the subconscious feeling of immemorial antiquity that the ultimate triumph of motherhood is from the female body to produce a male. Consequently, even in the unchallenged reign of the Great Goddess, her spectacular achievement was giving birth to a son. The primitive earth goddess of Central America had a plump infant son widely venerated as the mediator between his mother and humanity. In Japanese myth Ninigi descended from heaven in the form of a newborn babe wrapped in bed covers (cf. swaddling clothes of the baby Jesus).

Ephebe (Greek, "youth"). The valiant and admirable youth may be a young man's dream image, but he also springs from the female psyche. Who ever heard of an ugly, misshapen hero?[44] If in the folktales the youth first appears deformed and hideous, rest assured that the spell will be broken and the youth will prove to be the perfect Prince Charming.[45] Myth generally is silent about the male for the years between the puer aeternus and the young hero. Then the handsome young heroes are legion from Gilgamesh and Achilles to the latest matinee idol. Except in the hard-core patriarchal societies, an integral part of the ephebe's career is mating with a lovely maiden.

Father.[46] The authority figure has produced numerous gods: Jove, Zeus, Odin, Varuna, and other "Father of all" and "God the Father" figures. Most such paternal dignitaries in a patriarchal society are stern taskmasters like the implacable Yahweh of the early Hebrew scriptures. In a matrilineal society the authority figure may be the mother's brother.

Senex (Lat., "old man"). Quite unlike the archetype of the old woman, the archetype of the old man is highly favorable. The male elder is senator, the wise old man full of experience and wisdom, a Nestor, a Mentor. Understandably with the reverence for age, Chinese popular religion lists many white-bearded gods. The anonymous author of the Song of Roland purposely gave a long white beard to the beardless Charlemagne and extolled the emperor (who lived 72 years) as 200 years old.

The following seem the most acceptable archetypal patterns of the female:[47]

Nubile maiden. This figure looks like the Dream Girl of every male from the awkward boy to the senile magnate who divorces his wife of many years to marry the 19-year-old stenographer with the pretty legs. Females work hard to attain this image when they are still gangly, bony early teenagers; and pathetically aging matrons will strain every resource of hairdresser, cosmetician, couturier and plastic surgeon to retain the image of the vibrantly youthful maiden: Antigone, Anaxerete, Marpessa, Enid, Elaine, Mélisande. On the printed page they often become indistinguishable unless plucky like Antigone or very mysterious like Mélisande.[48] In the vivacious flesh of a charming ingenue, they will arouse the envy of every woman and the admiration of every man.

Seductress. The father figure can seem dreadfully stern and tyrannical, but the male archetypes cannot trouble and disturb as can this female figure or the crone. The femme fatale is simultaneously very attractive and very repelling. Her threat, as exemplified in Circe and Delilah, seems to be the ability to destroy masculine will and control. At the very least she dulls purpose or prevents the fulfilment of duty, like Calypso. Keat's "La Belle Dame Sans Merci" indicates the aftereffects of the male encounter with the seductress--let-down, weakness, frustration, hopelessness. Apparently the seductress figure suggests to the male psyche a female intent solely upon her own pleasure, physical and psychic, heedless of the fragile male ego.[49]

Magna mater[50] (Lat., "great mother"). As the father figure is the embodiment of the yang principle, the Great Mother epitomizes the yin principle. She is the Lotus goddess of Pre-Aryan India, Shaushka of the Hurrians, Erditse among the ancient Basques, Tanith from ancient North Africa, Pachamama to Peruvians, Hertha for the Teutons. Among some peoples such as the Cágaba or Kogi of Colombia she is so identified with life and fertility (and the male with death) that the Great Mother is totally, incorruptibly good and even a divine marriage is out of the question. With most societies, however, there is another side, the "terrible mother," discussed below.

Crone. While the aged male is an exalted symbol of wisdom, the aged female is stigmatized as the nasty witch. As the Great Mother is the revered symbol of feminine fertility, the sterile old woman seems a hideous caricature of womanhood. The Graeae are hideously depicted as three old crones with only one eye and one tooth among them. India has produced the most devastating representations of the aged woman as death and destruction. Camunda is one of the most terrifying forms of Durga; she is depicted as a withered, emaciated crone wearing an appalling garland of corpses. Dhumavati appears as a hideous old woman with long, bony nose and cruel, burning eyes; she personifies the final stage of cosmic obliteration by fire, only repellent smoke swirling upwards from dead ashes. An image within as well as a mirror outside compels a woman to conceal and deny the years, if she can.[51]

Myth and the Development of the Individual Psyche[52]

In normal process of growth, youth generally believes that its feelings, ideas, and reactions are unique, that no one else ever felt that way. Knowledgeable adults, sometimes amused, sometimes grievously irked, find youth quite predictable. Jungians claim that, in addition to the fixed archetypes above, each successive stage in the physical and psychic growth of the individual will evoke archetypal patterns shared by all mankind. Hence a relatively few basic myths from the "collective unconscious" dominate humanity, although the conscious rational mind will attempt variations, changes, and additions.

The unconscious stage. In the flush of youth, especially in the late teens and early 20's, sleep seems a nuisance when life is to be drained to the lees. The descent into the unconscious is reluctant, apparently adventitious, yielding to the abnormal. Consider the possibility that the unconscious is normality and consciousness is abnormal. Consciousness may really be a late, and still incomplete, supplement to the unconscious, an evolutionary quirk proving somewhat useful and therefore sustained. Certainly humanity has acted consciously only for a relatively few recent millenia of its millions of years; archaic societies still in existence are obviously quite dependent upon the unconscious, and many conditions (i.e. sleep, exhaustion, excitement, suffering, religious concentration) of the organism can today readily cause the upsurge and dominance of the unconscious. Possibly the organism has been peaked to consciousness as helpful to survival, but its real wish is to remain unconscious. Human sleep still is a bit puzzling to biologists, as it regularly entails unconsciousness at night when early man had most to fear from predators. Perhaps sleep arose from the more compelling bond of darkness and the unconscious. Every night we still drop down with relief to the welcome realm of the pre-natal and the pre-conscious.

The 9th century Tamil mystic Mānikkavācakar recalled each month in his mother's womb, but such precision is suspicious, for the distinct characteristics of the pre-natal condition are timelessness and eternity, totality and infinity. The Dreamtime[53] of the Australian aborigine and the Mythological Age of the Amerindian, both suggesting potential but unrealized form in the past, are myths of the pre-natal and pre-conscious period. The desire to escape from time into the timeless, to plumb back into the primal era, to regain the fresh unsullied start--all of these are desires for the womb where time does not exist or has not begun. The mystic's craving for eternity is a yearning for the pre-natal existence.

Aditi, the Vedic mother of the gods, is boundless Space, infinity. The concept of infinity seems to arise from the pre-natal condition, where there is naught else. The concept of unity, absolute oneness, again arises from the womb life. The burning desire in mystics and scientists to find a unity, a final definitive oneness, seems to spring from the totality of the womb where the fetus is the absolute one. Here are no opposites, none of the multiplicity of the world or of the adult self. All is self-contained, unified, seemingly indivisible.[54]

Such is the primal being according to Plato in the Timaeus (30-35). Its initial form is the symbol of perfection, the symbol of the unconscious: the circle,[55] sphere, round, egg, the World Egg in many myths. The circle is without beginning and without end. Within the primal World Egg, myth (India, Egypt, black Africa, New Zealand and Polynesia, Greece) situates the World Parents or, perhaps more accurately, the Bisexual World Parent, for in the original World Egg male and female are not separate but still one, as yin and yang spiral in the Chinese T'ai chi but are still a unity. In the Symposium (189-193) Plato ascribes to Aristophanes a mirthful portrayal of the primal hermaphrodite; instead of an Aristophanic fantasy, this description looks like the hermaphroditic myth of many archaic societies.[56] The mythic and very ancient theme of the hermaphrodite seems to originate in the concept of pre-natal bisexuality, the union of male and female physically in one: Egyptian Hapi and Nu, Cyprian Venus Barbata ("bearded"), the Navaho Ahsonnutli, Ometecuhli ("two-lord") of the Aztecs, the Germanic Twisto ("double-god"), Lamga ("double-god") of Ashur in Mesopotamia. Possibly the Hebrew plural Elohim arose from bisexual deities viewed as one. Especially momentous is Ardhanāri, the manifestation in Shiva of male-female. The left side of the body is female and the right is male. Collectively Ardhanāri generates the entire creative process. The splitting into a duality is the fall from unitary perfection.

The androgynous condition, conceived of symbolically rather than as physical hermaphroditism, intrigues "higher" religions which soft-pedal sexuality. Intellectuals of late ancient Egypt developed the idea of the androgynous supreme god, uniting in one person father, mother, and child.[57] Orphic hymns made the androgynous concept common in the later Roman empire. Unorthodox Christian writers early in the Christian era, the Gnostics, have now become better known from the Nag Hammadi documents which regard androgyny as the genuine nature of divinity.[58] Galatians 3:28 is explicit: "There is neither Jew nor Greek, there is neither slave nor free, there is neither male nor female; for you are all one in Christ Jesus." A traditional argument for the celibacy of Christian priests claims that thereby priests might display both masculine and feminine characteristics.

The circumference of the primal circle is visualized as a serpent (or dragon) with its tail in its mouth; quite literally its ending is its beginning, the eternal cycle as symbolized by the Yoruba of W. Africa, the Navaho Amerindians, and the ancients of

Mexico, India, Egypt, Mesopotamia. The Greek name for this "hoop snake" is ouroboros ("taileater"). In Orphic thought the ouroboros encircles the Cosmic Egg. The vastest employment of this theme in myth is the Midgard Serpent of Scandinavian accounts, the huge ouroboros completely girdling the earth. In the bloodstained Ragnarök, Thor and the Midyard Serpent mutually destroy each other; but, appropriate to a symbol of disintegration and reintegration, the giant ouroboros in perishing precipitates the new heaven and the new earth. Since the circle is powerfully associated with the womb and the eternal genetrix, the serpent is assigned to the Great Mother. Many archaic representations reveal the mother goddess with a serpent curled around her trunk or spiraling around one or both of her arms.

In the womb the fetus is normally head down with the umbilical cord the great lifeline to the mother. Many myths among Amerindians and other peoples tell of the descent of man from heaven via a rope, liana, or ladder. Possibly these accounts and even the axis mundi may be accounted for by the umbilical cord. Ascent to heaven may correspondingly be interpreted as the desire to return to the womb protection.

The pre-natal state is man's first and his lasting Paradise. The biblical concept of Paradise is revealing: a state of luxuriant food supply, total absence of predators or suffering or death, complete security and peace. Myths of all the world predicate the primal perfection, the unconscious delights of the womb from whence we are cast into the perils of the environment and the dubieties of consciousness. Over all our life is stretched this memory of the fetal unconscious and its surpassing excellence. The myth of "natural man" and the "noble savage," the nostalgia for the "good old days" by superannuates, and the eager hopes of Paradise Regained or the Marxist anarchistic paradise ahead are all symptoms of humanity's yearning for the unconscious. The Marxist perfection of the future, like the biblical vision of the past, is unstructured, uncomplicated, simple, the antithesis of the complication and diversity that human consciousness has generated.

Body consciousness. Reluctantly the human organism, dumped from the sheltering womb, accepts the realization of bodily existence, groping from the initial sense of still being part of the mother towards a sense of separate identity and a perception of the bodily structure. Unquestionably the most important and momentous of all human life experiences is birth, the sudden eruption of the organism from its nurturing womb into the bewildering world. Numerous reports of UFO "abduction" remarkably parallel the birth trauma.[59]

The myth establishing body consciousness is the myth of Creation.[60] The first four of the mythical theories about Creation in the list below all involve water, apparently the amniotic fluid surrounding the fetus. Probably the original water deities were female. Aphrodite was born of sea foam, and Thetis, mother of Achilles, was only one of numerous sea goddesses and nymphs. Japanese myth is especially replete with child water deities, probably again suggested by the amniotic liquid.[61] Early culture-bringers often emerged from the sea as half-fish, half-human, like Oannes of Babylonia. Swampy areas as mixtures of water and earth were often associated with the Earth Goddess. The Lernean Hydra, second labor of Heracles, inhabited the dread Lernean swamp under the patronage of Hera. This labor of Heracles has been interpreted as an attempt to suppress fertility rites of the Great Mother.[62] With many archaic peoples the deity of Creation is a goddess e.g.: Mawu (Fon of Dahomey), Maisö (Paressi of Brazil), Kokumthena ("our grandmother" of Shawnee N. Amerindians), Oppilamulaiyammai ("lady of the incomparable breast" of S. India). It is quite rare, however, for the Creator to be feminine in the last four theories of Creation discussed below; these latter myths, probably shaped by a patriarchal culture, strongly attribute Creation to divine consciousness.[63]

(1) Earth emerging from the waters. This idea certainly suggests the growing fetus within the amniotic fluid. The Egyptian myth of the Risen Land claims that the Primeval Hill rose above the waters of chaos. This fruitful earth, Ptah, springs from the Primeval Hill, the beginning of all earth and life. Vedic myth conceives of the primal waters bearing within themselves the germ of life which within a small clod of soil rises to the surface, expanding into a great mountain shouldering the sky. A variation is the Semitic proposal of coagulation of matter within primal chaos.

(2) Earth diver. Some animal plunges deep down into the primal waters in search of the smallest dollop of earth at the bottom of the sea. With the greatest difficulty, sometimes fatal to the diver, the tiny lump of soil is brought to the surface. The Creator is then able from the bit of earth to build up the entire land surface of the world. Note the life-enhancing effect (apparently deduced from the

growth of seeds) by which Christ multiplied five loaves of bread and two fish to feed 5000 (Matthew 14:16-21). The earth-diver account is widespread in America and in India, with strong representation in central Siberia, chiefly in food-gathering and hunting societies. The Seneca Amerindians even employ a separate term, oeh-da, for the little chunk of earth dredged up from the depths of the sea by Muskrat, the earth-diver. In Polynesia the Pacific Islands are explained as fished up from the ocean bottom by Tangaroa. An interesting and unusual version from Sumatra states that the god, Batāra Guru, sent a handful of earth down to his daughter, who had leaped from heaven into the landless sea.

Psychoanalysis suggests that the earth-diver theory represents cloacal birth. Freud interpreted all dreams of movement into or out of water as dreams of parturition, and further proposed that an early childhood concept believed babies are born anally like feces. The earth-diver myth may be considered male birth-envy of the female[64] or perhaps simply birth-anxiety.[65]

(3) Float and other objects added to the waters. One Indian myth has Prajāpati kindle a fire upon a floating lotus leaf, thus starting the earth amidst the waters. Another Indian myth[66] says that the Creator, Niranjan Dharma, formed the dry land from his own excrement. The Japanese co-creators, brother (Izanagi) and sister (Izanami) stood on the floating bridge of heaven stirring the formlessness below with a great jeweled spear; drippings from the spear point formed the island center of the emerging world.

(4) World egg. The Brāhmanas proclaim Prajāpati as supreme god; from the sweat of his body was formed an egg which floated for a year upon the primordial waters, then split apart to give birth to the world. The Dakkalwars of India suggest two primal humming sounds in the emptiness of space; the two humming sounds united into a huge ball from whence the universe arose. The Natha cult of Bengal claims that the impulse of creation caused a ripple in the void, forming a bubble, an egg. Taoism says that swirling of the original chaos took the form of an egg. The famous Orphic myth of Creation begins with the bursting of Phanes from the silver egg of the cosmos; within himself Phanes contained all heaven, earth, and life. The Kalevala ascribes Creation to a broken egg laid by a duck upon the knee of Ilmatar, mother of Vainamoinen.

(5) Purposeful divine fabrication. In Chinese myth the god P'an Ku chiselled the universe out of

chaos. The Rigveda (X.81.2-4) portrays Vishvakarman as physically constructing the entire universe with his hands. The Kachin of Burma insist that the god Shingrawa literally hammered out the present world. A major category of this theme is construction of the world from the body of a slain giant. The Mesopotamian myth of Marduk slaying the primordial female Tiamat and constructing the world from her corpse associates inchoate matter with the female and constructive will with the male. The Indo-European Creation myth details the sacrifice and dismemberment of a primal androgyne like Ymir of Scandinavian myth, but the same pattern appears in Iran, Russia, Rome, Germany and in non-Indo-European cultures such as China and Indonesia.[67]

(6) Divine Command. Archaic awe at the wonder of language causes reverence for the Word. As men by naming things feel a power over those things, so gods by utterance cause the things they named to be realities. Cuniraya Uiracocha of E. Peru created thus, simply by his order. Numi Tarem, the supreme being of the Vogul of W. Siberia, created the world solely by his spoken word. The Hebrew Yahweh commanded, "Let there be light," and there was light. By some Egyptian accounts Ptah thus verbalized the universe into being; by other Egyptian reports it was Thoth.

(7) Divine thought. When Anaxagoras of Clazomenae in Ionia c. 450 B.C. asserted that Mind was the principle that produced the cosmos from primordial chaos, he was stating in non-mythical language the archaic myth of god thinking the world into existence. Early Hinduism in the Laws of Manu (1. 74-75) proclaims that Mind "performs the work of creation by modifying itself." This notion, apparently so profound, may also be linked to wish fulfilment. Anyway, this idea is conceivable by the far from erudite Wijot of N. California who aver, "The Old Man Above did not use earth and sticks to make men. He simply thought, and there they were."[68]

(8) Divine inadvertence. Long before sophisticated modern "Black Comedy" perceived the universe as a bizarre accident, myth could humble and humiliate man, dismissing the entire world as wholly unintentional, a chance and random formation by heedless gods. Perhaps the least flattering of all is the Indian concept in the Satapatha Brahmana that the supreme deity created the cosmos unintentionally by merely drawing in and expelling air. Gods sprang into existence from the supreme mouth, men from the afflatus of the supreme anus. More flatteringly, his

devotees would see Vishnu as creating the kalpas or cycles by inhaling the universe to end the present dispensation and exhaling to form a new era. Artistic treatment of Creation as divine breath produces the aesthetic rendering of Genesis 2:7. One might think that a concept like Calderón's drama, La vida es sueño ("Life is a Dream"), is highly intellectual and self-conscious, but the Creation myth of the Witoto of Colombia long anticipates Calderón: Nainema ("he who is appearance only"), say the Uitoto, brought all things into being through a dream. The Vaishnava Creation myth suggests that the entire universe is merely an unpremeditated dream of Vishu. Shankara (fl. 800 A.D.), one of the greatest of Indian and world theologians, saw Creation as an off-hand, accidental game, a divertisement, by Brahma; since this Creation was not purposeful, Brahma is not to be blamed for the imperfections of the world.[69] We may think of the entire universe as a quite fortuitous spillage from the awesome plentitude of Brahma. Shaivites interpret Creation as produced by the dancing of Shiva, a dance of self-expression with no intention except vent of Shiva's monumental energy; the resultant universe is an unforeseen accident. The Iranian Mazdak (5th century A.D.) followed this mythological pattern but demythologized the account. The intermingling of light and darkness, he believed, produced the universe by purely random motions. Similarly, without any intentional plan, the total separation of light and darkness will bring the universe to an end. All of the myths in this category are asserting that the origin (and the conclusion) of all things will be found in the unconscious, not in conscious purpose or intent.

Even though some archaic societies have no myths about the creation of the earth, nonchalantly presuming that earth has always abided, every society is curious about how our species originated and universally propounds myths to account for the appearance of humanity.[70] Though immense in number, these myths fall into a handful of patterns:

(1) Man comes forth from living objects of earth. Many S. Asians and islanders (Formosans, Andamanese, Japanese, Tagalog of Philippines) say that mankind originated from a bamboo joint. Of course, this legend parallels the Western folklore theme of finding a child in a cabbage patch. All such reports assert that we are the products of Mother Earth. Similar is the Zulu myth of man's origin from a reed, and the Herero (also African)

myth that humanity sprang from a tree. When we tell
children that the stork brought them (if anybody
prattles this canard any longer), we are speaking
metaphorically. The stork is an aquatic bird associated with swampy, marshy places, the half-water
half-earth realm of the maternal.

(2) Ascent from below or descent from above
(such myths usually appear in settled agricultural
societies). The Trobriand Islanders relate elaborate
accounts of human emergence from underground. All
whose ancestors came from the same hole are related.
Clan and social status depend upon place and order of
ancestral ascent from the depths to the surface. The
Arunta of central Australia believe that great masses
of beings slept beneath the surface, finally waking
and breaking through. This and many parallel myths
from Amerindians obviously portray the birth trauma.

African and Amerindian myths of descent of man
from heaven also indicate the trauma of birth, here
the discharge of the infant, still attached by the
umbilical cord (most women in archaic societies give
birth upon their knees). Rather poignant is the
account from Tierra del Fuego of the mythical ancestor climbing down from the sky on a rope that
broke. After many vain attempts to reascend upwards,
humanity had to resign itself to living on this
sub-celestial world.

(3) Fashioning of man by god from earthly substance. The metaphor here seems to be mother earth
ultimately providing the material, and the male
element, the father, as the conscious shaper, the
formulator. Clay is the earth substance from whence
god fashioned man according to the Maoris, the Akkadians, and the Hebrews. Khnum of Egypt molded man
upon the potter's wheel. Norse mythology indicates
that the first human pair was carved from trees, an
ash and an alder. Odd sticks were joined together to
form man by Taikomol, the divine Creator, according
to the Yuchi of N. California. The Warikyana of
Brazil indicate that the deity fabricated mankind
from hunting bows. The Kachin of Burma believe that
the chief deity concocted the pumpkin, and other gods
made additions, eventually producing the first man by
committee. Amerindians and Australian aborigines
tell extensively of the pre-human era when the forms
of animals were tentative, unfixed. From these amorphous beings the gods or culture-bringers or first
ancestors shaped mankind. Many Australian myths
state that black lizards were the basis, with divine
reshaping of the lizards into human beings.

(4) Man made from divine substance. Man has always suspected that he is godlike, while ruing his lesser status. Quetzalcoatl sprinkled his own divine blood upon the dead of preceding worlds in order to create man. A Babylonian myth has Marduk fashion humanity from his own blood and the blood of other gods. Iranian myth claims that the first man, Gaya Maretan, was born from the sweat of Ahura Mazda. One Chinese account says that men descend from the parasites bred upon the body of P'an Ku, the primal dema deity constituting the earth. Of course, man egregiously deems himself in the image of god, as the first man, Tiki-ahua ("Tiki's image"), aver the Maoris, was the first man formed by the god Tiki.

(5) Mankind as an afterthought or wholly subsidiary creation. Could there be a less laudatory explanation of human creation than the myth of the Jicarilla Apaches? In his many acts of creation, states this account, God was followed by a patiently trotting dog. God considered Creation complete, but the disconsolate canine pleaded for a companion. To oblige the dog, God made man.

Probably the original versions of creation in very ancient matrilineal society indicated the first male as an afterthought. The Arosi of Melanesia declare that the first human was a woman and that the first male was fashioned from one of her ribs. Scholars do not think this myth indebted to Christianity. Could the Hebrew myth be an inversion of a previous account corresponding to that of the Arosi? Some S. Amerindian myths tell of primal mankind consisting only of males whose meat hoards were raided by women descending from the heavens. Cutting off the ladder or rope to the skies, the romantic males insured themselves spouses. Most of the extant mythological accounts are strongly patriarchal in orientation, therefore regarding women as an afterthought in Creation. The most misogynistic ploy is to suggest that god made man and left the making of woman to the devil. A Baltic story claims that the first woman was made from a dog's tail. The Tahiti myth, saying that Ta'aroa formed woman from a bone in the male body, may be derived from Christian teachings. Jungians would applaud the Cambodian myth that woman was born from the shadow of man, but they would politely point out that it is the anima, not the shadow.

The myths of Creation to archaic societies are sacred ritual. The Unambal of NW Australia begin any narrative concerning their life, customs, and viewpoints by starting with their Creation myth. When a

royal princess was pregnant in old Hawaii, the creation chant, Kumulipo, was continuously chanted until
the birth of the child. Although the formidable
Apache chieftain, Geronimo, became a member of the
Dutch Reformed Church in 1903, when he dictated his
autobiography in 1906, he began with the immemorial
Apache myth of Creation.[70] Every creation (child,
city, temple, nation, or any recognized or ceremonial
start) is an example of the eternal paradigm--the
birth of every human.

Chapter XII The Mythic Realm within Each Human (cont.)

Ejected from the paradisical womb, the human infant protests its independent existence and desperately desires to return to paradise (<u>regressus</u> <u>ad</u> <u>uterum</u>). Jungians say that to the unconscious the yearning to re-enter the womb is incestuous. Apparently in the unconscious is concentrated the ultimate irony: the urgent quest for rebirth in the womb of the mother is stigmatized as the most horrendous of human sins, incest.[1] The psychological struggle is brilliantly presented in the Maori version of the Maui legend. Significantly, Maui was rejected by his mother (the infant cannot regain the womb and consequently feels totally rebuffed). Seeking immortality, the adult Maui strove to re-enter the womb of Hine, Goddess of the Underworld and hence the Great Mother. The cruel Hine crushed Maui to death between her thighs as he had partially entered her womb. Significantly again, she is termed an Ancestress of Maui.

The regression to the womb is also an important element in male transvestism, for in wearing female garments the male is then "within" the mother. In many cultures female apparel, unlike the more spare male garments, has a wrapper quality, an enveloping effect, symbolic of maternal enclosing. The eunuch priests of Magna Mater in antiquity wore such all-covering feminine attire, and in many cultures priests wear feminized clothes, perhaps as being "within" the Great Mother. During fertility worship among the ancient Teutons, men donned women's clothing. Today in India the sacrificing priest of the Jalaris wears female garments to indicate that "he has been possessed by the goddess."[2] Freudians explain male transvestism as eroticism, having sexual relations not with a woman but with her clothing.[3] Such an attitude seems the unconscious identifying of <u>regressus</u> <u>ad</u> <u>uterum</u> with incest.

Love of mother is strongly emphasized almost universally, and its incessant repetition may be an attempt to override guilt feelings from deep-seated antipathy towards the mother. Neo-Freudians now theorize that the Terrible Mother concept arises from pre-natal experience. Recent techniques, permitting extensive observation of the fetus in the womb, disclose considerable movement by the fetus. If the placenta supplies rich red blood replete with nutrients and oxygen, it is a Nurturant Placenta to the fetus, which acts with joy and satisfaction. Thus arises the later love relationship to the mother.

If, however, the placenta produces dark blood polluted with carbon dioxide and wastes, it is a Poisonous Placenta to the fetus, which writhes in distaste,
even kicking the placenta in anger. Thus, presumably, from before birth emerges the concept of the
Horrible Mother.[4]
    The human infant is an egomaniac, interested
solely in itself. When it wants nourishment and
attention, its demands are imperative and tremendously vociferous. Even the slightest delay in
proffering satisfaction kindles an appalling infant
rage. When mother fails in instant attention, the
infant feels that she is not the "good mother" but
the Terrible Mother. Any thwarting generates this
image of the cruel and vicious mother to reinforce
the hostility arising from inability to return to the
womb. Furthermore, we always transfer to those we
dislike our own hostile feelings. Consequently, the
child attributes to the Terrible Mother its own
cannibalistic wishes towards her.[5] To all of this
syndrome is added the association of the female with
flowing blood in menstruation, defloration, and
parturition. From this brew are concocted the devastating hosts of witches and monstrous females.
Perhaps the deepest and darkest level of such hate
spawns the appalling animal females: snakes, dragons,
ogres, and other monsters of nightmarish conster-
nation.[6] The Egyptians retained a number of such
alarming female deities from a distant and infantile
past. Even if later granted beneficent roles,
Taueret the hippopotamus goddess, snake-headed
Renenet, Mertseger the snake-goddess of Thebes, and
scorpion-goddess Selket spring from infant fears and
bear the shivery blood-curse of the Terrible Mother.

    Interestingly, in the matrilineal areas of the
New Hebrides the Devouring Ghost is male, while in
the patrilineal areas the Devouring Ghost is female.
Actually the Terrible Mother is worldwide, and presumably this archetype is every whit as potent in the
female psyche as in the male. Until converted by
Buddha, the Chinese Kuei-tzu-mu had been the devouring ogress of children and the mother of 500
demons of illness and injury. Pot-tilter is the
abhorrent old woman of Crow Amerindian myth whose
pot, tilted in your direction, will engulf you in
boiling destruction. Tarn, a female deity of the
Ostyaks (W. Siberia), gloats over havoc by war,
sickness, famine, bad weather, or otherwise. Nhang
is the Armenian river goddess who delights in dragging swimmers to death. Rán in Norse mythology

(Sjöran in Swedish) dragged whole ships down to
watery annihilation; in early days sailors offered
human sacrifice to Rán before voyages.
    But the most repulsive of all Terrible Mothers
haunt Tibet and India. Lhamo of Tibet rides upon a
mule in a saddle made of her own son's skin which she
herself flayed. Her garments are assembled from
skins cut from her human victims. She lunches upon
human brains and quaffs human blood from a skull
drinking cup. The grim hosts of plague goddesses in
S. India cast a melancholy air upon their worshippers, resigned to the ceaseless toll of the inexorable Terrible Mother. Perhaps the ultimate horror is
Mahākālī, the epitome of carnage in female form. For
a garland she sports a string of human heads, and her
staff is fashioned of human bones. In cannibalistic
glee her teeth are gnashing, her livid tongue pro-
trudes, and blood courses from her lips. Mahākālī
shall preside at the final dissolution of the universe. No other deity is so ambivalent as Kālī. The
18th century Bengali poet-saint Rāmprasād deeply
sensed the abysmal horrors of Kālī but also revered
her benign motherliness, and the 19th century spiritual leader Ramakrishna especially revered Kālī as
the glorious and eternal Mother. The temple of
Kālīghat-Calcutta is the bloodiest temple in the
world, a slaughterhouse for huge numbers of male
beasts, creatures of the Great Mother--and her victims. Beyond all other deities, blessed is she who
brings life, and blessed is she who takes life in
blood and violence.
    Male masochism certainly enhances the image of
the Terrible Mother. The death of Pentheus at the
hands, quite literally, of his mother Agave looks
like a fantasy of the Terrible Mother derived from
male masochism. Lorelei, Sphinx, Judith, Delilah,
Salome, Lamia, and all the seductresses luring poor
males to their downfall and destruction similarly
appear to be versions of the archetypal Terrible
Mother. The growing and grown male, regardless of
his vocal support of equal rights, unconsciously
wants female passivity and acceptance. The assertive
female makes him fear impotence and subsequent womanly scorn of his inability to perform.[7]
    Probably the extreme mythical development of
this male masochism is the castrating vagina. The
Waspishiana and Tarumas Amerindians report that the
first woman had a carnivorous fish inside her
vagina.[8] The Medusa head has been suggested as a
castrating vagina.[9] Psychoanalysts report male
patients fantasizing a stare at the mother's genitals

with concurrent rigidity of the bodies of the patients, comparable to the freezing effect of the Medusa. This reaction is interpreted as castration impotence.[10] The most widespread version of the castrating vagina is the toothed vagina (vagina dentata). The vagina with masticating teeth to bite off the male genitals is reported in myths from many Amerindians, the Ainus of Japan, in Korea, Taiwan, Ryukyu, N. Asia, central India, and various Slavic peoples. The Shoshone N. Amerindians say that Coyote was puzzled when he observed an attractive girl dropping food down her body. His anus advised him that the girl had a toothed vagina that would chew off his penis. With his elkhorn scraper he broke off the teeth in her vagina, had intercourse with her, and thus fathered the first Shoshones. The Chaco of S. America say that the first men could not have sexual intercourse with their wives until their culture-bringer broke off the teeth in the women's vaginas. Clashing rocks, such as those encountered by the Argonauts, appear in many folk themes;[11] possibly these rocks could be a rather remote development of the vagina dentata theme. Another possibly related theme is the poison damosel, reported in the Gesta Romanorum as brought up by snakes, nurtured on poisonous herbs, and poisoning men whom she lures to her. An enemy sent the beautiful but lethal maiden to Alexander who was saved, however, by the shrewd Aristotle. The theme could also represent fear of venereal disease.

Body consciousness means no more unity and no more absolute harmony but, instead, the multiplicity and conflict of the world. All such struggle begins with the creation of polarities, opposites, first dramatically rendered mythically in the sundering of the World Parents. When Genesis 1:4 asserts that god separated the light from the darkness, it is recounting the separation of World Parents narrated in Sumerian myth as the splitting apart of previously united An (sky) and Ki (earth) by Enlil, the air god. Frequently it is the son who physically separates the parents. In Egyptian myth Shu pushes apart his mother Nut (sky) and his father Geb (earth). Probably the Greek myth of Kronos chopping up his father Uranus represents the separation of World Parents. One of the fullest accounts of this separation is the Maori myth of Rangi (sky-god) ripped apart from Papa (earth goddess) by their son Tane because all the offspring of sky and earth were jammed between their parents and needed breathing room. The Vedic recounting of this theme depicts Dyāvāpirthivī as one primal unit separated into the sky-god Dyaus and the Earth Goddess Pirthivī. The sundering of the former unity into a duality makes sense in the Jungian scheme of two major warring elements in each male and two different clashing elements in females. For all growing consciousness this sense of a splitting of one into two is a reality. Freudians attribute the savage violence of a son like Kronos to an infantile emergence of the Oedipal theme. Many myths, especially from Africa, report the sky as formerly pressing very close upon earth and then retreating upward because of human dereliction. All over the west coast of Africa appears the myth of a woman pounding meal and lifting the pestle on the upstroke so high that it poked the sky, who in a pique removed himself upward permanently. Whether male or female is to blame, there is a deep-seated sense of guilt about one's own birth as presumably a disruptive and divisive force. Perhaps we are chiding ourselves for emerging from the blissful unconscious and precipitating all the uncertainties and vagaries of consciousness.

The emergence of body consciousness may now be exalted by modern man as the beginning of rational observation and deduction, but it also means the development of magic. All magic requires motions and/or words. As infants explore their world, they have the delightful realization that when they want candy or a toy or other object, one of their own arms will quite magically snake out and convey the object to them. Magic has its rationale (if the term can here be employed) in this fulfilment of a wish by bodily motions. Thus a magician waves his baton, gestures, grimaces, shrugs, or in some manner performs a physical movement which is supposed to assure the desired end. Words may accompany or, in spells and incantations, supplant other bodily motions, for the infant discovers with glee that the utterance of certain specific sounds can magically cause mother to produce attention and cause other desirable things to happen. All the tales of all the world that involve magical feats and occurrences (Medea and Perseus, Sinbad and Faust, and so on) spring from this body consciousness of early childhood.

Freudians assert a sexual nature even within the fetus, and universally today we realize how erroneous was the older concept of sexual "innocence" in children. Sexuality in childhood is complex to the observer and confusing to the individual child. Everyone has noted "feminine" elements in some small boys and "masculine" elements in some young girls,

and modern psychologists frequently extoll the androgynous character (not physique) that will combine
elements of both sexes within one person. Jungians
insist that every male has the anima within him and
every female has the animus. Anxious parents, however, besiege the psychologists with fears that
children with certain characteristics usually attributed to the opposite sex will prove to be homosexual. The basic fear, however, seems a transgres-
sion of sexual sterotypes. All societies have concepts of what an adult male should be and do, and how
a grown woman should comport herself. Societies vary
considerably in their intensity of indoctrination,
but all societies exert some pressure to direct boys
toward the man's path and girls towards the woman's
path as the society interprets those paths. When the
breasts swell impressively on the girls and the
testicles on a boy, society then wants to squeeze the
youngsters definitively into the sexual grooves. At
this sexual crisis, the elements of the opposite sex
within each individual may precipitate a grave concern about sexual identity. At this time and later
the male may wish that he were a woman and the female
may wish she were a man. These wishes result in the
multitude of myths of sex change. Even the dextrous
surgery of today can as yet effect only a pseudo
change--a eunuch with simulated breasts and dosed
with estrogen or a woman with a hysterectomy and
false male organs and shots of testosterone. Myth
does better with spectacular (and fertile) sex
changes. The meaning behind these myths may be:
    (1) Physiological hermaphrodites switching sex
roles. No human has ever been established as a true
hermaphrodite, fertile in both sexes, but the term
has been applied to humans having observable organs
of both sexes. Extraordinarily rare as a human
hermaphrodite may be, folk fascination will insure
wide publicizing.
    (2) Actual physiological change of apparent
female into a male. A genetic defect can cause the
absence of a hormone that forms the male genitals
prenatally; at about the age of 11 or 12 the apparent
clitoris would gradually become a penis, and the
testicles would gradually descend.[12] Perhaps the
Indian story about Manu's offspring could thus be
explained. The Vishnu Parana (IV, 1) indicates that
the sacrifice to Mitra-Varuna suffered some ritual
flaw, and instead of the desired son, a daughter was
born. In course of time the exemplary piety of Manu
caused Mitra-Varuna to change the daughter into a
son. In Greek myth Leucippus may represent such a

374

physiological change. Lamprus had ordered his wife
Galatea to slay her child if it turned out to be a
girl. The daughter born to Galatea was brought up by
the mother as a male called Leucippus. As puberty
approached, the deception was in danger and Galatea
prayed to Leto, a benign goddess, who transformed the
disguised girl into a genuine male.

(3) Dramatizing the universal experience of
puberty. The Phaestians of antiquity annually commemorated the transformation of Leucippus. Significantly the ritual celebrated the ecdysia (shedding of
female raiment by the transformed male youth).
Perhaps this rite simply commemorates the normal
sexual development, with male childhood viewed as
feminine and puberty heralded as the start of male-
hood. Until recent generations infants and small
children were all garbed in feminine apparel; the
folk explanation was to fool malignant spirits into
believing that the small boy was only an inconsequential girl. The coming to manhood was always vigorously celebrated by an archaic society, and that
important ritual may be the real basis for the supposed sex change.

(4) Garb or mask accepted as sex transformation. On the island of Halmahera, Indonesia, un-
fruitful trees are deemed masculine. Trees supposedly can be made feminine and fruit-bearing by
tying a woman's skirt to the "male" tree. This
practice stems from an archaic belief that a mask or
clothing will not represent a mere pretense but is
the actual being. With the elaborate garments and
numerous secondary sexual trappings (cosmetics,
jewelry, foot gear, etc.) of many societies, the
pretense of sex change can be maintained. In
Japanese kabuki drama, the female impersonator
(onnagata) dresses and acts like a woman in everyday
life; the most accomplished of the onnagato
reportedly excel most women in feminine appearance
and deportment. In the traditional Chinese drama
actors and actresses were expected to take roles of
either sex.

(5) Warrior woman considered male. Poseidon
raped Caenis who requested as recompense that she be
transformed into a male. The resultant male,
Caeneus, was a valiant soldier, but at death the
corpse returned to female form. In Albania until
recently a woman could join a warrior band and fight
as a male with full recognition as a man.

(6) Castrated male considered female. Opera
seria of 18th century Italy extensively utilized the
castrato in female roles, and the castrato might also
appear off-stage in female garb. Stories from India,

Crete, and Germany report men changed to women as punishment for spying on the deities, especially the goddesses. Possibly this alleged sex change simply means castration. An Indian myth states that the altruistic Rūpavatī sacrificed her breasts to feed a starving person, and the god Indra thereupon transformed her into Prince Rūpavata. If loss of external male organs causes a man to be termed a woman, then logically the loss of both breasts could cause a woman to be deemed a male. Such amputation, however, has never been an established practice as castration has been.

(7) Ritual transvestism. The Matsya Purana presents a complicated tale about Ilā who unwittingly entered the forest of Shambhu. Pārvatī had been embarrassed by sages witnessing her nakedness there, and she persuaded her husband Shiva to transform into a woman any man who ventured into the forest. Thus far the change of Ilā into a woman would look like castration of a man impiously invading the privacy of a goddess. Extensive supplications to the deities, however, caused Shiva and Pārvatī to permit Ilā to alternate sex each month. Now the myth certainly sounds like a priest of the Great Mother commemorating female periodicity in female garb. To this day a male member of the Shaktībhava cult establishes his supreme goal as becoming a companion of Rādhā, the love-goddess; ritually he affects feminine garb and mannerisms, even to aping of the monthly cycle.[13] The transvestism of modern carnivals is a survival of ritual transvestism of fertility ceremonies in archaic societies, symbolizing a disruption of normality, a topsy-turvydom before a new cycle of sober commonplace is reasserted.[14]

(8) Non-ritualistic role reversal. Artists have found it titillating to portray Heracles in female dress spinning at the wheel while Queen Omphale, robed in the lion pelt garb of Heracles, stares down at him with a male-like condescension to "women's work." The servitude of Heracles to Omphale was punishment for his insane and utterly pointless murders. The Great Mother (and the Mistress of Animals) fully condones killing for food and for defense, and she will even demand the ritual sacrifice of human life, but pointless killing she stigmatizes. The punishment certainly indicates subservience to the female deity through her surrogate, Queen Omphale, and the role reversal seems an attempt to infuse into Heracles the Mother's attitudes (i.e. in womanly garb one thinks womanly thoughts). Taking a female role seems to explain why some deities shift

sex. Pales was the Roman protector of shepherds and flocks; hence this early male deity often became interpreted as a goddess. Similarly the male Buddhist deity Avalokitesvara symbolizing "compassion" was introduced into China in the 5th century A.D. as the male god Kuan Yin, but his nurturing role caused his transformation into a female as early as the 7th century.[15]

(9) Male castration anxiety. The Tiresias myth, according to Freudians, represents a terrifying fear of castration in the male. Freudians declare that to children, certainly the male child, the female is felt to be a castrated male.[16] Quite probably this concept is the underlying source of the male-into-female transformation theme, and the male fear of castration would account for the many examples of castration in myth and the fascination with sex change.

Ego consciousness. Jungian theory would interpret the anima as femininity and the unconscious in a man, and the animus as masculinity and consciousness in a woman. For both sexes, then, the striving for conscious selfhood, for self-formulation, and for creative action by the individual is considered masculine--the bold, heroic spirit that exalts the individual and changes the world.[17] In a poll of prominent people asked to name the important contemporary heroes, a determined feminist declared that there are no heroes today. That sounds like the conventional anti-hero of our time, but the feminist proceeded to say that ours is an era of heroic women. Perhaps the outstanding psychological event of this age is the conscious shaping of selfhood by modern women. The active assertion of forceful personality and demonstrable achievement in virtually the whole range of human performance has traditionally been a male prerogative, but in the 20th century the world's largest democracy and greatest reservoir of archaic myth, India, has been vigorously led by Indira Gandhi. The great mythical tradition of the past inserted a few women such as Semiramis, Zenobia, Fatima, into the pattern of the hero, but almost all the central figures in the mythical growth of ego consciousness have been males. In the future we may properly devise a term that includes men and women equally in the heroic myth.[18]

The food-gathering period in human society is the period of body consciousness. The hunting culture evoked in the male hunters the myth of the hero, emphasizing individual initiative, courage, daring, conscious stratagem, and, above all, the subordination of the body to the will.[19] Jungians consider the body associated with woman and mother; yielding to ease and security is yielding to the feminine. The masculine element trumpets the male power to "gut it out," compelling the flesh to obey the bidding of the conscious will. Accepting the challenge of a hostile environment and a highly competitive society accentuates the heroic attitude. The worldwide practice of male initiation in archaic cultures attempts to stimulate the heroic response in all adult males. Joseph Campbell sees this myth of the hero as so all-embracing in human thought that he terms it the "monomyth."[20] The contemporary anti-hero is a souring that is inevitable when global society faces numerous problems (overpopulation, dwindling natural resources, standardization, and so forth) that may diminish or obliterate the heroic concept. A psychoanalytical objection to heroism sounds from Otto Rank, who believes that the myth of the hero originates in the delusional structures of paranoiacs.[21]

Any theme of such universality manifests countless variations, but the ubiquitous myth of the hero[22] remarkably displays many uniform features:

(1) Miraculous parentage. The standard mythological rule asserts: gods and goddesses mating will produce deities, mortal males and females coupling will generate normal human beings, but the pairing of deity and human will create the hero. Achilles (Thetis) and Aeneas (Aphrodite) had goddesses as mothers, while their fathers were mortal. Romulus (Mars) and Cuchulainn (Lug) claimed gods as fathers and human mothers. Semiramis is a woman inserted into the hero myth as a daughter of the goddess Derketo. Hatshepsut claimed that her father was the god Amun. Some sort of record must have been established by the five Pandava princes of the Mahabharata. All five were sons of Kuntī and Mādrī, wives of Pandu, but each of the princes had a different god as father.[23]

The divine parentage of the hero is the first of many distinguishing features to elevate the hero above commonplace mortals. Humanity has zealously cultivated and sycophantically admired the hero because he is the luminous ideal incredibly bestowed upon our mundane world. In the individual psyche the fantasy that the genetic parents are not the "real" parents and that the individual possesses immensely noble but unacknowledged parents is rather unsatisfactorily labeled "Family Romance" (German Familien-Roman).[24] The Family Romance seems to start in the

378

juvenile resentment of parents who are felt to with-
hold the love and attention that the child wants; the
baffled child takes relief in believing that he is
not his parent's child but has been adopted. The
pre-adolescent youngster reinforces the Family
Romance by romanticizing his earliest years. In
those blessed days, he reflects, his father was the
strongest and noblest of men, his mother the love-
liest and most gracious of women. Since the parents
he now observes about him certainly don't match that
superb portrait, the youngster confidently asserts
that others were his true parents and these mediocre
adults about him only foster parents. With the
mounting ego consciousness of adolescence, the youth
is growingly certain that no one so wonderful as he
is could possibly be the offspring of the mundane
people who are supposedly his parents. A sort of
compromise is the dual paternity, "two fathers," one
father the man, the other father a god. This is the
pattern of Theseus (Poseidon the divine and Aegeus
the mortal father), Alexander the Great (Amun-Re the
divine and Philip the mortal father), Jesus (Yahweh
the god and Joseph the mortal father).[25]

(2) Extraordinary conception, fetal condition,
and birth. To be apart from average humans, the hero
must be rendered distinctly different from the outset. The mother of the Teutonic hero Volsung conceived by eating an apple sent by the gods, the
mother of the Dark King (founder of the Shang dynasty
of China) became pregnant from an egg dropped in her
mouth by a swallow (a divine messenger), the mother
of Quetzalcoatl conceived by swallowing an emerald
(symbol of youth and immortality), the mother of the
biblical Joseph seems to have become pregnant from
eating mandrakes (Genesis 30:14-24). Numerous heroes
are born to virgins:[26] Buddha, Lao-Tze, Deganawidah
(culture-bringer of Iroquois Amerindians), Jesus.
Frequently the conception is difficult and under
unusual circumstances, e.g. long barrenness or con-
tinence (Oedipus), incest (Siegfried), father visits
mother in disguise (Arthur).

The fetal development of the hero may be very
rapid so that he is born quite soon after conception,
or his embryonic state is incredibly protracted (some
W. African epic heroes were carried a century or more
in their mother's wombs). Often the hero speaks
while still a fetus. Fatima, daughter of Mohammed,
reportedly spoke from her mother's womb.

To demonstrate his extraordinary nature, the
hero often enters this world most unconventionally.
The Tinguin of the Philippines say that their hero

Kanag was born from his mother's little finger. The great Bon prophet of Tibet, Gsen-rabs-mi-bo, was born from his mother's right armpit. Karna of India was born from his mother's ear. One version has the Indian Ganesha born from his mother's feces. Psychoanalysts suggest that very young children think of conception arising from eating and birth as excretion.

Heroes at birth frequently bear objects of power. Mithra of Persia came forth from the womb armed with a knife and torch. W. African epic heroes emerge with scepters, spears, shoulder bags, and so on. Karna of India was wearing an unbreakable coat of mail at birth. An alternative is various body marks. Buddha's remarkable distinction was clear from a host of special marks upon his body at birth.

All of these notable demonstrations, from the difficult conception onwards, indicate the preexistent power and will of the hero, overcoming obstacles even before birth. The determination to be, to exist, is considered so puissant that the ego of the hero will assert itself even in getting himself conceived. The ego gloats in its triumphant birth, effectively thwarting the thwarters. As a logical extension, at birth the hero is extraordinarily precocious. Heracles could strangle serpents in his cradle, and Wol Fat (of Polynesia) could run about at birth. Other heroes at birth talk, prophesy, brandish weapons, and so forth. Lianja of the Nkundó in the Congo Basin, born soon after his father's murder, leaps fully grown and fully armed from his mother's womb to slay his father's killers.[27]

(3) Rejection by the father and the attempt to destroy the infant hero.[28] Frequently there are predictions of a hero's deeds before his birth, and usually these prophecies foretell injury or overthrow of the father or of an obvious paternal surrogate (wicked uncle, malicious relative, vicious tyrant, nasty usurper). The threatened adult male tries to kill the infant. Freudians immediately point out the Oedipal complex with the male infant congenitally hostile to the father and ascribing its own hatred to the father. It might equally be hazarded that the new born child is hostile to all outside itself and its mother. A child quickly realizes that its father expects attention from its mother, and the tyrannical infant is enraged at anyone who for a moment wants to take its mother away from it.

The standard attempt to destroy the child is exposure where mere lack of nurture, abetted by predators, is expected to eliminate the infant. The ostensible reasons for exposure can be: economic (culturally exposure superseded blatant infanticide), alleged illegitimacy, incestuous parentage, deformity, or avoidance of the fulfilment of a prophecy. Hou Chi of China, Attis, Cyrus of Persia, Paris of Troy, Telephos, Iamus, and Oedipus are a few of the numerous heroic infants exposed. The exposure of heroines as infants too scarily fitted a pattern of exposing female infants when a son was eagerly sought[29]: Semiramis, Atalanta, Cybele, Aërope. The most prevalent version of the exposure of the heroic infant is being cast adrift upon the waters: Sargon of Mesopotamia, Moses, Romulus and Remus, Darab of Iran, Perseus and his mother Danaë, Hiruko of Japan. Exposure in water is apparently symbolic of birth with water as the amniotic fluid and the basket, box, raft, or other floating device as the womb. Probably indicative of a very insecure and frightened ego is the theme of mass killings, huge slaughters of the innocents, from which the heroic infant is narrowly rescued: Sargon, Moses, Krishna, Christ. An extensive parallel in Zulu myth may be borrowed from the Christian account of Herod's Massacre of the Innocents. The mass destruction of other infants also boosts the importance and charmed life of the escaping hero.

Probably the overall motivation behind the supposed rejection by the father is the actual rejection by the son. To be a hero or a visionary or an artist or just any fully self-reliant person, one must break away from the routine family life and the dependence upon parents. Long before Stephen Dedalus of <u>Portrait of</u> the <u>Artist</u> as a <u>Young Man</u>, the adolescent male felt the need to renounce family restraints and independently forge his own destiny.

(4)Heroic infant is hidden or nurtured by animals or brought up by humble foster parents. To prevent his murder, Krishna was brought to the home of Nanda; Orestes was smuggled out of Argos by Elektra; Mwindo of the Nyanga (Zaïre) was concealed in a drum and sent to an aunt; Jesus was quickly borne off to Egypt.

A recurrent pattern is the nurture of the exposed infant by wild animals, apparently more sympathetic than savage man. The nursing beasts are extraordinarily varied: goat (Aegisthus), mare (Peleas), bitch (Neleus), doe (Telephos), "two gray-eyed snakes" (Iamus), the somurgh (a fabulous bird to mother Zal of Iran), eagle (Ptolemaös). A she-bear suckled the exposed infant heroine Atalanta, and doves fed Semiramis, daughter of a dove goddess. Nurturing by a female animal suggests a most lowly mother in contrast to the child's dream of a radiantly beautiful and sublimely noble mama. Turning mother into an animal vindicates the ingratitude of a son who denies her.

Humble foster parents often bring up the young hero: Amphion, Zethos, Cyrus of Iran, Romulus and Remus, Krishna of India, Siegfried. Here is the Family Romance with a vengeance, as the adolescent cannot possibly accept these mediocre and unimpressive people as the parents of such a unique and wondrous person as himself.

(5) After a blank period of at least a decade, the hero suddenly emerges as a redoubtable dragon slayer. While myth has much to say about the hero from even before his conception until he is safely ensconced in the home of humble herdsmen, fisherfolk, or farmers, then a strange silence descends. It is the anonymity of the young and immature; probably the blank period arises from the archaic assumption that the person is made by the initiation. The valorous career of the hero is so intertwined with the male initiation ritual that it is impossible to say which developed first. The concept of the hero and the male initiation rite mutually feed each other; both demand great deeds and dauntless determination.

In contrast to his precocity at birth, the hero is often portrayed as retarded in childhood growth, embarrassingly slow to develop: Parsifal, Ilya Muromets of Russia, Helgi (Edda), Hiruko of Japan, Offa of ancient Anglo-Saxons, Sunjata of the Mandingo folk of Guinea. Dramatically this retardation highlights the spectacular upsurge of the hero from obscurity. Adolescents are always annoyed at reports of their childhood, for they realize how trivial those earlier years appear in contrast to their teenage grandeur and glory.

Medieval romancers strained to devise the most bizarre of monsters to challenge heroes; more realistic eras settle for human enemies to be overcome by heroes, and science-fiction of this century has envisaged space monsters of the most outlandish and outglobish extravagance. The incredible ubiquity of this mythical pattern compels multiple interpretations of dragon slaying:

     (a) The animal nature, the supposed baser character within each person, is overcome.
     (b) The unconscious is subdued as the hero marks the triumph of consciousness.
     (c) The destruction of anonymity in favor of confident selfhood.

(d)   The assertion of culture against anarchy.
(e)   The victory of maturity over immaturity.
      The young male forcefully proves that he
      has thrown aside the childish role of
      dependence and is now independent and
      strong-willed.
(f)   The natural dangers of sea and land van-
      quished by the resolute hero. Note the
      labors of Heracles as reputedly eliminating
      a spectrum of natural adversaries. Archaic
      societies strongly apprehended this episode
      as inspiring young males to the heroic life
      of hunter and protector.
(g)   The overcoming of the mother figure within
      the young male (this theory is favored by
      depth psychologists). Of course, no youth
      consciously realizes such meaning.
In the process of ego development the male first
feels part of the mother, then separates but sees her
as a goddess, next degrades her to the nursing she-
animal, and finally fixes her as the autochthonous
creature of the unformed chaos.[30] To gain full
selfhood the hero must extirpate the last compulsive
monster within. Often the mythical monster is
female, like Tiamat in Mesopotamia, the Python at
Delphi, Kadru of India, and Grendel's dam in Anglo-
Saxon England.[31] Whether Marduk (according to
Babylon) or Ashur (according to the city of Ashur),
the slayer of the female monster Tiamat eliminates
chaos and thereafter insures the forming of order and
structure. Although the monster takes various forms,
the basic beast is the snake or dragon.[32]
     The deities who slew dragons read like a litany
of the heroic gods: Re of Egypt slew 'Apep, Indra of
India slew Virtra, Baal of Canaan slew Yanna, Hebrew
Yahweh slew Leviathan, Phoenician Zas slew Ophioneus,
Greek Zeus slew the Typhon. The list of dragon-
annihilating mortals is an honor roll of the valiant
heroes: Perseus, Heracles, Siegfried, St. Michael,
St. George, Beowulf, Arthur, Tristan. Multitudes of
less publicized males have also been redoubtable
dragon-killers. Cenchrius saved the inhabitants of
Salamis by slaying a dragon. Menestratus at Thespia
killed the man-eating dragon who ravaged a countryside and fed upon plump infants.[33]
     A variant in the struggle of the hero against
the Great Mother consists of the swallowing of the
hero by a monstrous female. A simple form of this
mythical theme comes from Arnhem Land, Australia.
Mutjingga, the Old Woman, swallowed children left in
her care and fled along a river. She was overtaken

and slain, and the children released from her belly were painted as initiated novices still are. Clearly this version shows the rampant Great Mother overpowered and youth delivered from her rule. Many initiation rituals worldwide share this pattern of swallowing by the monster and subsequent deliverance to ego consciousness. Standing in the open mouth of Tiamat, Marduk thrust his spear into her stomach, cut her heart asunder, and split her ravenous jaw into bits. Krishna, engulfed within a giant serpent, inflated himself into gigantic size, bursting the serpent. Note that Gilgamesh, Theseus, and Mithras all killed bulls within caves or building, i.e. within womb symbols.

A more straightforward rejection of the Great Mother appears in myth when Gilgamesh repulses the advances of Ishtar, Ugaritic Aqht refuses Anat, and Indian Arjuna rejects Urvashi. The dominance of Circe by Odysseus vigorously signalizes the heroic male. In body consciousness the chief role of the male was merely as the bearer of the phallus to impregnate the Great Mother; the male is then manipulated as the Great Mother wishes, and thereafter the male is discarded like the ex-lovers of Ishtar. Odysseus will not be a victim of the feminine unconscious, but will effectively assert his male will and consciousness.

(6) The hero releases the captive maiden and/or secures a treasure.[34] The multitudinous sterotyped heroes who so grippingly fascinated Don Quixote monotonously exterminated dragons, each time releasing a commendably beautiful and impeccably aristocratic young lady who had been languishing in durance vile just awaiting the all-conquering hero. Always the lovely maiden in gratitude marries her courageous rescuer. The Japanese god Susa-no-wo slew the ferocious serpent about to devour the beautiful Kushi-nada-hime. The god subsequently sired by this attractive lady a progeny that for a period ruled the entire world. From the belly of the serpent Susa-no-wo removed a sword which ever since has been an insignia of the imperial sovereignty; anyone doubting this account can see the actual sword still on display at the temple of Atsuta near Nagoya.

The classic version of this episode, often depicted by artists of antiquity and by numerous artists since the Renaissance, is the rescue of Andromeda by Perseus. The first part of the myth about the adult Perseus states that Hermes and Pallas Athene powerfully assisted him in the mission to slay the female Medusa. Aid from the gods means the highest counsciousness; Athene sprang from the brain of Zeus and therefore represents womanhood wholly independent of the Great Mother and, as Odysseus could eloquently testify, shrewd, rational power at its zenith. With these mentors Perseus slays the Great Mother within himself and turns her dread power to his own uses. While winging his way homeward with the severed Medusa head trussed up in his wallet, he spies the lovely Andromeda bound to the rocks, about to be a repast for a sea serpent. The direct threat to Andromeda is a chthonic creature of the Great Mother, a serpent and a being from the Mother sea. Andromeda is in bonds because of her boastful mother Cassiopeia and by the specific orders of her father Cepheus, a weak bully. The parents of Andromeda are unfavorably portrayed (by some ancient feminist?) as brutally circumscribing their daughter's life potential. The nubile Andromeda is herself a symbol of the emergent consciousness, but her silly, vain mother and petty tyrant father are attempting to force her into the old body conscious model, a mere instrument of the Great Mother. Andromeda needs desperately to be freed from these outmoded shackles. She demands of a would-be mate that he soar (and Perseus soars on winged sandals) above the old role as mere phallus-bearer. He must prove the utmost of ego consciousness: courage, intelligent planning, strong will, resolute action. Such assertion frees her from bondage to the Great Mother and permits their union on a new and more elevated psychic basis. Perseus has succeeded in transforming the concept of the feminine within himself, and Andromeda is now his anima. She is not the primordial female in rut but a new free woman, a companion, friend, associate, partner, of the animus within her and represented outwardly by Perseus. The mighty Mother Goddesses of the Middle East cared for nought save impregnation, gestation, parturition, and suckling. Those today who consider male-female association solely for the purpose of copulation and/or breeding are still worshippers of the Great Mother. The twofold liberation in heroic myth of both man and woman from the omnipotence of the Great Mother heralds the husband-wife association, a momentous psychic as well as physical union. The Great Mother has her poetry,[35] of course, but much of advanced Myth I and countless examples of the art and folklore of mankind have been generated by the new psychical-spiritual pairing of man and woman.

A variation upon this theme offers the active assistance of the woman to the man in the overpowering of the Great Mother. Medea aids Jason immensely in his dragon-slaying. Perhaps the unsavory character attributed to Medea springs from deep-seated sovereignty of the Great Mother, stigmatizing a woman who would aid a male in attacking tradition. Ariadne assists Theseus in the destruction of the Minotaur, apparently an agent of the Great Mother at the center (womb) of the Labyrinth. Theseus is the philandering male well known in our era; the anima within him looks impossibly romantic and idealistic. No human female will ever incarnate that superlative concept, and so he flits from one woman to another, quickly tiring of each, as do many 20th century Lotharios.

The treasure so often associated with the hero's deeds symbolizes not a beauteous maiden but the broad concept of ego consciousness realized. The point is not the treasure itself but the alteration of the psyche effected by the quest for the treasure. In Robert Louis Stevenson's Treasure Island the riches themselves are finally dismissed in a nonchalant sentence, for it is the seeking that is all important. In one of the oldest of heroic narratives, The Epic of Gilgamesh, the treasure is the fruit of immortality. Had Gilgamesh simply gobbled it upon receipt, he would have failed as a hero. The vast maturing that his struggles effect within him renders him thoughtful of others and fully conscious of how his actions will influence his fellows; he loses the physical object of fruit, but he has attained immense stature as a man. Later versions of the hero myth seem increasingly to miss the point, as the treasure is crudely presented as precious metals and jewels in the Rheingold account. When concentration is truly upon the material value of the treasure, the direction of the narrative changes, as in B. Traven's Treasure of Sierra Madre, to the paltry greed and petty selfishness of man. In the true hero myth, the treasure is puny in comparison to the enhanced inner stature of the hero.

(7) Journey to the underworld. Probably the eeriest passages in the accounts of heroes relate the descent into the bowels of the earth, into the realms of the dead. The descent may be unsuccessful, as with the Japanese Izanagi or the many global versions of the Orpheus account. The Great Mother in the form of Ishtar can reclaim Tammuz and triumphantly return with him to the surface. The heroes discover, however, that their wish to bring back physically those lost to death is as doomed as Hermod's quest for Balder in the depths. Hercules and Theseus descend and emerge apparently as the rather superficial

creatures they were from the outset. The grandeur of this quest below mounts, however, from Odysseus to Aeneas to Dante. The hero is actually descending into himself. The darkness is appropriate to slumber and the unconscious. Only by the fullest probing of the total personality down to the profoundest unconscious can the hero gain the inner completeness and full capability displayed by Aeneas after his descent. Aeneas truly realizes that he is not dropping down to pick up anything outside himself; he is exploring and amplifying within himself.

(8) Control over animals and Nature generally. Being licked by serpents is the usual way of learning the language of birds and animals, as with Melampus, but Siegfried secured this power by touching the blood of the dragon to his lips. Other heroes by potions, spells, or inherent gift obtain control over animals. Unquestionably this capability in part implies the skill of men in taming and domesticating animals. "Hector, tamer of horses" and even talking horses in the Iliad are tributes basically to the successful domestication by humans of creatures larger and muscularly far stronger than men. Beyond that flattery, however, is the symbol of self-mastery. The order that man imposes upon Nature represents man's inner creation of order, meaning, and purpose. As the Buddha may be mankind's supreme concept of man fully self-controlled, so in myth his power over the animals is supreme. The royal elephant had intentionally been made drunk and riotous by Devadatta, enemy of the Buddha, in whose path Devadatta placed the rampaging pachyderm. At the sight of the Buddha, the berserk beast immediately prostrated himself in what Buddhism terms "Submission of the Elephant." The stupa of the Buddha at Rāmagrāma was lost in the jungle as Buddhism lost its hold upon India. Nevertheless, travellers reported that wild elephants religiously decorated the abandoned stupa with garlands of flowers and meticulously swept and watered the sacred soil.

(9) Recognition by the father and/or gaining of the kingdom. Both of these accomplishments really indicate the public recognition of the hero's maturation into ego consciousness. While the initial rejection of the son by the father may be attributable to the Oedipus complex, it carries the larger meaning of general adult male scorn of the immature boy. The youth must prove himself before his initiation into manhood is completely and publicly celebrated. Sometimes the father figure is actually slain by the hero, as Perseus, supposedly loosing an

errant discus, killed his grandfather Acrisius and gained the kingdom. Theseus by sheer forgetfulness to change the black sails to white caused his father Aegeus to hurl himself into the sea and die (the suicide of Aegeus is especially suspect in a man who presumably had known his son for only a very few days and could not have worked up a profound affection in that time). Possibly these and similar accounts mask the Oedipal slaying of the father by the son, or the wish if not the deed.[36] The important point is that the rejected, like Mwindo of the Nyanga (Zaïre) who was smuggled out in a drum, now returns in victorious cavalcade to be acknowledged and to inherit the kingdom.

(10) Hero is the ideal male human of the era. Rāma of the Rāmāyana is the ideal Aryan and probably the most commendable of all heroes. His virtues reveal: faithful and wholly obedient son, affectionate brother, exemplary husband, brave hero, excellent monarch, pious and spiritual devotee. Like Hamlet he should be the king, but his father had been tricked into bestowing the throne upon a stepbrother of Rāma, and the noble hero accepts his father's blunder and voluntarily goes into forest exile. Moderns may detect a flaw in Rāma's suspicions about his wife Sīta when she was kidnapped. However, this distrust of women absent from their husband's bed was wholly characteristic of the aristocratic male of the period.

Other times and other cultures cannot be judged by our standards. We are wholly in error to brand Achilles as a sulky colonel mutinously defiant towards his general, Agamemnon. Achilles is positively without any obligation to fight; he took no vow as the suitors did, he owes no loyalty to any fighting man, and national ties simply do not exist in his era. He would appear a pathetic Milquetoast in contemporary eyes if he did not zealously defend his honor against the insults of Agamemnon. Roland certainly seems an inflated egotist in his grandiloquent grandstanding; the calm advice of Oliver would achieve the military objective with much more military effectiveness. Nonetheless, the anonymous author of The Song of Roland and his age valued impetuous valor and unthinking devotion far above sober stratagem and computerized logistics.

The most distinctive feature of the hero's ideal nature is his ability to impose his will, his ego consciousness, upon the outward world. The hero may alter his world as:

Physical hero. Victor over beast and man, winner of battles, conqueror of cities and nations, athletic champion, even a notable lady's man will be a famed physical hero. Such a hero glorifies his ego and awes his fellows with his prowess. Heracles seems basically such a physical hero, and the attempts to explain his labors as benefitting others look like an afterthought, perhaps a trifle lame.

Social hero. The hero who transforms society imposes his will and determination to change the course of human events. The founders of cities like Cadmus, the promulgators of laws like Solon, unifiers of peoples like Lacedaemon, and liberators from tyranny like Lucius Junius Brutus, change the direction of history and influence mankind many generations after their lifetimes.

Spiritual hero. The most remarkable heroes effect a powerful transformation within the personality of others, the ultimate imposition of a hero's psyche upon the world. Buddha, Jesus, Mohammed by implanting within others their spiritual visions have proved the most potent of heroes, influencing mankind for millenia.

(11) Unusual death of the hero.[37] Distinctive in birth, the hero must similarly meet an extraordinary death. Dying peacefully in bed is unthinkable for a hero, and cruel fate ended the heroics of Byron with a most unheroic death from disease. The hero may not suffer an actual death but be translated like Romulus. At apparent death the hero may experience transformation into another being, usually a bird. When Llew Llaw Gryffes of Brythonic myth was slain by his wife's lover, he flew away as an eagle. Semiramis, daughter of a dove-goddess, appropriately flies off as a dove. These are examples of the bird soul, with affinities to the motif of the separate soul. If the hero truly tastes of death, others are responsible: treachery as with Hamlet, cowardice of followers as with Beowulf. In The Song of Roland no enemy could despatch the incomparable Roland and Oliver, so they die by hitting each other while blinded with blood.

A frequent theme to kill off heroes is the vulnerability motif. Otherwise impervious to injury, the hero bears the curse of human limitations, though, of course, to a far lesser extent than the rest of us. Both Achilles and Krishna were vulnerable only in the heel. The explanation is clear with Krishna; it is Jara ("old age") that hits him there and slays him. Life is movement, "kicking up one's heels." The cessation of movement because of senility means death. Both the French hero Ferragus and the Swahili hero Liongo were vulnerable only in the navel. Perhaps the most arresting treatment of the vulnerability theme is mysterious. The faithless wife of Llew Llaw Gryffes revealed her husband's vulnerability to her lover, but what was the vulnerability? We shall never know. In fact the death of the hero, that creature of extraordinary and inexplicable potency, might best be clouded in mystery like the death of Theseus or remain unrecorded like the end of Odysseus.

(12) The hero is not dead but sleeps. Arthur, we are told, is the "once and future king." In the betrayal pattern he was betrayed by his wife and closest friend. But reportedly at Camlan he did not die, though sorely wounded. Arthur sleeps in Avalon to return eventually to regain rule of his kingdom. Hosts of other heroes similarly are not dead but are slumbering: Barbarossa (Germany), Charlemagne (France), Mucukunda (India), Meher (Armenia), Fionn (Ireland), Ogier the Dane, Marco (Serbo-Croats).

A familiar explanation for this pattern is the hope of defeated peoples for resurgence. The Arthurian legend is thus appraised as the yearning of the Britons for a return to power over the conquering Anglo-Saxons. For the most part, however, the formulation of the Arthurian account and its vast proliferation is a French (and non-British) creation. Probably the widespread theme arises from the mental image of the sleeper. Jung suggests that in dreams the sleeping hero for men and the Sleeping Princess (or Sleeping Beauty) for women represents the total Self. Each of us has the feeling that deep inside our prosaic selves lurks a hero capable of tremendous achievement, but for some unaccountable reason we are only partially productive: we are asleep. If only we could awake the sleeper and surge forward creatively with giant strength....

Ego transcendence. Almost universally mankind subscribes to the grandeur and towering magnitude of the tragic hero. Is it not pessimistic to contemplate the downfall of the high and the mighty? Again almost universally there seems agreement that after a great tragic myth such as Oedipus or Hamlet the spectator actually experiences an exultation, not a sense of bleak despair at death and destruction. The theater of the absurd proclaims the idiocy of a completely meaningless universe and its random annihilations. The death of the tragic hero, however, must have a resolute meaning.

Jungian psychology interprets the death of the tragic hero as symbolic of the move of the psyche towards individuation. The hero in carrying the conscious ego to its apogee emphasizes one and only one aspect of human nature while excluding many other aspects. He is guilty of hubris, the Greek word for "vaulting ambition," i.e. ego consciousness carried to its ultimate. While a necessary step in the development of the inner nature of man, such ego consciousness finally proves a blind alley, a dead-end, if cultivated to the ignoring of all else. Much as we admire the hero's assertion of his ego and his impact upon his fellow humans, we sense his incompleteness (a tragic flaw) and realize that this ego consciousness must be superseded by another and superior nature. The superior nature is a totality of absolutely all elements of the psyche, unconscious and conscious. All functions, all animae or animi, are fully operational, completely productive. Myth projects the hero as half-divine, and symbolizes the higher achievement of totality as altogether divine. The pattern is clear in Heracles, Krishna, Rāma. Their divinity following tragic death is the accomplishment of individuation--"putting it all together."

Genuine heroes always have a "moment of truth" before death. They are progressively and ultimately wholly aware of their relations to the Self. The experience of the Self is always perceived by the ego as a defeat. The overdeveloped ego must itself be overcome and supplanted as the only governor. To the ego this is destruction. But the death of the tragic comprehending hero is really the opening to a much fuller, truly divine existence. The human psyche will not predicate nihilism. Instead, it insists that death is merely the symbol of a transformed being, the rampant ego curbed and the god within wholly triumphant. The concept of a paradisical afterlife, living in fact the deity's existence eternally and victoriously, is mythologizing individuation. The Great Mother promulgated death-and-resurrection as the triumphant rebirth of fertility, the physical riches of earth. The amplified and transmogrified vision of the tragic hero is the death-and-resurrection of the psyche, the perfected Self ascendant and superbly alive after the "death" of the ego consciousness.[38]

We must experience vicariousness with the tragic hero, for he is, of course, our life and our psychic development. The criminal is dehumanized into an animal that talks; we recognize the criminal as the ego deformed and perverted, jettisoning all possibilities of growth to devote the being solely to survival, wholly at the expense of others. The purely physical hero is dangerously close to the criminal, as in the famous tale of the criminal accusing Alexander the Great (or any other noted military conqueror) of being simply a super-criminal. We must believe that the tragic hero genuinely strives to do what is right for himself and for others. His very thrust opposite to the selfish greed of the criminal forces him towards the defeat of the ego.[39] The Jungian conjecture discerns this entire pattern as essentially masculine in concept. Tragic heroines are definitely in the minority and the select group (e.g. Antigone, Brynhild, Hedda Gabler) is pictured for us by male authors.

Perhaps there is a fundamental difference between male and female psychology. Robert May has suggested that the myth of Phaëton is archetypal male. Eager self-assertion, aspiration, ambition, and hubris propel the exultant male on a great upward curve of exuberance, then collapsing in catastrophe and destruction. In contrast is the archetypal feminine myth of Demeter, which begins in deprivation, pain, and deep sorrow and ends in happiness and joy.[40] If this sex differential in archetypes is valid, then, understandably, tragic heroines are few and are largely male creations; and the whole tragic concept is basically masculine. Freudians propose that the difference arises from the different experiences in copulation. Male sexuality displays an initial intense activity, followed by a considerable let-down, a despairing feeling of being trapped by the female genitals. Conversely, the female in coitus at the outset feels thrust upon, passively suffering, but ends holding the diminished male organ in triumph.[41] Perhaps more generally it might be suggested that the feminine role is conditioned by evolution to nurture the young, aiding others and thereby encountering numerous problems but gaining great satisfaction from the outward reach. The male, under no such natural compulsion, is freer to exploit his ego and cultivate adventure, certainly subjecting himself to more dangers and, dashing far enough, to ultimate disaster. Self-made heroines of the future may totally traverse ego consciousness to ego transcendence, thereby dissipating any sexual sterotype or archetype.

Chapter XIII   Geomythology   and   Meteoromythology

Until Thales of Miletos in the 6th century B.C., human thought everywhere, so far as we can ascertain, was mythic; and, truthfully, much of man's thought to the present day still remains mythic. In trumpeting the glories of scientific knowledge we must nonetheless recognize the basic difference between the mythic and the scientific views as attitude rather than material. The mythic contention is that the universe and all in it are governed by conscious supernatural agency, by willful and capricious power, or by forces controllable by the counterpower of magic. The scientific position claims invariable, impersonal law as the governance of all things. Mesopotamian priests were charged from early Sumero-Akkadian times with precise observation of Nature in order to predict the intents of deity. Their astronomical studies resulted in a concept of ordered cosmic operation, still under divine superintendence. These carefully observant Mesopotamian sky-watchers devised astrology, essentially a mythic, non-scientific way of utilizing their exact observations. Science did not explode or mark a dramatic turnabout; the movement from primeval myth to modern science is a slow and often imperceptible evolution. Astronomers today continue to designate stars by the mythical names of constellations and rationally argue creation theories advanced millenia ago by myth.

The movement from myth to science is clearly revealed in the Egyptian medical documents. The earliest papyri about bandages treat prayers and incantations as paramount, with Isis as the provider and applier of bandages, and her quickening effect to render ointments and lotions truly healing. In late classical times the methods and materials were unchanged, but the prayers and incantations had become nominal or even superfluous. Astronomy and chronology in ancient Egypt originated solely in establishing holy days, prescribing relays of priests, calculating when Osiris would bring his divine moisture through inundation, and determining when the god would ritually die and leave the soil of Geb dry and sterile.

One might wrongfully assume that of all the sciences mathematics would be quite free of myth. The Egyptians employed fractions as successive halvings of ½. The "whole," the unit of one, was conceived as the eye of Horus ripped out and cut into pieces by Set. The eye of Horus was stylized in six parts, and therefore in mathematical references the fractions from 1/64 to 1/2 were each represented by one of the six parts of the eye of Horus. The total of these six fractions is 63/64; the Egyptians believed that the missing 1/64 was supplied by Thoth, the ibis-god who assembled and replaced the eye of Horus.

But the enormous strides of science in the 17th century, one might protest, are altogether different. No mythical influence there, one might aver. Perhaps we could have been more dogmatic here before 1940. Since that date the very bulky alchemical manuscripts of Sir Isaac Newton have been carefully examined, and sober researchers conclude that the hermetic tradition with all its mythological machinery united with mechanical philosophy in the 17th century to produce modern science.[1]

In earlier narrative, accounts of what we would consider scientific phenomena were stated in mythological terms. Hence, long before there was any geology there was geomythology.

Geomythology[2] and Meteoromythology[3]

The Mesopotamian myth of Creation reports the intermingling in primal chaos of the male Apsu (sweet water) and the female Tiamat (salt water). With brilliant accuracy this description indicates the mixture of the Tigris and Euphrates with the sea at the great delta on the western end of the Persian Gulf. Here silt is ceaselessly deposited amidst the reeds, and from this seeming chaos gradually land is formed. The observation is wholly accurate, and so is the entire account, though relating a geological process in mythical fashion.

Classification by archaic man can be as accurate as any system of ours, but again it is dominated by mythic technique. The Canaanite Poem of Baal tells of the fertility and moisture god Baal consigning his opponent, Môt, god of aridity and death, to the dark underworld. By trickery Môt persuaded Baal to eat of the food of the dead, thus trapping himself in the lower world. 'Ashtar, god of sluices and canals, proved a poor substitute for Baal; so the sun brought Baal back from the realm of the dead. In Arabic "land of Baal" means rain-moistened earth, "land of Môt" desert and barren soil, while "land of 'Ashtar" is irrigated land. This myth also states the problem of rainless periods and the way extensive rains will bring fertility to areas otherwise arable only by irrigation.

In Africa, Australia, and America the entire topography of an area is explained as a unit through the movements and actions of the culture-bringer. For instance, the Penobscot Amerindians of Maine identify every declivity and rise of ground, every beach and forest, as results of the activities of their culture-bringer Gluskabe. An elongated rock is pointed out as Gluskabe's canoe, while Mt. Kineo is his overturned cooking pot. Note in Greek myth how parallel is Poseidon's transformation of Odysseus' rescue ship into a rock at the harbor entrance to Ithaca.

The whole globe, of course, can be thought of as Mother Earth with every cave or valley considered her womb, every hill or mountain her breasts, mons Veneris, or limbs. Every feature of the earth's surface can be attributed to supernatural agency. Northern Europe is rife with accounts of primordial giants. When the earth was created, its surface was perfectly smooth, though the consistency of a brand new world was about that of dough. The male giants strode about playfully, gleeful at the great hummocks and gullies their sloshing was ripping up. Thus was created all the up and down of the landscape. The more fastidious female giants wept at the jumbled mess created by the males; the tears of the giantesses poured out as the streams and rivers of the world.

Man generally perceives the most significant and sinister of actions in border places, the liminal areas between opposites. In landscape perhaps the most myth-ridden territory is coastal, with every cape, promontory, shoal, reef, rocky islet, and so on associated with some demon, god, or hero. Scylla (SW Italy) and Charybdis (Sicily) are such border demons, as are the animated Symplegades at the entrance to the Black Sea and the Wandering Rocks, dire perils to the Argonauts. In our own day virtually every feature along the Greek coastline is personified by sailors or has some wondrous tale associated with it. Tides may be seen as the great systole and diastole of the living sea. Many Malaysians believe that tides are caused by the movements of a great crab who enters and leaves his cave at the foot of the world tree.

Basically the geomythological accounts are etiological. From the vast corpus of worldwide myth, the following seem the major categories:

(1) Land formations. The landscape is the product of willful supernatural beings, says mythology, from the heights to the depths. The highest of Indian glacier caps, Gaurishankar, seems to be embracing a jutting peak. Natives say that it is the earth mother, Gauri, divinely paired with Shiva to despatch precious waters of life from the dazzling top of the world to the famished plains below. The Asbyrgi Depression in NE Iceland is a huge horseshoe-shaped indentation, a fossil riverbed, which myth identifies as a hoofprint from Sleipnir, the gigantic eight-legged mount of Odin.

Water backed up from the Bonneville Dam east of Portland, Oregon, now conceals the rapids of the Columbia River at the Cascade Mountain range. Geologists say that the Cascades were formed by a huge landslide of rocks into the river. Amerindians in the vicinity claim that once there was a rock bridge over the Columbia River. A feud between giants to the north and south of the river caused Old Coyote to demolish the bridge and turn the warring giants to stone (i.e. the Cascade Mountains). Although geologists assert that no natural bridge ever existed here, the Amerindian legend is now perpetuated by a great metal bridge, the Bridge of the Gods.

The Gefion Fountain in Copenhagen appropriately honors the goddess supposedly responsible for the island Sjaelland on which Denmark's capital stands. Ingenious and observant Scandinavians noted long ago that Lake Vänern in SW Sweden has roughly the outline of Sjaelland. Poor King Gylfi of that Swedish area had no customary departure gift for the disguised goddess but offered Gefion whatever she could plough in a day and a night. With four magic oxen (her own sons by a giant) Gefion ripped out the block of land which she deposited in the sea as the island of Sjaelland.

Ancient Syracuse (Sicily) was a Greek colony, and, understandably, the colonists were nostalgic for their distant homeland. The ingenious myth they formulated stated that the fountain of Arethusa on the Sicilian island of Ortygia had originated in Greece. The beautiful young huntress Arethusa was bathing in the Alpheus River in S. Greece when the river-god assailed her. Praying to Artemis, she turned to water and flowed into the ground. In aqueous form Alpheus pursued her. Arethusa flowed under the Ionian Sea, emerging at Syracuse. This is the sort of sentimental and immensely artful story like the Eros-Psyche myth that appears quite late, smacking of Myth II.

(2) Earthquakes.[4] The mythical explanations for earthquakes fall into these categories:

(a) Subterranean beast whose movement shakes the earth. Basic is the world serpent, Ananta of India, whose yawn causes the earth to quake violently. In the Moluccas, Sumatra, and Fiji a snake is responsible. A Burmese Shan version postulates a huge slumbering fish beneath the earth with its tail in its mouth; when accidentally biting its tail, the fish shudders and the earth quivers. Other animals shaking the earth from underneath: hog (Celebes), buffalo (Bali, Malaya, Borneo, Bulgaria), tortoise (Algonquian Amerindians), elephant (another Indian myth), frog (Mongolia), catfish (Japan). A Vishnu myth insists that the gigantic boar Varāha causes earthquakes when shifting the earth from one tusk to the other tusk.

(b) The whole earth as a creature. Ancient Mexicans thought of the entire earth as a gigantic frog called Tlaltechuhli (or Tzontemoc). When the frog twitches his skin, that is a shaking of the earth. Kaffirs of S. Africa think of an earthquake as an ague shake by a feverish earth. Ancient Peruvians perhaps facetiously declared that an earthquake occurs when the earth kicks up its heels and dances.

(c) Subterranean humanoid. On the island of Timor a huge giant supposedly holds up the earth, occasionally shifting the burden from one shoulder to the other and thus shaking the world; amidst an earthquake natives shout to the giant not to drop the earth. Earthquakes near Mt. Etna were anciently explained as the thrashing about of Enceladus, a fettered Titan, straining to free himself. Because he was responsible for Balder's death, Loki was tied to a rock underground with a poisonous snake ceaselessly dripping venom upon his face. The faithful

397

wife of Loki, Sigyn, catches the venom in a bowl, but occasionally she must step aside to empty the bowl. Then the venom spatters upon Loki's face, causing Loki to squirm abruptly and the earth to tremble. As late as the 16th century Scévola de Sainte-Marthe of France explained earthquakes as the sudden exhalations of subterranean gnomes.

(d) Surface shaker. Although the Greeks believed that Atlas supported the earth on his shoulders, they attributed earthquakes to Poseidon, the Earthshaker. Greece is geologically a flooded mountain range with arms of the sea extending far inland so that Mediterranean waters are close to almost every Greek. Since the water levels and water movements in bays and inlets would alter most dramatically in an earthquake, it seemed logical to assume that water was the causative factor. Of course, many quakes experienced in Greece actually originate offshore underwater. The Basoga of Central Africa report an earthquake god Kitaba whose invisible strides can make the earth tremble.

(e) Divine visitation. Matthew 28:2 indicates an earthquake as subsidiary to an angel's descent to roll away the stone from the tomb of Christ, and presumably the earthquake of Acts 16:25-34 was divinely instigated for the benefit of Paul and Silas. The standard Old Testament as well as Medieval Christian concept considered earthquakes as the wrath of god. Such constituted the local explanation for the Lisbon earthquake of 1755. A Chickasaw Amerindian myth claims that the Great Spirit stamped his foot in anger at the behavior of Chief Redfoot and thus precipitated the New Madrid earthquake of 1811, one of the worst earthquakes in USA history.

An earthquake seems the most plausible explanation for the destruction of Sodom and Gomorrah, for no volcanic activity in recent geological eras is evident in this area. Bitumen is quite extensive in this area (made now into souvenir articles for the tourist trade) and apparently was used in ancient times as building material. An earthquake could easily scatter embers to burn up a city of bitumen blocks. The fire from heaven in Genesis 19:24-25 may have been lightning that started the fire or lightning from the thunder clouds often generated above earthquakes from the hurling upward of dust.[5]

(3) Volcanos.[6] The standard explanation for volcanic eruption is wrath of a fire god. The term _volcano_ comes from Vulcan, whose smithy was supposedly located under Mt. Etna. In the Valley of Mexico natives explain the constant plume of smoke from Mt. Popocatepetl ("smoking mountain") as "old man Popo puffing on his pipe." The Klamath Amerindians tell of a great battle between Llao, a chthonic deity inhabiting Mt. Mazama in Oregon, and Skell, the god inhabiting Mt. Shasta in California. They hurled flames and rocks upon each other until Mt. Mazama collapsed, forming the caldera containing Crater Lake. The description is remarkably accurate for an event datable about 6500 years ago. This account may therefore be the oldest myth in the world so far as we can assign a date to any myth.

Pacific islands, mostly volcanic in origin, are rich in volcanic myths. The most influential has been the story of Pele, fire goddess of Hawaii. From somewhere farther south (possibly Tahiti), Pele fled from her vindictive elder sister Namakaokahai and with her digging tool excavated for herself a volcanic residence at Kauai, one of the westernmost islands of the Hawaiian group. Namakaokahai pursued Pele eastward, successively dismembering her and each time exulting in the total destruction of Pele. But each time the immortal fire goddess resurrected herself from death, finally implanting herself triumphantly in Hawaii itself, the most eastern of all islands in the chain. The native observation is precise, for volcanic activity was oldest in the far west of the Hawaiian Islands, steadily progressing eastward until Mauna Loa and Kilauea on the easternmost island of Hawaii are the only active volcanos today in the island group. Wind-borne molten lava will solidify into droplets called "Pele's tears" or strands termed "Pele's hair"; both of these terms are employed technically by volcanologists and geologists.

New Zealand has extensive volcanic activity and has a myth to explain a great deal of it. According to the Maoris, Ngatoro, a noted medicine man (_tohunga_) and leader of the first Polynesian settlers, climbed Mt. Tongariro and found it bitterly cold. He prayed that his sisters, sorceresses remaining in the tropical homeland to the north (Tahiti?), would send fire to his aid. Fire demons were quickly despatched under water, surfacing first at White Island in the Bay of Plenty and there creating a still active volcano. Heading towards the chilled tohunga, the fire demons burrowed under the North Island, emerging in the Rotorua section to produce one of the world's most awesome thermal areas, lavish with geysers, hotsprings, steaming vents. Plunging farther, the fire demons swept to Mt. Tongariro. To prove the veracity of the Maori myth, the earth of Mt. Tongariro today is warm at high altitudes even though the surrounding air is cold.

(4) Floods.[7] Accounts about a gigantic flood are so prevalent throughout the world as to constitute one of the most ubiquitous themes of myth. The theme does not appear in obviously unfloodable areas such as the Sahara Desert, and there are far fewer indigenous flood myths in Western Europe than we might expect. The worldwide theme tends to greater uniformity in outline than most myths:

(a) Generally the flood is ascribed to divine wrath over human behavior. Most of the exceptions are myths stating no cause for the flood: it all just happened. About Lake Tyers in Victoria, Australia, the aborigines say that a colossal frog had swallowed all the water in the world. Animals sought to get the frog laughing to disgorge its waters, and finally a cavorting eel set the frog shaking with laughter. All the waters gushed forth, far more than expected, flooding the whole earth. The Younger Edda reports that Odin and his brothers, We and Wili, in slaying the giant Ymir caused vast outpourings of the giant's blood, inundating the world. The Kamars of Central India say that god in anger sent the flood to drown an insolent jackal, and unintentionally wiped out most of mankind. The overwhelming majority of flood myths blame human tabu violations, women's menstruation (a major concern with archaic peoples), human carelessness, or human viciousness. In Raiatea, Tahiti, it is reported that a fisherman snagged the hair of the sleeping sea-god Ruahatu, thus precipitating the god's flood of vengeance. The Tsimshian Amerindians blame the entire flood upon human mistreatment of a trout. Most of the accounts merely stigmatize humanity for general depravity, punishable by divinely instigated floods.

(b) Some human is warned to construct an escape device. The warning may originate from a fish, a bird, an animal, an angel, or a god. The means of survival is usually a raft, canoe, boat, even a coffin. Frequently the warning includes instructions to secure as cargo multitudes of animals to save from the flood for replenishing of the animal world afterwards. Quite unusual is the statement of the Arikena of Brazil that a few humans survived the flood by climbing upon the back of a huge roe deer or the assertion of the Guajiro S. Amerindians that their deity Maleiwa raised up a tall mountain upon which humans could take refuge.

(c) Almost all mankind is drowned in a universal deluge. Of course, if the limited realm of an archaic society is totally inundated, it is logical for natives to assume that all the world is flooded. Torrential rains, as in the biblical account, are the usual explanation for the flooding.

Sudden overflowing of rivers and streams, lakes and pools, is also suggested. The Murngin of Arnhem Land (N. Australia) say that one of the Wawilak sisters with her menstrual blood polluted the water-hole dwelling of the immense snake, Yurlunggur; enraged, the snake swirled upwards, bringing with it enormous volumes of underground water to drown the whole world. The Welsh flood legend declares that the lake of Llion burst to swamp the entire world. Rising water may cover with a shallow layer an enormous area of flat countryside, as in parts of the N. American plains, the interior of Australia, and Mesopotamia. Sudden flooding was most spectacularly exhibited in the northern hemisphere at the end of the ice ages. Natural ice dams suddenly giving way released vast deluges scouring out the Scablands of NW USA. Paleoclimatologists conclude that the enormous Laurentide ice sheet covering much of N. America during the last ice age melted with incredible rapidity, peaking c. 9600 B.C.[8]

Swelling of the ocean is a frequent explanation for flooding of Pacific islands and the entire coastal area touching the Pacific Ocean. More than any other ocean, the Pacific experiences submarine earthquakes that will generate a tsunami, the so-called "tidal wave." The only warning is a brief withdrawal of the sea out beyond the lowest of tidal retreats. Then an appalling wall of water can sweep inland to wreak monstrous destruction.

Chinese myth avers that the dragon Kung-Kung triggered a great deluge by knocking down the pillars

of the universe, i.e. an earthquake. Certainly a
severe quivering could displace all surface bodies of
water and perhaps rupture the earth to eject subterranean waters. Both Egyptian and Semitic myths
emphasize "waters under the earth." In lands of
drought and aridity, a spring is miraculous; the folk
mind will almost certainly magnify this anomaly and
predicate huge water reservoirs beneath the surface,
underground rivers or oceans, ready to surge upwards
and flood the dry land. The Benua-Jakun of Malaysia
claim that the ground beneath our feet is a thin
membrane over a vast sea. Anciently their deity,
Pirman, smote this tenuous membrane, causing total
inundation of all the earth. The Lenggong Negritos,
also of Malaysia, attribute the great deluge to the
"grandmothers" underground who spouted upwards the
vast flood waters to destroy iniquitous humanity.

(d) Replenishment of earth by the few
survivors. The standard mythical theme predicates
the pair or handful of survivors as the progenitors
of all present humanity. Sometimes the survivors are
tied into the incest theme; mother and son or brother
and sister are the only humans to survive the deluge.
Some N. Amerindians say that after the flood the Old
One or Chief made a new race of mankind from balls of
mud. The Deucalion concept of hurling stones over
the shoulder to create humanity anew is repeated
among Eskimos, some S. Amerindians, some Africans,
and elsewhere. This practice looks like the ritual
of Cadmus in sowing dragon's teeth; adults concealed
by undergrowth or crouched in shallow pits would leap
upwards upon signal in a fertility rite.

The world's most famous flood myth appears in
Genesis 6:5 - 9:17. The biblical account is a very
late recension of an old Mesopotamian legend. The
earliest known version is a Sumerian account in which
the god Enki warns the righteous king Ziusudra to
build a boat and stock it with animals and seeds to
float in the midst of the ensuing deluge. In the
Babylonian version the god Enlil advises the pious
king Atrahasis to construct a ship to weather the
storm ahead. The most literary and most exciting
treatment appears in the world's oldest epic, The
Epic of Gilgamesh, originally from Uruk on the
Euphrates, halfway between Babylon and Ur. Here the
god Ea warns Utnapishtim; the biblical account of
Noah summarizes the Gilgamesh legend and reduces the
host of deities to one god, Yahweh. A still later
account by Berossos, a priest of Marduk in the 3rd

century B.C., specifies Xisouthros as the hero of the flood.

Over millenia Mesopotamia has been devastated by several great deluges. Archeology finds amidst the ancient ruins of this valley evidence of three very large floods inundating early human settlements. Any one of these catastrophes of the 3rd and 4th millenia B.C. or a combination could lie behind the famous flood legends. The deep deposits of clay, as much as eight feet at Ur,[9] suggest that all these floods originated in torrential downpours in the mountains to the north, tumbling downstream many tons of soil. A tsunami is possible, as the area about the Persian Gulf has long been seismically active. A recent theory has hypothecated a giant meteorite plunging into the Persian Gulf and sending massive flood waves up the Mesopotamian valley.[10] This conjecture attempts to account for the propelling of Noah's ark NW to Mt. Ararat in the Caucasus, not, as one would expect, seawards towards the Persian Gulf. It should be borne in mind that, to Mesopotamians of that distant era, the most remote of known geography was the Caucasus. The narrator of the myth wanted to indicate the colossal dimensions of the flood and the far voyage of Noah by finding solid earth only at the uttermost extremity of the world.

Many archaic peoples have certainly been influenced by the Judeo-Christian account. It is difficult to say exactly how much of the Maori flood myth, with Parawhenuamea as the Polynesian Noah, is indebted to the biblical version. Throughout the world, however, the tale of a huge, catastrophic flood is probably the most uniform and consistent of all myths. Interpretations suggest:

(a) Universal flood. Finding the flood myth throughout the world, European explorers and missionaries from the Renaissance well into the 19th century assumed that the biblical account was wholly accurate in ascribing to the flood global dimensions and that local flood tales were mere confirmation. Such an opinion seems untenable, for there simply is not enough H_2O worldwide to flood the entire globe at any one time. Furthermore, while floods have inundated most parts of the land surface at one time or another, geology finds no one flooding that has been worldwide on land surfaces. Almost certainly we must conclude that many separate floods are enshrined in the many world flood myths.

(b) Melting of the ice sheet. During ice ages a tremendous portion of the earth's moisture is locked up in the massive glaciers and vast ice fields. About 12 millenia ago the sea level of the entire world was approximately 50 meters lower than at present. Many low-lying areas were then habitable, but were gradually, almost imperceptibly, drowned by the slow rising of the world's oceans. Slowness in the rise of sea level is the keynote here, for in any year the global lift of the world's oceans would be only a few centimeters at most. An occasional spillage over a natural obstacle and especially the sudden breaking of a natural barrier such as an ice dam could produce a dramatic and destructive deluge. In many cases settlers in the lowest areas would eventually be driven from their long-established residence by the inexorable rise of the waters; in retrospect they and their descendants could very well speed up the waters and render heartbreakingly fast what had been a quite gradual irritation mounting to the intolerable. Men recall the suddenness of despair, the celerity of flight, and make equally sudden the cause of that precipitate departure.

(c) Local flood or floods inspire each separate myth of the deluge. This is the rational approach best exemplified by Sir James Frazer who assembles a plethora of flood myths from all the world and contends that there was not a universal flood but distinctly different inundations.[11] All of this marshaling is eminently rational and undoubtedly correct, but it leaves unanswered a momentous question: why are all the versions from interior New Guinea to Pacific coastal America, from the Finns to S. Africa, so remarkably parallel? Separately induced flood myths should not, logic says, appear so similar.

(d) Flood as ritual. Since the ritualists hold that myth and ritual are inseparable, they have maintained that the flood myths are actually descriptions of the flood-inducing rituals in the great valleys of the Nile, Indus, and Mesopotamia where it was a royal and priestly duty to guarantee by ritual the annual river floodings essential for crops. In these river valleys floods occur at quite regular intervals. The flood myth, however, is quite strong in parts of the world where floods are highly irregular.

(e) The flood theme is symbolic of a tabula rasa, a wiping clean of creation to permit a fresh, unsullied re-creation. Before human technology disrupted much of Nature, archaic man very rarely witnessed gigantic floods or forest and grass fires. Several, perhaps many, generations would intervene between any of these great natural catastrophes. Once experienced, of course, such awesome and momentous disasters would be recounted across the centuries. Archaic man found short-term cycles clearly defined by lunar, solar, seasonal patterns. Man came to see long-term cycles defined by fire and flood.[12] Thus each Kalpa or Day of Brahma will end with a great flood, and thereafter begins a brand-new era. The Ragnarök, according to the Edda, will end with the entire earth submerged in the sea. From this watery grave the world will triumphantly emerge in a new creation led by the resurrected Balder.

The ancient Inca myth is reasonably explicit; the expression for deluge literally meaning "universal turning point worked by rain." The symbol seems clearly to mean that flooding represents a return to the unformed, fluid original of water, a condition ripe for a fresh start. S. Amerindian myth is rich in accounts of such epochal endings and new beginnings. The Mayas of Yucatán subscribe to a four-world theory with each world obliterated by total immersion in water. The Semitic versions, including the biblical account, note the destruction of one creation and the subsequent construction of a different and presumably much superior era. A. W. Nieuwenhuis, analyzing several hundred flood myths, concluded that the standard meaning is the wiping away of a long and less-then-perfect era, to be followed by a totally new dispensation.[13]

(f) The flood myth as a death-and-resurrection theme. The waters of life, amniotic fluid, seem destructive; though others perish, however, each of us is sublimely confident of his own survival. Every flood myth has a survivor sustained in the symbolic womb of boat, canoe, coffin, or whatever. The Self is carried safely through the great waters and emerges into a new world, a new life. The remarkable uniformity of most flood myths probably arises from such inner symbolic meaning of the deluge to every individual.

(5) Mythical islands and continents. In 1963 a new island surfaced close to Iceland, a product of

the grinding tectonic plates in that area of active volcanos and thermals. The name, Surtsey, bestowed upon this emergent island in 1963 may well cause learned scholars centuries hence wisely to pronounce the ancient Scandinavian religion still very much alive late in the 20th century. Surt was the ancient Nordic god of the underworld who at Ragnarök will be the last to expire. Flinging giant flames over the entire earth, Surt will annihilate gods and men, everything plunging downwards into the all-encompassing sea. Surtsey is a very real phenomenon, charted and photographed, but its naming unequivocally states its mythical nature to men. An island lifting out of the water is an emergence from the unconscious. Conversely, subsidence into the water is a descent into the unconscious. Standard in the mythology of lost continents is the death-and-resurrection theme, as the submerged continents are avowed to be the momentous contributors of civilization and culture to continents now above the water.

Perhaps the Happy Isles, the Islands of the Blest, far to the west beyond the Pillars of Hercules were the Cape Verde or Canary Islands. Whether purely imaginary or based upon faint rumors, these islands to the ancients meant liftings within the human psyche from the unconscious to the conscious. Apparently from their association with the unconscious, islands represent primal innocence and paradise, thus casting an enchanting fascination about Stevenson's Treasure Island and the tropical isles of Melville, Michener, and your travel agent. This same symbolic quality probably explains completely non-existent isles that mariners extensively reported for centuries. Floating islands might possibly be explained as masses of seaweed or, rarely, pumice from volcanic explosions; but, more likely, Delos was termed floating because of human interior symbols of the unfixed, the volatile, in the shadowy waters between our own consciousness and unconsiousness.

A most interesting subcategory of these mythical islands is the magnetic islands apparently first mentioned by Pliny and Ptolemy in antiquity. The Arabian Nights, Sir John Mandeville, Marco Polo, and other medieval writers similarly locate these remarkable islands in the Indian Ocean. So powerful was the reputed magnetism that ships with iron nails were irresistably drawn off their course to the islands. Editing the Arabian Nights, Richard Burton ventured strong currents as the drawing force and pointed out the construction on the E. African coast of boats without nails (presumably, observers would attribute this construction to fear of magnetic islands). Possibly this myth is simply a variation upon the marvelous islands amidst the vast seas of the human psyche.

Medieval speculation produced numerous islands westward across the Atlantic. St. Brandon, an Irish saint of the 6th century, purportedly found an earthly paradise far out in the Atlantic; here the very birds and beasts were punctilious Christians devoutly observing church festivals and fast days. As late as 1755 nautical charts depicted St. Brandon's Island or the Island of San Borandan west of the Canaries. The earliest known reference to Antilla is suspiciously late in the 15th century. The account states that the Islamic invasion of Spain caused seven Christian bishops to flee westward with numerous of the faithful in 734 A.D., finding refuge far to the west in the island of Antilla. Before Columbus set out on his voyage westward to Cathay, he was advised by the astronomer Toscanelli to make a stopover at Antilla. To this day the Antilles of the Caribbean bear the name of the mythical Antilla. After the voyages of Columbus numerous imaginary islands spotted maps like pustules on the faces of smallpox victims. The world map of Ortelius in 1570 depicted about a score of non-existent islands, some the confusion of cloud banks with land, some the product of grotesque navigational error, some wholly imaginary. The longest-lived of this coterie, not finally expunged from all maps until well into the 19th century, was the circular Isle of Brazil, re-portedly out in the central Atlantic SW of Ireland.[14]

Coastal lands lost to the sea are much closer to legend than to pure myth. All up and down the coastal regions of W. Europe circulate folk accounts of land formerly above the surface and now submerged under the sea. Some of these reports are probably fictitious, but there can be no question that with the rising of the ocean level from the melt of the world's ice cap at the end of the last ice age quite sizable areas of dry land were inundated. So sig-nificant a loss of inhabited soil could have been burnt into the folk memory. Even more recent sub-sidence seems genuinely to have flooded human settle-ments in what now are England and Wales. Supposedly the Lafan Sands in Caernarvonshire were once a kingdom engulfed by the sea because of the wickedness of King Helig. Farther south in Wales, the Lowland Cantref is reputedly a once rich area lost to the sea in Cardigan Bay when the king's drunken steward opened the flood gates.[15]

Romantic English writers from Malory and Spenser through the Victorians have waxed poetic over the lost kingdom of Lyonesse, supposedly dry terrain extending from Land's End out to the Scilly Isles. Shoals and reefs, here and northward along the Cornish and Welsh coasts, may be the basis for the myths. Nonetheless, the entire island seems to be lifting slowly on the eastward side and dropping slowly on the west side. Also, historical communities such as Old Sarum have unquestionably sunk beneath the waves. Apparently the Scilly Isles formed but one sizable island or almost a unified island as late as the Roman occupation, for ruins from Roman times have been excavated offshore below the water level. The glamour and glory of Lyonesse are the stuff of myth, but there truly was such a land above the sea and it was the residence of humans.

The most intense fascination of man is reserved, however, for supposedly lost continents.[16] While islands genuinely rise above the surface of the water and drop below, and coastal areas subside or lift upwards, geologists believe that the basic continents from primordial Pangea to the present have not in number increased or decreased. Sliding on the gummy magma far under the surface, tectonic plates have transported continents variously about the globe, sometimes jamming pieces together as apparently India once nuzzled against SE Africa and was gradually carried northward to be rammed into S. Asia. Certainly there is absolutely no evidence for lost continents since humanity came into existence, even if our species may be tracked backwards for four million years. Lost continents, therefore, are quite mythical and almost certainly have their great power to grip human minds as symbols of massive elements of consciousness slipping down or sucked down into the unconscious. As symbols of lost consciousness these now-submerged continents are highly touted for intellectual achievements or forceful manifestations of the conscious will.

The most recent of these lost continents is Mu, first proclaimed to the world in 1926 by James

Churchward and further detailed in two subsequent volumes.[17] The hypothetical Mu was reputed to extend over much of the vast Pacific from relative proximity to Japan and the Philippines to Easter Island off the Chile coast and from north of the Hawaiian Islands to south of Brisbane, Queensland. The numerous islands of this huge area are supposedly remnants of the once enormous land mass of Mu. Unfortunately, geologists insist that these are volcanic islands and that no continent has ever occupied that region. Churchward attributed to Muvians a noble monotheistic religion, an advanced civilization, and the cradle of all the world's culture. From Mu, colonies were zealously despatched to Atlantis, China, India, the Middle East, and Central America, thus precipitating all civilized societies everywhere. Lamentably the mother continent of Mu as well as the shining colony of Atlantis collapsed into the sea about 13,000 years ago when "gas belts," stupendous subterranean caves, suddenly collapsed. Churchward claimed to have uncovered Muvian inscriptions in many parts of the world and to have been inducted into hermetic lore of Mu by mysterious Oriental savants, but it appears that Mu and its marvels are wholly the child of Churchward's fertile imagination.

A somewhat earlier lost continent, not yet wholly scotched, was Lemuria. When 19th century biologists accepted the Darwinian concept of evolution, they were puzzled to explain related flora and fauna in widely separated locales. Noting that central India and South Africa had strong biological ties and lacking the 20th century tectonic plate concept, William T. Blanford in the 1870's conjectured that a land-bridge had at one time linked India and S. Africa. Ernst H. Haeckel postulated this land-bridge as the route for man's ancestors, the lemurs. Philip L. Sclater went the next step to label this hypothetical land-bridge as Lemuria. The lost continent of Lemuria might have languished in the esoteric library of scientific hypotheses if an even more esoteric and charismatic figure, Helena P. Blavatsky, had not seized upon it. In her major work[18] this founder of theosophy predicated seven cycles of global and human development. The Third Root Race (of the third cycle), Blavatsky asserted, consisted of the Lemurians, an absolutely vital rung of the ladder to the Fourth Root Race, the people of Atlantis, and the Fifth, ourselves. Theosophy is still supported by some of our contemporaries, and therefore some belief in Lemuria still continues.

Scientists, however, have wholly abandoned the idea in the light of tectonic plates.

Blavatsky designated a Second Root Race to inhabit Hyperborea. Of all the lost continents this is the most shadowy and the least likely to appear on any map. The ancient Greeks vaguely postulated a vast area beyond the cold north wind, a pleasant land of the Hyperboreans. Never visiting the far north, the Greeks could freely ascribe a balmy climate to the Arctic. They never clearly spelled out whether Hyperborea was an island, a continent (as Blavatsky assumed), or the remote northern fringes of Eurasia. Scholars are still puzzled--and still vent their puzzlement in extensive verbiage--about the classic Greek statements linking Apollo to the Hyperboreans, even to suggesting that the god wintered in salubrious Hyperborea.[19] Frankly, no one can do better than guess-work about the mysterious Hyperborea and its equally mystifying devotees of Apollo. The ancients always situated Hyperborea in the Arctic, but some modern scholars would locate Hyperborea just north of the Danube, the lengendary and most likely homeland of the Greeks before their southern migration. Possibly tribes along the lengthy amber route to the Baltic are the source of the Hyperboreans and their regular gifts to Apollo. The theory has even been advanced that the Greeks erred in their etymology of Hyperborea as "beyond the north wind." In Macedonia is a mountain named Bora, and perhaps Hyperborea means no more than on the other side of this mountain. Ancient allusions consistently, however, suggest that the Hyperborean area was the Arctic coast of N. Asia. From here or from the European Arctic coast there might be a considerable indebtedness to the shaman, especially flourishing in the circumpolar area. Apollo manifests decidedly shamanistic features perhaps attributable to Finno-Ugrian origins or to other peoples of the far north of Eurasia. A somewhat startling proposal has been brought forward on the basis of remains of human habitation along the Arctic coast of Eurasia during the last ice age. While a stupendous sheet of ice covered much of N. Eurasia, the Arctic Sea remained relatively clear and the coastal fringe of Arctic Eurasia proved actually inhabitable. Perhaps Eurasians south of the great sheet circulated rumors about human settlements north of the ice barrier. So wondrous a story might be transmitted through countless generations. Perhaps more likely is a hint of interesting and significant people to the north, who

410

then are given a most interesting mythological treatment.

While ancient Greece has varied references to Hyperborea, there is but one reference to fabled Atlantis, Plato. In his dialogues <u>Timaeus</u> and <u>Critias</u>[20] the Athenian philosopher briefly relates a tale, which, he says, was told by Egyptian priests of Neith (identified with Pallas Athene) to the visiting Athenian, Solon, about a century before Plato reports it. Atlantis, the aged hierophant declares, was a great island or sub-continent west of the Pillars of Hercules in the main Atlantic. A flourishing and powerful Atlantean society despatched waves of conquering troops across N. Africa almost to Egypt and across S. Europe into the Balkan Peninsula. Flatteringly, the Egyptian priest states that the city of Athens valiantly fought and defeated the invaders from Atlantis.[21] Later, violent earthquakes and floods shook Atlantis, and in a single day and night all Atlantis disappeared beneath the sea. The weighty tome by the American legislator Ignatius Donnelly, <u>Atlantis</u> (1882), is often reprinted today without clear indication of its hoary age. Donnelly's volume suggests a tremendous lore about Atlantis, but actually the brief statement by Plato is absolutely all we have to go on. All else is pure speculation.

The modern reader may feel that Plato's handling of the Atlantis myth is a palpable disclaimer. Plato says that the narrative was rendered a hundred years before by a old man far from Greece and was relayed to Plato by his senile grandfather at the age of 90. Plato therefore seems to be winking that the entire affair is babbling by superannuates. Not so, for these devices in Plato's time were to reinforce the story, claiming wise old men and tradition as staunch props. But perhaps Plato is straining too hard. Anyone of Plato's talents could certainly invent the entire story. His convincingness has impressed many generations of readers, and perhaps the over-all reputation of the illustrious philosopher has sanctified an account which could be as mythical as Plato's famous Myth of the Cave.

But an enormous sea of ink, perhaps enough to engulf Atlantis itself, has poured out, chiefly from believers in Atlantis.[22] Plato says that Atlantis was "larger than Libya and Asia put together." By Libya he meant N. Africa from the Atlantic through the present Libya, and by Asia he meant Asia Minor; that certainly is a great deal of territory. He seems to exclude the Americas by referring to a continent beyond Atlantis. Nonetheless Mercator, the famous cartographer; Alexander von Humboldt, the distinguished scientist; and Wegener, the noted meteorologist, thought that America was the lost Atlantis. Several theorists have specified Central America and Brazil. L. Sprague de Camp has compiled a list of 215 commentators on Atlantis from antiquity into the second half of the 20th century,[23] and the majority favor some Atlantic island from Bimini near N. America to Cape Verde and the Canary islands. The spectrum of guesses has been extraordinary: N. Africa, S. Africa, Spain, central France, Caucasus, Palestine, Belgium, the Netherlands, East Prussia and the Baltic, Greenland, the Arctic, Iran, Iraq, Ceylon, Crimea, Sweden, British Isles. Aristotle thought Atlantis was imaginary, Diogenes Laërtius termed the account an "ethical dialogue," and Plato's noted translator, Benjamin Jowett, considered it all a political allegory. The greatest number of appraisers branding Atlantis as wholly imaginary lived in the 18th and 19th centuries.

An interesting recent theory about Atlantis focuses upon the Dogger Banks in the North Sea. Trawlers have dredged up Stone Age axes and other signs of human occupancy from the bottom of the North Sea, an area well above sea level during the ice ages. Perhaps folk memory passed on for millenia the story of the appalling catastrophe that flooded out a very large hunting ground in the era when the oceans relentlessly shouldered upwards. The same epoch witnessed the flooding of the W. Mediterranean. The E. Mediterranean is a very old sea, part of the primordial Tetys Sea with some extraordinary depths. During the low sea level of the ice age the W. Mediterranean was apparently meadowland until the rising ocean burst through between Gibraltar and Ceuta and inundated the lowlands to juncture with the E. Mediterranean. Of course, this western area is inside the Pillars of Hercules, but the incredible spread of guesses makes this ascription no more improbable than many others.

In this century the proposed site of Atlantis has been closing in towards Greece. As early as 1900 James Baikie, an Egyptologist, favored Crete as the mythical Atlantis partly on the basis of a sudden and unaccountable setback of the Minoan civilization about 1900 B.C. The "in" theory of today points to Santorini, the collective name for five small islands in the Aegean Sea, the most southern of the Cyclades, due north of Crete. About 1450 B.C. this present island group constituted one large volcano that suddenly blew off its entire top down below sea level. At this time the era designated Late Minoan I by historians came to a disastrous smash-up in Crete. Careful archeological scrutiny confirms that this holocaust c. 1450 B.C. was a result of the Santorini explosion not too far to the north. Crete was buffeted by two major features of the explosion that look very similar to the Krakatoa disaster of 1883.

Tephra is the collective term for all the discharge of a volcano into the atmosphere. In the Krakatoa explosion the tephra ran the entire gamut, beginning with great boulders and rocks, hurled skyward and falling rather close to the volcano. Smaller expulsion would be fireballs, averaging several kilos in weight and guaranteed to strike fear in any beholder. Liquid lava squirted into the air, hardened quickly, trapped considerable air, and fell as pumice. Until waterlogged such airy stone would float upon the water, generally for a few days. Pele's tears and Pele's hair would, of course, be part of this discharge. An enormous quantity of dust particles would be jetted into the heavens. From some volcanos the dust is whitish, in others it is pink or red. The area within a radius of 70 kilometers of Krakatoa was midnight dark for three days. This colossal discharge into the atmosphere will trigger awesome thunder, lightning, and heavy rains. For several years after the Krakatoa explosion its suspended particles treated the entire globe to incredibly magnificent sunrises and sunsets. Volcanic tephra in recent Icelandic experience will, surprisingly, act as a helpful mulch for crops if the blanket of dust and pumice is only a few centimeters thick. However, if, as Crete encountered it, he tephra deposit exceeds ten or twelve centimeters, crops are destroyed and many trees and bushes broken by the weight. Frequently, as in Iceland, the tephra dust is poisonous, killing cattle and sheep that ingest the dust while feeding.

But the destruction of crops and herds was not the greatest man-killer for battered Crete. The tsunamis generated by Krakatoa smashed far inland upon neighboring Indonesian islands exacting an unknown toll, but probably around 35,000 humans.

Apparently the whole northern coast of Crete was thus inundated and virtually obliterated c. 1450 B.C. To any Mediterranean resident of the time it would truly seem that the great maritime island of Crete had in a day and night vanished into the sea. Putting together this real disaster of ancient Crete and the mythical Atlantis was the achievement of Galanopoulos in 1960.[24] Today this is the most widely accepted explanation for the lost Atlantis.[25]

At the same time that he advanced the theory about Crete-Atlantis, Galanopoulos theorized that the flood associated with Deucalion could be accounted for by the same tsunami that radiated out of Santorini to batter Crete. The straight, unimpeded shot south to Crete would wreak there the worst damage from the tsunami. The numerous islands, shoals, reefs, etc. of the Aegean would deflect and distort the tsunami, but undoubtedly the colossal waves created havoc along the east coast of Greece. If not this tsunami, then perhaps another one appears a very likely source for the Greek flood myth. Continuing the search for allusions to the Santorini explosion in Greek mythology, Galanopoulos further suggested that the Phaëton myth might refer to an awesome falling from the sky of a fireball from Santorini.[26] As early as the mid 1930's Jan Schoo had attributed the myth of Talus to volcanic fireballs.[27] As these eye-popping fireballs plummeted into the sea, sailors in the waters anywhere near Crete could assume that these missiles were hurled by some gigantic guard of the great Minoan power. Robert Brumbaugh proceeded to associated the fireballs with the myth of Icarus,[28] another flaming descent from the sky. Other applications of the Santorini episode to Greek myth may be the floating islands and wandering rocks of pumice, and the prolongation by Zeus of the night with Alcmene for a total of three nights.

J. G. Bennett extended the range still further by proposing the Santorini explosion to account for the plagues of Egypt[29] (Exodus 6:28 - 14:31) and Galanopoulos further extended the theorizing to the parting of the Red Sea because of a tsunami to permit passage of the Israelites and then to trap the army of Pharaoh.[30] The early chapters of Exodus certainly indicate a unique and unprecedented climatic disturbance in ancient Egypt, difficult to explain on any meteorological basis except something like this extraordinary volcanic eruption. The three days of darkness possibly arose from the mass of tephra borne to Egypt by the prevailing westerlies, and the plagues could have sprung from the incredible humidity suddenly shifting the balance of Nature in an otherwise eternally dry atmosphere. The river of blood might be pink pumice or reddish algae. The ground becomes quite shaky or swampy when the parting of the sea is tied to the Santorini explosion. This theory needs, first of all, the assumption that the Hebrews crossed a "reed sea" (i.e. estuary of the Mediterranean), not the Red Sea. The immemorial caravan routes from Egypt to Sinai certainly take this northern route, and the cut across the Red Sea looks rather unlikely. The crucial point is the time lapse between the retreat of the sea and then the annihilating wall of the tsunami hurtling landward. Half an hour is about the maximum, and it stretches credulity to assume that the fleeing Hebrews arrived at precisely the right moment to cross on the exposed sea bed and all effect the crossing before the tsunami would zoom in to drown the Egyptian pursuers.[31] Or course, by modern figures the fleeing Hebrews were pitifully few, perhaps no more than 300-500 in toto. Nonetheless, it seems more reasonable to suppose that the Egyptian cavalry, chariots, and heavily armed infantrymen were mired and bogged down in swampland, unknown and untraversable to the army of quite arid Egypt.

Chapter XIV Biomythology

A Lithuanian version of the flood myth states that god was eating walnuts at the time and randomly pitching away the shells; the righteous who climbed into the empty shells were saved. Such mythical employment of plants and trees seems incidental or tangential to us, but to societies completely enveloped in natural surroundings, trees and plants may well be the central figures of myth. The ancient Germans, the ancient Indians, and many other peoples worshipped under trees long before worshipping under roofs.[1]

At sowing, transplanting, and harvesting many peasants of S. India offer a coconut to the Goddess of Earth. In bygone days a human head was the offering to the goddess. The peasants are not stupid louts who think that they can pawn off something totally different and lesser upon a moronic deity. Instead, they and their deity both sense an identity, parallel growths upon human trunks and tree trunks. Both deity and worshipper know that a substitution has been made, but there has been no short-changing of the goddess with an inferior replacement. What we often interpret in archaic peoples as environmentalism or conservation is really a sense of sacral worth in all things, most especially in all living things, as much in trees as in humans. The five elements making up the entire universe according to the Chinese are: wood, fire, earth, metal, and water. The Rigveda asks what kind of wood it was and from what tree were heaven and earth so constructed that they stand forever, while days and mornings vanish. The Taittiriya Brahmana answers the question by affirming Brahman as the wood and Brahman as the tree from which all heaven and earth are formed. Metaphoric, yes, but a signal proof of the mythic importance of the tree.

The major mythic themes involving trees are:

(1) Etiology. There are numerous Indian explanations for the origin of the sacred tulsi tree. One version declares that Vishnu had promised eternal life to Jalandhara as long as his wife Vrinda remained faithful. Trusting his wife and therefore deeming himself invulnerable, Jalandhara tried to overthrow Vishnu. Unable to slay Jalandhara, Vishnu hit on the clever ruse of visiting Vrinda in the guise of her husband and then copulating with her.[2]

416

Jalandhara was immediately dispatched and the bewildered Vrinda informed of the deception. In chagrin at her unwitting infidelity, Vrinda committed suicide. Honoring an innocent victim, a truly virtuous woman, Vishnu caused the tulsi tree to grow from her ashes.

(2) Dendrolatry (tree worship). An evolutionary process seems to proceed thus--

Tree is deity. In the Rajput area of India peasants will never cut the sami tree because the god resides therein.

Tree represents the deity. Uzza, mentioned in Koran 53:19, was worshipped near Mecca in the pre-Islamic period. Her devotees symbolized the goddess as a sacred tree. Such a practice was widespread throughout the ancient Middle East, and it is difficult to say exactly how the worshippers associated trees and deities. Egyptian art shows goddesses within trees and the djed column of Osiris may have been a tree. Trees are regular in Cretan religious scenes. The yat tree of India does triple duty, representing Brahma in its roots, Vishnu in the trunk, and Shiva in the branches.

Tree favored by a deity. Apollo loved the laurel, Athene the olive tree, Attis the pine and almond. This ascription seems a fossil of the original tree worship, now separating a thoroughly anthropomorphosed deity from his or her original bonding with the tree.

Tree is inhabited by tree spirit. The major deities have all been discreetly removed from trees, but the sense of spirit possession of the tree cannot be expunged and a very minor supernatural being (dryad, hamadryad) is assigned to the tree.

Tree "veneration." Probably the most revered tree in the world today is the bodhi tree under which Buddha attained enlightenment. Probably the role of this tree stems from immemorial tree-worship and was attached to the Buddha account. Historical markers worldwide designate honorable trees associated with notable events and casting their divine shade even upon our iconoclastic times.

Idols and statues almost certainly developed in these stages: initial tree worship; carting about of

417

tree trunk as the deity; crude stylization of eyes, mouth, etc. upon log; approximation of human appearance in wooden statues; idealized human form in statue.

(3) Wholly mythical trees of life. In the royal garden of Indra grew the tree of eternity, and anyone eating the fruit of this tree was rendered immortal. The Nordic mythology correspondingly reports the apples of Idun which conferred immortality upon those eating this fruit. In the Judeo-Christian tradition the tree of life in Genesis 2:9, 15:3 ff. and in Revelations 22:1-2 is probably analogous to trees of life in African and Amerindian myth. All such mythical trees seem to represent a confluence of sacred themes: nourishment, fertility per se, phallicism, lasting life, cyclic renewal. The axis mundi, the shaman's ladder, and the magical curative powers of trees and their fruits are closely related. The folk practice of "knocking on wood" follows from the great tree of life.

(4) Man descended from tree. The tree of life concept would lead to a tree-ancestry for humanity. The Damara of S. Africa believe that the universal progenitor was a tree from which came the Damara people and, in fact, everything that lives. Oceanic myth assigned to Samoa the ancestral tree Kai-ni-tiku-aba from whence all mankind sprang. The Sioux Amerindians reported the first parents of humanity as trees rooted to the ground until the world serpent gnawed away the roots and permitted them independent movement. Since the Teutonic mythology depicts Woden and his two brothers forming mankind from trees, perhaps more than a happy figure of speech underlies British "hearts of oak."

(5) Transformation of human or humanoid into a tree. Mourning for their brother Phaëton, his three sisters were changed into poplar trees. Presumably it was a reward, a most gracious favor of the gods, to transform the aged humans Baucis and Philemon into trees.

(6) Tree as a savior. The famous anecdote about King Alfred taking refuge in a hollow tree and witnessing a spider spin a web across the opening to deceive the pursuing Vikings harks back to the idea of the tree as a protecting womb. The coffin probably so originated.

(7) Tree as destroyer. An Indian myth tells of a carpenter whose desire for superb wood overpowered his religious awe for a sacred tree and caused him to remove some branches. Later the mutilated tree pursued and slew his son.

(8) Tree as life token. Just as an animal life can be coterminus with a human life and the death of one means the death of the other, so with a tree. A version of this theme is the brand as a life token for Meleager.

(9) Tree marriage. In India the banyan and pipul trees, if planted together, will merge, apparently embracing each other. In many areas they are ceremonially married. Possibly the Apollo-Daphne myth is kindred. A favorite subject for painters and sculptors depicts Apollo embracing Daphne as she is already sprouting leaves and branches.

An interesting custom in India is the marriage of a man to a tree or bush. A bachelor marrying a widow is frequently publicly wed to a tree and then privately married to the widow. Some Indians explain it as deluding the ghost of the widow's dead husband, who will not be vengeful, for the living man is supposedly married to the tree not to the widow. The Kol of central India say that such a tree marriage, followed by the man's throwing of leaves or blossoms into the river, confers equal status, that of a widower, upon the subsequent husband of the widow. Since a third marriage (but not subsequent marriages) is considered very unlucky, an Indian male may make his third marriage to a tree and the fourth or subsequent marriage to a human female. All such tree marriages honor the life force in trees, according them equal status with humans.

(10) Flying or mobile trees. Probably the childish fears generated in the very young by whipping branches and swaying trees produce the extraordinary myths of moving trees. Examples appear in India and America. The Thonga of Zambia report the kakunka palm as a notable mobile dendrite, for this tree bears feathery leaves resembling wings.

The mythology about small plants and bushes parallels that of trees but tends to be more "cute," more the sort of quaint tale appropriate to coffee-table illustrated books and popular volumes of charming folk tales. Note these etiological myths about the violet:

While in a most compromising position with Io, a priestess of Hera, Zeus noted the approach of his jealous spouse, Hera. He transformed Io into a white heifer and created the violet as her special food, say the Greeks.

A Roman myth states that Venus, observing Cupid's fascination with dancing maidens, inquired whether he deemed the maidens more beautiful than Venus. Since Cupid preferred the maidens, the incensed goddess cudgeled them until they were purple. Pitying the battered maidens, Cupid changed them into violets.

Asia Minor myth claims that the violet sprang from the blood of Attis. The violet was regularly displayed at his adoration.

Christian myth states that the violet droops because the shadow of Christ's cross fell upon it.

Rare is divine grass, but the Indian durva grass is sacred and immortal. In the churning of the ocean, Vishnu grasped Mr. Mandara. Friction rubbed off some of the hairs upon Vishnu's body, hairs now constituting durva grass.

The one consistently exalted myth for plants celebrates entheogenic substances. Notable is the Crow Amerindian account about the movements of Transformer across the newly shaped earth. Transformer spotted a being whom he recognized as a star from the heavens above. As Transformer approached, the star-person changed himself into the tobacco plant.

Rarely is mankind descended from plants, but Iranian myth states that the first human couple issued from the ground in the shape of rhubarb. At first single, the rhubarb plant was later split into two. Note the hermaphroditic theme here. Reputedly Ormuzd inserted a human soul into each rhubarb stalk, and humanity was descended from this pair. The mythology of Armenia indicates that the war-god Vahagn emerged from a reed with hair of fire and eyes that were suns.

It is possible that some statuary originated in plant figures, i.e. human semblances formed by assembly of plant parts. In some areas of India Nabapatrika ("goddess of nine plants") originates in a life-size length of plantain. Eight other plant parts in a carefully prescribed pattern are attached as head, breasts, pudendum, limbs, etc. The resultant figure is ritually married to Vishnu.

Probably the most sacred flower in the world is the lotus. Archaic man, acutely observant, noted that the seedpod of the lotus has openings too narrow to permit the seeds to escape. Instead, the seedlings grow within the seedpod envelope until powerful enough to burst the pod and then proceed to an independent existence. The lotus clearly possesses a maternal womb, and therefore to the scrutinizer of archaic times the lotus flower represented the perfect symbol of womanhood.[3] Modern man can certainly appreciate the exquisite beauty of the flower itself and the aesthetic loveliness of the stylized lotus in painting and sculpture, but for the mythic mind, woman and lotus are true sisters, sharing the same divine function and identically fulfilling it. Western man vaguely senses that flowers are associated with women as beauty, fragility, fertility; but the hazy Western symbology seems nought beside the sacred lotus of the East.

The most publicized of sacred plants in W. Europe has been the mistletoe, highly revered by the ancient Celts. Probably Frazer was right in suggesting that to the ancients the evergreen mistletoe seemed the external soul of the oak tree to which it adhered as a parasite. Frazer further hypothecated that Balder was himself a personification of the oak tree and the god's death meant the snatching of the external soul (the mistletoe) from the oak tree.[4] Every reference to the death of Balder, however, tells of mistletoe killing the handsome youth by contact. The Saxo Grammaticus account claims that Hoder vehemently fought Balder and slew him with a sword named Mistletoe. The whole question of the origin and nature of Balder is really too complex and problematical to permit positive interpretation.[5]

In the Americas the most important sacred flower was the sunflower, apparently a native of S. America. The Inca priestesses bore on their breasts great sunflower discs made of gold. The observant Amerindians, seeing the giant flower daily follow the sun, deemed the flower the sacred image of the sungod himself.

During the Pleistocene era our species was quite rare. The world belonged to animals: the vast shoals of fish, the endless herds upon the steppes and veldts and prairies, the awesome clouds of birds. For us it is a world oriented to humans, but the world of early man was still oriented to animals. Early myth undoubtedly centered upon animals far more than has myth during historic times. Myth has also centered more upon animals than upon plants because of the carom effect of animals upon humans. Totemism certainly has influenced many stories about talking and otherwise remarkable animals. Animal masks, the wearing of animal pelts and hides, rituals and mural picturings to induce the Lord or Lady of Beasts to provide for the hunters, representations of animals upon weapons and ornaments, and the dramatic reports of hunters are other forces to reinforce myths about animals. The aegis of Zeus and Athene may have developed from an animal costume or the display of a portion of an animal as a totem insignia. While plants are living things, of course, animals in myth especially represent at all times the life force, psychic power both constructive and destructive.[7]

Water animals.[8] The astounding reproductive powers of fish obviously symbolize fertility. Psychoanalysts further suggest that fish are associated with the female in analogy to the amniotic fluid and to the piscine odor of the vagina. Male associations are to the penis and semen.[9]

Favorable associations with the female are indicated by the frequent representation of goddesses with fish: Freyja (Teutonic), Demeter (Greek), Kwan-Yin (Chinese). Dolphins were sacred to Aphrodite, and the Roman devotees of Venus (Latin counterpart of Aphrodite) ate fish on Friday, the day sacred to the goddess, as an aphrodisiac.

Unfavorable associations with the female arise from the Terrible Mother. From the dark unconscious surges the primeval female sea monster Tiamat of Mesopotamia, and, appropriately, the sea scourges, Scylla and Charybdis, are both female. The Egyptian hippopotamus goddess Retu had both beneficient and malevolent aspects, but she was chiefly a nightmarish horror to scare children. In Pacific myth the villainous crab seeking to snatch the souls of the dead on their way to paradise is usually the Terrible

Mother. It is possible, though not too likely, that the Medusa was suggested by basket stars, echinoderms related to starfish. Basket stars are restricted to the Mediterranean, usually resident between 150 and 1500 meters deep. The numerous branches of the basket star curl and twist upon one another like the coils upon the head of the dread Medusa. Significantly, basket stars have been termed <u>gorgonocephalus</u> ("Gorgon-headed").

Associations with the male seem a later and rather lighter layer upon the sea. The ability of tortoise and turtle to send retracted head and limbs out from the shell seems to suggest penile extension. In the Churning of the Ocean, a pivotal Indian myth, Vishnu appears in his tortoise or turtle incarnation. In the Indian flood myth Vishnu is manifested in his fish avatar as Matsya. Manu (the Indian Noah) while bathing was begged by a tiny fish (Matsya) to save him from sea predators. The tiny fish was placed in a bowl but quickly outgrew the bowl and successively larger containers. Eventually grown to huge size as a horned fish, Matsya towed the ship of Manu to safety. The rapid expansion of Matsya and his horn clearly seem phallic. The Greek Eros is frequently pictured with a fish in his hands or even with a fish between his legs. Reputedly, a fish swallowed the penis of Osiris, causing the type of fish involved to be sacred in Oxyrhynchites and elsewhere in Egypt. As frequently in human practice, the fish may be both sacred and "unclean," tabu. The association, however, of male with fish seldom reveals the unfavorable attitude frequent in the female association with fish. The fish-gods Dagon (Phoenicia), Oannes (Chaldeia), Ea (Babylonia) have no terrifying aspect such as female sea goddesses displayed. Consequently, Buddhists can enthusiastically designate their founder as the Great Fish, just as the Talmud labels the coming Messiah of the Hebrews. Christians explain the association of Christ with fish as the acronym ICHTHUS from the Greek words: "Jesus Christ, God's Son, Savior." The fish-savior (e.g. Dagon) theme of the Middle East may have had a potent influence here. A somewhat remote possibility may be the Tilapia fish of the Nile. The female Tilapia actually uses her mouth as a brooder for her fertilized eggs. The hatching small fry swim out of the mother's mouth but dash back into her mouth at the hint of danger. The process looks asexual and may underlie the fish symbol for Christ.

Unfavorable male association with sea creatures is relatively rare in myth. When it appears, it is primordial like the Hecatoncheires, the hundred-handed monstrous sons of Uranus and Gaea. The appalling Hecatoncheires suggest octopus tentacles or the many and frightening nudges upon a swimmer amidst sea creatures; in the broadest sense they are the crashing waves and general terrors of the deep.

Among the ancient Greeks the most mythicized sea creature seems to have been the dolphin, frequently playing around ships and traditionally promising good luck. Apollo Delphinius ("dolphin-like") may indicate a dolphin-god ancestry; the temple of Apollo at Delphi bore carvings of dolphins upon its walls. Supposedly Dionysus as a youth was abducted by pirates. Aboard ship he transformed himself into a lion; the terror-stricken pirates leaped into the sea and were therein transformed into dolphins. Telemachus, son of Odysseus, was reportedly saved from drowning by dolphins, and an even more famous dolphin rescue saved Arion when he was pitched overboard by murderous sailors.

Perhaps the most engrossing of myths about sea creatures in W. Europe for the past millenia have been tales about mermaids and mermen (mere means "sea"). The cry of a baby seal closely resembles that of a human infant, and the eyes of seals can be startlingly human in their expressiveness. In Iceland, Scotland, and W. Ireland certain families reputedly have a seal somewhere in the family line on the mother's side, from the strong association of the sea with the feminine. The surname Macnamara has been interpreted as "son of the seal." Among the Eskimos the seal is sacred to Sedna, goddess of the sea. Although the merpeople may be psychological formations of man-beast, the accounts of mermaids and mermen do seem localized to areas such as the N. Atlantic and N. Pacific where the seal is prevalent.

Although the world's largest animal, the whale receives meager mythic interest even among Eskimos and peoples of the Pacific. The identification of the biblical Leviathan with the whale is dubious. In Hebrew liwyāthān means "coiled" or "twisted" and originally must have referred to the world serpent. The gigantic Kraken, however, seems based upon the whale, although this monster reported off the Norwegian coast has been described as over a kilometer in length. In Erse mythology seven whales constituted a light lunch for Cirein Crôin, the immense sea serpent, largest of all living creatures.

Subterranean animals. Creatures below the earth or apparently emerging from it are chthonic beings. Such creatures are most certainly ambiguous, conferring sometimes bale and sometimes boon. Chthonic animals are generally messengers from the Great Mother, from the dead, from the depths.

The snake,[10] appearing in myth more frequently than any other animal, slithers from the water as well as from underground. Among the numerous water snakes in myth are: taniwah of New Zealand, the rainbow serpent of Australia, water serpents of the Kalihari Desert Bushmen, the damballah-wedo of Haitian voodoo, the great horned serpent of the Pueblo Amerindians, the Lernean Hydra slain by Heracles, and the sea serpents that crushed to death Laocoön and his sons at Troy.

Aquatic or terrestrial, snakes in myth display an extraordinary range:

(1) Fertility. The serpent is a phallic symbol; in the divine transformation of Moses' staff into serpent (Exodus 7:8-12), rod and snake are clearly interchangeable. Supposedly the mothers of Zagreus, Scipio Africanus, Alexander the Great, and Caesar Augustus were impregnated by serpents. Cernunnos, the Celtic god of fertility, was represented as a horned or ram-headed snake. Many Amerindians claim descent from serpents. Throughout the world the Mother Goddess is often represented with a snake encircling her trunk, her arm, or her wrist. The phallus is thus seen as her servant and protector.

In India snake groves, joining tree and serpent as fertility symbols, are often famed for aiding barren women to conceive.

(2) Healing. The brazen serpent erected in the wilderness by Moses at god's orders was a cure against snake bites (Numbers 21:8-9); i.e. homeopathy, "like cures like." The entwined snakes of the caduceus are still the world's best-known symbol of the healing arts.

(3) Wisdom. Christ commanded his disciples to "be wise as serpents" (Matthew 10:16). The uraeus or

425

cobra in the headgear of the pharaohs represents supreme wisdom of king and god. The ascription of wisdom to the snake probably arises in part from the lidless serpent eyes which suggest unbroken awareness and knowledge.

(4) Spirituality. Philo of Alexandria in the 1st century A.D. asserted that the snake was the most spiritual of all animals. The snake is eerie to mankind as it moves without legs or wings, implying a status above mere mundane creatures. Anything strange or enigmatic, as the snake certainly seems to man, is deemed spiritual.

(5) Prophetic and magical. Soothsaying world-wide is associated with snakes. Helenus of Troy and his sister Cassandra, according to one version, received the gift of prophecy when their ears were licked by serpents. Medea's steeds were serpents, appropriate to a witch and sorceress. Figures of enchantment such as the Erinyes, the Graeia, and Medusa have snakes for hair, the coiffeur of the uncanny.

(6) Guardianship and protection. The snake or its alter ego, the dragon, is the universal guardian of treasure, as Ladon was the dragon guardian of the apples of the Hesperides. The serpent is also the standard guard of the tree of life. These associations are generally unfavorable, but through much of Asia the snake is often treated as a worthy protector.

(7) Resurrected life. The sloughing off of a snake's skin obviously means regenerated life. In the Epic of Gilgamesh it was the snake that gobbled up the fruit of immortality.

(8) Symbol of cycles and latent energy. In coiled form the snake represents the cycles of the cosmos. In Yoga and Buddhist Tantric writings the kundalinī or latent energy is deemed a serpent coiled eight times at the base of the spinal column, arousable only by intensive Yoga techniques.

(9) Support of the world. Vishnu reclines upon the vast world serpent Shesha whose seven heads form a protective canopy over the head of Vishnu. Upon this ophidian couch the god sleeps the refreshing slumber that will re-create the cosmos. A quiver rippling through the colossal body of Shesha will make the world tremble with an earthquake.

(10) Creator serpent. Among the Fijians the Creator is a snake Kalori-Vu. Chinese myth makes a snake Pan Ku the creator of the world. The Fon of Dahomey report a female creator Mawu whose serpent mount was the primary agent in the forming of mountains and valleys, islands and continents.

(11) Supreme elevation of snake. The Ophites (from Greek ophis, "serpent") formed an early Gnostic sect which reversed the orthodox interpretation of the Fall of Man. The serpent in Genesis 3:1 ff., asserted the Ophites, was the actual savior of mankind, freeing humanity from the primal ignorance. This group may have been influenced by the cult of Agathos Daimon, the "good serpent," in Hellenistic Egypt.

(12) Death and the underworld. Some Amerindians believe that disease is caused by serpents, and some Australian aborigines regard the snake as causing death in many other ways beside snakebites. The Fijian god of the dead, Ratu-mai-mbulu, is himself a snake. The Egyptian underworld seems snake-ridden in all of its twelve divisions. In the seventh division Osiris commands fiery serpents to butcher the wicked. All through the watches of darkness the dreaded serpent of night, 'Apep, seeks to devour Re, the sun-god. In the twelfth division of the underworld Re enters the tail of the giant serpent named "Divine Life" and issues from the mouth of the serpent into the upper world. The very last portal of the underworld is guarded by Isis and Nephthys in the form of serpents.

Psychoanalysts suggest that the umbilical cord results in the Great Serpent of the Underworld.[11] The association of the snake with the Great Mother must have been awesome to early man but not necessarily repellant. As the Great Mother more sharply became the taker of life as well as the giver of life, the snake assumed more malevolent qualities.

(13) Snake as primal ancestor. Cecrops at the outset of Athenian myth and Fu Hsi and Nü Wa, the earliest Chinese ancestors, had serpent bodies and human heads. Again the umbilical cord looks like the origin.

(14) Snake as soul of the dead. Indian myth says that as Balarāma lay dying, a serpent issued from his mouth and glided towards the sea; hence

images of Balarāma often reveal him as a snake-man. Some Amerindians believe that snakes are their dead ancestors. Such belief was extensive among the ancient Greeks. The resident temple serpent in the Erechthion, atop the Athenian Acropolis, was considered an incarnation of Erechtheus. Because the gods highly regarded snakes, Cadmus of Thebes asked to be changed into a serpent; his loyal wife Harmonia, wanting to share his fate, sought the same boon, and both were transformed into serpents. Romans believed that a house snake was the genius and prophet of the family. Teutons felt that house snakes embodied the souls of ancestors and guarded children. Credence is given to such conjectures by the appearance of snakes from crevices and cracks, and their frequently quiet, unostentatious presence.

(15) God or demon in snake form. Zeus Ktesios ("household property") was a snake. In Vedic myth the demoniacal opponent of the gods was the vast serpent Virtra.

The most extensive series of myths about snakes consist of accounts about the nāgas in Brahmanic, Buddhist, Lamaistic, Cambodian, and Javanese literature. Dynasties of nāga kings, lavish descriptions of subterranean and submarine palaces of the snakes, weddings of nāgas and humans, and countless serpentine interventions in human affairs traverse almost all the known themes about snakes and are often bafflingly ambiguous. To confuse things further, the Nāgas of today are tribesmen from the pre-Aryan period. Understandably they are ascribed an ophidian ancestry and many snaky qualities.

Moderns often experience a scare, even horror, when encountering snakes but usually deem rats and mice mere pesky vermin. Earlier man associated many of the serpent themes above with rats and mice, though less extensively than with snakes. Mice issuing from the mouth were assumed to be the soul. The Germanic goddess Hludana was symbolized by the rat, and her successor St. Gertrude in medieval Christianity was similarly pictured with a rat. The sinister Pied Piper of Hamelin story may indicate archaic sacrifices to a rat-god. Apollo Smintheus ("mouse god") was an epithet of Apollo from the association of mice with disease; white mice were maintained in temples of Apollo as guards against plagues of other mice and diseases. Psychoanalysts interpret rats and mice as phallic symbols. To an even lesser extent, ants are also included in the category of the phallic and the chthonic, chiefly in tropical areas of huge anthills and vast swarms of ants.

Surface animals. Terrestrial animals lack the otherworldly character of chthonic creatures below and the flying birds and insects above. The animals of earth are our fellow dwellers upon the earth's surface. Where we have found in terrestrial animals capabilities surpassing ours, we have recognized the touch of divinity or, at least, of our parents. Where we have found in animals all too much of our own human nature, we have interpreted it as the baser element of ourselves.

The large and majestic beasts are fittingly celebrated. The mother of Buddha dreamt that a great white elephant with six tusks had entered her body. As diviners expertly interpreted, it meant that she would bear the savior of the world. For more northerly climes across all of Eurasia and N. America the bear was the creature of power and respect. The bear-god has awed worshippers among Amerindians and the Ainu of Japan. The bear cult belonged to the rituals of Artemis, and the British name of Arthur may mean "bear."

The cow is symbolic of feminine nurture, whether the Eddic Audhumla or the Egyptian Hathor. Jungians perceive the cow as the arch representative of mother and the bull as the symbol of the father. The epitome of bull worship is Apis, the sacred bull of Memphis, reportedly the incarnation of Osiris and Ptah. The slaying of the bull, whether by Mithras or in the Spanish bullring, is interpreted as Oedipal by Freudians.

Perhaps the highest consistent honor for animals in myth has been accorded horses for their power and speed. Apollo held the reins on the magnificent horses harnessed to the chariot of the sun, Poseidon was drawn by superb white horses, and Hades drove a span of black horses. In Indian myth the Ashvins were exalted horse gods born of the sun Surya in the guise of stallion and Ashvini in mare form. This myth remarkably parallels the liaison of Poseidon as a stallion with Demeter as a mare, the resultant offspring being the divine horse Areion. In the form of Kalki, a great white horse, Vishnu will end one of the vast cycles of the cosmos in order to inaugurate

a better age. Jungians think of the horse as a
primary symbol of sexual potency, especially the
stallion. Sexual assault is often dreamt of as
attack by horses.

Understandably the mythical attitude toward
monkeys and apes is ambiguous. On one hand is a
highly favorable viewpoint, as Hanuman, the Indian
monkey-god, is a noble and courageous figure in the
Ramayana. Hanuman means "heavy jawed"; possibly he
was a prognathous leader of an indigenous hill tribe
assisting the Aryans in their movement southward
through India. Many natives of Malaysia and Indonesia highly regard the monkey as a close relative to
man. Semitic myth, however, derogates the simians as
nasty caricatures of humanity. Jewish legend claims
that as punishment for building the tower of Babel,
some of the workers were transformed into monkeys.
Islamic legend claims that Allah turned into monkeys
the Jews at Elath who impiously fished on the Sabbath
Day.

Cats are the natural enemies of rat and mouse.
Appropriate, therefore, is the identification of the
cat with Demeter, goddess of vegetable food gnawed
upon by rats. In Egypt the cat-goddess was Bast,
again probably from the cat's destruction of rodents.
Freudians, however, propose that as the rat or mouse
is a phallic symbol, the cat in devouring the rodent
symbolizes the female genitals taking the male organ.
Cats are generally regarded as female in myth, and
there is a strong association with witches. The
goddess of the north, Freyja, was drawn in a chariot
by black cats. Much folk thought about tigers and
leopards seems parallel to the mythology about cats.
Everyone has observed the haughty independence of
felines; so it is logical that Libertas, the Roman
goddess of liberty, would be represented by a cozily
self-contented cat.

Saramā was the bitch who efficiently served as
Indra's watch-dog and messenger. Two of her offspring guarded the path of the dead to the afterworld. Here is the dual role of the canine as guard
for the living and guard or psychopomp of the dead.
T'ien K'on is the celestial dog in Chinese myth who
drives away evil spirits. The barking and howling of
dogs when man can detect nothing have led to the
belief that dogs sense the spirit realm. Hence
Cerberus as the sentry of Hades and the male votaries
of Hecate labeled as "dogs." In the Wild Hunt of N.

Europe, peasants hear the baying of hounds in the spectral lunge through the stormy heavens. In much of the East from Palestine to SE Asia dogs have a low reputation from scavenger packs. Dogs and harlots are lumped together in Deuteronomy 23:18, and Indian accounts ascribe a "dirty dog" image to canines.

The near relatives, fox, wolf, coyote, hyena, are never viewed affectionately as dogs can be. For Europeans the fox is crafty and unscrupulous, the wolf rapacious and diabolical. The Greek myth of Lycaon's slaying of his grandson and his subsequent transformation by Zeus into a wolf keynotes the werewolf theme. Perhaps the myth indicates a cannibalistic feast on Mr. Lycaeus, terminated by the enlightened rule of a triumphant Zeus.[12] Naturalists declare that the wolf has been given an unjustifiably bad reputation by man, but the eldrich howls of the wolf and the wolf's furtive habits have undoubtedly fostered this human judgment. As wolves in bygone days normally approached human dwellings only during famine and starvation, they were logically associated with the eating of human flesh. The fox holds in China and Japan somewhat the same position as the wolf in the West. In Japan foxes frequently transform themselves into beautiful women. In China the fox may appear as either sex, but generally the fox is a former woman in animal form because of her lewdness. Coyote is the sly trickster in many Amerindian accounts. In African myth the hyena is usually demoniacal.

Sheep receive scant attention in myth, but the ram as a figure of male will and strength symbolizes Amon-Re and Osiris in Egyptian myth. In India the fire-god Agni rides a great ram as a steed. The substitution of a ram for Isaac suggests the extensive sacrificial use of this animal by Hebrews. The goat was also a regular sacrificial animal in Greek myth, associated with Hera at Argos and especially with the rites of Dionysus where a live goat was torn to pieces and eaten raw. The cornucopia was a horn of plenty from Amaltheia, the she-goat who suckled Zeus when he was concealed from his father Kronos. The satyrs and Pan, sexually hyperactive, were goat-form. The medieval Christian devil is an obvious carry-over of this goat deity now viewed as lasciviously degraded.

The wild boar symbolizes savage violence and destruction as in the Calydonian Boar Hunt and the slaying of Adonis. The boar's head, worn atop warriors' helmets in the north of Europe, was the defiant symbol of paganism as Christianity was spreading. The sow apparently represented feminine fertility, as Isis, Demeter, and Persephone seem to have originated as sow-goddesses. The prohibition against pork probably started as a tabu on the sacred. Tabus often shift from the sacred delight to the forbidden filth. Patriarchal ascendency may have stigmatized the pig as base sexuality and grossness to counter the sow-goddess. The dangers of trichinosis in a warm climate may also affect the tabu. Gryllus was a man transformed by Circe into a pig; when given the opportunity to resume human form, Gryllus opted to remain a pig.

Creatures of the air.[13] As subterranean creatures have contact with the chthonic deities, so the birds and insects by flying are messengers of the gods above. Hugin and Munin are the two ravens perched upon the shoulders of Odin; every day they fly completely around the world and return at nightfall to caw in the god's ears a detailed report of what they have witnessed. The Japanese gods regularly dispatch the pheasant Na-naki-me to recite the divine orders to a waiting world.

As creatures of the heavenly gods, birds exemplify divine will and prophecy in movements and bird calls. The ancient Romans, Greeks, and Celts carefully studied the flights of birds for omens, as natives of Borneo do today. To understand the language of birds, as Siegfried did after tasting the blood of the dragon, is to know the future. Generally schizophrenics experience auditory hallucinations of human voices, but cases have been reported of schizophrenics claiming to understand bird language.[14] With their store of divine knowledge, birds may convey learning to mankind. The Menominee Amerindians attribute their medical knowledge to an owl, and Athene may have begun as an owl deity with a similar mission to teach humanity.

As lords of the sky it is logical that birds escort the sun across its great daily arc: the eagle of Zeus, the falcon of Re, Garuda of Vishnu, the huge three-legged crow of Chinese myth. Myths assert that tempests are caused by giant birds flapping their wings: Semites (Zu, whose name means "tempest"), the Eddas (Hroesvelger), Vedic myth (Garuda). In parts of Asia and among many Amerindians thunder is specifically attributed to a thunderbird.

Amerindians declare that the high-flying thunderbird is locked in ceaseless conflict with the horned water serpents at the great depths. This pattern is reproduced world-wide. According to Aztec myth their patron god Huitzilapotchli led the entire nation on a great migration with the promise of a mighty empire. Huitzilapotchli advised the Aztecs that they should establish their capital city where the god in eagle form would come winging with a serpent clutched in his talons. Thus was founded Tenochtitlan, the present Mexico City; to this day the flag of Mexico blazons the eagle grasping the snake. The Semitic myth about Etana, the king of Fish, states that the monarch released an eagle trapped in a pit by a serpent's ruse. In gratitude the eagle airlifted the king to heaven to obtain a magic "plant of birth" (i.e. the means of securing a son and heir). This Semitic account clearly is based on the mythic belief that both eagle and serpent possessed the secret of immortality. The eagle molts and renews its feathers, while the serpent sloughs off its old skin and grows another. The Indian version accounts for the implacable hatred of the magic bird Garuda towards serpents as a son's hostility to his mother's oppressor. Vinata, mother of Garuda, had been tricked into slavery by Kadrū, co-wife of Kashyapa along with Vinata. Kadrū's children, the nagas (snakes) perpetrated the chicanery for their mother and thus forever earned the enmity of Garuda. The 19th century tended to interpret the worldwide eagle-snake struggle as the sun (the bird as a solar figure) drying up the marshes and stagnant pools (the snake as a swamp symbol). Today we are far more likely to consider the conflict of eagle and serpent as the higher and more spiritual element within man himself struggling relentlessly against the lower and baser elements within the human psyche. If one prefers, it is the celestial vs. the chthonic. It might also be considered the battle of the patriarchal sky deity against the earth goddess.

With their celestial attributes birds do not in myth fall into the ambiguous roles of earth-bound creatures. Even the vulture is a spiritualized creature in myth. Among the Ashanti of W. Africa and among negroes of Guiana the vulture is the transmitter of sacrifices from man to god. The ultimate exaltation of the scavenger bird is the proud vulture headdress of Mut, the Egyptian mother-goddess. The mythical concept is powerfully ilustrated in the Parsee practice of exposing their dead upon high towers of silence; by voracious consumption of the body, the vultures hasten the glorious day of resurrection.

Although actually a mammal, the bat is regarded as a bird by archaic peoples, and is treated ambiguously. In the East the bat is favorably regarded, and in Samoa a potent war-god, Sepi Malosi, leads war parties in the form of a bat. The West tends to view the bat as diabolic from its appearance and from its nocturnal habits. The vampire bat especially sends shivers down human spines and results in the dreaded bat-god, Camazotz, of Guatemala. The frequent transformation of humans into birds in Greek myth (e.g. Ceyx, Alcyone, the Peirides, Procne) arises from the concept of a bird-soul, the human soul as a bird. Along the Ivory Coast of Africa the bat is believed to bear the soul of a dead human.

More than birds, insects represent the resurrected life. From ancient times the Chinese have regarded the cicada as the symbol of rebirth and immortality. After four years underground the pupa emerges to turn into an insect. Such remarkable rising from the grave caused the Chinese to insert into the mouths of corpses pieces of jade carved in the shape of the cicada. The scarab or beetle of ancient Egypt was a resurrection symbol because the beetle was born from dung, life miraculously resurgent from the dead refuse. Chaco Amerindians believe the Creator is a giant beetle; after forming the rest of the world, Beetle concocted humanity from leftovers. With the inordinate number of beetle species, it would be logical to see the Creator as a super beetle. The butterfly has been the Occidental symbol of rebirth among ancients and then among Christians. As caterpillar, chrysalis, then flying insect it represents mundane life, apparent death, triumphant rebirth.

Probably the most appreciated and celebrated of winged creatures is the bee. Outside of the tropics and its sugar cane, most of humanity until quite recent centuries depended entirely upon honey for all sweetening. Mead, an alcoholic beverage from honey, was long considered an aphrodisiac, as the term honeymoon still reveals. Beeswax long vied with tallow as the substance for candles. In Egypt bees supposedly sprang from the tears of Re, the sun-god; in Brittany bees are attributed to the tears of Christ on the cross. Indra, Krishna, and Vishnu are

434

all termed Madhava, "born of honey." The Indian god of love, Kama, employed a string of bees as his bow-string. The Tchuwashes of E. Russia worshipped a bee-god, and the epithet in Zeus Mellissaios ("honey-bee") suggests some local bee-god syncretically absorbed by the Olympian deity. Bees belong to the resurrection theme in the widespread folk idea of bees spontaneously generated in the carcases of dead oxen. Samson in Judges 14:8 concocted one of the most famous of all riddles from this notion, and country-wise Virgil accepts the idea in his lengthy treatment of bees in Book Four of the Georgics. Of course, the rib cage of a cattle skeleton is an ideal swarming place for wild bees. Honey as a restorer of life is a frequent theme; Lemminkainen is so reanimated in The Kalevala. The Orphics stated that the bee represented the human soul in generating sweetness from within, and the bees in the beehive symbolized souls clustering about the Unity of God.

Creatures of the imagination.[15] Myth offers three major categories of quite imaginary beings:

(1) Homanids modified.[16] Man fears the unknown and, to justify his cowardice, mythically portrays the unknown as terrifyingly different. Hottentot mythology tells of the Aigamuxa, a fabulous folk with eyes in the back of their feet. Irish myth attributes only one eye to Balor, king of the gigantic Fomorians; Balor seldom opened that one eye except on the battlefield, and it then required four normal men to lift Baylor's eyelid with a lever. One glance from that baleful eye struck dead anyone Balor glared upon.

Herodotus and Josephus in antiquity reported the Acephali ("headless"), supposedly a race of headless humans in Libya. The face was supposedly on the chest. Sir John Mandeville in medieval times repeated the same fabulous account. In Hindu myth Kabandha is a headless homanid with a mouth in the middle of his belly and a lone eye in his chest. A Tantric form of Durgā called Chinnamasta ("beheaded") probably explains this extraordinary concept. In Vedic ritual the sacrificial victim was always beheaded; since a sacrificial creature was automatically divinized, myth could credit a life still very active in a beheaded victim. But the weirdest of all would seem to be mouthless homanids. Australian aborigines report the wondjina without any mouth, and people today claiming contact with extraterrestrial beings have also reported mouthless homanids. Psychological tests with infants suggest that the very young ignore the mouth in adults and probably conceive of others as mouthless.

(2) Animals modified. Such imaginary creatures appear rather obvious exaggeration or far-fetched extrapolation from real-life animals. Such a mythical creature is the Eskimo qiqirn, a huge, hairless dog who throws men or sled dogs into fits; a silly and niggardly creature, the qiqirn runs away when it is shouted at. The kraken seems a whale extended to over a kilometer in length.

Perhaps the term cryptozoological should be applied to supposed creatures like the Loch Ness monster. It has been suggested that "Nessie" and "Champ" (Lake Champlain, USA) may be a zeuglodon, a primitive whale believed extinct for millions of years.[17] We must remember that other animals long believed extinct can surprisingly turn up, like the palaeotragus (giraffe-like) found in Congolese rain forests at the start of this century and the coelacanth netted from sea depths in 1939. The quite mysterious Mokele-Mbembe reported in the swampy jungles of west Africa may be some previously unknown large mammal, even a dinosaur.

The most beguiling of all imaginary creatures is the unicorn.[18] The oriental version, Chin-Lin, is basically a deer. The Occidental unicorn seems a beautiful white horse, though Pliny and others give varied descriptions of the unicorn. Perhaps the rhinoceros is behind the unicorn; narwhal horns have been pawned off as unicorn horns, but the horns of many two-horned creatures have also been substituted. A University of Maine biologist in 1936 reported that he had successfully implanted a horn in the center of a calf's forehead, and he further noted that transplantation was known to the ancients.[19] Supposedly a virgin was able to lure a unicorn; it all sounds like the usual snide stories implying the virtual non-existence of virgins. A deep seated enmity reputedly pits the unicorn against the lion. A lion pursued by a unicorn will duck behind a tree and the unicorn rams its horn into the tree. Stuck, the unicorn is easily despatched by the lion. In the nature myth tradition, 19th century theorists interpreted this struggle as the sun (golden male lion) against the moon (white female unicorn); the unicorn was trapped in the trees of darkness. The mass of unicorn lore is largely the product of medievalism and therefore highly allegorical, symbolizing purity and strength. The single horn suggests unification of all powers into one. Overall the unicorn apparently arises from the same tendency that produced Pegasus. Man idealizes the horse and must endow his mythical ideal with extraordinary attributes dramatically transcending those of the average horse. Freudians would explain both winged horses and unicorns as sexual symbolism, the unicorn as phallic and winged horses as coitus.

Certainly early man secured genuine survival value from extrapolation, "jumping to conclusions." A flash in the clearing or a barely discerned rustling in the trees would quickly be fleshed out within the mind into a full-fledged predator ready to leap upon the human passer-by. Such extrapolation probably accounts for gigantic sea serpents. Anyone witnessing a school of porpoises at sea is gripped by the spectacle of porpoises breaking the surface in effortless curves: the sight suggests one vast serpent rippling its coils. The "abominable snowman" of the Himalayas or its American manifestation as "bigfoot"[20] rests largely upon huge footprints in the snow. Tracks in snow or soft mud may well be altered by natural conditions and thereby seem the imprint of large and unknown creatures. With such a hint a poorly descried figure some distance away is at once registered as the astonishing yeti.

(3) Symbolic animals. Such creatures are consciously devised originals or are adapted from actual animals for moralistic or ritual reasons.[21] Such an extraordinary concept is Gu from Dahomey. At birth Gu was solid stone with a projecting metal blade; understandably Gu is the god of metal and of war.

Most prominent among these symbolic animals are bird-like creatures, for they suggest aspiration and soaring to the human mind. Most famous is the phoenix, which Herodotus skeptically reported from Egypt as burning up only to rise from its own ashes. The phoenix legend certainly looks like a solar myth, the bird representing the sun, which seems to perish each evening in its own fires, only to be reborn each dawn. Any one of numerous birds might be the original: egret, heron, stork, perhaps the hawk. The phoenix symbol of death and resurrection was quickly appropriated by Christians and has journalistically become a cliché for rebirth.[22] The Simurg of Iran

and the Ho-o of Japan are mythical birds volplaning
from the heavens to bestow benefits upon mankind and
then soaring back to their celestial home. Birds big
and strong enough to airlift humans are wholly mythical, from the eagle that transported Ganymede to Mt.
Olympus all the way to the Iranian and Arabic Roc
that carried entire elephants up to its nest for
dinner.

(4) Grotesqueries. For mankind there is the
intelligible circumambient world, the celestial world
above (with bird messengers to earth below) and the
sinister beings of the chthonic realm underground.
From this lower subterranean and submarine level,
eruptions all too often disturb or even destroy
humans. The monsters of this liminal stratum, partly
of this world and partly of the depths, are misshapen
combinations, horrible misjoinings, frightening
prodigies, vicious horrors. The only non-scary use
of such monsters is as steeds for gods, shamans, and
great visionaries. Mohammed ascended to heaven upon
a buraq, a creature not consistently portrayed, but
usually described as winged, white in color, larger
than a donkey but smaller than a mule. The implicit
symbolism is a mixture of bird and terrestrial
beasts, indicating the prophet's own union of earth
and heaven. Indian gods customarily possess distinctive mounts, none more extraordinary than the makara,
part crocodile and part something else, ridden by
Varuna. The something else may be a surface animal
or a bird. The symbolism parallels that of Mohammed's buraq with perhaps the strong suggestion of the
elevated sky deity fully controlling the baser elements and using them for his advantage.

Most of these grotesqueries, however, represent
dysmorphophobia, the fear of monsters. Such monstrous creatures are projections of the unconscious,
their bizarre mixture and terrifying behavior indicating the inability of man to control these beings.
Always these are frightfully threatening and destructive creatures. Today such monsters are probably
more numerous than in antiquity, but they now lurk on
remote planets and in distant galaxies of science
fiction.

The most obvious of these monsters, and perhaps
the only ones that normal mortals may observe and
still live, are animations of natural phenomena.
Aquatic monsters, dragging mortals to death are:
ahuizotl (Aztec), Grendel and Grendel's dam (Anglo-

Saxon), bunyip (Australian), kappa (Japanese). Creatures at the edge of sea and land are often monsters like Scylla and Charybdis. It is possible that the chimera killed by Bellerophon consisted of natural earth fires fed by gas seepage from the ground near Phaselis in Asia Minor.[23] All of these miscreations are inanimate natural perils conceived as rapacious wild beasts.

The major of the grotesqueries are nightmare anomalies, combinations of one animal's ferocity and another animal's vileness, symbolizing baseness in man and terrors beyond human power. The sphinx had a woman's head, a lion's body, and the tail of a serpent. The griffin had the head and wings of an eagle, the body of a lion, and a snake as tail. To compound things further, the griffin upon a mare sired the hippogriff, combining griffin and horse. The very youthful mind senses that the enormity of a creature is perhaps most emphasized by multiplying the number of its disagreeable features. Hence Cacus was three-headed, and Geryon was three-headed or three-bodied. The Cambodians report a three-headed Airavata. The Herren-Surge of the Basques is a snake with seven heads. These appalling monstrosities are clearly thrusts from the chthonic as indicated by their female nature like the Sphinx or by their origin from females of the depths. Consider the repulsive progeny of the monstrous female Echidna, dwelling beneath Arima, who by Typhon was the dam of: Orthus, Cerberus, Scylla, the chimera, the sphinx, the Lernean Hydra, the dragon guardians of Cochis and of the Hesperides, the Nemean lion, and the eagle or vulture that gnawed upon the liver of Prometheus.

But the most absymally terrifying are the monsters from the most frightening liminal area of the human psyche, the border of sanity. These are the creatures of blood-dripping, corpse-adorned Shiva and Durga, the monsters of ecstasy and death, the awesome horrors of madness. Germanic and Japanese myth summon up headless horses, crimson blood spurting from their neck stumps as they plunge into panic-stricken masses of men. Both of the great beasts of Revelations 13 rise from below, the first from the sea and the second from the earth, both from the dark unconscious. Here is the ultimate terror as these monsters of the unconscious rise to overpower consciousness and overrun humanity.

Notes to Preface

[1]Wendy Doniger O'Flaherty, The Origins of Evil in Hindu Mythology (Berkeley, 1976), pp. 9-10.

[2]Wendy Doniger O'Flaherty, Women, Androgynes, and Other Mythical Beasts (Chicago and London, 1980), p. 5.

[3]E.g., J.C. Cooper, An Illustrated Encyclopaedia of Traditional Symbols (London, 1978).

[4]Claude Lévi-Strauss, Structural Anthropology, trans. Monique Layton (New York, 1976), II, 65.

Notes for Chapter I
Some Basics about Myth

[1]Some general studies of mythology:
Thomas J.J. Altizer, ed., Truth, Myth and Symbol (Englewood Cliffs, New Jersey, 1962).
Mary Barnard, The Mythmakers (Athens, Ohio, 1967).
Franz Boas, "Mythology," Race, Language and Culture (New York, 1940), pp. 397-524.
Kees W. Bolle, The Freedom of Man in Myth (Nashville, Tenn., 1968).
I.R. Buchler and H.A. Selby, A Formal Study of Myth (Austin, Texas, 1968).
Joseph Campbell, The Flight of the Wild Gander (South Bend, Indiana, 1979).
Joseph Campbell, The Masks of God: Primitive Mythology (London, 1960).
Joseph Campbell, The Masks of God: Oriental Mythology (London, 1962).
Joseph Campbell, The Masks of God: Occidental Mythology (London, 1965).
Joseph Campbell, The Masks of God: Creative Mythology (New York, 1968).
Joseph Campbell, The Mythic Image (Princeton, 1974).
Joseph Campbell, Myths to Live by (New York, 1972).
Percy S. Cohen, "Theories of Myth," Man, IV (1969), 337-353.
Colloque sur les problèmes du mythe et de son interprétation (Chantilly, 1976).
Gilbert Durand, Les structures anthropologiques de l'imaginaire; introduction à l'archétypologie générale (Paris, 1969).
Mircea Eliade, Myth and Reality, trans. W.R. Trask (New York, 1963).
Mircea Eliade, Myths, Rites, Symbols: A Mircea Eliade Reader, ed. Wendell C. Beane and William G. Doty (New York, 1976). 2 vols.

Alexander Eliot, Myths (New York, 1976).

R. Firth, "The Plasticity of Myth," Ethnologica, N.S., II (1960), 181-188.

Robert A. Georges, Studies on Mythology (Homewood, Illinois, 1969).

Adolf E. Jensen, Ed., Myth, Mensch und Umwelt (New York, 1978).

Geoffrey S. Kirk, Myth: Its Meaning and Functions in Ancient and Other Cultures (Cambridge, England, and Berkeley, Calif., 1970).

Joseph Kitagawa and Charles H. Long, eds., Myths and Symbols: Studies in Honor of Mircea Eliade (Chicago, 1969).

Claude Lévi-Strauss, Myth and Meaning (New York, 1979).

Pierre Maranda, Mythology: Selected Readings (Harmondsworth, England, 1972).

John Middleton, ed., Myth and Cosmos (New York, 1967).

Henry A. Murray, ed., Myth and Mythmaking (New York, 1960).

Paul A. Olson, ed., The Uses of Myth (Champaign, Illinois, 1968).

Raphael Patai, Myth and Modern Man (Edgewood Cliffs, New Jersey, 1972).

Monique A. Piettre, Au commencement était le mythe genèse et jeunesse des mythes (Paris, 1968).

J. Rudhardt, "Mythe, langue et expérience religieuse," Numen, XXVII (1980), 83-104.

Thomas A. Sebeok, ed., Myth: A Symposium (Bloomington and London, 1965).

Bibliographies of mythology:

Donald Capps, et al., Psychology of Religion: A Guide to Information Sources (Detroit, 1976).

Katherine S. Diehl, Religion, Mythologies, Folklores: An Annotated Bibliography (New Brunswick, New Jersey, 1956).

Many other studies of mythology are cited in subsequent notes.

[2]Carol R. Ember, "Myths about Hunter-Gatherers," Ethnology, XVIII (1978), 439-448.

[3]Prime myth, primal myth, primitive myth are possible terms, but they all suggest "first." Every genuine myth is generations-old, perhaps millenia-old, when initially recorded. Pre-literate myth, while more accurate, seems slightly pejorative. True myth or pure myth sounds too commendatory and seems unnecessarily to derogate other varieties of myth. Archaic myth appears the most satisfactory label. The foundational material behind the familiar Greco-Roman mythology is most certainly archaic. Material from existing "primitives" also appears archaic to advanced societies.

Joseph Szövérffy, "Levels of Individual and Group Consciousness in Story-Telling," Fabula, XII (1971), 8-13, considers the "primitive" qualities in early story-telling and the transition to Myth II.

[4]F.R. Allchen, "The Reconcilation of Jñāna and Bhakti in Rāmacaritamānasa." *Religious* Studies, XII (1976), 81-91.

[5]Hans H. Penner, "Cosmogony as Myth in the Vishnu Parana," History of Religions, V (1966), 283-299.

[6]Robert Graves, Greek Myths (London, 1958), p. 331.

[7]Although this material was the original sacred myth of the English-speaking people (and is embedded in the language in such words as Wednesday--day of Woden--and Thursday--day of Thor), it was completely swept away by Christianity. When Thomas Gray published "The Fatal Sisters" and "The Descent of Odin" (both written in 1761), he had to explain the Teutonic mythology in footnotes.

[8]Many users of this word may not realize its reference to the Greek sea god Proteus. From Adonis to Zombi our language is enormously dependent upon mythical references to identify things or concepts vital to a highly rationalized era.

[9]Alan T. Davies, "The Aryan Myth: Its Religious Significance," Studies in Religion, X (1981), 289: "Nationalism, Marxism, and racism (as well as liberal humanism), the great competing secular 'isms' so familiar to everyone, all reveal the features of myth beyond the trappings of science."

[10]Eric Mottram, "Living Mythically: The Thirties," Journal of American Studies, VI (1972), 267-287, deems everyone in the 1930's from proletariat to intellectuals as governed by myth, i.e. imaginary concepts incapable of scientific proof. We are regularly admonished today by pundits who perceive all our lives controlled by mythical notions.

[11]"The malaise of culture is in reality the malaise of life in a world bereft of myth." Eric Neumann, "Die mythische Welt und der Einzelne," Eranos-Jahrbuch (Zürich, 1949), p. 222.

[12]Hans Vaihinger, Die Philosophie des Als Ob (Berlin, 1911).

[13]In Les deux sources de la morale et de la religion (Geneva, 1945).
Thumbnail definitions of "myth" words:
Mythical is the adjective for the myth-making faculty, the fonction fabulatrice, i.e. for any imaginary concept that is scientifically unverifiable.
Mythological is the adjective for specific references to any of the world's true body of Myth I and Myth II. It would be highly desirable if mythology could be retained as "study and analysis of myth," but usage has dictated its meaning.

Mythic is the adjective for qualities displayed in Myth I and Myth II. External features properly labeled as "mythic" could be: incantatory, poetized, reverent, incisive narrative even to the point of the cryptic. Internal features categorized as mythic could be: unconscious symbolism, post hoc ad propter hoc, free association, eidetic imagery, possible neurotic state.

[14]Louis Dupré, The Other Dimension (New York, 1972), p. 242, "Myths are verbally developed symbols."

[15]Ernst Cassirer, An Essay on Man (New Haven, Conn., 1944), pp. 23-6, defines man as a "symbol-making animal" and sees the principle of symbolism giving access to the specifically human world, the world of human culture.

[16]Also see David Bidney, "Myth, Symbolism, and Truth," Journal of American Folklore, LXVIII (1955), 379-392.

[17]"In all three [play, art, and religion] there is symbolism, a doing something which stands for something, but with a merging, in the mind, of the reality with the symbol; the act itself is of supreme importance. In all three there is thus an element of magic inherent in the symbol and its power, and in all there is a total surrender of the person, for the time being, to this symbol and this 'wholly other' power." Leroy E. Loemker, "Symbol and Myth in Philosophy," in Truth, Myth and Symbol, ed. Thomas J.J. Altizer et al. (Englewood Cliffs, N.J., 1962), p. 122.

[18]Archaic societies can outdo self-conscious artists in highly figurative language and symbolic themes. See:
Ralph L. Roys, The Book of the Chilam of Chumayel (Norman, Oklahoma, 1967), and,
Johannes Wilbert, "The Metaphoric Snare: Analysis of a Warao Folklore," Journal of Latin American Lore, I (1975), 7-18.

[19]Henri Frankfort, Kingship and the Gods (Chicago, 1948), pp. 30-31.

[20]"Myth is a verbal celebration of a sacred event." G. van der Leeuw, Religion in Essence and Manifestation, trans. J.E. Turner (London, 1938), p. 413.

[21]Robert Graves, "Introduction," Larousse Encyclopedia of Mythology (New York, 1959), p. v: "Mythology is the study of whatever religious or heroic legends are so foreign to a student's experience that he cannot believe them to be true."

[22]William A. Lessa, "Discoverer-of-the-Sun; Mythology as a Reflection of Culture," Journal of American Folklore, LXXIX (1966), 3-51.

[23]Kecizate Ashaninga, chief of the Campa Amerindians of Peru, told Dr. Fernando L. Porras: "All legends lead to purity, to the truth about man." "Epicycles: Myths, Stories, Parables," Parabola, II (Summer, 1977), 58.

[24]"The problem is not the material content of mythology but the intensity with which it is experienced, with which it is believed--as only something endowed with objective reality can be believed." Ernst Cassirer, Philosophy of Symbolic Forms, trans. Ralph Manheim (New Haven, Conn., 1953-1957), II, 5.

[25]Clyde Kluckhohn, "Myths and Rituals: A General Theory," Harvard Theological Review, XXXV (1942), 64.

[26]Raffaele Pettazzoni, Essays on the History of Religions (Leiden, 1954), pp. 11-13.

[27]Many other peoples make approximately the same classification of narratives. Among NW Amerindians myth is labeled:
adaorh--Salmon-Eaters
adaox--Tsimshian Indians
ik!anam--Chinook
nuyam--Kwakiutl
spetakl--Thompson Indians
There are corresponding labels for what we term "heroic tales" and "folklore."

[28]Other archaic peoples have varying but parallel classifications. See David Scorza, "Classification of Au Myths," Practical Anthropology, XIX (1972), 214-218.

[29]The familiar facetious rendition of this myth may be a thoroughgoing revision of an earlier serious conflict between smiths and soldiers, or some bitter row in heaven. Lucian of Samosata suggested that the story probably referred to the conjunction of Mars and Venus in the night sky.

[30]Nineteenth century religionists usually labeled as "religious" what they considered elevated and noble in other cultures, e.g. Buddhist contemplation. What they found distasteful, such as the blood-drenched Kali of Hinduism, was dismissed as "myth."

[31]"The religious conception uprises from the human intellect, in one mood, that of earnest contemplation and submission; while the mythical ideas uprise from another mood, that of playful and erratic fancy." Andrew Lang, Myth, Ritual and Religion (London, 1901), I, 4-5.

[32]Sartoris (New York, 1953), p. 25.

[33]Antti Aarne, The Types of the Folk-Tale, ed. and trans. Stith Thompson (Helsinki, 1928).
R.D. Abrahams, "Introductory Remarks to a Rhetorical Theory of Folklore," Journal of American Folklore, LXXXI (1968), 143-158.
W.R. Bascom, "Four Functions of Folklore," Journal of American Folklore, LXVIII (1955), 245-252.
Franz Boas, "The Development of Folk-Tales and Myths," Scientific Monthly, III (1916), 335-343.
Franz Boas, Primitive Art (Oslo and Cambridge, Mass., 1927).
H.R. Ellis Davidson, "Folklore and Myth," Folklore, LXXXVII (1976), 131-145.
Warren R. Dawson, The Bridle of Pegasus: Studies in Magic, Mythology and Folklore (London, 1930).
Richard M. Dorson, ed., Folklore and Folklife, an Introduction (Chicago, 1972).
Munro S. Edmonson, Lore: An Introduction to the Science of Folklore and Literature (New York, 1971).
Géza Róheim, "Myth and Folktale," American Imago, II (1941), 266-279.
Stith Thompson, The Folktale (New York, 1951).
Stith Thompson, Motif-Index of Folk-Literature (Bloomington, Indiana, 1932-1936), 6 vols.

[34]"Myth," Encyclopaedia of the Social Sciences (New York, 1933), XI, 178-179. In the more recent edition of this text, Victor W. Turner, "Myth and Symbol," International Encyclopedia of the Social Sciences (New York, 1968), X, 576, insists on clearly separating myth, legend, and folklore.

[35]"Folklore," Funk and Wagnalls Standard Dictionary of Folklore, Mythology and Legend (New York, 1949), I, 403. However, in the next entry, "Folklore and Mythology," Alexander H. Krappe suggests definite discrimination between these two terms.

[36]In the 19th century the term folklore was often applied to any mythical material outside of the respected Greco-Roman tradition.

[37]K.M. Briggs, "Possible Mythological Motifs in English Folktales," Folklore, LXXXIII (1972), 265-271, treats of several classical themes from ancient Greco-Roman mythology appearing in British folktales.

[38]Mac Linscott Ricketts, "The North American Indian Trickster," History of Religions, V (1966), 327-350.

[39]Robert M. Jacobs, "The Effects of Acculturation on the Traditional Narratives of Palau," Journal of American Folklore, LXXXIV (1972), 265-271.

[40]E. Thomas Lawson, "The Explanation of Myth and Myth as Explanation," Journal of the American Academy of Religion, XLVI (1978), 507-523. C.S. Burne and J.L. Myres, Notes and Queries on Anthropology, 4th ed. (London, 1912), pp. 210-211, so define myth that it is altogether etiological. Andrew Lang saw myth primarily as explanation, a sort of pseudo-science of the primitive. Today no major theorist would claim etiology as the sole type of myth.

[41]The Hero with a Thousand Faces (Princeton, 1968), p. 30.

[42]Two different men are bracketed under this name. The anonymous figure onward from Chapter 40 of Isaiah is designated as "Deutero-Isaiah."

[43]Various classification systems can be suggested. E.g. Rudolf Jockel, Götter und Dämonen: Mythen der Völker (Darmstadt und Genf, 1953), agrees with soteriological, eschatological, and etiological but further proposes cosmogonic myth (origin of world), cosmological (development of world and natural phenomena), and theogonic (dealing with the gods).
S.H. Hooke, Middle Eastern Mythology (Harmondsworth, England, 1963), pp. 11-16, lists as the types of Middle Eastern myth: ritual, etiological, cult (religious assertion of moral rather than magic import), prestige (glorifying family, clan, city), eschatological.
Lorraine Kisly, "Living Myths: A Conversation with Joseph Campbell," Parabola, I (Spring, 1976), 72, attributes to Joseph Campbell this classification: mystical, cosmological, sociological, pedagogical.

[44]Clyde Kluckhohn, "Recurrent Themes in Myths and Mythmaking," Myth and Mythmaking, ed. Henry A. Murray (New York, 1960), pp. 46-60, points out well-nigh universal myths: flood, slaying of monsters, incest, sibling rivalry, castration, androgynous deities. Joseph Campbell, The Hero with a Thousand Faces (Princeton, 1968), finds the myths of the hero worldwide. Mircea Eliade, Myth of the Eternal Return, trans. W.R. Trask (New York, 1947) finds "eternal return" in almost every mythology. Creation, death, war, and many other major topics of myths are generally found throughout the globe.

[45]Claude Lévi-Strauss, Anthropologie structurale (Paris, 1958), p. 29.

[46]Sri Aurobindo, Birth Centenary Library (Pondicherry, 1972), XV, 302. W. Norman Brown, K.A. Nilakanta Sastri, and S. Radhakrishnan are other Indologists confident that Christianity is deeply indebted to Buddhism.

[47]Dines Chandra Sircar, "Early History of Vaiṣṇavism," The Cultural Heritage of India, ed. Haridas Bhattacharyya (Calcutta, 1956), IV, 139.

[48]Lajos Boglár, "Creative Process in Ritual Art: Piaroa Indians, Venezuela" in The Realm of the Extra-Human: Ideas and Actions (The Hague and Paris, 1976), pp. 347-353.

[49]Karel Werner, "Symbolism in the Vedas and Its Conceptualisations," Numen, XXIV (1977), 229-30.

[50]See Robert A. Oden, Jr., "'The Contendings of Horus and Seth' (Chester Beatty Papyrus No. 1): A Structural Interpretation," History of Religions, XVIII (1979), 352-369. Another interesting multifaceted approach to a specific myth appears in Elli Köngäs Maranda, "Five Interpretations of a Melanesian Myth," Journal of American Folklore, LXXXVI (1973), 3-13. The myth from the British Solomon Islands involves a woman born of a snake mother in the earth.

[51]Charles P. Mountford, "The Rainbow-Serpent Myths of Australia," The Rainbow-Serpent: A Chromatic Piece, ed. I.R. Buchler and Kenneth Maddock, World Anthropology Series (The Hague, Paris, and New York, 1978), pp. 56-57.

[52]Jaroslaw T. Petryshyn, "The Nomenclature and Functions of Certain Lacandon Mayan Deities," The Realm of the Extra-Human: Agents and Audiences, ed. Agehananda Bharati (The Hague and Paris, 1976), p. 494.

Notes for Chapter II

The Beginnings to the Nineteenth Century

[1]Ernst Cassirer, Language and Myth, trans. Susanne K. Langer (New York and London, 1946).

[2]Raymond Dart, "The Makapansgat Australopithecine Osteodontokeratic Culture," Third Panafrican Congress of Prehistory, ed. J. Desmond Clark (London, 1957), pp. 161-171.

[3]Studies on early mythico-religious activity:
William F. Albright, From the Stone Age to Christianity; Monotheism and the Historical Process, 2nd ed. (Baltimore, 1957).
Jan van Baal, Symbols for Communication; An Introduction to the Anthropological Study of Religion (Assen, Netherlands, 1971).
F.M. Bergounioux and Joseph Goetz, Primitive and Prehistoric Religions, trans. C.R. Busby (New York, 1966).
R.B. Brockway, "Neanderthal 'Religion,'" Studies in Religion, VII (1978), 317-321.
John J. Collins, Primitive Religion (Totowa, New Jersey, 1978).
Wilhelm Dupré, Religion in Primitive Cultures; A Study in Ethnophilosophy (The Hague, 1975).

Mircea Eliade, A History of Religious Ideas. Volume I: From the Stone Age to the Eleusinian Mysteries, trans. Willard R. Trask (Chicago and London, 1978).
Edward E. Evans-Pritchard, Theories of Primitive Religion (Oxford, 1965).
William J. Goode, Religion among the Primitives (Glencoe, Illinois, 1951).
Hoffman R. Hays, In the Beginnings: Early Man and His Gods (New York, 1963).
Edwin O. James, Prehistoric Religion (New York, 1957).
Gertrude R. Levy, The Gate of Horn; A Study of the Religious Conceptions of the Stone Age, and Their Influence upon European Thought (London, 1963).
André Leroi-Gourhan, Les religions de la préhistorique (paléolithique) (Paris, 1964).
Robert H. Lowie, Primitive Religion (London, 1925).
Annemarie De Waal Malefijt, Religion and Culture; An Introduction to Anthropology of Religion (New York, 1968).
Johannes Maringer, The Gods of Prehistoric Man (New York, 1960).
Robert R. Marett, The Threshold of Religion (London, 1914).
Edward Norbeck, Religion in Primitive Society (New York, 1961).
Harald L. Pager, Stone Age Myth and Magic as Documented in the Rock Paintings of South Africa (Graz, 1975).
E.G. Parrinder, "The Origins of Religion," Religious Studies, I (1966), 257-261.
Charles Picard, Les religions préhistoriques (Paris, 1948).
Paul Radin, Primitive Religion; Its Nature and Origin (New York, 1937).
W.E.H. Stanner, On Aboriginal Religion (Sydney, 1966).
Guy E. Swanson, The Birth of the Gods; The Origin of Primitive Beliefs (Ann Arbor, Michigan, 1960).

[4]Isador H. Coriat, "Totemism in Prehistoric Man," Psychoanalytic Review, XXI (1934), 47.

[5]Marija Gimbutas, The Gods and Goddesses of Old Europe 7000 to 3500 B.C. (London, 1974), devotes but one of ten chapters to gods; goddesses dominate the rest of the book.

[6]See Joseph Campbell, "Renewal Myths and Rites of the Primitive Hunters and Planters," Eranos-Jahrbuch, XXVIII (1959), 407-457.

[7]Joseph Campbell, The Masks of God: Oriental Mythology (London, 1962), p. 15. Most of this volume is concerned with the distinctive features of Oriental myth and its difference from myth of the West.

[8]Géza Róheim, "La psychologie raciale et les origines du capitalisme chez les primitifs," Revue française de psychoanalyse, III (1929), 122-149.

[9]See Heinrich Zimmer, Maya: Der indische Mythos (Stuttgart/ Berlin, 1936) for an analysis of the Indian psyche through Indian mythology.

[10]Karl Jaspers, The Origin and Goal of History, trans. Michael Bullock (London, 1953).

[11]Geoffrey S. Kirk, Myth: Its Meaning and Functions in Ancient and Other Cultures (Cambridge and Berkeley, 1970).

[12]History of the study of myth: Pinard de la Boullaye, L'Étude comparée des religions (Paris, 1922), 2 vols.
Richard Chase, Quest for Myth (Baton Rouge, Louisiana, 1949).
Paul Decharmé, La critique des traditions religieuses chez les Grecs (Paris, 1904).
[Paullus] Otto Gruppe, Geschichte der klassischen mythologie und religionsgeschichte während des mittelalters im abendland und während der neuzeit (Leipzig, 1921).
Jan de Vries, Forschungsgeschichte der Mythologie (Freiburg/ München, 1961).

[13]Maurice M. Kaunitz, A Popular History of Philosophy (Cleveland and New York, 1943), p. 6: "the first man who tried to get away from supernatural beliefs." This echoes the appraisal by Diderot in the 19th century.

[14]UPI despatch of 29 August 1980 reports the perturbation of the Yungngara tribesmen of Western Australia because of contemplated oil drilling at Pea Hill where the Great Goanna dwells. Disturbance of the Great Goanna is expected to disrupt, perhaps to extinction, the physical goannas, lizards highly prized as delicacies.

[15]For Plato as a primitive philosopher see Mircea Eliade, Cosmos and History, trans. W.R. Trask (New York, 1959), pp. 34-35.

[16]Plato, Phaedrus, 229C ff.

[17]Plato, Apology, 26-28.

[18]Jacquetta Hawkes, Man and the Sun (London, 1963), and William T. Olcott, Myths of the Sun (New York, 1967), indicate some of the vast scope of solar mythology.

[19]Émile C.M. Senart, Essai sur la légende de Buddha, son caractère et ses origines, 2nd ed. (Paris, 1882).

[20]James C. Moloney, "Oedipus Rex, CuChulain, Khepri and the Ass," Psychoanalytic Review, LIV (1967), 234.

[21]Richard M. Dorson, "The Eclipse of Solar Mythology," Myth: A Symposium, ed. Thomas A. Sebeok (Bloomington and London, 1965), pp. 25-63.

[22]William A. White, "Moon Myth in Medicine," Psychoanalytic Review, I (1914), 241-256.

[23]John Tu Er-Wei, "The Moon-Mythical Character of the God Yü-huang," The Realm of the Extra-Human: Agents and Audiences, ed. Agehananda Bharati (The Hague and Paris, 1976), p. 509.

[24]W.K.C. Guthrie, Orpheus and Greek Religion (London, 1953).
Ivan M. Linforth, The Arts of Orpheus (Berkeley and Los Angeles, 1941).
G.R.S. Mead, Orpheus (London, 1896).
Joseph R. Watmough, Orphism (Cambridge, England, 1934).

[25]Homer has no specific biography like Valmiki, and is especially suspect as a "blind bard." Archaic people often attribute "second sight" to the blind, as to Tiresias. Of course, in Homeric society storytelling may have been about the only livelihood for a blind man.

[26]A.D. Pusalker, "The Rāmāyaṇa: Its History and Character," Cultural Heritage of India, ed. S. Radhakrishnan, et al. (Calcutta, 1962), II, 28.

[27]Bulfinch's Mythology (New York, n.d.), p. 241. This is the Modern Library edition.

[28]Mythology or Explication of Fables.

[29]Concerning the Wisdom of the Ancients.

[30]See C.W. Lemmi, The Classic Deities in Bacon (Baltimore, 1933).

[31]Jainism and Theravada Buddhism, similarly eschewing deities, are the other two heterodoxies.

[32]See Werner W. Jaeger, The Theology of the Early Greek Philosophers, trans. E.S. Robinson (Oxford, 1947) and Kathleen Freeman, The Pre-Socratic Philosophers (Oxford, 1946).

[33]Sophocles, The Theban Plays (Baltimore, 1947), pp. 135-136.

[34]Even Edward Tylor, the great anthropologist, considered a belief in gods basic to religion, but in light of Indian faiths the definer of religion today must carefully avoid that restriction.

[35]The euhemerism of Herodotus is eroded by his love of a good story which he often took from a glib narrator and repeated without criticism.

[36]See M.L.A.G. Boissier, La religion romaine d'Auguste aux Antonins (Paris, 1909), pp. 122 ff.

[37]Mircea Eliade, Cosmos and History (New York, 1959), pp. 39-46, cites extensive examples from eastern Europe of historical events and persons mythologized.

[38]G.C. Oosthuizen, "Isaiah Shembe and the Zulu World View," History of Religions, VIII (1968), 1-30. Reincarnation (a pre-existent deity assuming a human body) is a different condition, treated in Chapter IV.

[39]Gustav W. Gessmann, Die Sternenwelt und ihre mythologische Deutung (Leipzig, 1897).
Wilhelm Gundel, Sterne und Sternbilder im Glauben des Altertums und der Neuzeit (Bonn, 1922).
Gertrude and James Jobes, Outer Space: Myths, Name Meanings, Calendars from the Origin of History to the Present Day (New York, 1964).
Peter Lum, The Stars in Our Heaven, Myths and Fables (London, 1951).
Thassilo Fritz von Scheffer, Die Legenden der Sterne im Umkreis der antiken Welt (Stuttgart, 1939).
Oral E. Scott, The Stars in Myth and Fact (Caldwell, Idaho, 1947).

[40]See above in this chapter for myth derived from sun, moon, and other meteorological phenomena.

[41]Concerning Astronomy.

[42]Die Christus Mythe (Jena, 1911).

[43]See his entry, "Ages of the World (Babylonian)," Encyclopaedia of Religion and Ethics (New York and Edinburgh, 1908), I, 184.

[44]The sun is the eye of Ngai during the day. The familiar pattern worldwide is sun as the daytime eye of god, the moon at night.

[45]An Essay on Man, Epistle I, 99-112.

[46]Concerning the Ritual Laws of the Hebrews.

[47]Sir James Frazer, Folklore in the Old Testament (London, 1912), I, viii.

[48]See Jean Seznec, The Survival of the Pagan Gods: The Mythological Tradition and Its Place in Renaissance Humanism and Art, trans. B.F. Sessions (New York, 1961).

[49]Concerning the Genealogies of the Pagan Gods.

[50]Especially as presented by the influential Jacob Burckhardt, Die Kultur der Renaissance in Italien (1860).

[51]Ancient Likenesses of the Gods.

[52]Richard Chase, Quest for Myth (Baton Rouge, Louisiana, 1949), p. 73.

[53]E.g. A.B. Rooth, "Scholarly Tradition in Folklore Research," Fabula, I (1957), 195-196.

[54]The enthusiasm of Ganesha arose perhaps from his acceptance of the statement made in the Mahabharata itself: "What is not in the Mahabharata is not to be found anywhere else in the world."

[55]Gustav Bergmann, "Zur analytischen Theorie literarischer Wertmasstäbe (mit einer Bemerkung zur Grundlagendiskussion)," Imago XXI (1935), 498-504.
  Maud Bodkin, Archetypal Patterns in Poetry: Psychological Studies of Imagination (London, 1963).
  William Righter, Myth and Literature (London and Boston, 1975).
  K.K. Ruthven, Myth (London, 1976).
  William York Tindall, The Literary Symbol (Bloomington, Indiana, 1955).
  John B. Vickery, ed., Myth and Literature: Contemporary Theory and Practice (Lincoln, Nebraska, 1966).

[56]Burton Feldman and Robert D. Richardson, The Rise of Modern Mythology, 1680-1860 (Bloomington and London, 1972).
  Peter Gay, The Enlightenment: An Interpretation. The Rise of Modern Paganism (London, 1967).
  Edward B. Hungerford, Shores of Darkness (New York, 1941).
  Frank Manuel, The Eighteenth Century Confronts the Gods (Cambridge, Mass., 1959).

[57]About the Origin of Myths. In both French and English the word fable was often used in the sense of "myth" well into the 19th century.

[58]N.C.J. Trublet, Mémoires pour servir à l'histoire de la vie et des ouvrages de M. de Fontenelle, 2nd ed. (Amsterdam, 1759), believed the work written during the 1690's. This conjecture is generally accepted.

[59]Paul Radin, Primitive Religion: Its Nature and Origin (New York, 1937), p. 259.

[60]Wilhelm Schmidt, Der Ursprung de Gottesidee (Münster, Westphalia, 1926-1955), 12 vols.

[61]Works of Lucian of Samosata, trans. H.W. Fowler and F.G. Fowler (Oxford, 1905), II, 212-213.

[62]H.B.S. Ostermann, The Alaskan Eskimos, as Described in the Posthumous Notes of Dr. Knud Rasmussen. Report of the Fifth Thule Expedition 1921-24, trans. W.E. Calvert (Copenhagen, 1952), X, no. 3, pp. 97-99.

[63]The word is a portmanteau term devised by James Joyce, Finnegans Wake (New York, 1939), p. 581.

[64]See Andrew Ramsay, The Travels of Cyrus, 2nd ed. (London, 1728), pp. 116-126.

[65]Joseph Campbell, The Hero with a Thousand Faces (Princeton, 1949).

[66]Robert Graves, The White Goddess: A Historical Grammar of Poetic Myth (New York, 1948).

[67]Northrop Frye, "The Archetypes of Literature," Myth and Symbol (Lincoln, Nebraska, 1966), p. 94.

[68]Most present-day psychoanalysts are termed neo-Freudians because they modify Freud's views and utilize material ascertained subsequent to Freud's researches.

[69]Lloyd De Mause, "The Fetal Origins of History," The Journal of Psychoanalytic Anthropology, IV (1981), 24.

[70]New Science.

[71]The 18th century rash of interest in mythology produced a host of speculative mythologists of extremely fertile imagination, now forgotten. See Edward B. Hungerford, Shores of Darkness (New York, 1941). The misconceptions in William Stukeley's Stonehenge (1740) have been about the most persistent, perhaps not yet extinguished in our own day.

[72]Introduction to a Scientific System of Mythology.

[73]Theodor H. Gaster, Thespis: Ritual, Myth, and Drama in the Ancient Near East (New York, 1966), p. 383.

[74]Ibid., p. 394.

Notes to Chapter III

Myth and Religion: Personal Experience and Piety

[1]This and the next two chapters consider archaic myth and archaic religion. Many moderns will insist that their religion is an etherial and idealized experience quite removed from much that affected earlier man. It is eye-opening, however, to witness many of these archaic forces in the midst of today's most cosmopolitan cities; and, if we are honest, we will admit that many of these experiences have been encountered by all of us, though, of course, often secularized.

[2]"Myths are the most general and effective means of awakening and maintaining consciousness of another world, a beyond, whether it be the divine world or the world of the Ancestors." Mircea Eliade, Myth and Reality (London, 1964), p. 139.
    Through this and subsequent chapters the attitude will be that of Mircea Eliade, "Australian Religious: An Introduction. Part I," History of Religions, VI (1966), 17, "the myth is the ground of religion."
    Though Eliade is widely hailed, anyone of his prominence will arouse adverse criticism. See Robert F. Brown, "Eliade on Archaic Religion: Some Old and New Criticisms," Studies in Religion, X (1981), 429-449, for summaries of anthropological, philosophical, and other criticisms of Eliade.

[3]Gopi Krishna, Biological Basis of Religion and Genius (New York, 1972).
    Charles T. Tart, Altered States of Consciousness (New York, 1969).

[4]Are such alterations of consciousness pathological as some psychologists and psychoanalysts claim? Hans Selye, The Stress of Life (New York, 1950) and Robert K. Wallace, Altered States of Awareness: Readings from Scientific American (1971) both see dissociational states as but one segment of the response mechanism in normal personalities.

[5]The term is taken from R. Gordon Wasson, The Wondrous Mushroom: Mycolatry in Mesoamerica (New York, 1980).

[6]Jack O. Waddell, "The Place of the Cactus Wine Ritual in the Papago Indian Ecosystem," The Realm of the Extra-Human: Ideas and Actions, ed. Agehananda Bharati (The Hague and Paris, 1976), pp. 213-228.

[7]Johannes Wilbert, "Magico-Religious Use of Tobacco among South American Indians," Cannabis and Culture, ed. Vera Rubin (The Hague and Paris, 1975), pp. 439-461.

[8]The exact number is hard to determine because of classification. Are cannabis, hashish, marihuana, ganja, zamal, hemp all the same or several different plants?

[9]Hui-Lin Li, "The Origin and Use of Cannabis in Eastern Asia: Their Linguistic-Cultural Implications," Cannabis and Culture, pp. 51-62.

[10]David F. Aberle, The Peyote Religion among the Navaho (Chicago, 1965).
Weston La Barre, The Peyote Cult (New Haven, 1938).
James S. Slotkin, The Peyote Religion: A Study in Indian-White Relations (Glencoe, Illinois, 1956).

[11]Marlene Dobkin de Rios, "Man, Culture and Hallucinogens: An Overview," Cannabis and Culture, pp. 401-416.

[12]John M. Allegro, The Sacred Mushroom and the Cross (London, 1970).

[13]R. Gordon Wasson, Soma: Divine Mushroom of Immortality (London, 1971).

[14]See Theodore X. Barber, LSD, Marihuana, Yoga and Hypnosis (Chicago, 1970).

[15]Barbara G. Myerhoff, "The Huichol and the Quest for Paradise," Parabola, I (Winter 1976), 28-29.

[16]Julie Ann Miller, "Botanical Divinities," Science News, CXVIII (August 2, 1980), 75-78.

[17]Ibid., p. 76.

[18]Marlene Dobkin de Rios, "The Influence of Psychotropic Flora and Fauna on Maya Religion," Current Anthropology, XV (1974), 147-164.

[19]Alison Bailey Kennedy, "Ecce Bufo: The Toad in Nature and in Olmec Iconography," Current Anthropology, XXIII (1982), 273-290.

[20]William Braden, The Private Sea: An Enquiry into the Religious Implications of L.S.D. (Chicago, 1967).

[21]R.E.L. Masters and Jean Houston, The Varieties of Psychedelic Experience (New York, 1967), cautiously scrutinize subjects of these dosings and report quite a few cases definitely religiously negative. But also note:
Bernard Aaronson and Humphrey Osmond, Psychedelics (Garden City, New York, 1970).

Timothy Leary, The Politics of Ecstasy (New York, 1968). David Solomon, LSD: The Consciousness Expanding Drug (New York, 1964).

[22]Paul Radin, "The Religious Experiences of an American Indian," Eranos-Jahrbuch, XVIII (1950), 249-290.

[23]Ibid., p. 260.

[24]Aldous Huxley, The Doors of Perception (London, 1954).

[25]W.N. Pahnke, "Drugs and Mysticism," International Journal of Parapsychology, VIII (1966), 295-314.
   J.N. Sherwood, et. al., "The Psychedelic Experience," Journal of Neuropsychiatry, IV (1962), 69-80.
   H. Smith, "Do Drugs Have Religious Import?" Journal of Philosophy, LXI (1964) 517-530.
   Robert C. Zaehner, Drugs, Mysticism, and Make-Believe (London, 1972).

[26]The Varieties of Psychedelic Experience. Also see R.P. Marsh, "Meaning and the Mind-Drugs," ETC, XXII (1965), 408-430.

[27]Humphrey Osmund, "A Review of the Clinical Effects of Psychotomimetic Agents," Annals of the New York Academy of Sciences, LXVI (1957), 418-434.
   R. Gordon Wasson, Soma: Divine Mushroom of Immortality (New York, 1969).

[28]Philip Solomon, Sensory Deprivation (Cambridge, Mass., 1961).

[29]Breath control is especially emphasized in Yoga. Transformation of state is a likely consequence of a favored Yoga exercise in which inhalation, retention of breath, and exhalation are held to the ratio---1:4:2. Novices attempting this regimen are often quite affected.

[30]The magical or religious purposes of fasting include:
(1) Altered state of awareness, the only purpose here considered.
(2) Purification preparatory to ritual (e.g. fasting of priest before mass).
(3) Propitiation in mourning for dead. This practice is to assure the dead that we are also suffering and in fellow regret also pass up food and drink.
(4) Punishment in act of penitence.

[31]Alan Dundes, "Summoning Deity through Ritual Fasting," American Imago, XX (1963), 213-220.

[32]H.B.S. Ostermann, The Alaskan Eskimo, p. 99.

[33]Rudolf Arbesmann, Das Fasten bei den Griechen und Römern (Giessen, 1929).
A.M. Hocart, "Fasting," Encyclopaedia of the Social Sciences, ed. E.R.A. Seligman (New York, 1948), VI, 144-146.
J.A. MacCulloch, "Fasting (Introductory and non-Christian)," Hasting's Encyclopaedia of Religion and Ethics (New York, 1951), V, 759-765.
Joseph B. Tamney, "Fasting and Modernization," Journal for the Scientific Study of Religion, XIX (1979), 129-137.
Edward Westermarck, "The Principles of Fasting," Folk-Lore, XVIII (1907), 391-422.

[34]Arthur P. Stanley, Historical Memorials of Canterbury (London, 1906), p. 98.

[35]The entire Spring, 1979, issue of Parabola consists of articles on the sacred and mythical elements of the dance. Also note:
Eugène L. Backman, Religious Dances in the Christian Church and in Popular Medicine, trans. E. Classen (London, 1952).
Erika Bourguignon, Trance Dance (New York, 1968).
Clark Wissler, General Discussion of Shamanistic and Dancing Societies (New York, 1916).
Maria-Gabriele Wosien, Sacred Dance (London and New York, 1974).

[36]Ananda K. Coomaraswamy, The Dance of Shiva (New York, 1957), p. 67.

[37]K.V. Gajendragadkar, "The Mahārāṣtra Saints and Their Teachings," Cultural Heritage of India, ed. H. Bhattacharyya (Calcutta, 1956), IV, 375.

[38]W.O.E. Oesterley, The Sacred Dance (New York, 1968).

[39]Perhaps the limping was to demonstrate their inferiority to the god and to arouse pity in the deity for such handicapped mortals.

[40]A good short survey of the role of Dionysus can be found in Mircea Eliade, History of Religious Ideas (Chicago, 1978), I, 357-373.

[41]Ira Friedlander, Whirling Dervishes (New York, 1975).
Other less famed Islamic religious dancers are the Naqshbandi and Chishti dervishes.

[42]For a moderate position see Andrew M. Greeley, "Ecstasy through Sex," Ecstasy: A Way of Knowing (Englewood Cliffs, New Jersey, 1974), pp. 91-97. For a rather comprehensive picture of

457

general sexual manifestations in religion see Geoffrey Parrinder, Sex in the World Religions (New York, 1980).

[43]H.S. Darlington, "Ceremonial Behaviorism: Sacrifices for the Foundations of Houses," Psychoanalytic Review, XVIII (1931), 315.

[44]Prabodha-Chandra Bagchi, Studies in the Tantras (Calcutta, 1939).
S.C.V. Bhattacharya, Principles of Tantra, 4th ed. (Madras, 1969-1970), 2 vols.
Chintaharan Chakravarti, Tantras; Studies on Their Religion and Literature (Calcutta, 1963).
Nik Douglas, Tantra Yoga (New Delhi, 1971).
Omar V. Garrison, Tantra: The Yoga of Sex (New York, 1964).
Sanjukta Gupta, Dirk Jan Hoens, and Teun Goudriaan, Hindu Tantrism (Leiden, 1979).

[45]Literally the Greek word ascesis means athletic training. Asceticism in Christianity has followed the route (which can be a segment of athleticism) of renouncing the pleasures of the flesh and straining the body almost to the breaking point.

[46]Robert Ardrey, The Social Contract (London, 1970), pp. 361-364, ascribes religion ("a common body of assumptions") to animals and then denies it to mankind ("We are a species lacking a religion").

[47]Sue Mansfield, The Gestalts of War (New York, 1982).

[48]This is a border area between active and passive. Among archaic peoples emotive music is generally accompanied by physical movement ranging from energetic dancing to perhaps seated hip-slapping.

[49]Consult René Aigrain, La musique religieuse (Mayenne, 1929).
Jaap Kunst, ed., The Wellsprings of Music (The Hague, 1962).
Curt Sachs, The Rise of Music in the Ancient World, East and West (London, 1944).
Brian Wibberley, Music and Religion: A Historical and Philosophical Survey (London, 1934).

[50]More extensive discussion of ritual will appear later in this text in consideration of the social sciences.

[51]See Loomis Havemeyer, The Drama of Savage Peoples (New Haven, Conn., 1916).

[52]See Theodor H. Gaster, Thespis: Ritual, Myth and Drama in the Ancient Near East (New York, 1966) for early Egyptian, Canaanite, Hebrew, and Hittite drama.

See Bertha S. Phillpotts, *The Elder Edda and Ancient Scandinavian Drama* (Cambridge, 1920) for assertion of extensive drama in ancient Scandinavia.

[53]The quest theme, of course, is allied to the male initiation ritual and the myth of the hero, but is self-induced and voluntary. The young male being initiated into manhood undergoes a quest imposed upon him by adult males at one specific time. The hero similarly is forced to action by command, challenge, dare. Any adult--women, humble peasants, anyone--can become a pilgrim and at any time.

[54]Kamil Pecher, *Lonely Voyage: By Kayak to Adventure and Discovery* (Saskatoon, 1978), p. 1.

[55]Karl Abraham, *Dreams and Myths: A Study in Race Psychology*, trans. W.A. White (New York, 1913).

Helton G. Baynes, *Mythology of the Soul: A Research into the Unconscious from Schizophrenic Dreams and Drawings* (Baltimore, 1940).

Daniel Cohen, *Dreams, Visions and Drugs: A Search for Other Realities* (New York, 1976).

Mircea Eliade, *Myths, Dreams, and Mysteries*, trans. P. Mairet (New York, 1960).

Sigmund Freud and D.E. Oppenheim, *Dreams in Folklore*, trans. A.M.O. Richards (New York, 1958).

Sigmund Freud, *The Interpretation of Dreams*, trans. A.A. Brill (London and New York, 1927).

Erich Fromm, *The Forgotten Language: An Introduction to the Understanding of Dreams, Fairy Tales, and Myths* (New York, 1951).

Morton T. Kelsey, *Dreams: The Dark Speech of the Spirit, a Christian Interpretation* (Garden City, New York, 1968).

Jackson S. Lincoln, *The Dream in Primitive Cultures* (London, 1935).

Géza Róheim, *The Gates of the Dream* (New York, 1969).

David M. Schneider and Lauriston Sharp, *The Dream Life of a Primitive People: The Dreams of the Yir Yoront of Australia* (Ann Arbor, Mich., 1969).

Werner Wolff, *The Dream, Mirror of Conscience; A History of Dream Interpretation from 2000 B.C. and a New Theory of Dream Synthesis* (New York, 1952).

The Spring, 1982 (#2 of VII) issue of *Parabola* is wholly devoted to "Dreams and Seeing."

[56]E.g. Martin S. Bergmann, "The Impact of Ego Psychology on the Study of the Myth," *American Imago*, XXIII (1966), 263, insists that all myths "originated in the nightmare."

Also see Karl Abraham, *Dreams and Myths: A Study in Race Psychology* (New York, 1970).

[57]Western Christendom apparently accepted religious frenzy as supernatural and holy until late medieval times when such manifestation was increasingly termed "insanity" or "madness." See Judith D. Neaman, "Disorder in the Mind of the Middle Ages," Book Forum, V (1981), 251-258.

[58]Walter F. Otto, Dionysos (Frankfort-am-Main, 1933).

[59]See E.R. Dodds, "Maenadism in the Bacchae," Harvard Theological Review, XXXIII (1940), 155-176.

[60]Perhaps Actaeon's fate was similar, the myth veiling the actuality, as women's rites (those of Aphrodite) were accidentally stumbled upon by Actaeon.

[61]W.K.C. Guthrie, The Greeks and Their Gods (Boston, 1955), p. 145.

[62]James G. Frazer, The Golden Bough: A Study in Magic and Religion, Abridged edition (New York, 1947), p. 349.

[63]David Kinsley, "'Through the Looking Glass': Divine Madness in the Hindu Religious Tradition," History of Religions, XIII (1974), 270-305. Most of the subsequent discussion of the Indian religious madness (except for the Baul Cult) leans heavily upon this study. The quotation is from p. 270.

[64]Manikkavacakar, the 9th century Tamil poet, in the Tiruvacakam rejoices mightily in the madness induced by Shiva.

[65]Kinsley, p. 286 ff., lists numerous mad Hindu saints. Also see Ben-Ami Scharfstein, "Psychotic Mysticism," Mystical Experience (Baltimore, 1974), pp. 133-140.

[66]In the Bhagavata-purana (11. 18.29) Krishna says that his true devotees play like a child, behave like a dolt, and talk like a maniac.

[67]Piyushkanti Mahapatra, "The Baul Cult," Folklore (of India), XII (1971), 126-133, 167-175, 218-228, 258-267, 296-310, 333-349.

[68]Cf. Russell Noyes, Jr., "The Experience of Dying," Psychiatry XXXV (May 1972), 174-184. Note the bibliography.

[69]See M.D. Faber, "Suicide and the Ajax of Sophocles," Psychoanalytic Review, LIV (1967), 441-452.
Herbert Hendin, Suicide and Scandinavia: A Psychoanalytic Study of Culture and Character (New York, 1964), p. 19ff.
C.W. Wahl, "Suicide as a Magical Act," Clues to Suicide, ed. Edwin S. Schneidman and N.L. Farbelow (New York, 1957), pp. 22-30.

Gregory Zilboorg, "Considerations on Suicide, with Particular Reference to That of the Young," American Journal of Orthopsychiatry, VII (1937), 15-31.

[70]Moderns regard the Paleolithic cave paintings as aesthetic. It is almost certain that to the original artists the primary purpose was magico-religious. While a Westerner may find much in archaic religion that is aesthetic to him, to the member of archaic society it is primarily a sacral experience.

[71]Geddes MacGregor, Aesthetic Experience in Religion (London, 1947).
F. David Martin, "The Aesthetic in Religious Experience," Religious Studies, IV (1968), 1-24.
Thomas R. Martland, Religion as Art: An Interpretation (Albany, N.Y., 1982).

[72]An origin of art in play is possible. Consult the index under Huizinga.

[73]Frank Thompson, "The Splintered Glass: Painting and Religion in Modern India," Studies in Religion, X (1981), 177. The italics are Thompson's.

[74]George B. Sansom, Japan: A Short Cultural History (New York, 1962), p. 239.

[75]Arthur C. Headlam, Christian Theology: The Doctrine of God (Oxford, 1934).

[76]Georges Bataille, L'experience intérieure (Paris, 1943).
Richard M. Burke, Cosmic Consciousness, 7th ed. (New York, 1931).
Fritjof Capra, The Tao of Physics: An Exploration of the Parallels between Modern Physics and Eastern Mysticism (Berkeley, 1975).
B. Douglas-Smith, "An Empirical Study of Religious Mysticism," British Journal of Psychiatry, CXVIII (1971), 549-554.
J.N. Finlay, "The Logic of Mysticism," Religious Studies, II (1967), 145-162.
H. Fingarette, "The Ego and Mystic Selflessness," Psychoanalysis and the Psychoanalytic Review, XLV (1958), 5-40.
Sven S. Hartman and Carl-Martin Edsman, eds., Mysticism (Stockholm, 1970).
William R. Inge, Mysticism in Religion (Chicago, 1948).
Rufus M. Jones, et al., "Mysticism," Encyclopedia of Religion and Ethics (New York and Edinburgh, 1917), IX, 83-117.
Rufus M. Jones, Studies in Mystical Religion (London, 1936).
Thomas Katsaros and N. Kaplan, The Western Mystical Tradition (New Haven, Conn., 1969).

James H. Leuba, The Psychology of Religious Mysticism (London and New York, 1925).

Thomas Merton, Mystics and Zen Masters (New York, 1967).

Elmer O'Brien, Varieties of Mystic Experience (London, 1965).

Rudolf Otto, Mysticism East and West, trans. B.L. Bracey and R.C. Payne (New York, 1932).

Ben-Ami Scharfstein, Mystical Experience (Baltimore, 1973).

L. Schneiderman, "Psychological Notes on the Nature of Mystical Experience," Journal for the Scientific Study of Religion, VI (1967), 91-100.

Ninian Smart, "Interpretation and Mystical Experience," Religious Studies, I (1965), 75-87.

Frits Staal, Exploring Mysticism (Harmondsworth, England, 1975).

Walter T. Stace, Mysticism and Philosophy (Philadelphis, 1960).

Daisetz T. Suzuki, Mysticism: Christian and Buddhist (New York, 1957).

Evelyn Underhill, Mysticism (New York, 1961).

Alan W. Watts, Behold the Spirit: A Study in the Necessity of Mystical Religion (London, 1947).

John White, ed., The Highest State of Consciousness (Garden City, New York, 1972).

Robert C. Zaehner, Concordant Discord (Oxford, 1970).

[77]Richard Jefferies (1848-1887) may be the earliest vocal non-theistic mystic of Western society (the East, with Buddha and others, has a long tradition of such mysticism).

[78]Franz Alexander, "Buddhist Training as an Artificial Catatonia," Psychoanalytic Review, XVIII (1931), 137, in considering Eastern mysticism says that "the end goal of Buddhist absorption is an attempt at psychological and physical regression to the condition of intra-uterine life."

[79]Herbert Moller, "Affective Mysticism in Western Civilization," Psychoanalytic Review, LII (1965), 259-274.

[80]Richard Sterba, "Remarks on Mystic States," American Imago, XXV (1968), 85.

[81]Robert C. Zaehner, Mysticism: Sacred and Profane (London, 1961).

[82]Kenneth Wapnick, "Mysticism and Schizophrenia," The Highest State of Consciousness, ed. J. White (New York, 1972), pp. 153-174.

[83]Jack C. Carloye, "The Truth of Mysticism," Religious Studies, XVI (1980), 1-13.

[84]John G. Neihardt, Black Elk Speaks (Lincoln, Nebraska, 1961).

[85]Rudolf Otto, The Idea of the Holy, trans. John Harvey (Oxford, 1936).

[86]The examples are drawn from historical mystics because they are more articulate than primitives and more clearly recognizable to us. Archaic societies, from what we know, produced wholly parallel mysticism.

[87]St. John of the Cross, Dark Night of the Soul, trans. E. Allison Peers (Garden City, New York, 1959).

[88]William James, The Varieties of Religious Experience.

[89]K.V. Gajendragadkar, "The Mahārāṣṭra Saints and Their Teachings," Cultural Heritage of India, IV, 374.

[90]Op. cit.

[91]Many, including the distinguished anthropologist Edward Tylor, assert that a belief in a god or gods is basic to religion but Theravada Buddhism and other nontheistic faiths such as Jainism compel a definition of religion that omits deity as essential.

[92]Indian terminology suggests ātman as the true self of man and paramātman as the Cosmic Self. Many feel that ātman can be realized by concentrated contemplation or, as in Jungian individuation, by the fullest summoning of subconscious and unconscious elements to assemble the total self. Paramātman can only be secured by the mystic path.

[93]Op. cit.

[94]The Gospel of Sri Ramakrishna, trans. Swami Nikhilananda (New York, 1942), p. 396.

[95]Op. cit.

[96]Arthur J. Arberry, Discourses of Rūmī (London, 1961), pp. 55-56.

[97]Remember that what we mislabel as "primitive societies" are "traditional societies," and most of the members of that society express views and display behavior conditioned by millenia of tradition. Originally someone had to galvanize or at least direct primitive social units into paths that long have been routinized.

[98]Mircea Eliade, The Sacred and the Profane: The Nature of Religion, trans. Willard R. Trask (New York, 1961). Also see Mircea Eliade, Man and the Sacred (New York, etc., 1974). Challenge to the appropriateness of the terms "sacred" and "profane" appears in Jack Goody, "Religion and Ritual: The Definitional Problem," British Journal of Sociology, XII (1961), 143-164.

[99]Classification is imprecise at best, but this chapter will treat that which generally is concrete, sensual. Imaginary geography and cosmography will appear under psychology. Sacred beings will be discussed in the next two chapters.
For an interesting classification from the Indian viewpoint, consult Durga Charan Sahoo, "Components of Sacred Complex and Their Classification," Eastern Anthropologist, XXXI (1980), 79-82.

[100]There is a vast literature upon such places, most of it localized, like Christina Hole, English Shrines and Sanctuaries (London, 1954).
James J. Preston, "Sacred Centers and Symbolic Networks in South Asia," Mankind Quarterly, XX (1980), 259-293, reveals the immense breadth and complexity of the subject.

[101]See Virgil's Aeneid, XII. She was the sister and charioteer of Turnus, the Rutulian hero.

[102]John C. Irwin, "The Sacred Anthill and the Cult of the Primordial Mound," History of Religions, XXI (1982), 339-360.

[103]Sankar Sengupta, "Ideal of Toleration and Co-existence: A Study of Sacred Trees in India," Folklore (India), XXI (1980), 88, offers a page-length table of Indian deities associated with trees.

[104]Katherine Luomala, "A Dynamic in Oceanic Maui Myths: Visual Identification with Reference to Hawaiian Localization," Fabula, IV (1961), 137-162.

[105]See the next chapter for a discussion of religious specialists.

[106]The term is here employed not in the psychological but religious sense.

[107]Alfred C. Haddon, Magic and Fetishism (London, 1921).
John Miller, Fetish in Theology, or Doctrinalism Twin to Ritualism (Princeton, 1922).
Fritz Schultze, Der Fetischismus. Ein Beitrag zur Anthropologie und Religionsgeschichte (Leipzig, 1871).

[108]Charles R. Beard, Lucks and Talismans: A Chapter of Popular Superstitions (New York, 1972). Also see next note.

[109]Ernest A.T.W. Budge, Amulets and Talismans (New Hyde Park, New York, 1961).
    William T. Pavitt and Kate Pavitt, The Book of Talismans, Amulets, and Zodiacal Gems, 3rd ed. (New York, 1970).
    Elizabeth Villiers, Amulette und Talismane und andere geheime Dinge... (München, 1927).

Notes to Chapter IV

Religious Specialists

[1]H. L. Mencken, Treatise on the Gods (New York and London, 1930), p. 10.

[2]Das Volk ("the people") might be exalted by Romantics as having profound wisdom, even mystic glory, but the fact remains that in traditional societies effective creativity is rare and confined to a tiny elite.

[3]Mircea Eliade, From Medicine Men to Muhammad (New York, etc., 1974) and "Technicians of the Sacred," Myths, Rites, Symbols: A Mircea Eliade Reader, ed. W. C. Beane and W. G. Doty (New York, etc., 1976), I, 257-339.

[4]E.g.: prophet, seer, visionary, soothsayer, medicine man, exorcist, conjuror, fakir, guru, druid, bonze, lama, necromancer, wizard, charmer, mage, thaumaturgist, enchanter, witch doctor, and so on. Admittedly these roles display considerable overlapping and variation, and the terminology is frequently vague and confusing. In this chapter precise definitions are attempted, even though they may be rather arbitrary.

[5]Charles Ducey, "The Life History and Creative Psychopathology of the Shaman: Ethnopsychoanalytic Perspectives," The Psychoanalytic Study of Society, ed. Werner Muensterberger et al. (New Haven and London, 1976), VII, 173-230.
    Carl-Martin Edsman, ed., Studies in Shamanism (Stockholm, 1967).
    Mircea Eliade, Shamanism: Archaic Techniques of Ecstasy, trans. W. R. Trask (Princeton, 1964).
    Stephen Larsen, The Shaman's Doorway: Opening the Mythic Imagination to Contemporary Consciousness (New York, 1976).
    Andreas Lommel, Shamanism: The Beginnings of Art (New York, 1966).
    John L. Maddox, The Medicine Man: A Sociological Study of the Character and Evolution of Shamanism (New York, 1923).
    A. Ohlmarks, Studien zum Problem des Schamanismus (Lund and Copenhagen, 1939).

J. Silverman, "Shamans and Acute Schizophrenia," _American Anthropologist_, LXIX (1967), 21-31.

[6]See Brenda Z. Seligman, "The Unconscious in Social Heritage," _Essays Presented to_ C. G. _Seligman_ (London, 1934), p. 317, for "the beginning of shamanistic ritual in spontaneous personal dissociation."

[7]The English word ecstasy derives from this Greek word but is too slippery a term to employ precisely. In popular parlance ecstasy means "height of joy." In an analytical study such as Marghanita Laski, _Ecstasy_ (London, 1961) quite a few states, such as "knowledge ecstasy" and "Adamic ecstasy" do not really require the qualities referred to in the classic ekstasis. OBE ("out of body experience") is another label for ekstasis, but rather lacking the religious emphasis. In dreams probably a third or more of the adult population has at some time encountered OBE.

[8]Once again, note the many variations in individual cases. All the descriptions of this chapter examine basic religious specialists, but combinations and divergencies are extensive.

[9]Bruno Klopfer and L. B. Boyer, "Notes on the Personality Structure of a North American Indian Shaman: Rorshach Interpretation," _Journal of Projective Techniques_, XXV (1961), 170-178.

[10]Robert F. Kraus, "A Psychoanalytic Interpretation of Shamanism," _Psychoanalytic Review_, LIX (1972), 19-32.

[11]Mircea Eliade, _Shamanism: Archaic Techniques of Ecstasy_, trans. W. R. Trask (Princeton, 1964), pp. 33-144.

[12]Possibly related to the Sanskrit shramana ("ascetic").

[13]Erika Bourguignon, "World Distribution and Patterns of Possession States," _Trance and Possession States_, ed. Raymond Prince (Montreal, 1967), pp. 3-34.
Eric R. Dodds, _The Greeks and the Irrational_ (Berkeley, 1951).
H. E. Ennis, "Ecstasy and Everyday Life," _Journal for the Scientific Study of Religion_, VI (1967), 40-48.
Andrew M. Greeley, _Ecstasy: A Way of Knowing_ (Englewood Cliffs, New Jersey, 1974).
Bennetta Jules-Rosette, "Ceremonial Trance Behavior in an African Church: Private Experience and Public Expression," _Journal for the Scientific Study of Religion_, XIX (1979), 1-16.
Marghanita Laski, _Ecstasy: A Study of Some Secular and Religious Experiences_ (Westport, Connecticut, 1968).

I. M. Lewis, Ecstatic Religion: An Anthropomorphic Study of Spirit Possession and Shamanism (Harmondsworth and Baltimore, 1971).

Traugott C. Oesterreich, Possession, Demoniacal and Other Among Primitive Races, in Antiquity, the Middle Ages and Modern Times, trans. D. Ibberson (London, 1930).

Second Annual Conference, R. M. Bucke Memorial Society, "Universal Religions View Possession States, a Panel Discussion." Trance and Possession States, pp. 181-195.

Stewart Wavell, A. Butt, and N. Epton, Trances (London, 1967).

Alex Wayman, "The Religious Meaning of Possession States," Trance and Possession States, pp. 167-179.

[14]Many psychopomps are animals, or man-beasts. Possibly these are still shamans, as the ritual priest in Egyptian funeral rites wore the jackal mask of Anubis. Dogs are frequent psychopomps perhaps because, as in Egypt, they would frequent burial areas or because their unaccountable barking on occasion suggested perception of the supernatural.

[15]Marie Bonaparte, "Saint Christopher, Patron Saint of the Motor-Car Drivers," American Imago, IV (1947), 49 ff.

[16]The Avá-Chiripá of S. America appropriately term the shaman pai ("solitary one"), for he is on the threshold between men and gods.

[17]Géza Róheim, "Origin and Function of Culture," Psychoanalytic Review, XXIX (1942), 131-164, suggests that the dreams of the shaman are very similar to the conception dreams of women (i.e. spirit entry into body, especially the womb), and definitely indicate the androgynous character of the shaman.

[18]Consult the later psychological discussion of the androgyne to see justification for this behavior.

[19]Mircea Eliade, Shamanism, Archaic Techniques of Ecstasy (Princeton, 1964), p. 401.

[20]Dale A. Olsen, "Music-Induced Altered States of Consciousness among Warao Shamans," Journal of Latin American Lore, I (1975), 19-33.

[21]See Nora K. Chadwick, "Shamanism among the Tatars of Central Asia," Journal of the Royal Anthropological Institute of Great Britain and Ireland, LXVI (1936), 75-112.

[22]H. V Elwin, "Light Mysticism," Modern Churchman, XVII (1927), 69-86.

C. E. Stephen, Light Arising--Thoughts on the Central Radiance (Cambridge, 1908).

[23]Stanley Rosenman, "Black Magic and Superego Formation," Psychoanalytic Review, XLIII (1956), 272-319, suggests that all infants have some gastro-intestinal pains when the ego is just forming. The infant feels the ailment as non-ego, something of wholly alien origin. Hence the belief that the cause of all internal pains is some foreign substance.

[24]R. O. Manning, "Shamanism as a Profession," in The Realm of the Extra-Human: Agents and Audiences, ed. Agehananda Bharati (The Hague and Paris, 1976), pp. 73-94, treats shamanism seriously as a "proto-profession."

[25]Oskar Pfister, "Instinctive Psychoanalysis among the Navahos," Journal of Nervous and Mental Diseases, LXXVI (1932), 234-254.
    Also see Robert J. Beck, "Some Proto-psychotherapeutic Elements in the Practice of the Shaman," History of Religions, VI (1967), 303-327, for elaborate parallels between shaman and modern psychiatrist.

[26]Horst Nachtigall, "The Culture-Historical Origin of Shamanism," The Realm of the Extra-Human: Agents and Audiences, ed. Agehananda Bharati (The Hague and Paris, 1976), pp. 315-322.

[27]Ohlmarks, op. cit.

[28]Of course, the enormous pressure of Western civilization is destroying or modifying Amerindian religious tradition. Jordan Paper, "From Shaman to Mystic in Ojibwa Religion," Studies in Religion, IX (1980), 185-199, sees some evidence of increased spiritualization by alteration of shamanism without total capitulation to alien religions.

[29]Weston La Barre, The Ghost Dance: Origins of Religion (New York, 1970), p. 161.

[30]Ibid., p. 223.

[31]Julio Caro Baroja, The World of the Witches, trans. O.N.V. Glendinning (Chicago, 1964).
    A. Benitie, "Psychological Basis of Certain Culturally Held Beliefs," International Journal of Social Psychology, XXIII (1977), 204-208.
    Mary Douglas, Witchcraft: Confession and Accusations (London, 1970).
    Hans Peter Duerr, Traumzeit. Über die Grenze zwischen Wildnis und Zivilisation (Frankfort am Main, 1978).

Mircea Eliade, Occultism, Witchcraft, and Cultural Fashions: Essays in Comparative Religions (Chicago, 1976).
Julian Franklyn, Death by Enchantment: An Examination of Ancient and Modern Witchcraft (London, 1971).
Douglas Gifford, "Witchcraft and the Problem of Evil in a Basque Valley," Folklore, XCI (1979), 11-17.
Richard A. Horsley, "Further Reflections on Witchcraft and European Folk Religion," History of Religions, XIX (1979), 71-95.
Charles A. Hoyt, Witchcraft (Carbondale, Illinois, 1981).
Pennethorne Hughes, Witchcraft (Baltimore, 1967).
Thomas C. Lethbridge, Witches: Investigating an Ancient Religion (London, 1962).
Lucy P. Mair, Witchcraft (New York, 1969).
John S. Mbiti, "Mystical Power, Magic, Witchcraft and Sorcery," African Religions and Philosophy (Garden City, New York, 1970), pp. 253-265.
Leo L. Martello, Witchcraft: The Old Religion (Secaucus, New Jersey, 1973).
R. E. L. Masters, Eros and Evil: The Sexual Psychopathology of Witchcraft (New York, 1962).
Edward G. Parrinder, Witchcraft: European and African (London, 1963).
Elliot Rose, A Razor for a Goat: A Discussion of Certain Problems in the History of Witchcraft and Diabolism (Toronto, 1962).
Jeffrey B. Russell, Witchcraft in the Middle Ages (Ithaca, New York, 1972).
Montague Summers, The History of Witchcraft and Demonology (London and New York, 1926).
P. J. Wilson, "Outcast and the Prisoner: Models for Witchcraft and Schizophrenia," Man, XIII (March, 1978) 88-99.

[32]Lloyd De Mause, "The Fetal Origins of History," The Journal of Psychoanalytic Anthropology, IV (1981), 53, theorizes that the development of the "modern" viewpoint among the elitist class of this period in Western society stripped the lower classes of their traditional defenses. In the resultant perturbation the lower classes made scapegoats of the most peripheral and most helpless of society.

[33]Margaret Murray, The Witch-Cult in Western Europe (Oxford, 1921).

[34]Hermann Goetz, Epochen der indischen Kultur (Leipzig, 1929), p. 308 ff.

[35]Richard A. Horsley, "Further Reflections on Witchcraft and European Folk Religion," History of Religions, XIX (1979), 71-95.

[36]The English word <u>enthusiasm</u> derives from this Greek word, but the English term has come to mean no more than "to like exceedingly."

[37]P. Thankappan Nair, "Para Festival of the Nairs of Kerola," <u>Folklore</u> (of India), XI (1970), 177-187.

[38]See Felicitas D. Goodman, <u>Speaking in Tongues</u>: <u>A Cross-Cultural Study of Glossolalia</u> (Chicago, 1972).
Richard A. Hutch, "The Personal Ritual of Glossolalia," <u>Journal for the Scientific Study of Religion</u>, XIX (1980), 255-266.
John P. Kildahl, <u>The Psychology of Speaking in Tongues</u> (New York, 1972).

[39]Robert Flacelière, <u>Greek Oracles</u>, trans. D. Garman (New York, 1966).
Joseph E. Fontenrose, <u>The Delphic Oracle, Its Responses and Operations</u> (Berkeley, 1978).
Martin P. Nilsson, <u>Cults, Myths, Oracles, and Politics in Ancient Greece</u> (Lund, 1951).
Herbert W. Parke, <u>The Oracles of Zeus</u>: <u>Dodona, Olympia, Ammon</u> (Oxford, 1967).
John Pollard, <u>Seers, Shrines and Sirens</u>: <u>The Greek Religious Revolution in the Sixth Century, B.C.</u> (South Brunswick, New Jersey, 1967).
Philipp Vandenberg, <u>The Mystery of the Oracles</u>, trans. George Unwin (New York, 1982).

[40]Joseph Rock, "Sungmas, Living Oracles of the Tibetan Religion," <u>National Geographic Magazine</u>, CVII (October, 1929), 476-478, witnesses the descent of Chechin, one of the major guardian deities of Tibet, into a human oracle.

[41]John Koffend, "The Gospel according to Helen," <u>Psychology Today</u>, XIV (September, 1980), 74-90.

[42]H. R. H. Prince Peter of Greece and Denmark, "Tibetan Oracles," <u>The Realm of the Extra-Human</u>: <u>Agents and Audiences</u> (The Hague and Paris, 1976), p. 213.

[43]C. Kerényi, "Man and Mask," <u>Spiritual Disciplines</u>, ed. Joseph Campbell, Bollingen Series XXX, no. 4 (New York, 1960), pp. 151-167.

[44]Erika Bourguignon, "Spirit Possession Belief and Social Structure," <u>The Realm of the Extra-Human</u>: <u>Ideas and Actions</u> (The Hague and Paris, 1976), pp. 17-26.

[45]Sir James George Frazer, <u>The Golden Bough</u>: <u>A Study in Magic and Religion</u>, Abridged ed. (New York, 1947), especially

Chapter IV, pp. 48-60. Subsequent references to Frazer in this section on magic are from the same passage.

[46]F. E. Williams, "The Vailala Madness in Retrospect," in Essays Presented to C. G. Seligman, ed. E. E. Evans-Pritchard et al. (London, 1934).

[47]Henri Hubert and Marcel Mauss, "Esquisse d'une théorie générale de la magic," Année sociologique, VII (1902-1903), 1-446.

[48]The word is derived from the Magi, the wise men of the East (Iran). The reputation of the Magi plummeted after early Christianity, causing the derogatory connotation by medieval Christendom.
Some studies:
Eliza M. Butler, Ritual Magic (New York, 1959).
Arturo Castiglioni, Adventures of the Mind, trans. V. Gianturco (New York, 1946).
Warren R. Dawson, The Bridle of Pegasus: Studies in Magic, Mythology and Folklore (London, 1930).
Jan de Vries, "Magic and Religion," History of Religions, I (1962), 214-221.
R. B. Felson and G. Gmelch, "Uncertainty and the Use of Magic," Current Anthropology XX (1979), 587-589.
Francis King, Magic: The Western Tradition (New York, 1975).
Marcel Mauss, A General Theory of Magic, trans. R. Brain (London, 1972).
John Middleton, Magic, Witchcraft, and Curing (New York, 1967).
Géza Róheim, Animism, Magic and the Divine King (London, 1930).
Géza Róheim, Magic and Schizophrenia (New York, 1955).
George B. Vetter, Magic and Religion, Their Psychological Nature, Origin, and Function (New York, 1958).
Hutton Webster, Magic, a Sociological Study (Stanford, Calif., 1948).
Vol. I, no. 2 of Parabola is entirely devoted to the subject of magic.

[49]Morton Smith, Jesus the Magician (New York, 1978).

[50]Realize, as throughout this chapter, that the same person may simultaneously perform two or more of these religious functions, e.g. Magician-Exorcist. It is also true that any of these roles may be broken down into sub-specialists, e.g. magicians who specialize in mental disorders, or diviners who work only with beans or observe bird-flights.

[51]See Dominique Zohan, The Religion, Spirituality, and Thought of Traditional Africa (Chicago and London, 1979).

[52]See Adolf Rodewyck, Possessed by Satan: The Church's Teaching on the Devil, Possession, and Exorcism (Garden City, New York, 1975).
The fascination of the occult in recent decades has caused tremendous popular interest in exorcism. Malachi Martin, Hostage to the Devil: The Possession and Exorcism of Five Living Americans (New York, 1976), is an extensive case study of five recent exorcisms.

[53]This terminology and that of the sorcerer follow the recommendation of E. E. Evans-Pritchard, "Sorcery and Native Opinion," Africa, IV (1931), 26-28.

[54]I. Schapera, "Oral Sorcery among the Natives of Bechuanaland," Essays Presented to C. G. Seligman, ed. E. E. Evans-Pritchard et al. (London 1934), pp. 293-305.

[55]Max Marwick, Witchcraft and Sorcery (Harmondsworth and Baltimore, 1970).
John A. Rush, Witchcraft and Sorcery: An Anthropological Perspective of the Occult (Springfield, Illinois, 1974).

[56]Obeah is the most familiar name for the black sorcerer (a transplant from Africa) in Jamaica, but, according to F. G. Cassidy and R. B. Le Page, Dictionary of Jamaican English (Cambridge, England, 1967), pp. 326-327, there are 35 terms currently used for obeah: sure proof of a widespread practitioner.
In recent years some areas of Jamaica have legalized obeah. Many militant blacks in the West Indies regard Christianity as an alien imposition by white colonial administrators and support such practices as obeah as the authentic West Indian heritage. See West Indian Digest, III (February, 1974), p. 50.

[57]The doctrinal position of the institutionalized priest (see below in text for definition of this functionary) states that the church rituals are intercessory, i.e., requests to supernatural powers. The populace, at least in the past, has frequently considered such rituals as magical, that is, compelling the action to be accomplished.

[58]Claude Lévi-Strauss, The Savage Mind (Chicago, 1966), p. 221.

[59]Auguste Bouché-Leclercq, Histoire de la divination dans l'antiquité (Paris, 1879-1882), 4 vols.
Alfred Guillaume, Prophecy and Divination among the Hebrews and Semites (London, 1938).

William R. Halliday, Greek Divination: A Study of Its
Methods and Principles (Chicago, 1967).

O. K. Moore, "Divination--A New Perspective," American
Anthropologist, LXIV (1957), 69-74.

Friedrich Pfeffer, Studien zur Mantik in der Philosophie
der Antike (Meisenheim am Glan, 1976).

Richard F. Smith, Prelude to Science: An Exploration of
Magic and Divination (New York, 1975).

[60]Michel Gauquelin, The Scientific Basis of Astrology:
Myth or Reality, trans. James Hughes (New York, 1969).

Marc E. Jones, Astrology (Baltimore, 1971).

John A. West and Jan G. Toonder, The Case for Astrology
(Baltimore, 1973).

[61]Cf. Joseph Goodavage, Astrology: The Space Age Science
(New York, 1967).

[62]Eugene L. Mendonsa, "Characteristics of Sisala Diviners,"
The Realm of the Extra-Human: Agents and Audiences (The Hague
and Paris, 1976), pp. 179-195.

[63]See Mircea Eliade, The Forge and the Crucible, trans.
Stephen Corrin (New York, 1962).

[64]Stanley J. O'Connor, "Iron Working as Spiritual Inquiry
in the Indonesian Archipelago," History of Religions, XIV
(1975), 173-190.

[65]Dominique Zohan, The Religion, Spirituality, and Thought
of Traditional Africa (Chicago, 1979), p. 30.

[66]H. S. Darlington, "The Primitive Manufacture of Clay
Pots: An Exposition of the Psychology of Pot-Making," Psychoanalytic Review, XXIV (1937), 392-402.

[67]The devadāsī and bhāvinī of India as spouses of the god
were honored in older India. Probably such terms would be
advisable instead of "temple prostitute" or "sacred prostitute,"
but the Indian labels are completely alien to the West. It is
imperative that the term "sacred prostitute" be employed without
the usual pejorative attitude of the West.

[68]See Edwin O. James, The Nature and Function of Priesthood: A Comparative and Anthropological Study (New York, 1961).

Notes for Chapter V

Community Religion: Animatism to Lord of the Beasts

473

[1]A. R. Radcliffe-Brown, Structure and Function in Primitive Society (London, 1952), p. 157.

[2]Charles M. Leslie, Anthropology of Folk Religion (New York, 1960).

[3]This statement has been challenged because it leans chiefly upon Martin Gusinde, Die Feuerland-Indianer, 2 band, Die Yamana (Mödling bei Wien, 1937). Gusinde supported the contention of Wilhelm Schmidt that monotheism was the first human concept of god. Possibly Gusinde found what he was looking for.

[4]Edward Tylor advanced the term animism in 1866. While famous and useful, this term from the outset was too inclusive (and perhaps advanced) in deeming the first religious impulse to arise from assigning a personal soul to natural objects. R. R. Marett in 1897 coined animatism for the more limited and specific ascription of conscious volition in inanimate objects. This and subsequent terms are here employed as defined in this text. Also see R. R. Marett, The Threshold of Religion (London, 1914).

[5]T. K. Preuss, "Der Ursprung der Religion und Kunst," Globus, vols 86-87 (1904-1915).

[6]The Agency for Cultural Affairs, Japanese Religion (Tokyo and Palo Alto, 1972), p. 14.

[7]Géza Róheim, Panic of the Gods and Other Essays (New York, 1972), p. 87.

[8]Carveth Read, "Psychology of Animism," British Journal of Psychology, VIII (1915), 1-32.

[9]The Melanesians (Oxford, 1891).

[10]Human concepts of the supernatural can be extraordinarily complex and decidedly slippery. In discussing the African deity Ngai, G. J. Wanjohi, "An African Conception of God: The Case of the Gikuyu," Journal of Religion in Africa, IX (1978), 137, translates from S. Kiama Gathigira: "The Agikuyu not only conceive of Ngai as an animal but as the biggest of the animals. They also imagine Him to be a human being with animal characteristics; also that He is uncharacterizable, that is to say, He cannot be described as a true human being nor as a true animal." Gikuyu and Agikuyu are synonyms for the same tribe.

[11]George Catlin, The North American Indians (Edinburgh, 1903), I, 127-128.

[12]Michael Lowe, "Man and Beast: The Hybrid in Early Chinese Art and Literature," Numen, XXV (1978), 97-117.

The man-beast (half-man half-animal) is apparently the product of a hunting or a pastoral culture. An agricultural society may conceive of half-man half-plant, like the Millet Prince of ancient China. Possibly Daphne (a hominid changing into a laurel tree) may originally have been such a mixture of plant and woman. This human-cum-plant seems relatively rare and is likely in time to be fully humanized, explained away, or superseded, as the Millet Prince was displaced by the Celestial Overseer of the Five Cereals.

[13]The Reader's Digest 1980 brochure, "Gifts for Everyone on Your Christmas List," p. 34, advertising Animals Can Be Almost Human: "You'll swear these delightful animals possess the best qualities of people--loyalty, curiosity, a strong sense of family, a need for love and the ability to return it--and above all, an intelligence that is sometimes almost, well, human."

[14]Later ages are puzzled by this grotesque survival and offer even wilder mythical explanations. One Indian myth claims that Ganesha was decapitated and supplied with an elephant head. Another myth suggests that Shiva and Parvati as a jeu d'esprit transformed themselves into a pair of elephants and thus conceived Ganesha.

[15]Charlotte Olmstead Kursh, "Children of Capricorn: Pan and the Mermaid," Bucknell Review, XIV (1966), 14-25.

[16]I. G. Freeman and J. González Echegaray, "El Juyo: A 14,000-year-old Sanctuary from Northern Spain," History of Religions, XXI (1981), 16.

[17]See Alex Scobie, "The Origins of 'Centaurs,'" Folklore LXXXIX (1978), 142-147.

[18]H. J. Rose, A Handbook of Greek Mythology (London, 1964), pp. 4-5.

[19]Paul Kretschmer "Mythische Namen," Glotta, X (1920), 50-58, 211-212.

[20]Charlotte Olmstead Kursh, "Heracles and the Centaur," Psychoanalytic Review, LV (1968), 387-399.

[21]Maurice Besson, Le totémisme (Paris, 1929).
James G. Frazer, Totemism and Exogamy: A Treatise on Certain Early Forms of Superstition and Society (London, 1910).
Sigmund Freud, Totem and Taboo: Resemblances between the Psychic Lives of Savages and Neurotics, trans. A. A. Brill (New York, 1931).
Arnold van Gennep, L'état actuel du problème totémique (Paris, 1920).

Percival Hadfield, The Savage and His Totem (New York, 1977).

Edmund Leach, ed., The Structural Study of Myth and Totemism (London, 1967).

Claude Lévi-Strauss, Totemism, trans. R. Needham (Boston, 1963).

[22]Sigmund Freud, "The Return of Totemism in Childhood," Totem and Taboo, in The Standard Edition of the Complete Psychological Works of Sigmund Freud (London, 1955), XIII, 100-161. See discussion below under psychology of the Freudian analysis of the Oedipal complex.

[23]Godfrey Lienhardt, Divinity and Experience: The Religion of the Dinka (London, 1961), p. 110.

[24]Eli E. Burris, Taboo, Magic, Spirits: A Study of Primitive Elements in Roman Religion (New York, 1931).

Mary Douglas, Purity and Danger: An Analysis of Concepts of Pollution and Taboo (London, 1966).

Hutton Webster, Taboo, a Sociological Study (Stanford U. and London, 1942).

[25]The Tongan word seems close in meaning to the archaic concept of sacer ("sacred," "sacral") in Latin. It is possible that tabu derives from tupua ("menstruation"), rendering the menstrual flow the primal tabu.

[26]Sigmund Freud, Totem and Taboo.

[27]James Hillman, Re-visioning Psychology (New York, 1975).

James H. Leuba, The Belief in God and Immortality: A Psychological, Anthropological and Statistical Study (Chicago, 1921).

Otto Rank, Psychology and the Soul, trans. W. D. Turner (New York, 1961).

Erwin Rohde, Psyche: The Cult of Souls and Belief in Immortality among the Greeks, trans. W. B. Hillis (London and New York, 1925).

Victor White, Soul and Psyche: An Enquiry into the Relationship of Psychotherapy and Religion (New York, 1960).

[28]Also known as apparition, specter, spook, haunt. See discussion under psychology of souls in afterworld.

Also consult:

Thomas C. Lethbridge, Ghost and Ghoul (London, 1961).

Eric Maple, The Realm of Ghosts (New York, 1964).

George N. M. Tyrrell, Apparitions (London, 1953).

[29]The symbol / indicates a clicking sound in Bantu.

[30]James G. Frazer, The Belief in Immortality and the Worship of the Dead (London, 1913-1924), 3 vols.
James G. Frazer, The Fear of the Dead in Primitive Religion (New York, 1966).
William H. Newell, ed., Ancestors (The Hague and Chicago, 1976).
Lewis B. Paton, Spiritism and the Cult of the Dead in Antiquity (New York, 1921).

[31]Herbert Spencer, Principles of Sociology (London, 1876), I, 322 ff.

[32]Ruth Benedict, "The Concept of the Guardian Spirit in North America," Memoirs of the American Anthropological Association, XXIX (1923), 5-97.

[33]See Barbara Chesser, "The Anthropomorphic Personal Guardian Spirit in Aboriginal South America," Journal of Latin American Lore, I (1975), 107-126.
Guy E. Swanson, "The Search for a Guardian Spirit: A Process of Empowerment in Simple Societies," Ethnology, XII (1973), 359-378.

[34]Ronald Grambo, "The Lord of Forest and Mountain Game in the More Recent Folk Traditions of Norway," Fabula, VII (1964), 33-52.
Juan A. Hasler, "Chaneques und Tzitzimites. Ein Beitrag zum Problem des mesoamerikanischen Herrn der Berge und der Tiere," Fabula, X (1969), 1-68.
Calvin Martin, Keepers of the Game: Indian-Animal Relationships and the Fur Trade (Berkeley, 1978) focuses on Amerindians.
Edmund Mudrak, "Herr und Herrin der Tiere," Fabula, IV (1961), 163-173.
I. Paulson, "The Animal Guardian: A Critical and Synthetic Review," History of Religions, III (1964), 202-229.

[35]See Åke Hultkrantz, "The Owner of the Animals in the Religion of the North American Indians," The Supernatural Owners of Nature (Stockholm, 1961), pp. 53-64.
Harold A. Huscher, "The Keeper of the Game: A Demonstration of Old World-New World Acculturation," Anthropological Journal of Canada, X (1972), 13-21.

[36]See Ivar Paulson, Die primitiven Seelenvorstellungen der nord-eurasiatischen Völker (Stockholm, 1956), p. 137 ff.

Notes for Chapter VI

Anthropomorphic Gods to Present-Day Religious

View of Myth

[1]So-called "primitive" societies of today display many
logical patterns and also many apparent inconsistencies. All
have undergone considerable experience and influence over past
millenia. What seem aberrant religious manifestations can be
attributed to unknown complex history and to unknown spiritual
leaders. See Guy E. Swanson, The Birth of the Gods: The Origin
of Primitive Beliefs (Ann Arbor, Michigan, 1964).

[2]In practice rather than in theological theory, most Christians, as the designation suggests, actually worship Christ, a
god emerging from relatively recent Jewish nationalism. If
Christians are worshippng Yahweh (while admitting two other
aspects of his divinity), then like the Jews their god probably
originated in another Bedouin deity. Hinduism attempted to
assimilate Buddha into a long-established deity by making him an
avatar of Vishnu, and generally succeeded in India but not
beyond. In Mahayana Buddhism the Buddha is considered a god,
thereby representing another relatively recent deity of national
origin.

[3]Swami Vivekananda, Essentials of Hinduism (Mayavati,
1938).

[4]Doris Srinivasan, "The Religious Significance of Multiple
Body Parts to Denote the Divine: Findings from the Rig Veda,"
Asiatische Studien, XXIX (1975), 137-179.

[5]See Raffaele Pettazzoni, "On the Attributes of God,"
Numen, II (1955), 1-27.

[6]See Mircea Eliade, Myth and Reality (London, 1964), pp.
93-98.

[7]Wilhelm Schmidt, The Origin and Growth of Religion; Facts
and Theories, trans. H. J. Rose (London, 1931).

[8]Paul Radin, Primitive Religion (New York, 1937), p. 259.

[9]Rosemary Gordon, "God and the Disintegrates," Journal of
Analytical Psychology, VIII (1963), 25-43.

[10]Georg Widengren emphasizes the moral indifference of high
gods, while Raffaele Pettazzoni asserts the ethical character of
high gods. Many of Pettazzoni's examples may be high gods
dredged up to fill a modern need or gods influenced by other
religious impacts.

[11]P. R. McKenzie, "Yoruba Òrìsà Cults," Journal of Religion in Africa, VIII (1976), 200-206, indicates that these Nigerians have a pantheon strongly resembling that of ancient Greece. McKenzie was not attempting any parallel. Truthfully, many attempts at drawing such parallels mean wrenching to make things fit.

[12]Under each division only major or problematic examples can be considered. Also see Ernest Harms, "Five Basic Types of Theistic Worlds in the Religions of Man," Numen, XIII (1966), 205-240.

[13]Johann J. Bachofen, Myth, Religion, and Mother Right, trans. Ralph Manheim (Princeton, 1967).
Sibylle Cles-Reden, The Realm of the Great Goddess: The Story of the Megalith Builders, trans. E. Mosbacher (Englewood Cliffs, New Jersey, 1962).
Edwin O. James, The Cult of the Mother Goddess: An Archaeological and Documentary Study (New York, 1959).
Erich Neumann, The Great Mother: An Analysis of the Archetype (Princeton, 1972).
James J. Preston, ed., Mother Worship: Theme and Variations (Chapel Hill, North Carolina, 1982).
Because the greatest elevation of the Mother Goddess today is Hindu Shaktism, it boasts a large bibliography. Especially helpful are:
Wendell C. Beane, Myth, Cult and Symbols in Sakta Hinduism: A Study of the Indian Mother Goddess (Leiden, 1977).
Narenda N. Bhattacharyya, The Indian Mother Goddess (Columbia, Missouri, 1977).

[14]James E. Lovelock, Gaia: A New Look at Life on Earth (New York, 1980), is a modern version of this concept. Lovelock argues that organic and inorganic components of our planet's surface interact to form a single functioning system, Gaia.

[15]The standard mythic pattern is earth goddess and sky god, but the Egyptians startlingly reversed this situation to postulate an earth god Geb and a sky goddess Nut. Possibly this ascription arose from a female atop the male in sexual intercourse.

[16]"Song of Myself," 1. 105.

[17]James G. Frazer, The Golden Bough: A Study in Magic and Religion, Abridged ed. (New York, 1922), pp. 324-518, provides extensive illustrations of the following concepts.

[18]See Carl G. Jung, "Transformation Symbolism in the Mass," Pagan and Christian Mysteries, ed. Joseph Campbell (New York and Evanston, 1963), p. 99 ff.

[19]"Corn-god" is the term popularized by Frazer.

[20]Herbert Silberer, "Das Zerstückelungsmotiv im Mythos," _Imago_, III (1914), 502-523.

[21]Cf. the "seed" in the opening of "The Wasteland" by T. S. Eliot.

[22]The term is taken from Adolf E. Jensen, "The Dema-Deity," _Myth and Cult among Primitive Peoples_, trans. M. T. Choldin and W. Weissleder (Chicago and London, 1963), pp. 88-92. Jensen perceived myth as the quintessence of religion and culture. Also note Jan van Baal, _Dema: Description and Analysis of Marind-anim Culture (South New Guinea)_ (The Hague, 1966).

[23]Much of our information about the northern mythology comes from the Eddas, strongly influenced by Christianity and perhaps thereby unfairly despiritualizing the pagan myth. The Voluspá and other fully pagan works indicate a much more spiritualized concept of religion.

[24]See W. K. C. Guthrie, _The Greeks and Their Gods_ (Boston, 1950), for an interesting discussion on the backgrounds of Apollo, Athene, and other Greek deities.

[25]H. Rudolf Engler, _Die Sonne als Symbol; der Schlüssel zu den Mysterien_ (Küsnacht, 1962).
Peter Gelling and Helen E. Davidson, _The Chariot of the Sun, and Other Rites and Symbols of the Northern Bronze Age_ (London, 1969).
Jacquetta Hawkes, _Man and the Sun_ (London, 1963).
William T. Olcott, _Myths of the Sun_ (New York, 1967). When first published in 1914 the title was _Sun Lore of All Ages_.

[26]Mary E. Harding, _Woman's Mysteries, Ancient and Modern: A Psychological Interpretation of the Feminine Principle as Portrayed in Myth, Story, and Dreams_ (New York, 1955).
Marjorie H. Nicholson, _Voyages to the Moon_ (New York, 1948).
John E. Thompson, "The Moon Goddess in Middle America, with Notes on Related Deities," _Contributions to American Anthropology and History_, Carnegie Institution of Washington (Washington, 1939), V, 121-173.
Hamilton Wright, Helen Wright, and Samuel Rapport, eds., _To the Moon!_ (New York, 1968).

[27]Possibly one development of Aryan warfare arose from ritual hurling of the sun insignia at opponents.

[28]Gaston H. Halsberghe, _The Cult of Sol Invictus_ (Leiden, 1972).

[29]E.g. Jaiminiya Upanishad Brahmana, III, 10, 4-5.

[30]See E. S. Hartland, Primitive Paternity (London, 1910) for extensive impregnation by the sun. See Arthur B. Cook, Zeus: A Study in Ancient Religion (Cambridge, England, 1914-1940), 3 vols. in 5, for Zeus and sun-worship.

[31]Mircea Eliade, "Spirit, Light, and Seed," History of Religions, XI (1971), 1-30.

[32]See Martin P. Nilsson, The Mycenaean Origin of Greek Mythology (Berkeley, Calif., 1932); Minoan-Mycenaean Religion and Its Survival in Greek Religion (Lund, 1968); Greek Popular Religion (New York, 1940).
William F. Albright, Archaeology and the Religion of Israel (Baltimore, 1953), indicates from archeological evidence that ancient Jewish popular thought (as distinguished from the official Yahweh religion) similarly conceived of the dead as dwelling in the tomb and requiring offerings of food and drink.

[33]The Prelude (1850 ed.), XI, 140.

[34]See also the discussion of underworld geography under psychology.

[35]Georgius Agricola was the Latinized name of Georg Bauer (1494?-1555).

[36]If social crisis is the criterion, then Judaism should be the pre-eminent otherwordly faith, but all shades of Orthodox and Reformed Judaism emphasize their religion as the faith of the living for life.

[37]She may have originated as a goddess of darkness, a chthonic deity.

[38]Possibly Iacchus was a local dead-and-resurrected god who in time was identified with Dionysus.

[39]See Arthur B. Cook, Zeus, for an extended list.

[40]Often given the German label Augenblicksgötter.

[41]James Hastings, ed., Dictionary of the Bible, 2nd ed. (New York, 1963), entry for Moloch.

[42]James S. Van Teslaar, "The Death of Pan: A Classical Instance of Verbal Misinterpretation," Psychoanalytic Review, VIII (1921), 180-183.

[43]Maria Leach and Jerome Fried, eds., Funk and Wagnalls Standard Dictionary of Folklore, Mythology and Legend (New York, 1972), p. 1192.

[44]Alan Watts, The Joyous Cosmology: Adventures in the Chemistry of Consciousness (New York, 1965), p. 63.

[45]See the next chapter for discussion of the sacred king.

[46]See Percival Hadfield, Traits of Divine Kingship in Africa (London, 1949), pp. 12-15.

[47]Thomas A. Brady, The Reception of the Egyptian Cults by the Greeks (330-30 B.C.) (Columbia, Missouri, 1935).
Johan H. Croon, The Herdsman of the Dead: Studies on Some Cults, Myths and Legends of the Ancient Greek Colonization-area (Utrecht, 1952).
George W. Elderkin, Kantharos: Studies in Dionysiac and Kindred Cult (Princeton, 1924).
Mircea Eliade, History of Religious Ideas (Chicago, 1982), II, 277-305.
Otto Gruppe, Die griechischen Culte und Mythen in ihren Beziehungen zu den orientalischen Religionen (Hildesheim and New York, 1973).
Jane E. Harrison, Prolegomena to the Study of Greek Religion (New York, 1975).
Hugo Hepding, Attis, seine Mythen und sein Kult (Berlin, 1967).
Henri Jeanmaire, Le culte de Dionysus (Paris, 1951).
Walter F. Otto, Dionysus, Myth and Cult, trans. R. B. Palmer (Bloomington, Indiana, 1965).
Thassilo F. von Scheffer, Hellenische Mysterien und Orakel (Stuttgart, 1948).
Paul Stengel, Die griechisten kultusaltertümer (New York, 1975).

[48]See Wilhelm Koppers, "On the Origin of the Mysteries," The Mystic Vision, ed. Joseph Campbell, Bollingen Series XXX, no. 6 (Princeton, 1968), pp. 32-69 and Joseph Campbell, ed., The Mysteries, Bollingen Series XXX, no. 2 (New York, 1955).

[49]See Jeremiah 44:17-19; Isaiah 1:29, 46:17; Hosiah 4:13. Judaism and Sikhism are the only major religious traditions that have succeeded in complete displacement of the Great Goddess.

[50]Our information about the mystery cults is far from complete, for ancient initiates (even if later converted to Christianity) apparently took quite seriously their solemn oaths of secrecy. Early Christianity concentrated on deriding gross aspects of paganism and ignored any truly spiritualized elements in paganism.

[51]See C. Kerényi, "The Mysteries of the Kabeiroi," The Mysteries, ed. Joseph Campbell, pp. 32-63. Robert Graves, Hercules, My Shipmate (New York, 1945), pp. 155-161, offers an interesting fictional reconstruction. A Phoenician origin has been suggested but cannot be proved.

[52]A good brief summary appears in Mircea Eliade, A History of Religious Ideas (Chicago, 1978), I, 290-301.

[53]See Walter F. Otto," The Meaning of the Eleusinian Mysteries," The Mysteries, ed. Joseph Campbell, pp. 14-31.

[54]See Émile Durkheim, The Elementary Forms of the Religious Life (London, 1947), pp. 226-228. Also cf. the miracle of the Christian mass.

[55]Mircea Eliade, A History of Religious Ideas (Chicago, 1982), II, 180-209.
William K. C. Guthrie, Orpheus and Greek Religion: A Study of the Orphic Movement (London, 1935).
Otto Kern, Orpheus (Berlin, 1920).
Ivan M. Linforth, The Arts of Orpheus (Berkeley and Los Angeles, 1941).
Walter Wili, "The Orphic Mysteries and the Greek Spirit," The Mysteries, ed. Joseph Campbell, pp. 64-92.

[56]See Wendy D. O'Flaherty, "Dionysus and Śiva: Parallel Patterns in Two Pairs of Myths," History of Religions, XX (1980), 81-111.

[57]See George R. S. Mead, Orpheus (London, 1965).

[58]Paul Schmitt, "Ancient Mysteries and Their Transformation," The Mysteries, ed. Joseph Campbell, p. 105.

[59]Robert Eisler, Orpheus the Fisher (London, 1921).

[60]C. Bradford Welles, "The Discovery of Serapis and the Foundation of Alexandria," Historia (1962), 271-298, claims a pre-Alexander, Egyptian Serapis cult.

[61]Paul Van Buren, The Secular Meaning of the Gospel, Based on an Analysis of Its Language (New York, 1963).

[62]Martin Buber, Eclipse of God: Studies in the Relation between Religion and Philosophy (New York, 1952) and William Hamilton, The New Essence of Christianity (New York, 1961).

[63]Gabriel Vahanian, The Death of God: The Culture of Our Post-Christian Era (New York, 1961).

[64]Harvey Cox, The Secular City: Secularization and Urbanization in Theological Perspective (New York, 1965).

[65]Thomas J. J. Altizer, The Gospel of Christian Atheism (Philadelphia, 1966).

[66]David L. Miller, The New Polytheism: Rebirth of the Gods and Goddesses (New York, 1974).

[67]H. Richard Niebuhr, Radical Monotheism and Western Culture (New York, 1970), p. 24, so defines gods.

[68]William Hamilton, "The Discovery of Extraterrestrial Intelligence: A Religious Response," Extraterrestrial Intelligence: The First Encounter, ed. James L. Christian (Buffalo, New York, 1976), pp. 9-113.

[69]See Thomas J. J. Altizer, Radical Theology and the Death of God (New York, 1966).
    J. Kellenberger, "The Death of God and the Death of Persons," Religious Studies, XVI (1980), 263-282.
    Bernard Murchland, ed., The Meaning of the Death of God: Protestant, Jewish, and Catholic Scholars Explore Atheistic Theology (New York, 1967).
    Thomas W. Ogletree, The Death of God Controversy (Nashville, Tenn., 1966).

[70]For the background of 20th century demythologizing see Christian Hartlich and Walter Sachs, Der Ursprung des Mythosbegriffes in der modernen Bibelwissenschaft (Tübingen, 1952).

[71]Hans W. Bartsch, ed., Kerygma and Myth: A Theological Debate, trans. R. H. Fuller (London, 1953).
    Rudolf K. Bultmann, Jesus Christ and Mythology (New York, 1958).

[72]John Macquarrie, The Scope of Demythologizing: Bultmann and His Critics (Gloucester, Mass, 1969).

[73]Mircea Eliade, Myth and Reality (London, 1964). The italics are by Eliade.

[74]Franz Boas, The Religion of the Kwakiutl Indians (New York, 1930).

[75]Walter F. Otto, Die Gestalt und das Sein (Düsseldorf-Köln, 1955), p. 254.

[76]Joachim Wach, The Comparative Study of Religions (New York, 1958), p. 65. The same author in Types of Religious

Experience (Chicago, 1951), p. 39, terms myth "the first form of intellectual explanation of religious apprehensions."

[77]Peter Slater, "Parables, Analogues and Symbols," _Religious Studies_, IV (1968), 34.

Notes to Chapter VII

Myth as a Mirror of Society

[1]R. A. Oden, Jr., "Method in the Study of Near Eastern Myths," _Religion_, IX (1979), 185-190, presents the case against myth revealing social structure.

[2]Bryan S. Turner, "Sociological Founders and Precursors: The Theories of Religion of Émile Durkheim, Fustel de Coulanges, and Ibn Khaldûn," _Religion_, I (1971), 32-48.

[3]In _Les formes élémentaires de la vie religieuse_. Even earlier Franz Boas, "Tsimshian Mythology," _Bureau of American Ethnology, Annual Report for 1909-10_, XXXI, 29-1037, had given extensive demonstration of how myth is a reflection of social organization.

[4]Thus Henry VII and Richard III of England could be co-worshippers, for the rebellious Tudor sought no change in the system; he simply wanted to be king instead of Richard III. A Marxian cannot follow another religion, but must keep the faith of Marx, opposing all other social (and hence religious) systems.

[5]Talcott Parsons, _The Structure of Social Action_ (New York, 1937), p. 427.

[6]H. H. Farmer, _The World and God_ (London, 1963), p. 58.

[7]Although an energetic and creative religious movement, the Shakers of 19th century USA have vanished because they demanded celibacy of all members and therefore depended wholly upon converts from conventional society. By destruction of family structure such a sect dooms itself to early destruction.

[8]E. O. James, "The Influence of Folklore on the History of Religion," _Numen_, IX (1962), 6: "The purpose of myth...has been to stabilize the established order in society, to confirm the accepted beliefs, institutions, and sanctions and to vouch for the efficacy of the culture." James has been an important historian of religion rather than a social scientist.

[9]Joseph M. Kitagawa, "The Japanese _Kokutai_ (National Community) History and Myth," _History of Religions_, XIII (1974), 222.

[10]Harold B. Mattingly, "The Origin of the Name Christiani," Journal of Theological Studies, IX (1958), 26-37, suggests that early Christians may have been regarded, and may even have regarded themselves, as members of a quasi-political movement.

[11]William A. Lessa, "Discoverer-of-the-Sun; Mythology as a Reflection of Culture," Journal of American Folklore, LXXIX (1966), 3-51.

[12]Lloyd De Mause, "The Fetal Origins of History," The Journal of Psychoanalytic Anthropology, IV (1981), 34.

[13]See in text supra a discussion of the Great Earth Mother and bibliographical note.

[14]See Raphael Patai, The Hebrew Goddess (New York, 1967), and also David Biale, "The God with Breasts: El Shaddai in the Bible," History of Religions, XX (1982), 240-256.

[15]See Christine Allen, "Christ Our Mother in Julian of Norwich," Studies in Religion, X (1981), 421-428.

[16]Naomi R. Goldenberg, Changing of the Gods (Boston, 1979).

[17]The literal translation, "mother-right" is still employed for predominance of women in archaic societies.

[18]Berta Ekstein-Diener, Mothers and Amazons: The First Feminine History of Culture, trans. J. P. Lundin (New York, 1965).
Catherine G. Hartley, The Position of Woman in Primitive Society: A Study of the Matriarchy (London, 1914).
Robert H. Lowie, The Matrilineal Complex (Berkeley, Calif., 1919).
George R. Mead, The Matrifocal Family: Transition, Economics, and Stress (Greeley, Colorado, 1968).
Alice Schlegel, Male Dominance and Female Autonomy: Domestic Authority in Matrilineal Societies (New Haven, Conn., 1972).
David M. Schneider and Kathleen Gough, eds., Matrilineal Kinship (Berkeley, Calif., 1961).
William I. Thompson, The Time Falling Bodies Take to Light: Mythology, Sexuality, and the Origins of Culture (New York, 1981).

[19]Florence M. Anderson, Religious Cults Associated with the Amazons (New York, 1912).
Donald J. Sobol, The Amazons of Greek Mythology (South Brunswick, New Jersey, 1973).
Dietrich Von Bothmer, Amazons in Greek Art (Oxford, 1957).

486

[20]Much in Greek mythology is a result of false etymology. This tendency would explain the interpretation of Amazon as derived from a-mazos ("without breast"). The actual etymology of Amazon is unknown.

[21]Thus seem many imaginary depictions of general male-female shift of conventional roles as in Abbé Pierre François Guyot Desfontaines, Le Nouveau Gulliver (Paris, 1730). On the fictitious island Babilary in the East China Sea, SW of Japan, women are the rulers, soldiers, sailors, judges, authors, etc. to the total exclusion of men. Males are purposely kept uneducated so that they will perpetually be subordinate. Men spend all their time primping, dressing, and arranging their coiffures. While women are expected to be bold, dashing, and adventuresome, men are required to be modest, demure, and submissive. Desfontaines indicates precise reversal of expected sex roles among aristocratic French early in the 18th century.

[22]Note also that Omphale is queen monarch of Lydia.

[23]See Jeannie Carlier-Détienne, "Lez Amazones font la guerre el l'amour," L'Ethnographie, LXXVI (1980), 11-33.

[24]Significantly the Kato and Yuki Amerindians of California refer to the culture-bringer Coyote as "our mother's brother."

[25]The story of Eve created from Adam's rib may well be a belated male attempt to negate the earlier Lilith. The Arosi of Melanesia have a reverse myth. They say that the creator Hatuibwari first made woman from red clay and the heat of the sun, and from her rib made the first man. Experts doubt that the myth has been influenced by Christianity.

[26]Bronislaw Malinowski, The Father in Primitive Psychology (New York, 1927).

[27]E. S. Hartland, "Motherright," The Making of Man, ed. V. F. Calverton (New York, 1931), pp. 188-189, details a tragicomedy of European bureaucrats and African natives equally bewildered by the attempt to establish fathers for indigenes.

[28]David Bakan, And They Took Themselves Wives: The Emergence of Patriarchy in Western Civilization (New York, 1979).

[29]Dena Justin, "From Mother Goddess to Dishwasher," Natural History, LXXXII (February, 1973), 40-45, asserts that male womb envy and not female penis envy ousted women from their earlier dominance.

[30]Abdus Sattar, "Place of Menstruating Woman in Tribal World," Folklore (India), XX (1979), 111-118, provides extensive illustrations of the ostracizing of menstruating women, especially at menarche.

[31]Ronald M. and Catherine H. Berndt, The World of the First Australians: An Introduction to the Traditional Life of the Australian Aborigines (London, 1964), report numerous examples of female priority in sacred objects and rituals, but, significantly, no important religious doctrines and no notable cosmological myths have been ascribed to the women.

[32]Emile Durkheim, Incest: The Nature and Origin of the Taboo, trans. E. Sagarin (New York, 1963). Included in this volume is Albert Ellis, The Origins and the Development of the Incest Taboo.
R. E. L. Masters, Patterns of Incest: A Psycho-social Study of Incest, Based on Clinical and Historic Data (New York, 1963).
Lord Raglan, Jocasta's Crime: An Anthropological Study (New York, 1933).
Nikolaus Sidler, Zur Universalität des Inzesttabu: eine kritische Untersuchung der These und der Einwände (Stuttgart, 1971).

[33]Put positively, the social compulsion is to exogamy. Even in societies practicing endogamy there are usually strict tabus against certain matings.

[34]See Ernst Siecke, "Hermes der Mondgott," Mythologische Bibliothek (Leipzig, 1907), II, part I, p. 39.

[35]See discussion under psychology of ouroboric incest.

[36]One of the most telling arguments against such oddities as the Loch Ness monster, the abominable snowman, and their like is the need for a sizable genetic pool to sustain any organic species. Many types of animals now reduced to scores or even a very few hundreds may be biologically doomed. Probably an absolute minimum of 40-50 would be required to perpetuate the Loch Ness monster, and that number may only slightly delay an inevitable extermination. Also see Gardner Lindzey, "Some Remarks Concerning Incest, the Incest Taboo, and Psychoanalytic Theory," American Psychologist, XXII (December, 1967), 1051-1059.

[37]Exceptions abound, as unicellular organisms simply split into two; various worms fertilize themselves, and animals willingly accept the pairing of close relatives to provide breeds of dogs, cattle, etc.

[38]"Proper Prairie Dogs," Science '82, III (June, 1982), 6.

[39]Craig Packer and Anne E. Pusey, "Cooperation and Competition within Coalitions of Male Lions: Kin Selection or Game Theory?" Nature, CCXCVI (22 April 1982), 740-742.

[40]Claire Russell, "The Life Tree and the Death Tree," Folklore, XCII (1981), 59.

[41]A. M. Hocart, "Buddha and Devadatta," Indian Antiquary, LIV (1925), 98, indicates that the entire family and lineage of Buddha regularly practiced such cross-cousin matings.

[42]Bronislaw Malinowski, Sex and Repression in Savage Society (London and New York, 1927), p. 182. Also see J. R. Fox, "Sibling Incest," British Journal of Sociology, XIII (June, 1952), 128-150.

[43]Claude Lévi-Strauss, The Elementary Structures of Kinship, trans. J. H. Bell, R. von Sturmer, and R. Needham (Boston, 1969).

[44]Priestesses in early societies would be excluded from exogamy to prevent the group losing their knowledge and sacerdotal functions. To avoid incest, therefore, such priestesses would be enjoined to remain virgins. Hence Pallas Athene and Artemis in myth and the historic Vestal Virgins of Rome. Possibly the report of Mars impregnating Rhea Silvia (equivalent of Vestal Virgin) was purposely to forestall the accusation of incest, i.e., mating with a male from her own group.

[45]John Layard, "The Incest Taboo and the Virgin Archetype," Eranos-Jahrbuch, XII (1945), 253-307.

[46]Interestingly, it is a late account that claims that Hera became pregnant with Hebe by eating wild lettuce.

[47]See Luc de Heusch, Essais sur le symbolisme de l'inceste royal en Afrique (Bruxelles, 1958).

[48]"Mother-fucker."

[49]This story item seems to date from the French versions of 1200-1230. By Christian standards even royalty is not exempt from the incest tabu.

[50]Cf. the Tristan and Isolde legend.

[51]Jan Schoo, Hercules' Labors, Fact or Fiction? (Chicago, 1969).

[52]Monroe Edmonson, Lore: An Introduction to the Science of Folklore (New York, 1970) offers a helpful list of representative trickster figures and their traditions. An interesting specialized study is Robert D. Pelton, The Trickster in West Africa: A Study of Mythic Irony and Sacred Delight (Berkeley, Calif., 1980).

[53]Carl G. Jung, "On the Psychology of the Trickster Figure," in Paul Radin, The Trickster: A Study in American Indian Mythology (New York, 1956), p. 200.

[54]M. F. C. Bourdillon, "Religion and Ethics in Korekore Society," Journal of Religion in Africa, X (1979), 90.

[55]Laura Makarius, "Le mythe du 'Trickster,'" Revue de l'Histoire des Religions, CLXXV (1969), 17-46, perceives the trickster as a magician violating tabu.

[56]Barbara Babcock-Abrahams, "'A Tolerated Margin of Mess': The Trickster and His Tale Reconsidered," Journal of the Folklore Institute, XI (1975), 147-186.

[57]Trickster as High God--Raven on NW coast of USA
      Trickster as Creator--Coyote (among Pomo of Central Calif.)
      Trickster as assistant to High God--(Yuki of central Calif.)
      Trickster as counter-creator--(Maida of central Calif.)
Mac Linscott Ricketts, "The North American Indian Trickster," History of Religions, V (1966), 340.

[58]Christopher Vecsy, "The Exception Who Proves the Rules: Ananse the Akan Trickster," Journal of Religion in Africa, XII (1981), 161-177.

[59]Robert Graves, Greek Myths (London, 1965), pp. 148-149, suggests that Prometheus is a personification of the fire drill or the fennel stick which Greeks used to transport fire.

[60]Unless one agrees with Robert D. Pelton, The Trickster in West Africa: A Study of Mythic Irony and Sacred Delight (Berkeley, 1980), that Jesus Christ is a sly trickster.

[61]See James G. Frazer, Myths of the Origin of Fire (London, 1930).

[62]Sigmund Freud, The Acquisition of Fire (London, 1932), interprets the theft and transportation of fire as standing unconsciously for the renunciation of an exhibitionistic, basically homosexual, urination upon the hearth to extinguish the flame. Guilt feelings generated therefrom explain the punishment of Prometheus.

Karl Abraham, Dreams and Myths: A Study in Race Psychology (New York, 1970), claims that to the unconscious any theft is equated with sexual theft.

[63]The term "culture hero" is frequent, but confusing. The term "hero" is usually associated with the noble and valiant warrior of the hunting period and subsequent eras. The Culture-Bringer (German Kulturbringer) is often a rapscallion in the Trickster category, and at his best fosters crafts, arts, trade--a far cry from heroics. Culture-Bearer is also a good label.
Dale R. Bengtson, "Three African Religious Founders," Journal of Religion in Africa, VII (1975), 1-26, prefers the term "founder."
The traditional hero will be considered under psychology.

[64]The Greeks personified the five fingers as the Dactyls, consummate artisans.

[65]See diagram, Joseph Campbell, The Masks of God: Primitive Mythology (London, 1960), p. 167.

[66]Or it may, like the Abraham and Isaac account, explain the substitution of an animal for a human sacrifice.

[67]Perhaps his major enunciation appears in L'idéologie tripartie des Indo-Européens, Collection Latomus, XXXI (Brussels, 1958), but his bibliography is large.

[68]John Brough, "The Tripartite Ideology of the Indo-Europeans: An Experiment in Method," Bulletin of the School of Oriental and African Studies, XXII (1959), 68-86, claims that this pattern can be found in other social systems or can arbitrarily be imposed upon them.

[69]See below for the later figure of Quirinus, a somewhat hazy male deity.

[70]Donald Ward, "The Threefold Death: An Indo-European Trifunctional Sacrifice?" Myth and Law among the Indo-Europeans, ed. Juan Puhvel (Berkeley, 1970), pp. 123-142, and
David Evans, "Agamemnon and the Indo-European Death Pattern," History of Religions, XIX (1979), 153-166.

[71]C. Scott Littleton, The New Comparative Mythology: An Anthropological Assessment of the Theories of Georges Dumézil (Berkeley and Los Angeles, 1966).
Many supporters of Dumézil suggest modifications, as, for example, Emily B. Lyle, "Dumézil's Three Functions and Indo-European Cosmic Structure," History of Religions, XX (1982), 25-44, would incorporate his threefold concept into a fourfold pattern, suggestive of Jung's four functions.

[72] Luc de Heusch, "Myths and the Convulsions of History," Diogenes, LXXVIII (1972), 64-86.
H. R. Ellis-Davidson, "Folklore and History," Folklore, LXXXV (Summer, 1974), 73-92.

[73] Especially in Psychology and Ethnology (London, 1926).

[74] See M. F. C. Bourdellon, "The Manipulation of Myth in a Tavara Chiefdom," Africa, XLII (1972), 112-121, and
George Clement Bond, "Kinship and Conflict in a Yombe Village: A Genealogical Dispute," Africa, XLII (1972), 275-288.

[75] Bronislaw Malinowski, Myth in Primitive Psychology (New York, 1926), p. 58.

[76] Analytical psychologists would suggest that history appears in myth when historical events provide vivid examples of the archetype.

[77] Fritz M. Heichelheim, An Ancient Economic History (Leiden, 1968), I, 362-363.

[78] Claire Russell, "The Tree as a Kinship Symbol," Folklore, XCI (1979), 219-223.

[79] Kenelm Burridge, Mambu: A Study of Melanesian Cargo Movements and Their Ideological Background, 2nd ed. (New York, 1970).
Palle Christiansen, The Melanesian Cargo Cult: Millenarianism as a Factor in Cultural Change, trans. J. R. B. Gosney (Copenhagen, 1969).
Glynn Cochrane, Big Men and Cargo Cults (Oxford, 1970).
Freerk Ch. Kamma, Koreri: Messianic Movements in the Biak-Numfor Culture Area, trans. M. J. van de Vathorst-Smit ('s-Gravenhage, 1972).
Peter Lawrence, Road Belong Cargo: A Study of the Cargo Movement in the Southern Madang District, New Guinea (Manchester, 1964).

[80] The phenomenon seems confined to islands of the Pacific. The "cargo system" of Central Amerindians must not be confused with "cargo cult." In Central American aboriginal communities all males are expected to assume a series of "cargoes" or "burdens," i.e. public office or social responsibility. See Alexander Moore, "Initiation Rites in a Mesoamerican Cargo System: Men and Boys, Judas and the Bull," Journal of Latin American Lore, V (1979), 55-81.

[81] L. Hwekmarin, J. Jamenan, D. Lea, A. Ningiga, and M. Wangu, "Yangoru Cargo Cult, 1971," Journal of the Papua and New Guinea Society, V (1971), 3-28.

[82]See Roger Bastide, The African Religions of Brazil: Toward a Sociology of the Interpretation of Civilization, trans. Helen Sebba (Baltimore, 1978), and
Bryan R. Wilson, Magic and the Millenium: A Sociological Study of Religious Movements of Protest among Tribal and Third-World Peoples (New York, 1973).

[83]See Vittorio Lanternari, The Religions of the Oppressed: A Study of Modern Messianic Cults (New York, 1963).

[84]Weston La Barre chose the title of his book The Ghost Dance: Origins of Religion (New York, 1970) from this movement, for he conceives of every religion as just such a crisis cult. Under intense stress mankind will eagerly follow the visions and the teachings of a "vatic personality" (p. 343). Anthony F. C. Wallace had previously made this suggestion.
In the Freudian terms of Le Barre, god is the ego's projection of its reverie of omnipotence from prenatal perfection and self-centered infantilism. When the ego is gravely threatened, cults of messianic power reassure the ego of its omnipotence.

[85]Cf. the stone boat bearing the body of St. John from the Holy Land to Santiago de Compostela.

[86]Observe another predecessor of the cargo cults.

[87]F. E. Williams, "The Vailala Madness in Retrospect," Essays Presented to C. G. Seligman (London, 1934), pp. 369-379.

[88]Jeff Kessler, "Latin American Beat," World Press Review, XXVIII (March, 1981), 15.

[89]The Task, I, 749.

Notes for Chapter VIII

Social Scientists Theorize about Myth

[1]See, for example,
John Greenway, ed., The Anthropologist Looks at Myth (Austin, Texas, 1966).
Adolf E. Jensen, Myth and Cult among Primitive Peoples, trans. M. T. Choldin and W. Weissleder (Chicago, 1963).
Hans Kelsen, Society and Nature: A Sociological Inquiry (London, 1946).
Bronislaw Malinowski, Myth in Primitive Psychology (New York, 1926).
Werner Muensterberger, Man and His Culture: Psychoanalytic Anthropology after Totem and Taboo (New York, 1969).
Also consult the following:

493

M. P. Branton, ed., Anthropological Approaches to the Study of Religion (London, 1966).

Annemarie de Waal Malefÿt, Religion and Culture: An Introduction to Anthropology of Religion (New York, 1968).

W. G. Runciman, "The Sociological Explanation of 'Religious' Beliefs," Archives européennes de sociologie, X (1969), 149-191.

Anthony F. C. Wallace, Religion: An Anthropological View (New York, 1966).

Max Weber, Sociology of Religion (Boston, 1963).

[2]E.g. "pragmatism" or "structural-functionalist."

[3]In Les formes élémentaire de la vie religieuse.

[4]Anthropologists of the "structural-functionalist" school especially interpret myth as echoing the social structure of the community.

[5]Even if Radcliffe-Brown is categorized as a "structural-functionalist," there must be no confusion with structuralism as discussed at the end of this chapter.

[6]He defines: "The concept of function as here defined thus involves the notion of a structure consisting of a set of relations amongst unit entities, the continuity of the structure being maintained by a life-process made up of the activities of the constituent units."

"On the Concept of Function in Social Science," Structure and Function in Primitive Society (London, 1952), p. 180.

[7]Bronislaw Malinowski, "Myth in Primitive Psychology," The Frazer Lectures (London, 1932), p. 73.

[8]Ibid., p. 80.

[9]Annette Hamilton, "Snugglepot and Cuddlepie: Happy Families in Australian Society," Mankind, X (1975), 84-92.

[10]Anthony F. C. Wallace, Religion: An Anthropological View (New York,1966).

[11]Herbert Burhenn, "Functionalism and the Explanation of Religion," Journal for the Scientific Study of Religion, XIX (1980), 350-360, offers a summary and appraisal of the functionalistic approach. R. A. Oden, Jr., "Method in the Study of Near Eastern Myths," Religion, IX (1979), 183-185, presents the major challenges to functionalism.

[12]Representative of Neofunctionalism is Roy A. Rappaport, Pigs for the Ancestors (New Haven, 1968), which exhaustively

studies myths and rituals involving pigs in some New Guinea tribes.

[13]The disproportionate amount of space devoted to ritualism is not to suggest any preëminence of this theory. The necessity of considering many rituals vis-à-vis myth requires this extensive treatment.
  Erik Erikson, Toys and Reason (New York, 1975) uses "ritualisms" to refer to empty, arbitrary, perfunctory codes and behavioral patterns; but in this text the term ritualism is employed without prejudice.

[14]See Alice B. Kehoe, "Ritual and Religions: An Ethologically Oriented Formal Analysis," The Realm of the Extra-Human: Ideas and Actions, ed. Agehananda Bharati (The Hague and Paris, 1976), pp. 43-53.

[15]Jonathan Z. Smith, "The Bare Facts of Ritual," History of Religions, XX (1980), 124.

[16]E. O. James, "The Influence of Folklore on the History of Religion," Numen, IX (1962), 7: "ritual is at once a visual language and a vent of pent-up emotions and longings, hopes and fears. As in art a feeling or mood, an inner quality of life, an emotional impulse and interpretation of reality is externalized, so ritual gives visual and dramatic expression to the will to live, to the vital urge and rhythmic relations to life, in response to concrete situations and essential needs."

[17]Remember that deep religious impulse even in archaic societies is rare to the individual and is largely generated and directed by a religious specialist. The Romantic concept of individual rapture amidst the landscape is a very late phenomenon; if numerous 19th century followers were so stirred, it was chiefly because of the steering by a few Romantic leaders.

[18]Mircea Eliade, Cosmos and History (New York, 1959), p. 28. Also see "Rites--Birth, Renewal, Religious Experience, and Technique," Myths, Rites, Symbols: A Mircea Eliade Reader, ed. W. C. Beane and W. G. Doty (New York, etc., 1976), I, 131-255.

[19]See Evon Z. Vogt, "Rituals of Reversal as a Means of Rewiring Social Structure," The Realm of the Extra-Human: Ideas and Actions, ed. Agehananda Bharati (The Hague and Paris, 1976), pp. 201-211.

[20]Victor W. Turner, "Myth and Symbol," International Encyclopedia of the Social Sciences (New York, 1968), X, 577.

[21]Consult entries of "birth," "death," and so forth under psychology for discussion of other rites of passage and their effect on myth.

[22]Also see further under heading of "hero" under psychology.

[23]Brian M. DuToit, Configurations of Cultural Continuity (Rotterdam, 1976).
Ronald L. Grimes, Beginnings in Ritual Studies (Washington, 1982).
Theodor Reik, The Temptation (New York, 1961).
Simone Vierne, Rite, roman, initiation (Grenoble, 1973).
Vol. I, no. 4 of Parabola is entirely devoted to the subject of rites of passage. Vol. VII, no. 3 of Parabola is devoted who!ly to "Ceremonies."

[24]E.g. George Wechman, "Understanding Initiation," History of Religions, X (1970), 62-79, and
Frank W. Young, Initiation Ceremonies (Indianapolis, 1965).

[25]See J. W. M. Whiting, Richard Kluckhohn, and Albert Anthony, "The Function of Male Initiation Ceremonies at Puberty," Readings in Social Psychology, ed. Macoby, Newcomb, and Hartley (New York, 1958), pp. 359-370.

[26]Sigmund Freud, Totem and Taboo, trans. A. A. Brill (New York, 1931).

[27]Theodor Reik, Ritual: Psycho-analytic Studies, trans. D. Bryan (New York, 1946).

[28]Bruno Bettelheim, Symbolic Wounds: Puberty Rites and the Envious Male (New York, 1962).

[29]James G. Frazer, Totemism and Exogamy: A Treatise on Certain Early Forms of Superstition and Society (London, 1910).

[30]Leo Frobenius, The Childhood of Man, trans. A. H. Keane (New York, 1960).

[31]Mircea Eliade, Rites and Symbols of Initiation: The Mysteries of Birth and Rebirth, trans. W. R. Trask (New York, 1965).

[32]Johan Huizinga, Homo Ludens: A Study of the Play Element in Culture (Boston, 1955).

[33]F. B. Welbourn, "Keyo Initiation," Journal of Religion in Africa, I (1967), 212-232, includes a first-person narrative by a Keyo tribesman, D. K. Kiprono, who had already obtained his School Certificate and quite disliked the idea of initiation but underwent it (including circumcision) so that he could secure position and influence in his tribe.

[34]Vol. I, no. 3 of *Parabola* is entirely devoted to the subject of initiation.

[35]See Wendy Doniger O'Flaherty, "Sacred Cows and Profane Mares in Indian Mythology," *History of Religions*, XIX (1979), 1-25.

[36]See discussion of the hero under psychology.

[37]Paul Radin, "The Religious Experiences of an American Indian," *Eranos-Jahrbuch*, XVIII (1950), 255, tells of a Winnebago Amerindian youth who was properly briefed but returned to report honestly that he had not experienced any such vision.

[38]Another source of the drama is the mimetic dance to induce replication by Nature, e.g. a rain dance. The village revels of much of Europe until a few generations ago included very short, crude skits basically of fertility origin. These probably had the background of the mimetic dance, while the notable public drama of Europe and the world probably arose from the drama of the male initiation ritual.

[39]Sam D. Gill, "Disenchantment," *Parabola*, I (Summer, 1976), 6-13.

[40]H. S. Darlington, "Tooth Evulsion and Circumcision," *Psychoanalytic Review*, XVI (1929), 272-290.
Frank Zimmermann, "Origin and Significance of the Jewish Rite of Circumcision," *Psychoanalytic Review*, XXXVIII (1951), 103-112, lists eleven theories about circumcision but favors the theory stated in this text.

[41]Theodor Reik, *The Creation of Woman* (New York, 1960), p. 74. Jane Theodoropoulos, "Adam's Rib," *Psychoanalytic Review*, LIV (1967), 542-544, proposes that the rib is a displacement upward of a forbidden subject, the penis. The "bone" vanishes inside a woman, implying that she is made from it.

[42]The whole question of rituals restricted to women and of female behavior amidst male-dominated rituals in archaic society may need reinterpretation. Much of our information about archaic ritual has been obtained from male aborigines by male anthropologists and male ethnologists. A Margaret Mead or other female researcher finds a different picture. A challenging viewpoint appears in Henry Pernet, "Masks and Women: Toward a Reappraisal," *History of Religions*, XX (1982), 45-59.

[43]Steff Bornstein, "Das Märchen von Dornröschen in psychoanalytischer Darstellung," *Imago*, XIX (1933), 505-517.

[44]I. F. Grant Duff, "Schneewittchen. Versuch einer psycho-analytischen Deutung," Imago, XX (1934), 95-103.

[45]Perhaps another ancestor of this synthetic god-saint is the Hittite Weather-god whose battle against the dragon Illuyankas parallels the English St. George mummeries as a ritual overpowering of malevolent weather spirits.

[46]William Bascom, "The Myth-Ritual Theory," Journal of American Folklore, LIX (1957), 103-114.
     Samuel H. Hooke, Myth, Ritual, and Kingship: Essays on the Theory and Practice of Kingship in the Ancient Near East and in Israel (Oxford, 1958).
     E. O. James, "Myth and Ritual," Eranos-Jahrbuch, XVII (1949), 79-120; Myth and Ritual in the Ancient Near East: An Archaeological and Documentary Study (London, 1958).
     Alice B. Kehoe, "Ritual and Religions: An Ethologically Oriented Formal Analysis," The Realm of the Extra-Human: Ideas and Actions, ed. Agehananda Bharati (The Hague and Paris, 1976), pp. 43-53.
     Paul Radin, "The Esoteric Rituals of the North American Indians," Eranos-Jahrbuch, XIX (1950), 283-349.
     Robert A. Segal, "The Myth-Ritualist Theory of Religion," Journal for the Scientific Study of Religion, XIX (1979), 173-185.
     Victor Turner, The Ritual Process (Chicago, 1969).
     Herbert Weisinger, "Before Myth," Journal of the Folklore Institute, II (1965), 120-131.

[47]In Religions of Primitive Peoples (New York, 1899).

[48]In Völkerpsychologie (Leipzig, 1900).

[49]Edmund Leach, The Political Systems of Highland Burma (London, 1954), pp. 13-14.

[50]In Lectures on the Religion of the Semites.

[51]S. H. Hooke, Middle Eastern Mythology (Harmondsworth, Middlesex, 1963), p. 11 ff. Hooke was an Oxonian at U. of London, not a product of Cambridge.

[52]S. H. Hooke, Myth and Ritual (Oxford, 1933). Consult the index for the discussion elsewhere of other Hooke mythic themes.

[53]This is the usual designation for Fitzroy Richard Somerset IV, Baron Raglan. He was a product of Eton and Sandhurst, not of Oxbridge.

[54]Lord Raglan, "Myth and Ritual," Journal of American Folklore, LXVIII (1955), 454.

[55]Consult the index for treatment elsewhere of the mythic themes not discussed immediately below.

[56]Norman Cohn, "Monsters of Chaos," Horizon, XIV (Autumn, 1972), 42-46.

[57]James Frazer, The Golden Bough, Abridged ed. (New York, 1947), p. 501.

[58]This practice probably explains talking severed heads, a widespread folk concept.

[59]The word zombie may derive from zemi, although an African origin is often claimed for zombie.

[60]Hence the ban upon violence on the Greek stage, for the god was present.

[61]James Frazer, The Golden Bough, Abridged ed. (New York, 1947), pp. 74-75.

[62]Claude Lévi-Strauss, Structural Anthropology (New York, 1963), p. 232.

[63]Theodor H. Gaster, "Myth and Story," Numen, I (1954), 186, and Thespis (New York, 1966), pp. 24-25.

[64]"I remember how the late Gordon Childe, who liked to apply common sense to archaeological mystery, used to complain that archaeologists always say 'ritual' when they are stumped about the nature and purpose of some prehistoric monument." Georgery Grigson, Review of Prehistoric Avebury by Aubrey Burl, New York Review of Books, XXVI (22 Nov. 1979), 21.

[65]Trans. as Morphology of the Folktale (Austin, Texas 1968).

[66]Roman Jacobson and M. Halle, Fundamentals of Language (The Hague, 1956).

[67]"The Story of Asdiwal" was first translated by Nicholas Mann in The Structural Study of Myth and Totemism, ed. Edmund Leach (London, 1967), pp. 1-47.

[68]Marcel Detienne, Dionysos Slain, trans. M. Muellner and L. Muellner (Baltimore and London, 1979), p. 7.

[69]A good introduction is David H. Turner, "The Myth of Lévi-Strauss: An Introduction to Structural Analysis," Anthropological Forum, IV (1975-76), 3-18.

Also see Edith Kurzweil, The Age of Structuralism: Lévi-Strauss to Foucault (New York, 1980).

[70]Michael Grant, Myths of the Greeks and Romans (London, 1962), for example, details myths that deeply interest the author, then summarizes in an appendix numerous other myths.

[71]Claude Lévi-Strauss, "The Structural Study of Myth," Myth: A Symposium, ed. Thomas A. Sebeok (Bloomington, Ind., 1958), pp. 91-92.

[72]Ibid., p. 105: "the purpose of a myth is to provide a logical model capable of overcoming a contradiction."

[73]In English translation the series has appeared as:
Vol. I, The Raw and the Cooked (New York, 1969)
Vol. II, From Honey to Ashes (New York, 1973)
Vol. III, The Origin of Table Manners (New York, 1978)
Vol. IV, Naked Man (New York, 1981).

[74]How Natives Think, trans. L. A. Clare (New York, 1966).

[75]Emile Durkheim, Elementary Forms of Religious Life (New York, 1961), pp. 419-420.

[76]Ellen Rhoads, "Little Orphan Annie and Lévi-Strauss: The Myth and the Method," Journal of American Folklore, LXXXVI (1973), 345-357.

[77]See Peter Munz, When the Golden Bough Breaks: Structuralism or Typology (London and Boston, 1973). Dorothea Wender, "The Myth of Washington," Arion, III (1976), 71-78, is a witty spoof of structuralism.

[78]Joanne Punzo Waghorne, "A Body for God: An Interpretation of the Nature of Myth beyond Structuralism," History of Religions, XXI (1981), 23.

[79]John Middleton, "Some Social Aspects of Lugbara Myth," Myth and Cosmos, ed. John Middleton (New York, 1967), p. 55.

Notes for Chapter IX

Psychology Grapples with Myth and Some Mythic Concepts

[1]Material of this and the next two chapters is especially speculative. Most academic psychologists devote little attention to myth. Interesting studies are:
Joseph Campbell, The Flight of the Wild Gander: Explorations in the Mythological Dimension (New York, 1969).

Károly Kerényi, Die Eröffnung des Zugangs zum Mythos. Ein Lesebuch (Darmstadt, 1967).
Maynard Solomon, et al., eds., Myth, Creativity, Psychoanalysis: Essays in Honor of Harry Slochower (Detroit, 1978).

[2]Emmanuele Riverso, "Raison scientifique et explication mythique," XVIth World Congress of Philosophy (1978), Section Papers (Düsseldorf, 1978), pp. 551-554.

[3]James Hillman, The Dream and the Underworld (New York, 1979), p. 23: "Mythology is a psychology of antiquity. Psychology is a mythology of modernity."

[4]Mircea Eliade, "Kosmogonische Mythen und magische Heilungen," Paideuma, VI (November, 1956), 194-204.

[5]Paul Diel, Le symbolisme dans le mythologie grecque (Paris, 1966).

[6]James Bruner, "Myth and Identity," Myth and Mythmaking, ed. Henry A. Murray (New York, 1960), p. 286.

[7]John Z. Young, An Introduction to the Study of Man (Oxford, 1971), p. 8.

[8]John Stratton Hawley, "Thief of Butter, Thief of Love," History of Religions, XVIII (1979), 215.

[9]Kees W. Bolle, The Freedom of Man in Myth (Nashville, Tenn., 1968), p. 88.

[10]Howard L. Cox, "The Place of Mythology in the Study of Culture," American Imago, V (1948), 83-94.

[11]Shirley Park Lowry, Familiar Mysteries: The Truth in Myth (New York, 1982), finds the life-sustaining impact of myth upon the individual psyche to be "the truth in myth."

[12]Mark Shorer, William Blake: The Politics of Vision (New York, 1946), pp. 27-28.

[13]Joseph Rysan, "The Science of Folklore and Modern Society," Tennessee Folklore Society Bulletin, XXI (1955), 93-98.

[14]Clyde Kluckhohn, "Myths and Rituals: A General Theory," Harvard Theological Review XXXV (1942), 74.

[15]Heinz Werner, The Comparative Psychology of Mental Development (New York, 1948).

[16]Ernst Cassirer, The Philosophy of Symbolic Forms; Volume Two: Mythical Thought, trans. Ralph Manheim (New Haven and London, 1955).

[17]Mircea Eliade, Myth and Reality (London, 1964), p. 145.

[18]Johan Huizinga, Homo Ludens: A Study of the Play-element in Culture (Boston, 1962). Also note R.R. Marett, The Threshold of Religion (New York, 1914), p. 45: "The savage is a good actor who can be quite absorbed in his role, like a child at play; and, also like a child, a good spectator who can be frightened to death by the roaring of something he knows perfectly well to be no 'real' lion."

[19]See Frank Salamone, "Religion as Play," Journal of Religion in Africa, VII (1975), 201-211.
Edward Norbeck, "Religion and Human Play," The Realm of the Extra-Human: Agents and Audiences, ed. Agehananda Bharati (The Hague and Paris, 1976), 95-104.

[20]Stephen Larsen, The Shaman's Doorway: Opening the Mythic Imagination to Contemporary Consciousness (New York, 1976), p. 3.

[21]Roland Barthes, Mythologies (Paris, 1970), p. 265.

[22]Sigmund Freud, The Interpretation of Dreams (New York, 1927).

[23]Myth and dream are not identical. A dream employs fragments of myth in a personalized narrative. A myth is a consciously organized dream, a depersonalized dream.

[24]Carl G. Jung, "The Psychology of the Child Archetype," Essays on a Science of Mythology by C.G. Jung and C. Kerényi, trans. R.F.C. Hull (New York and Evanston, 1963), p. 73: "Myths are original revelations of the preconscious psyche, involuntary statements about unconscious psychic happenings, and anything but allegories of physical processes."

[25]Marie Bonaparte, "Psychoanalyse et Ethnographie," Essays Presented to C. G. Seligman, ed. E. E. Evans-Pritchard et al. (London, 1934), pp. 19-26.

[26]F.B.J. Kuiper, "Cosmogony and Conception: A Query," History of Religions. X (1970), 91-138.

[27]Smith E. Jelliffe and Zenia X--, "Compulsion Neurosis and Primitive Culture," Psychoanalytic Review, I (1914), 361-387, offers numerous illustrations from normal 20th century childhood paralleling the thinking and behavior of archaic peoples in symbol and myth.

[28]See Cora Du Bois, "Some Anthropological Perspectives of Psychoanalysis," Psychoanalytic Review, XXIV (1937), 246-263.

[29]J.E. Lovelock, Gaia: A New Look at Life on Earth (Oxford and New York, 1979).

[30]Jean Piaget, Language and Thought of the Child, trans. M. and R. Gabain (London, 1959).

[31]Peter Munz, When the Golden Bough Breaks (London and Boston, 1973), pp. 55-71.

[32]Ernest Jones, "Psycho-analysis and Anthropology," Journal of the Royal Anthropological Institute, LIV (1924), 47-66. Ernest Jones, "The Theory of Symbolism," British Journal of Psychology, IX (1916), 181-229.

[33]H.S. Darlington, "The Meaning of Head Hunting: An Analysis of a Savage Practice and Its Relationship to Paranoia," Psychoanalytic Review, XXVI (1939), 55-68.

[34]H.S. Darlington, "The Tooth-Losing Dream," Psychoanalytic Review, XXIX (1942), 71-79. He suggests that in dream symbolism the grave, the womb, and the house are all condensed or jammed into the mouth.

[35]Isador H. Coriat, "Totemism in Prehistoric Man," Psychoanalytic Review, XXI (1934), 41.

[36]Hyman S. Barahal, "The Psychopathology of Hair-Plucking," Psychoanalytic Review, XXVII (1940), 291-310.

[37]But an anthropologist also indicates a relatively limited number of mythic themes in Clyde Kluckhohn, "Recurrent Themes in Myths and Mythmaking," Daedalus, LXXXVIII (1959), 268-279.

[38]Géza Róheim, "The Study of Character Development and the Ontogenetic Theory of Culture," Essays Presented to C. G. Seligman, ed. E.E. Evans-Pritchard, et al. (London, 1934), pp. 281-292.

[39]Sigmund Freud, Totem and Taboo, Standard Edition of the Complete Psychological Works (London, 1955), XIII, 156.

[40]In The Interpretation of Dreams.

[41]Géza Róheim, Psychoanalysis and Anthropology (New York, 1950).

[42]Bronislaw Malinowski, Sex and Repression in Savage Society (London and New York, 1927).

[43]Charles Rado, "'Oedipus the King': An Interpretation," Psychoanalytic Review, XLIII (1956), 228-234, examines the entire Sophoclean Drama as a projection from the mind of Oedipus. The oracle of Delphi is the inner voice of Oedipus. The call to cleanse Thebes of pollution is the desire of Oedipus to confess and do penance. Blind Tiresias is termed "repressed memory." Polybus and Merope are part of the Family Romance in which a child invents fictitious parents.

[44]Thomas W. Moore, "Narcissus," Parabola, I (Spring, 1976), 50-55.

[45]Friedrich J.A. Wieseler, Narkissos (Göttingen, 1856).

[46]Daniel Whitman, "Africa and the Word," Parabola, II (Spring, 1977), 66, goes on to say, "For the African, the criterion for reality itself is contingent upon the Word, and the Word upon thought: thought creates the Word even as the Creator does."

[47]Also note Pedro L. Entralgo, The Therapy of the Word in Classical Antiquity (New Haven, 1970).

[48]Cf. the recital of Enuma elish by Mesopotamian priests, chanted at New Year's rituals.

[49]Theodor H. Gaster, Thespis (New York, 1966), p. 384.

[50]K.J. Narr, "Ursprung und Frühkulturen," Saeculum Weltgeschichte, ed. H. Franke et al. (Freiburg, 1965), p. 44.

[51]Felix Boehm, "Anthropophagy: Its Forms and Motives," International Journal of Psycho-analysis, XVI (1935), 9-21.

[52]Eric R. Dodds, The Greeks and the Irrational (Berkeley, 1963), p. 274 ff.

[53]Franciszek M. Rosiński, "Belief and Cult in Human Prehistory," The Realm of the Extra-Human: Ideas and Actions (The Hague and Paris, 1976), p. 434.

[54]Werner H. Stöcklin, "Die Kurukrankheit in ethnomedizinischer Sicht," Ethnomedicine, II (1972), 91-98.

[55]Also in forms wendigo or wiendigo.

[56]Joseph Campbell, "The Sacrifice," The Mythic Image, Bollingen Series C (Princeton, 1974), pp. 415-481.
René Girard, Violence and the Sacred, trans. Patrick Gregory (Baltimore and London, 1977).
Henri Hubert and Marcel Mauss, Sacrifice: Its Nature and Function, trans. W. D. Hall (Chicago, 1968).

Sylvain Lévi, <u>La</u> <u>doctrine</u> <u>du</u> <u>sacrifice</u> <u>dans</u> <u>les</u> <u>Brahmanas</u> (Paris, 1966).

[57]Maoris of New Zealand believe that a gift possesses a <u>hau</u>, a sort of mana, that compels the recipient to reciprocate lest the <u>hau</u> do him grave injury. Of course, this is the Maori sense of compulsive obligation.

[58]G. Heilbrunn, "The Basic Fear," <u>Journal</u> <u>of</u> <u>American</u> <u>Psychoanalytic</u> <u>Association</u>, III (1955), 447-466.

[59]Cottie A. Burland, <u>Myths</u> <u>of</u> <u>Life</u> <u>and</u> <u>Death</u> (London, 1974).
Edgar Herzog, <u>Psyche</u> <u>and</u> <u>Death</u>: <u>Archaic</u> <u>Myths</u> <u>and</u> <u>Modern</u> <u>Dreams</u> <u>in</u> <u>Analytical</u> <u>Psychology</u> (New York, 1967).

[60]Montague R. James, <u>Aprocryphal</u> <u>New</u> <u>Testament</u> (Oxford, 1926), p. 11.

[61]Jean Piaget, <u>The</u> <u>Child's</u> <u>Conception</u> <u>of</u> <u>the</u> <u>World</u> (New York, 1929), p. 362.

[62]Carl G. Jung, "The Soul and Death," <u>The</u> <u>Collected</u> <u>Works</u> (Princeton, 1960), VIII, 404-415.

[63]Especially note <u>Adonais</u> by Percy B. Shelley.

Notes for Chapter X

Times and Places of the Mind

[1]Mircea Eliade, <u>Cosmos</u> <u>and</u> <u>History</u>: <u>The</u> <u>Myth</u> <u>of</u> <u>the</u> <u>Eternal</u> <u>Return</u>, trans. W. R. Trask (New York, 1959), pp. 12-17. The work was first published in 1949 as <u>Le</u> <u>Mythe</u> <u>de</u> <u>l'éternel</u> <u>retour</u>: <u>archétypes</u> <u>et</u> <u>répétition</u>.
Mircea Eliade, <u>Patterns</u> <u>in</u> <u>Comparative</u> <u>Religion</u>, trans. Rosemary Sheed (New York, 1974), pp. 374-379.

[2]Judges 9:37.

[3]E. Burrows, "Some Cosmological Patterns in Babylonian Religion," <u>The</u> <u>Labyrinth</u>, ed. S. H. Hooke (London, 1935), p. 51.

[4]B. L. Gordon, "Sacred Directions, Orientation, and the Top of the Map," <u>History</u> <u>of</u> <u>Religions</u>, X (1971), 211-227.

[5]The 19th century overemphasis upon the solar myth understandably caused the 20th century disparagement of this interpretation. Nonetheless, the universality and symbolic power evoked by the course of the sun (here indicated in points of the compass) would certainly suggest the significant role of the sun in much mythology.

[6]Robin and Tonia Ridington, "The Inner Eye of Shamanism and Totemism," History of Religions, X (1970), 52-57, detail highly elaborate directional symbols for the Beaver Amerindians of British Columbia.

[7]Term suggested by William G. Niederland, professor of psychiatry at the Downstate Medical Center of the State University of New York in Brooklyn, N.Y.

[8]Patricia O'Toole, "The New Psycho-Disciplines," Change, XI (April, 1979), 38-39.

[9]Valerii I. Sanarov, "On the Nature and Origin of Flying Saucers and Little Green Men," Current Anthropology, XXII (1981), 163-167, believes that the reports of flying saucers represent modernized versions of the myths dealing with the great world tree. He equates the flying saucer with the nest of the eagle in the world tree.

[10]Stephen J. Reno, "Religious Symbolism: A Plea for a Comparative Approach," Folklore, LXXXVIII (1977), 76-85, gives 30 different interpretations of tree and axis mundi symbolism.

[11]F.B.J. Kuiper, "Cosmogony and Conception: A Query," History of Religions, X (1970), 125.

[12]In Yoga the serpent Kundalini is coiled at the base of the spine.

[13]Lietaert Peerbolte, Psychocybernetica (Amsterdam, 1968), p. 191.

[14]The label imago mundi ("cosmic image") may be given to these concepts. Somewhat complicated mental maneuvers are involved. The mind reads its own interpretations into the landscape and eventually postulates a supernatural condition of absolute perfection and absolute chaos. Belatedly man constructs communities and buildings which he claims are models of otherworldly, pre-existent structures. It might be best to restrict the term imago mundi to these late constructions or to term them imago coeli ("heavenly image"). The Latin mundus yields the English mundane, but this Latin word must bear an extensive load: "wild," "cosmos" (from the Greek), mankind."

[15]Paul Wheatley, The Pivot of the Four Quarters, a Preliminary Enquiry into the Origins and Character of the Ancient Chinese City (Chicago, 1973), extensively treats of the city as a symbol of cosmic order.
The concept is perhaps strongest in the Western mind through St. Augustine's De Civitate Dei ("Concerning the City of God").

[16]See Mircea Eliade, The Sacred and the Profane: The Nature of Religion, trans. W.R. Trask (New York and Evanston, 1961), pp. 42-54, 57-62.

[17]Isha Schwaller de Lubicz, Her-bak: The Living Face of Ancient Egypt, trans. C.E. Sprague (Baltimore, 1972), p. 417.

[18]For various concepts of afterlife consult:
James T. Addison, Life beyond Death in the Beliefs of Mankind (Boston and New York, 1932).
Ernest A.T.W. Budge, Egyptian Ideas of the Future Life (New York, 1959).
Franz V. M. Cumont, After Life in Roman Paganism (New Haven, Conn., 1922).
Mircea Eliade, Death, Afterlife, and Eschatology (New York, etc., 1974).
Hilda R. Ellis, The Road to Hel; A Study of the Conception of the Dead in Old Norse Literature (Cambridge, Eng., 1943).
Hilda R. Ellis-Davidson, ed., The Journey to the Other World (Totowa, New Jersey, 1975).
Alfred Jeremias, Hölle und Paradies bei den Babyloniern (Leipzig, 1900).
William F. J. Knight, Elysion: On Ancient Greek and Roman Beliefs Concerning a Life after Death (New York, 1970).
Jal D.C. Pavry, The Zoroastrian Doctrine of a Future Life, from Death to the Individual Judgment (New York, 1929).
Olof Pettersson, Jabmek and Jabmeaimo: A Comparative Study of the Dead and the Realm of the Dead in Lappish Religion (Lund, 1957).

[19]Buddhist hells are actually purgatories since souls there expiate sins before reincarnation. These hells are subterranean. It seems unlikely that the Buddhist concept, though previous to Christianity, had any influence upon the origin of the Christian Purgatory.

[20]Karl W. Luckert, "The Geographization of Death in Melanesia," Numen, XVIII (1971), 141-160.

[21]James Frazer, The Fear of the Dead in Primitive Religion (London, 1933), p. 123.

[22]Fairyland, presided over by a queen, is underground. It seems to stem from a matrilineal period.

[23]The oblique line in G/wai indicates a click.

[24]Mircea Eliade, Shamanism: Archaic Techniques of Ecstasy, trans. W.R. Trask (Princeton, 1974), pp. 482-486.

[25]See Robert Hughes, Heaven and Hell in Western Art (New York, 1968).

James Mew, Traditional Aspects of Hell (Ancient and Modern) (Ann Arbor, Mich., 1971).

[26]Cf. No Exit by Sartre.

[27]Snakes do not eat dust, but god so curses the tempting serpent because this is a Mesopotamian infliction upon the dead (Genesis 3:14).

[28]Bruce Lincoln, "The Lord of the Dead," History of Religion, XX (1981), 224-241.

[29]Significantly the dread torture of the Fifth Hell of Chinese Buddhist lore is memory of things past.

[30]Vedic myth considers the deities of earth and the underworld as the primal deities, closer to the primeval world of undifferentiated unity and the dark unconscious. The gods of heaven are "the younger brothers" of the ancient earth and are more agile in body and mind.

[31]John S. Dunne, Time and Myth (Notre Dame, Ind. and London, 1975).

[32]Such an explanation from normal human experience is preferable to the claim of Immanuel Velikovsky, Worlds in Collision (New York, 1965), pp. 39-46, that the earth actually ceased rotation. Carl Sagan, Broca's Brain: Reflections on the Romance of Science (New York, 1979), pp. 100-102, discusses the scientific difficulties of the Velikovsky hypothesis.

[33]English translation in 1916 of Detskie gody Bagrova vnuka (1856).

[34]Mircea Eliade, Australian Religions: An Introduction (Ithaca, N.Y., 1973), pp. 42-43.

[35]Cf. the short story "Metamorphosis" by Franz Kafka.

[36]Erudite astronomers theorize that the entire universe may go through a vast cycle of expansion followed by contraction that totally obliterates the former cosmos and inaugurates a completely new era of expansion. This scientific concept was long ago anticipated in myth.

[37]Ludwig Edelstein, The Idea of Progress in Classical Antiquity (Baltimore, 1967), is the one notable proponent of extensive ancient support for the idea of progress.

[38]"The self becomes the world. Thus the experiences which schizophrenics have of the destruction of the world are often only images of the revolution that is taking place in their

inner world. The shattering of the mental and physical self is reflected as a cosmic catastrophe." Robert A. Clark, "Cosmic Consciousness in Catatonic Schizophrenia," Psychiatric Review, XXXIII (1946), 494.

[39]Norman Cohn, "Monsters of Chaos," Horizon, XIV (1972), 42-47.

[40]A.J. Visser, "A Bird's-Eye View of Ancient Christian Eschatology," Numen, XIV (1967), 4-22.

Notes for Chapter XI

The Mythic Realm within Each Human

[1]See James W. Heisig, Imago Dei: A Study of C. G. Jung's Psychology of Religion (Lewisburg, Penna., 1979).

[2]Most practicing analytical psychologists today are termed neo-Jungians, since they modify or reinterpret the positions of Jung. Generally neo-Jungians are more in agreement with Jung than neo-Freudians are with Freud.

[3]Jung occasionally used the term "objective psyche."

[4]Henri Frankfort, "The Archetype in Analytical Psychology and the History of Religion," Journal of the Warburg and Courtauld Institutes, XXI (1958), 166-178, offers judicious criticism of the Jung theory.

[5]Carl G. Jung, Collected Works, trans. R.F.C. Hull, 2nd ed. (Princeton, 1968), Vol. 9, Part I, pp. 4-5, considers the term archetype "apposite and helpful, because it tells us that so far as the collective unconscious contents are concerned we are dealing with archaic or--I would say--primordial types, that is, with universal images that have existed since the remotest times."
The word archetype is two millenia in age and is still often employed in the original sense of "master plan." Note this older usage still followed, e.g., in Mircea Eliade, Patterns in Comparative Religion.

[6]Observe how in present-day dramatizations, especially in cartoons, the automobile may be animated, infused with will and purpose. Such myth-making has a remote ancestry.

[7]Jung, Collected Works, Vol. 12, pp. 208-211.

[8]Carl Kerényi, "Prolegomena," Essays on a Science of Mythology by C. G. Jung and C. Kerényi (New York and Evanston, 1963), p. 17.

[9]Richard Hubert Jones, "Jung and Eastern Religious Traditions," Religion, IX (1979), 141-155, states that Jung is quite challengeable in his interpretation of oriental concepts, which are bent to the Jungian viewpoint.

[10]Victor N. Mansfield, "Mandalas and Mesoamerican Pecked Circles," Current Anthropology, XXII (1981), 269-284, finds extensive employment of the mandala in Hindu, Buddhist, Oglala Sioux, and Nahuatl cultures. The Mansfield article is followed by comments from professional anthropologists, many of whom challenge the Jungian concept. H. J. Eysenck tartly objects to accepting an unprovable thesis and then delightedly discovering it to be widespread.

[11]Jung, Collected Works, Vol. 9, Part I, pp. 355-384. Also see:
José and Miriam Argüelles, Mandala (Berkeley, Calif., 1972).
Giuseppe Tucci, The Theory and Practice of the Mandala, with Special Reference to the Modern Psychology of the Subconscious, trans. A. H. Brodrick (London, 1961).

[12]John Layard, "Primitive Kinship as Mirrored in the Psychological Structures of Modern Man," British Journal of Medical Psychology, XX (1944), 118-134, finds considerable confirmation of the Jungian patterns in primitive societies. J. W. E. Newberry, "The Quality of Native Religion," Studies in Religion, IX (1980), 287-298, finds 1, 2, 3, 4, and 7 as extremely significant numbers in Amerindian religions.

[13]Jung, "Transformation Symbolism in the Mass," Pagan and Christian Mysteries, ed. Joseph Campbell (New York and Evanston, 1963), p. 97.

[14]Significantly, in Burmese mural art nari ("woman") is one of the four artistic elements. Nari is used for any depiction of the human body regardless of sex. Klaus Wenk, "The Paintings of Pagan," UNESCO Courier, XXXII (December, 1979), 39-40.

[15]Harold Jeffreys, "The Unconscious Significance of Numbers," International Journal of Psycho-Analysis, XVII (1936), 217-223.

[16]Karl Abraham, "Two Contributions to the Study of Symbols," The Yearbook of Psychoanalysis, ed. Sándor Lorand (New York, 1947), V, 219-224.

[17]The Charites (Graces) are a charming exception as three lovely sisters.

[18]Georges Dumézil, Jupiter, Mars, Quirinus: essai sur la conception indo-européenne de la société et sur les origines de

Rome. Collection "La Montagne Sainte-Geneviève," vol. 1 (Paris, 1941). The Jupiter-Mars-Ops trio discussed in Chapter VII comes from early Rome.

[19]James M. Robinson, ed., The Nag Hammadi Library (San Francisco, 1977), p. 99.

[20]The sexual partner to form a male-female pair is discussed below under "anima and animus."

[21]"A Poet's Epitaph," 11. 19-20. At the time of writing, 1799, the term scientist did not exist, and the profession was called "natural philosophy."

[22]All of these symbols indicate types of clicks in Bantu.

[23]See Howard H. Schlossman, "God the Father and His Sons," American Imago, XXIX (1972), 35-52.

[24]See George Devereux, "Mohave Beliefs Concerning Twins," American Anthropologist, XLIII (1941), 573-592.

[25]Mircea Eliade, Myths, Dreams, and Mysteries, trans. Philip Mairet (New York and Evanston, 1967), pp. 59-72.

[26]Géza Róheim, "Primitive High Gods," Psychoanalytic Quarterly, III (1934), 1-133.

[27]Carl G. Jung, Psychological Types, trans. H.G. Baynes (London, 1923), pp. 306-308.

[28]Arthur Evans, "The Earlier Religion of Greece in the Light of Cretan Discoveries," The Frazer Lectures (London, 1934), p. 286.

[29]E.g. Donald A. Mackenzie, Egyptian Myth and Legend (New York, 1978), p. 396.

[30]J. Duncan M. Derrett, "Greece and India: The Milindapañha, the Alexander-romance and the Gospels," Zeitschrift für Religions- und Geistesgeschichte, XIX (1967), 34.

[31]James H. Breasted, The Dawn of Conscience (New York and London, 1946).

[32]Karl Abraham, "Amenhotep IV (Ikhnaton). A Psychoanalytic Contribution to the Understanding of His Personality and the Monotheistic Cult of Aton," Psychoanalytic Quarterly, IV (1935), 537-569.

[33]Perhaps more cogent is the medical diagnosis of Froelich's syndrome, a hormonal deficiency which causes a male to have a sagging belly, widened hips, and the strangely elongated head apparent in the representations of Ikhnaton. Also see the discussion below on androgyne and hermaphrodite.

[34]Raffaele Pettazzoni, Essays in the History of Religions (Leiden, 1954), argues that monotheism is not the result of evolutionary process but is a revolution generated by great personalities like Ikhnaton.

[35]Kathenotheism is an alternate term.

[36]Of course, another possibility is the polite, formal reference, using the plural for a single personage; in English you, the plural form, has superseded the old singular form, thou.

[37]E. Bolaji Idowu, Olodumare (London, 1962), p. 202 ff.

[38]James W. Boyd and Donald A. Crosby, "Is Zoroastrianism Dualistic or Monotheistic?" Journal of the American Academy of Religion, XLVII (1979), 557-588.

[39]If militant feminists bristle at these contentions, it must be pointed out that Jung was a Middle European male powerfully conditioned by the 19th century of his youth.

[40]See Cuthbert Butler, Western Mysticism (New York, 1966), pp. 110-114, and Sidney Spencer, Mysticism in World Religion (London, 1966), pp. 253-256.

[41]The animus in a woman would be similarly structured but with four feminine figures for the four functions and a male figure, the animus, attached to each.

[42]Gustav Oppert, On the Original Inhabitants of Bharata-varṣa or India (London, 1893), p. 421, proposes the origin of Uma in Amma, designation for Dravidian mother goddesses. The mate of Shiva bears numerous names, such as Durga, Gauri, Mahakali, Parvati, etc.

[43]See Bholanath Bhattacharya, "Some Aspects of the Esoteric Cults of Consort Worship in Bengal: A Field Survey Report," Folklore (India), XVIII (1977), 310-324, 359-365, 385-397.

[44]Every version of the Paolo and Francesca tale dwells upon the ugly deformity of her husband Gianciotto and thereby strongly prejudices the reader or listener in favor of the adulterers.

[45]Cf. James C. Moloney, "The Origin of the Rejected and Crippled Hero Myths," American Imago, XVI (1959), 271-328.

[46]Bronislaw Malinowski, The Father in Primitive Psychology (New York, 1966).

[47]Less uniformly sympathetic than the male archetypes (except for the nubile maiden), these figures may not be universal at all but peculiar to a male-dominated society. Note that the archetypal infant is male, not female.

[48]Jung suggests that veiled or unapproachable or otherwise mysterious women are characteristic projections of the anima.

[49]The 18th century featured l'homme fatal, culminating in Byron who played the part to the hilt. The 20th century has emphasized the femme fatale. Perhaps all these are merely fads in sexual fantasies rather than IRM.

[50]Erich Neumann, The Great Mother: An Analysis of the Archetype, trans. Ralph Manheim (Princeton, 1972).
Edith Weigert-Vowinkel, "The Cult and Mythology of the Magna Mater from the Standpoint of Psychoanalysis," Psychiatry, I (1938), 347-378.

[51]Again, these "archetypes" look suspiciously like the value judgements of a male-dominated society rather than eternal imprints.

[52]See Erich Neumann, The Origins and History of Consciousness, Bollingen Series, XLII (Princeton, 1969).

[53]See Lucien Lévy-Bruhl, La mythologie primitive. Le Monde mythique des Australiens et des Papous (Paris, 1935).
Géza Róheim, The Eternal Ones of the Dream, a Psychoanalytic Interpretation of Australian Myth and Ritual (New York, 1945).

[54]A Taoist work by Huai-nan Tzu (d. 122 B.C.) states that at this primordial period "heaven and earth had not yet come into existence and yin and yang had not been distinguished. The four seasons had not yet separated and the myriad things had not yet been born. It was extremely peaceful and very tranquil. Forms were not yet visible. It was like light in the midst of non-being which retreats and is lost sight of." Daniel L. Overmyer, "Folk-Buddhist Religion: Creation and Eschatology in Medieval China," History of Religions, XII (1972), 63.

[55]See J.C. Cooper, "Circle," An Illustrated Encyclopaedia of Traditional Symbols (London, 1978), pp. 36-37.

[56]In Greek art Hermaphroditos was represented as a beauti-ful male with female breasts. Aphrodite with male genitals is the mother with a penis, the result of fantasizing by small boys in a society wearing clothing. The words hermaphrodite and androgyne can be synonymous, but recent usage seems to view the hermaphrodite as a half-male, half-female physiologically (very rare in the flesh) and the androgyne as more of a psychological combination. Often today's psychologists applaud the androgy-nous nature as truer to oneself and to the human image than an artificial polarity of macho male and clinging-ivy female. Archaic societies frequently regard the young of both sexes as androgynous, requiring rites of initiation to become fully sexed.

[57]Possibly contributory to the Christian trinitarian concept, especially if the Holy Spirit or Holy Ghost (Hagia Sophia) is to be regarded as female.

[58]Elaine H. Pagels, "The Gnostic Vision," Parabola, III (Fall, 1978), 6-9.

[59]Joel Greenberg, "Close Encounters: All in the Mind," Science News, CXV (February 17, 1979), 106-107.

[60]Charles Doria and Harris Lenowitz, Origins: Creation Texts from the Ancient Mediterranean (Garden City, New York, 1976).
Mircea Eliade, "Myths of the Creation of the World," Gods, Goddesses, and Myths of Creation (New York, etc., 1974), pp. 83-118.
Philip Freund, Myths of Creation (New York, 1965).
Barbara C. Sproul, Primal Myths: Creating the World (San Francisco, 1979).
Lawrence D. Trevett, "Origin of the Creation Myth: A Hypothesis," Journal of the American Psychoanalytic Association, V (1957), 461-468.
Raymond Van Over, Sun Songs: Creation Myths from around the World (New York, 1980).

[61]Ei'ichiro Ishida, "Mother-Son Deities," History of Religions, IV (1964), 31-34.

[62]In euhemeristic fashion Servius in late antiquity saw the Hydra as subterranean streams of water, breaking forth to inun-date the land until effectively shut off by Heracles. The flames, supposedly to cauterize the stumps of necks and thus prevent re-growth of Hydra heads, Servius interpreted as fires by Heracles to dry the ground.

[63]Analytic psychology (Jungian) consistently ascribes the unconscious to the feminine and consciousness to the male.

[64]Alan Dundes, "Earth Diver: Creation of the Mythopoeic Male," American Anthropologist, LIV (1962), 1032-1051.

[65]Michael P. Carroll, "The Rolling Head: Towards a Revitalized Psychoanalytic Perspective on Myth," Journal of Psychoanalytic Anthropology, V (1982), 31.

[66]Incredibly prolific in all myth, India is especially fertile in myths of creation. The Mahabharata, for instance, offers four theories in itself.

[67]Bruce Lincoln, "The Indo-European Myth of Creation," History of Religions, XV (1975), 121-145.

[68]David Steindle-Rast, "Views of the Cosmos," Parabola, II (Summer, 1977), 7.

[69]"Creation is, as it were, an incidental by-product of Brahma's yogic exercise of self-discovery." David R. Kinsley, "Creation as Play in Hindu Spirituality," Studies in Religion, IV (1974), 111.

[70]Mircea Eliade, "The Creation of Man," Gods, Goddesses, and Myths of Creation (New York, etc., 1974), pp. 130-138. Also consult the general studies on creation myth listed above.

[71]Geronimo, Geronimo: His Own Story, ed. S.M. Barrett (New York, 1970).

Notes for Chapter XII

The Mythic Realm Within (cont.)

[1]Many son-mother incest myths, including the Oedipal story, probably arise not from any actual incest but from the regressus ad uterum.

[2]A. C. Bouquet, "Beliefs and Practices of the Jalaris," Numen, VII (1960), 200-214.

[3]Otto Fenichel, "The Psychology of Transvestism," Psychoanalytic Review, XVII (1930), 490-491.

[4]Lloyd De Mause, "The Fetal Origins of History," The Journal of Psychoanalytic Anthropology, IV (1981), p. 16, also attributes the concept of the castrating father and even the punitive superego itself to the fetal reaction to the Poisonous Placenta.

[5]Philip Singer, Enrique Araneta, and Jamsie Naidoo, "Learning of Psychodynamics, History, and Diagnosis Management Therapy in a Kali Cult Indigenous Healer in Guiana," The Realm of the

Extra-Human: Agents and Audiences, ed. Agehananda Bharati (The Hague and Paris, 1976), pp. 345-369.

[6]Jacques Schnier, "Dragon Lady," American Imago, IV (1974), 78-98.

[7]Arnold H. Kamiat, "Male Masochism and Culture," Psychoanalytic Review, XXIII (1936), 84-91.

[8]The fish-like odor of the female genitalia may account for the powerful sexual associations of fish in human psychology.

[9]Géza Róheim, "The Dragon and the Hero," American Imago, I (1940), 40-69.

[10]Isador H. Coriat, "A Note on the Medusa Symbolism," American Imago, II (1941), 281-285.
Also see Sigmund Freud, "Medusa's Head," International Journal of Psycho-Analysis, XXII (1941), 69-70.

[11]See Ananda K. Coomaraswamy, "Symplegades," Studies in Comparative Religion, VII (1973), 35-56.

[12]"Sex Hormone Overrides Upbringing," Science News, CVII (28 June 1980), 406.

[13]Cheever Mackenzie Brown, God as Mother: A Feminine Theology in India (Hartford, Vermont, 1974), pp. 204-205.

[14]See Marie Delcourt, Hermaphrodite: Mythes et rites de la bisexualité dans l'antiquité classique (Paris, 1958). Transvestism is also a fertility symbol.

[15]John H. Chamberlayne, "The Development of Kuan Yin," Numen, IX (1962), 45-52.

[16]Ernest Rappaport, "The Tree of Life," Psychoanalytic Review, XXX (1943), 269.

[17]In the 19th century the solar mythologists claimed that the hero myth actually refers to the movement of the sun through the heavens, initially confronted by restraining clouds but eventually victorious over all obstacles. The tragic hero represents the setting sun. A lunar origin was also proposed for the myth of the hero, but neither solar nor lunar theory seems wholly tenable today.

[18]The term heroine is especially ambiguous.
Myth, epic, even folktales have bequeathed the concept of the passive "heroine" who is denied action, except for essentially passive performance like Penelope's delaying tactics with the suitors. Direct and forceful actions by women are therefore

often characterized as vicious and monstrous, as Medea kills and dismembers her brother Apsyrtus. Such anti-feminist attitudes spring from a determinedly patriarchal society in which women are categorized as childbearers and decorative appendages to heroes, even though peasant women and most women in the real world had to be a far cry from this limited image.

Nonetheless, courage and valorous accomplishment in women have always been celebrated, as in the goddess Artemis and the female hunter Atalanta. The extremely energetic heroine, Joan of Arc, has even been canonized in this century as a saint, while at her 15th century trial a major accusation was against her "non-feminine" and "male-like" actions. In the 20th century women, as in Israel, have been highly commended for heroic deeds in battle. Increasingly, characterization in Western drama, cinema, television, comics, etc. features role reversal with females as cool, daring, aggressive (i.e. the active heroine like Wonder Woman of the comics wholly superseding the traditional male hero).

Today there is general applause for the characterization of a woman who has long accepted a submissive, passive status but is stung by injustice and callousness to assert her independence and self-sufficiency. Countering this portrayal, however, is the reverse twist. In comics and television Col. Wilma Deering is depicted as a hard-nosed confident battle commander who becomes as "feminine" as Marilyn Monroe when enraptured with the heroic Buck Rogers.

[19]See Eckart von Sydow, "Träume und Visionen in der Religion der Indianer Nordamerikas," Imago, XXXI (1925), 96-111, for the predominance of the heroic myth in hunting societies.

[20]Joseph Campbell, The Hero with a Thousand Faces, Bollingen Series XVII (Princeton, 1968).

[21]Otto Rank, The Myth of the Birth of the Hero: A Psychological Interpretation of Mythology, trans. F. Robbins and S. E. Jelliffe (New York, 1952).

[22]Henri Brocher, Le mythe du héros et la mentalité primitive (Paris, 1932).
Lewis R. Farnell, Greek Hero Cults and Ideas of Immortality (Oxford, 1921).
Peter Heinegg, "The Agony of Nature: The Function of a Hero," Parabola, VI (February, 1981), 81-86.
Gertrude R. Levy, The Sword from the Rock: An Investigation into the Origins of Epic Literature and the Development of the Hero (London, 1953).
Vol. I, no. 1 of Parabola is entirely devoted to the subject of the hero.

[23]Even the twins Nakula and Sahadeva by some reports were sired by the Ashvins, the Indian version of the Greek Dioscori,

the Latin Gemini. Other reports make them the Ashvins themselves, reborn through the body of Madri.

[24]T. A. Walters, "Forms of the Family Romance," Psychoanalytic Review, XLIII (1956), 204-213.
Dorothy F. Zeligs, "The Family Romance of Moses," American Imago, XXIII (1966), 110-131.

[25]A "two fathers" pattern also appears in one twin with a divine father (Heracles the son of Zeus) and the other twin with a human father (Iphicles the son of Amphitryon), with one mortal mother (Alcmene).

[26]The meaning of "virgin" will differ considerably among various cultures.

[27]Juliette Boutonier, "Naissance des héros," Psyche (Paris), III (1948), 1335-1342.
Clémence Ramnoux, "Naissances divines et héroiques," Psyche (Paris), III (1948), 1343-1353.
M. R. C. MacWatters, "A Birth of the Hero Myth from Kashmir," International Journal of Psycho-Analysis, II (1921), 416-419.

[28]See A. J. Levin, "Oedipus and Samson: The Rejected Hero-child," International Journal of Psycho-Analysis, XXXVIII (1957), 105-116.

[29]In archaic societies a child is often nursed by the mother for several years before being weaned. Until recently Eskimos would frequently expose a girl if she were first born, impatient to start another pregnancy at once and secure a boy as a prospective hunter. Probably early hunting societies quite often resorted to such exposure of female infants.

[30]F. B. J. Kuiper, "Cosmogony and Conception: A Query," History of Religions, X (1970), 124, suggests that the origin of dragon slaying reaches back as far as the fertilization of the ovum by the spermatozoon. The bond to the maternal psyche must be "killed" for a distinct individual to come into being.

[31]A number of the dragons and assorted monsters are males. Psychologists explain this pattern as a sex change when a patriarchal society minimizes all femininity. Also, the male may very well be a servant of the Great Mother.

[32]Ernest Ingersoll, Dragons and Dragon Lore (Detroit, 1968).

[33]Heroes, of course, are aristocrats. Upper-class dragon-slayers always vanquish their opponents in straightforward manly fashion with conventional weapons, usually swords with prestigious names.

Lower-class (and non-heroic) dragon-slayers usually eliminate dragons by subterfuge. The tricking of the huge, rather befuddled, monster can easily become ludicrous.

Christian saints, instead of killing dragons, subdue the terrifying beasts by spiritual power (St. George overcame his dragon in proper heroic manner). Quelled by saintliness, the dragons are thereby rendered tame, often aiding the saints in commendable acts of charity and piety.

[34]This and subsequent elements of the hero myth (until death) may take various sequential patterns.

[35]See Robert Graves, The White Goddess: A Historical Grammar of Poetic Myth (New York, 1948).

[36]Of course, these killings of the father could also be ritual slayings of the king.

[37]Clémence Ramnoux, "Le carnage des héros," Psyche (Paris), V (1950), 880-903: "La mort du héros," Psyche (Paris), VII (1952), 46-52.

[38]Edward F. Edinger, "The Tragic Hero: An Image of Individuation," Parabola, I (Winter, 1976), 66-73.

[39]Leo Kaplan, "Der tragische Held und der Verbrecher," Imago, IV (1915), 96-124.

[40]Robert May, Sex and Fantasy: Patterns of Male and Female Development (New York, 1980). May holds that these different sex patterns in the mind are evident as early as six years of age and are well fixed at adolescence.

[41]Paul Schilder, "On Homosexuality," Psychoanalytic Review, XVI (1929), 377-389.

Notes for Chapter XIII

Geomythology and Meteoromythology

[1]Richard S. Westfall, Force in Newton's Physics: The Science of Dynamics in the Seventeenth Century (London and New York, 1971), pp. 377-391. Also see Betty J. Teeter Dobbs, The Foundation of Newton's Alchemy (Cambridge, 1975).

[2]Dorothy B. Vitaliano, "Geomythology: The Impact of Geologic Events on History and Legend with Special Reference to Atlantis," Journal of the Folklore Institute, V (1968), 5, identifies herself as the inventor of the term geomythology. Also see her book, Legends of the Earth: Their Geologic Origins (Bloomington and London, 1973).

[3]Since it is impossible to separate these two categories rigidly, they are treated together.

[4]Carey McWilliams, "The Folklore of Earthquakes," _American Mercury_, XXIX (June, 1933), 199-201.

[5]Frederich G. Clapp, "Geology and Bitumens of the Dead Sea Area, Palestine and Transjordan," _Bulletin of the American Association of Petroleum Geologists_, XX (1936), 881-909.
Archeologists have sought Sodom and Gomorrah for generations but apparently in vain. Now the early Bronze Age ruins of Bab edh-Dhra and Numeira on the east coast of the Dead Sea might be identified as those of Sodom and Gomorrah. See "Sodom and Gomorrah: Found Again?" _Frontiers of Science_, III (January-February, 1981), 5, 10.

[6]Lynn and Gray Poole, _Volcanoes in Action: Science and Legend_ (New York, 1962).

[7]François Berge, "Le mythe du deluge," _Psyche_ (Paris), II (1947), 711-719.
Theodor H. Gaster, "The Deluge," _Myth, Legend, and Custom in the Old Testament_ (New York, etc., 1969), I, 82-131. Much of the material is from James G. Frazer, _Folklore in the Old Testament_ (London, 1918).

[8]"Prehistoric Flood from Ice Surge," _Science News_, CVIII (4 October 1975), 214.

[9]See C. Leonard Woolley, _Ur of the Chaldees: A Record of Seven Years of Excavation_ (New York, 1930), pp. 26-32.

[10]"Did a Meteorite Cause the Biblical Flood?" _Second Look_, II (March-April, 1980), 10.

[11]James G. Frazer, _Folklore in the Old Testament_ (London, 1918). An updated incorporation appears in Theodor H. Gaster, _Myth, Legend, and Custom in the Old Testament_ (New York, etc., 1969), I, 82-131.

[12]Mircea Eliade, _Cosmos and History: The Myth of the Eternal Return_, trans. W. R. Trask (New York, 1959), pp. 86-88.

[13]Anton W. Nieuwenhuis, "Die Sintflugsagen als kausallogische Naturschöpfungsmythen," _Festschrift. Publication d'hommage offerte au P. W. Schmidt_ (Wien, 1928).

[14]William Babcock, "Legendary Islands of the Atlantic," _American Geographical Society Research Series_, no. 8 (1922), pp. 11-33.

[15]Glyn E. Daniel, "Lyonesse and the Lost Lands of England," *Myth or Legend?* (New York, 1968), pp. 11-19.

[16]Lyon Sprague de Camp, *Lost Continents: The Atlantis Theme in History, Science and Literature* (New York, 1970).

[17]James Churchward, *The Lost Continent of Mu* (New York, 1926), followed by *The Children of Mu* (New York, 1931) and *The Sacred Symbols of Mu* (New York, 1933). By the time of the latter volume popular interest, initially high, had considerably diminished.

[18]Helena P. Blavatsky, *The Secret Doctrine* (Pasadena, Calif., 1970), 2 vols. The first edition appeared in 1888.

[19]W. K. C. Guthrie, *The Greeks and Their Gods* (Boston, 1955), pp. 74-82, summarizes the conflicting opinions of classic scholars.

[20]All references are to the translation by Benjamin Jowett.

[21]Any such extensive military conquest would produce significant archeological evidence, but there is no indication whatsoever of any such invasion of S. Europe and N. Africa from the west.

[22]J. V. Luce, *Lost Atlantis: New Light on an Old Legend* (New York, 1969).
Edwin S. Ramage, ed., *Atlantis, Fact or Fiction?* (Bloomington, Indiana, 1978).
W. Scott-Elliot, *The Story of Atlantis and the Lost Lemuria* (London and Wheaton, Illinois, 1972).
Lewis Spence, *The History of Atlantis* (New Hyde Park, New York, 1968), and *The Problem of Atlantis* (New York, 1925).

[23]*Lost Continents*, p. 314-318. And this list does not include citations subsequent to Baikie.

[24]Angelos G. Galanopoulos, "On the Origin of the Deluge of Deukalion and the Myth of Atlantis," *Athenais Archaiologike Hetaireia*, III (1960), 226-231.

[25]Angelos G. Galanopoulous and Edward Bacon, *Atlantis: The Truth behind the Legend* (Indianapolis and New York, 1969).
Lois Knidlberger, *Santorin: Insel zwischen Traum und Tag* (München, 1975).
James W. Mavor, Jr., *Voyage to Atlantis* (New York, 1969).

[26]Angelos G. Galanopoulos, "Der Phaëton-Mythus im Licht der Wissenschaft," *Das Altertum*, XIV (1969), 158-161.

[27]Jan Schoo, "Vulkanische und seismische Aktivität des Ägaischen Meeresbeckens im Spiegel der Griechischen Mythologie," Mnemosyne, IV (1936-1937), 257-294.

[28]Robert S. Brumbaugh, "Plato's Atlantis," Yale Alumni Magazine, XXX, no. 5 (1970), 24-28.

[29]J. G. Bennett, "Geo-physics and Human History: New Light on Plato's Atlantis and the Exodus," Systematics, I (1963), 127-156.

[30]Angelos G. Galanopoulos, "Die ägyptischen Plagen und der Auszug Israels aus geologischer Sicht," Das Altertum, X (1964), 131-137.

[31]Immanuel Velikovsky, Worlds in Collision (New York, 1950), theorized that the planet Venus was generated somehow by the planet Jupiter and hurled sunward about 1500 B.C. Passing close to the Earth, this comet (at the time) supposedly exerted a stupendous gravitational pull that parted the Red Sea for the Israelites. Scientifically the Velikovsky conjecture seems untenable.
Velikovsky took literally the Greek myth of Pallas Athene (applied, however, to Aphrodite) leaping fully armed from the brain of Zeus. The perils of myth interpretation are twofold: the Scylla of the literal and the Charybdis of the allegorical.

Notes to Chapter XIV

Biomythology

[1]N. Venkata Ramanaiah, An Essay on the Origin of the South Indian Temple (Madras, 1930), p. 76, says of S. India: "The temple which is invariably associated with Gods, had at one time no connection with them. The Gods were worshipped in the form of trees."

[2]Note the close parallel to Zeus in the guise of Amphitryon coupling with Alcmene.

[3]Stella Kramrisch, "The Indian Great Goddess," History of Religions, XIV (1975), 251-252.

[4]James G. Frazer, The Golden Bough, One vol. abridged ed. (New York, 1947), p. 667.

[5]H. R. Ellis-Davidson, Gods and Myths of Northern Europe (Harmondsworth, England, 1964), pp. 182-189, offers a good summary of the difficulties in interpreting the Balder accounts.

[6]Jorge L. Borges and Margarita Guerrero, The Book of Imaginary Beings, trans. N. T. di Giovanni (New York, 1970).

Colin Clair, Unnatural History (London, 1967).

John Block Friedman, The Monstrous Races in Medieval Art and Thought (Cambridge, Mass., 1981).

Angelo De Gubernatis, Zoological Mythology; or, The Legends of Animals (Chicago, 1968).

Peter Lum, Fabulous Beasts (New York, 1951).

Anthony S. Mercatante, Zoo of the Gods: Animals in Myth, Legend and Fable (New York, etc., 1974).

Heinz A. Mode, Fabulous Beasts and Demons (London and New York, 1975).

J. R. Porter and W. M. S. Russell, Animals in Folklore (Totowa, New Jersey, 1978).

Northcote W. Thomas, "Animals," Encyclopaedia of Religion and Ethics, ed. James Hastings.

The multiplicity of imaginary creatures requires an extensive dictionary, Jean P. Clébert, Bestiaire fabuleux (Paris, 1971).

[7]Carl G. Jung, "On the Psychology of the Unconscious," Collected Works (Princeton, 1960), VII, 1-201.

Smith Ely Jelliffe and Louise Brink, "The Role of Animals in the Unconscious with Some Remarks on Theriomorphic Symbolism as Seen in Ovid," Psychoanalytic Review, IV (1917), 253-271.

Nolan D. C. Lewis, "Theriomorphic Symbolisms and Mechanisms in Ancient Literature and Dreams," Psychoanalytic Review, L (1964), 535-556.

[8]All creatures of the water are lumped together by archaic peoples. Hence whales and dolphins, otters and beavers, are termed "fish."

[9]Robert Eisler, "Der Fisch als Sexualsymbol," Imago, III (1914), 165-196.

[10]M. Oldfield Howey, The Encircled Serpent: A Study of Serpent Symbolism in All Countries and Ages (Philadelphia, 1926).

Balaji Mundkur, The Cult of the Serpent (Albany, New York, 1982).

[11]Lloyd De Mause, "The Fetal Origins of History," The Journal of Psychoanalytic Anthropology, IV (1981), 44: "the placental serpent-goddess."

[12]Robert Graves, Greek Myths (London, 1961), p. 140.

[13]Edward A. Armstrong, The Folklore of Birds (New York, 1970).

Ernest Ingersoll, Birds in Legend, Fable and Folklore (Chicago, 1968).

[14]L. Kerschbaumer, "Bird Language in Schizophrenics," Psychoanalytic Review, XXXI (1944), 195-196.

[15]See Willy Ley, The Lungfish and the Unicorn: An Excursion into Romantic Zoology (New York, 1941).

[16]See index for animal deities, shapechangers, man-beasts.

[17]George W. Earley, "The Lake Champlain Monster," Frontiers of Science, III (May-June, 1981), 33.

[18]Rüdiger R. Beer, Einhorn: Fabelwelt und Wirklichkeit (München, 1972).
Nancy Hathaway, The Unicorn (New York, 1980).
Odell Shepard, The Lore of the Unicorn (London, 1930).
Adolf Zeckel, "The Totemistic Significance of the Unicorn," Psychoanalysis and Culture, ed. G. Wilbur and W. Muensterberger (New York, 1951), pp. 344-360.

[19]W. Franklin Dove, "Artificial Production of the Fabulous Unicorn," Scientific Monthly, XLII (1936), 431-436.

[20]J. Richard Greenwell and James E. King, "Attitudes of Physical Anthropologists toward Reports of Bigfoot and Nessie," Current Anthropology, XXII (1981), 79-80, report the following responses from 71 professionals:

	The Loch Ness Monster	"Bigfoot" of NW USA
"imagination, hoaxes, myths"	56.7%	74.4%
"ordinary animals misidentified"	20.0%	12.8%
"living animal still unknown to science"	23.3%	12.8%

[21]The unicorn as we know it falls into this category, but its early employment seems euhemeristic, probably from the rhinoceros.

[22]Jean Hubaux and Maxime Leroy, Le mythe du phénix dans les littérateurs grecque et latine (Liège et Paris, 1939).
Barbara Renz, "Sphinx, Greif und Phönix," Zeitschrift für Sexualwissenschaft, XII (1925), 137-143.
R. Van den Broek, The Myth of the Phoenix, According to Classical and Early Christian Traditions, trans. I. Seeger (Leiden, 1972).

[23]Richard Hennig, "Altgriechische Sagengestalten als Personifikation von Erdfeuern und vulkanischen Vorgangen," Deutsches Archäologisches Institut Jahrbuch, Band 54 (1939), 230-246.

Index

All dates are A. D. unless otherwise indicated.

Underlined numbers indicate the chief entry under a subject.

To conserve space very extensive subjects (i.e. Greece and India as locales of myth) are indexed only for the major discussions. Individual tribes and regional groups are indexed under the heading: "myth, geographical distribution of."

Roman deities are indexed under their corresponding Greek figures, e.g. Mars appears under Ares.

In looking for an entry, keep in mind alternate spellings, as in Firdausi/Firdusi/Firdousi.

Aaron (biblical), 106.
Abaris, 111.
Abel (biblical), 224, 241, 301, 345, 347.
Abraham (biblical), 227, 491.
Abraxas, 195.
Abydos Passion Play, 81
Acephali, 435.
Achi Zoschan, 115.
Achilles, 13, 17, 114, 153, 172, 285, 326, 356, 362, 378, 388, 389.
Acrisius, 388.
Actaeon, 460.
Acts of St. John, 73.
Adad/Addu, 184-185.
Adam (biblical), 138, 151, 180, 217, 220, 262, 306, 487.
Adapa, 24, 309.
Adharma, 194.
Adī ibn Musāfir (Islamic religionist) (12th cent.), 199.
Aditi, 30, 147, 172, 359.
Adler, Alfred (Austrian psychiatrist) (1870-1937), 292.
Admetus, 323.
Adonis, 54, 113, 147, 177, 180, 202, 213, 226, 355,

432.
Adrastos, 217.
Adri, 194.
Aeacus, 191, 327.
Aegeus, 218, 237, 379, 388.
Aegisthus, 381.
Aeneas/Aeneid, 76, 101, 122, 137, 139, 142, 162, 190, 239, 325, 378, 387.
Aeolus, 37, 185.
Aërope, 381.
Aeschylus (Greek dramatist) (525-456 B.C.), 5, 95, 199, 234, 247.
Aeshmadaeva, 28.
Aesir, 7, 241.
aesthetics/esthetics (religious), 89.
Aethra, 218.
afflictions (sacred), 85-88.
Afrekete, 233.
Agag, 304.
Agamemnon, 101, 304, 388.
Agastya, 50, 97.
Agathos Daimon, 427.
Agave, 74, 371.
Age of Fable, 41.
Agenor, 47.
Agnes, St. (Christian martyr) (c.300) 195.
Agni, 171, 182, 301, 313, 353,

431.
Agricola, Georgius, i.e. Georg
  Bauer (German mineralogist)
  (1494-1555), 192.
Agrippa, Cornelius
  Heinrich/Agrippa von
  Nettesheim (German
  occultist) (c. 1486-1535),
  321.
Ahania, 354.
Ahriman, 348.
Ahsonnutli, 360.
ahuizotl, 438.
Ahura Mazda, 41, 186, 233,
  348, 367.
Aigamuxa, 435.
Aiol, 218.
Airāvata, 439
aition, 4, 36.
Ajax, 17.
Aksakov, Sergei (Russian
  novelist) (1791-1859), 333.
Ala, 177
Aladdin, 106
Alastor, 191
Albigensians, 70, 348
Alcaeus, 196
Alcestis, 323
Alcmaeon, 133, 292, 518, 522
Alcmene, 22, 414
Alcyone, 284, 434
Alexander of Abonutichos
  (Greek religionist) (2nd
  cent.), 57.
Alexander the Great
  (Macedonian conqueror)
  (356-323 B.C.), 47, 139,
  194, 268, 347, 350, 372,
  379, 392, 425.
Alfred the Great (Anglo-Saxon
  ruler) (849-899), 418
Algaloa, 184
al-Halladj/Hallāj (Moslem
  mystic) (10th cent.), 79,
  196
Ali (Islamic religionist) (c.
  600-661), 197
Allah, 126, 168-169, 193, 197,
  213, 233, 320, 329
Allat, 329

allegory, intellectual, 41-43
allegory, moral, 39-41, 53
allegory, nature, 37-39, 53
Allegro, John Marco (American
  scholar) (1923-   ), 68.
Alpheus, 397
Althaea/Althea, 105-106, 217.
Amakandu, 225
Amala, 316
Amalthea/Amaltheia, 180, 431
Amarāvati, 331
Amaterasu, 115, 186, 216, 228
Amazons/female warriors/
  warrior women, 215-217
Amenhotep III (Egyptian
  pharaoh) (c. 1411-1375
  B.C.), 138, 351.
Amenophis (Egyptian statesman
  (c. 1400 B.C.), 46.
Ameritat, 41
Amesha Spentas, 41
Amirani, 32
Ammon (biblical), 227
Am-mut, 191
Amon/Amun, 47, 139, 196, 350,
  351, 352, 378, 379, 431
Amphiaraos, 192, 217
Amphion, 382
Amphitryon, 196, 348, 518, 522
amulet, 106, 162
Amycus, 302
An, 372
Anahita, 139, 176, 350
Anahuac, 322
Anaitis, 139
Anansi, 233
Ananta, 397
Anaxagoras of Clazomenae
  (Greek philosopher) (c.
  500-428 B.C.), 38, 364
Anaxerete, 357
ancestor worship, 161-162
Anchises, 137, 139, 190, 328
Ancient Mariner, 83
Andal, 271
Andromeda, 177, 355, 384, 385
anima/animus, 353-356, 377
animatism, 143-145
Aningakh, 165
Anseïs, 218

Anshar, 50
Anthony of Padua, St.
   (Portuguese theologian)
   (1195-1231), 109
Antigone/Antigone, 44, 217,
   357, 392
Antilla/Antilles, 407
Antiope, 215
Antisthenes (Greek
   philosopher) (c. 444-c. 371
   B.C.), 247
Antony, Marc (Roman
   militarist) (c. 83-30
   B.C.), 135.
Anu, 24, 184
Anubis, 111, 112, 149, 467
Anunit, 52
'Apep, 383, 427
Aphrodite/Venus, 17, 42, 50,
   54, 139, 150, 169, 176,
   184, 202, 238, 264, 271,
   343, 350, 355, 362, 378,
   420, 422, 444, 460, 514
      Uranian Venus, 184
      Venus Barbata, 360
      Venus Genetrix, 176
      Venus (planet), 49, 50,
      522
Apis, 350, 429
Apocalyse/Book of Revelations,
   26
Apollo/Apollonian, 14, 27, 38,
   52, 63, 69, 75, 88-89, 111,
   125, 170, 172, 183-184,
   186, 213, 263, 313, 343,
   347, 350, 351, 352, 410,
   417, 419, 429
      Apollo Belvidere, 343
      Apollo Delphinius, 424
      Apollo Lykeios, 147
      Apollo Smintheus, 154,
      428
Apollonius of Tyana (Greek
   philosopher) (1st cent.),
   109, 130
Apollyon, 52
Apology (of Socrates), 38
Apophis, 191
Appar (Indian musician) (7th
   cent.), 42

Apsu, 295, 394
Apsyrtus, 6, 302, 517
Apuleius, Lucius (Roman
   author) (2nd cent.), 149,
   202
Aqht, 384
Aquila, 51
Aquinas, St. Thomas (Italian
   theologian) (c. 1225-1274),
   89
Arabian Nights/1001 Nights
   Entertainment, 11, 111, 406
Aralū, 328
Arcturus, 52
Ardhanāri, 360
Areion, 429
Ares/Mars, 17, 23, 42, 78,
   139, 150, 182-183, 238,
   239, 267, 345, 378, 444,
   489
Arethusa, 396-397
Argo, 51
Argonauts, 6, 17, 51, 215,
   302, 347, 372
Ariadne, 386
Aries, 52
Arion, 424
Aristeas, 109, 112
Aristophanes (Athenian
   dramatist) (c. 448-c. 380
   B.C.), 117, 228, 360
Aristotle (Greek philosopher)
   (384-322 B.C.), 13, 14, 36,
   49, 74, 277, 372, 412
Arjuna, 384
Armageddon, 338
Ārmaiti, 41
Arnobius (Christian Latin
   writer) (c. 300), 47
Arta, 41
Artak, 225
Artemis/Diana, 14, 39, 101,
   165, 172, 213, 264, 304,
   344, 350, 397, 429, 489,
   517
      Brauronian Artemis, 147
      Diana (Artemis) of
      Ephesus, 66, 86, 165,
      176, 289, 328
Arthur/Arthurian, 145, 211,

527

science-fictionist) (1920-
), 25
Brahma, 42, 47, 51, 97, 170,
220, 227, 294, 310, 322,
335, 338, 342, 344-345,
346, 349, 350, 355, 365,
405, 417, 515
Brahman, 349, 416
<u>Brāhmanas</u>, 363
Brahmanaspati, 137
Brahmānda, 322
Brahmashiras, 145
Brahmo Samāj, 353
Brandon/Brendan/Borandan
(Irish saint) (484-577),
407
Brentano, Klemens (German
author) (1778-1842), 8
Br'er Rabbit, 233
Bres, 295
Brian, 180
Brigit, 235
Brinton, Daniel Garrison
(American anthropologist)
(1837-1899), 266
Britomartis, 165
Brotherhood of the
Flagellants, 72
Brumbaugh, Robert Sherrick
(American educator) (1918-
), 414
Brutus (Briton), 239
Brutus, Lucius Junius (Roman
patriot) (c. 500 B.C.), 389
Bryant, Jacob (English
theologian) (1715-1804), 27
Brynhild/Brunhild, 392
Buddha/Buddhism/
Gautama/Gotama/ Siddhartha
24, 28, 38, 39, 44, 45, 47,
65, 70, 91, 93, 98, 102,
103, 104, 105, 107, 110,
115-116, 141, 146, 192,
194, 209, 223, 243, 299,
300, 313, 317, 318, 319,
327, 330, 342, 344, 346,
353, 370, 377, 379, 380,
387, 389, 417, 423, 429,
444, 446, 462, 489, 507,
510

Mahā-Vairochana
Buddha/Dainichi, 321
Mahayana Buddhism, 478
Theravada Buddhism, 450
Zen Buddhism, 246
Bulfinch, Thomas (American
mythologist) (1796-1867),
41
Bultmann, Rudolf K. (German
theologian) (1884-1976),
206
Bunyan, Paul, 8
bunyip, 439
Burāq/Burak, 84, 111, 438
Burton, Sir Richard Francis
(English orientalist)
(1821-1890), 406-407
Būshyāsta, 194
Bwana Jezu Kristo, 345
Byron, George Gordon Noel/Lord
Byron (English poet) (1788-
1824), 389
Cabiri, 200
Cacus, 439
Cadmus, 23, 50, 289, 389, 402,
428
caduceus, 425
Caeculus, 192
Caenis/Caeneus, 375
Caesar Augustus/Gaius Julius
Caesar Octavianus (Roman
emperor) (27 B.C.-14 A.D.),
425
Caesar, Gaius Julius (Roman
statesman) (100-44 B.C.),
135
Caf/Kaf/Qaf, 315
Cain (biblical), 138, 224,
241, 262, 301, 345, 347
Cairbre, 295
Caitanya (Indian religionist)
(15th-16th cent.), 197
Calderón de la Barca, Pedro
(Spanish dramatist) (1600-
1681), 365
Callisto, 50
Calypso, 313, 357
Camazotz, 434
Campbell, Joseph (American
mythologist), (1904-   ),

Julian (Roman emperor) (331-363), 43
Julian of Norwich (English mystic) (14th cent.), 214
Jung, Carl Gustav (Swiss psychologist) (1875-1961)/Jungian/neo-Jungian, 59, 90, 162, 230, 288, 311, 315, 340-392, 429, 430, 463, 491, 509, 514
Justin Martyr/St. Justin (Patristic writer) (c. 100-c. 165), 52
Juturna, 96
Ka, 194
Kaaveri, 97
Kabandha, 435
Kabat, 236
Kabbala/Kabbalists/Cabbala/Cabbalists, 228, 343
Kadluna, 243
Kadru, 383, 433
Kahu, 307
Kai-ni-tiku-aba, 418
Kālachakra, 198
Kalevala, 8, 137, 180, 183, 228-229, 317, 329, 363, 435
Kali, 16, 87, 304, 371, 444
Kalki, 429
Kalori-Vu, 427
Kalvaitas, 137
Kama, 435
Kamatha, 347
Kanag, 380
Kang, 173
Ka'nini, 244
Kant, Immanuel (German philosopher) (1724-1804)/neo-Kantian, 280
kappa, 439
Karna, 380
Kartikeyta, 347
Karu, 228
Karusakaibe, 173
Kashyapa, 433
Kazantzakis, Nikos (Greek author) (1885-1957), 8
K'daai Maqsin, 137
Keats, John (English poet) (1795-1821), 241, 357

K'êng-san-ku, 183
Kerényi, Károly/Carl Kérenyi (Hungarian mythologist) (1897-1973), 342
Kesil, 50
Khnum, 138, 366
Khonsu, 188
Ki, 225, 372
Kimpurushas, 149
King Henry (Jamaican legend), 152
"King Orfeo," 20
Kinnaras, 149
Kircher, Athanasius (German polymath) (1601-1680), 27
Kitaba, 398
Kluckhohn, Clyde (American anthropologist) (1905-1960), 16, 253, 279
Knaritja, 184
Kokumthena, 362
Koran, 84, 126, 329
Korybantes, 74
Kouretes, 74
kraken, 424, 436
Kresnik, 265
Krishna, 87, 101, 106, 197, 220, 271, 351, 355, 381, 382, 384, 389, 391, 434-435, 460
Krishnamurti, Jiddu (Indian mystic) (1895-   ), 58
Krohn, Kaarle Leopold (Finnish folklorist) (1863-1933), 28
Kronos/Saturn, 40, 46, 139, 169-170, 241, 298, 299, 372, 373, 431
Kuan Yü (Chinese general later deified) (2nd cent.-3rd cent.), 47
Kubera, 190
Kuei-tzu-mu, 370
Kukitat, 173, 347
Kullervo, 228-229
Kunapipi, 177
Kung-kung, 401-402
Kuntī, 378
Kur'an'up, 321
Kushi-nada-hime, 384

181, 209, 238, 250, 263, 281, 295, 320, 352, 364, 367, 383, 384, 402 (planet), 50
Marīchī, 198
Maringer, Johannes (German prehistorian) (1902-   ), 33
Marpessa, 357
The Marriage of the Moon God, 265, 268
Marsham, Sir John (English scholar) (1602-1685), 27
Marx, Karl (German theorist) (1818-1883)/Marxism, 9, 27, 59, 142, 291, 361
mask, sacred, 126-127
Mastamho, 234
Masters, Robert E. L. (American psychologist) (20th cent.), 70
Masubi, 32
Matanga, 117
matriarchy, 214-215
Matronit, 228
Matsya, 423
Matsya Pūrana, 376
Matus, Don Juan (Castañeda's mentor) (20th cent.), 122
Maui, 15, 23, 52, 104, 295, 369
Mawu, 362, 427
May, Robert (American psychologist) (1940-   ), 392
Mayuel, 66
Mazdaism/Mazdean, 49, 192
Mazdak (Persian religionist) (5th cent.), 365
Mbumba Philippe (African religionist) (20th cent.), 197
Medb, 78
Medea, 6, 134, 190, 237, 292, 302, 373, 386, 426, 517
Medusa, 134, 171, 286, 323, 371-372, 384, 385, 423, 426
Mehabub-uddaula, 236
Meher, 390
Melampus, 113, 387

Meleagant, 177
Meleager, 105-106, 217, 419
Meletinskij, Eleazar Moiseevich (Russian folklorist) (20th cent.), 272
Meletus (Athenian politician) (5th-4th cent. B.C.), 38
Melgart, 195
Mélisande, 357
Melvas, 177
Melville, Herman (American novelist) (1819-1891), 406
Menasseh (biblical), 347
Mencken, Henry Louis (American author) (1880-1956), 44, 107
Menelaus, 17
Menestratus, 383
Mentor, 357
Mephistopheles, 232, 233
Mercator, Gerhardus/Kremer, Gerhard (Flemish cartographer) (1512-1594), 412
mermaid/merman/merpeople, 149, 424
Merope, 504
Mertserger, 370
Metamorphoses, 12
Meyer, Elard Hugo (German mythologist) (1837-1908), 159
Michener, James Albert (American novelist) (1907-   ), 406
Mictlan, 167
Midas, 149.
Middlemarch, 27, 62.
Middleton, John (English anthropologist) (1921-   ), 276.
Midgard, 317.
Midgard serpent, 50, 361.
Midsummer Night's Dream, 54.
Miki, Tokuharu (Japanese religionist) (1871-1938), 125.
Milaraspa, 133.
Milky Way, 51.

Milton, John (English poet) (1608-1674), 52, 296.
Milu, 326-327.
Mimir, 127, 251,317.
The Mind of Primitive Man, 284.
Minos, 191, 264, 289, 327.
minotaur, 146, 149, 151, 305, 386.
Mirabai, 271.
Mirganka, 145.
Mirtyu, 194.
Mirza Ghulām Ahmad (Islamic religionist) (1835-1908), 197.
Mishna, 314.
Mitra/Mithra/Mithras/ Mithraism, 147, 186-187, 192, 202, 238, 240, 317, 374, 380, 384,429.
Mjollnir, 166.
Mnemosyne, 55.
"Modest Proposal," 297.
Mohini, 233.
Mokele-Mbembe, 436.
Moller, Herbert (American historian) (20th cent.), 90.
Moloch, 195, 302.
Moloney, James Clark (American psychologist) (1900-   ), 38.
Moma, 178.
Momotaro, 7.
Momus, 189.
monomyth, 23, 58-60.
monotheism, 173, 174-175, 205, 210.
    primeval/ur-monotheism, 56, 57.
Monroe, Marilyn (American actress) (1926-1962), 356.
Montanists, 70.
Mordred, 229.
Mormonism, 208-209.
Morpheus, 284.
mortification, 71-73.
Moses (Hebrew leader) (c. 1200 B.C.)/ Mosaic, 250, 306, 320, 350, 352, 381, 425.

Môt, 394.
mother god/great mother/earth mother/earth goddess/magna mater, 20, 33, 35, 38, 59, 86, 100, 104, 107, 111, 113, 114, 125, 161, 165, 166, 168, 175-176, 177, 180, 184, 200-202, 212-214, 225, 285, 288, 289, 290, 304, 315, 319, 323, 330, 342, 344, 349, 351, 355, 356, 358, 361, 362, 365, 369, 376, 383-384, 385, 391 395, 425, 427, 518.
    Also consult named god- dess of fertility such as Cybele, Mã, Rhea.
Mt. Purgatory, 331.
Mountford, Charles Pearcy (Australian anthropologist) (1890-   ), 32.
Mpadi Simon (African religion- ist) (20th cent.), 197.
Mu, 315, 408-409.
Mucukunda, 390.
Mugive, 28-29.
Muhammed al-Mahdi/Mohammed Ahmed ibn-Seyyid Abdullah (Islamic religionist) (c. 1843-1885), 197.
Muhammed, Elijah (American Black Muslim) (1897-1975), 197.
Müller, Friedrich Max (British philologist) (1823-1900), 38, 56, 63-64, 187, 296, 352.
Müller, Karl Otfried (German scholar) (1797-1840), 62- 63.
Mulungu, 173.
Mungu, 345.
Munin, 432.
Munz, Peter (New Zealand philosopher) (1921-   ), 287.
Muqaddimah, 208.
Murray, Margaret Alice (English historian) (1863- 1963), 122.

552

Naraka, 322, 329.
Narcissus/Narcissism, 293.
Narmer (Egyptian pharaoh) (c. 3000 B.C.), 78.
The Natural History of Religion, 60.
Nechepso, 49.
necromancy, 136-137.
Neihardt, John G. (American author) (1881-1973), 91.
Neith, 411.
Neleus, 381.
Nemesis, 189.
Nephthys, 427.
Nergal, 50, 191.
Nessus, 63.
Nestor, 17, 357.
New Atlantis, 9.
New System (Jacob Bryant), 27.
Newton, Sir Isaac (English physicist) (1642-1727), 2, 47, 394.
Ngai, 51, 451, 474.
Ngatoro, 399.
Ngorieru, 191-192.
Nhang, 370.
Nibelungs/Nibelungenlied, 18, 62, 290.
Nicholas (German religionist) (13th cent.), 10.
Nieuwenhuis, Anton W. (Dutch mythologist) (20th cent.), 405.
Niflheim, 317.
"A Night on Bald Mountain," 189.
Nikkal, 265.
Nimrod (biblical), 147.
Ningirsu, 84.
Ninib, 50.
Ninigi, 356.
Ninmah, 240.
Niobe, 14, 172.
Niraikanai, 321.
Niranjan Dharma, 363.
Nirvana, 331.
Nisus, 289.
Niu-t'on, 149.
Noah (biblical), 222, 402-403, 423.

N!odima, 347.
non-theistic religion, 45.
Norns, 317, 343.
Norok, 329.
Novalis (pseudonym of Baron Friedrich von Hardenberg) (1772-1801), 62.
Ntjikantja, 318.
Nu (Egyptian deity), 360.
Nü Wa, 427.
Nuada, 251.
Nü-kua, 235.
Numbakulla, 318.
Numi Tarem, 364.
Nusku, 182.
Nut (Egyptian deity), 228, 372, 479.
Nyx, 189.
Nzambi, 306.
Oannes, 235, 362, 423.
Obassi, 168.
Oberon, 355.
Obrik, Axel (Finnish mythologist) (20th cent.), 28.
Oceanus, 37.
Ocnus, 194.
Odhroerir, 180.
Odysseus/Ulysses, 8, 15, 24, 105, 122, 137, 189, 230, 233, 261, 281, 295, 296, 323, 333, 384, 385, 387, 390, 395, 424.
Odyssey (Homer), 69, 98, 137, 189, 295, 301.
Odyssey (Kazantzakis), 8.
Oedipus/Oedipus Rex/Oedipal, 21-22, 72, 213, 217-218, 225, 274, 286, 291, 292, 294, 351, 373, 379, 380, 381, 387, 388, 390, 429, 504, 515.
Oeneus, 264.
Oesterley, William Oscar Emil (English scholar) (1866-1950), 73.
Offa, 382.
O'Flaherty, Wendy Doniger (American Indologist) (1940-   ), vi.
Ogier, 218, 390.

Ogun, 137, 240.
Ohrmazd, 313.
Ojin, Penno (Japanese emperor) (c. 200-310), 48.
Oko, 115, 240.
Oliver, 354, 388, 389.
Olympic games, 40.
Ometecuhli, 322, 360.
Omphale, 217, 376.
omphalos/navel, 313-314, 319.
Oorpazhassi, 229.
Ophion, 289.
Ophioneus, 383.
Oppilāmulaiyammi, 362.
Ops, 238.
oracle, 67, 69, 78-79, 85, 123-128, 129, 196.
Orationes, 352.
Orcus, 191.
Oresteia, 247.
Orestes, 292, 381.
Orestheus, 23.
Origen (Greek Christian theologian) (c. 185-c. 254), 40, 75.
The Origins of Religion, 269.
Orion, 50, 185.
Ormuzd, 420.
Orpheus, 74, 86, 122, 127, 147, 298, 323, 350, 386.
Orphism/Orphic cult, 40, 42, 75, 158, 178, 189, 195, 203-204, 224, 247, 298, 346, 360, 361, 363, 435.
Ortelius/Oertel/Ortell, Abraham (Flemish cartographer) (1527-1598), 407.
Orthus, 439.
Oserapis, 204.
Osiris, 11, 12, 24, 30, 52, 64, 77, 81, 99, 162, 179, 180, 192, 193, 202, 204, 219-220, 228, 237, 255, 264, 269, 296, 318, 327, 350, 352, 393, 417, 423, 427, 429, 431.
Otto, Rudolf (German scholar) (1869-1937), 91.
Otto, Walter F. (German

historian) (1874-1958), 85, 207.
Ovid (Latin poet) (43 B.C.-17 A.D.) 5, 12.
Ozolae Greeks, 23.
Pachacámac, 181.
Pachamama, 358.
Packer, Craig (American biologist) (20th cent.), 223.
Paguk, 167.
Pakrokitat, 173, 347.
Palaiphatos/Palaephatus (Greek historian) (4th cent. B.C.), 150.
Pales, 377.
palladium, 105-106.
Pan, 52, 79, 195, 351, 431.
Pan Ku, 427.
Pan-Babylonians, 49.
Pandu/Pandava, 378.
Pan-Egyptionists, 27.
Panj Phul, 106.
P'an-ku, 181, 363, 367.
Papa, 372.
Paracelsus, Philippus Aureolus/Theophrastus Bombastus von Hohenheim (Swiss occultist) (c. 1493-1541), 321.
Parawhenuamea, 403.
Parcae, 343.
Paris (Troy), 238, 381.
Pārshvanātha, 347.
Parsifal/Perceval, 382.
Paruxti, 185.
Parvati, 182, 376, 475.
Pasiphaë, 147, 151.
Pātāla, 322.
Pathen, 168.
patriarchy, 219-222.
Patroclus/Patroklus, 285.
Paul, St. (Christian apostle) (1st cent.), 39, 52, 76, 85, 141, 201, 398.
Pausanias (Greek traveler) (2nd cent.), 99, 192.
Pegasus, 111, 437.
Pehar, 198, 271.
Peirides, 434.

Pekai, 268.
Pele, 32, 182, 198, _399_, 413.
Peleas, 381.
Peleus, 153, 218, 237.
Pelias, 302.
Penelope, 217, 337, 516.
Penitentes, 72.
Pentheus, 74, 86, 247, 298, 371.
Perceval le Gallois, 218.
Percy, Thomas (English antiquary) (1729-1811), 62.
Perfect Liberty Organization, 76.
Perimbó, 187.
Perkunas, 9.
Perry, William James (English anthropologist) (1868-1949), 27.
Persephone/Proserpine/Kore /Libera, 37, 99, 177, 190, 201, 202, 224, 266, 323, 344, 432.
Perseus, 18, 43, 122, 187, 265, 292, 373, 381, 383, 384, 385, 387-388.
Peter Pan, 343.
Petosiris, 49.
Phaedo, 60-61.
Phaedre, 7.
Phaedrus, 38.
Phaëton, 287, 392, 414, 418.
Phanes, 298, 363.
Philemon, 41, 270, 355, 418.
Philip II (Macedonian ruler) (382-336 B.C.), 379.
Philistines, 6.
Philo of Alexandria/Philo Judaeus (Jewish philosopher) (1st cent. B.C.-1st cent. A.D.), 39, 426.
Phobos, 194.
phoenix, 437.
Phrixus, 237, 302, 305.
Phyllis, 270.
Phytius, 23.
Piaget, Jean (Swiss psychologist) (1896-1980), 36, 287, 310.

piety, 96-106.
Piggott, Stuart (English prehistorian) (1910-   ), 33.
Pimiku/Himiko, 215.
Pirman, 402.
Pirthivī, 373.
Pisacha, 299.
Pisces, 50.
Plato (Greek philosopher) (c. 427-347 B.C./Platonism, 36, 37, 43, 76, 228, 286, 341, 346, 349, 359, 360, _411-412_.
Pleïades, 49, 50.
Pliny/Gaius Plinius Secundus (Roman author) (23-79), 293, 406, 436.
Plutarch (Greek biographer) (c. 46-c. 120), 43, 195.
Pluto, 189.
Poe, Edgar Allan (American author) (1809-1849), 228, 311.
Poem of Baal, 394.
Poetics (Aristotle), 13.
Polo, Marco (Venetian traveler) (c. 1254-c. 1324), 215, 406.
Polyaenus (Greek scholar) (2nd cent.), 117.
Polybus, 504.
Polydorus, 101.
polygenesis (of myth), 27-28.
Polynices, 217.
Polyphemus, 230, 296.
polytheism, 174-196, 205.
Pompey the Great (Roman militarist) (106-48 B.C.), 135, 186, 202
Pope, Alexander (English poet) (1688-1744), 53.
Poře, 187.
Portrait of the Artist as a Young Man, 381.
Poseidon/Neptune, 105, 264, 347, 375, 379,395, 398, 429.
Poseidon Hippios, 146.
Prajāpati, 117, 195, 353, 363.

Reik, Theodor (German
psychologist) (1888-1970),
258, 262.
Reinga, 323.
Reliques of Ancient English
Poetry, 62.
Remus, 45, 139, 381, 382.
Renenet, 370.
Retu, 422.
Reuben (biblical), 347.
Reynard, 233.
Rhadamanthus, 191, 327.
Rhea, 40, 176.
Rhea Silvia, 23, 139, 489.
Ridgeway, Sir William (British
archeologist) (1853-1926),
48.
Rigveda, 5, 10, 30, 57, 117,
137, 162, 172, 173, 195,
216, 227, 294, 321, 329,
353, 364, 416.
Les rites de passage, 257.
rites of passage, 118, 257.
ritual artificers, 137-140.
ritualistic theory of
myth/ritualism, 22, 31, 77,
254-272, 404.
Rivers, William H.R. (English
anthropologist) (1864-
1922), 239.
Robin Hood, 214.
Roc, 438.
Róheim, Géza (Hungarian
psychologist-
anthropologist) (1891-
1953), 35, 290-291.
Roland/Song of Roland, 145,
218, 239, 302, 354, 357,
388, 389.
Romulus, 6, 23, 45, 47, 135,
139, 378, 381, 382, 389.
Ruahatu, 400.
Rudra, 63, 350.
Rūmī, Julāl al-Dīn (Islamic
religionist) (13th cent.),
74, 94, 95.
Rumpelstiltskin, 296.
Rūpāvatī/Rūpāvata, 376.
Rustum, 11, 23.
Saci/Sacipati, 195.

sacred king, 199, 236-237.
Sacred Writings, 46.
sacrifice, 189, 299-306.
foundation sacrifice, 189,
303, 304.
substitution, 285-286.
Saehrimnir, 167.
Sagara, 116.
Salome, 308, 371.
Sambandha (Indian saint) (c.
639), 42.
Samkhya, 45.
Sämpsä Pellervo, 225.
Samson, 6, 38, 289, 435.
Sansom, Sir George Bailey
(English Orientalist (1883-
1965), 89.
Sarah (biblical), 227.
Saramā, 430.
Sarasvati, 144, 238, 344, 355.
Sargon, 381.
Sartoris, Bayard, 18.
Satan, 348.
Satapatha Brahmana, 364.
Satī, 103.
Satyr, 52, 112, 149.
Saul (biblical), 304.
Savitr, 353.
Savonarola, Girolamo (Italian
religionist) (1452-1498),
58.
Saxo Grammaticus (Danish
historian) (c. 1150-c.
1220), 47, 421.
Sayo, Kitamura (Japanese
religionist) (20th cent.),
74.
Scaevola, Mucius, 251.
Scathač , 216.
Scévola de Sainte-Marthe
(French philosopher) (16th
cent.), 398.
Schelling, Friedrich (German
philosopher) (1775-1854),
62.
Schlegel, August (German
author) (1767-1845), 62.
Schlegel, Friedrich (German
author) (1772-1829), 62.
Schmidt, G. Elliot (19th cent.

mythologist), 27.
Schmidt, Wilhelm (Austrian ethnologist) (1868-1954), 28, 57, 173, 349.
Schoo, Jan (20th cent. mythologist), 414.
Schucman, Helen (American psychologist) (20th cent.), 126.
Schweitzer, Albert (French polymath) (1875-1965), 94.
Scienza Nuova, 61.
Scipio Africanus, Publius Cornelius (Roman leader) (237-183 B.C.), 425.
Sciron, 7.
Sclater, Philip L. (English scientist) (19th cent.), 409.
Scylla, 163, 170, 289, 395, 422, 439.
Seb, 350.
Secret Book of John, 345.
Sedna, 165, 181, 191, 424.
Segal, Dmitry/Dimitri Segal (Russian folkorist) (1938-), 272.
Selene, 38, 188.
Selket, 370.
Semele, 298.
Semiramis/Sammu-ramat (Assyrian ruler) (9th cent. B.C.), 215, 225, 226, 377, 378, 381, 382, 389.
Senart, Émile C.M. (French Orientalist) (1847-1928), 38.
senex, 357.
Sennacherib (Assyrian king) (705-681 B.C.), 21.
Sepi Malosi, 434.
Serapis, 204, 350.
Servius/Servius Marius Honoratus (Latin scholar (4th cent.-5th cent.), 514.
Set/Seth, 30, 31, 64, 77, 394.
sex (sacred), 75.
Sforza, Caterina (Italian countess) (1462-1509), 216.
Shahnamah, 9.

Shaibyā, 250.
Shakers, 74.
Shakespeare, William (English dramatist) (1564-1616), 54.
Shakti/Shaktism, 87, 107, 173, 176, 202, 213, 354.
shaman, 4, 20, 34, 48, 58, 66, 69, 71, 78-79, 83, 85, 91, 107, 108-122, 128, 129, 131, 132, 137, 138, 140- 141, 142, 145, 149, 151, 160-161, 171, 185, 212, 215, 229, 230, 231, 243, 258, 260, 270, 273, 275, 298, 303, 323, 325, 326, 332-333, 410, 418.
Shamash, 188, 289.
Shango, 48, 185.
Shang-ti (T'ien), 184.
Shankara/Shankaracharya (Hindu theologian) (c. 788-c. 820), 25, 365.
shapechanger/shapeshifter, 123, 151-152.
Shastradevatā, 145.
Shatadhanu, 250.
Shatapatha Brāhmana, 326.
Shaushka, 358.
Shelley, Percy Bysshe (English poet) (1792-1822), 8, 277.
Shenrab, 187.
Shên-tsung (Chinese emperor) (11th cent.), 84.
Sheol, 50, 328.
Shesha, 426.
Shingrawa, 173, 364.
Shinto/Shintoism, 74, 102, 105, 135, 198, 315, 328, 336, 346.
Shipap, 328.
Shir ā t, 326.
Shirokogorov, Sergei Mikhailovich (Russian anthropologist) (20th cent.), 121.
Shiva/Shaivite, 42, 47, 51, 63-64, 73, 87, 97, 100, 102, 103, 114, 116, 139, 145, 150, 165, 175, 179, 182, 193, 197, 213, 220,

561

Yanna, 383.
Yashoda, 106.
Years of Childhood, 333.
yeti, 437.
Yggdrasil, 66, 300, 317, 318.
Yima, 228, 235.
Yimaha, 228.
Ymir, 11, 15, 181, 364, 400.
Yogini, 299.
Yü Huang/Jade Emperor, 195,
    249.
Yurlunggur, 401.
Yuvanāha, 220.
Zadkiel, 1.
Zaehner, Robert Charles
    (English scholar) (1913-
    1974), 93-94.
Zagreus, 192, 203, 224, 267,
    298, 425.
Zal, 381.
Zalmoxis, 45, 303.
Zas, 383.
Zeno of Citium (Greek
    philosopher) (4th cent.-3rd
    cent. B.C.), 40, 42.
Zenobia, 377.
Zethos, 382.
Zeus/Jupiter/Jove, 13, 37, 38,
    40, 42, 46, 47, 50, 52, 78,
    95, 96, 100, 101, 102, 136,
    139, 151, 161, 168, 170,
    171, 180, 184, 187, 189,
    194, 196, 202, 203, 204,
    220, 224, 225, 227, 238,
    241, 262, 264, 267, 281,
    298, 305, 343, 345, 347,
    348, 350, 357, 383, 385,
    414, 420, 422, 431, 432,
    518, 522.
    Jupiter Dolichenus, 350.
    Zeus Acraeus, 193.
    Zeus Averter of Flies, 193.
    Zeus Georgios, 265.
    Zeus Kappotas, 98-99.
    Zeus Ktesios, 428.
    Zeus Lykaios, 147.
    Zeus Mellissaios, 435.
    Zeus Picus, 193.
Zeus, 267.
Ziusudra, 402.

Zlotababa, 176, 177-178.
Zohar, 157, 343.
Zoroaster/Zoroastrianism, 25,
    41, 158, 186, 194, 209,
    213, 225, 314, 326, 339,
    348, 352.
Zu, 432.